Agribusiness

Agribusiness offers a unique introduction to the business of agriculture: what agribusiness is, why it matters, what the role of technology is, how trade fits into the picture, what its key risks are, who is lending and investing and why and what returns they are getting. It is both practical in orientation – focusing on the role of managers in the industry as well as that of lenders and investors – and international in scope – drawing on case studies and interviews with key figures all over the world.

The text ranges across various agricultural commodities to stress that there is no 'one size fits all' solution and successful management, lending or investment in agribusiness requires understanding specifics. Readers are introduced to the economics of the supply and demand of food, the role of agricultural trade, agricultural marketing and farm management along with key business aspects including:

- Main drivers of agribusiness value;
- Principal risks of agribusinesses;
- Agribusiness as an investment class; and
- Agribusiness lending: why, who and how.

This engaging textbook offers a complete guide to the international business of agriculture which is ideal for all students, scholars and practitioners.

A selection of eResources is also available to supplement this text, and instructors will find PowerPoint slides, discussion questions, case studies and further teaching materials available to them.

Julian Roche is an international financial trainer and consultant who has taught agribusiness and finance worldwide for over two decades. After serving many years as a consultant to the United Nations Conference on Trade and Development (UNCTAD), he is currently on the Adjunct Faculty at the University of Western Australia.

Agribusiness

An International Perspective

Julian Roche

Routledge
Taylor & Francis Group

LONDON AND NEW YORK

First published 2020
by Routledge
2 Park Square, Milton Park, Abingdon, Oxon OX14 4RN

and by Routledge
52 Vanderbilt Avenue, New York, NY 10017

Routledge is an imprint of the Taylor & Francis Group, an informa business

British Library Cataloguing-in-Publication Data
A catalogue record for this book is available from the British Library

Library of Congress Cataloging-in-Publication Data
Names: Roche, Julian, author.
Title: Agribusiness : an international perspective / Julian Roche.
Description: Abingdon, Oxon ; New York, NY : Routledge, 2019. |
Includes bibliographical references and index.
Identifiers: LCCN 2019017065 (print) | LCCN 2019019819 (ebook) |
ISBN 9781351039741 (Ebook) | ISBN 9781138488656 (hardback : alk. paper) |
ISBN 9781138488663 (pbk. : alk. paper)
Subjects: LCSH: Agricultural industries. | Agriculture–Economic aspects.
Classification: LCC HD9000.5 (ebook) |
LCC HD9000.5 .R5792 2019 (print) | DDC 338.1–dc23
LC record available at https://lccn.loc.gov/2019017065

ISBN: 978-1-138-48865-6 (hbk)
ISBN: 978-1-138-48866-3 (pbk)
ISBN: 978-1-351-03974-1 (ebk)

Typeset in Helvetica and Bembo
by Newgen Publishing UK

Visit the eResources: www.routledge.com/9781138488663

Every effort has been made to contact copyright-holders. Please advise the publisher of
any errors or omissions, and these will be corrected in subsequent editions.

Contents

Figures

Tables

Preface

The central challenge in writing this book has been how to select what to include from the vast quantity of information out there. Examples rather than catalogues are the rule in this book, not the exception. No doubt every reader will want an inclusion here, a changed emphasis there. It is the risk that every author embarking on a general introduction to a massive topic such as agribusiness must inevitably take. I have tried to indicate wherever possible where further information on particular topics is to be found. But the lesson to be learned, especially so far as agtech is concerned, is that it is now no more possible to corral all the investments taking place in agribusiness, or the available information, than it would be in telecoms or finance, or than it would be possible to assemble all the relevant scientific information about agriculture itself. All I can hope is that there is nothing major missed, whilst I sincerely hope that readers will take the trouble to send me, and through me all those who have bought the book, any additional information or thoughts – initially, at least, for the accompanying eResources for the book. This is especially valuable at a time of such rapid change in agribusiness, agtech in particular.

The eResources are an essential part of this book, especially from a teaching perspective. I have included there four types of resources:

- A set of PowerPoint slides for each chapter;
- The documents referenced in each chapter, except for those protected by copyright such as academic articles not available under open access;
- Some suggested questions for discussion; and

■ Additional case studies and other materials, such as Excel files not referenced in the chapter but relevant to the subject matter and which I believe may be useful as teaching resources. As time goes on the number of these additional case studies and files can be expected to rise.

The eResources tab can be accessed at: www.routledge.com/9781138488663

Acknowledgements

My thanks to Mark Blundell, without whose decision to employ me decades ago in the agricultural futures market I would not have conceived an interest in agribusiness. Also to my editor at Woodhead Publishing, Neil Wenborn, who guided me through successive commodity and international trade books with tact and skill. I owe much to the wisdom and foresight of my colleagues in the Commodity Division at UNCTAD, with whom I worked for many years, especially Lamon Rutten and Leonela Santana-Boado. More recently my colleagues at the University of Western Australia, where I have had the privilege to be an Adjunct, are an inspiration. Especial thanks therefore to Professor David Pannell, who originally brought me on board.

During this project I have been helped by many.

I would also like to thank my farming neighbours, both in the Western Australian wheatbelt and in the Highlands of Scotland, whose daily endeavours to provide food are a source of inspiration for agribusiness academics everywhere.

My final thanks are to my wife Gowri and daughter Tabitha for their support during this project.

1

The need for agribusiness

Introduction: what is agribusiness?

One of the most vexing questions about agribusiness is, perhaps alarmingly, its definition. Or more accurately, what are its boundaries? We might usefully paraphrase Wittgenstein's famous point about games, that there is nothing that all agribusinesses have in common, yet all are agribusinesses nonetheless. In an effort to throw a ring around the subject matter, there have however been over time a number of attempts to define an agribusiness.

The most successful, at least judged by frequency of citation, is still the original definition:

> the sum total of all operations involved in the manufacture and distribution of farm supplies; production operations on the farm; and the storage, processing and distribution of farm commodities and items made from them (Davis & Goldberg, 1957:9).

However there have been a number since:

- In a revised definition that included retailers, Sonker & Hudson (1999) defined agribusiness as a sequence of interrelated sub-sectors made up of: (1) genetic and seedstock firms, (2) input suppliers, (3) agricultural producers, (4) merchandisers or first handlers, (5) processors, (6) retailers and (7) consumers. Notably still absent from this definition were trading companies and land and timber investors.

- The Missouri Department of Agriculture's definition from 2003 was similar: farmers and ranchers producing food, fibre and other raw materials, but also processors, handlers, transportation agents and operators, wholesalers, and finally retailers (Ricketts & Ricketts, 2009:5). Again, traders and investors were left out.

- The Agribusiness Council of Australia said that it welcomed all definitions, because it is the commonly held perceptions about agribusiness that is relevant to its acceptance throughout the wider community. In summary, though, it says, the two concepts are:

(i) 'In the context of agribusiness management in academia, each individual element of agriculture production and distribution may be described as agribusiness. However, the term 'agribusiness' most often emphasises the 'interdependence' of these various sectors within the production chain'; and

(ii) 'Among critics of large-scale, industrialized, vertically integrated food production, the term agribusiness is used negatively, synonymous with corporate farming. As such, it is often contrasted with smaller family-owned farms.' (ACA, 2018)

Generally, definitions have become wider over time, and as farming has become more technical and capital-intensive, it has been increasingly recognised as agribusiness, practitioners even being described as 'production agriculturalists' rather than 'farmers'. In accounting for the heterogeneity of the agribusiness sector, it would at least be wise to distinguish between primary and manufacturing agribusiness products, most obviously by using the Standard Industrial Classification (SIC) system. Primary agribusiness includes three categories (agriculture; livestock; forestry), whereas manufacturing agribusiness includes ten categories to reflect the variety of traded products (canned; cereals; drinks; leather; meat; oils; paper; tobacco; wood; other). In addition, there are service agribusinesses, notably supermarkets. Finally, there are the traders and the investors, especially in farmland.

Agribusiness now includes all businesses whose raw materials are primarily products of the land and the sea. Finally, it is worth noting that not all 'businesses' are there to make a profit, or exclusively to do so, especially those owned by the public sector. But however broad the definition, there is no escaping the negative connotations of 'agribusiness' in certain quarters, which should neither be ignored nor celebrated. Rather, advocacy and criticisms of large-scale production should be treated alike, as calls for empirical analysis and evidence-based policymaking wherever possible. As with any contentious subject, this path is not easily trod.

The development of agriculture

The history of agriculture and farming should be swiftly summarised in a contemporary perspective on agribusiness.

Homo sapiens began as nomadic hunters and gatherers, eating wild vegetables, fish and fowl, using fire for cooking. This was followed by farming, and for millennia, agriculture *was* farming – following the seasons in planting and harvesting crops and domesticating animals – to which should be added fishing. Wooden sickles and ploughs gave way to metal in the Bronze Age, which although rainfall appears to have been higher than now also saw irrigation in Egypt and Mesopotamia (Araus *et al.*, 2014), and the use of the wheel; in the Iron Age crops first became part of a commercial system, with the Roman Empire for example prospering on a substantial Mediterranean grain trade (Kessler & Temin, 2007). In the Middle Ages in Europe, crop rotation, fencing, and even limited selective breeding began (Parain, 1966). Increasing efficiency was paralleled by progressively more crops and different animals introduced into agriculture (*National Geographic*, 2018). The use of grains and the development of more productive crops were central to population growth. And grow population did. When farming began, somewhere around 10–15,000 years ago, global human

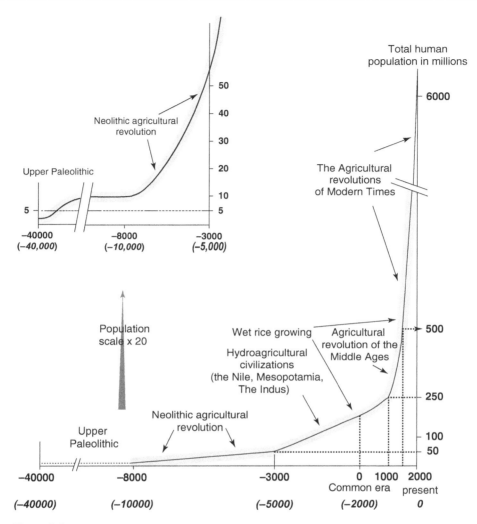

Figure 1.1 Population growth and agricultural systems
Source: Mazoyer & Roubart (2006:63)

population was probably only 1–10 million. Reaching 300 million around the time of Jesus' birth, it doubled in the next millennium and a half. It then rose from 1.5 billion in 1900 to about 7 billion now, and is still rising. True, fertility has declined in most countries, as the 'demographic transition' cuts in, especially in cities, but there are still important exceptions (Zaidi & Morgan, 2017), and the strategic trend is quite dramatic, as Figure 1.1 amply demonstrates. Although it does not include the additional billion people already added since the turn of the century, the figure demonstrates the close correlation between population growth and change in the agricultural systems necessary to support it:

In the later 20th century, artificial insemination for livestock, electric fencing, better ploughs, chemical fertilisers, insecticides and pesticides were all introduced into production

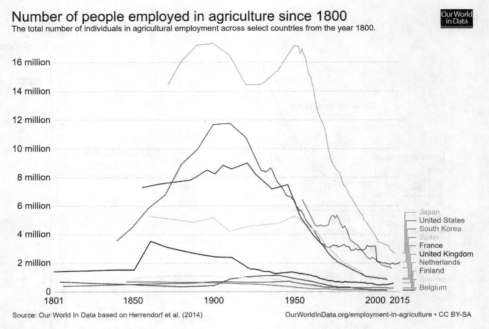

Figure 1.2 Number of people employed in agriculture over time
Source: Roser (2015)

agriculture (Federico, 2005). Risk management techniques improved and agricultural finance became far more widespread. Production grew dramatically, as Figure 1.1 shows, but the effect of the mechanisation that primarily drove production growth was also a dramatic decline in the number of people working in agriculture in advanced economies.

In the 20th century, economies of scale underlay the consolidation of farms that became the norm in developed economies. Whereas in 1900 in the USA there were 5.7 million farms covering 839 million acres, giving an average size of 146 acres (59 hectares), little changed by 1930, in 1997 there were 1.9 million farms covering 932 million acres, giving an average size of 487 acres (197 hectares) (USDA, 2017a). This compares to the EU-28, where in 2013 there were 10.8 million agricultural holdings covering 175 million hectares (some 40.0% of the total land area), giving an average size of 16.1 hectares per agricultural holding (Eurostat, 2015). In France the average farm size is around 50 hectares. And in Australia, home of the largest farm in the world at almost 2.5 million hectares, of all farms with grain in their enterprise mix, the national average for the annually cropped area per farm is just over 800 hectares (ABS, 2018).

In China, however, the average farm size is still just 1 hectares, whilst in Africa smallholders are working with even smaller landholdings (FAO, 2018). In the poorest 20% of countries the average farm size is 1.6 hectares, while in the richest 20% of countries the average farm size is 54.1 hectares, a 34-fold difference. In poor countries, very small farms (less than 2 hectares) account for over 70% of total farms, whereas in rich countries they account for only 15%. In

Table 1.1 ABARES categorisation of Australian broadacre dairy farms

	Small	**Medium**	**Large**
Turnover	<A$450,000	A$450,001–A$1m	>A$1m
% number	70%	20%	10%
% total value of sales	24%	27%	49%
Capital value	<A$5m	A$5–9m	A$9m+
% off-farm income	>50%	<50%	Small percentage

Source: ABA RES (2017:155)

poor countries, by contrast, there are still virtually no farms over 20 hectares, while in rich countries these account for 40% of the total number of farms (Adamopoulos & Restuccia, 2014).

The debate over the survival of family farms has been prolonged. On the one hand is the belief that only massive subsidies are preventing their total eclipse. 'Using smallholdings agriculture as a development policy is like promising an automobile to everyone in the world, but limiting construction to hand labor' (Blumenthal, 2013:112). On the other is the contention that many company farms are family companies, incorporated only for taxation purposes, and that even in developed countries, most farms continue to be operated by families, employing labour in addition to family members. But even Brookfield & Parsons (2007), the last celebrated enthusiasts for family farms, recognised that in what was for them the future there will be fewer of them than before, albeit that some farms will continue to grow whilst others ebb.

This is a far larger definition of 'small' than even the current USDA definition of a farm, which is 'any place from which $1,000 or more of agricultural products were produced and sold, or normally would have been sold, during the year' (USDA, 2014). The USDA's Economic Research Service (ERS) divides farms into four, based on turnover:

- Small family farms both low <$150,000 and medium $150–349,000;

- Mid-size family $350–999,000;

- Large-scale family $1m+, very large $5m+; and

- Non-family farms – primary operator's family does not own 50% or more of the business.

In the 2010s, the USA depended on 7% of its farms, about 155,000 farmers, to produce 80% of the country's agricultural production, and this percentage seems more or less to have stabilised. Dividing farms by income probably makes more sense than by size, especially in countries such as Australia: whilst in Victoria the minimum viable farm size is probably still around 50–100 hectares, even in the more fertile western part of the Wheatbelt of Western Australia 3000 hectares is probably an equivalent, whilst some farmers have more, especially in the East of the Wheatbelt, where the bush becomes the Outback. Generalising across large geographic areas is dangerous, though – parts of the WA Wheatbelt are very fertile, while in others, where the same production requires twice the area or even more, 'low rainfall eastern wheatbelt of Western Australia may cause the optimal farm plan to shift away from strategic cropping to a more extensive grazing system with opportunistic cropping' (Kingwell & Payne, 2015:32–33).

Now, in developed countries, farming is increasingly dominated by technology (Viviano, 2017) and there are sub-disciplines – agricultural production, agroscience and agribusiness. Employment is mainly in the supply chain, not working on farms themselves – in feeds, seeds, farm machinery, fertiliser, biotechnology, chemical supply, food-processing, finance, distribution and marketing (Ricketts & Ricketts, 2009:4) with more no doubt to come as agtech takes hold of production agriculture. But elsewhere in the world, these Organisation for Economic Cooperation and Development (OECD) definitions, and sub-disciplines, however much they may differ from one another, are still relatively alien. That does not however mean that the consequences for employment, a decline in farm employment in particular, seem just as likely, and are already starting to happen – even in Africa (Tschirley *et al.*, 2015).

Yield growth, varietal improvements and the effects of the Green Revolution

The term 'Green Revolution' was coined in 1968 by the US Agency for International Development and encompasses, *inter alia*, breeding of high-yielding crops that positively respond to fertilisers and irrigation. The crops that led the Green Revolution were wheat and rice. Agricultural production more than tripled between 1960 and 2015, owing in part to productivity-enhancing Green Revolution technologies and a significant expansion in the use of land, water and other natural resources for agricultural purposes (FAO, 2017:4). The International Rice Research Institute (IRRI) bred rice in similar ways to those of pioneer Norman Borlaug when he bred wheat in Mexico in the middle years of last century. A key feature was to shorten and strengthen the stems (straw) such that the plant could bear more grain without collapsing, since it is difficult to achieve a realised higher yield when the heads of grain fall to the ground. This shortening of the stem was the result of introducing 'semidwarfness' genes, which allowed the plant to make much better use of fertiliser and water in producing higher recoverable yields. Borlaug also bred for resistance to wheat diseases such as the devastating stem rust, a serious problem at the time but eventually overcome by the use of genes to provide resistance. Green Revolution technology has been extended to many other developing-country crops, including sorghum, millet, maize, cassava and beans. For many years, optimism about increased yields was the global norm.

But in fact, earlier rates of growth slowed: 'Since the 1990s, annual average increases in the yields of maize, rice and wheat at the global level have been slightly more than 1%, whilst those of soybeans and sugarcane have been even less (FAO, 2017a:48). Then in 1998 a new strain of stem rust was detected and reported in Uganda (known as Ug99). An estimated 80–90% of the world's wheat varieties are susceptible to this strain, and the pathogen was spreading to other countries. A huge effort was mounted to develop resistant varieties, largely funded by the Bill & Melinda Gates Foundation. Several varieties were eventually made

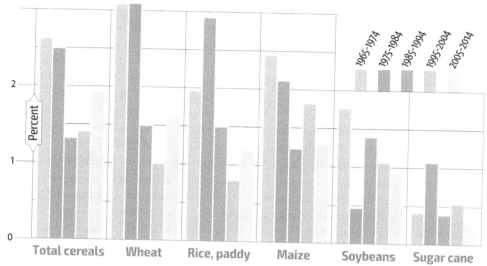

Note: Calculations based on FAOSTAT production statistics (downloaded on 20 September 2016). Growth rates estimated using the ordinary least squares (OLS) regression of the natural logarithm of crop yields on time and a constant term. The commodity group 'Cereals (total)' is from FAOSTAT and includes: wheat, rice (paddy), barley, maize, rye oats, millet, sorghum, buckwheat, quinoa, fonio, triticale, canary seed, as well as grains and mixed cereals not elsewhere specified.

Figure 1.3 The end of the Green Revolution? The slowing of yield growth over time
Source: FAO (2017a:48)

available for Africa with a reasonable degree of resistance to Ug99, but the problem was an early warning sign that the Green Revolution needed to be, at best, a permanent kind of revolution if it were to continue to succeed.

Optimism needed to come from another quarter. In low income countries, livestock production has been one of the fastest growing sectors. The increased use of land, irrigation and agrochemicals all played a major role. However, 'It is now recognised that the gains were often accompanied by negative effects on agriculture's resource base, including land degradation, salinization of irrigated areas, over-extraction of groundwater, the build-up of pest resistance and a decline in biodiversity. The challenge of any further 'Green Revolution' is to avoid these negative effects whilst still raising productivity' (FAO, 2011a). Here lay, and continues to lie, the real opportunities, which certainly still do exist: yields for the majority of crops and vegetables vary substantially across regions. Estimated yield gaps – the difference between actual and possible yields – exceed 50% in most developing countries. The cause is the difference between agriculture using technology, and that which does not.

Agribusiness matters because food matters

Notwithstanding this rapid growth in population, therefore, the overall picture, now relatively stable for many years, is that production is keeping pace with consumption globally. The importance of the sector is underlined by the fact that, globally, 30% of all employment is still in primary agriculture. The share rises to over 50% in India (Indian Government, 2018) and around 60% in sub-Saharan Africa and – perhaps surprisingly – still in China (Huang *et al.*, 2017:192), but falls to less than 10% in developed countries.

Volatility notwithstanding, in developed countries, the good news is that food is vastly cheaper in relative terms than in the past. In the USA, the USDA estimated that in 1960, 17.5% of household income was spent on food, falling to less than 10% in the 2000s. This compares to about 40% of household consumer expenditures in Guatemala and the Philippines and over half in Nigeria, whilst even the French and the Japanese spend about double US averages (World Economic Forum, 2016; USDA, 2018a).

The bad news is that sufficient production globally is not enough on its own to replicate this trend universally, or to prevent hunger, even starvation. This is now usually expressed in terms of a problem of food security in regions and countries. Africa has the highest levels of severe food insecurity, reaching over a quarter of the population, four times as many as any other region – and as the century wears on, the problem has appeared to grow (FAO, 2017:17). By the tail end of the second decade of the new century, the FAO reported that, after a prolonged decline, world hunger, the elimination of which is the principal goal of the FAO, appeared to be on the rise again. The estimated number of undernourished people increased dramatically and threatened to reach a billion. The worrying trend in undernourishment is not reflected in levels of chronic child malnutrition (stunting), at least, which continue to fall – but at a slower rate in several regions. Stunting still nevertheless affects well over 100 million children, in some regions one-third of children under five. Wasting continues to threaten the lives of over 50 million children, whilst almost one-third of women of reproductive age worldwide have suffered from anaemia, which also puts the nutrition and health of many children at risk (FAO, 2017:1). The World Food Programme, which has produced an annual report on food insecurity, reported that an estimated 124 million people in 51 countries were facing crisis-level food insecurity. However, the usual definition, 'a situation that exists when all people, at all times, have physical, social, and economic access to sufficient, safe, and nutritious food that meets their dietary needs and food preferences for an active and healthy life' (FAO, 2003:296; Tadele, 2017) is relatively hard to achieve, as even in an advanced country such as the UK there is still poverty, and an estimated one in ten people do not eat properly (Taylor & Loopstra, 2016), a figure that rises to one in seven in the USA (USDA, 2017c).

Severe and persistent drought in eastern and southern Africa, and other climatic events, such as hurricanes in the Caribbean, have also reinforced food insecurity: 90% of production losses in sub-Saharan Africa were linked to droughts between 2003 and 2013. Since the production agriculture sector in sub-Saharan Africa on average contributes to a quarter of GDP (rising to a half when all sub-sectors of agribusiness are included), droughts have a clear negative multiplier effect on the economy (i.e. that when agricultural production falls, other sectors decline as well). Other regions affected by drought are Latin America (30%), the Far East (50%) and Asia (10%). Droughts directly affect agriculture through decreased yields and production, and have indirect socio-economic impacts such as unemployment, food scarcity or increased costs, lower tax revenues and increased loan foreclosures (World Bank, 2017:14).

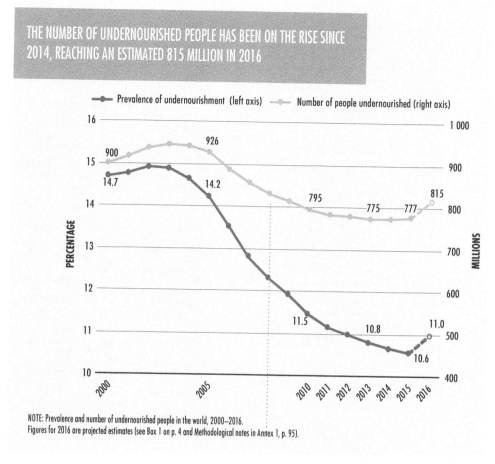

Figure 1.4 FAO reporting on world hunger in recent years
Source: FAO (2017:5)

Conflict and insecurity, however, exacerbated by climate change, continued to be the primary drivers of food insecurity in dozens of countries, such as the Yemen, the Democratic Republic of the Congo and South Sudan, where millions of food-insecure people remain in need of urgent assistance (WFP, 2018). South Sudan is a good example of the real problem and the reason for it.

Most — almost all, actually, although international organisations are wary of pointing blame — of the recent increase in food insecurity can therefore be traced to the greater number of conflicts, often exacerbated by climate-related shocks, as the number of UN interventions testifies. The remainder, especially in developed countries, can be ascribed to economic policies that permit widening inequality alongside freedom in individual decision-making that can frequently put family nutrition low on personal agendas.

South Sudan is an example of how conflict can affect the lives and livelihoods of the population in multiple ways, resulting in a humanitarian catastrophe on an enormous scale and with destructive longer-term impacts on livelihoods, as well as on the agriculture and food systems upon which these depend. In December 2013, two and half years after South Sudan gained its independence, large-scale violence erupted in the Greater Upper Nile Region and by 2016 had spread to Greater Equatoria and Western Bahr el Ghazal.

The ongoing conflict caused acute food insecurity to increase dramatically, with famine declared in parts of Greater Upper Unity State in February 2017 (see figure). More than 4.9 million people (over 42 percent of the population) are currently severely food insecure (IPC Phases 3–5), a number that is projected to increase to 5.5 million in 2017 if the situation is left unaddressed.[1]

Widespread acute malnutrition is giving rise to a major public health emergency: one in three children is acutely malnourished in the southern part of Unity State, and out of 23 counties, 14 have global acute malnutrition (GAM) at or above the emergency threshold of 15 percent. Rates of GAM of more than 30 percent were observed in Leer and Panyijiar and of 27.3 percent in Mayendit. These high levels are caused by reduced food access and by child, maternal and public health factors. The situation is exacerbated by a number of factors, including inadequate diets, low quality and coverage of water and sanitation facilities, as well as poor access to and levels of basic health services.

Armed conflict and communal violence are destroying rural livelihoods, decimating assets, deepening poverty and increasing the vulnerability of millions of people. Agricultural production and food systems have been disrupted, livestock production has declined significantly, and the spread of violence to cereal surplus-producing areas in Equatoria is severely affecting crop production. Violence is limiting market access and disrupting trade flows, affecting livestock

producers, consumers and traders alike. The economic impact of the current conflict on the livestock sector – which constitutes 15 percent of GDP – has been extensive, as livestock have been direct targets of insurgency and counterinsurgency warfare. It is estimated that the loss of GDP attributed to the livestock sector is between US$1.4 billion and US$2 billion (2014–16).[2]

Food access has been hampered by sharp increases in prices, with inflation driven by shortages, currency devaluation and high transport costs owing to insecurity along major trading routes. The year-on-year inflation rate peaked at 836 percent in October 2016: the value of the South Sudanese pound (SSP) depreciated from SSP16 to the US dollar in August 2015 to SSP74 in November 2016. The conflict in Juba in July 2016 restricted inflows of imported food through the main southern supply corridor from Uganda, reducing food supplies and further driving up prices. In July 2016, cereal prices were more than double those of June and almost ten times higher than 2015 levels.[3]

A lack of financial and physical access to food is limiting individual and household food consumption, with real labour incomes and the relative price of livestock falling dramatically. Meanwhile, violence and insecurity have led to the depletion and loss of assets such as livestock and key household food sources such as standing crops and grain stocks.

In the worst-affected areas, food is being used as a weapon of war, with trade blockades and security threats leaving people marooned in swamps with no access to food or health care. Humanitarian access to the worst-hit areas is limited, as warring factions are intentionally blocking emergency food, hijacking aid trucks and killing relief workers. A lack of protection of civilians against violence has led to 1.9 million internally displaced persons and more than 1.26 million refugees, who have lost their livelihoods and are dependent on support for their survival.[3]

[1] IPC. 2017. *Key IPC findings: January–July 2017. The Republic of South Sudan.*
[2] Y.A. Gebreyes. 2016. *The impact of the conflict on the livestock sector in South Sudan.* FAO.
[3] FSIN. 2017. *Global Report on Food Crises 2017.*
SOURCES: IPC. 2013. *Acute food insecurity overview. Republic of South Sudan;* IPC. 2015. *Food security and nutrition analysis – key messages;* IPC. 2016. *Communication summary. The Republic of South Sudan;* and IPC. 2017. *Key IPC findings: January–July 2017. The Republic of South Sudan.*

Figure 1.5 South Sudan: FAO facts
Source: FAO (2017:42)

Agricultural production: sub-sectors

The structure of agricultural production globally is itself an increased focus of attention. Since the early 1970s, global per capita consumption of milk, dairy products and vegetable oils has almost doubled, fish has more than doubled (almost all from aquaculture), whilst meat consumption has almost tripled, the consequences of which influence the whole of agribusiness worldwide.

The generally agreed taxonomy of flowering plants is as shown in Figure 1.6.

Amongst the major staples

Rice.

Worldwide there are more than 40,000 different varieties of *Oryza sativa*, classified into four major categories: indica, japonica, aromatic and glutinous. *Oryza sativa* contains two major subspecies: the sticky, short grained japonica or sinica, and the non-sticky, long-grained indica. Japonica varieties are usually cultivated in dry fields, in temperate East Asia, upland areas of Southeast Asia and high elevations in South Asia, while indica varieties are mainly lowland varieties, grown mostly submerged, throughout tropical Asia (Ricepedia, 2018).

Is rice production stable? Yes, and growing slowly. It is the most produced food crop and makes up more than 20% of human calories (Giraud, 2013). In Asia, where 90% of rice is grown, it is of course a dietary staple. China is the leading producer: Hunan is the largest rice-producing province, and most rice production is in the Yangtze River Valley (or farther south) where ample supplies of water are available. However, rice production in northern China has increased substantially in recent years, in Heilongjiang and the other two north-eastern provinces of Jilin and Liaoning, but also in Henan and Shandong (CGIAR, 2012). In the USA, rice production is concentrated in the Southern States: California and along the Mississippi River. Rice forms a vital part of food aid programmes. Information on rice is plentiful: the Food and Agriculture Organisation of the United Nations (FAO), the international system's food intergovernmental organisation, maintains a large database on rice production and trade, and reports regularly on the rice market (FAO, 2018a). Information is also readily available from the International Rice Research Institute (IRRI) in the Philippines. Private sector databases and subscription services also provide information on production, trade, prices and deals even more frequently, intra-day, as well as a regular newsletter and consult (Oryza, 2018). Making sense of the information, however, is not easy.

Wheat. There are thousands of wheat varieties (KSU, 2018), but wheat taxonomy has generally divided them into six. It is a robust crop which can be grown in many different climates, for example the north-western USA and Pakistan, as it can survive in dry and cold weather. China produces most, India next, the USA third. Hard wheat has high protein and is used for bread, buns, pasta, pizza crusts, etc. Soft wheat is the opposite, and is used for biscuits, cakes, pastries, crackers, noodles and steam bread. White wheat, which needs no breaching, is also the least bitter in taste, and is used for making bread (Kansas Wheat, 2014). Overall, although worldwide wheat demand is softening, it is still sown on more land than any other crop.

As an example of what information is publicly available, Figure 1.9 shows what the United States Department of Agriculture (USDA)'s monthly report had to say about the global wheat market in May 2018.

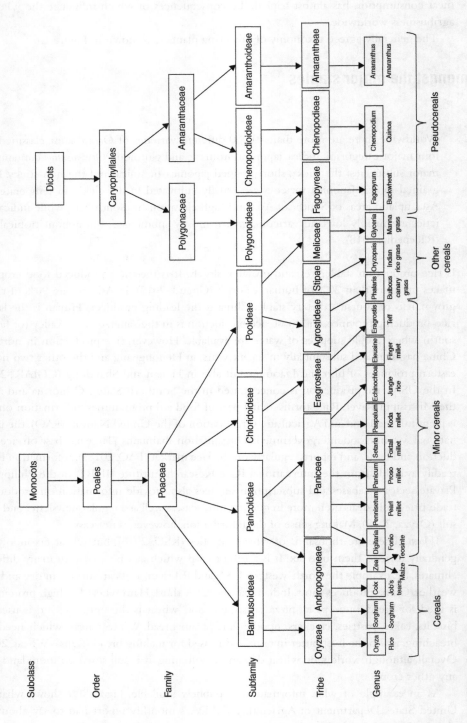

Figure 1.6 Plant taxonomy
Source: Moreno et al. (2014)

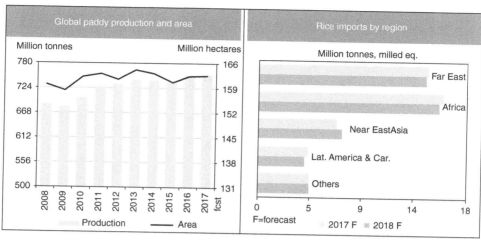

Figure 1.7 FAO rice statistics
Source: FAO (2018a)

Similar reports are produced by the International Grains Council (International Grains Council, 2018). Actual production in the EU, by comparison, has been relatively stable for almost a decade; Eurostat (the EU's statistical service) provides detailed information on production and use.

Maize, or corn, *Zea mays*, is the world's most important grain based on production volume, with around 1 billion tonnes harvested annually. Less than 0.2% is the 'sweet corn' consumer product. The remainder is field or dent corn, for animal feed, ethanol and corn products (corn syrup, starch, etc). Just over a third is grown in the USA, mainly in Iowa, Illinois and Nebraska, and most of the remainder in China, Ukraine, Argentina and Brazil. The USA is the world's leading corn exporter, though exported volumes have been relatively stable (Statista, 2018). Importing countries use US corn mainly to feed livestock, as in China where it is used to feed pigs, but also poultry and fish – a sharp contrast with US domestic use, where almost half goes for ethanol production (see the section below). Analysis drew attention to the potential risk that climate change poses to maize yields worldwide (Tigchelaar *et al.*, 2018), which in turn could have significant effects on the cost of raising livestock.

Soybeans (Glycine max) are of the legume family, which includes dried beans, peas and lentils. An annual crop, they are used for food and oils, and add nitrogen to soils, often alternating with corn. They are high protein producers – twice other crops, and many more than animals. Production is now greater than maize in the USA, although there are held to be significant environmental risks from soy production, especially connected with deforestation in the Amazon.

Animal husbandry refers to the best – most cost-effective and yet sympathetic – method of keeping animals for agricultural production. In developed countries, the main animal enterprises with the greatest value of production are beef cattle and calves, dairy cattle, sheep, hogs and poultry. There are, for example, about a billion head of cattle in the world,

The Six Classes of Wheat

A look at the six classes of wheat grown in the U.S. and the food products made from them.

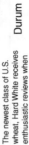

Hard Red Winter

Versatile, with excellent milling and baking characteristics for pan bread, Hard Red Winter is also a choice wheat for Asian noodles, hard rolls, flat breads, general purpose flour and cereal.

Hard Red Spring

The aristocrat of wheat when it comes to "designer" wheat foods like hearth breads, rolls, croissants, bagels and pizza crust. Hard Red Spring is also a valued improver in flour blends.

Soft Red Winter

A versatile weak-gluten wheat with excellent milling and baking characteristics, Soft Red Winter is suited for cookies, crackers, pretzels, pastries and flat breads.

Soft White

A low moisture wheat with high extraction rates, providing a whiter product for exquisite cakes, pastries and Asian-style noodels. Soft White is also ideally suited to Middle Eastern flat breads.

Hard White

The newest class of U.S. wheat, Hard White receives enthusiastic reviews when used for Asian noodles, whole wheat or high extraction appications, pan breads and flat breads.

Durum

The hardest of all wheats, Durum has a rich amber color and high gluten content, ideal for pasta, couscous and some Mediterranean breads.

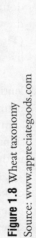

Figure 1.8 Wheat taxonomy
Source: www.appreciategoods.com

United States Department of Agriculture

ISSN: 1554-9089

World Agricultural Supply and Demand Estimates

Office of the Chief Economist	Agricultural Marketing Service Farm Service Agency	Economic Research Service Foreign Agricultural Service
WASDE - 577	Approved by the World Agricultural Outlook Board	May 10, 2018

Note: This report presents USDA's initial assessment of U.S. and world crop supply and demand prospects and U.S. prices for 2018/19. Also presented are the first calendar-year 2019 projections of U.S. livestock, poultry, and dairy products. Due to spring planting still underway in the Northern Hemisphere, and being several months away in the Southern Hemisphere, these projections are highly tentative. Forecasts for U.S. winter wheat area, yield, and production are from the May 10 *Crop Production* report. For other U.S. crops, the March 29 *Prospective Plantings* report is used for planted acreage. Methods used to project 2018/19 harvested acreage and yield are noted in each table.

WHEAT: The 2018/19 U.S. wheat crop is projected at 1,821 million bushels, up 5 percent from the prior year. The year-over-year increase is due to greater harvested area and slightly higher yield. Reduced beginning stocks and imports bring total supplies down 49 million bushels from the previous year. The all wheat yield is projected at 46.8 bushels per acre, up slightly from 2017/18. Winter wheat yields are below average in the drought affected states of Kansas, Oklahoma, and Texas. Combined spring wheat and Durum production for 2018/19 is projected to increase 34 percent from the previous year's low, which is due to both increased area and yield.

Total 2018/19 use is projected up 3 percent on higher food, feed and residual, and exports. Food use is projected at a record 965 million bushels, up 2.0 million bushels from the previous year's revised estimate. U.S. feed and residual use is projected at 120 million bushels, up 50 million bushels from last year's low level but still below the 5-year-average. Exports are projected at 925 million bushels, up 15 million bushels from the revised 2017/18 total. Ending stocks for 2018/19 are projected down 115 million bushels to 955 million, which if realized would be a 4-year-low. The season-average farm price is projected at a range of $4.50 to $5.50 per bushel. The midpoint of this range is up $0.30 per bushel from the previous year and the highest since 2014/15.

Global wheat supplies for 2018/19 are projected to increase fractionally as higher beginning stocks are partially offset by a production decline following last year's record. Global wheat production is projected at 747.8 million tons, down 10.6 million from the previous year's record. Most of the year-over-year production decline stems from a 13.0-million-ton reduction for Russia. Global wheat consumption is projected at a record 753.9 million tons, up 10.1 million from 2017/18. Global imports are expected to increase 3.5 million tons in 2018/19 for the sixth consecutive record. With total use rising faster than supplies, global ending stocks are projected to decline 6.1 million tons to 264.3 million.

Figure 1.9 World agricultural supply and demand estimates
Source: USDA (2018)

of which just under a third are for dairy. India has over 30% of the total,[1] Brazil 23%, China 10% and the USA and the European Union both around 9% (Beef2Live, 2018). In the USA approximately 750,000 ranchers command $500 billion in annual revenue, but production is very fragmented: only 5,000 ranches own more than 500 cattle. Breeding cattle for dairy production is a relatively recent activity, less than a century old, but dairy has risen in importance: milk production has been, in the 2010s, the main purpose of selecting breeds and evaluating individual cow performance, with the poor-performing cows – and many calves – sent for slaughter. Although most dairy operators are still small family farms, they contribute less than a fifth of annual US dairy production. Milk production is rising, using more cattle, in regions such as South-East Asia, including countries not traditionally noted for their milk consumption, and China, which now has over 12% of its total cattle stock as

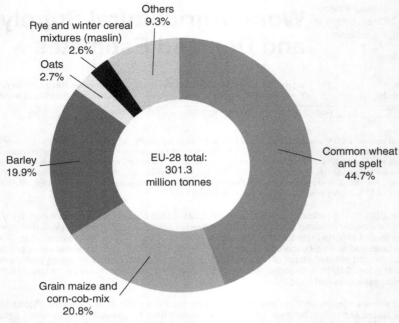

Note: 'Total cereals' includes cereals for the production of grain (including seed).
'Others' includes rice, triticale, sorghum and buckwheat, millet, canary seed, etc.)

Figure 1.10 EU production and use of cereals
Source: Eurostat (2015)

dairy. As for sheep, kept not only for meat (an A$3–billion industry, increasing annually) but also for their wool and, increasingly, their milk. Australia still leads the way in numbers and experience, although China is now the world's leading wool producer. Most notably in Australia, too, grain farmers have lost the fences and shearing sheds they need to return to livestock. Shearing labour is now also at a premium (Barrett & Packham, 2018).

Keeping animals is neither easy, nor cheap.

The main issues in Africa, for example, are:

- Limited amount of feed – availability of feed is low, especially during the dry season. Preservation of animal feed is very rarely practised.
- Susceptibility to parasites and diseases – due to a lack of closer management attention, insufficient feeding and unfavourable weather and housing conditions common in many systems, animals are very susceptible to disease and parasite infections.
- Limited knowledge on proper animal breeding – in many situations, animals move together in mixed groups of females and males. They mate randomly without much control from the farmer, hence propagating inferior traits (Organic Africa, 2018).

Just bringing African and other developing country animal husbandry practices into line with best international practice, as agribusiness firms seek to do, can alone significantly improve productivity, as well as animal welfare, which is already of great importance to consumers in the developed world (Heise & Theuvsen, 2017) and which eventually will become a concern of the whole world.

Fibre. Not all agriculture is for food. The most well-known agricultural fibres are *cotton* and *wool*, where volume and price information are plentiful. Cotton is the most produced and used natural fibre worldwide.

Specifically, 50% more cotton is produced worldwide today on the same amount of land as compared to 40 some years ago. And though cotton occupies less than 3% of the world's agricultural land, cotton production provides two crops with each seasonal harvest: cotton fiber, which currently supplies 30% of the world's textile fiber needs; and cottonseed, a source of nutritious cooking oil and a protein-rich supplement for dairy cattle and aquaculture feeds (Cotton Today, 2018).

India, China and the USA are the largest producers, responsible for more than the half of the world's total production volume. Though part of agribusiness, cotton is also an important component of the textile industry, and the global market is dominated by China (Quark & Slez, 2014; Gu & Patton, 2018).

There are, however, many other types of natural fibre:

Natural fibres have been used to reinforce materials for over 3000 years. More currently they have been employed in combination with plastics. Many types of natural fibres have been investigated for use in plastics including flax, hemp, jute, and banana. Natural fibres have the advantage that they are renewable resources and have marketing appeal (Sakthivei & Ramesh, 2013:1).

One of the most important of these is *jute*, a versatile fibre which can be used either on its own or combined with other fibres and materials, mainly for sacking. Although threatened by synthetic materials in many of its uses, its biodegradable nature, is of benefit in, for example, containers for planting young trees, or geotextiles for soil and erosion control where the application is designed to break down after some time and where no removal is required. Limited price statistics for jute and other minor fibre markets are available from the FAO, but jute is an example of a highly specialised and not especially transparent market, especially as the majority of transactions take place in the Indian subcontinent.

Another very detailed market is that for *silk*. Silk is claimed to be 'the most elegant textile in the world with unparalleled grandeur, natural sheen, and inherent affinity for dyes, high absorbance, light weight, soft touch and high durability and known as the "Queen of Textiles" the world over' (Central Silk Board, 2016:1). On the other hand, it provides millions of jobs in China and India, as it is labour-intensive in cultivation. India is the only country producing all the five known commercial silks, namely mulberry, tropical tasar, oak tasar, eri and muga, of which muga is largely only produced in India.

Horticulture is the culture of plants for food, as well as for general welfare purposes. The word itself derives from the Latin for garden culture. It now includes several distinct divisions, each with its own key performance indicators. Planting, harvesting, storing, processing and marketing – vegetable food crops like sweetcorn, lettuce or tomatoes is *olericulture*. *Pomology* refers to an analogous activity with fruit and nuts. Amongst fruits, in the USA the leaders are grapes, oranges and apples, whilst amongst nuts almonds lead the production table, although Asia-Pac now produces more fruit and vegetables than any other region. To this can be added *viticulture,* the same for grapes and the production of wine, where traditional production countries such as France, Spain and Italy have now for decades been challenged by New World wines from Australia, the USA and Argentina, themselves now facing new competition even from China. *Ornamental* horticulture is about decoration, including both flowering and foliage plants for internal and external use – think garden centres or nursery production: a huge business in developed countries, $41 billion in the USA alone in 2016.

Fruit and vegetables are of huge alimentary benefit, although the quantity consumed is almost universally lower than the 400g daily recommended by the World Health Organisation. Largely this is for reasons of taste: generally, people do not enjoy eating fruit and vegetables so, unfortunately, they do not feature highly either in ready meals or in dining out. Urban areas are often not well served, whilst the picture in at least some rural areas, especially in agricultural regions, is quite different. Demand for all-year round supply of a wide range of fruits and vegetables is increasing worldwide, along with demand for 'organic' produce and associated concerns about conventional production methods. Developing markets will end up where OECD consumers already are, highly aware of the health benefits and risks of particular foods, even if they do not always, or even frequently, act accordingly.

Aquaculture is the farming and husbandry of aquatic organisms under controlled or semi-controlled conditions. These organisms may be plants, fish or shellfish – clams, crayfish, mussels, oysters, prawns, shrimps, etc. Aquaculture is used for a variety of ends, not just intensive food production: fish may be raised for leisure or commercial fishing, for example. In developed countries, sophisticated systems enable each fish cage to receive its own supply of feed depending on the number and size of the fish, temperature and time of year. This has enabled the production time for salmon from 100g to harvest size, 4–5 kg, to be cut drastically, from three years to just 18 months (Adoff, 2018). Whilst aquaculture is already well established in developed countries, its biggest opportunities probably lie elsewhere. It is little wonder that the Russian government, for example, is anxious to encourage it (USDA, 2017b). Most aquaculture in Africa is still in Egypt, where 80% of the continent's farmed fish production takes place. Although most African countries have water to support aquaculture, historically development has been in inland countries like Zambia, where the population has a custom of eating fish and the fish in rivers and lakes have been exploited to the maximum. The species fish-farmed in South Africa have been very different from in Europe – abalone, yellowtail and dusky cob – as the country has legislation that makes it difficult to bring in other species that are not indigenous and farm them there. In the rest of Africa, the most commonly farmed fish is the indigenous tilapia, which are easy to cultivate even on a small scale; a smallholder can dig out a pond and fertilise it and fish live off natural production from nutrients and sunlight (Karen, 2012).

Forestry. In virtually no area of agribusiness has the impact of land values, public policy, including taxation, and that of climate change been greater than in the case of silviculture. Commercial forestry for pulp and paper as well as for tourism, specific production uses (e.g. sandalwood) and the use of forestry for carbon offsets are the principal drivers of the industry. It is a straightforward argument that over the last 30 years, the context of forest management in the USA, along with other developed countries, has gone through one of its most dynamic periods in history. Record accumulation of fuel loads (the aboveground organic biomass components that can contribute to wildland fires), extreme fire events (megafires), and epidemic insect outbreaks, often as a result of extended drought, fire exclusion and management policies (Rego *et al.*, 2018), have affected forests, especially in the West. In addition, during this period, changing ownership and land tenure patterns, rural land urbanisation, increased globalisation of forest markets, decreases in demand for wood products, operational-scale adoption of forest certification standards and best management practices (BMPs), and conservation easements have all influenced silvicultural decision-making. With the exception of private, intensively managed forestlands, forest management objectives have been broadened and go beyond the historical importance of managing for sustained timber yield. Contemporary silvicultural prescriptions for a range of land ownerships may also include elements of invasive species management; conserving old forest ecosystems and riparian reserves; enhancing water quantity and quality; recreation; aesthetics; augmenting biological diversity; and the restoration of endangered, threatened and sensitive species and ecosystems' (D'Amato *et al.*, 2018). None of these objectives, however laudable, are necessarily easily compatible with high financial returns.

Bioenergy and biofuels have been the subject of much debate. According to the FAO (2017), about two-thirds of the bioenergy used worldwide is for cooking and heating, mainly by burning wood inefficiently. Biofuel production itself has risen, more than doubling in the last decade with continued growth expected. The FAO pointed out that in the first decade of the new century, world cereal consumption increased by 1.8% annually – almost a third went to US biofuel production, which has also taken much vegetable oil production. The FAO also noted that 'the greater competition between food and non-food uses of biomass has increased the interdependence between food, feed and energy markets' (FAO, 2017a:35).

Ethanol production. Ethanol, derived mainly from sugarcane and corn, but which can be extracted from a wide range of crops, can be blended with gasoline for gasohol, to be used for fuel. Brazil is the second-largest bioethanol producer and the greatest exporter. E85, the main product, is 85% ethanol and 15% gasoline. The USA (the greatest producer) and Brazil have together been responsible for 70% of the world ethanol, with the sugar cane industry accounting in the last decade for as much as 2% of Brazil's GDP: Brazil's sugarcane in the 2010s accounted for about 20% of world supply and 60% of global trade. One of the biggest domestic uses of sugarcane is ethanol. Almost all passenger vehicles in Brazil are flex-fuel; they run on gasoline or a biofuel with as much as 85% ethanol (Kostreva, 2014). Europe follows, supplying around 5%, followed by Canada supplying 2%. This is an example of a complex political issue within agribusiness: the US Renewable Fuel Standard (RFS) programme in relation to ethanol was introduced in the Energy Policy Act of 2005 and the Energy Independence and Security Act of 2007, and has in fact prompted significant changes in agricultural markets (Sant'Anna *et al.*, 2016). But in 2016, after a lengthy battle, the Renewable Fuel Standard (RFS) was finally put 'back on track' when the Environmental Protection Agency (EPA) announced blending requirements would be returned to statutory levels. Meanwhile, farmers harvested a record corn crop, ensuring ample feedstock supplies. Excessive production costs have continued to limit the quantity of non-corn-based biofuels, placing a greater burden on corn to fulfil the mandated ethanol production requirement and leading to a reallocation of corn away from its traditional uses in domestic livestock and poultry feed. Technological advances that allowed a corn-ethanol by-product – distillers' dried grains (DDGs) – to be used as a supplement to livestock feed became a partial saving grace during this market transformation. The result was a quickly emerging domestic market (and more recently an international market) for DDGs (Bekkerman & Tejeda, 2017:175). However, this remains a volatile industry and ethanol producers continued to face a number of important challenges.

- **Biodiesel.** This is a domestically produced, renewable fuel that can be manufactured from vegetable oils such as soybeans, animal fats or recycled restaurant grease, either pure or in e.g. an 80:20 blend with oil-based diesel, for use in diesel vehicles. It is the most widely used renewable agricultural energy source.

- **Methane.** This amounts to approximately two-thirds of biogas production. Feed or dairy is the main source of production, and its use as fuel eliminates the need for its disposal. Even the residue, humus, is a good fertilizer.

- **Wood burning.** Millions of people worldwide rely on wood-burning stoves for some or all of their home heating and cooking. The rising cost of home fuel together with social trends towards 'natural' fuel use is responsible, although there is medical evidence to suggest that prolonged exposure to fumes from burning wood is highly undesirable (Taleb *et al.*, 2014).

International distribution of production and consumption of major agricultural commodities

This changes constantly and is most frequently reported from monthly to annually. Information can be found in publicly available research documents, such as those published by agencies including the USDA (USDA, 2018), FAO (FAO, 2017) and private sector organisations such as Rabobank (2016, 2017, 2018). But for anyone attempting to understand the progress of agricultural markets, e.g. for trading purposes, there is simply too much information produced from too many sources to make an overall view of agricultural commodities even possible for one person. AI systems can do it: but developing reliable investment or trading algorithms on the basis of publicly available information is hard to do. The best advice possible is to start by specialising – by commodity, and then by market.

Some examples:

- At 157 million hectares, India holds the second largest amount of agricultural land in the world. Agriculture plays a vital role in India's economy. Almost 60% of rural households depend on agriculture as their principal means of livelihood. The share of primary sectors (including agriculture, livestock, forestry and fishery) was estimated to be about a fifth of gross value added (GVA) in the 2010s. India's food grain production reached 276 million tonnes in 2016. With at least 20 distinct climate regions, all the major climates in the world exist in India. The country also possesses 46 of the 60 soil types in the world. India is the largest producer of major agricultural and horticulture crops: spices, pulses, milk – India has been the world's largest producer of milk for the last two decades and contributes 19% of the world's total milk production – tea, cashew and jute; and is the second-largest producer of wheat, rice, fruits and vegetables, sugarcane, cotton and oilseeds (IBEF, 2017, 2018).

- In Nigeria, the northern region supports grains (such as millet, sorghum and maize) and groundnuts; the centre, which produces most of the country's food, rice, tubers (crops such as potatoes and sweet potatoes, as opposed to roots such as beets and carrots), fruits and vegetables; the eastern belt, tubers as well as oil palm; and the west, cocoa. Cattle graze in the open fields of the north, fishing is concentrated along the coast and rivers, and poultry are everywhere. On the one hand, agriculture is the mainstay of the economy, contributing 24.18% to real gross domestic product in Q4 2015 (PwC, 2016:3). On the other hand, of an estimated 71 million hectares of cultivable land in Nigeria, only half is currently used for farming; there is similar potential for an expansion of irrigation, which now only covers 7% of irrigable land. Most of the rural population farms on a subsistence scale, using small plots and depending on seasonal rainfall. A lack of infrastructure such as roads further exacerbates food-poverty in rural areas by isolating rural farmers from needed inputs and profitable markets. Pressure from growing populations, and in the north, conflict, is also impacting already diminished resources, further threatening food production in Nigeria. As a result, food insecurity in Nigeria is of major concern (Omatayo et al., 2018).

- For China, the USDA reported on the publication of China's annual agricultural goals that the bottom line for the Chinese government was 'absolute security' in the area of staple grains (i.e. rice and wheat). Parts of the country have been reserved for specific crops, partly to maintain production, but also to take advantage of economies of scale. Policies are in place for specific crops and sub-sectors, obviously pigs but even wine as well. 'Production of grass-fed cattle and sheep will be encouraged. In an effort to revive the dairy industry, the government will support the development of family ranches and foster domestic dairy brands' (USDA, 2017).

  The USDA observed that, whilst food security remains a top priority in China, the focus seems to have shifted from quantity to quality, which is also the core of the so-called supply-side structural reform. In other words, the government encourages farmers to improve product quality or to produce commodities that meet the increased

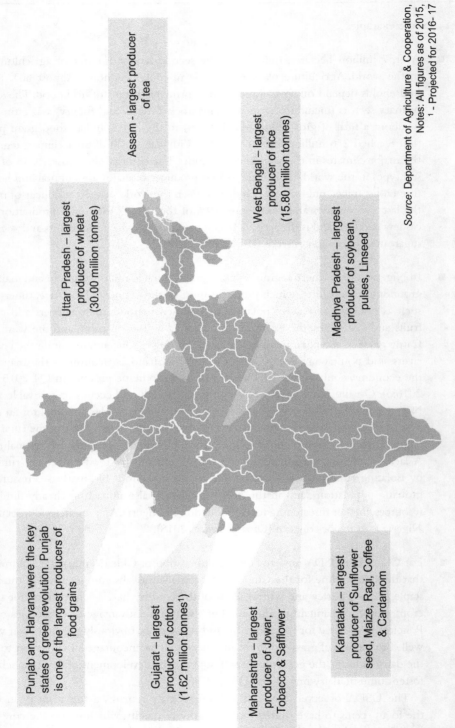

Assam - largest producer of tea

Uttar Pradesh – largest producer of wheat (30.00 million tonnes)

West Bengal – largest producer of rice (15.80 million tonnes)

Madhya Pradesh – largest producer of soybean, pulses, Linseed

Punjab and Haryana were the key states of green revolution. Punjab is one of the largest producers of food grains

Gujarat – largest producer of cotton (1.62 million tonnes[1])

Maharashtra – largest producer of Jowar, Tobacco & Safflower

Karnataka – largest producer of Sunflower seed, Maize, Ragi, Coffee & Cardamom

Source: Department of Agriculture & Cooperation,
Notes: All figures as of 2015,
[1] - Projected for 2016- 17

Figure 1.11 Agricultural production in India by state – key indicators

demand from local consumers for better and more varied agricultural products. For example, the government encourages farmers to plant premium rice varieties and wheat varieties with high/low gluten content. While the government guides farmers to reduce corn acreage, with millions of hectares fewer planted at the end of the 2010s than the outset, China also encourages farmers to expand areas for feed crops, such as silage corn and alfalfa in order to increase grass-fed cattle and sheep production. Farmers are also encouraged to increase production of food-grade soybeans, tuber crops and coarse grains.

Agriculture and the environment in a time of climate change

Climate is the primary determinant of agricultural productivity. Food and fibre production, in turn, are essential for sustaining and enhancing human welfare. Inevitably, therefore, agriculture has been a major focus in discussions about the effects of climate change. This has now been the case for decades: the United Nations Framework Convention on Climate Change (United Nations, 1992) viewed the sustainability of food production as paramount in the objectives for stabilising greenhouse gas (GHG) emissions, with the view that emissions should be stabilised at a level that 'ensures that food production is not threatened' (Muldowney *et al.*, 2013). Clearly, agronomic and economic impacts from climate change depend primarily on two factors:

(1)   The rate and magnitude of change in climate variables and the biophysical effects of these changes; and

(2)   The ability of agricultural systems to adapt to changing environmental conditions (Adams, 2009).

Environmentalists point out that expanding food production and economic growth have often come at a heavy cost to the Earth's natural environment. Croplands cover 12% of the available land and they have, no doubt, a massive environmental impact. Almost one-half of the forests are now gone. Groundwater sources are being depleted rapidly and sometimes irretrievably, for example in Australia, where feeble and largely competitive local government policy has entirely failed to prevent it. Biodiversity on Earth has been deeply eroded, with consequences that are not yet fully understood. Every year, the burning of fossil fuels produces billion of tonnes of greenhouse gases, which are responsible for global warming and climate change. Notably, deforestation, mainly for plantations and farming, produces a significant share of global GHG emissions. Natural resources are being depleted, as much in the Punjab in India (Singh, 2011) as in Africa, ecosystem services are being degraded and there may be pollution of groundwater with pesticide or fertiliser residues, or the atmosphere with nitrous oxide, a potent greenhouse gas. The presence of pesticides in the environment can contribute to adverse ecological effects ranging from fish and wildlife kills to more subtle effects on reproduction and fitness. Due to the toxic effects that pesticides have on pests and potentially to the environment and human health, national regulatory agencies regulate their use and exposure. For example, the EPA has set standards for pesticide residues in drinking water for approximately 200 organic chemicals. All of these negative trends are at least not diminishing, and agriculture is an important part of the problem (FAO, 2017:4).

Agriculture is also a significant direct contributor to climate change. This is because agribusiness uses significant quantities of energy, taking up somewhere between 10–20% of US energy production a decade ago (Ricketts & Ricketts, 2009:53), of which farms, which both produce and consume energy, took about one-third. Globally, estimates of energy use from international agencies are close. The FAO reported that the food sector (including input manufacturing, production, processing, transportation marketing and consumption) accounted for around 95 exajoules – approximately 30% of global output – and produces over 20% of GHG emissions (FAO, 2011), whilst the World Bank estimated 25%, including land use change for agriculture (World Bank, 2015:13).

Whilst the comparative energy efficiency of developed farming in the USA is note-worthy, future energy production will undoubtedly be more decentralised, so statistics of this kind may become obsolete, especially as the energy will be predominantly generated from renewables. But for the time being, there is still reason to be concerned on this score as well.

Moreover, not all agricultural production is created equal. The global shift to meat consumption currently entails far less efficient utilisation of energy than plant-based products. In the USA, though climates vary, one hectare would be enough to feed an individual if wheat, potatoes or another high-producing grain were used. For comparison, it takes an estimated 2–3 calories of fossil fuel to produce 1 calorie of protein from soybeans, corn or wheat. For beef it takes 54 calories of fuel to produce 1 calorie of protein. The result is that almost 50% of the world's harvest is fed to animals. Globally, 90% of the ever-increasing soybean harvest goes for animal feed. Online it is now possible to see real-time estimates of meat consumption, as part of the global concern with the environmental consequences of meat production and consumption (World Counts, 2019). Inevitably, as worldwide demand for animal protein rises, there will be increased derived demand on natural resources, disproportionate to the nutritional benefit.

Soil erosion is a natural geological phenomenon resulting from the removal of soil particles by water or wind. This natural process can be accelerated by human activities creating soil loss that exceeds the soil formation rate in a given area. Human activities that change land use from a comparatively higher form of permanent vegetation cover, to a state of lesser vegetation cover, have increased soil erosion. In developing countries in particular, for example Ethiopia, soil erosion has become an alarming problem over several decades, and it is now considered to be the major factor affecting the sustainability of agricultural production in the country. The leading factors causing erosion are the usual culprits: increased population pressure resulting in forest/woodland clearance for wood and smallholding agriculture, traditional agricultural practices, and declining land productivity – partly as a result of bringing marginal land into production and partly as a result of intensive use of the land (Wolka *et al.*, 2015). But the problem is by no means confined to developing countries: soil erosion is a major environmental problem on Prince Edward Island in Canada as well (PEI Department of Agriculture and Fisheries, 2018). The loss of topsoil has obvious implications for the loss of agricultural productivity, but there are also wider environmental concerns, e.g. for wildlife in wetlands.

Hence, although Brazilian agribusiness stands out globally for its competitiveness in exporting products such as sugar, coffee, orange juice, ethanol, soybean and derivatives, and beef, pork and chicken meat – which has been attributed mainly to three measures: the management of natural resources, the use of genetic engineering in the development of new varieties, and the adoption of new management practices (Oliveira & Alvim, 2017:46) – environmental criticisms have emerged. 'Soybeans have particularly impacted Brazil's agricultural landscape and environment. Since 1970, almost 20% of the Amazon rainforest has been cleared to make way for agriculture in Brazil' (Pullman & Wu, 2012:88). An even more dramatic, but much more longstanding, reduction in forestry has occurred in the Wheatbelt of Western Australia, but the politics appear very different when the destruction of the forests occurred over a century ago, and there is no NGO campaigning for *reforestation* although the rainfall effect is equally significant – the Amazon, similar to other forests, produces over half its rainfall via the moisture it releases into the atmosphere, so cutting its trees reduces rainfall, which in turn dries out the remaining trees, a vicious cycle that eventually leads to salinated soils, vegetation loss and a decline in agricultural production itself.

There are models aplenty of the interaction of all these issues and problems.

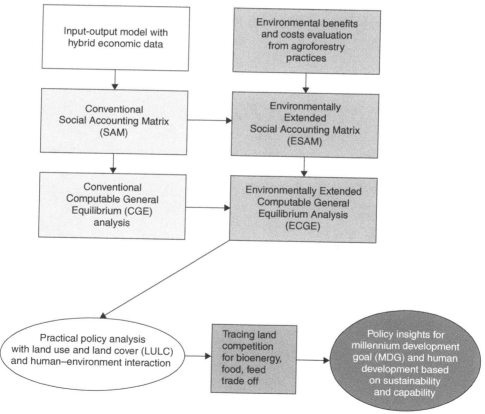

Figure 1.12 Millennium development goal (MDG) development
Source: Das (2014)

Perhaps even more significant going forward, however, is the fact that as arable land available for farming diminishes, substantial gains in production of higher value foods are most likely to come from intensive production systems in which animals are raised in confinement systems, and reared, to a large extent, on grains. This has a multiplier effect on grain consumption due to the increased demand for grains which are used as feed for livestock. To produce one gram of animal weight requires many grams of grains to be used as feed:

For example, approximately 8.3 grams of grain are required to produce 1 gram of beef, while 3.1 grams of grain are required for 1 gram of pork. Further, the energy produced by one gram of beef is 2.78 kcal, which is much less than the energy produced by the 8.3 grams of grain required to produce it, which is approximately 25 kcal. This multiplier effect means that as dietary patterns shift to include a greater proportion of higher value foods a much greater volume of grains is required to maintain the amount of energy consumed (Macquarie, 2010:3).

Doubt has been expressed over the accuracy of these figures, on the grounds that they refer only to OECD animal husbandry and moreover overlook the price effects of switching away from animal production and the equally important question of land use for protein production (Flachowsky *et al.*, 2017).

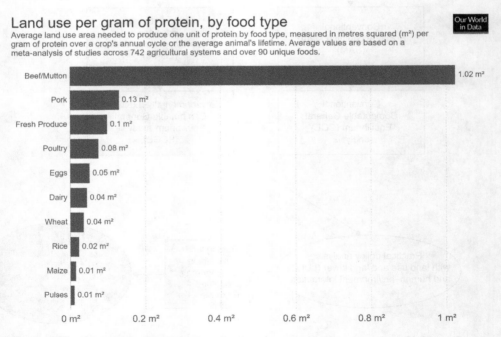

Land use per gram of protein, by food type

Average land use area needed to produce one unit of protein by food type, measured in metres squared (m²) per gram of protein over a crop's annual cycle or the average animal's lifetime. Average values are based on a meta-analysis of studies across 742 agricultural systems and over 90 unique foods.

Our World in Data

- Beef/Mutton — 1.02 m²
- Pork — 0.13 m²
- Fresh Produce — 0.1 m²
- Poultry — 0.08 m²
- Eggs — 0.05 m²
- Dairy — 0.04 m²
- Wheat — 0.04 m²
- Rice — 0.02 m²
- Maize — 0.01 m²
- Pulses — 0.01 m²

0 m² 0.2 m² 0.4 m² 0.6 m² 0.8 m² 1 m²

Figure 1.13 Grains required for animal production
Source: Ritchie (2017)

Serious consideration has already been given to grain diversion, even through regulation (Locke *et al.*, 2013).

The disparate nature of individual initiatives and the way in which some of them counteract each other should shine through these pages. Unfortunately, although a plethora of integrated assessment models (IAMs) have been constructed and used to estimate the social cost of carbon (SCC) and evaluate alternative abatement policies, it has been argued, at least, that these models have crucial flaws that make them close to useless as tools for policy analysis: certain inputs, e.g., the discount rate (the rate at which future values are reduced in value by comparison to present ones, see Harrison (2010) are arbitrary, but small changes in their values have huge effects on the SCC estimates the models produce; the models' descriptions of the impact of climate change are completely ad hoc, with no theoretical or empirical foundation; and the models can tell us nothing about the most important driver of the SCC, the possibility of a catastrophic climate outcome. IAM-based analyses of climate policy, and government policy papers on environmental assessment and the impact of agriculture, create a perception of knowledge and precision, but that perception is illusory and potentially even misleading.

Climate change and water use

Warnings from international organisations have continued over the decades. The World Economic Forum, regarding 2018, declared that:

> Rising temperatures and more frequent heatwaves will disrupt agricultural systems that are already strained. The prevalence of monoculture production heightens vulnerability to catastrophic breakdowns in the food system – more than 75% of the world's food comes from just 12 plants and five animal species, according to the FAO, and it is estimated that 'there is now a one-in-twenty chance per decade that heat, drought, and flood events will cause a simultaneous failure of maize production in the world's two main growers, China and the United States (Kent *et al.*, 2017).

Global water use doubled in the last four decades of the last century and is projected to grow at least twice as fast as oil consumption over the next two decades (United Nations, 2018). Maybe even more. Agriculture and land use change, construction and management of reservoirs, pollutant emissions and water and wastewater treatment have a critical influence on water resources in terms of both quantity and quality. None of this is new: the Intergovernmental Panel on Climate Change said decades ago that the principal drivers of these pressures are the result of demographics and the increasing consumption that comes with rising per capita incomes, and in fact rapid population growth had already led to a tripling of water withdrawals in the second five decades of the last century (IPCC, 2001). Agriculture takes 70% of all water withdrawal, whilst almost half the world's rural population lives in or around river basins that are water scarce. Countries are considered 'water-stressed' if they withdraw more than 25% of their renewable freshwater supplier, 'water scarce' at 60% and severely stressed after 75%. An alternative approach is to define 'water stress' as having less than 1,000 m^3 per capita per year (based on long-term average runoff), since this volume is usually more than is required in a basin for domestic, industrial and agricultural water uses. It was estimated a decade ago that the population living in water-stressed basins – from Africa through America and Asia – ranged from 1.4 billion to 2.1 billion, so this number will undoubtedly have risen since. Fast-forward a decade, and an estimated 3.6 billion people (nearly half the global population) live in areas that are potentially water-scarce at least one month per year, and this population could increase to some 4.8–5.7 billion by 2050 (United Nations, 2018). Drought, the next stage of water deprivation, is defined as a sustained and regionally extensive occurrence of below-average natural water availability, and both more intense and more widespread droughts affecting more people and linked to higher temperatures and decreased precipitation, have been observed in the 21st century. The problem is exacerbated by depletion of water tables beyond their – declining – renewable levels, sending water supplies into a downward spiral from which they cannot recover, e.g. in West Asia, North Africa and even in parts of Australia. This in turn reduces water quality, which is negatively impacted by chemical, microbiological and thermal pollution.

Eutrophication, defined as the excessive richness of nutrients in a lake or other body of water, frequently due to runoff from the land, which causes a dense growth of plant life mainly due to high phosphorus and nitrogen loads in water, is the most prevalent water quality problem globally, substantially impairing the beneficial uses of water. Inorganic nitrogen and phosphorus within river systems have increased several-fold over the last two centuries. Moreover, chemical contamination is occurring as a result of excess nutrients, acidification, salinity, heavy metals and other trace elements, persistent organic pollutants and changes in sediment loads. Microbiological contaminants, bacteria, viruses and protozoa in water pose one of the leading global human health hazards, and when water heats, biological functions can be impaired. All these contaminants can operate together, reinforcing their collective impact.

The politics of environmental control at national level

Almost every country devolves environmental legislation to an agency. The USA has the Environmental Protection Agency (EPA), but a great deal of the responsibility is devolved to state level. Constraints on agricultural production to reduce pollution discharges typically arise at the state level in response to local concerns, and how to manage agricultural sources has been a prominent issue in several locations, such as the Chesapeake Bay and Florida. Most environmental regulations, in terms of permitting, inspection and enforcement, are implemented by state and local governments, often based on federal EPA regulatory guidance. In some cases, agriculture is the direct or primary focus of the regulatory actions. In other cases, agriculture is one of many affected sectors. Traditionally, farm and ranch operations have been exempted or excluded from many environmental regulations. Given the agricultural sector's size and its potential to affect its surrounding environment, there is interest in both managing potential impacts of agricultural actions on the environment and also maintaining an economically viable agricultural industry. Of particular interest to agriculture are a number of regulatory actions affecting air, water, energy and pesticides.

Agricultural production practices from both livestock and crop operations generate a variety of substances that enter the atmosphere, potentially creating health and environmental issues. Water quality issues also are of interest to the agricultural industry, as water is an input for production and can also be degraded as a result of production through the potential release of sediment, nutrients, pathogens and pesticides. But recent actions by the EPA to regulate emissions and pollutants have drawn criticism, including GHG emission reporting and permitting requirements, and National Ambient Air Quality Standards (NAAQS) related to dust. The criticism, however, is divided, reflecting a fundamental political division. On the one hand, some claim that the EPA is overreaching its regulatory authority and imposing costly and burdensome requirements on society. In general, the agriculture community, among others, has been vocal in its concerns, contending that the EPA appears to be focusing some of its recent regulatory efforts on agriculture. On the other hand, many public health and environmental advocates support many of the EPA's overall regulatory efforts, even suggesting that the EPA has not taken adequate action to control the impacts of certain agricultural activities.

The Nutrient Management Program (NMP) is directed by the Delaware Nutrient Management Commission (DNMC) and administered by the Delaware Department of Agriculture (DDA). Delaware's Nutrient Management Program is broad in coverage, requiring NMPs for all animal feeding operations (AFOs) with greater than eight animal units (AUs) and for any farmer who applies nutrients to more than 10 acres under their control. All NMPs must be developed by a certified nutrient consultant. In FY2013, the Nutrient Management Program had a total budget of $103,335 and approximately 1.625 full-time employees dedicated to it.

In 2015, there were approximately 1,072 AFOs and crop land farm operations in Delaware regulated by the Delaware Nutrient Management Law, representing approximately 57% to 68% of the farms that meet the USDA definition of a farm in Delaware over 10 acres or with more than $10,000 in sales, respectively. The DNMC reported that 100% of cropland and nutrient-applied acres were managed under a current NMP developed by a certified consultant.

Source: EPA (2015)

Another contrasting example: in Zambia, for instance, the Zambian Environmental Management Agency (ZEMA) has developed sector guidelines, including air and water quality guidelines, for Environmental Impact Assessments (EIAs) for major projects in fisheries and forestry, amongst others, examples of which are available (ZEMA, 2018).

So far as agriculture is concerned, there are six criteria for schemes requiring EIA: (a) Land clearance for large-scale agriculture; (b) introduction and use of agrochemicals new to Zambia; (c) Introduction of new crops and animals, especially exotic ones new to Zambia; (d) Irrigation schemes covering an area of 50 hectares or more; (e) Fish farms, of which production is more than 100 tonnes annually; and (f) Aerial and ground spraying on an industrial scale.

Similar organisations and procedures exist in virtually every country in the world.

There must, for example, be integration with water use. Water is now an especially important factor for agriculture and one of the keys to understanding agribusiness worldwide.

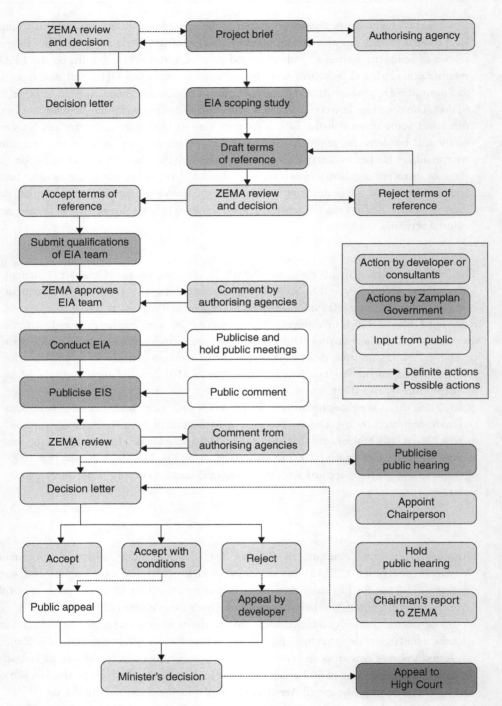

Figure 1.14 The EIA process in Zambia
Source: ZEMA (2018)

Irrigation is a good example of why, in the last 50 years, the worldwide area under irrigation has grown at approximately 1.6% annually, more in developing countries. But the growth in agricultural water use is decelerating, partly due to encouraging developments in the performance of irrigation systems themselves, but also because increased urbanisation is compressing water demand. There is now more competition for water, so for example the construction of dams and water diversion is affecting fish migration and inland fisheries. Urban settlement is dominating water use, and agriculture has been forced to adapt. Large levels of investment are needed to solve the problem.

Meteorology and climatology

This reinforces the need for accurate understanding of the weather. Demand is growing worldwide for forecasts of storms, floods and droughts in particular, as the risks and consequences of environmental change are rising. Modes of collecting and delivering weather and climate information are evolving. Businesses and non-profits are increasingly supplying weather services to farmers. And data now stem from a broader range of sources, such as for Android mobile-phone apps (e.g. Yahoo Weather) and other smart devices.

Typical publicly available snapshots of climate as it relates to agriculture are shown in Figure 1.15a–b.

To make the task of agribusiness that much more complex in coming decades, significant average crop yield declines are projected with higher temperatures. There are suggestions that this is already happening, for example stalled wheat yields in Australia (Hochman *et al.*, 2017). Declines of 5–10% in the concentrations of iron, zinc and protein in crops such as wheat, rice, and soybeans with increased CO_2 concentrations, would certainly place people at greater health risks due to potential malnutrition as well as posing social risks, which are again arguably already happening (Fuller *et al.*, 2018). Projected global shifts in consumption patterns to yet more livestock and dairy products, which are more emissions-intensive than cereals, will further increase the challenge of lowering the aggregate emissions intensity in the sector.

There are in many countries meteorological services provided to farmers to warn them of the dangers of climate to agricultural production.

Obviously, what is needed are innovative systems that protect and enhance the natural resource base, while increasing productivity – but this may be an impossible combination. Equally needed is a transformative process towards 'holistic' approaches, such as agroecology, agroforestry, climate-smart agriculture and conservation agriculture, which also build upon indigenous and traditional knowledge (FAO, 2017a:xi) – and equally obviously, if these approaches do not provide value for money, they will not be taken up. To be charitable, the FAO argument excludes research and development (R&D) improvements to seed and varieties. It does not even take a position on genetically modified (GM) crops. It mainly refers to environmental issues in developing countries, which are very real, such as the depletion of rainforests in Indonesia as a result of commercial palm oil, timber and rubber plantations.

Palm oil is the most widely used vegetable oil in the world, appearing in the ingredients list of many consumer goods, from chocolate to soap. Indonesia, the world's largest

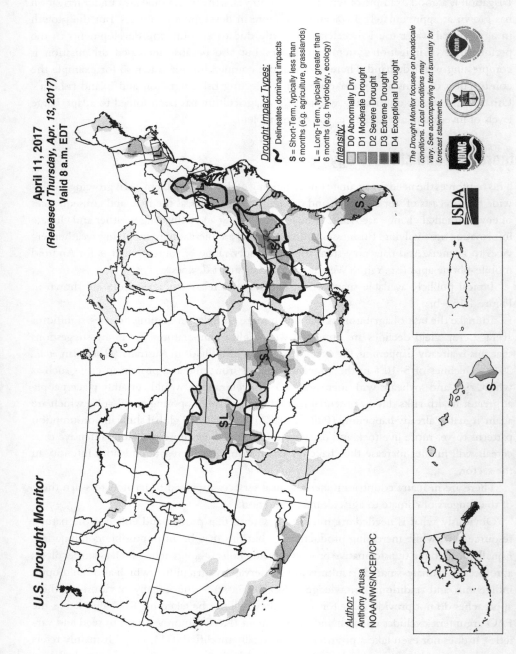

Figure 1.15a Weather map for the USA

Source: Rabobank (2017:5); Climate Prediction Center (2019)

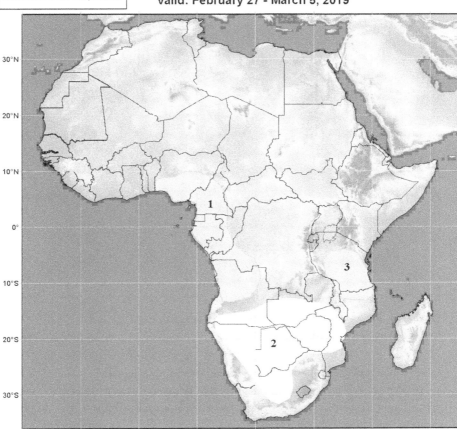

Figure 1.15b Weather map for Africa
Source: Rabobank (2017:5); Climate Prediction Center (2019)

producer of palm oil, has seen large swathes of rainforest cleared away and replaced by oil palm plantations at rates that exceed those of Brazil. On the island of Sumatra, which has had the highest loss of native rainforest in all of Indonesia, the changes in land use have meant a substantial loss of animal and plant diversity (Science Daily, 2017).

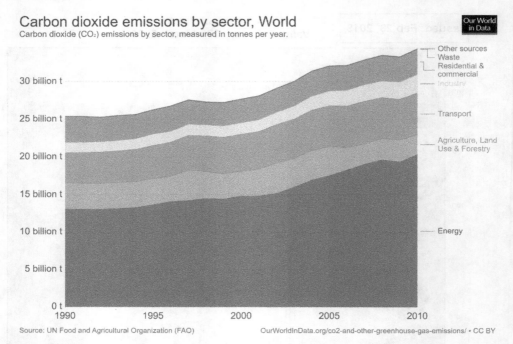

Carbon dioxide emissions by sector, World
Carbon dioxide (CO₂) emissions by sector, measured in tonnes per year.

Source: UN Food and Agricultural Organization (FAO)   OurWorldInData.org/co2-and-other-greenhouse-gas-emissions/ • CC BY

Figure 1.16 Summary of greenhouse gas effects of agriculture
Source: Ritchie & Roser (2017)

But it not just in Indonesia that commercial farming is replacing subsistence agriculture, or that farm sizes are rising: the average size of farms in developed countries is rising. And even in Indonesia, all is not lost: the rate of depletion of rainforests has declined, largely thanks to government action following NGO pressure. The large international trading companies (the largest known as the ABCD companies, discussed in Chapter 7 as well as other chapters) are now also active in the sustainability space: for example, January 2017 saw the major international trading firm Louis Dreyfus Company (LDC) join the World Business Council for Sustainable Development. They reported this example of collaboration, as shown in Figure 1.17.

Commercial farming and agribusiness operations

Agriculture is still one of the world's largest industries. More people work in agriculture than all other occupations combined. Based upon applying the definition of agribusiness to global data, the food and agribusiness system is the largest economic sector in the world economy, representing 50% of global assets, 50% of the global labour force and 50% of global consumer expenditures. The sheer scale of agriculture in countries such as the USA, Brazil and Russia should never blind us to the continued importance of agriculture elsewhere. For example, Tunisia is one of the world's biggest producers and exporters of olive oil and it exports dates and citrus fruits that are grown mostly in the northern parts of the country.

REA Kaltim

Global demand for segregated palm oil products has increased over the past few years as end consumers have become progressively more aware of the importance of whole supply chain sustainability. REA Kaltim is a grower and producer of crude palm oil in the East Kalimantan region of Borneo, Indonesia. The company currently produces crude palm oil and palm kernel oil under the mass balance supply chain model but is committed to moving towards producing segregated palm oil, notwithstanding certain challenges.

In 2016, 16% of the oil palm fruit processed by REA's three mills was sourced from independent smallholder farmers neighbouring the Group's own plantations. REA's relationship with these farmers was initially purely commercial, but over time REA has become more involved in the socio-economic welfare of neighbouring communities and now works closely with independent smallholders to improve their farming practices and make them more sustainable. Despite considerable efforts in this regard, the independent smallholders that supply oil palm fruit to REA's mills are not yet

RSPO certified. To achieve the objective of producing segregated palm oil products, REA would therefore have to either refuse to accept palm fruits from non-certified smallholders or reconfigure the production and transport logistics of the operations to allow for the production of some segregated palm oil, while maintaining the current mass balance system so that fruit from non-certified farmers can still be accepted.

REA does not consider the rejection of fruit from neighbouring smallholders to be a desirable option given the negative economic impact on local communities that would ensue, inevitably harming the good relationships with these communities that have built up over recent years, and likely to lead to a gradual return to less sustainable farming practices by smallholders. Until local independent smallholders have achieved RSPO certification, REA's strategy for producing segregated crude palm oil products must therefore be the reconfiguration of its business logistics. This is a significant challenge for REA that is unlikely to be overcome in a reasonable timeframe without support. So how can other members of REA's

supply chain help the Group to achieve its objectives, and as a grower, what does REA expect from its partners further down the supply chain?

REA sees its relationship with LDC as analogous to its relationship with independent smallholders. The partnership with LDC began as a commercial relationship, with each company solely responsible for the sustainability of its own operations. Now, however, REA and LDC have the opportunity to further develop this relationship and work more closely together in order to improve the sustainability of our shared supply chain and meet the market demands for palm oil that is produced according to stricter sustainability standards. LDC can assist REA in two ways. First, by providing logistical support as REA reconfigures its business to produce segregated oil and, secondly, by collaborating with us to help the independent smallholders that comprise part of the shared supply chain to achieve RSPO certification. In providing this support, LDC would not simply be benefitting REA's operations, but enhancing the sustainability of a product from the base of the supply chain through to the end consumer.

As a grower at the base of the palm oil supply chain, REA also expects downstream elements of its supply chain to maintain the sustainability of the palm oil products that began with us in order to uphold the international sustainability standards to which the group is committed through capital investment, biodiversity conservation and the socio-economic improvement of local communities.

Dr Ben Godsall
Sustainability Consultant
REA Holdings plc

Figure 1.17 Partner testimony between Louis Dreyfus Company and REA Kaltim
Source: Dreyfus (2017)

In the Lebanon, agriculture is the third most important sector after the tertiary and industrial sector. It contributes nearly 7% to the country's GDP and employs around 15% of the active population. The main crops are cereals (mainly wheat and barley), fruits and vegetables, olives, grapes, and tobacco (Agra ME, 2017:4).

In sub-Saharan Africa, the agribusiness sector is about half the economic size of farming; in Asia and Latin America, it is about two to three times the size; while in some industrial countries it is more than ten times as large. As economies grow, the agribusiness share of GDP relative to the farming share of GDP increases even as the overall share of agriculture in GDP declines. In agriculture-based economies (most of sub-Saharan Africa), this relative share is about 0.6; in transforming economies (most in Asia), it is 2; in urbanised countries (mostly in Latin America), it is 3.3; and in the USA, it is 13 (World Bank, 2013). The trajectories of developing countries are therefore readily apparent.

Hence the significance of the most important insight raised by Davis & Goldberg in *A Concept of Agribusiness* (1957), which was that what was happening *on* the farm in the USA, and in other developed countries, even by the mid-20th century, was utterly dependent on what was happening *off* the farm. A reviewer almost six decades later was surely right, though, that 'So many people seem to have missed this point, however, that even today when most people hear the term "agribusiness" they think not of food processors, fertilizer manufacturers, or supermarket chains but instead of large-scale commercial farms' (Hamilton, 2016:543) Farms produce output, but it is processed, marketed and distributed by agribusiness companies. A range of service companies is also part of agribusiness: transportation, storage, refrigeration, credit, finance and insurance, plus now agtech throughout the sector.

What is different, this century, is the globalisation of agribusiness. Already by 2013, agribusiness had taken hold in India, where there was a rising trend in *marketable surplus*. For major staple crops it had already risen to high levels: 81% for rice and 73% for wheat. Even for 'inferior' staples, it had reached high levels such as 62% for sorghum and 67% for pearl millet. This growth in marketed surplus brought substantial agribusinesses development – for handling it, including procurement/purchase, transport, storage, processing and marketing, as well as providing services such as finance, information and management. Just as important, commercialisation has also led to *diversification* in production, as farmers respond to market signals, needs and prices, and seek profits. Inevitably, there has been a shift to high value crops/products such as fibres, spices, vegetables, fruits, flowers and livestock products. This has stimulated the development of various agribusinesses which support and facilitate their production, undertake processing, and do the special supply chain management, marketing and trade arrangements they require (Gandhi, 2014).

A significant share of agricultural commodities is traded internationally (OECD-FAO, 2016). The larger this share, the more local production conditions are codetermined by global socio-economic and environmental conditions and political interventions mainly through price signals from world markets, although there are still significant price distortions at national and again at local level. The intensely political nature of agriculture explains why political decisions, e.g. on agricultural policies, as well as demographic and technological developments – and now environmental pressures as well – trigger feedback between global markets for agricultural commodities and local land use decisions which, in turn, eventually affect global prices, stocks, consumption and planting decisions. Virtually every individual producer, with very rare exceptions in highly regulated markets (Obasanjo Farms in Nigeria, perhaps (Ngex, 2018) are price-takers, and do not therefore control prices through their own investment and planning decisions. This is especially so for agricultural production

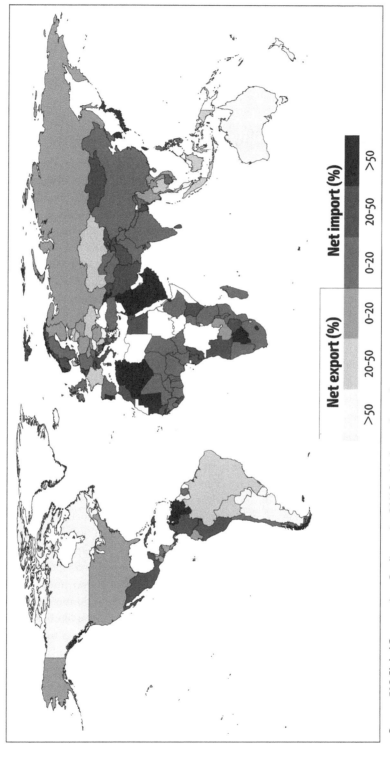

Source: FAO Global Perspectives Studies, using 2011 food balance sheets from FAO, 2016a.

Figure 1.18 International agricultural trade patterns

Source: FAO (2015a)

for export. Although more than 90% of food consumed in the USA is produced there, for example, countries such as the USA, as well as Argentina and Australia, export more than 50% of their domestic food supply. At the opposite extreme, the Near East/North Africa region imports more than half of its food supply (FAO, 2017a:29).

The pattern of a world divided is very clear: the USA, Australia, Russia and the former CIS countries, and South America, are now feeding the world.

What drives commodity volatility?

The volatility of the price of an agricultural commodity can be associated with the standard deviation or error of price fluctuations of the commodity with respect to the mean value or to the trend. It is also possible to conceptualise volatility more straightforwardly as the rate at which asset prices change. Volatility affects prices, production and inventories in agricultural commodities by directly affecting the marginal value of storage (the marginal convenience yield), i.e. the flow of benefits from an extra unit of inventory. When prices – and hence production and demand – are more volatile, there is a greater demand for inventories, which are needed to smooth production and deliveries and reduce marketing costs. Thus, an increase in volatility can lead to inventory build-ups and raise prices in the short run (Pindyck, 2004). But note Pindyck's second process, that of the option premium, does not apply as agricultural commodities are a largely renewable resource, albeit with exceptions and bottlenecks. And with respect to the predictability of agricultural commodity market volatility, at least one study (Giot, 2003) suggested that the best way to predict volatility is to look at the price of options (see Chapter 8), although this work would require constant updating to be reliably used as the basis for any action.

International agribusiness organisations

Agriculture – not so much agribusiness in its widest sense, but certainly production agriculture – is also characterised by a number of international organizations that undertake much of the global research and co-ordination effort. Most of them would resist very strongly the suggestion that they were, or even could ever become, global trade associations for agribusiness. The most well-known, and important, is the Food and Agriculture Organisation of the United Nations, the FAO – a vast collection of expertise, data, policies and experience on global food and agriculture questions. Figure 1.19 shows how it was described in a report from 2013.

The FAO has come in for much criticism in recent decades. An independent review of its policies in 2007 said the agency had lost the confidence of donors, who had steadily reduced funding to the organisation and at least one director-general has been forced out as a result (Christoffersen *et al.*, 2008). Since then the FAO has attempted to pursue a middle line between the market advocacy of organisations such as the World Bank and the criticism of NGOs, for example of its attitude towards and plans to deal with agriculture and climate change (e.g. Oxfam, 2015). With the receding of the food crisis of that time, criticism has also become less vocal, although the internal struggle within the FAO between supporters and critics of market solutions continues to rumble on, with no sign of resolution any more than in the world at large.

The oldest of the Rome food agencies, the Food and Agriculture Organization of the United Nations (FAO) was born in 1945 in the post-World War II burst of international institution building. It is the only global intergovernmental organization today with a broad mandate in governing the world's food and agriculture system. FAO is charged with four goals: improving nutrition, increasing agricultural productivity, raising the standard of living in rural populations, and contributing to global economic growth.

Given this comprehensive mandate, FAO's work spans an array of activities, including gathering and analyzing statistics; providing policy assistance to countries; engaging in advocacy and capacity building; implementing field projects; contributing to international agreements and guidelines; and responding to emergencies. These activities fall into numerous areas—crops, livestock, fisheries, forestry, and water and land management.

FAO's notable historical achievements include:

■ Adopting the International Plant Protection Convention (1951), the framework for rules to prevent the spread plant pests through international trade.

■ Establishing the Codex Alimentarius Commission with the World Health Organization (1961), regulating international food safety standards.

■ Creating the Global Information and Early Warning System for detecting food crises and enabling timely response (1975).

■ Pioneering integrated pest management, which reduces losses to pests without exposure or reliance on excessive pesticides, and the farmers' field schools approach used to disseminate integrated pest management through farmer participation (1980s).

More recently, FAO's achievements include:

■ Leading successful campaigns to eradicate rinderpest (1998–2011) and to control avian flu (2004) and desert locust (2003–2005).

■ Adopting the International Treaty on Plant Genetic Resources for Food and Agriculture.

Figure 1.19 About the FAO
Source: Center for Global Development (2013:xiii)

The FAO is not the only organisation active in the space: the Consultative Group on International Agricultural Research (CGIAR) states that its objective is a world free of poverty, hunger and environmental degradation. They say that they work to advance agricultural science and innovation to enable poor people, especially women, to better nourish their families, and improve productivity and resilience so they can share in economic growth and manage natural resources in the face of climate change and other challenges. Their claim is that, by 2030, the action of CGIAR and its partners will result in 150 million fewer hungry people, 100 million fewer poor people – at least 50% of whom are women – and 190 million hectares less degraded land. They aim to:

■ Improve the rate of yield increase for major food staples from the current <2.0 to 2.5%/year;

■ Ensure 150 million more people, 50% of them women, are meeting minimum dietary energy requirements;

■ Enable 500 million more people, 50% of them women, to be without deficiencies of one or more of the following essential micronutrients: iron, zinc, iodine, vitamin A, folate and vitamin B12;

■ Achieve a 33% reduction in women of reproductive age who are consuming less than the adequate number of food groups;

■ Enable a 20% increase in water and nutrient (inorganic, biological) use efficiency in agro-ecosystems, including through recycling and reuse; and

■ Reduce agriculture-related greenhouse gas emissions by 8 $GtCO_2$ eq per year (15%), compared with a business-as-usual scenario in 2030.

These are ambitious goals, for sure, and they may not all be mutually compatible, let alone achievable.

CGIAR and its member centres have led studies concerning the adoption of new technologies in agricultural production by farmers in emerging economies. A leading member is the International Food Policy Research Institute (IFPRI), which 'provides research-based policy solutions to sustainably reduce poverty and end hunger and malnutrition in developing countries. Established in 1975, IFPRI currently has more than 600 employees working in over 50 countries' (IFPRI, 2018). Another member is the Technical Centre for Agricultural and Rural Cooperation (CTA), a joint international institution of the African, Caribbean and Pacific (ACP) Group of States and the European Union (EU). A similar organisation for West Africa is the West and Central African Council for Agricultural Research and Development (CORAF) – for their programme, see CORAF (2018). The promotion of the maize sector through collaborative and innovative research is one of the primary areas of the work of CORAF. For this specific project, CORAF worked jointly with the National Institute of Agricultural Research of Benin (INRAB), the Institute of the Environment and Agricultural Research of Burkina Faso (INERA), the National Center for Agronomic Research of Cote d'Ivoire (CNRA) and the Institute of Rural Economy of Mali (IER).

In addition, the international development banks perceive themselves as having a role in agricultural development. The Asian Development Bank (ADB), for example, has a five-year plan in the agriculture and natural resources sector, which prioritises four areas:

■ Increasing the productivity and reducing pre- and postharvest losses of food harvests;

■ Improving market connectivity and value chain linkages;

■ Enhancing food safety, quality and nutrition; and

■ Enhancing management and climate resilience of natural resources (ADB, 2015).

Generally, the ADB has focused on asset creation and access to markets and inputs in the poorest regions. For example, it has looked to replicate small-scale planting innovations in forestry, bringing them into the mainstream of forestry practice.

Conclusion

The current position of the FAO, in a tightrope walk between increasing production and conserving the environment, is that high-input, resource-intensive farming systems, which have caused massive deforestation, water scarcities, soil depletion and high levels of greenhouse gas emissions, cannot deliver sustainable food and agricultural production without huge alterations in practice.

Yet, the inefficiencies of small farm operation have been regularly reported, for example that small farm sizes and growing wheat in the mixed production zone in Punjab in Pakistan tend to have greater technical inefficiencies (Battese & Smale, 2017). Moreover, whilst in rich countries farms are consolidating, although the trend has slowed, the opposite is found elsewhere: the average size of an Indian farm keeps shrinking, falling by 50% over the last half of the 20th cCentury. If this continues any potential comparative advantage to Indian agriculture will be lost. Only large-scale investment and entirely commercial agribusiness stands any chance of reversing this trend.

The need for commercial agribusiness to feed a growing world is clear. One indication of rising interest by government and the private sector worldwide in the sector is the proliferation of conferences devoted to agribusiness. For example, Agra ME (www.agramiddleeast.com), delivered a conference in Dubai in April 2017 focusing on issues surrounding production and import of agricultural commodities in the MENA (Middle East and North Africa) region. The annual Global AgInvesting Conference for investors in New York has hundreds of participants, more every year. There are many other such events. Regulators and governments confronting agtech and international trade are similarly beset with problems and issues surrounding agriculture, food and livelihoods.

Agribusiness has a huge task ahead of it this century. *How it will achieve it is the subject of the rest of this book.*

Note

1 The cattle inventory in India includes water buffalo.

Bibliography

Adamopoulos, T. and Restuccia, D. (2014) The size distribution of farms and international productivity differences. *American Economic Review*, 104(6):1667–1697.

Adams, R. (2009) Climate change and agriculture. In Yotovaay, A. (ed.) *Climate Change, Human Systems and Policy.* Volume 1. EOLSS [on line], 309–327. Available at: www.eolss.net/sample-chapters/C12/E1-04-03-06.pdf. Retrieved 6 June 2018.

Adoff, G.A. (2018) Guide to Marine Aquaculture. Available at: www.aquafima.eu/export/sites/aquafima/documents/WP4/Guide-to-marine-aquaculture.pdf. Retrieved 6 June 2018.

Agra ME (2017) *Agriculture Market in the MENA Region.* Presentation [unpublished]. Agra ME Conference, 10–12 April 2017.

Agribusiness Council of Australia (ACA) (2018) Advancing Agribusiness in Australia. Available at: www.agribusiness.asn.au/. Retrieved 5 June 2018.

Amin, M., Amanullah, M. and Akbar, A. (2014) Time series modelling for forecasting wheat production in Pakistan. *Journal of Animal and Plant Sciences* 24(5), 1444–1451.

Araus, J.L., Ferrio, J.P., Voltas, J., Aguilera, M. and Buxó, R. (2014) Agronomic conditions and crop evolution in ancient Near East agriculture. *Nature Communications* 5, 3953. Available at: www.nature.com/articles/ncomms4953. Retrieved 17 July 2018.

Asian Development Bank (ADB) (2015) The Operational Plan for Agriculture and Natural Resources: Promoting Sustainable Food Security in Asia and the Pacific in 2015–2020. Available at: www.adb.org/documents/operational-plan-agriculture-and-natural-resources-2015–2020. Retrieved 13 July 2018.

Australian Bureau of Agricultural and Resource Economics and Sciences (ABARES) (2017) *Agricultural Commodities*. March. Canberra, ABARES. Available at: www.agriculture.gov.au/abares/Documents/agricultural-commodities-report-march-2017.pdf. Retrieved 5 July 2017.

Australian Bureau of Statistics (ABS) (2018) 7121.0 – Agricultural Commodities, Australia, 2016–17. Available at: www.abs.gov.au/ausstats/abs@.nsf/cat/7121.0. Retrieved 8 June 2018.

Australian Wheat Board (n.d.) *Global Wheat Trends*, Melbourne, AWB.

Barnard, F.L., Akridge, J.T., Dooley, F.J., Foltz, J.C., and Yeager, E.A. (2016) *Agribusiness Management*, 5th edition. London and New York, Routledge.

Barrett, J. and Packham, C. (2018) Falling off the sheep's back: Why Australia can't capitalize on record wool prices. Reuters. 9 March. Available at: www.reuters.com/article/us-australia-wool/falling-off-the-sheeps-back-why-australia-cant-capitalize-on-record-wool-prices-idUSKCN1GK36S. Retrieved 17 July 2018.

Battese, G. and Smale, M. (2017) Factors influencing the productivity and efficiency of wheat farmers in Punjab, Pakistan. *Journal of Agribusiness in Developing and Emerging Economies* 7(2), 82–98.

Beef2Live (2018) *World Cattle Inventory: Ranking of Countries*. Available at: beef2live.com/story-world-cattle-inventory-ranking-countries-0-106905. Retrieved 5 June 2018.

Bekkerman, A. and Tejeda, H.A. (2017) Revisiting the determinants of futures contracts success: the role of market participants. *Agricultural Economics* 48(2), 175–185.

Blumenthal, G.R. (2013) Investors' perspectives. In Kugelman, M. and Levenstein, S.L. (eds.) *The Global Farms Race: Land Grabs, Agricultural Investment, and the Scramble for Food Security*. Washington DC, Island Press, 99–112.

Brookfield, H. and Parsons, H. (2007) *Family Farms: Survival and Prospect. A World-Wide Analysis*. London and New York, Routledge.

Cargill (2009) *Annual Report 2009*. Minnetonka, Cargill.

Center for Global Development (2013) Time for FAO to Shift to a Higher Gear. A Report of the CGD Working Group on Food Security. Available at: www.cgdev.org/sites/default/files/FAO-text-Final.pdf. Retrieved 13 July 2018.

Central Silk Board (India) (2016) *Note on the Performance of the Indian Silk Industry and the Functioning of the Central Silk Board*. Delhi, Ministry of Textiles.

Christoffersen, L.E., Bezanson, K., Lele, U., Davies, M., del Castillo, C.P. and Awori, T. (2008) FAO: The Challenge of Renewal. Helsinki, Ministry of Foreign Affairs of Finland. Available at: www.oecd.org/derec/finland/40800533.pdf. Retrieved 13 July 2018.

Climate Prediction Center (USA) (2019) Week 1 Outlook for Africa 20–26 February 2019. 19 February. Available at: www.cpc.ncep.noaa.gov/products/international/africa/expert/week1.jpg Retrieved 24 February 2019.

Consultative Group on International Agricultural Research (CGIAR) (2012) *China*. Available at: http://ricepedia.org/china. Retrieved 12 July 2018.

CORAF (2018) New Program Seeks Lasting Changes to Agriculture System of West and Central Africa. Available at: www.coraf.org/en/2018/02/16/new-program-seeks-lasting-changes-to-agriculture-system-of-west-and-central-africa. Retrieved 6 June 2018.

Cotton Today (2018) *Land*. Available at: https://cottontoday.cottoninc.com/agriculture-4/land/. Retrieved 27 July 2018.

D'Amato, A.W., Jokela, E.J., O'Hara, K.L. and Long, J.N. (2018) Silviculture in the United States: An amazing period of change over the past 30 years. *Journal of Forestry* 116(1), 55–67.

Das, G. (2014) Land use, land cover, and food-energy-environment trade-off: Key issues and insights for Millennium Development Goals. In Van Alfen, N. *Encyclopaedia of Agriculture and Food Systems*, 2nd edition. Volume 4, 114–133.

Davis, J.H. and Goldberg, R.A. (1957) *A Concept of Agribusiness*. Boston, Harvard Business School.

Devia, G.K., Ganasri, B. P. and Dwarakish, G.S. (2015) A review on hydrological models. *Aquatic Procedia* 4, 1001–1007. Available at: www.sciencedirect.com/science/article/pii/S2214241X15001273. Retrieved 6 June 2018.

Dreyfus (2017) Louis Dreyfus Company. Available at: www.ldc.com/files/7814/9935/8354/LDC_SR_2016-Partners.pdf. Retrieved 5 July 2018.

Drummond, H.E. and Goodwin, J.W. (2004) *Agricultural Economics*, 2nd edition. New Jersey, Prentice Hall International Journal of Economics, Finance and Management Sciences.

EPA (2015) Delaware Animal Agriculture Program Assessment. Available at: www.chesapeakebay. net/channel_files/22592/delawareanimalagricultureprogramassessment.pdf. Retrieved 16 May 2019.

Eurostat (2015) Farm structure statistics. Available at: http://ec.europa.eu/eurostat/statistics-explained/index.php/Farm_structure_statistics. Retrieved 8 June 2018.

FAO (2003) *Trade Reforms and Food Security: Conceptualizing the Linkages*. Rome, FAO.

FAO (2011) *"Energy-Smart" Food for People and Climate*. Rome, FAO. Available at: www.fao.org/docrep/014/i2454e/i2454e00.pdf. Retrieved 27 July 2018.

FAO (2011a) *Save and Grow: A Policymaker's Guide to The Sustainable Intensification of Smallholder Crop Production*. Rome, FAO. Chapter One. Available at: www.fao.org/ag/save-and-Grow/en/1/index. html Retrieved 26 February 2019.

FAO (2015) Cropland Data (FAOSTAT). Available at: www.fao.org/faostat/en/#data/GC/metadata. Retrieved 4 June 2018.

FAO (2015a) Global Perspectives. Available at: www.fao.org/global-perspectives-studies/en/. Retrieved 16 May 2019.

FAO (2017) *The State of Food Insecurity and Nutrition in the World*. Rome, FAO. Available at: www.fao. org/3/a-I7695e.pdf. Retrieved 30 October 2017.

FAO (2017a) *The Future of Food and Agriculture: Trends and Challenges*. Rome, FAO. Available at: www. fao.org/3/a-i6583e.pdf. Retrieved 5 February 2018.

FAO (2018) Smallholders Datapoint. Available at: www.fao.org/family-farming/data-sources/dataportrait/farm-size/en/. Retrieved 8 June 2018.

FAO (2018a) FAO Rice Market Monitor. Available at: www.fao.org/economic/est/publications/rice-publications/rice-market-monitor-rmm/en/. Retrieved 6 June 2018.

Federico, G. (2005) *Feeding the World: An Economic History of Agriculture, 1800–2000*. Princeton, Princeton University Press.

Flachowsky, G., Meyer, U. and Südekum, K-M. (2017) Land use for edible protein of animal origin – A review. *Animals (Basel)* 7(3), 25. Available at: www.ncbi.nlm.nih.gov/pmc/articles/PMC5366844/ Retrieved 23 February 2019.

Fuller, T. L., Sesink Clee, P.R., Njabo, K.Y., Trochez, A., Morgan, K., Mene, D.B., Anthony, N.M., Gonder, M.K., Allen, W.R., Hanna, R. and Smith, T. B. (2018) Climate warming causes declines in crop yields and lowers school attendance rates in Central Africa. *The Science of the Total Environment* 610–611, 503–510.

Gandhi, V.P. (2014) Growth and transformation of the agribusiness sector: Drivers, models and challenges. *Indian Journal of Agricultural Economics* 69(1), 44–73.

Giot, P. (2003) The information content of implied volatility in agricultural commodity markets. *Journal of Futures Markets*, 23(5), 441–454.

Giraud, G. (2013) The world market of fragrant rice, main issues and perspectives. *International Food and Agribusiness Management Review* 16(2): 1–20.

Gu, H. and Patton, D. (2018) China cotton imports to reach up to 3 million tons by 2019/20: trader. Reuters [on line]. 7 June . Available at: www.reuters.com/article/us-china-cotton/china-cotton-imports-to-reach-up-to-3-million-tons-by-2019-20-trader-idUSKCN1J30UA. Retrieved 31 July 2018.

Hamilton, S. (2016) Revisiting the history of agribusiness. *Business History Review* 90(3), 541–545.

Harrison, M., (2010) *Valuing the Future: The Social Discount Rate in Cost-Benefit Analysis.* Canberra, Australian Government Productivity Commission. April. Available at: www.pc.gov.au/research/supporting/cost-benefit-discount/cost-benefit-discount.pdf. Retrieved 5 July 2018.

Heise, H. and Theuvsen, L. (2017) What do consumers think about farm animal welfare in modern agriculture? Attitudes and shopping behavior. *International Food and Agribusiness Management Review* 20(3), 379–399.

Hochman, Z., Gobbett, D.L. and Horan, H. Climate trends account for stalled wheat yields in Australia since 1990. *Global Change Biology* 23(5), 2071–2081.

Huang, Z., Guan, L. and Jin, S. (2017) Scale farming operations in China. *International Food and Agribusiness Management Review* 20(3), 191–200.

IBEF (2017) Agriculture. Indian Brand Federation. Available at: www.ibef.org/download/Agriculture-May-2017.pdf. Retrieved 6 June 2018.

IBEF (2018) Agriculture in India: Information About Indian Agriculture & Its Importance. Available at: www.ibef.org/industry/agriculture-india.aspx. Retrieved 6 June 2018.

Indian Government (2018) Annual Report 2017–18. Department of Agriculture, Cooperation & Farmers Welfare Ministry of Agriculture & Farmers Welfare. Available at: http://agricoop.nic.in/sites/default/files/Krishi%20AR%202017-18-1%20for%20web.pdf. Retrieved 13 July 2018.

International Food Policy Research Institute (IFPRI) (2018) About IFPRI. Available at: www.ifpri.org/about. Retrieved 18 July 2018.

International Grains Council (2018) Grain Market Report Number 498. 2 July 2018. Available at: www.igc.int/downloads/gmrsummary/gmrsumme.pdf. Retrieved 5 July 2018.

IPCC (2001) Third Assessment Report. Available at: www.grida.no/publications/267. Retrieved 9 July 2018.

Kansas Wheat (2014) Which Wheat for What? 2 December. Available at: http://kswheat.com/news/2014/12/02/which-wheat-for-what. Retrieved 13 July 2018.

Karen, K. (2012) Profitable aquaculture now a reality for investors. 19 September. Available at: www.matchdeck.com/article/371-profitable-aquaculture-now-a-reality-for-investors#/index. Retrieved 6 June 2018.

Kent, C., Pope, E., Thompson, V., Lewis, K., Scaife, A.A. and Dunstone, N. (2017) Using climate model simulations to assess the current climate risk to maize production. *Environmental Research Letters* 12(5). Available at: http://iopscience.iop.org/article/10.1088/1748–9326/aa6cb9/meta. Retrieved 18 July 2018.

Kessler, D. and Temin, P. (2007) The organization of the grain trade in the early Roman Empire. *Economic History Review* 60(2), 313–332.

Kingwell, R. and Payne, B. (2015) Projected impacts of climate change on farm business risk in three regions of Western Australia. *Australian Farm Business Management Journal* 12, 32–50. Available at: www.agrifood.info/AFBM/2015/Kingwell_Payne.pdf. Retrieved 27 July 2018.

Kostreva, O. (2014) *Brazil's Sugarcane Industry.* Borgen. 6 August. Available at: www.borgenmagazine.com/brazils-sugarcane-industry/. Retrieved 31 July 2018.

KSU (2018) Wheat Taxonomy. Available at: www.k-state.edu/wgrc/wheat-tax.html. Retrieved 6 June 2018.

Locke, A. Wiggins, S. Henley, G. and Keats, S. (2013) *Diverting Grain from Animal Feed and Biofuels. Can it Protect the Poor from High Food Prices?* London, Overseas Development Institute. April. Available at: www.odi.org/sites/odi.org.uk/files/odi-assets/publications-opinion-files/8343.pdf. Retrieved 10 July 2018.

Macquarie (2010) *The Case for Investing in Agriculture.* Macquarie Agricultural Fund Management. Available at: www.macquarie.com/dafiles/Internet/mgl/com/agriculture/docs/white-papers/case-for-investing-in-agriculture.pdf. Retrieved 9 July 2018.

Mazoyer, M. and Roubart, L. (2006) *World Agriculture: From Neolithic Times to the Present Crisis.* New York, Columbia University Press.

Moreno, M., Comino, I. and Sousa, C. (2014) Alternative grains as potential raw material for gluten-free food development in the diet of celiac and gluten-sensitive patients. *Austin Journal of Nutri Food Sciences* 2(3), 1016. Available at: http://austinpublishinggroup.com/nutrition-food-sciences/fulltext/ajnfs-v2-id1016.php. Retrieved 23 February 2019.

Muldowney J., Mounsey, J. and, Kinsella L. (2013) Agriculture in the climate change negotiations; ensuring that food production is not threatened. *Animal* 7 Supplement 2, 206–211.

Murphy, K., Burch, D. and Clapp, J. (2012) Cereal secrets: The world's largest grain traders and global agriculture. Oxfam Research Reports. August. Available at: www.oxfam.org/sites/www.oxfam.org/files/rr-cereal-secrets-grain-traders-agriculture-30082012-en.pdf. Retrieved 14 November 2013.

National Geographic (2018) The Development of Agriculture. Available at: https://genographic.nationalgeographic.com/development-of-agriculture/, Retrieved 17 July 2018.

Ngex (2018) Obasanjo Farms. Available at: www.ngex.com/bd/b/Obasanjo-Farms-Ota-Ogun-Nigeria/. Retrieved 5 June 2018.

Nijs, L. (2014) *The Handbook of Global Agricultural Markets: The Business and Finance of Land, Water, and Soft Commodities.* Basingstoke, Palgrave Macmillan.

OECD-FAO (2016) *Agricultural Outlook 2016–2025.* Rome, FAO. Available at: www.fao.org/3/a-i5778e.pdf . Retrieved 16 May 2019.

Oliveira, A.L.R. and Alvim, A.M. (2017) The supply chain of Brazilian maize and soybeans: The effects of segregation on logistics and competitiveness. *International Food and Agribusiness Management Review* 20(1), 45–61.

Omatayo, A., Ogunniyi, A.I., Tchereni, B.H.M. and Nkonki-Mandleni, B. (2018) Understanding the Link between households' poverty and food security in South-West Nigeria. *Journal of Developing Areas* 52(3), 27–38.

Organic Africa (2018) *Training Manual.* Available at: www.organic-africa.net/training-manual.htm. Retrieved 5 June 2018.

Oryza (2018). About Rice. Available at: https://oryza.com/about-rice. Retrieved 6 June 2018.

Oxfam (2015) Global alliance on climate smart agriculture: solution or mirage? Oxfam blog. Available at: https://blogs.oxfam.org/en/blogs/15-09-26-global-alliance-climate-smart-agriculture-solution-or-mirage/. Retrieved 13 July 2018.

Parain, C. (1966) The evolution of agricultural technique. In Postanm M.M, Rich E.E. and Miller, E. (eds.) *The Cambridge Economic History of Europe from the Decline of the Roman Empire. Volume One.* Chapter Three. Cambridge, Cambridge University Press, 125–179.

PEI Department of Agriculture and Fisheries (2018) Soil Organic Matter Status on PEI. Available at: www.princeedwardisland.ca/en/information/agriculture-and-fisheries/soil-organic-matter-status-pei. Retrieved 31 July 2018.

Pindyck, R.S. (2004) Volatility and commodity price dynamics. *Journal of Futures Markets* 24(11), 1029–1047. Available at http://web.mit.edu/rpindyck/www/Papers/Volatility_Comm_Price.pdf. Retrieved 7 February 2018.

Pullman, M. and Wu, Z. (2012) *Food Supply Chain Management*. London and New York, Routledge.

PwC (2016) AgTech – don't wait for the future, create it. Africa Agribusiness Insights Survey 2016. Available at: www.pwc.co.za/en/assets/pdf/agri-businesses-insights-survey-may-2016.pdf. Retrieved 12 July 2016.

Quark, A.A and Slez, A. (2014) Interstate competition and Chinese ascendancy: The political construction of the global cotton market, 1973–2012. *International Journal of Comparative Sociology* 55(4), 269–293.

Rabobank (2016) *Outlook 2017 – Bear in Mind, Stocks Remain Large*. London, Rabobank.

Rabobank (2017) North American Agribusiness Review. Available at: https://research.rabobank.com/far/en/sectors/regional-food-agri/NA-ag-april-2017.html. Retrieved 16 June 2017.

Rabobank (2018) Outlook 2018: Good Buy, Low Prices. Available at: https://research.rabobank.com/far/en/sectors/agri-commodity-markets/outlook-2018-good-buy-low-prices.html. Retrieved 6 June 2018.

Rego, C.C.F.N., Rodríguez, J.M.M., Calzada, V.R.V, and Xanthopoulos, G. (2018) *Forest Fires – Sparking Firesmart Policies in the EU*. Publications Office of the European Union. Available at: https://ec.europa.eu/info/sites/info/files/181116_booklet-forest-fire-hd.pdf.

Ricepedia (2018) Cultivated Rice Species. Available at: http://ricepedia.org/rice-as-a-plant/rice-species/cultivated-rice-species. Retrieved 13 July 2018.

Ricketts, K. and Ricketts, C. (2009) *Agribusiness Fundamentals and Applications*. New York, CENGAGE Delmar Learning.

Ritchie, H. (2017) How much of the world's land would we need in order to feed the global population with the average diet of a given country? *Our World in Data*. 3 October. Available at: https://ourworldindata.org/agricultural-land-by-global-diets. Retrieved 23 February 2019.

Ritchie, H. and Roser, M. (2017) CO_2 and other greenhouse gas emissions. *Our World in Data*. May. Available at: https://ourworldindata.org/co2-and-other-greenhouse-gas-emissions Retrieved 24 February 2019.

Roche, J. (1995) *Commodity Forecasting*. London, Probus.

Roser, M. (2015) Employment in Agriculture. *Our World in Data*. Available at: https://ourworldindata.org/employment-in-agriculture Retrieved 26 February 2019.

Sakthivei, M. and Ramesh, S. (2013) Mechanical properties of natural fibre (banana, coir, sisal) polymer composites. *Science Park* 1(1), 1–6.

Salerno, T. (2017) Cargill's corporate growth in times of crises: How agro-commodity traders are increasing profits in the midst of volatility. *Agriculture and Human Values* 34(1), 211–222.

Sant' Anna, A.C., Shanoyanb, A., Bergtoldc, J.S., Caldasd, M.M. and Grancoe, G. (2016) Ethanol and sugarcane expansion in Brazil: What is fueling the ethanol industry? *International Food and Agribusiness Management Review* 19(4), 153–181.

Satterthwaite, D., McGranahan, G. and Tacoli, C. (2010) Urbanization and its implications for food and farming. *Philosophical Transactions of the Royal Society B* 365, 2809–2820. Available at: http://pubs.iied.org/pdfs/G03152.pdf. Retrieved 27 February 2018.

Science Daily (2017). Deforestation linked to palm oil production is making Indonesia warmer, study finds. 25 October. Available at: www.sciencedaily.com/releases/2017/10/171025090524.htm. Retrieved 6 June 2018.

Singh, K. (2011) Groundwater depletion in Punjab: Measurement and countering strategies. *Indian Journal of Agricultural Economics* 66(4), 573–589.

Sonker, S.T. and Hudson, M.A. (1999): Why agribusiness anyway? *Agribusiness* 14, 305–314.

Statista (2018) U.S. exports of corn from 2001 to 2017 (in million bushels). Available at: www.statista.com/statistics/191026/us-exports-of-corn-since-2001/. Retrieved 6 June 2018.

Tadele, Z. (2017) Raising crop productivity in Africa through intensification. *Agronomy* 7(1), 22; doi:10.3390/agronomy7010022. Available at: www.mdpi.com/2073–4395/7/1/22/htm. Retrieved 7 June 2018.

Taleb, M., Hariri, I., Ali, A., Anandan, V. and Yoon, Y. (2014) Pulmonary hypertension caused by constrictive bronchiolitis secondary to exposure to wood burning fumes. *Chest* 146(4), 880A.

Taylor, A. and Loopstra, R. (2016) *Too Poor to Eat: Food Insecurity in the UK*. Food Foundation. Available at: https://foodfoundation.org.uk/wp-content/uploads/2016/07/FoodInsecurityBriefing-May-2016-FINAL.pdf. Retrieved 9 July 2018.

Tigchelaar, M., Battisti, D.S., Naylor, R.L. and Ray, D.K. (2018) Future warming increases probability of globally synchronized maize production shocks. *Proceedings of the National Academy of Sciences of the United States of America* 115(26), 6644–6649. Available at: www.pnas.org/content/115/26/6644/. Retrieved 17 July 2018.

Tschirley, D.L., Snyder, J., Dolislager, M., Reardon, T., Haggblade, S., Goeb, J., Traub, L., Ejobi, F. and Meyer, F. (2015) Africa's unfolding diet transformation: Implications for agrifood system employment. *Journal of Agribusiness in Developing and Emerging Economies* 5(2), 102–136.

United Nations (1992) *United Nations Framework Convention on Climate Change*. New York, United Nations. Available at: https://unfccc.int/resource/docs/convkp/conveng.pdf. Retrieved 6 July 2018.

United Nations (2018) *Nature Based Solutions for Water. World Water Development Report 2018*. New York, United Nations. Available at: www.unwater.org/publications/world-water-development-report-2018/. Retrieved 21 July 2018.

USDA (2012) Farm Level Data. Available at: www.agcensus.usda.gov/Publications/2012/index.php. Retrieved 6 June 2018.

USDA (2014) 2012 Census Highlights. Available at: www.agcensus.usda.gov/Publications/2012/Online_Resources/Highlights/Farm_Economics/. Retrieved 17 July 2018.

USDA (2017) *China's Annual Agricultural Policy Goals. The 2017 No. 1 Document of the CCCPC and the State Council*. GAIN Report CH17006. 15 February. Washington DC, USDA. Available at: https://gain.fas.usda.gov/Recent%20GAIN%20Publications/China's%202017%20Agricultural%20Policy%20Goals_Beijing_China%20-%20Peoples%20Republic%20of_2-15–2017.pdf. Retrieved 5 June 2018.

USDA (2017a) Farms and Land in Farms. 2016 Summary. February. National Agricultural Statistics Survey. Available at: http://usda.mannlib.cornell.edu/usda/nass/FarmLandIn/2010s/2017/FarmLandIn-02-17-2017.pdfv. Retrieved 8 June 2018.

USDA (2017b) Russian Federation. Aquaculture Production Update. GAIN Report Number 1718. Available at: https://gain.fas.usda.gov/Recent%20GAIN%20Publications/Aquaculture%20Production%20Update_Moscow_Russian%20Federation_3-20–2017.pdf. Retrieved 20 December 2017.

USDA (2017c) Food Security in the U.S. Key Statistics and Graphics. Available at: www.ers.usda.gov/topics/food-nutrition-assistance/food-security-in-the-us/key-statistics-graphics.aspx#foodsecure. Retrieved 17 July 2018.

USDA (2018) World Agricultural Supply and Demand Estimates. Available at: www.usda.gov/oce/commodity/wasde/latest.pdf. Retrieved 6 June 2018. See also: www.usda.gov/oce/commodity/wasde/Secretary_Briefing.pdf where there may be slight differences.

USDA (2018a) *Food Expenditures*. 26 July. Available at: www.ers.usda.gov/data-products/food-expenditures.aspx. Retrieved 27 July 2018.

US Environmental Protection Agency (EPA) (2015) Delaware Animal Agriculture Program Assessment. Available at: www.epa.gov/sites/production/files/2015-09/documents/delawareanimalagriculture programassessment.pdf. Retrieved 11 June 2018.

Viviano, F. (2017) This tiny country feeds the world. *National Geographic*. September. Available at: www.nationalgeographic.com/magazine/2017/09/holland-agriculture-sustainable-farming/. Retrieved 8 June 2018.

Wolka, K., Tadesse, H. Garedew, E. and Yimer, F. (2015) Soil erosion risk assessment in the Chaleleka wetland watershed, Central Rift Valley of Ethiopia. *Environmental Systems Research* 4(5), doi 10.1186/s40068-015-0030-5. Available at: https://link.springer.com/article/10.1186/s40068-015-0030-5. Retrieved 12 February 2018.

World Bank (2013) *Growing Africa: Unlocking the Potential of Agribusiness*. Washington DC, World Bank.

World Bank (2015) *Ending Poverty and Hunger by 2030: An Agenda for the Global Food System*. Washington DC, World Bank.

World Bank (2016) *The Future of Food: Shaping the Global Food System to Deliver Improved Nutrition and Health*. Washington DC, World Bank.

World Bank (2017) *Options for Increased Private Sector Participation in Resilience Investment. Focus on Agriculture*. Washington DC, World Bank.

World Counts (2019) Global Meat Consumption Statistics. Available at: www.theworldcounts.com/counters/world_food_consumption_statistics/world_meat_consumption_statistics. Retrieved 7 June 2018.

World Economic Forum (2016) Which countries spend the most on food? This map will show you. Available at: www.weforum.org/agenda/2016/12/this-map-shows-how-much-each-country-spends-on-food/. Retrieved 27 July 2018.

World Food Programme (WFP) (2018) 2018 Global Report on Food Crises. Available at: www.wfp.org/content/global-report-food-crises-2018. Retrieved 6 June 2018.

World Health Organisation (2015) Healthy Diet. 14 September. Available at: www.who.int/newsroom/fact-sheets/detail/healthy-diet. Retrieved 27 July 2018.

World Health Organisation (2018) Increasing fruit and vegetable consumption to reduce the risk of noncommunicable diseases. Available at: www.who.int/elena/titles/fruit_vegetables_ncds/en/. Retrieved 27 July 2018.

Zaidi, B. and Philip Morgan, S. (2017) The second demographic transition theory: A Review and appraisal. *Annual Review of Sociology* 43, 471–492.

Zambian Environmental Management Agency (ZEMA) (2018) Available at: www.zema.org.zm/index.php/download/eis-proposed-agriculture-development-lukulu-farm-kasama-district-northern-province/. Retrieved 10 July 2018.

Agricultural economics

Introduction: resources, scarcity, economic policy and systems

Agricultural economics, a long-established discipline (Runge, 2006), covers areas such as production economics (farm management), the supply and demand for food and other agricultural products, as well as agricultural finance, rural development, price analysis, agricultural policy, the impact of macroeconomic activity on agriculture, international development and marketing (Ricketts & Ricketts, 2009:36).

A leading textbook suggested that:

> Agricultural economics is an applied field of economics that focuses primarily on food and fiber production and consumption. Defining the boundaries of agricultural economics can be difficult, however, because issues outside these traditional areas have become increasingly important to the profession in recent years. Agricultural economists engage in work ranging from farm-level cost accounting to assessing the consumer impact of food safety and nutrition labeling to analyzing worldwide agricultural trade patterns and a host of other real-world issues (Duffy, 2010: 598).

Alternatively:

> Agricultural economics is the social science that deals with the allocation of scarce resources among those competing alternative uses found in the production, processing, distribution and consumption of food and fiber (Drummond & Goodwin, 2004:11).

However defined, agricultural economics draws on the basic concepts of market economics: scarcity, markets, supply and demand, opportunity costs, diminishing marginal returns (and rising marginal costs), costs and returns, timescales, externalities and concepts of value, and then applies these concepts specifically to agriculture.

It is accurate enough to say, as economists do, that all societies must decide what to produce, how much of it, how and when to produce, and who should get the benefits. It is also quite reasonable to distinguish between macro- and micro-economics, to distinguish between the national and international economies and the decision-making processes of individual firms and people. This chapter addresses both the macro and micro issues, with farm management analysed in Chapter 5, but trade, considered in Chapter 3, is also a macro issue, whilst the economics of supply and demand, costs of production and such issues as economies of scale and market structure are deeply relevant to the success or failure of the firms analysed in Chapters 7, 12 and 13, at least over a prolonged period of time. *How relevant these issues are to the decision-making process of firms themselves, however, is a different question.*

Traditional agricultural macroeconomics sets out its stall as follows. The existence of linkages between the agricultural sector and the rest of the economy points to the specificity of that sector and justifies why a macroeconomics of agriculture is even possible. From an economic perspective, the primary sector is, or was, characterised by relative product homogeneity, a pre-condition for the absence of imperfect competition, as basic agricultural products are more likely to be homogenous or largely indistinguishable from each other than are other products in the market (Duffy, 2010), although the power of branding in the 21st century, when combined with the rise of canned, chilled and frozen food sales, has arguably diminished that homogeneity. Also, agricultural prices are volatile, and subject to seasonal fluctuations that affect stocks, demand and prices. That much is set to continue. Moreover, farming activities are in some countries the occupation of a majority of the population and are very geographically dispersed. This, however, is also changing and diminishing, even in developing countries. Finally, traditional agricultural macroeconomics argued that the production of commodities relied on a relatively static irreproducible factor of production – land – whose availability is finite and whose productivity cannot be individually infinitely increased. Often ignored in this argument is the fact that in the USA, as in many developed countries, 'Even though the number of acres of farmland is decreasing, the economic land base is increasing. The productivity of land is increasing faster than the acres are decreasing' (Ricketts & Ricketts, 2009:42), a trend which has continued in the decade after they wrote, for example with the rise of vertical farms which has now placed in serious question the whole concept of a fixed supply of land (Al-Kodmany, 2018).

Even with these doubts over the traditional model, it is reasonable just on the twin assumptions of price volatility and the importance of agriculture to governments worldwide (both from a production/export perspective and in terms of consumption by the population) that macroeconomic policy should affect the agricultural sector, and agricultural prices and markets will through linkages affect other sectors and the macroeconomy in a specific way, and vice versa. Models and studies attempting to quantify the linkages have then discussed in terms of theoretical constructs, structural econometric models, computable general-equilibrium models and time-series models (Ardeni & Freebairn, 2002).

Two traditions, meanwhile, have co-existed within growth economics (Engel, 2010). One of them has its roots in traditional development economics. It draws a sharp, arbitrary distinction between the 'traditional' and 'modern' sectors of the economy, typically characterised as agriculture and industry, respectively. The neoclassical model, on the other hand, presumes different types of economic activity are structurally similar enough to be aggregated into a single representative sector. As agriculture morphs into agribusiness, the idea of any country migrating 'away' from agriculture becomes less realistic, and the idea that agriculture as a sector within developed countries is in some sense 'traditional' becomes entirely inappropriate. Rather, the question in any country becomes the degree of industrialisation within the agricultural sector (and many other factors such as the value chain) which determine the relative position of the sector for development purposes. But this will come at a cost. In the past, according to the World Bank, overall, growth originating from agriculture has been two to four times more effective at reducing poverty than growth originating from other sectors, without costing any more to achieve than income gains in other sectors. Smallholder productivity has recently increased even in the poorest regions such as sub-Saharan Africa, where higher cereal yields have been closely correlated with a higher share of the population above the poverty line (World Bank, 2015:7). However, this optimism and relative advantage of agriculture, specifically, may well change. If industrialisation brings with it a decrease in jobs, as has definitely been the case in developed countries notwithstanding statistics that conceal the rise in part-time and semi-employment, then without active policies to redistribute wealth, future increases in agricultural productivity driven by agtech, as with other industries, will *not* necessarily continue to bring the same kind of reduction in poverty, unless the increased wealth it generates is redistributed through taxation. If the International Monetary Fund (IMF) is worried, so should be policymakers everywhere (Berg *et al.*, 2018)

Microeconomic analysis

The other persistent strand of agricultural economics is the attempted application of microeconomic theory to farm management. It has been contended that production theory is used in farm management applications, estimations of productivity growth, and formulation of estimates of the response of agricultural output to changes in economic conditions. The basis of production theory in microeconomics is undoubtedly the production function, which attempts to show the relationship between inputs (traditionally land, labour, capital and an amorphous 'entrepreneurship', in fact more often management) and outputs, in physical terms. To produce an agricultural output such as rice or cotton, for example, land, fertiliser, labour and other inputs are required. A production function analyses the theoretical way these different inputs combine to produce rice or wheat, usually in a specific geographic area and type of production for which statistics are available, testing a specific production function, i.e. relationship between inputs and outputs (e.g. Kea et al., 2016; Ghoshal & Goswami, 2017)

In principle, costs can be broadly categorised as fixed and variable. The difference is entirely obvious: fixed costs do not vary with the level of production. Rents, insurance, the salaries of administrative staff and depreciation on capital equipment (an expenditure, just not a *cash* expenditure) are all examples of expenditures which do not directly vary with the level of production. In other words, if the output of the farm in a given time period were zero, these costs still have to be met. In contrast, variable costs are those expenditures which vary in direct relation to the volume of farm output. Examples of this class of cost include fertiliser (except where bought on a regular supply contract), casual labour on the farm and packaging costs.

If total fixed costs (TFC) are divided by the number of units produced then the average fixed cost (AFC) per unit of output is obtained. Similarly, dividing the total variable cost (TVC) by the number of units of output gives the average variable cost (AVC). Average total cost (ATC) is obviously the sum of AFC + AVC. As production increases, fixed costs are spread over a larger output and so AFC falls. AVCs also fall, over a certain range of production levels, as the farm benefits from economies of scale. However, at some point AVCs will start to rise again as diseconomies of scale take effect: Given these cost patterns, an agribusiness, like every other business, is naturally interested in identifying the point at which AVCs are at their lowest. It does not necessarily follow, however, that the agribusiness will stop production at that point, because it may be the case that the market is willing to pay a higher unit price to secure supplies of the product. Ideally, the agribusiness would like to find the point at which supply, demand, prices and costs would allow it to maximise profits.

To this end, marginal analysis should be employed. In some cases, an input may be limited so that the profit-maximising point cannot be reached for all possible uses. *A limited input should in principle be allocated among competing uses in such a way that the marginal value products of the last unit used on each alternative are equal.*

Production functions are therefore largely dependent on assumptions regarding diminishing marginal returns from particular inputs, e.g. the reduced returns to increased applications of fertiliser, the inefficiency of deploying labour beyond the required level of a given quantity of land.

Supply and demand curves

Agricultural microeconomists have also sought to create supply and demand curves for particular agricultural commodities based on neoclassical assumptions regarding perfect markets, traditional assumptions about the elasticity of demand for food staples and the largely price-taking position of the overwhelming majority of agricultural producers.

The theoretical laws of supply and demand are even more widely known and understood. Price theory holds that *ceteris paribus*, as prices increase so demand falls and supplies increase, i.e. a downward-sloping demand curve. Conversely, supply increases with price. Where the two curves intersect, the market clears, equilibrium is reached, and the quantity of the agricultural product supplied and bought by the market can be identified. The theory can accommodate some dynamics. If incomes rise, more will be demanded. And the price will rise. If the product suddenly acquires a substitute product, as butter did with margarine, or certain locally-produced fruits did in Western markets with the introduction of hitherto unknown tropical fruits, then the opposite will occur. Similarly, a supply curve can shift as a result of climate change, alterations in input prices (fertiliser, fuel prices, the cost of farm labour, etc), regulatory pressure, or, considering a local market, a change in import levels.

It is certainly a reasonable argument that any agribusiness must be concerned with how the level of demand for its product will change in response to a price change. This is the question of *price elasticity*. Supermarkets, as well as wholesalers, face price questions all the time. If the cost of coffee rises, for instance, should the supermarket raise its price to consumers? Total revenue could either rise or fall depending on how big the increase in demand is in relation to how much the supermarket raises the price of a packet of coffee on the net or on the shelf. When the price elasticity of demand is greater than unity (one), it is 'elastic', as for many luxury goods it undoubtedly is. Staples, on the other hand, tend to have much lower elasticities of demand. A raise in price will cut total revenue revenue only if demand is elastic, and vice versa if demand is inelastic. Price elasticity of demand therefore measures by how much buyers change their behaviour in response to price changes. It is measured by the percentage change in the quantity of a product demanded divided by the percentage change in its price. Similarly, the elasticity of price with respect to supply is a measure of how much the amount supplied to the market changes when price alters. The price elasticity of supply of a product is therefore the percentage change in the quantity of product supplied divided by the percentage change in its price.

There are also cross-elasticities, which measure the change in demand or supply as a result of changes in price or supply of other commodities or products. For many food products, however, it is very difficult to calculate cross-elasticities. What, for example, are the likely fruits or vegetables for which it would make any sense to calculate cross-elasticity of demand for avocados? The problem is, every consumer has a slightly different substitute for avocados. The task may well be simply impossible. Government intervention, for example in restricting imports, granting subsidies or setting floor prices, further complicates consumer decision-making and makes the determination of elasticities that much more difficult. Compounding all these problems are the continually changing characteristics of markets for agricultural produce, even for cotton and wool. The market in reality will not stand still long enough for a detailed elasticity calculation to be made, albeit that decision-makers must make decisions which would be vastly improved if elasticities could not only be calculated, but *accurately forecast*. Efforts none-theless are made to make estimates, even in fluid regulatory environments (e.g. Odemero, 2013).

Many agricultural management texts refer to the idea of *pricing strategies* for agribusiness either based on costs or on the market. One set of approaches to pricing are those which start from a consideration of internal factors, i.e. the agribusiness's costs structures and target profit margins. When a more realistic set of assumptions is made about market-based pricing, agricul-tural economists come much closer to how in practice most agribusinesses have to price their products, as there are few businesses of any sort, and certainly not production agriculturalists, that are able to charge based on their costs. Rather, they are price-takers and must accept whatever the market throws at them from season to season. Agricultural economists frequently suggest the importance of the break-even point is where the number of units of the product sold, at a given price, is just sufficient to cover both the fixed and variable costs incurred. Deducting the variable costs from the selling price gives us the contribution each unit, whether a tray of avocados or a ready meal, when sold, makes towards fixed costs.

How agricultural economists envisage pricing decisions being made

An avocado farm has fixed costs of $500,000. Assume that the variable cost of production, per tray of avocados, is $10 and that the farmer is considering selling to local wholesalers at $20. The farm needs to sell 50,000 bags of avocados before it breaks even. The farmer considers the size of the potential market, the prices of other close competitors (if there are any) and the elasticity of demand for avocados. The farmer will also wish to estimate total sales, and therefore the farm's total profitability. Suppose that the demand for avocados is best represented by a normal downward sloping demand curve (i.e. demand increases as the selling price falls) and that three possible wholesale prices are being considered: $15, $20 and $25. As the selling price is raised, the break-even point falls and the per tray contribution to fixed costs increases. However, it is achieving the right balance between the per tray contribution and demand that matters. So, whilst the $25 price is the best per tray contribution and the $15 price obviously maximises demand, possibly it is the $20 price that returns the best profit.

The demand for food

Agricultural commodities have three main uses: food, feed and fuel. Demand for each of these uses is increasing, competing with each other and putting pressure of varying degrees on supply to meet this demand. Researchers for the Australian Bureau of Agricultural and Resource Economics (ABARES) summarised the issues neatly at mid-decade:

> Food consumption at the national level relates to the size of the population and the amount of food consumed by each person. Changes in per person food consumption, as well as in the mix of foods consumed, are largely influenced by growth in household incomes and by factors such as the age structure of the population, lifestyle, and the proportion of the population living in urban and rural areas (Gunning-Trant *et al.*, 2015:2).

The starting point for the analysis of demand is population growth, which is the most fundamental factor driving an increase in the consumption of agricultural products. As noted in Chapter 1, global population has grown substantially over the past few decades, and will grow from its current level of around 7 billion. In studying future food demand, Lutz *et al.* (2014) recommended adopting, with some caveats, the United Nations Population Division projections with the 'medium fertility' assumption (United Nations, 2004), which forecast global population of 9 billion by 2050. However, they argued that this would only be achieved by lowering the UN projection of approximately 1.8 children per adult female, which they argued overestimated fertility in China and which they thought more likely to be 1.5 (though not as low as the official estimates of 1.2). China, and India, are large enough that changes in assumptions of this kind make a difference. With this adjustment, they argued that global population growth was predicted to decelerate and reach just over 9 billion in 2050; without, it could be expected to grow to almost 10 billion by 2050, boosting agricultural demand – in a scenario of modest economic growth – by some 50% compared to 2013 (FAO, 2017:x). Subsequent United Nations population estimates (United Nations, 2017) revised these estimates upwards, with the current world population of 7.6 billion in 2017 then expected to reach 8.6 billion in 2030, 9.8 billion in 2050 and 11.2 billion in 2100. The UN also noted that, from 2017 to 2050, it was expected that half of the world's population growth will be concentrated in just nine countries: in descending order of their contribution, India, Nigeria, the Democratic Republic of the Congo, Pakistan, Ethiopia, Tanzania, the USA, Uganda and Indonesia.

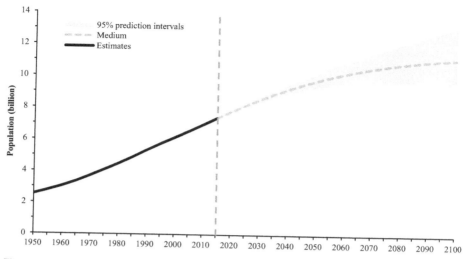

Figure 2.1 Long-term global population growth
Source: United Nations (2017:2)

Either way, there is no doubt about the need for extra agricultural production, with roughly 80 million more people to feed each year, and in countries that require food imports. In the longer term, most assumptions (e.g. the FAO, USDA) are, and have been for some time, that population growth will slow, for which there is already evidence (May, 2017), but the medium term is quite long enough to be looking at the future of agribusiness, especially given the kind of discounted cash flow (DCF) valuations that are in usual use for valuations (see Chapters 5, 12 and 13).

Increasing affluence: dietary change

Bennett's law describes how, as people become wealthier, they switch from simple starchy plant-dominated diets to a more varied food input that includes a range of vegetables, fruit, dairy products, and especially meat (Godfray, 2011). As people who are initially under-nourished obtain access to more food calories, they first go through an expansion phase where diets contain just more food – typically, grains, roots, tubers and pulses – and then a substitution phase, where the latter are replaced by more energy-rich foods such as meat and those with a high concentration of vegetable oils and sugar. This change in dietary habits is most pronounced in emerging economies, where, according to PwC amongst many other forecasts, the strongest economic growth is expected over the next decades (PwC, 2017). The developing world has more than doubled its per capita meat consumption in the last three decades and is widely expected to continue this comparatively greater growth than the developed world. The World Health Organisation expects annual meat production – almost all beef, pork and chicken – to reach 376 million tonnes by 2030, compared to 262.8 million in 2017, twice as much meat as in 1986 (Beef2Live, 2018).

The result is what is called *nutritional transition,* which has major implications for food supply, and which organisations have tried to model (Trinh Thi *et al.,* 2018). One recent study came to the conclusion that, whilst overall food demand could be expected to rise by roughly half between 2010–2050, this single statistic would conceal an almost doubling in demand for animal-based calories and a much smaller one-fifth increase in demand for starchy staples (Gouel & Guimbard, 2017). Typically, the production of high-energy food such as beef requires more resources (for example, instead of grain being directly consumed by humans, it is used as animal feed for livestock production which is then consumed by humans, overall a much more inefficient process). Increased consumption of high-energy foods can also increase the risk of obesity and the chronic diseases associated with being overweight: indeed, as the FAO pointed out, child and adult obesity are on the rise, including in low- and middle-income countries. In addition, 'it is anticipated that more animal production facilities will end up located close to urban areas due to urban sprawl, thereby increasing public health risks' (Pullman & Wu, 2012:35), a trend that only reduced transport costs will curb.

Further, in the next few decades, population growth is expected to be concentrated in developing and emerging economies, so some countries that have previously been self-sufficient will need to start food imports. Although the rate of growth is slowly decelerating, the absolute annual increases are undeniably large. Secondly, urbanisation is also closely linked to economic growth and rising incomes. Global dietary patterns are also being influenced by a complex and changing pattern of socio-economic trends and drivers. Most obviously, ever more people live in cities where they often have relatively sedentary occupations and often have relatively high disposable incomes, certainly in real terms and by comparison to previous generations. Increasing urbanisation and urban spread has a direct, though sometimes exaggerated, effect on the land available for agriculture, but many more indirect effects. Urban populations can access a greater diversity of foods, though this may include meat, dairy and convenience foods – types of food that may have required more resources for their production or be less healthy – as many studies, from Japan to Australia suggest (Smil & Kobayashi, 2012; Martin *et al.,* 2017), although it would be wrong to conclude that the case is yet proven. Urbanisation can also have very positive effects on rural areas and food production, in general by increasing national wealth and more specifically by creating markets for food producers. In developing countries in particular there are often strong financial links between people living in cities and the countryside, with remittances from urban households financing innovation and yield growth in farming (Satterthwaite *et al.,* 2010). It is a 'wicked problem' – multiple forms of malnutrition are actually coexisting, with countries experiencing simultaneously high rates of child undernutrition and adult obesity (FAO, 2017:1).

The factors that underpin urbanisation include the search for employment or higher paying employment, access to better health and education services, and greater entertainment and lifestyle options. Urbanisation usually leads to higher per capita income and an increase in living standards, including for example greater access to refrigeration, which, in turn, results in urban populations consuming a higher number of calories demanding better quality and a greater variety of food products. The UN estimated in 2014 that, by

2050, 66% of the world's population is projected to be urban, up from around half currently. Projected global shifts in consumption patterns to more livestock and dairy products, which are more emissions-intensive than cereals, will also increase the challenge of lowering aggregate emissions intensity in the sector (World Bank, 2015:13).

There are also expected to continue to be marked regional variations: Europe's population will decline, despite immigration, Africa's will double – more than that, in many areas already suffering from malnutrition – while China will peak in about 2030 and may well already have been overtaken by India around 2020. Migration, changes in religious affiliations and even tourism will be key demographic characteristics of the near future (Sardak et al., 2018). Populations will age – quickly in developed countries, more gradually in the developing world – but the old will be healthier and attitudes to old age, already very different from even a generation ago, can be expected to change further. Growth in food demand is reflected in projected rejuvenation of demand for wheat, which is one of the primary food grains, demand for which grew, according to the FAO, at around 1.6% annually during the 2000s and 2010s (Enghiad et al., 2017). No doubt, economic growth in the emerging markets is the prime source of growth in the demand for agricultural products, wheat amongst others, as rising per capita incomes and urbanisation are resulting in greater consumption of food, as well as a shift in the dietary patterns in these countries. Increasing demand for food is caused not only by a rise in population size but, as many including Kearney (2010) observed, a rise in per capita consumption.

Beyond this, it is important to know the full *distribution* of per capita income and how this is reflected in food purchases, which is an area of active research in behavioural economics (Just, 2016). Engel's law states that, as income increases, households' demand for food increases less than proportionally. As may be expected, demonstrating the veracity of this law in practice is difficult, especially as the Engel curve is nonlinear. One also cannot just use *per capita* behaviour either, as the size of households, the number of children and different tastes between cultures alter the income/food demand relationship. What seems certain, however, is that distribution of income between households and countries affects the rate of growth of food demand. One review of the literature (Cirera & Masset, 2010) therefore suggested that existing models of food demand fail to incorporate the required Engel flexibility when aggregating different food budget shares among households; and budget share changes as income grows. Their use of simulations of a fairer and less equal scenario of income inequality suggested that world food demand in 2050 would be 2.7% higher and 5.4% lower than distributional-neutral growth, respectively. Not all food requires the same resources for its production, and to understand the full consequence of increased wealth, there is a need to couple Engel's law with Bennett's law.

On the supply side, economic growth, regulatory liberalisation, the encouragement of foreign direct investment and globalisation in general has allowed a burgeoning fast-food and supermarket sector to develop to meet this demand. In the last decade of last century, the service and retail sectors in Latin America made changes that had previously taken 50 years in North America, and much of Asia and Eastern Europe are only a few years behind and catching up fast. This increased economic activity in the food sector brought advantages such as employment and investment opportunities, and often increased the availability and safety

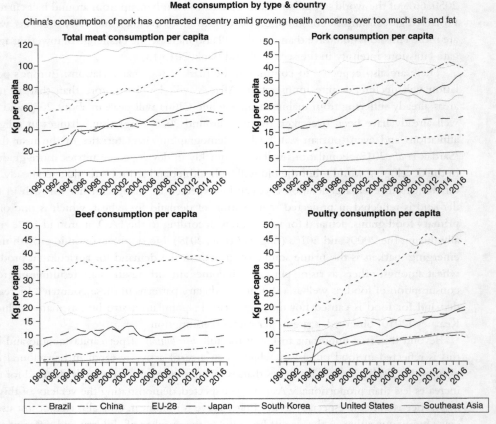

Meat consumption by type & country

China's consumption of pork has contracted recentry amid growing health concerns over too much salt and fat

Total meat consumption per capita

Pork consumption per capita

Beef consumption per capita

Poultry consumption per capita

- - - - Brazil   — · — China   EU-28   — · Japan   —— South Korea   United States   —— Southeast Asia

Figure 2.2 Meat consumption by type and country
Source: FAO (2015a)

of the food on offer to its consumers. But by making cheap foods rich in fats and sugars easily available (many processed foods contain as much as 30% fat), there were important health implications. Significantly, South Korea, which has vigorously promoted local foods rather than a Western diet, has lower rates of obesity than similar countries, although how long it can continue the fight remains to be seen.

This pessimistic outlook is not the whole story, for three main reasons. First, worldwide, chicken is the huge winner – the world produces twice as much chicken as two decades ago, but only a fifth more beef and two-fifths more pork. Even in the USA, it was identified in the early 2010s that 'beef has lost ground due to health concerns and pricing. Chicken has gradually replaced beef as the meat of choice whilst pork has made gradual inroads and lamb has stagnated' (Pullman & Wu, 2012:34). These trends have continued, and intensified, in the subsequent decade. Second, the overall pattern of the nutritional transition hides many interesting local variations. For example, while China has seen a very strong increase in the consumption of high-energy foods, in India, for cultural and religious reasons, the rise has been much less marked, for equivalent levels of income. Third, the trend may now have peaked. Chinese pork demand seems to have hit a ceiling, well ahead of most official forecasts. Sales of pork have now fallen by around 1–5% annually, with expectations that they would continue to fall (Reuters, 2017) or at least remain relatively flat.

But despite all this alleged progress, and certainly a great deal more convenience, variety and consumer choice for the majority, 800 million people still go to bed hungry every night, and an even greater number live in poverty (defined as living on less than $1.25 per day). Agricultural economics cannot explain the causes of why these people still are not getting the minimum dietary energy needs. The majority of these people are in sub-Saharan Africa, in which – figures vary, but approximately – 1 in 4 people are hungry; and in South Asia, in which 1 in 6 people are hungry. More than 2 billion people are deficient in key vitamins and minerals that are necessary for growth, development and disease prevention. Most are in rural areas. Last decade, over 900 million poor people (78% of the poor) lived in rural areas, with about 750 million working in agriculture (63% of the total poor). Mid-decade, the World Bank forecast that about 200 million rural poor could migrate to urban areas by 2030, based on urbanisation projections and assuming migration of a proportional share of the rural population that is poor (World Bank, 2015:5–6). Since then, there are some limited suggestions that the drift from the countryside may be slowing, at least, partly due to concerted government policy in some cases, at least in China, where a cap on population in 2035 has been placed on two of its biggest cities, Beijing (23 million) and Shanghai (25 million). But this does little to stop urban growth in megacities as geographically diverse as Bogota, Lagos and Dhaka. Meanwhile, globally, over 2 billion people are overweight or obese, two-thirds of whom live in developing countries.

Distributional problems evidently abound. But the central Malthusian problem, that of the total volume of agricultural production, is not the world's central concern – at least, not to date. More area has been devoted to agriculture, even last century, whilst productivity has increased too, in some cases quite dramatically. Data on production and yields to support this contention can be found on FAOSTAT and from the USDA (2018, 2018a, 2018b), whilst world population data are available from the World Bank.

Modelling food demand – an example

A typical modelling framework for agribusiness now looks like that shown in Figure 2.3, which indicates just how difficult an industry it is to model and forecast

When ABARES wanted to analyse Indonesian food demand long-term, they updated and used the ABARES agri-food model (Linehan et al., 2012). This model was a partial equilibrium economic model of global agricultural production, consumption and trade with a base year of 2009. The agri-food products in the model included both primary and lightly transformed agricultural products, such as flour and meat. Uses of agri-food products include direct food use, feed use and industrial use. Highly processed food items, such as beverages and packaged foods, were not included, nor are non-food agricultural commodities and cash crops, such as natural rubber, copra, palm kernels, coffee, cocoa and

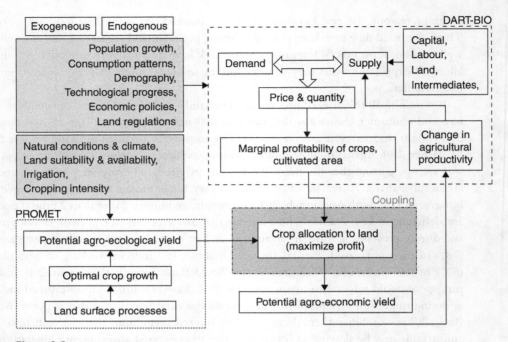

Figure 2.3 A model for agribusiness
Source: Mauser *et al.* (2015)

spices. In addition, Indonesia's targeted consumer subsidy for rice, Raskin, was built into the model baseline.

Their conclusions were as follows:

Continued strong income and population growth, combined with greater urbanisation, are driving Indonesia's increasing demand for not only more food but for a wider variety of foods. This demand growth is projected to be met by increases in both domestic production and imports.

Assuming no major changes to Indonesia's existing agricultural policies to 2050, the real value of food consumption in Indonesia is projected to increase more than four times between 2009 and 2050. The increase will be characterised by a move towards more diverse diets, with higher intake of meat, dairy products, fruit and vegetables. Between 2009 and 2050, the real value of beef consumption is projected to rise more than 14 times, dairy tenfold, and fruit and vegetables to more than triple. These projected increases are from a relatively low base and are driven by a rise in the quantities consumed, rather than any significant projected rise in real prices. To support this rise in demand, imports of many agrifood commodities are projected to increase to 2050.

The contribution of meat, dairy products, fruit and vegetables in Indonesian diets will increase more quickly than cereals and staples to 2050. While cereals and starchy staples will remain important components of Indonesian diets, their relative contribution will decline – the continuation of a trend that began around 1990.

The upward trend in food demand is most pronounced among urban households, whose income growth is assumed to be more than double that of rural households. A declining rural population and relatively lower incomes will result in slower growth in food consumption compared with the urban population.

For most agricultural commodities, assuming no significant change to historical TFP [total factor productivity] growth for total agriculture, production is projected to increase at a slower rate than consumption. As a result, food imports will be an important component of Indonesia's food and feed supply towards 2050. The real value of Indonesia's agrifood imports is projected to rise more than 20 times from 2009 to US$152bn (in 2009 US dollar terms) in 2050.

The projected significant increases in consumption and import demand for food in Indonesia are based on the assumption of relatively strong income growth to 2050. Under a lower growth scenario, consumption of protein-based food products, such as meat and dairy products, is projected to be around 14 to 17% lower than the reference case at 2050. While consumption of domestically produced products is also projected to be lower in 2050 in the lower-income-growth scenario, the declines are less significant compared with the baseline case.

While not included in the modelling in this report, there is scope for increased production of non-food agricultural commodities and cash crops in Indonesia, in which it has a comparative advantage. These include natural rubber, copra, palm kernels, coffee, cocoa and spices. Indonesia's current policies on food self-sufficiency favour investment in food industries rather than the non-food and cash crops industries. This has the effect of allocating resources away from their most efficient use (Gunning-Trant *et al.*, 2015:31).

Whilst it would be unreasonable to judge the performance of these models without a comprehensive, retrospective cross-sectional analysis, there are clear difficulties in forecasting food demand in this way. Some of the forecasting based on demographics is reasonably reliable. It is the fine-tuning of the forecasts where policy considerations (e.g. import restrictions, subsidies to domestic producers, and many other examples) can make a large difference. Macro analysis is much easier than the kind of micro analysis to where we next turn. Yet only the successful combination of both types of analysis can deliver value for individual investors.

Conclusion

Descriptive economic analysis at the macro level can accurately portray consumer government expenditure on food. Poverty, hunger and affluence can all be modelled, even if the multiplier is now more difficult to estimate than in the past. On the other hand, microeconomic analysis is subject to the same limitations as the assumptions on which it is based, e.g. that all agribusinesses seek to maximise profits, when in practice, they do not necessarily do. Moreover, it is difficult, if not sometimes impossible, to estimate demand curves. The supply side of the pricing equation is less difficult since costs can usually be calculated fairly reliably, but demand must be estimated from market research. In practice, most agribusinesses aim to price at a level where they will achieve complete clearance of their products, which is rendered easier, in a sense, by the fact that they are price takers who cannot determine market prices. However, as Chapter 5 will show, farmers generally do not take opportunity costs properly into account in their decision-making processes as they 'ought' to according to economic theory. Nor are demand schedules, the structure of diminishing returns, price or cross-elasticities of demand, or exact marginal costs of additional production, very clearly known by either producers or others in the agribusiness value chain. Clearly, there is a real need for understanding of process, policy and practice in the development of agricultural economic theory.

A place for agricultural economics, even for macro and micro theory within it, no doubt remains. But a wider economics of agribusiness, applying the principles of economics to the wider areas of crop and livestock production, distribution, manufacture and consumption, investment and financial performance, is already emerging to complement it.

Bibliography

Alexandratos, N. and Bruinsma, J. (2012) *World Agriculture Towards 2030/2050*, ESA Working Paper 12-03. Rome, FAO. Available at: www.fao.org/docrep/016/ap106e/ap106e.pdf. Retrieved 6 June 2018.

Al-Kodmany, K. (2018) The vertical farm: A review of developments and implications for the vertical city. *Buildings* 8(24). Available at: www.mdpi.com/2075–5309/8/2/24. Retrieved 13 July 2018.

Ardeni, P.G. and Freebairn, J. (2002) The macroeconomics of agriculture. In Gardner, B.L. and Rausser, G.C. (eds.) *Handbook of Agricultural Economics*. Amsterdam, Elsevier, Volume 2(1), 1455–1485.

Beef2Live (2018) World Meat Production by Year. Available at: http://beef2live.com/story-world-meat-production-year-0-111818. Retrieved 6 June 2018.

Berg. A., Buffie, E.F. and Zanna, L. (2018) *Technology and the Future of Work*. Washington DC, IMF. Available at: www.imf.org/en/Publications/WP/Issues/2018/05/21/Should-We-Fear-the-Robot-Revolution-The-Correct-Answer-is-Yes-44923. Retrieved 31 July 2018.

Cirera, X. and Masset, E. (2010) Income distribution trends and future food demand. *Philosophical Transactions of the Royal Society B: Biological Sciences*, 365(1554), 2821–2834.

Drummond, H.E. and Goodwin, J.W. (2004) *Agricultural Economics*, 2nd edition. New Jersey, Prentice Hall International Journal of Economics, Finance and Management Sciences.

Duffy, P. (2010) Agricultural economics. In Free, R.C. (ed.) *21st Century Economics: A Reference Handbook*: Thousand Oaks, SAGE Publications, 597–606.

Engel, S.N. (2010) Development economics: From classical to critical analysis. In R. A. Denemark and R. Marlin-Bennett (eds.) *The International Studies Encyclopedia,* Volume Two. West Sussex, Blackwell Publishing, 874–892.

Enghiad, A., Ufer, D., Countryman, A.M. and Thilmany, D.D. (2017) An overview of global wheat market fundamentals in an era of climate concerns. *International Journal of Agronomy* 2017(19), 1–15.

FAO (2015) Global Perspectives. Available at: www.fao.org/global-perspectives-studies/en/. Retrieved 16 May 2019.

FAO (2017) *The State of Food Insecurity and Nutrition in the World*. Rome, FAO. Available at: www.fao. org/3/a-I7695e.pdf. Retrieved 30 October 2017.

Godfray, C. (2011) Food for thought. *Proceedings of the National Academy of Sciences of the United States of America* 108(50), 19845–19846. Available at: www.pnas.org/content/108/50/19845. Retrieved 27 July 2018.

Ghoshal, P. and Goswami, B. (2017) Cobb-Douglas production function for measuring efficiency in Indian agriculture: A region-wise analysis. *Economic Affairs* 62(4), 573–579.

Gouel, C. and Guimbard, H. (2017) *Nutrition Transition and the Structure of Global Food Demand*. Centre d'Etudes Prospectives et d'Informations Internationales. Working Paper Number 2017-05. March. Paris, CEPII. Available at: www.cepii.fr/PDF_PUB/wp/2017/wp2017-05.pdf. Retrieved 27 July 2018.

Gunning-Trant, C., Sheng, Y., Hamshere, P., Gleeson, T. and Moir, B. (2015) *What Indonesia Wants. Analysis of Indonesia's Food Demand to 2050*. Canberra, ABARES.

Just, D.R. (2016) Food and consumer behavior: Why the details matter. *Agricultural Economics* 47(S1), 73–83.

Kea, S., Li, H. and Pich, L. (2016) Technical efficiency and its determinants of rice production in Cambodia. *Economies* 4(4), 1–17.

Kearney, J. (2010) Food consumption trends and drivers. *Philosophical Transactions of the Royal Society B (Biology)* 365(1554). Available at: https://royalsocietypublishing.org/doi/full/10.1098/rstb.2010.0149. Retrieved 16 May 2019.

Linehan, V., Thorpe, S., Andrews, N. and Beaini, F. (2012) *Food Demand to 2050: Opportunities for Australian Agriculture*, paper presented at ABARES Outlook conference, Canberra, 6–7 March. Available at: daff.gov.au/abares/publications.

Lutz, W., Butz, W.P. and Samir, K.C. (eds.) (2014) *World Population and Human Capital in the Twenty-First Century*. Oxford, Oxford University Press.

Martin, J.C., Moran, L.J., Teede, H.J., Ranasinha, S., Lombard, C.B. and Harrison, C.L. (2017) Exploring diet quality between urban and rural dwelling women of reproductive age. *Nutrients* 9(6), 586. Available at: www.ncbi.nlm.nih.gov/pmc/articles/PMC5490565/pdf/nutrients-09-00586.pdf. Retrieved 31 July 2018.

Mauser, W., Klepper, G., Zabel, F., Delzeit, R., Hank, T., Pulzenlechner, B. and Calzadilla, A. (2015) Global biomass production potential exceeds expected future demand without the need for cropland expansion. *Nature Communications* 6, 8946.

May, A. (2017) Population Growth and the Food Supply. Available at: https://wattsupwiththat.com/2017/12/11/population-growth-and-the-food-supply/. Retrieved 6 June 2018.

Odemero, A.F. (2013) Price transmission and households demand elasticity for frozen fish under fuel subsidy reform in Delta State, Nigeria. *International Journal of Food and Agricultural Economics* 1(1), 119–127.

PriceWaterhouseCoopers (PwC) (2017) The Long View. How will the global economic order change by 2050? Available at: www.pwc.com/gx/en/world-2050/assets/pwc-the-world-in-2050-full-report-feb-2017.pdf. Retrieved 31 July 2018.

Pullman, M. and Wu, Z. (2012) *Food Supply Chain Management*. London and New York, Routledge.

Reuters (2017) China's pork demand hits a peak, shocking producers, as diets get healthier. Reuters. 20 June. Available at: www.reuters.com/article/us-china-meat-demand-insight/chinas-pork-demand-hits-a-peak-shocking-producers-as-diets-get-healthier-idUSKBN19A31C. Retrieved 6 June 2018.

Ricketts, K. and Ricketts, C. (2009) *Agribusiness Fundamentals and Applications*. New York, CENGAGE Delmar Learning.

Runge, C.F. (2006) Agricultural Economics: A Brief Intellectual History. Center for International Food and Agricultural Policy. Research Paper WP06-1. University of Minnesota Department of Applied Economics. Available at: https://ageconsearch.umn.edu/bitstream/13649/1/wp06-01.pdf. Retrieved 18 July 2018.

Sardak, S., Korneyev, M., Dzhyndzhoian, V., Fedotova, T. and Tryfonova, O. (2018) Current trends in global demographic processes. *Problems and Perspectives in Management* 16(1), 48–57. Available at: https://businessperspectives.org/images/pdf/applications/publishing/templates/article/assets/9946/PPM_2018_01_Sardak.pdf. Retrieved 18 July 2018.

Satterthwaite, D., McGranahan, G. and Tacoli, C. (2010) Urbanisation and its implications for food and farming. *Philosophical Transactions of the Royal Society, Series B*, 365. Available at: www.iufn.org/wp-content/uploads/2013/08/Satterthwaite-2010-Urbanisation-and-its-implications-for-food-and-farming.pdf. Retrieved 18 July 2018.

Smil, V. and Kobayashi, K. (2012) *Japan's Dietary Transition and Its Impacts*. Cambridge, MA, MIT Press.

Trinh Thi, H., Simioni, M. and Thomas-Agnan, C. (2018) Assessing the nonlinearity of the calorie-income relationship: An estimation strategy – With new insights on nutritional transition in Vietnam. *World Development* 110, 192–204.

United Nations (2004) *World Population Prospects. 2004 Revision*. New York, United Nations. Available at: www.un.org/esa/population/publications/WPP2004/2004Highlights_finalrevised.pdf. Retrievsed 31 July 2018.

United Nations (2017) *World Population Prospects. 2017 Revision*. New York, United Nations. Available at: https://esa.un.org/unpd/wpp/Publications/Files/WPP2017_KeyFindings.pdf. Retrieved 31 July 2018.

USDA (2018) U.S. All Wheat Planted Area Projected to Rise in 2018 on Sizable Other Spring Wheat Expansion. 12 April. Available at: www.ers.usda.gov/webdocs/publications/88417/whs-18d.pdf?v=43202. Retrieved 6 June 2018.

USDA (2018a) Rice Outlook. 12 February. Available at: www.ers.usda.gov/webdocs/publications/87382/rcs-18b.pdf?v=43143. Retrieved 6 June 2018.

USDA (2018b) Rice Outlook: April 2018. Available at: www.ers.usda.gov/publications/pub-details/?pubid=88421. Retrieved 6 June 2018.

World Bank (2015) Ending Poverty and Hunger by 2030. An Agenda for the Global Food System. Available at: http://documents.worldbank.org/curated/en/700061468334490682/pdf/95768-REVISED-WP-PUBLIC-Box391467B-Ending-Poverty-and-Hunger-by-2030-FINAL.pdf. Retrieved 6 June 2018.

International agricultural trade

Introduction: a need for change in approach

An initial observation: there is an imbalance in most discussions of global agricultural trade, which in turn produces an informational asymmetry that in turn can generate unique, and sometimes very profitable, investment opportunities. To some extent this imbalance can be observed in other industries, but for agriculture it is very obvious. The imbalance is between, on the one hand, generalised discussions of commodities of trade, which are plentiful, and on the other, detailed analysis of specific trade opportunities and performance, which are, unfortunately, much rarer. Most of the 'analysis' amounts to little more than marketing, either from firms or from governments or international donors and agencies. Much of this chapter concerns the former, but the difficulty for this chapter, and for all discussions of agricultural trade, is to extract useful, consistent, reliable information from the mass of available data, not all of it of the highest quality. The value of many, almost all, of the companies mentioned in Chapters 12 and 13 will be determined, to a greater or lesser extent, on the outcomes for prices and traded volumes discussed in this chapter, but a balanced commercial perspective on international agribusiness must always analyse the plethora of discussion, statistics and policies of international agricultural trade only as one input into the value of a company. Many agribusinesses depend mostly on domestic markets which are still regulated, and which are still little affected by even significant changes in trading conditions outside their own markets.

Size and scope of international agricultural trade

That said, agricultural trade *matters*. The USDA's Economic Research Service (ERS) estimated that each dollar of agricultural exports stimulated another $1.27 in business activity. The $133 billion of agricultural exports in calendar year 2015 produced an additional $169 billion in economic activity for a total economic output of $302.5 billion. Every $1 billion of US agricultural exports required approximately 8,000 American jobs throughout the economy (Barnard *et al.*, 2016:101). Agricultural exports required 1.067 million full-time civilian jobs, which included 751,000 jobs in the non-farm sector (USDA, 2018). A similar story could be told, were the statistics as readily available, for the agricultural export sector of every country.

Major agricultural commodities – feed grains and feed grain products, soybeans and soybean products, wheat/wheat products, live animals, meat and meat products, and vegetables – remain the main components of international agricultural trade. Agricultural trade follows global economic trends, but recently the overall tendency is for trade as a whole to grow less than global GDP. Figure 3.1 shows how international trade in agricultural products accelerated rapidly from the start of the new millennium, but slumped with the global financial crisis (GFC) of 2008–09. Some recovery has taken place since then, but growth has been sluggish since. These developments are now commonly referred to as part of the 'global trade slowdown' (Gros, 2017; Federal Reserve, 2016). The net result was that between 1995 and 2017, world agricultural trade more than tripled in nominal terms (not adjusted for inflation) and roughly doubled in real terms (adjusted for inflation). Key factors driving this expansion include a more than 25% increase in the world's population and about a 75% increase in the real size of the world's economy. Other factors have also stimulated agricultural trade, including falling trade barriers and technological advances in agricultural production, transportation, information and communications.

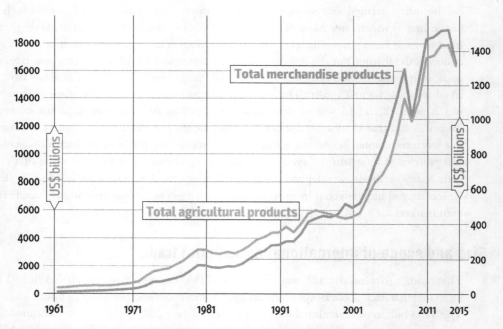

Source: Data from 1961–2013 are based on FAO, 2016a; data for 2014 and 2015 are based on ITC, 2016.

Figure 3.1 A comparison between global agricultural and all international trade
Source: FAO (2017:28)

Trade structure

Agricultural trade has therefore expanded, but most food is still supplied domestically. Despite the generally fast growth of agricultural trade, most of the food consumed in many countries is produced domestically; net imports are within the range of 0–20% of the domestic food supply in many instances. Some countries, such as Argentina, Australia and the USA, have net exports of more than 50% of their domestic food supply, while the Near East/North Africa region imports more than 50% of its food supply. Sub-Saharan Africa, South Asia and China are also net importers of food.

Trends in trade are mainly explained by business cycles in the global economy. Trade policies and trade agreements also play a role, but their impact is more difficult to assess. For example, although total world grain trade has not grown significantly in the past few decades, the grade train patterns have changed dramatically' (Ricketts & Ricketts, 2009:47). This observation has continued to be correct: for example, in 2010, China made its first sizeable purchase of US corn for more than a decade. In the past, China exported corn but with successive issues such as drought and dietary changes, there is now a need for imports. Another example: trade is now frequently counter-seasonal. So, for example, grapes and avocados are imported into the USA during January-April. Then, during the US summer, apples, grapes and stone fruits are exported. The many varieties of wheat and their different uses also necessitate trade. The USA, for example, despite being a formidable wheat exporter, imports wheat for bread, pasta and biscuits. On the other hand, other countries are structural wheat importers, hence US flour exports have increased continually. Trade has also, importantly, been responsible for a shift in agricultural production in the Global South away from traditional agricultural products such as coffee, tea and cacao to agricultural exports such as fruits, vegetables, cut flowers and fish, in order to meet customer demands and increase producer livelihoods by serving high-value food chains. As a result, many developing and transition export countries have become heavily dependent on a few high-income countries. The EU, for instance, is a major player in the international fresh fruit market (Sonntag et al., 2016).

The continuing growth of the middle class in Indonesia has meant a move towards higher levels of meat consumption. As a majority Muslim country, chicken and beef are the main meats consumed. As a highly price-sensitive market, Australian beef has to compete with Indian buffalo meat, especially for wet markets and the manufacturing sector. Australian exporters must also master complex import regulations, including an import permit system and a '5+1 feeder-breeder' policy for live cattle imports. On top of this, live animal exports have gradually become a politically sensitive subject in Australia and other OECD countries.

Source: Meat and Livestock Australia (2016)

To understand development of this kind, the most immediate place to turn is to the USDA, which produces monthly updates on the international trade in key commodities,

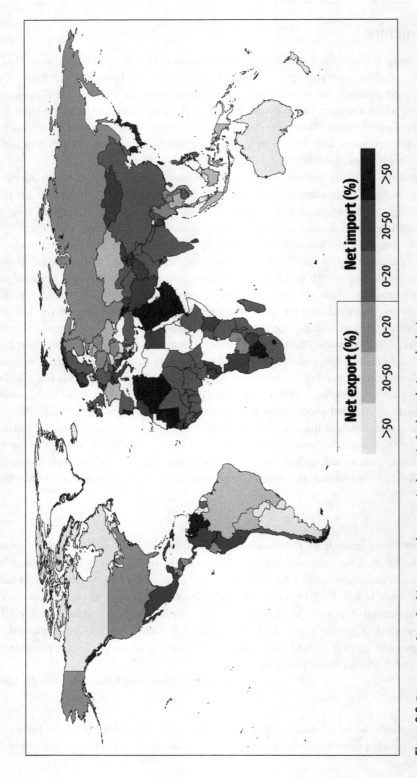

Figure 3.2 Percentage of net food imports and exports in domestic food supply, in total calories

Source: FAO (2017:29)

notably grains (USDA, 2018a, 2018b). The USDA also produces interactive charts that are both interesting and reliable (USDA, 2018c). For 2017–18, for example, the USDA reported in January 2018 that its global grain production forecast had been raised to a new record based on a larger crop for Russia. Russia's days of importing wheat are firmly over: about one-third of Russian grain production is already now exported, generating more competition in international markets than in previous decades (Medetsky, 2018).

Global agricultural exports are still dominated by the developed countries. Amongst exporters, the USA is an international agricultural powerhouse. It is the third-largest producer of agricultural commodities globally, after China and India, yet with a far lower population than either, it is the world's largest agricultural exporter. Its agribusinesses dominate world markets, and will continue to do so, at least for the immediate future. Among the developing countries the top exporters are in Latin America and East (including Southeast) Asia.

Value-added agribusiness trade versus bulk commodities

Whilst much more follows on the value chain in Chapter 6, it is significant that agricultural trade is divided into value-added products and bulk agricultural commodities. The former category includes either those that have been processed, like meat products, or at least branded. An ideal value-added product for export should exhibit many of the following characteristics, which have not changed for decades and which are probably permanent features of the international agricultural trade market:

- Be a differentiated product recognised as such by buyers;

- Be a 'protected' technology not readily available to others;

- Require a unique labour skill not easily learned;

- Be surrounded by a specialised support network;

- Have economies in research, handling and selling that are difficult to duplicate elsewhere;

- Be capable of easy change to meet shifts in consumer preferences;

- Have an effective market intelligence system; and

- Have a processing system that is relatively less sensitive to competition from producers with low cost labour (Moulton, 1986).

It is these products that are forming a steadily larger percentage of international agribusiness trade.

Distribution for foreign markets is the most concentrated part of the global value chain, both in developed and developing countries. This applies to commodities market structures, where the export trade is highly concentrated, as well as logistics and trade in widely traded commodities (grains, vegetable oils) which is also dominated by a few distribution companies, handling both export and import sides of the business. Hence, for example, Fuglie *et al.* (2012) presented concentration measures for the global agricultural input trade. The specialised input companies rely heavily on foreign sales, but this does not necessarily imply domination of cross-border trade, as the sales may have been generated through foreign direct investment (FDI) in overseas markets. The limiting case of monopoly can be observed where government regulation still reserves either the export or import trade to parastatals. But for the most part, the observed horizontal concentration in international commodities and agricultural trade arise from economies of scale together with entry barriers. These factors are becoming progressively more important worldwide, including in developing countries, and include biotechnology, IT, inventory and logistical systems, production and processing technologies. Likewise, all the usual demand drivers favour sophisticated production and distribution systems which are really only available to highly capitalised exporters. This leads to the last driver, institutional change, namely the transition from spot markets to the formation of supply chains characterised by the components discussed in Chapter 5: vertical co-ordination, outsourcing and contracting, and quality standards.

In absolute values *primary* and *manufacturing* agribusiness trade has expanded substantially around the world from 1990 to 2014 – *primary* agribusiness from $195 billion to $963 billion and *manufacturing* agribusiness from $498 billion to $2,812 billion of constant 2010 US dollars. However, the shares of primary and manufacturing agribusiness in total trade have been mostly stable during that period, shrinking from 6% to 5% and 16% to 14% respectively.

As countries' income increases, the ratio of *manufacturing* to *primary* agribusiness decreases for imports and increases for exports. Therefore, this ratio can be considered as a proxy for the degree of sophistication of agribusiness trade. Whereas the share of *primary* agribusiness imports in total imports has been small, *manufacturing* agribusiness imports have played a

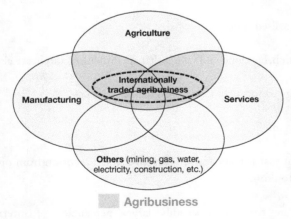

Source: World Bank staff.

Figure 3.3 The intersection of sectors within international agribusiness trade
Source: Mendez-Ramos & Paustian (2017:1)

major role, especially in low-income economies where they have accounted for almost 25% of their total imports from 1990 to 2014. Moreover, *primary* agribusiness exports have been a major component of total exports in low-income countries, greatly exceeding their *manufacturing* agribusiness exports.

There are numerous constraints to the development of agricultural trade in developing countries. The capacity of developing countries to expand agricultural trade is first of all related to their ability to produce and thus to factors affecting agricultural productivity. While the agricultural supply capacity of a country is first of all determined by comparative advantage factors, such as rural labour and machinery, arable land or fresh water availability which are not amenable to aid interventions, productive capacity is often significantly restricted by a number of constraints which can and should be addressed by policy and aid interventions. Institutional and regulatory issues as well as lack of infrastructure indeed often result in sub-optimal access to agricultural inputs, such as fertilisers and improved seeds, modern machinery, adequate irrigation systems and energy, appropriate storage capacity, or agricultural extension services. This in turn may render very difficult the required compliance with global good agricultural practice (GAP) that, for example, sub-Saharan African smallholders that target global food markets, usually producing under contract for medium or large agribusinesses, must achieve to access international markets for conventional fresh products.

This most recent analysis demonstrates an end even to this disparity, whilst the likelihood is that, within a few decades, this entire line of research will have declined in significance. Countries with comparative advantage in agribusiness will dominate agribusiness exports, but this will no longer be a question of relative or absolute GDP. Rather, as is already the

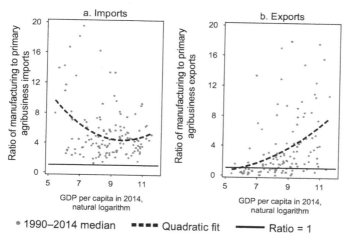

Source: COMTRADE, World Development Indicators, and World Bank staff estimates.
Note: GDP per capita, exports, and imports are in constant 2010 U.S. dollars. The median values of the ratios are estimated from annual country observations from 1990 to 2014.

Figure 3.4 Agribusiness to manufacturing import and export ratios, regressed on GDP by country
Source: Mendez-Ramos & Paustian (2017:2)

case with Australia, the USA, and now Brazil and Russia as well, it will be a matter of comparative advantage. The extent of correlation between the percentage of agribusiness exports and imports and GDP can therefore be expected to decline.

Trade of *manufacturing* agribusiness has expanded faster than *primary* agribusiness, especially in low-income countries. Across all income classifications, the growth rates of imports and exports of all defined categories have been positive, indicating the constant expansion of the sector. However, the expansion has been uneven across the different categories and income groups. On average, growth rates in *primary* and *manufacturing* agribusiness imports and exports have been higher in low-income countries than in high-income countries or middle-income countries, and lowest in high-income countries. For *manufacturing* agribusiness, for example, oils, meat and cereals exports have increased at annual growth rates of more than 20% in low-income countries, compared to annual compound growth rates of around 10% in high-income countries (Mendez-Ramos & Paustian, 2017).

Finally, it should be noted that not all data on trade are recorded. Informal trade takes different forms and is called various things: unrecorded trade, illegal trade, unofficial trade, underground trade, part of parallel market activity, the black market, trade subject of over- and under-invoicing, smuggling or hoarding. Whatever it is called, it is not included in the national accounts of a country or region in terms of its domestic and International trade (Aryeetey, 2009; Nkendah, 2014). Informal trade is not necessarily illegal, but it is also not really legal – and yet it is vital to country economies. Research on informal trade, which remains important in developing countries, especially in sub-Saharan Africa, has been substantial but has been bedevilled by data lack and inconsistencies. According to the FAO, the informal economy includes legitimately produced goods and services that do not necessarily follow formal processes such as standards regulations, business registration or operational licences. The informal sector generates up to 90% of employment opportunities in some sub-Saharan African countries, while also accounting for a significant share of GDP. Whilst the International Labour Organisation (ILO) estimated that more than 66% of total employment in sub-Saharan African is in the informal sector (Kathage, 2018). The sector often supports the most vulnerable people in society, including women, youth and the rural poor. In 2012, the African Development Bank (AfDB) estimated that 75% of intra-regional trade in sub-Saharan Africa is informal, a substantial share of which constitutes staple foods, whilst 43% of the African population gained income via informal cross-border trade (ICBT). AfDB also estimated that around 60% of informal traders at the borders of West and Central African countries are women. The IMF has suggested that similar trends prevail in the Caribbean, where the informal sector also accounts for a substantial share of national GDPs. Thus, informal trade has a direct impact on food security and, according to the IMF, it represents 'a safety net, providing employment and income to a large and growing working-age population'. Likewise, the AfDB said that:

> ICBT can have positive macroeconomic and social ramifications such as food security and income creation, particularly for rural populations, who would otherwise suffer from social exclusion... if properly harnessed, ICBT has the potential to support Africa's ongoing efforts at poverty (African Development Bank, 2012).

However, informal trade often results in substantial loss of revenue for states, so the key question is how can countries take advantage of the informal economy to create jobs, and support growth and sustainable development (Ramos, 2017).

Price determination in international agricultural markets

In the presence of strong monopsony power of agricultural intermediaries with sufficiently convex cost functions, one should expect an asymmetric price transmission which is consistent with the use of this monopsony power by intermediaries. Indeed, as international prices fall, local prices will fall proportionally more than when international prices increase. This prediction is confirmed when confronted with a sample of 161 agricultural products produced in 117 countries over a period of 35 years. Moreover, the asymmetry seems to be driven by the results for markets where large international intermediaries are present or when exports represent a large share of total production which increases the monopsony power of international intermediaries (McLaren, 2013).

International agricultural policy also affects domestic prices and, in turn, the calorie consumption of households in rural and urban areas. Unfortunately, the economic support provided for farmers in OECD countries benefits domestic farmers as much as it reduces competitiveness in production and consumption of farmers in sub-Saharan Africa. Arguably, the support from OECD countries is a deliberate action to prevent farmers in sub-Saharan Africa from accessing international and domestic markets because it impairs competitiveness in the subregion. However, this dominance has been achieved at a cost; in several of the agricultural commodities in which the USA is a major supplier to world markets, the prices at the point of export from US ports are less than the cost of producing the crop. According to Institute for Agriculture and Trade Policy (IATP) calculations, in 2015 US wheat was exported at 32% less than the cost of production, soybeans at 10% less, corn at 12% less and rice at 2% less. So, 'With US corn subsidies in place, encouraging high growth and enabling a sales price of about 30% below the true cost of production, US corn can now essentially be "dumped" into Mexico' (Pullman & Wu, 2012:86), despite the North American Free Trade Agreement (NAFTA). Dumping is also encouraged by the favourable loan rates made available to Mexican corn importers from US export agencies, which have mainly been taken up by corporate farming operations.

Trade constraints and issues (export/import quotas, tariffs, phytosanitary issues)

A lot depends on the state of play of international agreements on trade. The General Agreement on Tariffs and Trade (GATT) formed the basis for agricultural trade after its signature. GATT can hardly be counted as much of a victory for free trade, any more than can the World Trade Organisation (WTO), as agriculture as always been a sticking point for trade negotiations. Some success has been achieved regionally, however: NAFTA is a large, regional cooperative trade policy agreement between the USA, Canada and Mexico, originally signed in 1994. NAFTA ended Mexican quotas on imported grains, especially corn.

Box: What about cotton?

Dumping also undermines the ability of exporters in developing countries to compete in global markets. U.S. dumping of cotton has been the subject of formal WTO complaints by Brazil, a countervailing duty ruling by Turkey, as well as ongoing pressure by several African countries demanding changes in WTO rules to address the problem. In 2004, the Dispute Settlement Body of the WTO found in favor of Brazil, ruling that government subsidies gave U.S. producers an unfair advantage and suppressed the world market price, which damaged Brazil cotton farmer interests. After multiple appeals the WTO upheld the original ruling, and in 2009, the U.S. agreed to pay Brazil compensation and to revise its cotton program.[9] Those changes still fail to address the very real problems confronting African cotton farmers, most of whom are smallholder farmers from some of the world's poorest countries and depend heavily on export markets. While global prices are affected by changing production and consumption patterns in China and other countries, there is little doubt that U.S. policies continue to contribute to artificially low global prices.

IATP's earlier calculations showed persistent levels of dumping of cotton, ranging from 16 percent in 1996 to a whopping 65 percent in 2002. Unlike the other calculations presented in this paper, the same sources of information as we used in the earlier periods are not available. Still, based on USDA information on the cost of production, and International Monetary Fund data on the global prices of cotton, the evidence of dumping persists:

	Cost Production[1]	Export Price[2]	% Dumping
2005	0.67	0.56	16%
2006	0.81	0.59	27%
2007	0.73	0.73	0%
2008	1.08	0.61	44%
2009	1.11	0.78	30%
2010	0.94	1.64	-75%
2011	1.51	1.00	34%
2012	1.21	0.88	27%
2013	1.38	0.91	35%
2014	1.22	0.71	42%
2015	0.92	0.71	23%

1. USDA Commodity Costs and Returns: Cotton. May 1, 2017 update

2. USDA Cotton and Wool Yearbook, Table 13--Index of selected cotton price quotation offerings, c/f Far Eastern, monthly, 2003/04-present. A Index.

Figure 3.5 What about cotton?
Source: Murphy & Hansen-Kuhn (2017:7)

Where tariffs and quotas remain, particularly on sensitive agricultural commodities, market access talks are focused on the target of comprehensively eliminating restrictions on trade at the border. Border protection for agricultural imports of the countries negotiating these agreements range considerably, from close to zero for Australia and New Zealand to high on certain commodities imported by Japan and Canada. Except for the EU and the USA, many of the countries involved in the Trans-Pacific Partnership (TPP) and the Regional Comprehensive Economic Partnership (RCEP) have already entered into bilateral reciprocal trade agreements (RTAs) that have eliminated tariffs on many commodity and food imports or are in the process of phasing them out. Some low-income countries fear that the elimination of tariffs and quotas on agricultural products, being negotiated among RTA partners, could erode the tariff preferences that have given their agricultural exports a competitive edge in those countries. The rules of origin crafted in each of the mega-regions could affect the extent to which agricultural commodities from third countries are utilised as inputs by each trade bloc's food-processing sectors. Another fear is that strengthened TPP and Transatlantic Trade and Investment Partnership (TTIP) regulatory disciplines and processes would institutionalise how rules on sanitary and phytosanitary measures and technical barriers to trade are applied, and set the stage for more rigorous standards that third-country exporters of agricultural products might find more difficult and costly to meet.

Customs duties on merchandise imports – tariffs – can give a price advantage to locally-produced goods over similar goods which are imported, and they also raise revenues for governments. One result of the WTO Uruguay round of negotiations was countries' commitments to cut import tariffs and to bind their tariff rates to levels which are difficult to raise. Ongoing negotiations continue efforts in that direction in agriculture, albeit with not much immediate hope of success. Tariff rates can be set in a number of different ways. The most common type is an 'ad valorem' tariff, in which the amount paid is a percentage of the price of the item being imported. Ad valorem tariffs are widely used by the EU and by many other countries. An alternative is to set a tariff at a fixed amount in monetary terms per unit (usually based on weight). Tariffs may also be a mix of ad valorem and fixed amounts. Some tariffs may vary seasonally, usually for products where supply levels, either globally or within the importing country, depend on the time of year. Tariffs for processed products are sometimes more complex, being based on a formula which takes account of the quantity of different components which are used to make up the product. EU tariffs on processed products are typically higher than those for raw materials, as this makes it more cost-effective to import raw materials and process them within the EU, giving some protection to processing industries.

The share of agriculture in trade disputes is large and shows few signs of declining. For the first 50 years of the GATT/WTO multilateral trade system one could have put this down to imprecise rules and inadequate enforcement mechanisms in that sector (Josling, Tangermann & Warley, 1996). With the introduction of the Uruguay Round Agreement on Agriculture (URAA) much of the ambiguity was removed, but this did not stem the flow of disputes (Josling, 2009). Under its reform programme, WTO members converted some of their non-tariff measures to equivalent bound tariffs. The new rule for market access in agricultural products is 'tariffs only'. Before the URAA, some agricultural imports were restricted by quotas and other non-tariff measures. These have been replaced by tariffs that provide more-or-less equivalent levels of protection – if the previous policy meant domestic prices were 75% higher than world prices, then the new tariff could be around 75%.

The proliferation of agricultural cases in the WTO reflects both the ambivalent nature of the multilateral trade rules in the sector and the sensitive nature of the trade itself. In addition, the perceived vulnerability of the major farm programmes of industrial countries to challenge under the URAA and the Subsidies and Countervailing Measures Agreement (SCM) has led to some high-profile disputes. The nature of technological changes in food production, particularly the uneven adoption of biotech seeds, has led to other disputes. Countries are still grappling with the trade policy consequences of the search for attributes in production that are desirable to consumers. The dividing line between providing consumers with adequate decisions on which to base decisions and cooperating with domestic producers to restrict imports is often difficult to determine.

Tariff rate quotas (TRQs) allow a specified quantity of produce to enter the market at a reduced (or zero) tariff. Once the limit has been reached, the tariff reverts to the standard external tariff rate. TRQs are used to protect industries which would be vulnerable to international competition but where there is a desire to allow a certain level of imports, for example to ensure market stability. Quotas can be specific to one exporting country, a group of specified countries or can be open to all suppliers. The EU currently operates a number of TRQs covering agricultural products.

Recent agreements, such as the EU-Canada trade deal, have included TRQs for some sensitive agricultural products. This allows products from the exporting country to gain some access to the importing market, while still providing a degree of protection to domestic production. This would usually be balanced by similar concessions on access for other sensitive products in reverse.

Non-tariff barriers include sanitary and phytosanitary (SPS) measures and technical barriers to trade. WTO rules state that SPS measures should be applied only to the extent necessary to protect human, animal or plant life or health. Therefore, there is a balance between ensuring imported food is safe to eat for domestic consumers, while at the same time ensuring that regulations put in place are not being used to protect domestic producers. Also, they should not arbitrarily or unjustifiably discriminate between countries where identical or similar conditions prevail. In practice these measures are often the hardest to agree in trade agreements, as seen in debates over the TTIP, where issues such as anti-microbial treatments and hormone-treated beef became highly contentious.

Technical barriers to trade can also become obstacles, but they are often deemed necessary for a range of reasons, from environmental protection, safety and national security to consumer information. The same basic question arises again: how to ensure that standards are genuinely useful, and not arbitrary or an excuse for protectionism. Examples of technical barriers to trade include country of origin labelling and restrictions on importation of genetically modified products.

The lack of progress in multilateral trade negotiations under the auspices of the WTO, notably the failure to conclude the Doha Development Agreement and a partial relapse into protectionist policies after the global financial crisis, may have compounded the slowdown in global trade (WTO, 2018). Recently negotiated regional trade pacts (RTPs), such as the much-maligned TPP, include, or at least affect, agriculture. RTPs aim at further liberalising agricultural trade, changing rules on food safety, animal and plant health, and harmonising food product standards. Successful RTAs will also address legal rights and obligations associated with the use of names of certain foods and wines in international trade, such as port wine, basmati rice or types of cheese (Mandala Projects, 2018) and address the scope of patent protections available for plants. Also on the negotiating table are additional regulations on the use of subsidies for agricultural exports and the circumstances under which agricultural export restrictions could be imposed.

Much now also depends on bilateral or X+1 negotiations: how agricultural trade between the UK and EU develops post-Brexit – assuming it happens – will depend on whether a trade deal is in place and on what terms. One possibility, if there is no such deal, is that import tariffs will be imposed on trade between the UK and the rest of the EU. As the UK is such a major net importer of horticultural produce, for example, this will have a bigger impact on its imports than on exports. If the UK chooses to impose the same tariffs as the EU currently applies to imports from third countries, it would effectively increase the price of imported produce. This should mean that domestic produce becomes more competitive and could allow UK production of some horticultural crops to expand and displace some imports, depending on how rapidly and sustainably domestic industry can respond. Current EU tariffs on horticultural imports offer a degree of market protection but not enough to deter non-EU imports. UK tariffs on imports could make domestic produce more competitive but also raise prices for consumers. Any opportunities to expand production to displace imports may be tempered by labour availability and the seasonal nature of production. Finally, any disruption such as Brexit causes uncertainty around continued collaboration and investment between UK producers and overseas partners.

Changing tastes and heightened demand have led to counter-seasonal trades, especially in fresh produce. Generally, regulation of imported foods is outsourced to the exporting country, although in the USA foreign meat processors are regulated by the USDA, the FDA tests imported food products on an irregular basis, and labelling laws are domestically regulated. The consequences when this process goes wrong can be fatal. In Australia, after a scandal (Smith, 2016), then Deputy PM Barnaby Joyce was allegedly furious at the lack of hepatitis A and *E. coli* testing on imported frozen berries. (*E. coli* is considered the best indicator of a country's hygiene practices.) The public of developed countries is now hyper-alert to risks from imported food, but it is impractical to test every imported food, and the uneasy compromise goes on.

Since 2012 Kenya, for example, had faced challenges in the EU over excess pesticides and quarantine pests that cost the country billions in export losses leading to the new development. Developing countries have responded to this pressure by issuing export standards. In 2015 Kenya issued KS 1758 Part One – Flowers and Ornamentals, followed by KS 1758 Part Two – Fruits and Vegetables, issued in 2017. The standards bring all exporters and handlers under a standard practice and have become the basis on which export permits are issued (Africa Business Community, 2017; US Government, 2018).

Perhaps in the USA arguments are still necessary for agribusiness to justify participation in international trade (Barnard *et al.*, 2016:101–104) but for the rest of the world, it is largely a necessity. The arguments put for US business – to expand sales, garner economies of scale, get the benefits of a global brand, diversify to reduce risk, lower production costs (including from international sourcing of raw materials), broaden access to credit and generally lever domestic expertise, are persuasive.

All along the chain there are risks. Leading agribusiness brands are recognised in virtually every country in the world (Barnard *et al.*, 2016:102). But a food safety scandal can lead to severe reputational damage, with social media eagerly disseminating the bad news very quickly indeed: the 2013 horse meat story drew parallels with the 1990 Perrier benzene contamination scandal. Both avian flu and BSE negatively impacted international trade; e.g. after

STEP 1: Selling your grain

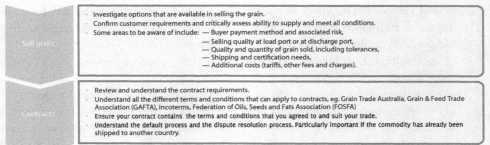

STEP 2: Harvest, storage and outturn quality

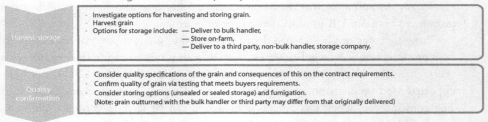

STEP 3: Quality and market (Country) considerations

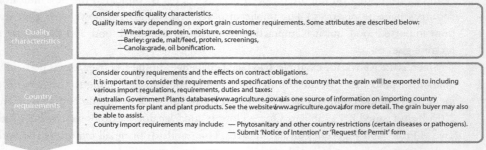

Figure 3.6 Australian grain export process
Source: Australian Export Grains Innovation Centre (2016)

STEP 4: Payment considerations

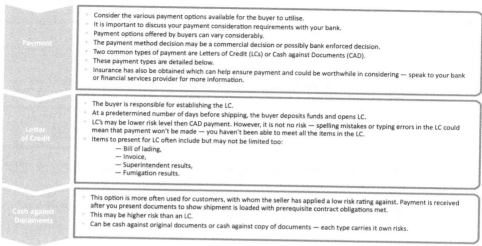

Payment
- Consider the various payment options available for the buyer to utilise.
- It is important to discuss your payment consideration requirements with your bank.
- Payment options offered by buyers can vary considerably.
- The payment method decision may be a commercial decision or possibly bank enforced decision.
- Two common types of payment are Letters of Credit (LCs) or Cash against Documents (CAD).
- These payment types are detailed below.
- Insurance has also be obtained which can help ensure payment and could be worthwhile in considering — speak to your bank or financial services provider for more information.

Letter of Credit
- The buyer is responsible for establishing the LC.
- At a predetermined number of days before shipping, the buyer deposits funds and opens LC.
- LC's may be lower risk level then CAD payment. However, it is not no risk — spelling mistakes or typing errors in the LC could mean that payment won't be made — you haven't been able to meet all the items in the LC.
- Items to present for LC often include but may not be limited too:
  — Bill of lading,
  — Invoice,
  — Superintendent results,
  — Fumigation results.

Cash against Documents
- This option is more often used for customers, with whom the seller has applied a low risk rating against. Payment is received after you present documents to show shipment is loaded with prerequisite contract obligations met.
- This may be higher risk than an LC.
- Can be cash against original documents or cash against copy of documents — each type carries it own risks.

STEP 5: Logistic considerations

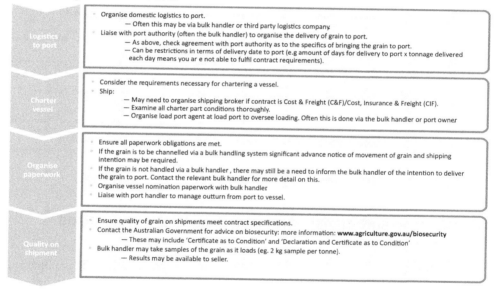

Logistics to port
- Organise domestic logistics to port.
  — Often this may be via bulk handler or third party logistics company.
- Liaise with port authority (often the bulk handler) to organise the delivery of grain to port.
  — As above, check agreement with port authority as to the specifics of bringing the grain to port.
  — Can be restrictions in terms of delivery date to port (e.g amount of days for delivery to port x tonnage delivered each day means you ar e not able to fulfil contract requirements).

Charter vessel
- Consider the requirements necessary for chartering a vessel.
- Ship:
  — May need to organise shipping broker if contract is Cost & Freight (C&F)/Cost, Insurance & Freight (CIF).
  — Examine all charter part conditions thoroughly.
  — Organise load port agent at load port to oversee loading. Often this is done via the bulk handler or port owner

Organise paperwork
- Ensure all paperwork obligations are met.
- If the grain is to be channelled via a bulk handling system significant advance notice of movement of grain and shipping intention may be required.
- If the grain is not handled via a bulk handler , there may still be a need to inform the bulk handler of the intention to deliver the grain to port. Contact the relevant bulk handler for more detail on this.
- Organise vessel nomination paperwork with bulk handler
- Liaise with port handler to manage outturn from port to vessel.

Quality on shipment
- Ensure quality of grain on shipments meet contract specifications.
- Contact the Australian Government for advice on biosecurity: more information: **www.agriculture.gov.au/biosecurity**
  — These may include 'Certificate as to Condition' and 'Declaration and Certificate as to Condition'
- Bulk handler may take samples of the grain as it loads (eg. 2 kg sample per tonne).
  — Results may be available to seller.

Figure 3.6 Continued

the USDA's 2003 BSE announcement, most countries banned or restricted imports of US beef and cattle.

Aside from food safety and other risks associated with production, the risks of international agricultural and agribusiness trade are held in common with most other sectors of international trade.

STEP 6: Shipment considerations

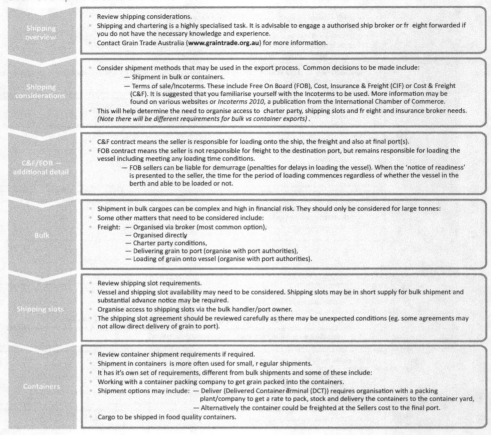

Shipping overview
- Review shipping considerations.
- Shipping and chartering is a highly specialised task. It is advisable to engage a authorised ship broker or fr eight forwarded if you do not have the necessary knowledge and experience.
- Contact Grain Trade Australia (**www.graintrade.org.au**) for more information.

Shipping considerations
- Consider shipment methods that may be used in the export process. Common decisions to be made include:
  — Shipment in bulk or containers.
  — Terms of sale/Incoterms. These include Free On Board (FOB), Cost, Insurance & Freight (CIF) or Cost & Freight (C&F). It is suggested that you familiarise yourself with the Incoterms to be used. More information may be found on various websites or *Incoterms 2010*, a publication from the International Chamber of Commerce.
- This will help determine the need to organise access to charter party, shipping slots and fr eight and insurance broker needs. *(Note there will be different requirements for bulk vs container exports)* .

C&F/FOB — additional detail
- C&F contract means the seller is responsible for loading onto the ship, the freight and also at final port(s).
- FOB contract means the seller is not responsible for freight to the destination port, but remains responsible for loading the vessel including meeting any loading time conditions.
  — FOB sellers can be liable for demurrage (penalties for delays in loading the vessel). When the 'notice of readiness' is presented to the seller, the time for the period of loading commences regardless of whether the vessel in the berth and able to be loaded or not.

Bulk
- Shipment in bulk cargoes can be complex and high in financial risk. They should only be considered for large tonnes:
- Some other matters that need to be considered include:
- Freight: — Organised via broker (most common option),
  — Organised directly
  — Charter party conditions,
  — Delivering grain to port (organise with port authorities),
  — Loading of grain onto vessel (organise with port authorities).

Shipping slots
- Review shipping slot requirements.
- Vessel and shipping slot availability may need to be considered. Shipping slots may be in short supply for bulk shipment and substantial advance notice may be required.
- Organise access to shipping slots via the bulk handler/port owner.
- The shipping slot agreement should be reviewed carefully as there may be unexpected conditions (eg. some agreements may not allow direct delivery of grain to port).

Containers
- Review container shipment requirements if required.
- Shipment in containers is more often used for small, r egular shipments.
- It has it's own set of requirements, different from bulk shipments and some of these include:
- Working with a container packing company to get grain packed into the containers.
- Shipment options may include: — Deliver (Delivered Container Terminal (DCT)) requires organisation with a packing plant/company to get a rate to pack, stock and delivery the containers to the container yard,
  — Alternatively the container could be freighted at the Sellers cost to the final port.
- Cargo to be shipped in food quality containers.

Figure 3.6 Continued

Licences, export quotas, exchange controls, payment and transfer risk

Firms frequently require licences from domestic governments as well as importing ones (NIbusinessinfo.co.uk, 2018; Government of Malta, 2018; USDA, 2018d) in order to carry on agricultural trade. In some cases, especially in developing countries, the imposition of exchange controls provides further risk to the exporter (Reserve Bank of South Africa, 2018). Finally, monies and even goods may not be satisfactorily transferred internationally.

Documentary issues and contracts

International trade often begins with a tender, frequently generated by a government, for example in rice (see box).

Tender for procurement of Indian parboiled rice

Tender No.MMTC/AGRO/EXP/Par.boil.rice/2015–16/1 dated Dated 10, April 2015 and Closes on 17$_{th}$ April 2015 at 1500 Hrs IST Tender Opening on 17$_{th}$ April 2015 1630 hours IST

Terms and Conditions of Tender

MMTC Limited invites Bids from Local Suppliers for Supply of Parboiled Rice for Export by MMTC FROM Kakinada Anchorage Port [East Coast], India

The bids are invited from prospective local indigenous suppliers for supply of Indian Origin parboiled rice. The prospective suppliers are requested to submit their bid(s) as per the detailed terms and conditions of the Tender given below.

I.   Commodity Indian par boiled rice of Quality IR-64 & 1001 & 1010 of Current Crop
II.   Packing In 50kg Polypropylene bags Quality print as per design of final buyer
III. Specifications **Indian long grain100%sortexed 5% broken of quality IR-64 & 1001 & IR1010**

Particulars	Value
AV Length of Whole Grain	6mm Min
Broken	5.0 Max
Moisture	14.0% Max
Damaged / Dis-coloured Kernels	2.0% Max
Foreign Matter Incl Paddy	1.0% Max
Red / Red Streakad	1.0% Max
Paddy Per Kg	15 Pcs Per kg
Yellow Kernels	2.5% Max
Chalky Grains	6% Max
Milling Degree	Well Milled and Polished

(IV)   **QUANTITY:** Maximum quantity that may be quoted by the Bidder for Kakinada anchorage **Port is 13000** MT plus/ minus 10%. on FOB ST or CIF basis.

(V)   **SHIPMENT PERIOD:** Prompt – Firm dates to be intimated later

(VI)   **PRICE:** To be quoted in Indian Rupees PMT FOB ST **Kakinada Anchorage Port [East Coast], India** & CIF to **DURBAN** and **CAPE TOWN** in **50kg poly propylene bags.**

(VII) **BID VALIDITY**: Price Bids must remain valid up to one month after Tender **Update Validity upon confirmation till final shipment**

(VIII) **FUMIGATION:** The cargo will be fumigated with Methyl Bromide @ 32 gm / cu. m at 21 degree centigrade and above under NAP and the treatment to be endorsed on Phytosanitary Certificate by any other fumigant / substance in the manner approved by the plant protection advisor for the purpose at godown if required in vessel after completion of loading.

(IX) **BID BOND/EARNEST MONEY DEPOSIT**

All bidders are required to submit a BID BOND in INR, as per MMTC's standard format (**Annexure-I**) or Bank Draft for at least 2% value of the total bid. The Bid Bond must be valid for 30 days. In case of unsuccessful bidders, the BID BOND shall be returned. No interest would be paid on EMD amount. Original Bid bond/Bank draft should be submitted to MMTC on or before closing of the tender i.e. **1500 Hrs (IST) of 17th APRIL 2015**

(X) **PERFORMANCE BANK GUARANTEE:** The successful bidder is required to establish Performance Bank Guarantee (PBG) strictly in the prescribed format for 3% value of the contract within 5 working days from the date of issuance of LOI and upon acceptance of PBG the bid bond/Bank Draft will be returned. The PBG should be valid and enforceable **upto 31st December, 2015.** BG should be in the prescribed format (**Annexure-II**) from/ through scheduled bank in India and the PBG to be encashable at the counter of scheduled bank in India on first demand.

(XI) Suppliers must be having all valid permit/ licence/statutory clearances for export of rice through Kakinada Port.

Source: MMTC Ltd. (2015)

Types of documents (title, bills of lading, bankers' acceptances, charters, receipts, bills)

Export documentation lies at the heart of all international trade transactions. It provides exporters and importers with an accounting record; shipping and logistics companies with instructions of what to do with freight information; and banks with instructions and accounting tools for collecting payments. Export documents are understandably more complex than those used for domestic sales due to the special characteristics of international trade: geographical distance, different customs laws, different means of transport, greater risks, etc. The documents required for each shipment will depend on the conditions of sale (Incoterms) agreed between seller and buyer. These are the key documents required for international trade:

■ *International Purchase Order (IPO).* Once the transaction details have been agreed, the seller may issue an informal price quote or a more detailed proforma invoice. If the buyer accepts the seller's price and other conditions, the buyer issues an IPO, which may constitute a binding offer or a binding acceptance; where a large commercial buyer is involved, the purchase order is often the main contract form and constitutes the first legally binding offer. In such cases, signature of the purchase order by the seller will constitute the acceptance of the offer.

- The *International Commercial Invoice* (ICI) is the main document of export documentation, containing all data on the international sale. The item, quantity, price for the products/services sold, delivery and payment conditions, as well as the taxes and other expenses that might be included in the sale, are detailed in an ICI. Tax and regulatory compliance depend on it. Usually an ICI is prepared by the exporter and addressed to the importer and the import customs clearance.

- The *Packing List (PL)* is a more detailed version of the commercial invoice, prepared by the exporter, but without price information. It should include, *inter alia*, the invoice number, quantity and description of the goods, weight of the goods, number of packages, and shipping marks and numbers. Although not required in all transactions, it is required by some countries and some buyers.

- The *CMR transport document* is an international consignment note used by drivers, operators and forwarders alike that governs the responsibilities and liabilities of the parties to a contract for the carriage of goods by road internationally.

- A *Bill of Lading* (B/L) is a document issued by the agent of a carrier to a shipper, signed by the captain, agent or owner of a vessel, furnishing written evidence regarding receipt of the goods (cargo), the conditions on which transportation is made (contract of carriage), and the engagement to deliver goods at the prescribed port of destination to the lawful holder of the B/L. A B/L is, therefore, both a receipt for merchandise and a contract to deliver it as freight. Very importantly, as it is a negotiable instrument, the B/L may be endorsed and transferred to a third party while the goods are in transit. This document is prepared by the shipping company and addressed to the exporter, the shipping company through the agent, and the importer.

- The *Certificate of Origin* certifies the country in which the goods originated or in which the preponderance of manufacturing or value was added. It also constitutes a legal declaration by the exporter. Its importance derives from trans-shipment issues as well as tax and regulatory exemptions for particular countries.

- The *Inspection Certificate* for pre-shipment inspection is a document issued by an authority indicating that goods have been inspected (typically according to a set of industry, customer, government or carrier specifications) prior to shipment and the results of the inspection. Inspection certificates are generally obtained from neutral testing organisations (e.g. a government entity or independent service company such as SGS, www.sgs.com, or Bureau Veritas, www.bureauveritas.com).

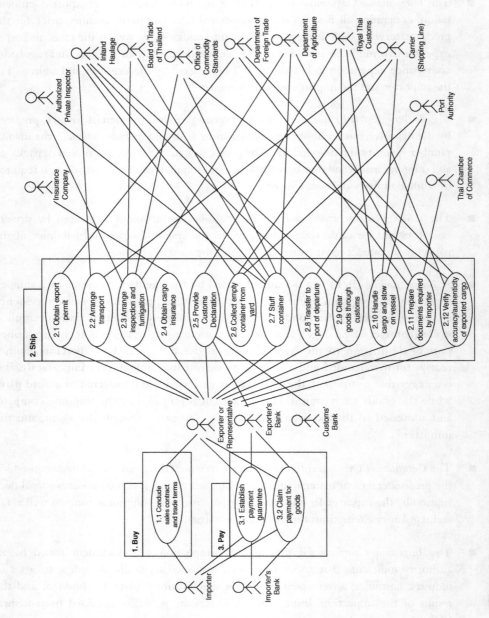

Figure 3.7 UNESCAP diagram of business processes in jasmine rice exportation from Thailand
Source: UNESCAP (2011)

The emergence of blockchain technology threatens to reduce the time and cost involved throughout this process, rendering agricultural trade much easier and – just possibly – improving the competitive position of smaller exporters, especially in developing countries, who have difficulty accessing the necessary services.

Full freight forward, free alongside ship and other transport arrangements and terms

- CIF (cost, insurance and freight): An agreement whereby the seller pays for all costs, insurance and freight to the designated delivery point.

- FAS (free alongside ship): The seller's obligations are fulfilled when the goods have been placed alongside the ship on the quay or in the lighters. This means that the buyer has to bear all costs and risks of loss or damage to the goods from that moment. Note that unlike FOB, FAS requires the buyer to clear the goods for export.

- FOB (free on board): An agreement whereby the seller pays for loading the ship or other means of transportation at the designated point of delivery, with the buyer paying freight charges.

A comparison of terms is available at AirSeaGlobal.com (2018) *Incoterms are useful and sensible, but they may not be accepted everywhere. In any event they represent a good due diligence tool when reviewing other contracts.*

Examples of contracts and issues between the parties

Good sales contracts should include, at minimum:

- Parties (buyer and seller);

- Commodity;

- Quality and grade;

- Price and method of payment;

- Time, place and method of delivery;

- Shipping documents required for payment (L/C);

- Default factors;

- Remedies for injured parties; and

- Forum for disputes (GAFTA, 2018).

There are several widely known international contracts, including the much-used North American Export Grain Association four-page, standard-use contract for FOB purchases of bulk grain and oilseeds called the NAEGA standard contract No. 2 (AG). It has 26 separate clauses delineating the various aspects of grain purchase. There is also the Grain and Feed Trade Association of London (GAFTA) contract for C&F and CIF grain transactions, and the Federation of Oils, Seeds and Fats Associations (FOSFA) standardised contract for CIF and C&F sales of soybeans (FOSFA, 2018).

Conclusion

It seems likely that the future will bring continued growth in agricultural trade. Inadequate agricultural production in high population growth countries will be the main driver, but the greater availability of solar and other renewable energy sources and reduced dependence on the energy supply grid may also be expected to have a positive impact on agricultural trade over the coming decade. Advances in technology, notably the blockchain, may also make certification easier to achieve and quality issues easier to resolve, further paving the way for an expansion of agribusiness trade from, and between, developing countries.

Bibliography

ABARES (2017) *Agricultural Commodities March 2017.* Canberra, Australian Bureau of Agriculture and Research Economics and Sciences. Available at: www.agriculture.gov.au/abares/Documents/agricultural-commodities-report-march-2017.pdf. Retrieved 5 July 2017.

Africa Business Community (2017) Kenya unveils new standards for fruit and vegetable exports. Available at: http://africabusinesscommunities.com/news/kenya-unveils-new-standard-for-fruits-and-vegetable-exports/. Retrieved 6 June 2018.

African Development Bank (2012) Informal cross border trade in Africa: Implications and policy recommendations. Available at: www.sdgfund.org/informal-cross-border-trade-africa-implications-and-policy-recommendations. Retrieved 16 May 2019.

AirSeaGlobal.com (2018) Incoterms. Available at: http://airseaglobal.com.au/img/AirSea-incotables.pdf. Retrieved 9 July 2018.

Aryeetey, E. (2009) The Informal Economy, Economic Growth and Poverty in Sub-Saharan Africa. Paper prepared for the AERC Project Workshop on Understanding Links between Growth and Poverty Reduction in Africa. Available at: www.africaportal.org/publications/the-informal-economy-economic-growth-and-poverty-in-sub-saharan-africa/. Retrieved 1 May 2018.

Australian Export Grains Innovation Centre (2016) Exporting grain from Australia – some considerations. Available at: www.aegic.org.au/wp-content/uploads/2016/08/AEGIC_Exporting-Grain.pdf. Retrieved 23 February 2019.

Bank of China (2018) Re-issuance of Letter of Guarantee. Available at: www.bankofchina.com/nl/en/cbservice/cb2/cb23/201110/t20111022_1567734.html. Retrieved 6 June 2018.

Barnard, F.L., Akridge, J.T., Dooley, F.J., Foltz, J.C. and Yeager, E.A. (2016) *Agribusiness Management*, 5th edition. London and New York, Routledge.

Dy, R. (2009). *Food for Thought: How Agribusiness is Feeding the World. (With Special Focus on the ASEAN)*. Manila, University of Asia and the Pacific and Comprehensive Initiative for the Transformation of Organizations Foundation.

EBRD (2018) Agricultural Finance. Available at: www.ebrd.com/what-we-do/legal-reform/access-to-finance/agricultural-finance.html. Retrieved 6 June 2018.

FAO (2017) *The Future of Food and Agriculture: Trends and Challenges*. Rome, FAO. Available at: www.fao.org/3/a-i6583e.pdf. Retrieved 5 February 2018.

Federal Reserve (2016) Causes of the Global Trade Slowdown. Available at: www.federalreserve.gov/econresdata/notes/ifdp-notes/2016/causes-of-the-global-trade-slowdown-20161110.html. Retrieved 6 June 2018.

FOSFA (2018) FOSFA 26 Oilseeds Contract. Available at: www.pastrade.com/contracts/fosfa-en/cif-fosfa-26-european-oilseeds/44-contracts/fosfa-en.html. Retrieved 6 June 2018.

Fuglie, K.O., Heisey, P.W., King, J. and Schimmelpfennig, D.E. (2012) Rising concentration in agricultural technology industries influences new farm technologies. *Amber Waves* 10(4), 1–6. Available at: www.researchgate.net/publication/235341940_Rising_Concentration_in_Agricultural_Input_Industries_Influences_New_Farm_Technologies. Retrieved 20 March 2018.

GAFTA (2018) All Contracts. Available at: www.gafta.com/All-Contracts. Retrieved 6 June 2018.

Government of Malta (2018) Import Licence AGRIM (AGRicultural IMports). Available at: https://servizz.gov.mt/en/Pages/Environment_-Energy_-Agriculture-and-Fisheries/Agriculture/Agriculture/WEB245/default.aspx. Retrieved 6 June 2018.

Gros, D. (2017) Globalisation: The hype, the reality, and the causes of the recent slowdown in global trade. Available at: https://voxeu.org/article/hype-reality-and-causes-global-trade-slowdown. Retrieved 6 June 2018.

HKTDC (2015) Common Import/Export Documents. Available at: http://hong-kong-economy-research.hktdc.com/business-news/article/Small-Business-Resources/Common-Import-Export-Documents/sbr/en/1/1X000000/1X006MLL.htm. Retrieved 6 June 2018.

Josling, T. (2009) Agricultural trade disputes in the WTO. In Hartigan, J.C. (ed.) *Trade Disputes and the Dispute Settlement Understanding of the WTO: An Interdisciplinary Assessment*. Frontiers of Economics and Globalization, Volume 6. London, Emerald Group Publishing Limited, 245–282

Josling, T., Tangermann, S. and Warley, T.K. (1996) *Agriculture in the GATT*. London and New York, Houndmills.

Kathage, A.M. (2018) Understanding the informal economy in African cities: Recent evidence from Greater Kampala. World Bank [blog]. Available at: http://blogs.worldbank.org/africacan/understanding-the-informal-economy-in-african-cities-recent-evidence-from-greater-kampala. Retrieved 6 June 2018.

Mandala Projects (2018) Geographic Indications and International Trade (GIANT). Available at: http://mandalaprojects.com/giant-project/basmati.htm. Retrieved 6 June 2018.

McLaren, A. (2013) Asymmetry in price transmission in agricultural markets. WPS 13-04-1 Working Paper Series. Geneva, University of Geneva. Available at www.unige.ch/ses/dsec/repec/files/13041.pdf. Retrieved 5 January 2018.

Meat and Livestock Australia (2016) Market Snapshot: Beef Indonesia. Available at: www.mla.com.au/globalassets/mla-corporate/prices–markets/documents/os-markets/red-meat-market-snapshots/mla-indonesia-beef-snapshot-2017.pdf. Retrieved 6 June 2018.

Mendez-Ramos, F. and Paustian, N. (2017) Measurement and Patterns of World Agribusiness Trade. Kuala Lumpur, World Bank. Available at: http://documents.worldbank.org/curated/en/296411485179723309/pdf/112195-BRI-Policy-5.pdf. Retrieved 28 May 2018.

Medetsky, A. (2018) *Russia Is Exporting More Wheat Than Any Country in 25 Years*. Bloomberg. 16 February. Available at: www.bloomberg.com/news/articles/2018-02-16/russia-is-exporting-more-wheat-than-any-country-in-25-years. Retrieved 6 June 2018.

MMTC Ltd. (2015) Tender for Procurement of Indian Par-Boiled Rice. For export by MMTC. Available at: http://mmtclimited.com/app/webroot/upload/tenders/Rice_Tender_Vizag.pdf. Retrieved 6 January 2018.

Moulton, K. (1986) *The Potential for Value-Added Exports. Increasing Understanding of Public Problems and Policies*. USA, University of Minnesota, Farm Foundation, 61–67. Available at: https://ageconsearch. umn.edu/bitstream/17555/1/ar860061.pdf. Retrieved 6 June 2018.

Murphy, K. and Hansen-Kuhn, K. (2017). *Counting the Cost of Agricultural Dumping*. IATP. June. Available at: www.iatp.org/sites/default/files/2017-06/2017_06_26_DumpingPaper.pdf. Retrieved 6 June 2018.

NIbusinessinfo.co.uk (2018) Applying for a Common Agricultural Policy import licence. Available at: www.nibusinessinfo.co.uk/content/applying-common-agricultural-policy-import-licence. Retrieved 6 June 2018.

Nkendah, R. (2014) The Informal Cross-Border Trade of agricultural commodities between Cameroon and its CEMAC's Neighbours. Paper for the NSF/AERC/IGC Conference. Available at: www. theigc.org/wp-content/uploads/2014/08/nkendah.pdf. Retrieved 30 April 2018.

North American Export Grain Association (2018) Free On Board Export Contract. Revised as of 1 May 2000. Available at: https://78462f86-a-17e36604-s-sites.googlegroups.com/a/hotgrain.com/ www/contracts/naega2000.pdf?attachauth=ANoY7cr14RK3jg_NP4xnW5wsF5xS3 KGcxJ1rFKov9wk3UNyq_J-CN02Pdb0vBy 6iVsqaF9pmHK0DZSsTnykHm5OVn1MHemyzg meD7hZ4XmVITo 2LGe6haO3IEZHafNE9hJo7JtrEChpwh4CKyVCGIPavrbLTwLzTcZX9Eia vYQ4vwXArl1J7tUjN6Ie 6iVEocDdU1VBdnmN_jRbLLRiN 9dsJGuWAqGJwjQ%3D%3D&a ttredirects=0. Retrieved 6 June 2018.

Pullman, M. and Wu, Z. (2012) *Food Supply Chain Management*. London and New York, Routledge.

Ramos, F.M. (2017) Agribusiness trade as a pillar of development: Measurement and patterns. Available at: https://blogs.worldbank.org/developmenttalk/trade/ppps/sustainablecities/developmenttalk/ climatechange/agribusiness-trade-pillar-development-measurement-and-patterns. Retrieved 6 June 2018.

Reserve Bank of South Africa (2018) Exchange Control Legislation. Available at: www.resbank. co.za/RegulationAndSupervision/FinancialSurveillanceAndExchangeControl/Legislation/Pages/ default.aspx. Retrieved 6 June 2018.

Ricketts, K. and Ricketts, C. (2009) *Agribusiness Fundamentals and Applications*. New York, CENGAGE Delmar Learning.

Smith, J. (2016) Frozen berries still on the shelf after Hep A scare a year ago. Available at: www. smh.com.au/national/frozen-berries-still-on-the–shelf-as-a-choice-20160124-gmd6qd.html. Retrieved 6 June 2018.

Sonntag, W., Theuvsen, L., Kersting, V. and Otter, V. (2016) Have industrialized countries shut the door and left the key inside? Rethinking the role of private standards in the international fruit trade. *International Food and Agribusiness Management Review* 19(2), 151–170.

Thoopal, V. (2013) Collateral Management in Agriculture Finance in India. Available at: http:// agrifinfacility.org/resource/collateral-management-agriculture-finance-india. Retrieved 6 June 2018.

UNCTAD (2008) *COCOA STUDY: Industry Structures and Competition*. Geneva, UNCTAD. Available at: http://unctad.org/en/Docs/ditccom20081_en.pdf. Retrieved 20 March 2018.

USDA (2018) Agricultural Multipliers. Available at: www.ers.usda.gov/data-products/agricultural-trade-multipliers/. Retrieved 6 June 2018.

USDA (2018a) Grain: World Markets and Trade. April 2018. Available at: www.agrochart.com/en/news/6723/wheat-world-markets-and-trade-april-2018-usda.html. Retrieved 6 June 2018.

USDA (2018b) Outlook for U.S. Agricultural Trade. Available at: www.ers.usda.gov/topics/international-markets-us-trade/us-agricultural-trade/outlook-for-us-agricultural-trade/. Retrieved 6 June 2018.

USDA (2018c) Agricultural Trade. Available at: www.ers.usda.gov/topics/international-markets-trade/us-agricultural-trade/interactive-chart-the-evolution-of-us-agricultural-exports-over-the-last-two-decades. Retrieved 6 June 2018.

USDA (2018d) Dairy Import Licensing Program. Available at: www.fas.usda.gov/programs/dairy-import-licensing-program. Retrieved 6 June 2018.

UNESCAP (2011) *Business Process Analysis Guide to Simplify Trade Procedures*. Bangkok, United Nations Economic and Social Commission for Asia and the Pacific.

US Government (2018) Kenya – Standards for Trade. Available at: www.export.gov/article?id=Kenya-trade-standards. Retrieved 6 June 2018.

WTO (2018) Strong trade growth in 2018 rests on policy choices. 12 April. Available at: www.wto.org/english/news_e/pres18_e/pr820_e.htm. Retrieved 6 June 2018.

4

The role of technology

Introduction: a difference in approach

I imagine that most readers of this book are interested in the *business* of agriculture, in one or more capacities of regulator, lender, investor, supplier or adviser. It is always necessary to decide, even for scientists and certainly for business people, what research is needed, and for what purpose, and then to select only the latest and/or most relevant research. Agricultural scientists are often, it must be recognised, not especially well versed or even interested in economics or finance. Even basic concepts such as cost-benefit analysis are often alien, whilst on the other hand scientific jargon is rife. The best way to approach the dichotomy between their vast experience, dedication, research and achievements, and their oft-evidenced disinterest in finance, is to regard agricultural research as a data resource for financial decision-making. Certainly, the application of agricultural science has major financial impacts. This chapter has been written as an introduction to agtech and agricultural science with that aim in mind.

Principles of agricultural science and technology

What is agricultural science? Agricultural *research* – the Australian government tells us – is not an actual scientific discipline in its own right. Rather, it is a broad term to describe the application to agriculture of many *different* scientific disciplines and endeavours, combined with the objective of achieving improvements in agricultural output, sustainability and, sometimes, profitability. Primarily, but perhaps regrettably, agricultural science integrates scientific disciplines in which research may have been carried out without an explicit end-point application. Traditionally this has involved all of botany, zoology and soil science including, *inter alia*, genetics, chemistry, biochemistry, plant physiology, microbiology, soil nutrition and statistics. More recently, the range of contributing disciplines and associated sub-components has broadened further – advances in molecular biology, but imminently now also from technology, as with every other industry – so now engineering, robotics, automation, weather forecasting, informatics and 'big data' manipulation are all playing a role in 'agricultural science' (Australian Academy of Science, 2016). The old image of 'just' plant breeding is now way out of date. One immediate conclusion: the task of keeping on top of every aspect of this fast-growing science is simply impossible, at least for a person: selecting particular crops or animals for research is imperative – a problem now complicated by the development of agtech spread out amongst many individual firms.

The key role of agricultural science is illustrated by the age-old struggle against plant disease. The earth accommodates a staggering number of microbes: they include viruses, bacteria, oomycetes and nematodes. Even closely related plant species may vary greatly in their exposure or susceptibility to pathogens, ranging from highly susceptible to completely immune (resistant). Environmental conditions, including temperature, humidity and availability of nutrients, can also influence whether the plant-pathogen interactions lead to disease or resistance (Prabha *et al.*, 2016; Kushalappa *et al.*, 2016). Another example: the role of carbon sequestration in curbing, or reversing, soil erosion, aquifer depletion and other negative effects of agriculture on the ecosystem, as well as biodiversity (Powlson *et al.*, 2016). These types of requirement in turn shows the need for statistical analysis. Because of the variability inherent in biological and agricultural data, knowledge of statistics is necessary for their understanding and interpretation. The importance of statistical science in agriculture is obvious, where the collection, analysis and interpretation of numerical data are concerned. Statistical principles apply in all areas of experimental work and they have a very important role in agricultural experiments (Cobanovic, 2002:1) which cannot ever be expected to diminish.

In the course of what follows it might well be imagined that pedestrian advice on the choice of particular species, crop husbandry, weeding, pollination, harvesting and storage is unimportant. Far from it – agricultural scientists will be the first to admit that the advice provided by professional companies and even brokers to farmers is invaluable. At the other extreme, the long-heralded promise of nanotechnology may be about to bring significant advances across a range of agricultural applications. Striking the right balance is imperative, and the often-derived result of the process is the adage that the importance of agricultural science, at least in terms of yields, profitability and investment success, is much higher in developed economies than in the developing world. Part of the problem is low adoption rates, which have been found significantly to depend on membership in a group (such as a co-operative), the number of agricultural assets in each household and participation in production training. As we shall see subsequently, this is a litany of *economic*, not technical, factors that repeats itself again and again.

The evolving role of agricultural science

The technical purpose of agricultural research and science overall is clear. It is hard to disagree with the contention that crop (and livestock) technology needs to address more than just calories and yields, much as it needs to do that; it also needs to address sustainability (Weiner, 2017), because of the importance of greenhouse gas emissions by agriculture, which accounts – sources vary – for anywhere between 12–35% of the emissions produced by agriculture worldwide, through the use of pesticides and fertilisers, animals, transport methods that are still largely reliant on oil, energy-intensive food processing, and packaging and distribution networks. The relationship between these objectives and profitability, however, is not straightforward.

On the one hand there are plenty of good stories to tell. Hence, for example, new maize varieties, which have been found to be high-yielding, adaptable and resistant to different pests and diseases, and could potentially increase the revenue of those involved in the sector, have an 88% adoption rate in Benin, Burkina Faso, Côte d'Ivoire and Mali, countries which have maize as their primary crop (CORAF, 2018). On the other hand, Pakistani basmati price is a good example of the overall problem with R&D and production. As the Asian Development Bank (ADB) observed:

> New pest-resistant varieties of basmati have not been introduced due to inadequate support for research and development. At the same time, the pressure to generate greater revenue has focused attention on high-yield rice varieties, whose cultivation has infringed on the basmati heartland of Punjab (ADB, 2017).

Economic pressure does not therefore *necessarily* coincide with optimum economic results.

To this conundrum must be added a gradual slippage in the quantity and even quality of local agricultural R&D. It does seem – although there are very understandably no data to back up this assertion – that globalisation is effectively centralising agricultural research in key locations worldwide, mainly in developing countries – e.g. the fabulous University of Wageningen in the Netherlands, the University of Reading in the UK or the US universities with agricultural extensions – with agencies, especially international development agencies, then responsible for their introduction to specific countries and adoption by farmers.

Government policy

The USDA had this to say about the future of Chinese agricultural technology policy:

> China will establish resource-sharing platforms on agricultural technology, with independent development and innovation in the seed industry being a priority. Joint efforts will be made to develop seeds for major crops. (Note: China would like to consolidate resources in the area of agricultural technology by establishing information-sharing platforms and high-tech development zones in agriculture. It is important to emphasise that, for the first time in many years, the No. 1 Document does not address China's plans in the field of biotechnology. Such a lack of acknowledgement in this important field of agricultural innovation may indicate China's intent to lower the profile of its agricultural biotechnology efforts by, for example, continuing research in this area, but slowing the pace of commercialization.) (USDA, 2017:1).

Similarly, the Indian Department of Agriculture provided the FAO with the following comprehensive list of objectives of agricultural research (see box). Notice how many of these are either broad principles or in fact concern the application of agricultural science, and even policy, rather than having much to do with pure science or research, still less directly to do with improving the financial returns of investment in agribusiness. That which does, value-addition, has little to do with research and much to do with investment and finance.

- Increasing agricultural production and productivity, to ensure food security for the rising population.
- Developing areas of untapped potential, thereby correcting emerging imbalances in growth in eastern, hilly, rain-fed and drought-prone regions.
- Meeting challenges of degradation of land and water resources, and emerging ecological imbalances, due to increased biotic pressure on land.
- Compensating for diminishing size of land holdings and fragmentation, leading to restricted management options and lower income levels.
- Addressing problems of underemployment, unemployment and malnutrition in rural areas through diversification of agriculture and promotion of horticulture, fisheries, dairy, livestock, poultry, beekeeping, sericulture, etc.
- Value addition in agriculture can only be achieved by a concerted thrust being made in increasing processing, marketing and storage facilities. These are imperative for the development of agro-processing industries, which are the key areas for development in agriculture.
- Revitalising and democratising the cooperatives for providing credit, inputs and extension support as well as enhanced marketing and processing.
- Focusing the agricultural research system to develop economically viable and location-specific technologies in rain-fed, drought-prone and irrigated areas, and strengthening institutional frameworks for farmers' education and training in improved farm techniques.
- Harnessing of scientific research, in frontier areas of science and technology, for all sections of the farming community.
- Addressing technology training and input needs of farm women, farmers living in tribal areas and other disadvantaged sections of rural society, with a view to remove the drudgery and burdens of their lives and augmenting their income.
- Accelerating the development of rain-fed and irrigated horticulture, floriculture, aromatic and medicinal plants production, and plantation crops, with full back-up support of processing and marketing, both for the domestic market and for exports.
- Encouraging efficient use of marginal lands and augmentation of biomass production through agroforestry and farm forestry.
- Increasing the utilisation of irrigation potential and promoting water conservation and its efficient management.
- Providing improved variety of seeds, agricultural implements and machinery and other critical inputs to farmers in or near their village.
- Reviving and strengthening local institutions of the farming community as legitimate instruments of decentralised planning with full participation of the local community.
- Increasing the involvement of non-governmental organisations in agricultural development and village upliftment programmes.
- Correcting the terms of trade to make them favourable for agriculture, thereby increasing the flow of resources and augmenting the rate of capital formation in agriculture substantially.

Source: FAO (n.d.)

The relative importance of agricultural research, and public policy towards agriculture generally, in countries such as the USA, China and even India can be compared with Africa, where for example even in its largest economy, and where data are still scarce and out-of-date, 'Public spending on agriculture in Nigeria is exceedingly low. Less than 2% of total federal expenditure was allotted to agriculture during 2001 to 2005, far lower than spending in other key sectors such as education, health, and water' (IFPRI, 2008:vii). About half of these figures would be expended on running the bureaucracies of the agricultural ministries and their related agencies of forestry, rural development and water resources, among others. The same dismal picture has continued with more recent federal budgets, and compares poorly with the 2003 AU-Maputo Declaration's Comprehensive Africa Agriculture Development Programme (CAADP), pledge to spent around 10% (UN, 2018). The litany of problems besetting Nigerian public agricultural spending that IFPRI found included concentration on just a few programmes, inadequate budgeting processes, political interference and 'an urgent need to improve internal systems for tracking, recording, and disseminating information about public spending in the agriculture sector. Consolidated and up-to-date expenditure data are not available within the Ministry of Agriculture, not even for its own use' (IFPRI, 2008:vii). For a limited period, the Central Bank of Nigeria attempted to direct a more co-ordinated agricultural policy, but this too foundered amidst political disagreements. With this kind of problem, and the importance of public spending for yield improvement, disparities in agricultural performance between countries such as Nigeria and others are inevitable, unless international agribusiness can fill the void.

Legal, commercial and regulatory aspects

Scientific advances, particularly in agriculture, were traditionally driven by universities and public institutes, and therefore treated largely as public goods. By contrast, in recent decades, the growth of intellectual property (IP) rights, held by the private sector, has overturned this practice, e.g. with respect to patents for genetics. The logic for the change is economic: whilst in the past there may have been economic logic behind as rapid and substantial as possible a distribution of information, today information dissemination is inexpensive and can be extremely rapid, but the cost of research and development is simply too high to envisage much of an alternative to the continued growth of the private patent system, despite arguments to the contrary (Mathews, 2012). Even academic research is not protected by an 'experimental use' exemption from patent infringement and may become increasingly entangled in issues involving access to IP. Unfortunately, although the importance of IP in agriculture is becoming better appreciated in both the public and the private sectors, many researchers, business people, R&D decision-makers and policy-makers are still relatively uninformed about how to find, understand and utilise IP information, including published patents and patent applications (Alandete-Saez *et al.*, 2014).

An example of the interface between science and law in agriculture

A local entrepreneur, Ibrahim, with support from the international agency CTA, is using participatory three-dimensional modelling (P3DM) events to help settle disputes over land and resource ownership between the local and indigenous communities in the district of

Baïbokoum, Chad. With support from the FAO, a pastoral code has also been developed that recognises the land rights of the nomadic M'Bororo people. Ministry of livestock allocated 6,000 km of land corridors through which herders can now move their cattle.

Population growth and climate change have exacerbated tensions between M'Bbororo herders and sedentary farmers. One particularly contentious issue was herders' ability to access water (rivers, dams, etc.) for their cattle. In 2011, as clashes threatened to spiral out of control, Ibrahim approached the CTA to help her employ P3DM in southern Chad.

P3DM is a community-based method for mapping landscapes using local and traditional knowledge of the surrounding environment. Natural features, such as ridges and plateaus, are mapped out on a board by the community, which leads to the creation of an intricate 3D landscape model from which data about the surrounding area can be extrapolated.

Source: CTA (2018)

Agriculture and the environment in a time of climate change

Agricultural science has a vital role to play in correcting the imbalances that production brings. Much starts with understanding, and therefore being able to influence, how below-ground interactions involving plants and the soil environment can generate significant productivity and sustainability gains for agriculture. For example, there are many ways in which agricultural science's research into soil-plant interactions can deliver further benefits for agriculture (Werner & Dubbert, 2016). The development of new crop varieties with greater nutrient and water foraging abilities, for instance, could be significantly advanced by a better understanding of root architecture and how plants explore and exploit different soil environments. But the complexities of soils – their geological origins, chemistry, diverse biological content and the ways in which conditions can alter dramatically over extremely small areas – renders research and application, as with so many aspects of agricultural science, only really effective when diverse multidisciplinary teams involving biologists, biogeochemists, ecologists, agronomists and spatial modellers, among others, all work together (Australian Academy of Science, 2016:51). Hence, it tends to happen only in developed countries, and serves further to widen the yield gap between developed and developing countries.

There is plenty else that very basic agricultural science or, rather, the application of scientific knowledge to agricultural production can bring to agricultural production during a prolonged period of climate change. Decades ago, the UN identified the following as highly desirable in the South African context:

(1)   Agricultural management practices needed to change, e.g. more logical planting dates, row spacing, planting density and cultivar choice, and other measures to counteract the effects of limited moisture. Already the UN had recognised that although irrigation is currently used to supplement low levels of precipitation, it could well become very expensive and less effective, giving conditions of increasing aridity. This would require a phasing out of irrigation farming and a relocation of the production

areas eastwards, if practicable. To reduce the risk of famine, marginal production areas could be kept economically viable by, for example, decreasing input costs or planting drought-resistant crops, such as sorghum or millet. Alternatively, land use could be changed to grazing. Many current agricultural practices, such as conservation tilling, furrow diking, terracing, contouring and planting vegetation as windbreaks, protect fields from water and wind erosion and assist in retaining moisture by reducing evaporation and increasing water infiltration. Management practices that reduce dependence on irrigation would reduce water consumption without reducing crop yields, and would allow for greater resiliency in adapting to future climate changes. Such methods include water harvesting (Lloyd & Dennison, 2018).

(2)   Reduced use of some pesticides could directly reduce greenhouse gas emissions and also reduce water pollution, thereby contributing to both adaptation and mitigation. The UN advocated the use of agricultural management practices that recognise drought as part of a highly variable climate, rather than a natural disaster (Gómez & Blanco, 2012).

(3)   Farmers should be provided with information on climatic conditions, and incentives should be given to those farmers who adopt sound practices for drought management, and therefore do not rely on drought relief funds. Land use planning can be used to identify trends in land use that would be advantageous in the event of climate change. Suitable measures could be incorporated in national agricultural policy directed towards farmers, those most affected (Masud *et al.*, 2017).

(4)   Although this remains highly contentious, the UN advocated a reduction of reliance on industrialised monocropping, such as practised by coffee growers in East Timor, albeit with a measure of jackfruit intercropping (Dos Santos *et al.*, 2017).

(5)   Quite obviously, the development of more and better heat- and drought-resistant crops would help fulfil current and future national food demand by improving production efficiencies in marginal areas, with immediate effect.

(6)   Seed banks to preserve biological diversity could also provide farmers with an opportunity to make informed choices and could be used to counteract the effects of climate change, maintain food security and establish possibilities for profitable specialisation (United Nations, 2002).

All of these remain priorities today. Information is much more plentiful than then, thanks mainly to far wider mobile internet access, even in Africa and other developing parts of the world. Knowledge, too, is better disseminated. The problem, as ever, is implementation. Moreover, the problems are becoming more acute.

Water technology

Water scarcity and the fragility of water supplies is a global reality, and has accelerated in importance over the past two decades. A good starting point is to recognise that different crops have radically different 'water footprints', whilst animal husbandry is vastly more water-intensive. The methane emitted by cattle and sheep, generated during digestion – enteric fermentation – accounts for 40% of agricultural greenhouse gas emissions in the EU-28 plus

Iceland, roughly 4% of all emissions in the EU. Similar data are available for other developed jurisdictions, such as Australia (DPIRD, 2018).

Hydrogen fuel cell power is a definite possibility with – possibly – unique applications on farms. At the forefront of new innovations to meet the challenges of water scarcity are improved irrigation techniques (via drip systems), software designed to improve water reservoir retention, multiple cropping and the use of seed varieties that produce more drought-tolerant crops (PwC, 2016:13). Simple drip irrigation can stabilise soil moisture during the day and in the plant root zone, and brings other benefits including highly efficient water use, requires only little effort in land levelling, fertilisers can be applied at one go with irrigation, produces uniform products, reduces pest and wild attacks, and reduces soil salinity. The technology of rain shelter protects plants from heavy rains, as well as from pest and disease attacks. The end results of the application of both technologies in crop production are that they increase quantity and quality of production (Uddin & Sjah, 2017:79).

Technology must be supplemented by well-regulated markets. Worldwide, water distribution is inefficient and many countries are grappling with problems of market-based solutions to address water rights and allocation. They might look to Australia for a solution. The Murray-Darling Basin, which covers 14% of Australia's land area and accounts for 40% of the country's agricultural production, is one of the most well-established global water markets. Legislation passed in 1994 created a potential separation between water and land rights. By the 2000s the market was active. The water trading market has driven the trend towards high value farming activities reflecting water availability, the cost of supply and the general importance of water resources (Colliers, 2016; Aither, 2017).

Greenhouse technology – an example

Dozens of crops benefit from stable temperatures, higher than otherwise found, in greenhouses, where plants are grown in a controlled micro-environment. These structures range in size from small sheds (cold frames) to very large buildings. They can have different types of covering materials, such as a glass or plastic roof and frequently glass or plastic walls; they heat up because incoming visible solar radiation (for which the glass is transparent) from the sun is absorbed by plants, soil and other things inside the building. Air warmed by the heat from hot interior surfaces is retained in the building by the roof and walls. All this reduces the possibility of disease infection and also raises the temperature. So, for example, tomatoes require an optimum temperature range of 20–25°C during the day and 15–17°C at night, which may well be quite impossible outside the greenhouse. Greenhouse construction requires a range of different materials quite inaccessible to the smallholder – not only plastic, but polycarbonate, row or thermal covers, steel structures, heating, ventilation, electrical, plumbing, irrigation and anchoring systems, temperature, humidity and irrigation monitoring devices, and other related building supplies. Construction standards must be suitable for all relevant weather conditions (Dutch Greenhouses.com, 2018). The Netherlands is a global leader in modern greenhouse design and implementation (Runkle, 2012). There, nearly all large Dutch growers had even by the turn of the decade invested in a combined heat and power (CHP) system, which uses natural gas to create heat,

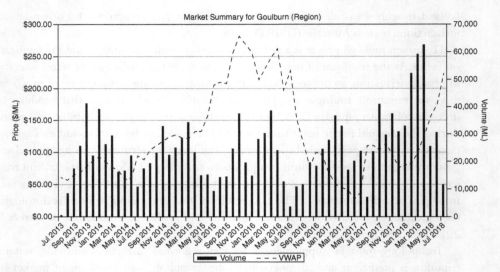

Figure 4.1 Allocation market summary for the Goulburn catchment, July 2013 to July 2018
Source: Australian Government (2018)

electricity, carbon dioxide and water. It is a very clean and efficient way to heat a green-house, supply power for supplemental lighting, and generate CO_2 to increase plant photosynthesis. They use light-emitting diodes (LEDs) for lighting plants indoors, or geothermal heating in a greenhouse, where water warmed during the summer is used for heating in the winter. The Dutch are leading the way in automation, with technologies to transplant, water, grade, sort and transport plants, as well as control the environment; nearly all growers in the Netherlands capture and store rain water, then treat it and use it on plants, many also capture water runoff so that nothing leaves their facility. Growers are also using biological techniques to control greenhouse pests, rather than relying on chemicals. Active research in the USA on commercial greenhouses now includes modifying the glass roof panels to become solar panels themselves, as greenhouses are currently very energy-intensive, as well as to improve photosynthesis by selectively filtering light (Purdy, 2017). In developed countries, and increasingly in developing ones also, millions of acres are now under greenhouses.

Nursery and greenhouse production is often very intensive. Vegetable transplants and bedding plants can be finished anywhere from three to six weeks, depending on the season. This short crop cycle sometimes militates against the success of plant growth stimulants and other natural products (Glinicki *et al.*, 2010). Other products might confer an advantage when plants are stressed, but, under optimal conditions, there are often no advantages to using these products (Villavicencio, 2012). Promising developments of systemic acquired resistance (SAR) it was initially thought might substantially reduce these disadvantages (Durrant & Dong, 2004), but this kind of technology has been in implementation for over a decade and although there have been some achievements there has not been any breakthrough (Science Direct, 2018). Mention should also be made of plant retardants, as there are circumstances where rapid or extensive plant growth may be undesirable (Currey & Lopez, 2010). Finally, moderate and difficult-to-root plant species can prevent producers from realising their full potential as propagators. It has been suggested that application of auxin-based, commercially available rooting hormones may be the key to overcoming this challenge, which ultimately leads to an increase in product diversity (Cerveny & Gibson, 2005).

Hazard and control measures for animal waste

Statistics are now available on, for example, ammonia emissions by type of animal. These data, included in free screening tools from university extensions, makes the process of calculation easier in developed economies. Simple Calculation of Atmospheric Impact Limits from Agricultural Sources (SCAIL-Agriculture), for example, assesses the impact from pig and poultry farms on human health and on semi-natural areas. The model provides an estimate of the amount of acidity and nitrogen deposited as a consequence of ammonia emissions from a farm as well as predictions of air concentrations of ammonia (NH_3), odour and particulate matter with an aerodynamic diameter of less than 10 microns (PM10). These values can then be used to assess whether impact limits for human health or habitats are exceeded or not (SCAIL, 2014). Animal housing is now also an important area of technical study (Michigan, 2016). Manure utilisation practices are now very well catalogued and promoted within the USA (EPA, 2018). There is devolution to state level for the collection, transportation, storage, processing and disposal of animal manure and other livestock operation wastes. State Feedlot Programs implement rules governing these activities, and provide assistance to counties and the livestock industry. The feedlot rules apply to most aspects of livestock management, including the location, design, construction, operation and management of feedlots and manure handling facilities (Agriculture and Food Development Authority, 2017).

Fertiliser, growth stimulants, retardants, and rooting hormones

Fertilisers are manufactured materials, mainly inorganic in nature (nitrogen, phosphate and potash). The majority of the fertilisers used in developed countries are straight or compound fertilisers applied mainly in a solid form. Straight fertilisers contain only one nutrient, e.g. calcium ammonium nitrate (27.5% N). Compound fertilisers contain two or more nutrients – e.g. 18% N, 6% P, 12% K – used for silage and hay. Most fertilisers are sold in granular or prill form so that they can be broadcast using mechanical spreaders. Although genetics often steals the limelight, and certainly molecular biology has led to significant achievements through both selective breeding and genetic manipulation, crop production can also be increased through conventional measures such as innovations in crop production or the better use of these fertilisers and other chemicals. These measures are rapid and can be applied to existing varieties.

But, at least currently, pesticides are only effective against invertebrates (insects, nematodes, etc.) or fungi, not bacteria or viruses. They are not cheap, so they do not get used by smallholders in developing countries unless subsidised, they may have side-effects, and their targets develop resistance over time (Gould et al., 2018). Horticulturalists are regularly offered newly developed natural products instead, which have mixed results but which will no doubt continue to be developed (Ganesan et al., 2015).

Crops, animals and science

Plant science is key. We know that in nature genetic variety is the result of mutation, which enables species to adapt to, for example, urbanisation, acid rain or rising temperatures, all driven by Darwinian natural selection. Each organism has a *phenotype*, with its genetic traits, which mutation can alter over time. Breeders try to select or reject traits that are deemed desirable, and eliminate those that are not. Humanity has made use of this basic kind of agricultural science since land was cultivated and livestock bred, millennia ago, creating a perceived distinction between natural selection and human intervention – though in reality they interact (García-Ballesteros *et al.*, 2017), and resulting in tremendous improvements in plant cultivation through crop domestication, breeding and selection. Then Gregor Mendel discovered the laws of genetic inheritance, and selective breeding became widespread. *Population genetics* is broadly the extension of Mendelian genetics to the species population (a collection of organisms of a single species, the individuals of which interact with each other in some way). Population genetics provides the mechanics or mathematics underlying the evolutionary process, and is highly relevant to agriculture, although both genetic mutation in general and mutagenesis in particular seem now to be covered by restrictive EU law, to the displeasure of the USA, a point to be born in mind in the discussion that follows (Farmfutures, 2018).

Then, with the discovery of DNA, and recombinant DNA, agricultural scientists were able to 'cut and splice' DNA molecules together. This led to *transgenesis*, whereby genomes are altered by the integration of exogenous (i.e. from other genomes) DNA fragments (e.g. genes). This new technology of genetic modification allows the transfer of genes between even very distantly related organisms. It was developed first in bacteria and the viruses which infect them, and subsequently applied to multicellular organisms, including plants and vertebrates. The emergence of transgenic approaches involving the introduction of defined DNA sequences into plants by humans has increased the gene pool used by plant breeders for plant improvement. Transgenesis became a powerful tool in research for a better understanding of gene functions and physiological mechanisms, and for breeders by providing access to the full potential of biodiversity. Two major limitations of transgenesis in plants and (non-laboratory) animals should however be noted. First, most phenotypic traits are complex, requiring more than a single gene, and second, transgenesis offers no control over where the added genes are inserted into the genome (Nuffield Council on Bioethics, 2016).

Genetic engineering (GE) speeds up selective breeding of livestock and crops. Using GE, specific genes from one plant or embryo are introduced into the chromosome of another to develop a desired trait, such as disease, salt or drought resistance, toxicity to insects not humans, herbicide tolerance, taste or size. Traditional breeding relied on crossing (ADHB, 2009) and backcrossing many generations of plants – and only those that are cross-fertile – to achieve the same, or reduced, results. The same applies to animals (Hazel *et al.*, 2017). GE by comparison achieves instant results, with no need for investment in trial and error, and an enormous range of possible donor organisms, e.g. bacteria to plants, plants to bacteria, or animals to plants. Gene mapping locates and records where genes are located on a chromosome: there are millions to map and then develop restriction enzymes for, these allow for extraction and gene splicing. There are continued rapid advances in DNA sequencing technology, so it is now relatively straightforward to identify genes in crops and species, to link genomic DNA sequences with traits (Baulcombe, 2013:3) and generate sequence data for a genome, the RNA molecules in its cells. The result: improved accuracy in crop breeding. Genome-wide panels of genetic markets can now be used to forecast species performance and breeding value with much greater precision than hitherto (Josephs *et al.*, 2017; Su *et al.*, 2018; Sant'Ana *et al.*, 2018).

Genome editing allows the selective mutation of one or a few genes exclusively and the precise modification or replacement of entire genes, whether from closely or distantly related organisms. Other techniques are not intended to alter the genome at all, but rather to temporarily change gene expression patterns in order to adjust the traits of an organism. Cellular structure can now be seen in 3D. Using immunodetection of proteins, scientists can now see changes in subcellular structures at much better levels of view than normal light microscopy. Chemical analysis of plants has also made progress: mass spectrometry can monitor proteins within cells. Although there has been a succession of these kinds of different techniques, they have complemented, not replaced, each other. For example, the recently acquired ability to precisely edit plant genomes by modifying native genes without introducing new genetic material offers new opportunities to rapidly exploit natural variation, create new variation and incorporate changes with the goal to generate more productive and nutritious plants. But transgenic approaches in food plants have raised concerns about the merits, social implications, ecological risks and true benefits of plant biotechnology (Francis *et al.*, 2017).

Gene editing can certainly help meet that challenge of production, along with making food more flavourful and nutritious. The path to widespread usage is currently complicated – from the science to consumer acceptance. For example, CRISPR, a gene-editing tool, evolves varieties using the best native characteristics already available within the crop's DNA. The goal of using CRISPR is to make plants more resilient, more productive or more nutritious, while changing consumers' expectations and experience of food. Unlike genetic modification, gene editing does not involve a transfer of foreign genetic material between species. CRISPR has already dodged two potentially fatal bullets – a 2017 claim that it causes sky-high numbers of off-target effects was retracted in March, and a report of human immunity to Cas9 (CRISPR associated protein 9) was largely shrugged off as solvable. But the risks should be taken seriously. One of the biggest restrictions to the global commercial use of gene editing is uncertainty around regulation. The USDA ruled it would not regulate plants that could otherwise have been developed through traditional breeding techniques, as long as they are not developed using plant pests. Companies interested in using CRISPR, such as Tropic Biosciences, a UK-based start-up using gene-editing technology including CRISPR to optimise coffee and banana crops, need to carefully navigate the opportunity, balancing obtaining the correct licence, protection of brand equity and attention to global trade barriers, to make sure they get a return on investment in a reasonable time frame.

Hormones can be modified (synthetic hormones) to promote qualities in animals, notably growth (Vivo, 2018). An animal's hormonal balance can also be changed, either by injection or implant/pessary. This can improve breeding rates: the breeding period can be reduced. Hormones can be added to feed or injected directly. In the USA, artificially produced bovine somatotropin (BST), for example, is permitted (if labelled). It can increase dairy cow milk production with no noticeable deterioration in quality. The modern dairy cow can produce about 35–50 litres of milk per day – about ten times more milk than her calf would need. Attempts to reproduce this with pigs remain at the experimental level (Rabassa *et al.*, 2018). Transgenic fish are still opposed, although the FDA approved transgenic salmon in 2015, and technicians have painstakingly created fertilised Atlantic salmon eggs that include growth-enhancing DNA from two other fish species. The eggs were to be shipped to ponds in the high rainforest of Panama, where they will produce fish that mature far more quickly than normal farmed salmon (Bender, 2017). But, generally, early enthusiasm for growth hormones in agriculture has now receded amid lingering health concerns.

Hybrids are created by pollinating plants back to themselves and planting the seed, removing undesirable plants successively. Biotechnology enables hybrids from plants that cannot be crossed using pollen. An example is the development of the New Rices for Africa (NERICAs) through tissue-culture assisted hybridisation of a traditional African rice species with Asian rice, combined with agrochemicals to enhance endogenous plant defence pathways.

Cloning is the process of producing genetically identical plants or animals. The nucleus of an unfertilised ovum from one plant or animal is replaced with the cell nucleus from the plant or animal to be cloned. The result is identical in genetic composition. Plant cloning occurs when a single plant cell divides. The cell is changed temporarily so it does not have any particular structure or function. If from leaves, hormones are added to the culture medium to enable the genes to function as previously (callus). Nutrients and hormones are added, the genes operate in succession and the plant develops (tissue culture). Cloning, especially when combined with gene splicing, can produce endlessly more useful plant varieties. The first animal thus produced (embryo splitting) was Dolly the sheep (Feltman, 2016). Embryo splitting is now common in the dairy and beef cattle industries. Embryos can be implanted in surrogate mother animals (embryo transfer). Cattle again are the most frequent recipients. Cloning allows multiple copies of prize animals and, using split embryos implanted in surrogate cows, the development of disease-resistant animals. Progress has been rapid: gender selection is now possible through the differentiation of DNA. Flow cytometers can identify X and Y chromosomes and select them (Yadav *et al.*, 2017). Embryos themselves can be removed and sorted by gender. Dairy farmers can keep females, and beef producers the opposite. Aquaculture, similarly: meiosis (whereby a single cell divides twice to produce four cells containing half the original amount of genetic information) can be modified through UV light, generating only female fish which in turn can be treated to act as males, yet producing only females. Needless to say, this complex procedure is explained by economic demand: for some fish species, such as trout, the female is preferred (Manor *et al.*, 2015) and in other cases, such as Nile tilapia, it is the male (Biró *et al.*, 2010).

Tissue culture systems are where plant cells can be grown in isolation from intact plants. The cells have the characteristics of callus cells, rather than other plant cell type. The exact conditions required to initiate and sustain plant cells in culture, or to regenerate intact plants from cultured cells, are different for each plant species. Each variety of a species will often have a particular set of cultural requirements. Despite all the knowledge that has been obtained about plant tissue culture during the 20th century, these conditions have to be identified for each variety through experimentation (University of Liverpool, 2018). Provided contamination can be avoided, tissue culture is a proven method to speed up plant production.

Practical technologies: freezing often cripples fruit and vegetable productivity, so if plants can be prevented from freezing – e.g by bacteria – production can be increased. Hydroponics – growing plants without soil – is a growing area of agriscience (Simply Hydro, 2018). There are also opportunities to combine aquaculture in a symbiotic joint production process. Farmers must add additional nutrients to plants grown this way, notably macronutrients such as nitrogen, phosphorus, potassium, magnesium, sulfur and calcium, and micronutrients such as iron, boron, zinc, copper, chlorine, molybdenum and manganese. A connected technology is vertical farming,

Unfortunately, especially in Africa, there is longstanding evidence that take-up rates for new technology are lamentable. The reasons are predictable and have been frequently established. They are closely correlated with the take-up rates for improved grain varieties noted above. One study found that the determinants of adoption of new seed varieties in Uganda and Tanzania include farm size, contact with government agencies, number of improved seed varieties and credit. Other factors included age, distance to the market, contact with other extension agents and access to off-farm activities, family size, participation of soil and water conservation, farmers association and access to media (Kinuthia & Mabaya, 2017). Another similar study for Kenya found that the combined use of improved seed and fertiliser increased productivity and improved household welfare, though liquidity constraints and other barriers still limit overall use of improved technologies (Njagi *et al.*, 2017). It is clear enough – *the problems of agricultural productivity in developing countries, particularly but not exclusively in Africa, are economic and financial, not technical or scientific.*

Entomology, the use of pesticides and insecticides

Insects can be beneficial for pollination of crops, and as parasites and predators of destructive species. They are also important as food for birds, fish and other animals, and provide products of commercial value such as honey, shellac, silk and wax. But some are very destructive: they may damage or kill cultivated plants, and they may damage or contaminate stored foods and other products. Crops suffer from insects either directly or because the insect transmits viral disease to the plant. Either insect-resistant breeds or the use of insecticides is the usual method of defence. In terms of best management practices (BMPs) for the use of pesticides, there are a wide range of possibilities. Most pesticides also have adjuvants, which are broadly defined as any substance added to the spray tank, separate from the pesticide formulation, that will improve the performance of the pesticide. The proper adjuvant may reduce or even eliminate application problems, thereby improving overall pesticide effectiveness (Penn State, 2018). The extent of concern about pesticide use is now widespread: the legal position even of plant food, which might be considered a pesticide, is now of importance to environmental law.

Buffers, water treatments and conservation tillage are the most effective methods for reducing off-site movement of pesticides, along with improving irrigation and the specialised construction of wetlands and water return systems, although these may be

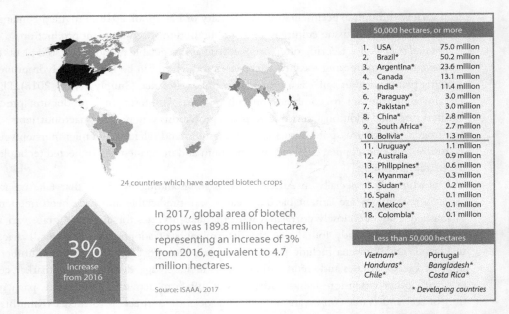

In 2017, global area of biotech crops was 189.8 million hectares, representing an increase of 3% from 2016, equivalent to 4.7 million hectares.

Source: ISAAA, 2017

50,000 hectares, or more	
1. USA	75.0 million
2. Brazil*	50.2 million
3. Argentina*	23.6 million
4. Canada	13.1 million
5. India*	11.4 million
6. Paraguay*	3.0 million
7. Pakistan*	3.0 million
8. China*	2.8 million
9. South Africa*	2.7 million
10. Bolivia*	1.3 million
11. Uruguay*	1.1 million
12. Australia	0.9 million
13. Philippines*	0.6 million
14. Myanmar*	0.3 million
15. Sudan*	0.2 million
16. Spain	0.1 million
17. Mexico*	0.1 million
18. Colombia*	0.1 million

Less than 50,000 hectares	
Vietnam*	Portugal
Honduras*	Bangladesh*
Chile*	Costa Rica*

Developing countries

Figure 4.2 Global area (in million hectares) of biotech crops, 1996–2017, by country, mega-countries, and for the top ten countries
Source: ISAAA (2017)

uneconomic. The use of conservation tillage must be undertaken with great care to prevent trade-offs between a surface water quality problem and a groundwater quality problem. Pesticide use can also be reduced with sensor spray technology compared with the use of standard sprayers. The reduction in pesticide use will result in reduced inputs to surface waters and a significant cost saving for the grower (Zhang & Goodhue, 2010). In Zambia, conservation farming – a system of minimum or no-till agriculture with crop rotations – has reduced water requirements by up to 30% and uses new drought-tolerant hybrids to produce up to 5 tons of maize per hectare, five times the average yield for sub-Saharan Africa (Tadele, 2017).

Improving yields: methods and results

Agricultural biotechnology has been successful in providing resistance to various pests in maize, sorghum, cowpeas, groundnuts and cotton. It has also been possible to provide disease-resistance in maize and bananas, as well as in livestock. Such methods can help rapidly build resilience. Scientists are working on combining them with biotechnology-based improvements in yield through improved photosynthesis, nitrogen uptake, resistance to drought and other climate change impacts (University of Queensland, 2012). A splendidly detailed analysis of developments to date is available from the EU (European Commission, 2017). One difficult-to-face technology is the use of plastic in agricultural production (Horti Daily, 2014):

Mulch film has become the core technology in vegetable and berry production. It serves so many purposes and has proven to more than pay for itself in most high value crops. The grower can choose different mulches to accomplish different objectives depending on his/her particular needs. Mostly, however, mulch serves to; suppress weed growth, control bed temperature, protect against leaching of fertilisers, increase the efficacy of fumigation and protect the crop from touching the soil directly. By altering a mulch film's color, barrier properties, thickness and other characteristics (surface, construction, resin type, etc.) different benefits can be achieved (Intergro, 2018).

In China, some 1.45 million metric tons of polyethylene are spread in razor-thin sheets across 20 million hectares of farmland. The plastic sheets, used over as much as 12% of China's farmland, are growing in popularity because they trap moisture and heat, and prevent weeds and pests. Those features can bolster cotton, maize and wheat yields by up to 30%, while enabling crops to be grown across a wider area. The material enables crops to be grown in both drier and colder environments. In Xinjiang, which accounts for almost 70% of the country's cotton output, plastic mulch is used on all cotton farms, and across 93% of the country's tobacco fields. The film reduces water demand by 20-30%. Unfortunately, the polypropylene film is environmentally dangerous, not biodegradable and often not recycled. 'White pollution' has therefore become an important issue as the country pursues more sustainable forms of food and fibre production, the agriculture ministry has admitted. The government aims for 80% of polyethylene mulch to be recycled by 2020 in provinces where it is used intensively, but the recycling rate was less than 66% in the 2010s (Bloomberg, 2017).

The GM crops debate

Gene sequencing technology also enables the molecular isolation of genes associated with traits, enabling GM to transfer them between varieties. There are essentially two main methods for introducing new DNA into plant cells: indirect and direct delivery. In indirect delivery, genes of interest are introduced into the target cell via bacteria, whereas with direct delivery there is no intermediary. Biolistic and protoplast methods are used instead (DHA, 2012). Monsanto introduced genetically modified organisms (GMO) as long ago as 1996, with Roundup Ready. There was particular concern over the terminator gene, which generated sterilised plants, requiring farmers to buy new seed annually, and which has been commercially suppressed, although the patents remain. More recently the transplanted genes have been plant genes themselves, although there is no in-principle distinction between cis- and trans-genesis: they have the same nucleotide composition and use the same genetic code (Baulcombe, 2013:3). A good example is GM squash (see box).

Squash, also known as pumpkin (Foodofy, 2018), improved through biotechnology brings important benefits to growers and consumers. By protecting the plant against specific viruses, biotech squash provides better harvests and more attractive produce for consumers when virus conditions are present. Squash growers continually battle the viral plant diseases spread by aphids, or small plant-eating insects. Virus-infected plants develop fruits that are distorted and discoloured, making the squash unmarketable, therefore negatively affecting both yield and grower profitability. While biotech protection does not prevent all viruses, it does dramatically reduce the incidence of virus infection and yield loss. Growers – especially growers in the eastern USA – value the virus-resistant (VR) squash product and their experience has been that protection delivered through biotechnology offers some of the highest possible protection against infection from viruses. Seeds, plants and produce improved through biotechnology are subject to government regulations (Monsanto, 2014).

GM crop varieties have been developed to meet different breeding aims, including:

■ Herbicide resistance – crops that show minimum damage following herbicide spraying regimes that are designed to eliminate weeds;

■ Disease resistance – crops that are less prone to be damaged by fungal, bacterial or viral diseases;

■ Pest resistance – crops that are less attractive to natural predators such as insects;

■ Stress resistance – crops that are more tolerant to various environmental stresses such as drought, salinity and extreme temperatures;

■ Varieties with altered composition – crops that show improved nutritional values, e.g. 'Golden Rice' which has an increased level of vitamin A by comparison to conventional rice species;

■ Elimination of pollutants to be used in bioremediation – crops that have the ability to decontaminate land by assimilating hazardous pollutants and toxic compounds. These plants can then be harvested and forwarded for industrial use or incinerated; and

■ Pharming (biopharming/molecular farming for the production of pharmaceuticals, enzymes, etc.) – crops that produce increased yields of desirable compounds for industrial and pharmaceutical use, e.g. starch, fuel, antibodies, hormones, etc.

Data on the global status of GM crops show very significant net economic benefits at the farm level, amounting to about $17.7 billion in 2014 and $150.3 billion for the 19-year period 1996–2014. Around 65% of the gains have derived from yield and production gains, with the remaining 35% coming from cost savings. Overall, studies from 1995–2014 confirmed multiple and significant benefits that have been generated by biotech crops over the past 20 years. On average, the adoption of GM technology has reduced the use of chemical pesticides by 37%, increased crop yields by 22% and increased farmer profits by 68% (Klümper & Qaim, 2014).

The growth in their use has as a result been remarkable. In 1996, only 1.7 million hectares were planted with GM crops globally, but by 2015 GM crops were grown in 28 countries and on 180 million hectares of land, over 10% of the world's arable land. Despite the growing area of GM crops planted worldwide, GMO crops pose several important economic as well as environmental risks, which are increased by a lack of capacity in developing countries to assess and manage associated risks. Additionally, recent activities in the area of policy development have shown a growing recognition of potential negative environmental impacts of GM, e.g. a potential loss of biodiversity and a hastening of the development of pest resistance (Taheri et al., 2017). But although some developing countries' authorities have not given farmers official permission to plant GM crops due to concerns about their biological safety, the majority of GM crops *are* now cultivated in the developing world: in 2014, around 53% of the 182 million hectares (nearly 2 million km²) of GM crops grown. Brazil and Argentina are way out in front, planting nearly 70 million hectares of GM soy, maize and cotton. India had 11.6 million hectares of GM cotton alone. China had a broader spread but much smaller quantities, while in sub-Saharan Africa there were 2.7 million hectares of GM soy, maize and cotton in South Africa, and 0.5 million hectares of cotton in Burkina Faso. Bangladesh and Australia also grow GM crops (The Conversation, 2015).

See also James (2016) for a detailed, if biased, examination of the state of GM research, trials and crops by country at the end of 2016. By far the most common GM crops are those that can tolerate herbicides. They suit the large monocropping farming systems found in the

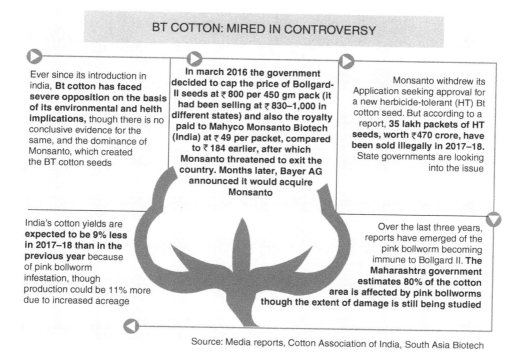

BT COTTON: MIRED IN CONTROVERSY

Ever since its introduction in india, **Bt cotton has faced severe opposition on the basis of its environmental and helth implications,** though there is no conclusive evidence for the same, and the dominance of Monsanto, which created the BT cotton seeds

In march 2016 the government decided to cap the price of Bollgard-II seeds at ₹ 800 per 450 gm pack (it had been selling at ₹ 830–1,000 in different states) and also the royalty paid to Mahyco Monsanto Biotech (India) at ₹ 49 per packet, compared to ₹ 184 earlier, after which Monsanto threatened to exit the country. Months later, Bayer AG announced it would acquire Monsanto

Monsanto withdrew its Application seeking approval for a new herbicide-tolerant (HT) Bt cotton seed. But according to a report, **35 lakh packets of HT seeds, worth ₹470 crore, have been sold illegally in 2017–18.** State governments are looking into the issue

India's cotton yields are **expected to be 9% less in 2017–18 than in the previous year** because of pink bollworm infestation, though production could be 11% more due to increased acreage

Over the last three years, reports have emerged of the pink bollworm becoming immune to Bollgard II. **The Maharashtra government estimates 80% of the cotton area is affected by pink bollworms** though the extent of damage is still being studied

Source: Media reports, Cotton Association of India, South Asia Biotech

Figure 4.3 Bt cotton: mired in controversy
Source: Seetharaman (2018)

USA, Argentina and Brazil. Among smallholdings, notably in India, China and South Africa, the biggest GM crop has been Bt cotton, which incorporates a toxin that kills pests. It has been at the centre of the debate about the extent to which GM can help the poor – or even work (LiveMint.com, 2018).

It has been argued that different GM crops in different countries lead to very different outcomes (Stone & Glover, 2016). In India, this argument suggests that the effects of GM cotton have been largely a function of India's particular problems with agricultural de-skilling

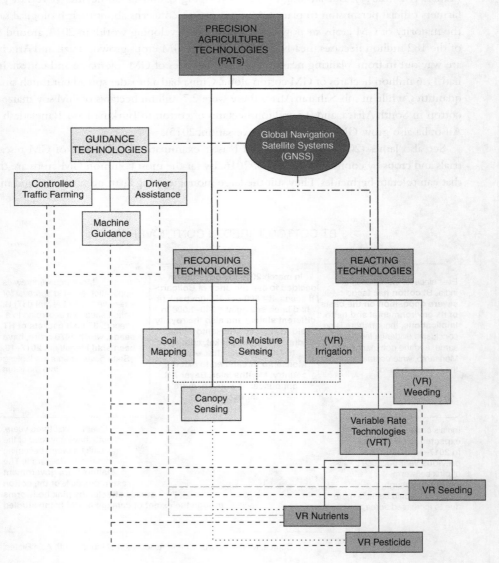

Figure 4.4 A schema of precision agriculture technologies
Source: Balafoutis *et al.* (2017)

(Stone, 2011), and the fate of GM eggplant (brinjal, aubergine) was partly determined by India's Ayurveda establishment (Kudlu & Stone, 2013). On the other hand, the adoption and impacts of GM cotton in Burkina Faso and South Africa have been strongly shaped by specific economic relationships between growers and gins (Dowd-Uribe *et al.*, 2014).

Poorer countries might also benefit from crops being developed to resist drought, heat, frost and salty soil – drought-tolerant maize is seen as a promising answer to 'climate-smart' farming in Africa, for instance. Also promising are crops with enhanced nutritional value, such as vitamin A-enriched Golden Rice:

> As part of the Golden Rice initiative, researchers introduce genes into existing rice strains to coax these GMO plants into producing the micronutrient beta carotene in the edible part of the grain. The presence of beta carotene gives the genetically modified rice a yellow hue, which explains the 'golden' in its name (Everding, 2016).

But there has been huge opposition from NGOs, especially Greenpeace, to its introduction (Miller, 2018). Golden Rice, cited above, still remains in development. In the UK, field trials of GM wheat were approved by the government in 2017 (Novella, 2017). Trials under greenhouse conditions have found that the introduction of a wild gene allows the modified wheat to photosynthesise more efficiently, resulting in yields increasing by 40%. The trials were conducted by researchers at Rothamsted, working in conjunction with the universities of Essex and Lancaster (Rothamsted, 2016).

Research has shown that wild oilseed populations, for example, containing GM traits could be due not only to the 'one-off' escape of GM material, but also due to GM persistence among field plants, acting as a 'relay' to disseminate GM traits in crop fields (Bailleul *et al.*, 2016). Cross-pollination remains a major concern: genetically modified canola has been found in North Dakota. Amid furious debate continues over the health consequences of human consumption of GM crops, unbiased scientific research and balanced conclusions are at a premium. The UK's Royal Society came down in their favour (Royal Society, 2016), and so perhaps more predictably has the USA (NAS, 2016), although even their conclusions have been challenged by passionate critics (Verkerk, 2016; Robinson, 2016). Consensus does seem to be emerging, and along the lines of KPMG in New Zealand – a country known for its promotion of food quality – which concluded that: 'The conversation is no longer about whether or not these technologies will be adopted, given the benefits they can deliver, but about the regulatory framework that needs to be built around their use' (KPMG, 2017:17).

The role of technology in agribusiness (e.g. automation, GPS, drones)

Generally, agribusiness now refers to 'precision agriculture' (PA) (Oliver *et al.*, 2013; Lal & Stewart, 2015; Pedersen & Lind, 2017). This includes three main categories: hardware and sensors (i.e. positioning and guidance, crop sensing for water stress, nutrients and yield sensing, environmental sensing, seed bed preparation, and fertiliser placement in the soil profile); data analysis and decision support systems (DSS) (i.e. protocols and standards for field data layers production, methods for data analysis for delineation of management zones and easy-to-use software) and commodity and whole-farm focus (i.e. development of DSS to apply commercially in farms including environmental impact assessment, and apply PA at farm level and not at field level). Or one could categorise precision agriculture technologies (PATs) for crop and livestock farming in a linear manner following the timeline of use of the technologies ending up in three categories, namely guidance systems, remote sensing and reacting technologies.

■ Guidance systems (i.e. hard- and software that guide tractors and implements over a field) include all forms of automatic steering/guidance for tractors and self-propelled agricultural machinery, such as driver assistance, machine guidance, controlled traffic farming.

■ Recording technologies (i.e. sensors mounted on ground-based stations, rolling, airborne or satellite platforms, and gathering spatial information) include soil mapping, soil moisture mapping, canopy mapping, yield mapping, etc.

■ Reacting technologies (i.e. implements, hard- and software that together can vary the placement of agricultural inputs in the field), include technologies such as variable rate irrigation and weeding and variable rate application of seeds, fertiliser and pesticides.

Guidance technologies can be used for any agricultural practice application (including traditional practices), generating instructions for precise machinery movement within and between fields with tangible results in reduced overlapping, causing lower input use (seeds, fertilisers, and pesticides) in parallel with decreased self-propelled machinery fuel consumption. Recording technologies are required in order to receive information from the field (before, during and after the crop period) and after processing, extract the data useful for any kind of PA application and generating positive feedback loops. Reacting technologies should then use the data produced by the recording systems and minimise all inputs (seeds, fertilisers, pesticides and water) in the optimum quantity required by the particular crop to grow. The right combination of these three categories is expected to increase or at least maintain yield with the advantage of higher quality and reduced environmental impact (Balafoutis et al., 2017).

Computerisation is now ubiquitous in the agriculture of the West, just as it is in agribusiness firms more generally. Software applications track milk productivity in dairy herds and use models to determine the right way forward for the farmer or feed manufacturer; tax, accounting and landscaping applications drive farm decision-making; the academic world is replete with econometric and other analysis of agricultural production, decision-making, profitability and agriscience. Automation is now expanding into farms through, for example:

■ *Robotic milking systems.* Northern Europe, Holland, Germany and France have been leading this paradigm shift in milking. Around 90% of new equipment installations in Sweden and

Table 4.1 Environmental impact of best management practices (BMPs)

BMPs	Environmental component					
	Water quality		Air quality	Farm worker/wildlife		All
	Mode of impact					
	Runoff	Leaching	VOCs[a]	Drift	Exposure	Use reduction[b]
Buffers	X					
Windbreaks			X			
Constructed wetlands/ tailwater ponds	X					
Water treatments: PAM, Landguard™	X					
Conservation tillage	X					
Application: timing	X	X			X	
Application: handling					X	
Application: low drift sprayers/equipment				X		
Application: sensor sprayer						X
Biological control						X
Pesticide choice: low risk and formulation			X			X
Habitat removal						X
Barriers						X
Optimal irrigation	X	X				X
Optimal fertilisation						X
Cover crop	X					X
Trap/intercrop						X
Synthetic mulches						X
Variety choice						X

a) Volatile organic compounds

b) Interpreted as a reduction in use of higher risk pesticides – overall pesticide use may not be reduced if alternative lower risk controls are used, such as for BMP 'pesticide choice'.

Source: Seetharaman (2018)

Finland, and 50% in Germany, include robotic milkers – showing that these systems have become a reliable technology for small and medium farms. In North America, automated milking began making its appearance in the mid-1990s. A growing lack of high-quality, affordable labour, in combination with the demand for higher efficiency, lower costs and flexible lifestyles, has created demand for robotic milking and other automated systems on dairies. Today, many US states use robots as do farms in Germany, Russia, Canada and Mexico with herd sizes ranging from 600 to 2,400 cows – more than 600 robots, milking 75,000+ cows in North America, with 1–2 units per farm, an average of 2.5. It is still far from being generally adopted, however, even in wealthy countries like Australia, and sheep shearing has so far defied an AI solution. However, progress has apparently been made in respect of robotic fruit-picking. Fieldcraft Robotics, a spin-off from the University of Plymouth, has already conducted trials with raspberries (Proactive Investors, 2019), whilst the University of Cambridge is developing a robot lettuce picker (Haridy, 2019). Within a decade, robotic fruit picking may start to become commercially viable.

- *Sensors on animals*, such as ultrasound, can be used, for example, to monitor imminent births, X-ray scanners of meat quality, red/white tissue identification, insect pest detection, fruit damage location. Again, even in the Australian Wheatbelt, these are far from ubiquitous.

- *GPS* uses satellites to view fields and crops. Field conditions may vary from one square metre to the next: individual fields may contain different soil types, each of which has its own fertility, drainage, organic content and nitrogen levels. GPS enables seeding, irrigation, fertilisation and cultivation practices to be varied across a single field. The farmer uses a GPS receiver to locate preselected field positions to collect soil samples. Then a lab analyses the samples, and creates a fertility map in a geographic information system (GIS). A GIS is in essence a computer database program handling geographic data and mapping. Using the map, a farmer can then prescribe the amount of fertiliser for each field location that was sampled. Variable-rate technology (VRT) fertiliser applicators then dispense exactly the amount required across the field. Satellite infrareds can e.g. distinguish crop diseases, identify problems, and, through artificial intelligence and vehicle-mounted sensors, recommend and implement solutions. The general term is *precision farming*. Arguably it reduces the use of fertilisers and pesticides and supports more efficient water use and management. Precision farming is no longer restricted to the West: it is being introduced into the more advanced developing countries, such as Kenya (Corral, 2017).

- More recently, *drones* are being used. In the USA, specific legislation (Part 107) has encouraged their use, with over 100,000 now having applied for licences according to the Federal Aviation Administration (FAA, 2018). The difference a drone can make is around the speed of that information, rendering information in real time and allowing growers to make immediate and hopefully therefore better decisions. Physical sensors and bands of light identifying stress in plants have been around for a long time. The challenge becomes to operationalise that solution with drone data extracted even beyond visual range, feeding to mobile devices in real time. From there, it should be a short step to calculating the return on investment (ROI) from data (Karpowicz, 2017).

- *Lasers* can alter land for drainage, irrigation, for building terraces and walls, and for mapping using light detection and rangefinding (LIDAR) laser systems

- *Weather modification* is at an early stage, but although scientists are not sure if cloud seeding actually consistently works, China and the USA in particular have made progress (Weather Modification History, 2018). In 2017, vineyards in Burgundy in eastern France were the first in the country, which is the world's second-largest producer of wine (behind Italy), to be extensively protected by a 'shield' to help mitigate against damaging hail storms that have blighted the area and caused losses of up to 100% in recent years (Samuel, 2017).

Food safety

Food safety scandals seem to be more frequent and severe than ever before, although statistics would suggest that, in fact, it is simply that news about them spreads more rapidly than in the past. The World Health Organization (WHO) estimated that one in ten people fall ill every year from eating contaminated food and 420,000 die as a result. African and South-East Asian regions have the highest incidence and highest death rates, including among children under the age of five. Diarrhoeal diseases are responsible for more than half of the global burden of foodborne diseases, causing 550 million people to fall ill and 230,000 deaths every year. Children are at particular risk of foodborne diarrhoeal diseases, with 220 million falling ill and 96,000 dying every year. Diarrhoea is often caused by eating raw or undercooked meat, eggs, fresh produce and dairy products contaminated by norovirus, *Campylobacter*, non-typhoidal *Salmonella*, *Shigella dysenteriae* and pathogenic *E. coli* are the main threats by number of outbreaks and affected persons (generally, 'Category B agents'). Other major contributors to the global burden of foodborne diseases are typhoid fever, hepatitis A, *Taenia solium* (a tapeworm), and aflatoxin (produced by mould on grain that is stored inappropriately). Certain diseases, such as those caused by non-typhoidal *Salmonella*, are a public health concern across all regions of the world, in high- and low-income countries alike. Even more dangerous are 'Category A' agents such as anthrax and botulism (WHO, 2018), but these are thankfully very rare. Other diseases, such as typhoid fever, foodborne cholera, and those caused by pathogenic *E. coli*, are much more common to low-income countries, while *Campylobacter* is an important pathogen in high-income countries (WHO, 2015). Raw foods of animal origin are the most likely culprits, because of their high protein and moisture content as well as potential self-contamination. *One may reasonably ask why there is so much more attention placed on the alleged threat posed by GM crops than these very real, very large numbers of deaths, almost exclusively in developing countries.*

A problem with peanuts

In 2008, a specific brand of peanut butter used as an ingredient by many of the USA's largest food manufacturers was identified as the likely source of a *Salmonella* infection outbreak that led to one of the largest, most complex, and costliest food recalls in US history.

The tainted peanut butter sickened hundreds of people in 46 states, and was blamed for at least nine deaths. More than 3,900 food products manufactured by more than 200 companies had to be removed from retailers' shelves.

The economic losses from the *Salmonella* outbreak are estimated to have topped $1 billion, excluding the cost of medical treatment for those infected by the bacteria and the cost of the related lawsuit settlements.

Source: Thompson *et al.* (2012)

Another small but well-documented example was the US sprout *Salmonella* outbreak in 2009, eventually traced to the sprout seeds themselves, which could have been tainted through contaminated water, improperly composted manure, contaminated runoff from animal-processing facilities or wild animals, a failure properly to clean harvesting or processing equipment, or poor storage (Pullman & Wu, 2012:13). The US Food Safety Modernization Act 2011 aimed to establish standards to prevent contaminated food products from entering the market. 'With today's intense focus on food safety, innovation is now honing in on issues like bacterial growth inhibition, micro-element pollutant detection, food stabilization and general contaminant prevention' (Pullman & Wu, 2012:10). A further documented example was the Serbian aflatoxin M1 outbreak in 2013–14, which lasted almost two years and was estimated to have cost the sector almost €100 million (Popoviç *et al.*, 2017).

Far worse was the 2008 melamine infant formula scandal in China, which caused babies' kidneys to malfunction – it killed six infants and hospitalised 300,000 others (BBC News, 2010). BSE (Creutzfeldt-Jakob Disease or CJD) had by 2012 killed 266 people in the UK and elsewhere since the late 1980s (Meikle, 2012). In 2017, the Fipronil egg scandal caused millions of eggs to be withdrawn from the shelves in Europe and Hong Kong (BBC News, 2017). Probably the worst event remains what happened in 1981 in Spain, when 600+ people died from drinking industrial rapeseed oil illegally passed off as olive oil. Or from something else: conspiracy theories have abounded (Woffinden, 2001). The list of major scandals is depressingly long. Responses to the problem include the widespread adoption of hazard analysis and critical control points (HACCP) during production, so that potential hazards and contamination can be identified and if possible eliminated. Further principles include traceability, transparency, testability, time, trust and training (Pullman & Wu, 2012:23–24). Yet again, the problem remains implementation, especially in developing countries.

Food contamination is a widespread problem, but the risk can be mitigated through successful risk-management programmes that include stringent processes and controls, traceability and transparency measures, and detailed recordkeeping, at which the US Food and Drug Administration (FDA) excels, but which of course is far more difficult in developing countries without the same administrative infrastructure.

Most recently there has been global concern over avian flu. In the UK the Department for Environment, Food and Rural Affairs (DEFRA) has put an interactive map on its website, showing the higher risk areas (DEFRA, 2018).

Conclusion

Agtech and agricultural scientific research are making considerable strides annually and there is no substitute for regularly trawling the relevant scientific journals as well as keeping track of what innovative companies are doing. Each technique has advantages and disadvantages in specific situations, depending, for example, on the respective species, the purpose, the environment and other conditions.

Critics present biotechnology as being inevitably linked to multinational corporations and as being inconsistent with the interests of smallholders and the developing world generally. In fact, biotechnology presents numerous opportunities for precisely those categories, although certainly there are huge disparities in the application of science to farming and agribusiness more widely. Large organisations may be the most obvious beneficiaries, but important benefits may derive from biotechnology (and GM) linked to traditional cultivation and techniques such as integrated pest management (IPM). The problem so far as agribusiness is concerned is uncertainty. Most crop genetics and food production companies operate globally: shipping seeds, plant materials or final foods worldwide. Regulatory authorities such as the EU must rule if gene-edited crops fall under the genetically modified organism rule, although there is some indication that may change. Until this is clear, many crop genetics companies will not risk the potential trade barriers of using gene-editing technology. Equally, consumers must accept gene-editing technology as they have GM crops, which may be a prolonged process given the rise in fear of genetic modification in food generally.

The stark reality is, however, that the potential benefits from adopting BMPs, such as those outlined for the UK by the Department for Environment, Food and Rural Affairs (DEFRA, 2009), have the potential to deliver at least as great, and possibly much greater, benefit to agricultural production as scientific developments, especially in developing countries. Organic farming stands as the next stage after widespread adoption of BMPs. Both apply as much to the environmental benefits of carbon sequestration, water conservation and soil preservation as to yield enhancement. Integrating advances in agtech science with BMPs is, of course, the best possible combination, but for all of that, I argue, *agriculture must be a business*. With that, science can be utilised for profitability.

Bibliography

Aguilera, E., Lassaletta, L., Gattinger, A. and Gimeno, B.S. (2013) Managing soil carbon for climate change mitigation and adaptation in Mediterranean cropping systems: A meta-analysis. *Agriculture, Ecosystems & Environment* 168, 25–36.

Alandete-Saez, M., Chi-Ham, C.L., Graff, G.D. and Bennett, A.B. (2014) Intellectual property in agriculture. In Van Alfen, N.K. (ed.) *Encyclopedia of Agriculture and Food Systems*, Volume 4. London, Elsevier, 31–43.

Adams, R. (2009) Climate change and agriculture. In Yotovaay, A. (ed.) *Climate Change, Human Systems and Policy*, Volume 1. EOLSS, 309–327. Available at: www.eolss.net/sample-chapters/C12/E1-04-03-06.pdf. Retrieved 6 June 2018.

ADB (2017) Pakistan's fragrant basmati rice at a crossroads. Asian Development Blog. Available at: https://blogs.adb.org/blog/pakistan-s-fragrant-basmati-rice-crossroads. Retrieved 6 June 2018.

Agriculture and Food Development Authority (2017) World renowned animal behaviour expert Professor Temple Grandin at ICoMST 2017. Available at: www.teagasc.ie/news–events/news/2017/animal-behaviour-expert.php. Retrieved 7 June 2018.

AHDB Dairy (2009) The pros and cons of crossbreeding. 1 July. Available at: https://dairy.ahdb.org.uk/news/technical-article-archive/july-2009/the-pros-and-cons-of-crossbreeding/#.WW7vfIh97IU. Retrieved 7 June 2018.

Aither (2017) Water markets in New South Wales. Available at: www.industry.nsw.gov.au/__data/assets/pdf_file/0006/155859/Water-markets-in-nsw-aither-report-for-dpi-water.pdf   Retrieved 24 February 2019.

Arizona (2008) Guide to Agricultural PM10 Best Management Practices. Agriculture Improving Air Quality. Available at: http://legacy.azdeq.gov/environ/air/plan/download/webguide.pdf. Retrieved 7 June 2018.

Australian Academy of Science (2016) Decadal Plan for Australian Agricultural Sciences 2017–26. Available at: www.science.org.au/files/userfiles/support/reports-and-plans/in-progress-decadal-plans/decadal-plan-agricultural-sciences-final-draft-nov16.pdf. Retrieved 6 June 2018.

Australian Government (Environmental Water Office) (2018) Goulburn Water Allocation Sale. Available at: www.environment.gov.au/system/files/media-releases/a472d0bc-37aa-4bc4-a058-254e3f08a07b/files/goulburn-market-information-2018.pdf. Retrieved 18 March 2019.

Bailleul, D., Ollier, S. and Lecomte, J. (2016) Genetic diversity of oilseed rape fields and feral populations in the context of coexistence with GM crops. *PLOS One* 11(6), e0158403, doi:10.1371/journal.pone.0158403. Available at: http://journals.plos.org/plosone/article?id=10.1371/journal.pone.0158403. Retrieved 7 June 2018.

Balafoutis, A., Beck, B., Fountas, S., Vengeyte, J., van der Al, T., Soto, I., Gómez-Barbero, M., Barnes, A. and Eory, V. (2017) Precision agriculture technologies positively contributing to GHG emissions mitigation, farm productivity and economics. *Sustainability* 9(8), 1339, doi:10.3390/su9081339. Available at: www.mdpi.com/2071-1050/9/8/1339/htm. Retrieved 27 February 2018.

Baulcombe, D. (2013) Introduction. In Bennett, D.J. and Jennings, R.C. (eds.) (2013) *Successful Agricultural Innovation in Emerging Economies*. Cambridge, Cambridge University Press.

BBC News (2010) Timeline: China milk scandal. Available at: http://news.bbc.co.uk/2/hi/7720404.stm. Retrieved 8 June 2018.

BBC News (2017) Eggs containing fipronil found in 15 EU countries and Hong Kong. 11 August. Available at: www.bbc.com/news/world-europe-40896899. Retrieved 8 June 2018.

Bekkerman, A. and Tejeda, H.A. (2017) Revisiting the determinants of futures contracts success: tThe role of market participants. *Agricultural Economics* 48(2), 175–185.

Bender, E. (2017) Transgenic fish are ready for us. Are we ready for them? Available at: https://geneticliteracyproject.org/2017/07/10/anti-gmo-ngos-sharpen-attacks-aquabountys-aquadvantage-worlds-sustainable-salmon-edges-market/. Retrieved 7 June 2018.

Biró, J., Hancz, C., Szabó, A. and Molnár, T. (2010) Effect of sex on the fillet quality of Nile tilapia fed varying lipid sources. *Italian Journal of Animal Science* 8(S3), 225–227, doi: 10.4081/ijas.2009.s3.225. Available at: www.tandfonline.com/doi/abs/10.4081/ijas.2009.s3.225. Retrieved 7 June 2018.

Bloomberg (2017) Plastic Film Covering 12% of China's Farmland Pollutes Soil. Bloomberg News. 6 September. Available at: www.bloomberg.com/news/articles/2017-09-05/plastic-film-covering-12-of-china-s-farmland-contaminates-soil. Retrieved 7 June 2018.

Case, P. (2015) 'Push-pull' strategy boosts maize yields for Ugandan farmers. *Farmers' Weekly*. 5 March. Available at: www.fwi.co.uk/news/push-pull-strategy-boosts-maize-yields-ugandan-farmers. Retrieved 8 June 2018.

Cerveny, C. and Gibson, J. (2005) Grower 101: Rooting Hormones. Available at: https://gpnmag.com/article/grower-101-rooting-hormones/. Retrieved 7 June 2018.

Cobanovic, K. (2002) Role of Statistics in the Education of Agricultural Science Students. Available at: https://iase-web.org/documents/papers/icots6/4i2_coba.pdf. Retrieved 11 February 2018.

Colliers (2016) Ripe for the picking: A new dawn for agribusiness. *Colliers Edge*. Available at: www.colliers.com.au/colliersedge. Retrieved 12 July 2016.

CORAF (2018) Farmers are adopting new maize varieties, preliminary results of a new study show. 25 January. Available at: www.coraf.org/en/2018/01/25/farmers-are-adopting-new-maize-varieties-preliminary-results-of-a-new-study-show/. Retrieved 31 July 2018.

Corral, C. (2017) Precision agriculture for development. 20 May. Available at: www.atai-research.org/wp-content/uploads/2017/06/PAD_CC_presentation-for-ICED-2017.05.24_Carolina_Corral.pdf. Retrieved 7 June 2018.

CTA (2018) Climate change and conflict in Chad – using p3dm to secure peace. 24 January. Available at: www.cta.int/en/article/2018-01-24/climate-change-and-conflict-in-chad-using-p3dm-to-secure-peace.html?utm_source=CTA+corporate+newsletter+-+CTA+Flash&utm_campaign=e31b12ff1a-CTA-flash-en-june-2016&utm_medium=email&utm_term=0_17518d6256-e31b12ff1a-78701821&goal=0_17518d6256-e31b12ff1a-78701821&mc_cid=e31b12ff1a&mc_eid=d83951eb05. Retrieved 6 June 2018.

Currey, C.J. and Lopez, R.G. (2010) Commercial Greenhouse and Nursery Production. Available at: www.extension.purdue.edu/extmedia/HO/HO-248-W.pdf. Retrieved 7 June 2018.

Department for Food, Environment and Rural Affairs (DEFRA) (2009) Protecting our Water, Soil and Air. A Code of Good Agricultural Practice for Farmers, Growers and Land Managers. Available at: https://assets.publishing.service.gov.uk/government/uploads/system/uploads/attachment_data/file/268691/pb13558-cogap-131223.pdf. Retrieved 4 July 2017.

Department for Food, Environment and Rural Affairs (DEFRA) (2018). Avian Influenza (Bird Flu): Interactive map. Available at: www.gisdiseasemap.defra.gov.uk/intmaps/avian/map.jsp. Retrieved 8 June 2018.

DeBano, L.F. (1990) The Effect of Fire on Soil Properties. Available at: https://forest.moscowfsl.wsu.edu/smp/solo/documents/GTRs/INT_280/DeBano_INT-280.php. Retrieved 8 June 2018.

DHA (2012) Risk Assessment Reference: Methods of Plant Genetic Modification. Department of Health and Office of the Gene Regulator. December. Available at: www.ogtr.gov.au/internet/ogtr/publishing.nsf/Content/plant-modifications-ref-1-htm/$FILE/Methods%20of%20plant%20Genetic%20Modification.pdf. Retrieved 7 June 2018.

Devia, G.K., Ganasri B.P. and Dwarakish, G.S (2015) A review on hydrological models. *Aquatic Procedia* 4, 1001–1007. Available at: www.sciencedirect.com/science/article/pii/S2214241X15001273. Retrieved 6 June 2018.

DPIRD (2018) How Australia accounts for agricultural greenhouse gas emissions. Department of Primary Industries and Rural Development (Australia). Available at: www.agric.wa.gov.au/climate-change/how-australia-accounts-agricultural-greenhouse-gas-emissions. Retrieved 7 June 2018.

Dos Santos, T., Koestiono, D., and Wahib Muhaimin, A. (2017) Feasibility study of coffee monoculture farming and jackfruit intercropping in Emera District of East Timor. *Scholars Journal of Agriculture and Veterinary Sciences* 4(12), 513–521. Available at: http://saspjournals.com/wp-content/uploads/2018/01/SJAVS-412513–521.pdf. Retrieved 7 June 2018.

Dowd-Uribe, B., Glover, D. and Schnurr, M. (2014). Seeds and places: The geographies of transgenic crops in the global south. *Geoforum* 53, 145–148.

Durrant, W.E. and Dong, X. (2004) Systemic acquired resistance. *Annual Review of Phytopathology* 42, 185–209. Available at: www.annualreviews.org/doi/abs/10.1146/annurev.phyto.42.040803.140421. Retrieved 7 June 2018.

Dutch Greenhouses.com (2018) Dutch Greenhouse Technology. Available at: https://dutchgreenhouses.com/technology. Retrieved 11 June 2018.

EPA (2018) A. Permit Provisions and Program Elements. Available at: www.epa.gov/sites/production/files/2017-01/documents/a_minnesota_feedlot_registration.pdf. Retrieved 7 June 2018.

European Commission. (2017) New techniques in Agricultural Biotechnology. High Level Group of Scientific Advisors. Explanatory Note 02/2017. Available at: https://ec.europa.eu/research/sam/pdf/topics/explanatory_note_new_techniques_agricultural_biotechnology.pdf. Retrieved 7 June 2018.

Everding, G. (2016) Genetically modified Golden Rice falls short on lifesaving promises. St Louis, Washington University. 3 June. Available at: https://source.wustl.edu/2016/06/genetically-modified-golden-rice-falls-short-lifesaving-promises/. Retrieved 7 June 2018.

FAO (2017) *The Future of Food and Agriculture: Trends and Challenges*. Rome, FAO. Available at: www.fao.org/3/a-i6583e.pdf. Retrieved 5 February 2018.

FAO (n.d.) *Objectives and Organization of Agricultural Research*. Rome, FAO. Available at: www.fao.org/3/w7501e/w7501e04.htm. Retrieved 15 May 2019.

FarmFutures (2018) EU Court rules in mutagenesis case. 27 July. Available at: www.farmfutures.com/regulatory/eu-court-rules-mutagenesis-case. Retrieved 31 July 2018.

Federal Aviation Administration (2018) *Unmanned Aircraft Systems*. Available at: www.faa.gov/uas/. Retrieved 31 July 2018.

Feltman, R. (2016). Dolly the sheep died young – but her clones seem perfectly healthy as they turn 9. *Washington Post*. 26 July. Available at: www.washingtonpost.com/news/speaking-of-science/wp/2016/07/26/dolly-the-sheep-died-young-but-her-clones-seem-perfectly-healthy-as-they-turn-9/. Retrieved 7 June 2018.

Foodofy (2018) How to identify squash – different squash types you didn't know about! Available at: www.foodofy.com/how-to-identify-squash-different-squash-types-you-didnt-know-about.html. Retrieved 7 June 2018.

Francis, D., Finer, J. and Grotewold, E. (2017) Current opinion in biotechnology challenges and opportunities for improving food quality and nutrition through plant biotechnology. *Current Opinion in Biotechnology* 44, 124–129.

Ganesan, S., Vadivel, K. and Jayaraman, J. (2015). *Sustainable Crop Disease Management Using Natural Products*. Wallingford, CABI.

García-Ballesteros, S., Gutiérrez, J.P., Varona, L. and Fernández, J. (2017) The influence of natural selection in breeding programs: A simulation study. *Livestock Science* 204, 98–103.

Glinicki, R., Sas-Paszt, L. and Jadczuk-Tobjasz, E. (2010) The effect of plant stimulant/fertiliser "Resistim" on growth and development of strawberry plants. *Journal of Fruit and Ornamental Plant Research* 18(1), 111–124. Available at: www.insad.pl/files/journal_pdf/journal_2010_1/full10%202010_1_.pdf. Retrieved 7 June 2018.

Gómez, C.M. and Blanco, C.D.P. (2012) Do drought management plans reduce drought risk? A risk assessment model for a Mediterranean river basin. *Ecological Economics* 76, 42–48.

Gould, F., Brown, Z.S. and Kuzma, J. (2018) Wicked evolution: Can we address the sociobiological dilemma of pesticide resistance? *Science (New York)* 360(6390), 728–732.

Haridy, R. (2019) Machine learning helps robot harvest lettuce for the first time. *New Atlas*, 8 July 2019. Available at: https://newatlas.com/robot-harvest-lettuce-vegetable-machine-learning-agriculture/60465/. Retrieved 15 July 2019.

Hazel, A.R., Heins, B.J. and Hansen, L.B. (2017) Fertility, survival, and conformation of Montbéliarde × Holstein and Viking Red × Holstein crossbred cows compared with pure Holstein cows during first lactation in 8 commercial dairy herds. *Journal of Dairy Science* 100, 9447–9458, doi:10.3168/jds.2017-12824.

Horti Daily (2014) Philippines: Agri-plastic, the new farming tech. Available at: www.hortidaily.com/article/11723/Philippines-Agri-plastic,-the-new-farming-tech. Retrieved 7 June 2018.

IFPRI (International Food Policy Research Institute) (2008) *Agricultural Public Spending in Nigeria*. Washington DC, IFPRI. Available at: www.ifpri.org/publication/agricultural-public-spending-nigeria. Retrieved 3 December 2012.

Intergro (2018) Plastic Mulch Films. Available at: www.intergro.com/en/products/plastic-mulch-films/. Retrieved 7 June 2018.

International Service for the Acquisition of Agri-Biotech Applications (ISAAA) (2017) Global Status of Commercialized Biotech/GM Crops in 2017: Biotech Crop Adoption Surges as Economic Benefits Accumulate in 22 Years. Available at: http://isaaa.org/resources/publications/briefs/53/download/isaaa-brief-53-2017.pdf. Retrieved 18 March 2019.

James. C. (2015) *20th Anniversary (1996–2015) of the Global Commercialization of Biotech Crips and Biotech Crops Highlights in 2015*. ISAAA Brief Number 51. Ithaca, NY, ISAAA. Available at: www.isaaa.org/resources/publications/briefs/51/download/isaaa-brief-51-2015.pdf. Retrieved 23 February 2018.

James, C. (2016) *Global Status of Commercialized Biotech/GM Crops: 2016*. ISAA Brief Number 52. Ithaca, NY, ISAAA. Available at: www.isaaa.org/resources/publications/briefs/51/download/isaaa-brief-52-2016.pdf. Retrieved 12 February 2018.

Josephs, E.B., Stinchcombe, J.R. and Wright, S.I. (2017) What can genome-wide association studies tell us about the evolutionary forces maintaining genetic variation for quantitative traits? *New Phytologist* 214(1), 21–33.

Karlen, D.L., Mausbach, M.J., Doran, J.W., Cline, R.G., Harris, R.F. and Schuman, G.E. (1997) Soil quality: A concept, definition, and framework for evaluation. *Soil Science Society of America Journal* 61, 4–10.

Karpowicz, J. (2017) How are Precision Agriculture Professionals Using Drones in 2017? Available at: www.expouav.com/wp-content/uploads/2017/03/free-report-precision-agriculture-professionals-using-drones-2017.pdf.

Kinuthia, B.K. and Mabaya, E. (2017) Impact of Agriculture Technology Adoption on Farmers' Welfare in Uganda and Tanzania. Available at: http://barrett.dyson.cornell.edu/staars/fellows/files/Kinuthia_Mabaya%201%20Jan%202017%20abstract.pdf. Retrieved 21 February 2018.

Klümper, W. and Qaim, M. (2014) A meta-analysis of the impacts of genetically modified crops. *PLOS One* 9(11). Available at: http://journals.plos.org/plosone/article/file?id=10.1371/journal.pone.0111629&type=printable. Retrieved 31 July 2018.

KPMG (2017) Agribusiness Agenda 2017: The Recipe for Action. Available at: https://home.kpmg.com/au/en/home/insights/2017/06/agribusiness-agenda-2017-the-recipe-for-action.html. Retrieved 7 June 2018.

Kudlu, C. and Stone, G.D. (2013) The trials of genetically modified food: Bt eggplant and Ayurvedic medicine in India. *Food Culture and Society* 16(1), 21–42.

Kushalappa, A.C., Yogendra, K.N. and Karre, S. (2016) Plant inate immune response: Qualitative and quantitative resistance. *Critical Reviews in Plant Sciences* 35(1), 38–55.

Lal, R. and Stewart, B.A. (2015) *Soil-Specific Farming: Precision Agriculture*. Oakville, CRC Press.

LiveMint.com (2018) Bt cotton doubled production, minimised harm by pest: Govt. 5 February. Available at: www.livemint.com/Politics/vrG4Um2ZXJd7yDzzR33lVI/Bt-cotton-doubled-production-minimised-harm-by-pest-Govt.html. Retrieved 7 June 2018.

Lloyd, B.J. and Dennison, P.E. (2018) Evaluating the response of conventional and water harvesting farms to environmental variables using remote sensing. *Agriculture, Ecosystems and Environment* 262, 11–17.

Manor, M.L., Cleveland, B.L., Brett Kenney, P., Yao, J. and Leeds, T. (2015) Differences in growth, fillet quality, and fatty acid metabolism-related gene expression between juvenile male and female rainbow trout. *Fish Physiology and Biochemistry* 41(2), 533–547. Available at: https://link.springer.com/article/10.1007/s10695-015-0027-z. Retrieved 7 June 2018.

Masud, M.M., Azam, M.N., Mohiuddin, M., Banna, H., Akhtar, R., Ferdous Alam, A.S.A. and Begum, H. (2017) Adaptation barriers and strategies towards climate change: Challenges in the agricultural sector. *Journal of Cleaner Production* 156, 698–706.

Mathews, J.A. (2012) Reforming the international patent system. *Review of International Political Economy* 19(1), 169–180.

Meikle, J. (2012) Mad cow disease – a very British response to an international crisis. *The Guardian.* 25 April. Available at: www.theguardian.com/uk/2012/apr/25/mad-cow-disease-british-crisis. Retrieved 8 June 2018.

Michigan (2016) *Generally Accepted Agricultural and Management Practices for Manure Management and Utilization.* Michigan Department of Agriculture and Rural Development. January. Available at: www.michigan.gov/documents/mdard/2016_MANURE_GAAMPs_516117_7.pdf. Retrieved 7 June 2018.

Miller, H. (2018) Viewpoint: Misguided activism imperils potential of Golden rice. Genetic Literacy Project. 10 January. Available at: https://geneticliteracyproject.org/2018/01/10/misguided-activism-imperils-potential-golden-rice/. Retrieved 7 June 2018.

Monsanto (2014) Squash – User Guide. Available at: www.monsantoglobal.com/SiteCollection Documents/squash-TUG.pdf. Retrieved 7 June 2018.

Muldowney J., Mounsey, J. and Kinsella L. (2013) Agriculture in the climate change negotiations; ensuring that food production is not threatened. *Animal* 7(S2), 206–211.

NAS (2016) *Genetically Engineered Crops: Experiences and Prospects.* National Academies of Sciences, Engineering, and Medicine. Available at: www.nap.edu/catalog/23395/genetically-engineered-crops-experiences-and-prospects?utm_source=NAP_embed_book_widget&utm_medium=widget&utm_campaign=Widget_v4&utm_content=23395. Retrieved 7 June 2018.

Njagi, T., Mathenge, M., Mukundi, E. and Carter, M. (2017) *Maize Technology Bundles and Food Security in Kenya.* Available at: https://basis.ucdavis.edu/publication/policy-brief-maize-technology-bundles-and-food-security-kenya. Retrieved 26 June 2017.

Novella, S. (2017) New GM wheat trials set. Neurologica [blog]. 7 February. Available at: https://theness.com/neurologicablog/index.php/first-gm-wheat-trials-set/. Retrieved 7 June 2018.

NSW Office of Water (2016) Water Markets in New South Wales. Available at: www.industry.nsw.gov.au/water/licensing-trade/trade. Retrieved 24 February 2019.

Nuffield Council on Bioethics (2016) Genome Editing: An ethical review. Available at: http://nuffieldbioethics.org/wp-content/uploads/Genome-editing-an-ethical-review.pdf. Retrieved 15 May 2019.

Oliver, M.A., Bishop, T. and Marchant, B. (2013) *Precision Agriculture for Sustainability and Environmental Protection.* London, Routledge.

Pedersen, S.M. and Lind, K.M. (eds.) (2017) *Precision Agriculture: Technology and Economic Perspectives.* Cham, Springer International Publishing.

Penn State (2018) Spray Adjuvants. Available at: https://extension.psu.edu/spray-adjuvants. Retrieved 7 June 2018.

Popoviç, B.R., Radovanov, B. and Dunn. J.W. (2017) Food scare crisis: The effect on Serbian dairy market. *International Food and Agribusiness Management Review* 20(1), 113–127. Available at: www.wageningenacademic.com/doi/pdf/10.22434/IFAMR2015.0051. Retrieved 20 July 2018.

Powlson, D.S., Stirling, C.M., Thierfelder, C., White, R.P. and Jat, M.L. (2016) Does conservation agriculture deliver climate change mitigation through soil carbon sequestration in tropical agro-ecosystems? *Agriculture, Ecosystems and Environment* 220, 164–174.

Prabha, S., Yadav, A., Sharma, A., Yadav, H.K., Kumar, S. and Kumar, R. (2016) Plant immune system: Plant disease resistance genes and its applications. *Journal of Pure and Applied Microbiology* 10(2), 1269–1276.

Proactive Investors (2019) Frontier IP's Fieldwork Robotics sees success in initial trials of fruit-picking robot. 28 May 2019. Available at: www.proactiveinvestors.co.uk/companies/news/221014/frontier-ips-fieldwork-robotics-completes-initial-trials-of-raspberry-picking-robot-221014.html. Retrieved 15 July 2019.

Pullman, M. and Wu, Z. (2012) *Food Supply Chain Management.* London and New York, Routledge.

Purdy, C. (2017) Want a greenhouse that can fight climate change? Make it pink. 4 November. Available at: https://qz.com/1121386/new-greenhouse-technology-can-grow-food-and-generate-electricity/. Retrieved 11 June 2018.

PwC (2016) AgTech – don't wait for the future, create it. Africa Agribusiness Insights Survey 2016. Available at www.pwc.co.za/en/assets/pdf/agri-businesses-insights-survey-may-2016.pdf. Retrieved 12 July 2016.

Rabassa, V.R., Feijó, J.O., Perazzoli, D., Pereira, C.M., Schild, A.L.P., Lucia Júnior, T., Corcini, C.D., Schmitt, E., Schneider, A., Pino, F.A.B.D., Bianchi, I. and Corrêa, M.N. (2018) Effect of porcine somatotropin on metabolism, testicular size and sperm characteristics in young boars. *Arq. Bras. Med. Vet. Zootec,* 70(1), 73–81. Available at: www.scielo.br/pdf/abmvz/v70n1/0102-0935-abmvz-70-01-00073.pdf. Retrieved 7 June 2018.

Reddy, P.P. (2016) Push–Pull Strategy. In Reddy, P.P. (ed.) *Sustainable Intensification of Crop Production.* Singapore, Springer, 323–336.

Ricketts, K. and Ricketts, C. (2009) *Agribusiness Fundamentals and Applications.* New York, CENGAGE Delmar Learning.

Robinson, C. (2016) How the National Academy of Sciences misled the public over GMO food safety. GM Watch. 26 May. Available at: www.gmwatch.org/en/news/latest-news/16976. Retrieved 7 June 2018.

Rothamsted (2017) Application for permission to carry out field trial with GM wheat plants with increased photosynthetic efficiency. Available at: http://resources.rothamsted.ac.uk/sites/default/files/attachments/2016-11-04/QandAfortheweb_3_11_2016F%20%28Henry%20Osim%29.pdf. Retrieved 7 June 2018.

Royal Society (2016) GM Plants. Questions and Answers. Available at: https://royalsociety.org/~/media/policy/projects/gm-plants/gm-plant-q-and-a.pdf. Retrieved 7 June 2018.

Runkle, E. (2012) Cutting Edge Greenhouse Technology. Available at: https://gpnmag.com/article/cutting-edge-greenhouse-technology/. Retrieved 11 June 2018.

Samuel, H. (2017) Entire Burgundy wine region to be covered by hi-tech 'hail shield' to kill storm clouds. *Daily Telegraph.* 20 April. Available at: www.telegraph.co.uk/news/2017/04/15/entire-burgundy-wine-region-covered-hi-tech-hail-shield-kill/?WT.mc_id=tmgliveapp_androidshare_AlsCVWKwF5nX. Retrieved 7 June 2018.

Sant'Ana, G.C., Pereira, L.F.P., Pot, D., Ivamoto, S.T., Domingues, D.S., Ferreira, R.V., Pagiatto, N.F., da Silva, B.R.S., Nogueira, L.M., Kitzberger, C.S.G., Scholz, M.B.S., de Oliveira, F.F., Sera, G.H., Padilha, L., Labouisse, J-P., Guyot, R., Charmetant, P. and Leroy, T. (2018) Genome-wide association study reveals candidate genes influencing lipids and diterpenes contents in *Coffea arabica*. *Nature: Scientific Reports* 8, 465.

SCAIL (2014) SCAIL-Agriculture: User guide. Available at: www.scail.ceh.ac.uk/agriculture/ Sniffer%20ER26_SCAIL-Agriculture%20USER%20GUIDE%20Final%20Issue%2011032014. pdf. Retrieved 7 June 2018.

Science Direct (2018) Systemic Acquired Resistance. Available at: www.sciencedirect.com/topics/ agricultural-and-biological-sciences/systemic-acquired-resistance. Retrieved 7 June 2018.

Seetharaman, G. (2018) These two issues could put the brakes on the Bt cotton story. *The Economic Times (India)*. 21 January. Available at: https://economictimes.indiatimes.com/news/economy/ agriculture/the-brakes-are-applied-on-the-bt-cotton-story/articleshow/62583116.cms. Retrieved 24 February 2019.

Simply Hydro (2018) What is hydroponics? Available at: www.simplyhydro.com/whatis.htm. Retrieved 7 June 2018.

Singh, K. (2011) Groundwater depletion in Punjab: Measurement and countering strategies. *Indian Journal of Agricultural Economics* 66(4), 573–589.

Stone, G.D. (2011) Field versus farm in Warangal: Bt cotton, higher yields, and larger questions. *World Development* 39(3), 387–398.

Stone, G.D. and Glover, D. (2016) Disembedding grain: Golden Rice, the Green Revolution, and heirloom seeds in the Philippines. *Agriculture and Human Values* 34(1), 87–102.

Su, J., Li, L., Zhang, C., Wang, C., Gu, L., Wang, H., Wei, H., Liu, Q., Huang, L. and Yu, S. (2018) Genome-wide association study identified genetic variations and candidate genes for plant architecture component traits in Chinese upland cotton. *Theoretical Applied Genetics* 131(6), 1299–1314.

Tadele, Z. (2017) Raising crop productivity in Africa through intensification. *Agronomy* 7(1), 22, doi:10.3390/agronomy7010022. Available at: www.mdpi.com/2073–4395/7/1/22/htm. Retrieved 7 June 2018.

Taheri, F. Azadi, H. and D'Haese, M. (2017) World without hunger: Organic or GM crops? *Sustainability*, 9(4), 580. Available at https://biblio.ugent.be/publication/8526688. Retrieved 7 September 2017.

The Conversation (2015) GM crops and the developing world: Opposing sides miss the bigger picture. 13 November. Available at: http://theconversation.com/gm-crops-and-the-developing-world-opposing-sides-miss-the-bigger-picture-50479. Retrieved 7 June 2018.

Thompson, H., Nishio, E. and Cryer, C. (2012) *Peanut Butter Recall: A Case Study in Food Safety*. Cobank. May. Available at: www.cobank.com/Knowledge-Exchange/~/media/Files/Searchable%20PDF% 20Files/Knowledge%20Exchange/2012/Front%20Page%20%20Peanut%20Butter%20Recall%20 Report%20May%202012%201.pdf. Retrieved 8 June 2018.

Uddin, J. and Sjah, T. (2017) Integration of the technologies of simple drip irrigation and rain shelter for sustainable chili production in East Lombok, Indonesia. *Asian Academic Research Journal of Multidisciplinary Research* 4(6), 79–88. Available at: www.asianacademicresearch.org/2017_paper/ june_md_2017/9.pdf. Retrieved 26 June 2017.

United Nations (1992) *United Nations Framework Convention on Climate Change*. New York, United Nations. Available at: https://unfccc.int/resource/docs/convkp/conveng.pdf. Retrieved 6 July 2018.

United Nations (2002) Agriculture and Rural Development. Available at: www.un.org/esa/agenda21/ natlinfo/countr/safrica/agriculture.pdf. Retrieved 7 June 2018.

United Nations (2018) Comprehensive Africa Agriculture Development Programme (CAADP). Office of the Special Adviser on Africa. Available at: www.un.org/en/africa/osaa/peace/caadp. shtml. Retrieved 20 July 2018.

University of California (2008) Soil Solarization for Gardens & Landscapes. Available at: http://ipm.ucanr.edu/PMG/PESTNOTES/pn74145.html. Retrieved 8 June 2018.

University of Liverpool (2018) Plant Tissue Culture Case Study 1. Available at: www.liverpool.ac.uk/~sd21/tisscult/case_study_1.htm. Retrieved 7 June 2018.

University of Queensland (2012) Agricultural Science. Available at: http://downloads.realviewtechnologies.com/Luna%20Media/UQ/Agricultural%20Science.pdf. Retrieved 7 June 2018.

USDA (2017) *China's Annual Agricultural Policy Goals. The 2017 No. 1 Document of the CCCPC and the State Council.* GAIN Report CH17006. 15 February. Washington DC, USDA. Available at: https://gain.fas.usda.gov/Recent%20GAIN%20Publications/China's%202017%20Agricultural%20Policy%20Goals_Beijing_China%20-%20Peoples%20Republic%20of_2-15–2017.pdf. Retrieved 5 June 2018.

Verkerk, R. (2016) UK Royal Society whitewash on GM crops. GM Watch. 20 June. Available at: www.gmwatch.org/en/news/latest-news/17042-uk-royal-society-whitewash-on-gm-crops. Retrieved 7 June 2018.

Villavicencio, L. (2012) Plant growth stimulants: Do they work? Recent research shows that the use of certain supplements may be worth consideration. Available at: https://gpnmag.com/article/plant-growth-stimulants-do-they-work/. Retrieved 12 February 2018.

Vivo (2018). *Growth Hormone (Somatotropin).* Vivo Pathophysiology. Available at: www.vivo.colostate.edu/hbooks/pathphys/endocrine/hypopit/gh.html. Retrieved 7 June 2018.

Weather Modification History (2018). Interactive Timeline. Available at: https://weathermodificationhistory.com/interactive-timeline/. Retrieved 15 May 2019.

Weiner, J. (2017) Applying plant ecological knowledge to increase agricultural sustainability. *Journal of Ecology* 105, 865–870. Available at: https://besjournals.onlinelibrary.wiley.com/doi/epdf/10.1111/1365–2745.12792. Retrieved 31 July 2018.

Werner, C. and Dubbert, M. (2016) Resolving rapid dynamics of soil-plant-atmosphere interactions. *New Phytologist* 210(3), 767–769.

Woffinden, R. (2001) Cover up. *The Guardian.* 25 August. Available at: www.theguardian.com/education/2001/aug/25/research.highereducation. Retrieved 8 June 2018.

World Bank (2013) *Turn Down the Heat: Climate Extremes, Regional Impacts, and the Case for Resilience.* Washington DC, World Bank.

World Counts (2019) Global Meat Consumption Statistics. Available at: www.theworldcounts.com/counters/world_food_consumption_statistics/world_meat_consumption_statistics. Retrieved 7 June 2018.

World Health Organisation (2015) WHO's first ever global estimates of foodborne diseases find children under 5 account for almost one third of deaths. Available at: www.who.int/mediacentre/news/releases/2015/foodborne-disease-estimates/en/. Retrieved 8 June 2018.

World Health Organisation (2018) Specific diseases associated with biological weapons. Available at: www.who.int/csr/delibepidemics/disease/en/. Retrieved 8 June 2018.

Yadav, S.K., Gangwar, D.K., Singh, J., Tikadar, C.K., Khanna, V.V., Saini, S., Dholpuria, S., Palta, P., Manik, R.S., Singh, M.K. and Singla, S.K. (2017) An immunological approach of sperm sexing and different methods for identification of X- and Y-chromosome bearing sperm. *Vet World* 10(5), 498–504, doi: 10.14202/vetworld.2017.498–504. Available at: www.ncbi.nlm.nih.gov/pmc/articles/PMC5465762/. Retrieved 7 June 2018.

Zhang, M. and Goodhue, R. (2010) Agricultural Pesticide Best Management Practices Report: A Final Report for the Central Valley Regional Water Quality Control Board. Award # 06-262-150-0 Task Eight. Available at: www.waterboards.ca.gov/rwqcb5/water_issues/tmdl/central_valley_projects/central_valley_pesticides/ag_practices/final_22mar10_bmp_rpt.pdf. Retrieved 4 July 2017.

5

Farm management

Introduction: the proper place of farm management in agribusiness

Production agriculture has been defined as, or at least includes, the crop and livestock products that provide inputs to the food and fibre sector (Barnard *et al.*, 2016:25). Much has been written elsewhere about the conduct of production agriculture, often still called farm management, including a surprising amount that is to be found in agribusiness analysis. Several initial points are surely worth making. First, best practice in farm management is generally still only found in developed countries. Most of the advances in farm management that are needed in developing countries are simply catch-up, and will be greatly assisted by the type of technology described in Chapter 4, and the investment analysed in Chapter 12. Second, farms are only one component of agribusiness: the significance of the entire value chain in creating investment value is rising. Too much focus on farm management to the detriment of other parts of the value chain is an imbalance, especially in the academic study of agribusiness, that should be remedied. Third, much of effective farm management trespasses on other disciplines, such as accounting, crop science and general management, all of which deserve their own separate study, and which are only summarised in this chapter.

Structure and form of farm operation

How a farm or other agribusiness is regulated, taxed and organised depends significantly on its legal structure, worldwide. There are many legal structures, but Western practice (which is becoming gradually universal) has three dominant types: the sole proprietorship, the partnership (including limited liability partnerships) and the corporation (or company). In the past, sole proprietorships remained 'the major type of legal structure in the agricultural industry' (Ricketts & Ricketts, 2009:124) and so far this generalisation continues to hold. In Kenya, an adviser suggested the following list to decide on which structure would be best:

■ Life of business: do you wish for the business to continue, without interruption, after your death?

- Estate planning: what will happen to the business if you or another owner were to die?

- Sources of capital: how much exposure to debt can you tolerate? Is combining of funds from multiple owners an option?

- Management: how much control of the business do you want?

- Inter/intra family issues: how involved do you want your family to be in the business?

- Termination of business: how easily do you want to be able to terminate the business or transfer ownership?

- Taxes: is tax management an issue for your operation? What are the capital gain tax implications?

- Risk management: how concerned are you about liability?

- Multiple entities: in risk management, income tax management, estate and retirement planning, multiple entities can be effective tools.

- Income sharing: is there a requirement to distribute income between multiple parties? (Kennas, 2018).

It is striking how global this list now seems: the gap in decision-making between developed and developing countries is shrinking at last. A sole proprietorship – or its equivalent in a developing country where even such a formal characterisation may not be appropriate – is easy to manage, but the farmer should maintain a separate bank account for the farming enterprise, and if the farmer wants to bring children into the business, it may be advantageous to consider a partnership, which works better in most jurisdictions as an estate-planning tool. Alternatively, where the option is available, a trust may be used as the legal form of the business. The tax rate for trusts is much higher, but continuity can be achieved through the use of beneficiaries.

Sometimes, too, in the USA, Limited Liability Partnerships (LLPs) and Limited Liability Companies (LLCs) are used, especially in order to protect assets where separate LLCs or LLPs may be created – one for the holding of assets which are then leased to another LLC or LLP that governs the operations of the farm. There are advantages and disadvantages to every legal form: jumping from one legal form to another requires a regulatory and tax impact analysis. There could be taxable events on distributions and liquidations of prior entity structures as when a corporation decides to become an LLC, or a sole proprietorship goes to the trust level (Bradley, 2017). It must be severely qualified, though, by noting that in Australia, for instance, most farms are run as companies for tax reasons: even though taxation is theoretically payable twice, once at the corporate and again at the individual level, the permissible level of expenses to be deducted *against* tax makes the corporate form attractive. Detailed advice is available from governments and advisers in developed countries on the choices, and their consequences. Unfortunately, this kind of information is neither available, nor necessarily accessible, in many other countries where farms are run, with the consequence that many are run in the informal economy.

More widespread in the agricultural industry are cooperatives: for supply, which buy in bulk supplies such as fertilisers, feed, seed and fuel, for resale to their members; and marketing, assisting farmers (mostly) to sell (Horwath, 2014); but rarely actual farms. There are also franchises, which in theory can be of any kind, but are much more usually seen at the retail end of the agribusiness value chain, not farms.

Entrants to the market who do not have the resources for a mortgage deposit (see Chapter 9) have to rent, at least to start with. Tenants pay a fixed rent, but may be faced with the need to come up with rental payments in advance – sometimes years. Sharecropping, by comparison, is widespread in developing countries, e.g. in West Africa, where it was suggested that in the 2000s, 'the normal rent share is either one-half or one-third of the principal crop. There is a variety of arrangements, and in some of them two-thirds of the main crop goes to the landlord, and less or none of the minor crops' (Brookfield & Parsons, 2007:35–36). But there are still occasional examples even in Australia, where it represents almost the only way into the market to own a farm for those without capital. Larger farms, too, can acquire additional land by 'reverse tenancies' whereby the smallholder can earn rental income whilst exiting farming.

Empirical evidence on farm size and efficiency

Agricultural inputs provide farmers with the feed, seed, fertilisers, credit, machinery, fuel, chemicals, etc. that they need to operate. Measurements of farm efficiency vary: one measure is the number of persons supplied by the average farmworker: by the mid-2000s, one US farmer could feed 150 people and the trajectory is still upwards. US farm efficiency is certainly remarkable: with less than 0.3% of the world's farmers, the USA is the third largest agricultural producer. The mantra for increased productivity is simple: output rises, inputs do not, or at least by less than output, so profitability rises as well as production. In the USA, and in many other developed countries, agriculture has certainly delivered: agricultural productivity rose three times faster in the USA than industrial productivity in the last decades of the 20th century (Ricketts & Ricketts, 2009:45). However, there is now evidence that this process has faltered. In Australia, for instance, for grain production, 'productivity improvements have halved in broadacre farming from 1.8% per annum between 1980 and 2000 to 0.9% per annum between 2000 and 2013 (ANZ, 2016:13).

Megafarms are a particular aspect of the new century. They sometimes approach several hundred-thousand hectares of land, the integration of multiple stages of production and processing, and the increasing influence of outside investors with no background in primary agricultural production. In a number of developing countries, such enterprises resulted from foreign direct investment (FDI), often called 'land grabs' and discussed in succeeding chapters. But in industrialised and emerging market economies around the world, such megafarms have reached a substantial share of production as well (Byerlee & Deininger, 2013). Critics and policymakers worry about the governance of megafarms, but they appear to be here to stay (Hermans et al., 2017).

The rise in value of farms over the same period is unmistakable. However, what has largely driven this increase in value has not directly been increased production, but, rather, increases in land values which have only an indirect connection with farm efficiency. *This is a point of extreme importance to agribusiness investment.*

This is not intended to minimise the significance of the huge efforts made by farmers into farm efficiency noted below, just to recognise that farm management must always take land values into account. Expenditures on different agricultural inputs from the USA are available from the USDA's National Agricultural Statistics Service.

But these data do not explain *how* efficient any of these inputs actually are. Emphasis in efficiency analysis studies in agricultural production has historically focused on technical inefficiency as a single concept, avoiding this problem altogether, until methodological advances enabled it to be decomposed into pure technical inefficiency and scale inefficiency. But even this advance was insufficient to identify what one study at least concluded was the major source of inefficiency in agricultural production, namely 'mix inefficiency' (Hadley *et al.*, 2013). We now know that several technologies and management techniques can increase agricultural input efficiency. A good example of current thinking is the movement towards *precision farming*, discussed in Chapter 4, where nutrient and pesticide inputs are applied in varying quantities at specific times and in specific places within fields, based on soil type and quality, matching crop requirements, which has increased fertiliser input efficiency and farmer profits without decreasing crop yields across many different crops and areas. Another example *is conservation tillage* and *cover cropping*, particularly with nitrogen-fixing crops because they simultaneously reduce required nitrogen inputs, which have been held also to increase fertiliser input efficiency by reducing nutrient loss from agricultural systems. Likewise, feed input efficiency in livestock systems can also be increased – e.g. pork from pigs that were fed diets supplemented with amino acids required less feed and emitted

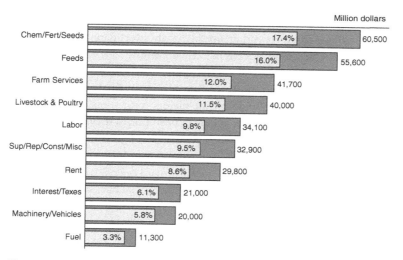

Figure 5.1 Major input expenditures by total, and percent of total – the USA: 2016
Source: USDA (2017a)

5% fewer GHGs with 28% lower eutrophication (creating too many nutrients in water) potential than pork from pigs fed with unsupplemented diets. Similar benefits have also been found in poultry, beef and dairy systems. In addition, it is thought that using agricultural waste and by-products as animal feeds could reduce the environmental impacts of livestock production by 20% without reducing food quality or farmer profits (Clark & Tilman, 2017). But the evidence continues to point to the need for much more basic utilisation of assets. A study in Tanzania demonstrated that the variables that affect efficiency in tobacco growth were 'modern' inputs provided to tobacco farmers, such as fertiliser, high variety seeds, credit availability, extension advice and marketing outlets. Based on an evaluation of the tobacco and other crops, the study suggested that the efficiency of tobacco, maize, groundnuts and rice were 75.3%, 68.5%, 64.5% and 46.5% respectively. So, despite the infusion of massive agricultural input allotted to it, tobacco is still just 75.3% efficient. Put another way, tobacco farmers should have produced the same amount by utilising only 75.3% of realised inputs (Kidane *et al.*, 2013). The figures for the other crops and, even worse, the under-half figure for rice are especially noteworthy. It is important to recognise that regulation is also now biting into yields worldwide. In 2015 in the UK, for example, the ban on neonicotinoid insecticides made its mark, and some oilseed crops were completely destroyed by flea beetle, or at least had significantly reduced yields (Bidwells, 2016).

Production functions and profitability

Farm management economics (i.e. economic analysis applied to the choices confronting farmers) provides the general disciplinary basis for farm-level systems analysis (ignoring land valuation and concentrating on cash flow). The standard theoretical approach, as noted in Chapter 2, is that of demand and supply, even though the textbook version is seldom encountered (Barnard *et al.*, 2016:65) and is indeed rarely even analysed in practice. This is because whilst farmers are usually aware of current or imminent structural changes in their industry, such as tax changes or technical developments, in agribusiness particularly prices change rapidly as a result of factors (weather, notably) that distort (largely theoretical) supply and demand curves, and which in practice render their construction entirely otiose. In addition, most theoretical demand curves for agribusinesses are derived not from consumer preferences, but from intermediate steps. Larger agribusinesses further up the value chain, especially those who are in market conditions of oligopoly or monopolistic competition, must consider pricing very carefully. Farms generally need not, as they are price takers in all but the most extreme examples; perhaps Obasanjo Farms in Nigeria may have qualified, but probably not even then. Although it has been claimed that 'Agribusiness managers must have a clear understanding of economics to be successful' (Barnard *et al.*, 2016:73), I am not myself at all sure that this is true. A clear understanding of business, yes, but economics? *I have never known a single production agribusiness actually construct a demand curve.*

Obviously other farm and family-related disciplines will be involved in building a decision-making system and organising for profitability: construction, building and vehicle maintenance, agronomy, animal husbandry, soil and water conservation/management, forecasting, marketing and sales, etc. However, except in the case of special-purpose technical systems (e.g. when the farm-household unit is analysed in terms of nutritional or energy flows among its different components), textbooks often argue that all these other disciplines should play subordinate contributing roles, with farm management economics as the lead discipline. That in fact this often does not is, I argue, because of a confusion between economics and business. So, although the disciplinary basis of farm management remains economics – but economics of a special wide-ranging kind, the core of which is production economics supported by other branches of economics of which marketing, resource economics, agricultural credit and data analysis (including operations research, econometrics and risk analysis) are probably the most important – farmers do not really need to be economists to run their business well. On the other hand, they do need – and often do not, by no means exclusively only in developing countries – to understand how to run a business. Information on herd size, yields, prices and overall performance is now widely available in developed countries, including from some apparently unlikely sources, such as chartered surveyors specialising in agricultural properties, such as Savills in the UK (Bailey, 2017). This is the kind of information farmers need to benchmark their performance and determine the value of their farms. But no amount of information can force a good decision.

Decision-making in farm analysis

Because farms *are* businesses, most of what is said and written about the success and failure of businesses in general applies to them. Failure to understand, to plan, to forecast accurately, to have people skills, to appreciate and manage risks: all these account for the majority of farm failures as they do with all agribusinesses, and firms generally. All agribusiness managers must plan, organise, direct control and execute. Basic concepts like feedback are highly relevant. Financial, HR, chemical, material, technical, IP and above all land and mechanical resources must be combined to produce output efficiently. Farmers, though, do have a set of particular problems, and it would also seem, particular prejudices. Of these the worst does appear to be an inability to recognise a *good* year, and therefore to plan to put aside financial resources during good times in order to be prepared for *bad* years. Rising farm debt, including in developed countries, has been a major issue connected with failure, whilst inadequate record-keeping, the failure to appreciate the need for capital expenditure, forgetting tax payments that are due, and treating the business like a personal piggy-bank are all really significant problems for farmers, whether in Australia, India or anywhere else in the world.

Crucial, therefore, to the success of any farm is a business plan, although as the farm is often family-owned (FAO, 1997), there is – as with many family-owned businesses – no set cycle for planning and, often, no specific financial targets. Farms are often run as inadvertent lifestyle businesses as a result. Australian government at state level in particular has provided numerous online resources to try to prevent this (e.g. Business Queensland, 2018), but if there is no corporate control it is hard to combat for any family business, farms are just more susceptible than most. Credit, as will be discussed in more detail in Chapter 9, is the main constraint on farm development in developing countries. There are plenty of online examples of business plans for farms, notably from University Agricultural Extension programmes and banks, and not only in developed countries, but it is adopting them consistently that is lacking. Plans should not, however, only guide decision-making. They also need to provide feedback on success and failure along the way. Planning for a farm, certainly, should be done on a 'day-to-day, year-to-year and long-term basis' (Ricketts & Ricketts, 2009:113), an injunction that is scarcely likely to alter. Perhaps one of the best economic definitions of aristocracy is an indifference to wealth between generations, inflation excluded.

Cost structures

Every organisation, including farms, must consider its costs when making pricing decisions. Sometimes, in regulated markets, selling prices are set as a fixed mark-up on costs, but these markets are a slowly dying breed, albeit that the rise of protectionism in the 2010s gave them a filip. But for most agribusinesses, costs are treated as only one determinant, albeit an important one, in establishing selling prices. Fixed costs are extremely difficult to shift, and often cannot be changed inside one growing season. Maximising sales volumes and maximising profits are therefore not identical in practice, as maximising sales revenues does not always lead to the highest profit, especially where the expansion of production on the farm requires taking on a further large range of fixed costs, such as employing a new manager, acquiring – as opposed to leasing, although as noted below even leasing will be seen as capex (capital expenditure) in International Financial Reporting Standard (IFRS) accounts – a new tractor or even buying or leasing a plot of land. Variable costs are often a function of how much the farm has produced, e.g. the cost of leasing machinery for harvesting, and not an input into decision-making in an abstract way. Either way, the calculation of production and marketing costs is essential, but not always easy to achieve, since farm costs are slippery and not easy to allocate, especially on farms that are both dairy and crop, or which simply grow a range of crops. Only sometimes is it possible to identify not only economies of scale but also diseconomies, i.e the higher rates of workers' pay for overtime and sometimes premium prices paid for hard-to-find inputs, that there is only so much fertiliser or labour a farm can absorb, and ultimately, only so many hectares a single farmer can manage.

The utilisation of existing resources

Agricultural textbooks do not always follow their own logic. Yes, if choosing between dairy and horticulture, the temptation for a farmer will always be to use existing greenhouses, as opposed to the need for barn construction, silos, tractors, equipment and the cows themselves. Yes, if borrowed, the interest cost for all these expenses would have to be deducted from revenue to make a comparison. But no, that should not be the end of the story, although it often is, because the idea of using existing resources before acquiring others presupposes that these resources cannot be either sold or leased out instead of being used, which may well be a false assumption. So, the notion that 'it is wise to make production decisions based on resources that already exist' (Ricketts & Ricketts, 2009:36) is something of a curse in production agriculture, unless it is backed up by analysis of transaction costs and proper forecasting, as it can obviously lead to inefficient utilisation of resources and is closely linked to production agriculture still being based on culture and tradition.

Equally, however, constant switching from arable to livestock and back again based on short-term price trends can result in unnecessary capex and poor risk management, which is a better basis for a campaign for continuity. Even worse is the utilisation of existing resources without paying proper attention to the investment implications of depreciation: it may seem smart to avoid expenditure on fencing, for example, and let it deteriorate gradually, and certainly expenditure tomorrow is more cost-effective than expenditure today, but eventually there will be a need to repair or replace the whole fencing system, and the illusion of profitability may evaporate at that point, especially with livestock farming in a country like Australia, which requires vast amounts of fencing. Similarly, farmers are often not good managers of decision-making options. It might appear to make sense to let the fences run down, as the farm has now switched entirely to arable, but it precludes the ability, without substantial capex, of moving back into livestock quickly. Sometimes it is better to pay for flexibility in agricultural production decision-making.

The mention of fixed costs such as machinery obliges one to note that agricultural production does often require significant investment in assets, such as tractors, irrigation systems and especially land. Though expensive, these types of assets are typically expected to produce economic returns for many years into the future. Before acquiring capital assets, farm managers should use budgeting and forecasting techniques to assist with the decision-making process. Athough these cannot provide an entirely reliable view of the future, they give producers the capacity to analyse different management strategies and scenarios, aiming at the best management decisions possible given 'Neutral, Balanced, Central and Reasonable' (NBCR) expectations of the future. Capital budgeting is therefore a projection method that can prove especially useful when considering large capital investment decisions, e.g. the purchase of additional farmland.

A note on net present value analysis

The essence of capital budgeting is, or rather ought to be, net present value (NPV) analysis, which forms the core of financial analysis worldwide. NPV operates on the principle of the time value of money, i.e. that the owner of an agribusiness values a dollar, shilling or rupee more today than tomorrow. How much more, for each period, depends on the wealth, expectations and other resources of the farmer. Using NPV analysis, every year (or quarter), the value of cash received is devalued by the *discount rate*, which reflects several factors. First, inflation erodes purchasing power. The cost of goods and services in the future will be more expensive than their costs today. Second, opportunity costs must be considered as well: farmers have many other uses for their capital, so it makes sense to recognise that investment of capital into one project means that an alternative project cannot be undertaken – even if that alternative project is just keeping capital in a range of shares approximately equivalent to the risk of the agribusiness, gaining diversification benefit in the process. Capital is moreover not the only resource that has an opportunity cost. The argument is presented in a popular agribusiness text (Barnard *et al.*, 2016:62) that *foregone earnings* are also an opportunity cost. In this view, the calculation of economic profit for a small agribusiness should take into account as a cost the marginal difference between salary extracted from the business and a salary that could be earned elsewhere. In principle, taking opportunity costs into account is right, although I do not know any farmers (or many businesspeople generally) who do, except when they take a dramatic decision to sell up or – just about – in the choice between different crops. The problem is that for many farmers, it is simply impossible for them to calculate what those opportunity costs really are: wedded to the land, the disruption that would be caused if they decided to work elsewhere must be factored in. Plus, off-farm income already happens in many cases – diversification would not be well served if everyone decided to do it and abandon the farm. What is correct, however, is to take into account the opportunity cost of facilities, such as barns that could be rented out or even sold for real estate use. Farmers are becoming progressively more aware of the opportunities that real estate provides, which has led in some cases to the construction and letting of dwellings on farmland, and in other cases to the careful evaluation and frequent adoption of solar and wind farm opportunities, all of which are excellent sources of diversification, but which may pose problems for agribusiness production itself. In sum, *the economic profit concept is hard to apply to farms*. Finally, the time value of money also factors into account risk. Crops may fail, markets are volatile. In conclusion, a discount rate can be thought of as a farmer's cost of capital, which is presumed to be the same as the farmer's opportunity cost of choosing to invest in one project in lieu of another. Discount rate assumptions will therefore vary from country to country, from region to region and even individual to individual. The smaller the assumed discount rate, the greater the potential net present value of the investment and vice versa, which is why it is such a shame that, all things considered, risks are higher in developing countries and therefore so are discount rates, especially when expensive bank loans are also figured into the farmer's overall cost of capital. The cost of capital is an essential ingredient to farm decision-making and analysis, but it is no easy friend of the farmer in a developing country, and many, even if they understand the concept, prefer to turn a blind eye to its – often brutal – consequences. More formal approaches to the discount rate will be presented in Chapter 7.

Capital budgeting – also referred to as investment analysis – using DCF is, notwithstanding these limitations, in principle extremely useful for evaluating the potential profitability of a new business investment, such as the acquisition of a new tractor or the purchase of farmland. The procedure is relatively simple, especially now that almost every farmer in the developed world at least has access to a laptop running Excel or its equivalent. NPV is the present value – the value today – to the farmer of projected cash inflows less the present value of the investment's projected cash outflows. NPV works on the premise that we will likely make an initial investment at the onset of a 'project'. In other words, we will have a capital outlay of some amount at the time it is being considered whether to spend the initial cash outlay. To determine the potential profitability of the 'project', especially if it is expected to run over multiple years, estimates of expected cash inflows and outflows occurring as a result of the initial investment are discounted back to the present time using the farmer's assumed discount rate.

Why environmentalists and policymakers distrust NPV

There have been studies of the application of discounting to climate change. Whatever discount rate is chosen, apart from zero, discounting eventually reduces the value of the environment to virtually nothing. After 200 years, a 0.1% deterioration in the value of Global GDP for ever reduces to just $1 at a discount rate of only 4.1%. DCF is no friend of the environment, and this problem explains a lot about farming, the environment and the dilemmas faced by governments and international agencies like the World Bank, striving for long-term social benefits yet confronted with business need for immediate return and sometimes very high costs of capital, especially in developing countries.

Both how much and when cash flows will occur must be projected, usually either quarterly or annually. The initial capital expenditure must be compared with net inflows over time. These are net, because of ongoing capex and maintenance costs associated with the 'project', which are usually projected annually or seasonally, and which include, e.g. for wheat production, seed, fertiliser and chemicals as well as wages. Once the cash flows have been projected, the NPV is straightforward enough to calculate. A positive NPV is an indication to go ahead with the 'project' and vice versa, and the larger the NPV, the better. A parallel, relevant decision-making process is the calculation of the internal rate of return (IRR), which is defined as *that discount rate which with a given set of forecast cash flows results in a zero NPV.* A healthy capex project generates an IRR perhaps around 3% or more higher than the discount rate. Farms should be no different from other agribusinesses in setting *hurdle rates* around this level (Ben-Horin & Kroll, 2017; Shockley *et al.*, 2017).

Additional considerations

Excel, as well as specialised farm management software, has built-in functions for investment analysis, including the calculation of NPV and IRR analysis. NPV analysis is especially useful when considering investment in depreciable assets, which have a limited useful life. Assumptions regarding the expected useful economic life of the asset can be incorporated into the analysis. This often involves an additional cash inflow inclusion for the expected salvage value, which the asset could be sold for once fully depreciated. In many NPV analyses, cash transactions, including the initial investment, are often assumed. However, the reality is that many capital acquisitions will be financed. If this is the case, it is important to note initial cash-down payments, and then also include annual principal and interest payment estimates in the cash outflows, as these payments will affect the overall profitability of the investment. The effect of taxes should not be ignored, as these are also cash outflows, which will affect profitability. Finally, because businesses always have competing uses for capital, multiple potential projects may be considered at the same time. Performing multiple NPV analyses for each project, especially those with very different projected cash flows and time horizons, is often useful for profitability comparison.

Agribusiness textbooks share with corporate finance investment banks and real estate developers a warm endorsement of NPV analysis. Yes, it is a powerful planning tool which allows producers to accurately estimate the potential profitability from an investment. Although there is no way to perfectly simulate projected returns, investment analysis provides a concise way to quickly examine the benefits versus costs of a multitude of capital investment options. Using NPV and IRR analysis represents a quantum leap in accuracy, professionalism and valuation for agribusiness. But no, it cannot accurately reflect the problems of managing a farm on an ongoing basis, because farmers are usually not engaged in 'projects' or 'investments', they are making day-to-day decisions about inputs, fertilisers and harvesting, amongst other things. It does make sense to have a business plan, and that requires a start point, at which time the value of the farm should be assessed. But in practice, even if a farm generates a negative NPV based on the market value of the land, farmers will not simply sell the farm. Cash flow, rather than NPV, often rules the roost, for right or wrong. And practical choices about crops and livestock will determine profitability.

Crop and livestock management plans

A crop management plan is a form in which the farmer each year records a plan concerning the use of his/her arable land and, after harvest, notes how the plan has been followed. The plan includes information on soil quality, use of crops on each plot, as well as the amounts of seed, fertiliser and plan protection chemicals used. The plan should be drafted and followed up, sometimes with the help of consultants who also perform the necessary tests to establish, for example, the quality of soil as well as the need for fertilisers and plant protection chemicals (CTIC, 2018). Part of a good crop management plan is therefore a crop nutrient management plan, presented here as an example of how crops must be managed successively for a farm to be profitable. The plan needs to contain the following elements:

- *Field map.* The map, ideally generated from a source such as Google, should include general reference points (topography, buildings, etc.), the number of hectares and soil types. It is is the base for the rest of the plan.

- *Soil test.* How much of each nutrient (N-P-K and other critical elements such as pH and organic matter) is in the soil profile? The soil test is a key component needed for developing any accurate nutrient rate recommendation.

- *Crop sequence.* Did the crop that grew in the field last year (and in many cases two or more years ago) fix nitrogen for use in the following years? Or did it remove it? Has long-term no-till increased organic matter? Did any test indicate a nutrient deficiency?

- *Estimated yield.* Factors that affect yield are numerous and complex. Rainfall, both in absolute quantity and timing, the soil types, drainage, fertiliser, insecticide and pesticide use, crop rotation and many other factors determine the yield of any individual field. Accurate yield estimates can significantly improve nutrient use efficiency.

■ *Sources and forms.* The sources and forms of available nutrients can vary from farm-to-farm and even field-to-field. For instance, manure fertility analysis, storage practices and other factors should need to be included in the plan.

■ *Sensitive areas.* These may be environmentally protected, legally questionable, capex-intensive, hard-to-farm or loaded with externalities for the rest of the farm.

■ *Recommended rates.* Ideally, all of the above points lead to logical conclusions as to the optimum nutrient deployment throughout the growing cycle, structured for the crop and the field.

■ *Recommended timing.* Depending on resources, weather forecasting and crop analysis, a sequence for field management will be generated.

■ *Recommended methods.* There are surface and injection methods, the of which may differ between fields, even with the same crop.

■ *Feedback.* Every crop management plan is a vital resource for its successors.

Clearly the main obstacle to developing effective farm management of this kind in most developing countries is a combination of lack of education (leading, for example, to poor record-keeping) and inefficiencies of scale. This also applies to a further range of ways to improve yields. For example, freezing often cripples fruit and vegetable productivity, so if plants can be prevented from freezing, e.g by bacteria, production can be increased.

This is not to ignore that there are traditional soil and water conservation practices to conserve the environment whilst maintaining or even increasing yields. These include, in alphabetical order rather than that of importance:

■ Brush management pastures and ranges;

■ Contour farming;

■ Fallow fields;

■ Farm ponds (including summer/winter ponds);

■ Field windbreaks planting and management;

■ Grassed waterways;

■ Irrigation systems;

■ Minimum tillage;

- No-till practices;

- Pasture and hay land seedings;

- Range reseeding;

- Rotation cropping and grazing;

- Strip cropping;

- Subsurface drainage;

- Surface drainage;

- Tree and hedge planting and management; and

- Use of natural pests and insects.

An example is the traditional Zai system used in Burkina Faso and neighbouring nations, where crops are planted in manure-filled pits in which termites make porous tunnels that store water. Another example is the companion crop approach, where crops are fertilised and protected from insects and parasitic weeds by legumes and forage grasses cultivated between and around the main crop (Baulcombe, 2013:2). A third example, widely used worldwide, is the orchard, where trees are often propagated by grafting, budding or cuttings, as opposed to being grown from seeds, as these enable faster, more consistent growth.

The same applies to livestock, which involve an animal health plan as much as a livestock plan, or ought to. Plenty of thought needs to be put into what to do in case of drought or flood, as well as operational considerations such as the need for (and condition of) buildings associated with livestock, the mass of veterinary information (e.g. vaccinations) and planning that running an effective livestock farm involves (at least in developed countries), which in turn may need consultations with a vet, as well as soil and water testing, disease and biosecurity planning (e.g. conformity with regulations, disaster planning), managing the process of bringing new animals to the farm or back from shows or stud services (e.g. testing, quarantine), rodent, parasite and other pest control, how to manage visitors to the farm (e.g. farriers, vets, haulers, delivery trucks, neighbours, officials, etc.), decisions regarding pasture, range and arable land, fencing, everything to do with feeding (e.g. supplements) and water (e.g. dams, troughs) and drainage, as well as soils, manure, grazing rotation, fencing, stock densities and even how to deal with wildlife (foxes, for example, are a continual threat to sheep in Australia and elsewhere). All this requires, in the well-run farm, extensive documentation, all of which is best managed through specialised software, although many farms in developing countries get by with a laptop or even written records of everything from individual animal health, culling and fertility records to pasture health (forage height and density), rainfall, temperature, soil coverage and exposure. Effective use of data is a virtually essential component of successful farm management. Large commercial farms build these processes almost instinctively as part of hierarchical management structures. Small family farms do not.

What is perhaps remarkable, from the perspective of other industries, is how farming, at least in developed countries, is *assumed* to make a profit, and the remarkable degree of accuracy that public institutions are able to deploy in assessing that level of profit. This applies overwhelmingly in the USA. The annual Farm Management Planning Guide issued by North Dakota State University extension service held that:

> The profitability budget accounts for full economic opportunity costs for land and machinery investment, regardless of farm operator equity position. The bottom line is the return to labour and management. This is the expected 'payment' to the producer for the labour and managerial efforts required by the crop enterprise. Each agribusiness must make the decision whether it is sufficient. The budget can be changed to conform to the more common definition of accounting profit (return to unpaid labour and management, and owner equity) by replacing the machinery investment and land charge cost items with your per acre interest and rental expense of machinery and land, and real estate tax if land is owned. The budget can be used for long-run decisions if the revenues and costs are realistic for several years. (Crop prices, direct costs, and the land charge are best estimates for only the 2018 crop year, but crop yields are historic averages and machinery ownership costs are an average for the total length of ownership). If the budget shows a high return to labour and management, and is representative for several years, increased acreage and corresponding investment should be considered. However, if long-run returns to labour and management are unsatisfactory the best decision may be to exit the crop enterprise and employ the machinery and land investment, and labour and management, in a different enterprise or investment [how exactly this could possibly be done, the NDSU document does not specify]. For short-run planning decisions, the NDSU says, it is fine [and I agree] to omit the indirect costs if the land and machinery required to produce the different enterprises are in place. Simply compare the crop enterprises by calculating return over direct costs. Labour requirements and risk should also be considered. Insurance is not available for some crops, even in the USA (Swenson, 2017).

Few other businesses can enjoy this luxury in their financial and management planning.

HR management on the farm

This is a tale of different economies. In developed countries, HR specialists in developed economies look to a future in which HR will become a bigger issue in farming, as farms get bigger and employment becomes more of an issue. In this self-interested but plausible view, even if one overlooks automation, farmers still do not look at human resources as something they can manage and save costs on, with the oft-expressed view from production or farming based businesses in relation to recruitment or salary benchmarking that, if you are a farmer or in farm production, recruiting and retaining staff is somehow different to a downstream agribusiness or a corporate.

HR professionals are right in that, unless the farm is being run by an enormous extended family (which brings its own problems), a family farm or a partnership is competing for talent with corporates, as well as family farms. It is also competing for talent from other sectors within agribusiness such as retail distribution (e.g. in Australia, firms such as Wesfarmers, Landmark, Elders, etc.) and supply companies (fertiliser and seed companies, etc.). And, of course, in countries such as Australia and South Africa, farming is competing with other sectors such as mining, albeit that they are more cyclical. There is no separate talent market for family farms; employee satisfaction is the main driver for people of all ages and industries in staying in their roles. The other misconception is that human resource management (HRM) is a separate work practice or role within a business. Sometimes it can be, but most small businesses and even large businesses generally weave HRM into their standard business practices rather than maintain separate individuals responsible for HR functions such as strategy (future workforce requirements), compensation (salaries and benefits), safety, liability, training and development and compliance. For most farms, good HR is an instinctive way of doing business, rather than a function of the business (Real Agriculture, 2017). Put in HR-speak, people should be looked at the same way, as a balance sheet item rather than a cash flow item. But what does that mean in practice, other than a need for 'maintenance', which may include pay rises, holidays, medical insurance, training or other retention incentives? What makes people stay working for the same farmer, year after year? Or choose one vineyard to work in as a student rather than another? No one is quite sure.

At the other end of the scale, basic agricultural labour demand is highly seasonal. In some cases, labour is still 'swapped' between farms with different planting or harvesting times. In most cases, however, unskilled farm workers have been employed on a casual basis either from other local farms, or from seasonal workers. Frequently 'farm labour contractors' arrange, for example, accommodation, transport and other services from their often immigrant workforce, a system officially but often critically described in Europe as the 'gangmaster' system, in countries throughout the EU (Palumbo & Sciurba, 2018) and in the UK (UK Government, 2018). The gang system favours larger growers who can provide more secure business. However described, the numbers of casual workers in agriculture are immense: in West Bengal, for example, there was in the 2000s a seasonal workforce of over half a million in one of several districts alone during the monsoon rice harvest (Brookfield & Parsons, 2007:52). It is worth comparing this with the hiring process in the USA and other developed countries, where HR recruitment techniques are increasingly using technology, including robots. Recruitment even in developing countries, however, is following very similar pathways, especially given the proliferation of inexpensive mobile devices.

Recruitment is just one aspect of HR in farm management. The other vitally important question is how the people of the business itself are managed. Family farms not only have to ensure that individual family members know what they can do, allocate them manageable tasks and ensure they are adequately remunerated, but they also have to deal with the thorny question of inheritance and succession. What if there are multiple children in the next generation, and they all want to farm? And what if one does not – how are they to be fairly, or at least effectively, compensated?

Farm insurance

Insurance is often one of the most overlooked aspects of running a farm business. Knowing what to insure, what types of insurance are available, what policies cost, and what level of coverage is needed to reduce risks on a farm can be a daunting task. However, insurance is one of the best ways to manage and reduce risk: it can help the farm weather disruptions from natural disasters, accidents and market devaluation. In some cases, insurance may be required by a lender. Farmers ought to analyse what could happen, what the consequences are and what should be insured, e.g. through a SWOT analysis (Strengths, Weaknesses, Opportunities, Threats, in case this term is unfamiliar). Although insurance coverage can be found for nearly any farm activity, as costs vary, and not every eventuality should necessarily be insured against, a detailed plan is needed to determine optimum risk appetite and hence what insurance will be bought. Amongst available insurances are:

- Premise liability insurance, which covers the farm in the event of accident or physical injury to anyone visiting the farm.

- Product liability insurance, which provides coverage against injury or illness resulting from ingesting your farm products.

- Limited liability coverage is for products that your customers are ingesting.

The recommended amount of coverage for property and liability is based on the farm's net worth and at least five years of earnings. Commercial general liability policies combine liability insurance with property insurance. This might meet the needs of farms that process foods, sell flowers, non-edibles, or have the public on the farm. Commercial insurance for fire, crop damage or otherwise should not be confused with government or private crop insurance, which provides protection for a particular crop or to cover any losses due to crop failure or, in some cases, market failure.

Livestock on the farm

Sheep are hardy, well covered animals, usually kept in the open all year round. They are at present not so intensively farmed as either pigs, poultry or cattle. The most important and the most profitable produce of British sheep is their lambs; wool is secondary. The reverse applies in Australia, where the Chinese wool trade is central to agricultural profitability (Rural Bank, 2018).

Australian farmers, with their focus on sheep (Rural Bank, 2018a) and an A$3.7 billion industry to look after, would no doubt beg to differ, but generally, *cattle* are the most productive farm livestock. They produce not only milk but also meat of different types at various stages in their lives. Although there are distinct beef and dairy types, there is no clear line between them. There are hundreds of cattle breeds, each with their own particular qualities (Cumming, 2007). Dairy cows can often only produce very high milk yields for an average of three years, after which they are slaughtered and the meat is normally used for beef. In intensive dairy farms, cows are confined to indoor housing, but this reflects a drive to increase the amount of milk produced by each cow. The Holstein-Friesian, the most common type of dairy cow in the UK, Europe and the USA, has been bred to produce very high yields of milk. Milk production per cow has more than doubled in the past 40 years. An average of 22 litres per day is typical in the UK, with some cows producing up to 60 litres in a day during peak lactation. The average yield in the USA is even higher, at over 30 litres per day. Given a natural healthy life, cows can live for 20 years or more, but high-yielding dairy cows will typically be slaughtered after three or four lactations because their milk production drops and/or they are chronically lame or infertile.

Pigs are kept for meat production. For both pork and bacon, the same type of long, lean pig is needed. For manufacturing, a broader and heavier type may be suitable. The modern quality type of pig, formerly called the bacon type, is suited to all purposes, is long, lean and fast-growing. The main breeds are Large White, Landrace and Welsh.

Pigs, historically, were born in the spring, left to forage in the wild, then rounded up and slaughtered in the autumn. Currently, with a short gestational period of about 110–120 days, and with twice yearly litters of six to 13, pigs are very productive. In the UK, for instance, the industry has a large variety of production systems, ranging from indoor units, outdoor units, straw-based accommodation and slatted accommodation. This mixture makes the industry very different from its global counterparts. There are some 30,000 premises with pigs on (including pets) and 10,000 pig farms. However, 92% of production comes from about 1,600 assured farms including ten corporate companies which account for 35% of breeding sows. The UK is also unusual in that 40% of its herd is outdoors. Generally, feed costs make up some two-thirds of pork production costs: in the past, therefore, production was generally close to feedstock, but scale and specialisation have moved hog farming to other less densely populated and less regulated states in the USA. With fewer purchasers, farmers' margins are increasingly under pressure. Specialisation is increasing because efficiencies (i.e. more weight per kg of seed) occur with age division for feeding, so smaller farms that rear hogs across the whole of their life cycle, from farrow to finish, are falling progressively further behind.

The *poultry* industry in the West is now also segmented – egg vs. meat or broiler production. Supply chain specialisation has also entered the industry with, at the level of production agriculture, breeding companies, hatcheries (incubators for fertile eggs) and broiler, pullet or grow-outhouses, where chickens are fed to egg-laying or slaughter weights. Breeder hens lay eggs for hatching, typically 250–300 eggs annually, which are sent to the hatchery. After hatching, chicks go to layer houses, containing up to 1 million chicks, for their lives, usually two seasons. There they are placed in cages over conveyor belts that take the eggs to collection In the USA, 'the typical breeds in the egg supply chain are White Leghorns, which produce white eggs, and the Rhode Island Red, New Hampshire and Plymouth Rock breeds, which produce brown eggs' (Pullman & Wu, 2012:47). For broilers, the fertile eggs from breeder hens also go to a hatchery, but thereafter when the chicks are a day old, they go to broiler farms. They are then raised until ready to be sent for slaughter. There are huge biosecurity issues because of, for example, avian flu.

Poultry are kept for five main reasons. Egg and meat production are the main ones, with chickens being kept either specially for one of those purposes or for dual egg and meat production. Poultry is also kept for maternal instincts (i.e. broodies), and sometimes for showing and pedigree breeding. There are two main turkey breeds, the American Bronzewing and the White Holland, bred entirely for meat for human consumption.

Other animals kept are geese, ducks and goats, which are kept for meat, milk, angora and cashmere fibre production. Common breeds of dairy goat are Anglo-Nubian, British Alpine, Saanen and Toggenburg. Common indigenous goats, e.g. Boer, are usually dual or even multipurpose. Still more include horses, donkeys, deer, rabbits and even some exotic species kept for commercial reasons, including ostriches, kangaroos, reindeer, rheas and wild boar. Some animals have been farmed for their fur, such as mink, but this is mostly illegal now.

Feeding, fencing, transport and working

Primary food products must be protected against contamination, having regard to any processing that they will subsequently undergo. Producers must therefore comply with appropriate community and national legislative provisions relating to the control of hazards in primary production and associated operations, including measures to control contamination arising from the air, soil, water, feed, fertilisers, pesticides, herbicides, biocides, veterinary products and waste, measures relating to plant health, animal health and welfare, and the environment, which all have implications for feed safety or human health, including programmes for the monitoring and control of zoonoses and zoonotic agents. An example of a full compliance suite is given by the Vale of Glamorgan council in the UK (Vale of Glamorgan, 2018).

Fencing for livestock is another significant cost, at almost $10 per metre in advanced economies (Farming Forum, 2017), although in some countries, such as the UK, the cost can be reclaimed if it meets certain standards (Scottish Government, 2017). If not, the cost of fencing, and keeping it intact, may itself be a disincentive to keep livestock by comparison to arable farming, as is the case for example in Western Australia.

On top of this, most farms require internal transport, usually in the form either of animals or vehicles, the ubiquitous farmer's pick-up being the most commonly observed. Whilst the vehicle itself, fuel, ongoing registration costs and repairs and maintenance, are of course deductible expenses, time spent on these issues is diverted from direct attention to crops, which in turn has seen the growth of vehicle cooperatives, and leasing services for vehicles, even in developing countries (Okinda, 2017).

All of these represent employment areas that intersect with farm operations themselves. In most cases farmers do not employ these experts themselves but, rather, buy their services as appropriate. Most recently, questions of work on farms and farm management can best be studied using a human capital approach.

Veterinary science

The FAO, understandably, is very keen on animal health, not least because, it argues, changes in livestock production increase the potential for new pathogens to emerge, grow and spread from animals to humans on a global scale. Healthy animals are closely related to healthy people and a healthy environment. The FAO wants an integrated approach with greater emphasis on agro-ecological resilience, the protection of biodiversity, the efficient use of natural resources and the safety of food supply chains, particularly in areas

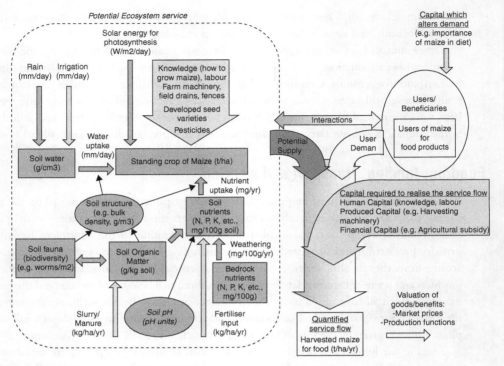

Figure 5.2 Provisioning service e.g. maize production
Source: Jones *et al.* (2016:156)

worst afflicted by poverty and animal disease. They point to the kind of success that can be achieved with this approach, such as the global elimination of rinderpest in 2011 (FAO, 2018a).

From our standpoint, it must be noted that veterinary science has an important economic impact. For example, in the USA, 'A revolutionary fowl cholera vaccine invented by Clemson researchers has saved the international turkey industry more than $300 million' (Clemson University, 2018). A similar story from the UK is a £10 million deal to boost the impact of animal science innovations from Edinburgh University:

> The investment in the new company Roslin Technologies...will allow researchers to explore the commercial potential of technologies that enable low-cost manufacturing of new medicines using chicken eggs. Methods of preserving frozen stocks of reproductive material from bird species are set to benefit from the funding. Such technologies aim to safeguard the future of rare bird species, which may carry useful genetic information that makes them resistant to existing – and future – diseases. The company will also bring to market new veterinary vaccines and tools for diagnosing diseases that affect farmed animals (Edinburgh University, 2017).

These positive impacts are on top of the preventative effect of veterinary research, identified by a research report for the UK in 2013. Recurring foodborne diseases such as campylobacteriosis and salmonelliosis cost the UK respectively £538 million and £14 million per annum. In one year alone, at the height of the BSE crisis, more than £3.5 billion was spent in the UK to control and deal with the disease, whilst the foot-and-mouth epidemic in 2001 cost the UK £8 billion in just 7.5 months. Whereas financial losses associated with zoonotic outbreaks are measured in billions of pounds, research investment is limited to the low millions. Even so, UK veterinary teams have been performing remarkably well – it is estimated that the Bluetongue vaccination programme in 2008 saved £460 million and 10,000 jobs in the UK, not to mention countless animal lives. This is in contrast to the unsatisfactory position in China, where, in 2013, hundreds of pigs that had died from unknown causes were dumped into a tributary of the Shanghai river, the source of much of Shanghai's drinking water (Kelly *et al.*, 2014). This incident was symptomatic of larger problems with animal health care in China and prompted Jia Youling, head of the Chinese Veterinary Medical Association and former head of the Ministry of Agriculture's Bureau of Veterinary Medicine, to observe that the Chinese veterinary medical system is nowhere near adequate. Jia further remarked that, in China, veterinary medicine is barely recognised as a profession (Nan, 2013). Change in this area, which is to be expected, will improve Chinese and other countries' economic performance, as well as animal health.

Sustainable farming

The concept of integrated pest management (IPM) has general acceptance amongst environmentally aware researchers. The basic idea is simple: integrate many methods – chemical, biological, mechanical and organisational – to control pests, rather than relying on one, particularly environmentally insensitive chemicals. The objective of IPM is to keep pest levels below economically damaging levels while concurrently minimising the adverse effects of pest control on human health and the environment. Pests, for this purpose, are simply undesirable plants or animals, e.g. insects, nematodes, pathogens, vertebrates or weeds. Together, crops and pests are part of an agro-ecosystem, sharing the same biological processes. So, IPM protagonists assert, attempts to control one pest species without regard for the entire ecosystem can be counterproductive. IPM therefore depends on a detailed understanding of the interrelationship between different elements of the ecosystem, which poses a difficulty where knowledge is at a premium. 'Integrated' implies the use of a broad interdisciplinary approach, using scientific principles of plant protection to:

- Strive for maximum use of naturally occurring control forces in the pests' environment, including weather, pest diseases, predators, and parasites;

- Focus first on non-chemical measures that help prevent problems from developing, rather than relying on chemicals to kill infestations after they have occurred; and

■ Use chemical pesticides as a last resort, i.e. only if close inspection shows they are needed to prevent severe damage

IPM is probably therefore best thought of as a decision-making process aimed at keeping pest numbers and impact to below financially unacceptable levels. Just as with insecticides, however, pests can develop resistance to IPM, whether biological, physical or chemical, although it develops much more frequently, it must be conceded, in response to herbicides, insecticides and pesticides, especially amongst insects. Resurgence is the term used when insecticide works initially but eventually the pest reaches higher levels than before; replacement (secondary pest outbreak) is sometimes a consequence of attacking an individual pest.

The five principles of IPM

• There is no silver bullet to pest control;
• Tolerate, do not try to eradicate;
• Treat the causes of pest outbreaks, not the symptoms;
• If you kill the natural enemies, you inherit their job; and
• Pesticides are not a substitute for good farming.

Farmers put these IPM principles into practice by following three general steps:

■ Step 1 – use cultural methods, biological controls and other alternatives to conventional chemical pesticides.

■ Step 2 – use field scouting, pest forecasting and economic thresholds to ensure that pesticides are used for real (not perceived) pest problems.

■ Step 3 – match pesticides with field site features so that the risk of contaminating water is minimised.

Economically viable pest management. With consumer resistance (and insect resistance) to insecticides continually rising, farmers everywhere are under pressure to adopt methods such as frequent cultivation, changing around planting and harvesting dates, crop rotation, using better seeds/varieties, water management and solarisation, i.e. heating the land (University of California, 2008) to reduce pest losses. Farmers have for many decades also used techniques such as screens and netting, artificially controlled temperatures (such as in greenhouses), shredders, rollers, ploughs and soil pulverisers, soil sterilisation and soil flaming (Litzinger, 1969). In addition, the use of parasites, predators and pathogens on the insects can reduce their effect, as can interfering with insect life cycles, e.g. through pheromones, the introduction of other species, and the production of natural insecticides (semiochemicals) which can influence the feeding or breeding pattens of insects. One strategy, known as 'push-pull' or companion cropping, uses a push plant grown between the crop that repels, and another trap

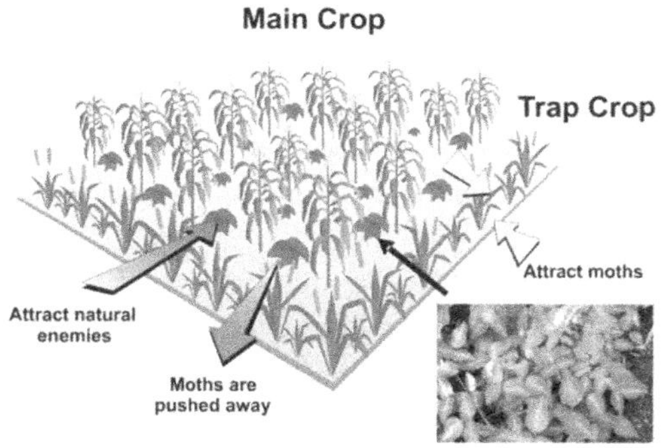

Figure 5.3 Push-pull cropping
Source: Pickett (2017); Pickett & Khan (2016)

crop on the outside: it has doubled crop yields in East Africa. Push-pull strategies have been developed for the management of stem borers in maize and sorghum, boll worms in cotton, pea leaf weevil in beans, Colorado potato beetle in potatoes, pollen beetle in oilseed rape maggot on onions, and thrips on chrysanthemums (Reddy, 2016).

Together, all these strategies reduce, but rarely eliminate, the need for pesticides, which are for many crops still essential. There is debate over the economic benefits of this kind of strategy, moreover: on the one hand a claim that 'even when fully optimised, a companion cropping system would produce less than an intensively cultivated crop with fertiliser inputs' (Baulcombe, 2013:11). Innovations include 'the development of methods and products to rebuild topsoil, such as direct seeding into field stubble, which prevents erosion as there is no tilling. Dairies and other animal facilities are experimenting with bio-digesters to convert animal and plant wastes into useful fuels on the farm' (Pullman & Wu, 2012:10).

There are many possible environmental fate processes for a pesticide. These processes can be grouped into those that affect persistence, including photodegradation, chemical degradation, and microbial degradation, and those that affect mobility, including sorption, plant uptake, volatilisation, wind erosion, runoff and leaching. Pesticide persistence is often expressed in terms of field half-life. This is the length of time require for one-half of the original quantity to break down or dissipate from the field. Pesticide mobility may result in redistribution within the application site or movement of some amount of pesticide off site. After application, a pesticide has the potential to:

■ Dissolve in water and be taken up by plants, move in runoff, or leach through the soil column.

■ Volatilise or erode from foliage or soil with wind and become airborne.

■ Attach (sorb) to soil organic matter and soil particles and either remain near the site of deposition or move with eroded soil in runoff or wind.

Organic farming

Organic farms often sustain higher species diversity and cultivate locally adapted varieties. This enhances the resilience of agro-ecosystems against adverse climate conditions, such as extreme weather events. Studies indicate that organic systems out-produce conventional under extreme drought conditions, that there is 15–20% greater movement of water through soils down to the groundwater level, and therefore higher groundwater recharge in organic systems. Water capture and retention capacity in organically managed soils is up to 100% higher than in conventional soils. Organic farming systems are more resilient to changing weather conditions, such as extreme droughts and extreme rainfall. Currently there is a vocal debate about the extent to which hydroponics can be organic (Nosowitz, 2017).

So why is organic farming not universal? The problem is straightforward: lower yields. Based on the rules of organic production, agricultural land can only sustain a limited number of animals, since there are clear rules on how many head of livestock are allowed per hectare. Further, there is currently an insufficiently nuanced public policy structure anywhere in the world to take account of these kinds of externalities to price organic fruit, vegetables and other crops with greater social accuracy.

Most farm-related greenhouse gas emissions come in the form of methane (CH_4) and nitrous oxide (N_2O). Cattle belching (CH_4) and the addition of natural or synthetic fertilisers and wastes to soils (N_2O) represent the largest sources, making up 65% of agricultural emissions globally. Smaller sources include manure management, rice cultivation, field burning of crop residues, and fuel use on farms. At the farm level, the relative size of different sources will vary widely depending on the type of products grown, farming practices employed, and natural factors such as weather, topography and hydrology (Russell, 2014). For Australia, agriculture was responsible for about 16% of greenhouse gas emissions in 2013, and the sources were:

- 66.3% from enteric fermentation in ruminant livestock (eructation and flatulence);

- 15.5% from agricultural soils;

- 10.8% from prescribed burning of savannas;

- 3.9% from manure management; and

- 2.4% from liming and urea application.

The remainder came from rice cultivation and field burning of agricultural residues (Sudmeyer, 2018).

Supporters of organic farming pointed to studies such as Aguilera *et al.*, (2013) of two dozen comparison trials in Mediterranean climates between organic systems and non-organic systems without organic supplements, and the conclusions drawn by the Louis Bolk Institute in its study to calculate soil carbon sequestration at Sekem, the oldest organic farm in Egypt (Leu, 2016). In the EU, it has been claimed that the universal adoption of organic agriculture by 2030, through soil carbon sequestration and the avoidance of mineral fertilisers in organic agriculture, could reduce or offset emissions equivalent to about 35% of total agricultural emissions (IFOAM, 2016:41). Indeed, if sequestration rates attained by exemplar cases were achieved on crop and pastureland across the globe, the claim is that regenerative agriculture could sequester more than our current CO_2 emissions, roughly 52 gigatonnes of carbon dioxide equivalent (52 $GtCO_2$ eq). All this could be achieved through techniques such as longer rotations, catch-crops, cover crops, green manures, legumes, compost, organic mulches, perennials, agroforestry, permaculture, agro-ecological biodiversity and livestock on pasture through holistic grazing.

The rise in organic farming has been well documented. Its benefits include soil composition, plant strength, reduced erosion and less contamination and risk from chemicals. But it takes time and effort, labour costs in particular being higher, with the time taken often reducing off-farm income. So far as animals are concerned there are major choices for farmers. So, for example, the major alternative to single lots for sows is group pens: the latest versions use electronic ear tags linking sows to feeding systems that dispense the proper meal dose based on the animals' needs, but the machinery is expensive and requires expert workers, whilst there is still some debate over the efficacy and even welfare of the two systems (Jackson & Marx, 2016). Already, however, improvements in cage-free production systems, driven by science and engineering, are increasing productivity, reducing production costs and moving consumer prices lower, a trend likely to continue into the future.

Wildlife, ecoscience and the boundaries of agribusiness

Food security consultants have promoted wildlife farming as a way to boost rural incomes and supply protein to a hungry world. So are public health experts, who view properly managed captive breeding as a way to prevent emerging diseases in wildlife from spilling over into the human population and to protect endangered species. Conservationists doubt these benefits (Conniff, 2016). On the other hand, in developed countries where there is precious little wildlife left (witness the sad story of the wildcat in Scotland), charities such as the Royal Society for the Protection of Birds (RSPB) see the catastrophic loss of farmland wildlife as one of the big conservation challenges of our time. And in countries like the UK, where agriculture covers three-quarters of the total land area, this means wildlife is seriously depleted across most of the countryside (Ceci, 2018). The causes of farmland wildlife loss are well understood: wide-ranging and pervasive changes in a suite of farming practices have removed or degraded the key resources and habitats on which wildlife depends. In the case of birds, this means the removal of safe places to nest, and the loss and degradation of food-rich habitats. Ecoscience and wildlife-friendly farming aim to reverse this trend. Ultimately, however, societies worldwide obviously need to find a balance between cheap food and farming productivity and profitability on the one hand, and wildlife and other environmental concerns on the other.

Structure and plant management

Farm structures may be used to house livestock, grow farm products, protect equipment and farm supplies, and store wastes.

Barns are usually large buildings used to house livestock. Livestock are housed for a number of reasons: to shelter animals from the elements, to make animal handling more convenient and to increase productivity and efficiency. Barn design varies. Specific designs depend on the type and quantity of livestock to be housed, the space they require and the local climate. Barns can be built of various construction materials. Livestock may be kept in barns year-round or kept on pasture or range during the late spring, summer or early autumn months. Barns can be naturally or mechanically ventilated. Most large-animal structures are naturally ventilated whereas many poultry barns are typically mechanically ventilated. Appropriate methods of collecting and removing wastes generated within a barn must be included in an overall design. Wastes may be handled as a solid, semi-solid or liquid. Exhaust fans should be located on the sides of buildings facing away from urban dwellings; the Canadians even require that barns located close to neighbours' residences should have their fans hooded to direct exhaust air down towards the ground.

Farm buildings are typically subject to a low human occupancy load, are often located in remote areas, and are often special in nature with respect to the occupancies involved. Any activity designated as a farm use includes the construction, maintenance and operation of a building, structure, driveway, ancillary service or utility necessary for that use. For livestock or poultry kept outdoors, confinement with adequate fencing is essential.

The Canadian Ministry of Agriculture provides useful information on the design of structures and farmstead planning considerations. These are available in the form of farm building plans, fact sheets and other publications. In addition, the Canada Plan Service offers publications and plans for those contemplating farm building construction. No such regulations are usually enforced in developing countries, nor is such helpful information available, but this indifference on the part of governments in Africa, for example, is gradually changing, and best practice information from governments such as Canada is free for all to see, if expensive to implement (Agriculture Canada, 1988; Ontario Government, 2019).

Relevant power and machinery operation

Agricultural implements may be towed behind or mounted on a tractor, and a tractor may also provide a source of power if the implement is mechanised. Tractors are the versatile workhorses of the 21st century, now playing a key role in ploughing, tilling, disking, harrowing, planting, etc. Amongst the machines that are used are:

Cultivating

■ A *cultivator* which stirs and pulverises the soil before planting, or to remove weeds and loosen the soil after plants. Many are equipped with hydraulic wings that fold up to make road travel easier and safer.

■ A *plough* is used for initial cultivation of soil in preparation for sowing seed or planting. The primary purpose of ploughing is to turn over the upper layer of the soil, bringing fresh nutrients to the surface, while burying weeds and the remains of previous crops, allowing them to break down. It also aerates the soil, and allows it to hold moisture better. In modern use, a ploughed field is typically left to dry out, and is then harrowed before planting.

- (A set of) *harrows* is an implement for cultivating the surface of the soil. It is different in its effect from the plough, which is used for deeper cultivation. Harrowing is often carried out on fields to follow the rough finish left by ploughing operations. The purpose of this harrowing is to break up lumps of soil and to provide a finer finish, a good soil structure that is suitable for seeding and planting operations. Harrowing may also be used to remove weeds and to cover seed after sowing. There are nominally three types of harrows: spike harrows, drag harrows, disk harrows.

- A *rotary tiller*, also known as a rototiller, rotavator, rotary hoe, power tiller or rotary, is a motorised cultivator that works the soil by means of rotating tines or blades. Rotary tillers are either self-propelled or drawn as an attachment behind a tractor.

Planting

- A *broadcast seeder* (or broadcast spreader or fertiliser spreader) is a tractor implement commonly used for spreading seed, lime or fertiliser.

- A *seed drill* or grain seeder is a tool that is used in crop sowing/planting. Its purpose is to sow the seeds evenly over the entire surface. A seeder needs a machine that pulls it because it is not self-propelled. Row spacing and the depth of sowing can be controlled.

Fertilising and pest control

- A *fertiliser spreader* or manure spreader is an agricultural machine used to distribute fertiliser or manure over a field as a fertiliser. A typical modern spreader consists of a trailer towed behind a tractor with a rotating mechanism driven by the tractor's power.

- A *slurry tank* is a trailer with a tank and pump which is used for slurry (a combination of manure and water) to fertilise the fields.

- A *sprayer* is a piece of equipment that applies herbicides, pesticides, and fertilisers to agricultural crops. Sprayers range in size from man-portable units (typically backpacks with spray guns) to self-propelled units similar to tractors.

Harvesting/post-harvest

- A *combine harvester*, or simply a combine, is a machine that combines the tasks of harvesting, threshing and cleaning grain crops. The objective is the harvest of the crop – corn (maize), soybeans, flax (linseed), oats, wheat, rye… The waste straw left behind on the field is the remaining dried stems and leaves of the crop with limited nutrients which is either chopped and spread on the field or baled for feed and bedding for livestock.

The FAO defines mechanisation as the application of these kinds of tools, implements and machinery in order to achieve agricultural production, replacing hand-held implements such as sickles. These can all be operated by manual, animal or engine (fossil fuel or electric) power. Essentially, agricultural mechanisation represents technological change through the adoption of non-human sources of power to undertake agricultural operations. Mechanised agricultural operations can be grouped into power- and control-intensive functions. Mechanisation of power-intensive agricultural operations, such as land preparation, threshing, grinding and milling, is characterised by non-human sources of energy input to replace human and animal ones required in the operations. On the other hand, mechanised control-intensive operations, such as planting, weeding, winnowing and fruit harvesting, require greater human judgement and mental input in addition to energy. Hence grain harvesting, for example, can be thought of as both a power- and control-intensive operation. Some literature also separates stationary operations, such as milling, water lifting and threshing, from mobile operations, which include ploughing, weeding and harvesting. Distinctions between power- and control-intensive operations, and stationary and mobile operations, are important for understanding the demand for mechanisation.

Following pressure from the FAO, in 2012 the UK government picked up on the importance of agricultural engineering; but a year later the FAO opined that farm mechanisation seemed to have become, to a certain extent, the 'neglected waif' of agricultural and rural development. The benefits of mechanisation are clear enough – it can transform farm family economies by facilitating increased output and reducing the drudgery of hand-powered production. Tractor manufacturers have provided evidence for the effectiveness of mechanisation: if horses were still the major source of power on the farm, they would consume the output of approximately 25% of grain acreage. Even a 100hp tractor 'can do the work of more than 1000 workers without machine or animal power' (Ricketts & Ricketts, 2009:17). It is therefore depressing to realise that Africa, in particular, has the lowest farm power base, with an incredible still lower than 10% of mechanisation services provided by engine-powered sources. At the same time approximately 25% of farm power is provided by draught animals and over 70% still comes from human effort, mostly from women, the elderly and children. The FAO noted that this human power source often only has rudimentary tools and equipment at its disposal for soil preparation, crop care, transport of goods and bucket irrigation. As Chapter 4 showed, effective irrigation or water and soil management can help protect natural capital and the environment at the same time, especially when combined with the latest technology. But agricultural engineering departments in the CGIAR's international research centres have been wound down, even expertise within the FAO is not widely dispersed, and there is little international pressure to move towards universal mechanisation (FAO, 2013).

The positive impact of precision farming is equally clear. Too much, as well as too little, irrigation is poor farm management. Not only does it waste scarce water supplies, but excessive irrigation can also reduce soil aeration and provide a favourable habitat for soilborne pathogens, which may increase crop vulnerability to disease. Done right, however, international technology transfer can dramatically improve agricultural performance; here is an example:

Mango trees, like people, need a good start in life and continuing care as they grow up, to enable them to reach their full potential and have a long and productive life. The 'mango production project', part of the Australia-Pakistan Agriculture Sector Linkages Program (ASLP) portfolio, looked systematically at the pests and diseases that were adversely affecting the productivity of mango trees in Pakistan and the quality of the fruit coming to market.

The researchers concluded that many of the problems started in the nursery and were compounded by neglectful or inappropriate management of most orchards. Traditionally, mango seeds are planted in dense seedbeds in the soil, under the parent trees, where they become infected with fungal diseases such as those implicated in mango sudden death and mango malformation disease by the trees above. A high proportion of the seedlings die from these diseases or from root damage when they are dug up and transplanted to their final position in a new orchard. A concerted research and training effort by the project team resulted in the establishment of well-managed, dedicated mango nurseries. Mango seeds were carefully selected, planted in polythene pots, in well-drained, soil-less growing media (formulated from locally available materials such as sugarcane waste and coconut peat), grafted with defined, market-preferred varieties, and carefully raised with adequate water and fertiliser. Almost all the trees survived subsequent field planting – with a strong root system undamaged by the planting process – and quickly started to bear good-quality fruit. A manual on nursery practices, jointly produced with the citrus project, has been widely used in an extensive effort to train nursery operators and farmers.

As to improving existing mango orchards, the project team focused their efforts on 'canopy management' – pruning to achieve an open structure of highly productive branches – and on more efficient irrigation. Irrigation in response to the need of the trees reduces the amount of water needed by 40% and avoids salt build-up and waterlogging. Farmers using these best practices were able to increase the yield of their trees by at least 60%. The researchers were able to diagnose the fungi causing mango sudden death and mango malformation disease in Pakistan (*Ceratocystis fimbriata* and *Fusarium mangiferae*, respectively). They developed a treatment for the former that involved injecting fungicide directly into the trunks of the trees. Tree losses were reduced by this practice from 10% a year to virtually nil, and in some cases whole orchards were saved. Perhaps the project's most important legacy will be a new generation of well-trained researchers, extension officers and farmers (Markham, 2016:1–2).

A similar strategy was adoped by CGIAR in Vietnam to combat climate change effects on rice:

Rising sea levels have caused salt-water intrusion further up-river and into rice paddies, hurting the rice industry. Using spatial data, the project maps the risks of sea-level rise to

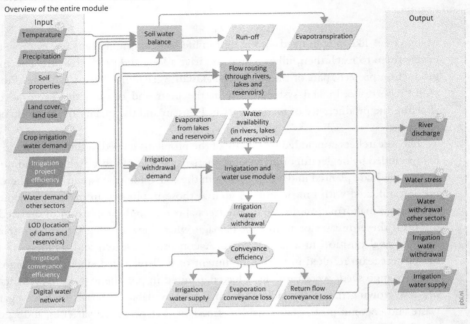

Water module of LPJmL, in IMAGE 3.0
Overview of the entire module

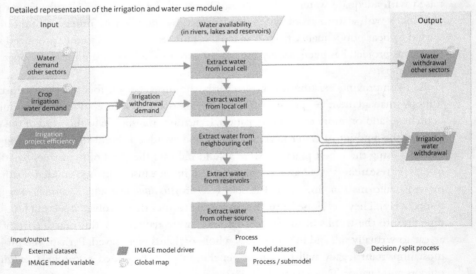

Detailed representation of the irrigation and water use module

Input/output
- External dataset
- IMAGE model variable
- IMAGE model driver
- Global map

Process
- Model dataset
- Process / submodel
- Decision / split process

Figure 5.4 Key inputs to irrigation decision-making
Source: PBL Netherlands (2014)

predict future flooding. The project is also working on salt-tolerant and high-yielding rice varieties through the marker-assisted backcrossing plant breeding technique.

A total of 300 traditional and improved rice varieties were screened for survival and recovery potential, and new breeding lines were developed. Four rice lines were submitted for varietal release across the four target provinces in 2014. These included varieties for short growth duration, submergence and salinity-tolerance, and high yield. A total of five tonnes of seed of improved breeding varieties, comprising either four or eight varieties for each province, was distributed to the four provinces. Reduced phosphorus requirements for all varieties without affecting yield have also enabled farmers to increase their net incomes. In addition to breeding work, climate-smart agricultural practices and technologies, such as alternate wetting and drying to reduce greenhouse gas emissions, were implemented and are now influencing new climate change policies (ACIAR, 2018).

New irrigation strategies for limited water resources, such as site-specific variable rate irrigation, are required to maintain modern irrigated agricultural cropping systems. Recently, moving sprinkler systems have been modified for spatially variable water and chemical applications. Onboard sensor packages, such as infrared thermometers and spectral reflectance sensors, have been installed to provide near real-time field maps of water status, vegetation and nutrient indices. Linking information on spatial and temporal development of abiotic and biotic stresses with instructions for site-specific sprinkler irrigation systems allows producers to maximise irrigation water-use efficiency, improve sustainability and diminish negative effects on the environment.

In 2013, Thanet Earth – the UK's largest greenhouse complex, based in Kent – used controlled-environment agriculture to produce around 225 million tomatoes, 16 million peppers and 13 million cucumbers, which equated respectively to 12%, 11% and 8% of the UK's entire annual production of these crops.

Ploughing, sowing, threshing, tilling and harvesting

Crops are essentially similar, at least in requiring to be planted (sown), tended, harvested and stored.

Rice can be grown either as lowland or upland. For lowland rice, suitable for rainy climates, the seeds are put into small seedbeds, being transplanted into paddy fields in early spring. The water therein must have high nutrition, so the paddies are dammed and channelled, usually with about 12 cm or so water depth. Labour intensity is high, for the time being, although in Japan robotics is being tested for paddy rice growing (Kurita *et al.*, 2017). For regions with less moisture, upland rice is grown, which is planted like other crops. With either type of cultivation, harvesting is four months after planting, again labour-intensive, by cutting plants with a knife and tying into bundles to dry. In the Philippines, robotics is being tested for drying (Frejas *et al.*, 2016). In the West, rice harvesting is mechanical with a combine, which removes and cleans the grain, it being dried in storage bins or columnar dryers.

Crops such as wheat are highly suited to large-scale, highly mechanised planting, tending and harvesting processes. Wheat planting seasons vary with varieties, with spring wheat planted in the spring and harvested after about 90 days' growth, ideally with sunshine, in the summer, and winter wheat planned in autumn and again harvested in the summer. Wheat needs time to dry: warmer weather means an early harvest, and vice versa: once mature, wheat must be harvested quickly, as moisture content is critical. For the highest quality, wheat must be harvested early, and usually first, and then artificially dried. Harvesting involves a combine cutting and feeding wheat; it is then threshed, separating the wheat grain from straw, and cleaned. The grain is then stored in silos.

Corn seed is usually planted in the early spring, after any last frost, and takes 70–90 days to mature, depending on variety and climate. Once the kernels reach a particular moisture content, the crop is harvested, either by combine (removing the corn but leaving the stalk), or all of it (for silage and animal feed). Or it can be threshed (kernels separated). Drying is essential, as undried corn is perishable and must be distributed immediately. With field corn, it is least costly to be dried on the stalk before harvesting, if weather permits.

Soybeans are also planted some time in spring, depending on the variety, climate and region. Up to a dozen varieties may be planted to extend the growing season. Soybeans may even be able to grow after early-harvested wheat. Most have two to three beans per pod. When dry, they are harvested, usually in autumn. Similar to other commodities, soybeans are harvested by a combine that pulls off the pods, threshes the beans out of the pods and moves the beans into a transport truck (Pullman & Wu, 2012:75).

Fruit and vegetables are usually field crops, grown from seeds. Some, like asparagus, are perennial, and others like cucumbers are annual. In the West, most are planted mechanically. Orchards of perennial trees (apples, oranges, apricots, peaches) may also be used, a particular issue being to protect against birds. Orchard layout is crucial. Berries (blueberries are the most widely cultivated, but also strawberries, raspberries and even blackberries, which often grow wild) are perennial and, for the time being, very labour-intensive to harvest when ripe – and the more labour-intensive, the more expensive. Melons, for instance, are still picked manually. If harvesting is not quick yet efficient, utilising the shade and cooler hours of the day, the product deteriorates and can only be sold for frozen, canned, juiced or pulped goods, and the price falls commensurately. Strawberries, for instance, must be sold within three days of picking. Grading and sorting follow immediately on picking, or after harvest. Such is the rate of deterioration-rate of fruit and vegetables, they are often picked before they are completely ripe.

New types of berries are merging the markets and are opening new opportunities.

Honeyberry is a novelty on the supermarket shelves but definitely not a novelty on our planet. Honeyberries, also called Haskap berries, have been growing wild in Siberia for millennia and were treasured for their nutritional value by the ancient Ainu tribes in Northern Japan. This berry can only thrive in the Northern hemisphere or in the southern part of the Southern hemisphere. Haskap literally means 'the little gift at the end of the branch'. Today it is cultivated on farms and it is sold as a fresh or frozen produce, or used for juices, syrups, jams or even wine and gin production. Honeyberry is already called a super berry for being three times richer in antioxidants than wild blueberries and packed with vitamin C. There are already well-established producers of such berries in Canada, Netherlands, Slovenia, Germany, China and Poland.

Source: Octofrost (2017)

Energy conservation at the farm level

That there is a major problem with carbon loss through agricultural production is virtually undeniable.

Soil carbon loss from existing cropland and grassland, from managed drained peatlands and from conversion of other land use to cropland, together in the EU led to emissions of 2–3% of total EU GHG emissions (roughly equivalent to 25% of agriculture emissions). Existing forests and land conversion to forest, on the other hand, represent a significant sink in the magnitude of about 10% of total emissions (and roughly equivalent to 100% of EU agriculture emissions). Emissions from deforestation embodied in imported goods, primarily concentrate feed, equal to an amount of 3–5% of total EU emissions. The production of mineral fertilisers is another important contributor, amounting to 1.75% of total EU emissions.

Source: IFOAM (2016)

Farm accounting

The right place is to start from the accounts, not from an everyday use of the words. Income belongs on the income statement of the accounts. An *income statement* always represents a period of time like a month, quarter or a year, to be contrasted with a *balance sheet*, which shows account balances for one exact date. Income and expenditure for an income statement can be generated using either a cash or an accrual accounting method. Cash accounting for income is simply to record income (revenue) and expenditure when it arrives or leaves a bank account; the more sophisticated, but hard-to-handle, accruals version involves recording both when they occur, leaving debts aplenty in the accounts. *Gross profit* is derived by subtracting *direct expenses* (known as 'cost of goods sold', essentially wholesale costs, where they apply) from revenue, i.e. before expenses categorised as 'overheads' or 'general expenses'. Production agribusinesses do find intense difficulties in calculating cost of goods sold, so *gross profit figures make little sense for farms. Operating profit*, however, calculated by subtracting overheads from gross profit, makes much more sense for a farm, as it sweeps up both variable and fixed costs. For most agribusinesses it is possible to identify overheads, such as head office staff, office rent etc., but farms just do not work in this way. *Depreciation* is another key accountancy concept – capital items such as tractors age and have to be replaced eventually, which is why cash accounting cannot properly explain the long-term trajectory of any business that requires regular injections of – often very expensive indeed – items of capital. A *depreciation schedule* identifies these items and, in accordance with local accountancy practice, reduces their value on the balance sheet. Other accountancy items worth noting include interest expense and income, any non-recurring expenses (such as acquisition costs) and income taxes, which, when deducted from corporate income, become reported profits. It is important to note that for partnerships (and in the USA, LLCs and S-Corps), there are no taxes – business income flows through to the partners' or owners' personal tax statements. Due diligence on a farm often logically begins with studying an income statement, identifying radical changes (e.g. sudden increases in costs) or trends such as how costs are being controlled or how operating profits are holding up by comparison to revenues.

Balance sheets, on the other hand, record assets and liabilities of the business. They are dominated by the accountancy concept of 'fair value', which is aimed at reflecting the current market conditions for any asset, the price at which a willing buyer and seller would enter into a transaction. The fair value of a biological asset or agricultural produce is not affected by forward contracts the entity entered into (so use the current market value). If an active market does not exist, an entity uses one of the following in determining fair value:

■   The most recent market transaction price;

■   Market prices for similar assets with adjustment to reflect differences; and

■   Sector benchmarks such as the value of the value of cattle expressed per kilogram of meat.

If fair value cannot be determined using the above methods, use the present value of expected net cash flows from the asset discounted at a current market to estimate fair value, i.e. a DCF calculation.

Background and objectives of international accounting standards (IAS)/US generally accepted accounting practices (GAAP)

IAS 41 prescribes the accounting treatment, financial statement presentation, and disclosures related to agricultural activity. IAS 41 contains the following accounting requirements:

*   bearer plants are accounted for using IAS 16;
*   other biological assets are measured at fair value less costs to sell;
*   agricultural produce at the point of harvest is also measured at fair value less costs to sell;
*   changes in the fair value of biological assets are included in profit or loss; and
*   biological assets attached to land (for example, trees in a plantation forest) are measured separately from the land (IFRS, 2018).

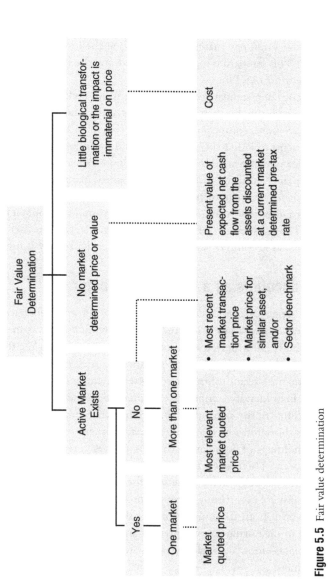

Figure 5.5 Fair value determination

Source: Malaysian Institute of Accountants (2010)

So, a biological asset shall be measured on initial recognition and at the end of each reporting period at its fair value less costs to sell, except where fair value cannot be measured reliably. If fair value cannot be measured reliably, measure biological assets at cost, less accumulated amortisation and accumulated impairment losses. Once the fair value of such a biological asset becomes reliably measurable, measure it at its fair value, less costs to sell. Agricultural produce harvested from an entity's biological assets shall be measured at its fair value less costs to sell at the point of harvest. After point of harvest, it is measured using IAS 2 inventories (i.e. harvested cotton becomes raw material for clothes) at the lower of cost or net realisable value (Deloitte, 2018). This standard is regularly updated, and the information is readily available, including online from IAS Plus.

Other relevant accounting standards across relevant issues including income recognition, leasing, intangible assets, forex, business combinations and grants (e.g. IAS 16, 17 and 40, IPSAS 27), the measurement, composition and depreciation of biological assets (including 'bearer plant' amendments to IAS 2014) and agricultural inventory. Mature bearer biological assets, which no longer undergo significant biological transformation and are used solely to grow produce, were perceived to be more akin to property, plant and equipment and their operation similar to that of manufacturing, and are now within the scope of IAS 16 Property, Plant and Equipment rather than using the fair value measurement approach prescribed by IAS 41 Agriculture. These issues are set to become progressively more significant in agribusiness going forward, so keeping IFRS and agriculture under review is highly desirable.

What to look for in accounts as a lender or investor

Whilst the standard range of accountancy inputs is mostly applicable to agribusinesses (including farms), there is also a range of other ratios in which farmers may have especial interest. Ratios are the most widely used tools for financial analysis. Yet their function is often misunderstood and, consequently, their significance may easily be overrated. A ratio expresses the mathematical relationship between two quantities. Ratios are analysis tools that provide clues to help identify symptoms of underlying conditions. Analysts, depending on their needs, may differ in the ratios they find useful when examining a business's financial position, whereas short-term creditors are primarily interested in the business's current performance and its holdings of liquid assets that can provide a ready source of cash to meet current cash requirements. These assets include cash, marketable securities, accounts receivable, inventory, and other assets which can be sold for cash or can become cash through the normal course of a business cycle. Long-term creditors and member/owners, on the other hand, are concerned with both the long-term and short-term outlook. Management will also find ratios useful in measuring its own performance.

Standard financial ratios – four categories of ratios are typically used in analysing the financial position of a business:

- Liquidity;

- Leverage;

■ Activity; and

■ Profitability.

Liquidity ratios measure the ability to fulfil short-term commitments with liquid assets. Such ratios are of particular interest to the cooperative's short-term creditors. These ratios compare assets that can be converted to cash quickly to fund maturing short-term obligations. The current ratio and the quick ratio are the two most commonly used measures of liquidity. For most cooperatives, these two ratios provide a good indication of liquidity. However, these ratios do not address the quality of liquid assets.

Leverage ratios measure the extent of the firm's 'total debt' burden. They reflect the cooperative's ability to meet both short- and long-term debt obligations. The ratios are computed either by comparing earnings from the income statement to interest payments or by relating the debt and equity items from the balance sheet. Creditors value these ratios because they measure the capacity of the cooperative's revenues to support interest and other fixed charges, and indicate if the capital base is sufficient to pay off the debt in the event of liquidation.

Activity ratios show the intensity with which the firm uses assets in generating sales. These ratios indicate whether the firm's investment in current and long-term assets is too large, too small or just right. If too large, funds may be tied up in assets that could be used more productively. If too small, the firm may be providing poor service to customers or inefficiently producing products.

Profitability ratios measure the success of the firm in earning a net return on its operations. Poor relative performance indicates a basic failure that, if not corrected, would probably result in the firm going out of business.

Compare this US list to an Indian analysis suggesting these additional (somewhat more production-orientated) ratios:

■ *Return on inputs.* Calculated by dividing the net returns by annual inputs and multiplying the result by 100. This ratio shows the efficiency of the management in using various inputs. The higher the ratio the better, if in relation to benchmarks or comparables, some changes in the proportion of inputs or varieties of corps may be required.

■ *Value of Production* (VOP). VOP = Farm Cash Receipts + (Change in Value of Product Inventory + Change in Value of Accounts Receivable) − Livestock Purchases. This amount should be equal to the accrued value of commodities produced during the year.

■ *Cash Operating Margin* (COM). COM= (VOP − Production Inventory Change − Accounts Receivable Change) − (Direct Costs − Supplies Inventory Change − Accounts Payable (Change) − (Capital Costs − Depreciation). The COM removes accruals from the agribusiness income statement. It represents cash available to cover principal payments, net cash capital acquisitions and family living expenses.

(> = greater than; < = less than)				
Liquidity Analysis	**Calculation**	**Strong**	**Stable**	**Weak**
Current Ratio	Total Current Farm Assets ÷ Total Current Farm Liabilities	> 1.50	1.00 - 1.50	< 1.00
Working Capital	Total Current Farm Assets − Total Current Farm Liabilities	Compare with business expenses; amount varies by size of operation		
Working Capital Rule**	Working Capital ÷ Total Expenses	> 50%	20 - 50%	< 20%
Solvency Analysis	**Calculation**	**Strong**	**Stable**	**Weak**
Owner Equity	Total Farm Assets ÷ Total Farm Liabilities	> 30%	30 - 70%	< 70%
...or Debt / Asset Ratio	Total Farm Liabilities ÷ Total Farm Assets	< 30%	30 - 70%	> 70%
Equity / Asset Ratio	Total Farm Equity ÷ Total Farm Assets	> 70%	30 - 70%	< 30%
Debt / Equity Ratio	Total Farm Liabilities ÷ Total Farm Equity	< 42%	42 - 230%	> 230%
Profitability Analysis	**Calculation**	**Strong**	**Stable**	**Weak**
Rate of Return on Farm Assets (ROA) *(mostly owned)*	(NFIFO* + Farm Interest Expense − Operator Management Fee) ÷ Average Total Farm Assets	> 5%	1 - 5%	< 1%
Rate of Return on Farm Assets (ROA) *(mostly rented or leased)*	(NFIFO* + Farm Interest Expense − Operator Management Fee) ÷ Average Total Farm Assets	> 12%	3 - 12%	< 3%
Rate of Return on Farm Equity (ROE)	(NFIFO* − Operator Management Fee) ÷ Total Farm Equity	Look at trends and compare to other farm and non-farm investments		
Operating Profit Margin	(NFIFO* + Farm Interest Expense − Operator Management Fee) ÷ Gross Revenue	> 25%	10 - 25%	< 10%
Financial Efficiency	**Calculation**	**Strong**	**Stable**	**Weak**
Asset Turnover Ratio	Gross Revenue ÷ Average Total Farm Assets	Depends heavily on type of operation and whether it is owned / leased		
Operating Expense / Revenue Ratio *(mostly owned)*	Operating Expenses (less interest & depreciation) ÷ Gross Revenue	< 65%	65 - 80%	> 80%
Operating Expense / Revenue Ratio *(mostly rented or leased)*	Operating Expenses (less interest & depreciation) ÷ Gross Revenue	< 75%	75 - 85%	> 85%
Depreciation Expense Ratio	Depreciation Expense ÷ Gross Revenue	compare to capital replacement and term debt repayment margin		
Interest Expense Ratio	Interest Expense ÷ Gross Revenue	< 12%	12 - 20%	> 20%
Net Farm Income From Operations Ratio	NFIFO* ÷ Gross Revenue	Look at trends; varies with cyclical nature of agricultural prices & income		
Repayment Analysis	**Calculation**	**Strong**	**Stable**	**Weak**
Term Debt and Lease Coverage Ratio	[(NFIFO* + Gross Non Farm Revenue + Depreciation Expense + Interest on Term Debts and Capital Leases) − Income Tax Expense − Family Living Withdrawals)] ÷ Scheduled Annual Principal and Interest Payments on Term Debt and Capital Leases	> 150%	110 - 150%	< 110%
Debt Payment / Income Ratio**	Scheduled Annual Principal and Interest Payments on Term Debt and Capital Leases ÷ (NFIFO* + Gross Non-Farm Revenue + Depreciation Expense + Interest on Term Debts & Capital Leases)	< 25%	25 - 50%	> 50%

Developed by Dr. David Kohl, Agricultural Economist, Virginia Tech University. Modified by Greg Blonde, Waupaca County UW-Extension Agricultrue Agent. *NFIFO = Net Farm Income From Operations, excluding gains or losses from disposal of farm capital assets. ** Not an official standard or benchmark, but widely used in the financial industry.

Figure 5.6 Farm financial ratios and benchmarks, calculations and implications
Source: Blonde (2009)

■ *Net Farm Income less Net Government Transfers.* It is equal to NFI − (Government Program Receipts − Government Program Premiums). This ratio is a measure of a farm's dependence on government transfers for income. As the level of government support in India continues to drop, this ratio will become less significant.

■ *Net Earnings per Acre.* (NEA). NEA per acre may be calculated by dividing the net returns by the total acres in the farms. It is a figure which reflects the productivity of the farm business and is not a measure of farm business and is not a measure of farm

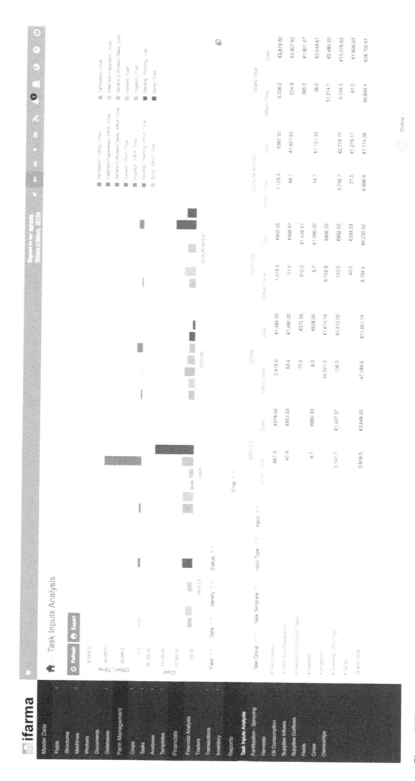

Figure 5.7a Screenshots from farm management software
Source: IFARMA (2019)

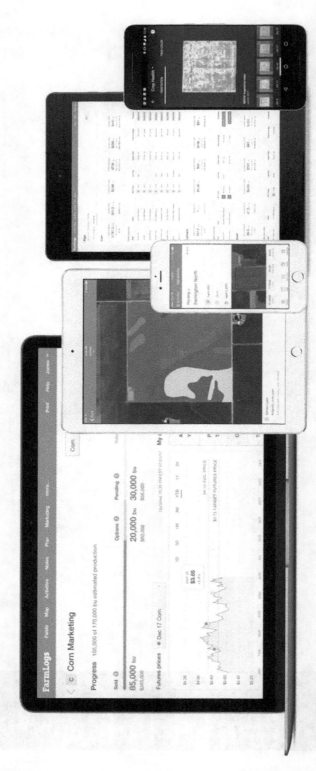

Figure 5.7b Screenshots from farm management software
Source: Shiffler (2017)

efficiency unless the farm in question is compared with other farms similar in size, organisation, and land quality.

A final caveat in relation to accounts is that, of themselves, they do not take account of risk. A farm supplying under contract, for example, may be less vulnerable than one entirely at the mercy of market conditions. Or not, depending on those conditions and the credit-worthiness of the off-taker.

Accounting software for farms

Farm-relevant software is much more extensive than just accounting. The UK's Gatekeeper, for example, claims to be 'a complete crop recording and field management solution for growers, agronomists and consultants' (Farmplan, 2019), whilst there is a range of software solutions from the same company for different livestock. The space is crowded and there are plenty of reviews of the alternatives available (Capterra, 2018).

In Africa, PwC reported software use as shown in Figure 5.8.

Conclusion

Efficient farm management, which has traditionally been at the centre of conception of agribusiness, now encompasses a wide range of disciplines. The starting point is the combination of agronomy and economics, but effective financial management in its broadest sense, including both capital budgeting and accounting, is necessary for the commercial success of production agriculture. The injection of best international practices in terms of soil, water and livestock management, capital investment in items as varied as fencing and genetics, software and mechanisation, and business organisational forms that transcend smallholdings, are the basis for effective production at the farm level.

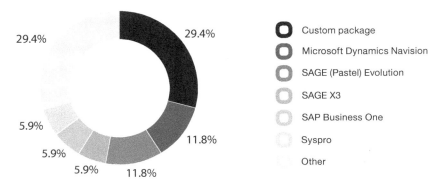

Figure 5.8 What software package/ERP system is your agribusiness currently using?
Source: PwC (2016:52)

Bibliography

ACIAR (2018) $2 billion 'white gold' industry at risk. Available at: https://aciar.exposure.co/2-billion-white-gold-industry-at-risk. Retrieved 4 June 2018.

Agriculture Canada (1988) Canadian Farm Buildings. Available at: http://publications.gc.ca/collections/collection_2014/aac-aafc/agrhist/A15-1822-1988-eng.pdf. Retrieved 29 June 2019.

Aguilera, E., Lassaletta, L., Gattinger, A. and Gimeno, B.S. (2013) Managing soil carbon for climate change mitigation and adaptation in Mediterranean cropping systems: A meta-analysis. *Agriculture, Ecosystems & Environment* 168, 25–36.

ANZ (2016) The Grains Muster. Infocus, March 2016. Sydney, ANZ Bank. Available at: www.ausgrainsconf.com/sites/default/files/files/ANZ.pdf. Retrieved 11 June 2018.

Bailey, I. (2017) Where Dairy Farm Cash Flows. Savills Rural Research. 5 July. Available at: https://pdf.euro.savills.co.uk/uk/rural---other/spotlight-where-dairy-farm-cash-flows---june-2017.pdf. Retrieved 11 June 2018.

Barnard, F.L., Akridge, J.T., Dooley, F.J., Foltz, J.C. and Yeager, E.A. (2016) *Agribusiness Management*, 5th edition. London and New York, Routledge.

Baulcombe, D. (2013) Introduction. In Bennett, D.J. and Jennings, R.C. (eds.) *Successful Agricultural Innovation in Emerging Economies*. Cambridge, Cambridge University Press.

Ben-Horin, M. and Kroll, Y. (2017) A simple intuitive NPV-IRR consistent ranking. *Quarterly Review of Economics and Finance*, 66, 108–114.

Bidwells (2016) Our View on Contract Farming Results. Available at: www.bidwells.co.uk/assets/Uploads/downloads/contract-farming-results/contract-farming-results-summer-2016.pdf. Retrieved 11 June 2018.

Blonde, G. (2009) Farm Financial Ratios and Benchmarks. Calculations and Implications. Available at: www.grainnet.com/pdf/FarmFinancialRatiosBenchmarks.pdf. Retrieved 24 February 2019.

Bradley, J. (2017) *Selecting the Best Business Structure for Your Farm*. Noble Research Institute. 1 June. Available at: www.noble.org/news/publications/ag-news-and-views/2017/june/selecting-best-business-structure-for-farm/. Retrieved 11 June 2018.

Brookfield, H. and Parsons, H. (2007) *Family Farms: Survival and Prospect. A World-Wide Analysis*. London and New York, Routledge.

Business Queensland (2018) Support Services for Agricultural Businesses. Available at: www.business.qld.gov.au/industries/farms-fishing-forestry/agriculture/overview/support. Retrieved 30 July 2018.

Byerlee, D. and Deininger, K. (2013) The rise of large farms in land-abundant countries: Do they have a future? In Holden, S.T., Otsuka, K. and Deininger, K. (eds.) *Land Tenure Reform in Asia And Africa: Assessing Impacts on Poverty and Natural Resource Management*. Basingstoke, Palgrave Macmillan, 333–353.

Capterra (2018) Farm Management Software. Available at: www.capterra.com/farm-management-software/. Retrieved 11 June 2018.

CBH (2018) Available at: www.cbh.com.au/.

Ceci, C. (2018) Wildlife-friendly farming schemes are working for birds. Royal Society for the Protection of Birds [blog]. 3 January. Available at: ww2.rspb.org.uk/community/ourwork/b/biodiversity/archive/2018/01/03/wildlife-friendly-farming-schemes-are-working-for-birds.aspx. Retrieved 11 June 2018.

Clark, M. and Tilman, D. (2017) Comparative analysis of environmental impacts of agricultural production systems, agricultural input efficiency, and food choice. *Environmental Research Letters* 12(6), 064016. Available at: http://iopscience.iop.org/article/10.1088/1748-9326/aa6cd5/pdf. Retrieved 27 February 2018.

Clemson University (2018) Animal and Veterinary Sciences. Available at: www.clemson.edu/degrees/animal-and-veterinary-sciences.

Conniff, R. (2016) Wildlife Farming: Does It Help or Hurt Threatened Species? Yale Environment 360. 30 August. Available at: https://e360.yale.edu/features/wildlife_farming_does_it_help_or_hurt_threatened_species. Retrieved 11 June 2018.

CTIC (2018) *What is a Crop Nutrient Management Plan?* Conservation Technology Information Center, Purdue University. Available at: www.ctic.purdue.edu/resourcedisplay/325/. Retrieved 11 June 2018.

Cumming, B. (2007) Cattle Breed Types. Primefact 623, May 2007. Available at: www.dpi.nsw.gov.au/__data/assets/pdf_file/0003/148080/Cattle-breed-types.pdf. Retrieved 11 June 2018.

Deloitte (2018) IAS 41 – agriculture. Available at: www.iasplus.com/en/standards/ias/ias41. Retrieved 11 June 2018.

DiPietre, D. (1999) Vertical Integration – Sometimes a Solution to Market Failure. Available at: www.nationalhogfarmer.com/mag/farming_vertical_integration_sometimes Retrieved 11 June 2018.

Edinburgh University (2017) £10m deal to boost impact of animal science innovations. Available at: www.ed.ac.uk/vet/news-events/archive/2017-news/ps10m-deal-to-boost-impact-of-animal-science-innov. Retrieved 11 June 2018.

FAO (1997) Farm Management and Farm Types. In McConnell, D.J. and Dillon, J. (eds.) *Farm Management for Asia: A Systems Approach*, FAO Farm Systems Management Series – 13. Rome, FAO. Available at: www.fao.org/docrep/w7365e/w7365e05.htm. Retrieved 11 June 2018.

FAO (2013) Mechanization for Rural Development: A review of patterns and progress from around the world. *Integrated Crop Management,* Volume 20. Available at: www.fao.org/docrep/018/i3259e/i3259e.pdf. Retrieved 11 June 2018.

FAO (2018a) Animal Health. Available at: www.fao.org/animal-health/en/. Retrieved 11 June 2018.

Farming Forum (2017) Post and rail fencing costs. 29 May. Available at: https://thefarmingforum.co.uk/index.php?threads/post-and-rail-fencing-costs.174148/. Retrieved 11 June 2018.

Farmplan (2019) Time to Grow. Available at: https://farmplan.co.uk/. Retrieved 16 May 2019.

Frejas, J.L., Donnell, A.M., Danica Frejas, J.L., Donnell, A.M., Lumanlan, D.M., Pacis, M.M., Subido, E.D.C. and Bugtai, N.T. (2016) *Design and Implementation of an Automated Stirring Robot for Rice Paddy Sun Drying.* Paper presented at the 4th DLSU Innovation and Technology Fair 2016, De La Salle University, Manila, Philippines, 24–25 November. Available at www.dlsu.edu.ph/conferences/ditech/2016/_pdf/paper-12.pdf. Retrieved 18 October 2017.

Goedde, L., Horii, M. and Sanghvi, S. (2015) Pursuing the global opportunity in food and agribusiness. McKinsey. July. Available at: www.mckinsey.com/industries/chemicals/our-insights/pursuing-the-global-opportunity-in-food-and-agribusiness. Retrieved 11 June 2018.

Horwath, C. (2014) *Business Structures for a Successful Family Farm.* Australia, Grains Research and Development Council. 9 October. Available at: https://grdc.com.au/resources-and-publications/grdc-update-papers/tab-content/grdc-update-papers/2014/10/business-structures-for-a-successful-family-farm. Retrieved 11 June 2018.

Hadley, D., Fleming, E., Andrin, R., Villiano, A. and Andrin, R. (2013) Is input mix inefficiency neglected in agriculture? A case study of pig-based farming systems in England and Wales. *Journal of Agricultural Economics* 64(2), doi10.1111/1477–9552.12003.

Hermans, F.L.P., Chaddadb, F.R., Gagalyukc, T., Senesid, S. and Balmanne, A. (2017) The emergence and proliferation of agroholdings and mega farms in a global context. Editorial. *International Food and Agribusiness Management Review* 20(2), 175–186.

Huang, P.C. (2011) China's new-age small farms and their vertical integration: Agribusiness or co-ops? *Modern China* 37(2), 107–134.

IFARMA (2019) Farm Management. Available at: https://ifarma.agrostis.gr/index_en.php. Retrieved 24 February 2019.

IFOAM (2016) Organic Farming, Climate Change Mitigation and Beyond. Available at: www.ifoam-eu.org/sites/default/files/ifoameu_advocacy_climate_change_report_2016.pdf. Retrieved 11 June 2018.

IFRS (2018) IFRS 41 – Agriculture. Available at: www.ifrs.org/issued-standards/list-of-standards/ias-41-agriculture/. Retrieved 11 June 2018.

Ito, N.C. and Zylbersztajnb, D. (2017) Vertical integration in the Brazilian orange juice sector: Power and transaction costs. *International Food and Agribusiness Management Review* 21(1), doi:10.22434/IFAMR2016.0071. Available at: http://ageconsearch.umn.edu/record/266446/files/ifamr2016.0071.pdf. Retrieved 11 June 2018.

Jackson, D. and Marx, G. (2016) Pork producers defend gestation crates, but consumers demand change. *Chicago Tribune*. Available at: www.chicagotribune.com/news/watchdog/pork/ct-pig-farms-gestation-crates-met-20160802-story.html.

Jones, L, Norton, L., Austin, Z., Browne, A., Donovan, D., Emmett, B.A., Grabowski, Z., Howard, D., Jones, J., Kenter, J., Manley, W., Morris, C., Robinson, D., Short, C., Siriwardena, G.M., Stevens, C.J., Storkey, J., Waters, R. and Willis G.F. (2016). Stocks and flows of natural and human-derived capital in ecosystem services. *Land Use Policy* 52, 151–162.

Kelly, A., Osburn, B. and Salman, M. (2014) Veterinary medicine's increasing role in global health. *The Lancet* 2(7), e379–e380. Available at: www.thelancet.com/journals/langlo/article/PIIS2214-109X(14)70255-4/fulltext. Retrieved 11 June 2018.

Kennas (2018) Farm Ownership Structures. Available at: www.kennas.com/services/agribusiness/farm_ownership_structures. Retrieved 31 July 2018.

Khan, Z.R., Midega, C.A.O., Bruce, T.J., Hooper, A.M. and Pickett, J.A. (2010) Exploiting phytochemicals for developing a 'push–pull' crop protection strategy for cereal farmers in Africa. *Journal of Experimental Botany* 61(15), 4185–4196. Available at: https://academic.oup.com/jxb/article/61/15/4185/428504. Retrieved 23 February 2019.

Kidane, A., Hepelwa, A., Tingum, E. and Hu, T.W. (2013) Agricultural inputs and efficiency in Tanzania small scale agriculture: A comparative analysis of tobacco and selected food crops. *Tanzanian Economic Review* 3(1–2), 1–13. Available at: www.ncbi.nlm.nih.gov/pmc/articles/PMC5256986/. Retrieved 27 February 2018.

Kurita, H., Iida, M., Cho, W. and Suguri, M. (2017) Rice autonomous harvesting: Operation framework. *Journal of Field Robotics* 34(6), 1084–1099.

Leu, A. (2016) *Regenerative Organic Agriculture Can Reverse Climate Change*. IFOAM. 21 July. Available at: https://permaculturemag.org/2016/07/regenerative-agriculture-reverse-climate-change/. Retrieved 11 June 2018.

Litzinger, D. (1969) *Insect Pest Management and Control*. Washington DC, National Academy of Sciences. Available at: https://jameslitsinger.files.wordpress.com/2016/11/insect-pest-management-and-control.pdf . Retrieved 15 May 2019.

Malaysian Institute of Accountants (2010) Applying IAS 41 in Malaysia. *Accountants Today*. March, 32–33.

Markham, R. (2016) *Breaking the Mango Disease Cycle*. Australian Centre for International Agricultural Research. Available at: http://aciar.gov.au/files/partners1606_pakistan_p14_breaking.pdf. Retrieved 12 July 2016.

MIT (2015) Hydroponics. Available at: http://web.mit.edu/12.000/www/m2015/2015/hydro_agriculture.html. Retrieved 11 June 2018.

Nan, X. (2013) Shanghai pig scandal shows Chinese veterinary system is failing. China Dialogue. 8 April. Available at: www.chinadialogue.net/article/show/single/en/5873-Shanghai-pig-scandal-shows-Chinese-veterinary-system-is-failing. Retrieved 11 June 2018.

Nosowitz, D. (2017) Can hydroponic farming be organic? The battle over the future of organic is getting heated. *Modern Farmer*. 5 June. Available at: http://modernfarmer.com/2017/05/is-hydro-organic-farming-organic/. Retrieved 8 June 2018.

Octofrost (2017) GBC part 4: berries market – a market of change and dynamics. 20 April. Available at: www.octofrost.com/news-room/berries-market. Retrieved 11 June 2018.

Okinda, B. (2017) Don't modify your car for farm use, get the right machine and maintain it well. Daily Nation. 4 August. www.nation.co.ke/business/seedsofgold/get-the-right-machine-and-maintain-it-well/2301238-4044942-5ugw3s/index.html. Retrieved 11 June 2018.

Ontario Government (2019) Constructing a Farm Building in Ontario. Ministry of Agriculture and Rural Affairs. Available at: http://www.omafra.gov.on.ca/english/engineer/facts/07-007.htm. Retrieved 29 June 2019.

Palumbo, L. and Sciurba, A. (2018) *The Vulnerability to Exploitation of Women Migrant Workers in Agriculture in the EU: The Need for a Human Rights and Gender Based Approach*. European Parliament. Available at: www.europarl.europa.eu/RegData/etudes/STUD/2018/604966/IPOL_STU(2018)604966_EN.pdf. Retrieved 31 July 2018.

PBL Netherlands Environmental Assessment Agency (2014) Flowchart Water. Available at: https://models.pbl.nl/image/index.php/Flowchart_Water. Retrieved 24 February 2019.

Pickett, J.A. (2017) Push-pull cropping: fool the pests to feed the people. Available at: www.rothamsted.ac.uk/push-pull-cropping. Retrieved 19 March 2019.

Pickett, J.A. and Khan, Z.R. (2016) Plant volatile-mediated signalling and its application in agriculture: successes and challenges. *New Phytologist* 212, 856–870.

Pullman, M. and Wu, Z. (2012) *Food Supply Chain Management*. London and New York, Routledge.

PwC (2016) AgTech – don't wait for the future, create it. Africa Agribusiness Insights Survey 2016. Available at: www.pwc.co.za/en/assets/pdf/agri-businesses-insights-survey-may-2016.pdf. Retrieved 12 July 2016.

Real Agriculture (2017) Re-thinking finding farm labour in the face of expansion [podcast]. 6 February. Available at: www.realagriculture.com/2017/02/re-thinking-finding-farm-labour-in-the-face-of-expansion/. Retrieved 11 June 2018.

Reddy, P.P. (2016) Push–Pull Strategy. In Reddy, P.P., *Sustainable Intensification of Crop Production*. Singapore, Springer, 323–336.

Ricketts, K. and Ricketts, C. (2009) *Agribusiness Fundamentals and Applications*. New York, CENGAGE Delmar Learning.

Rural Bank (2018) Australian Lamb and Sheep Meat Annual Review. Available at: www.ruralbank.com.au/for-farmers/ag-answers/sheep-and-wool. Retrieved 30 July 2018.

Rural Bank (2018a) Australian Wool Annual Review. Available at: www.ruralbank.com.au/assets/responsive/pdf/publications/wool-review-apr18.pdf. Retrieved 30 July 2018.

Russell, S. (2014) *Everything You Need to Know About Agricultural Emissions*. World Resources Institute. Available at: www.wri.org/blog/2014/05/everything-you-need-know-about-agricultural-emissions. Retrieved 4 June 2018.

Scottish Government (2017) Stock Fence. 17 November. Available at: www.ruralpayments.org/publicsite/futures/topics/all-schemes/agri-environment-climate-scheme/management-options-and-capital-items/stock-fence/. Retrieved 11 June 2018.

Sharma, S. (2006) Corporate agriculture: Transplanting failure. *India Together*. 3 May. Available at: http://indiatogether.org/contract-agriculture--2. Retrieved 17 July 2018.

Shiffler, A. (2017) 10 companies building the future of farm management software. *Disruptor Daily*. 29 December. Available at: www.disruptordaily.com/10-companies-building-future-farm-management-software/. Retrieved 23 February 2019.

Shockley, J., Mark, T. and Dillon, C. (2017) Educating producers on the profitability of precision agriculture technologies *Advances in Animal Biosciences* 8(2), 724–772.

Sudmeyer, R. (2018). How Australia accounts for agricultural greenhouse gas emissions. Department of Primary Industries and Regional Development. Available at: www.agric.wa.gov.au/climate-change/how-australia-accounts-agricultural-greenhouse-gas-emissions. Retrieved 4 June 2018.

Swenson, C. (2017). Projected 2018 Crops Budgets. Available at: www.ag.ndsu.edu/farmmanagement/documents/18-ec-budget. Retrieved 11 June 2018.

UK Government (2018) Agricultural Workers' Rights. Available at: www.gov.uk/agricultural-workers-rights/gangmasters. Retrieved 31 July 2018.

University of California (2008) Soil Solarization for Gardens & Landscapes. Available at: http://ipm.ucanr.edu/PMG/PESTNOTES/pn74145.html. Retrieved 8 June 2018.

USDA (2017a) Charts and Maps. Available at: www.nass.usda.gov/Charts_and_Maps/Farm_Production_Expenditures/arms3cht2.php. Retrieved 11 June 2018.

Vale of Glamorgan (2018) Food & Feed Hygiene: A guide for livestock farmers. Available at: www.valeofglamorgan.gov.uk/Documents/Working/Business%20Support/Trading%20Standards/Food%20and%20feed%20hygeine%20gudie%20for%20livestock%20farmers.pdf. Retrieved 11 June 2018.

Van Zyl, H (2017) Measurement of biological assets. *Accounting Weekly*. 17 October. Available at: https://accountingweekly.com/measurement-biological-assets/. Retrieved 10 July 2018.

The agricultural value chain

Introduction: definitions

First, some points of definition. A *supply chain* can be visualised as a sequence of (decision-making and execution) processes and (material, information and money) flows that aim to meet final customer requirements, that take place within and between different stages along a continuum, from production to final consumption. The agribusiness supply chain therefore not only includes the producer and its suppliers, but also, depending on the logistic flows, transporters, warehouses, retailers and consumers themselves. In a broader sense, agribusiness supply chains include also new product development, marketing, operations, distribution, finance and customer service (Vorst *et al.*, 2007:7). And, as Deloitte pointed out, the agribusiness supply chain has a considerable range of participants, including you and me, as consumers at least, who are often far apart geographically, culturally and economically.

By comparison, the *value-added* of a sector is defined as the difference between its *gross output* (total production value of the sector) and its *intermediary inputs* (costs of production inputs). It measures the amount of value created by the sector, to be then shared between labour (wages and compensations), capital (remuneration of capital and profits) and taxes. The value-added of a sector is a reasonable proxy for its economic importance in anything approximating to a capitalist economy, and its evolution therefore provides insights on the sector's level of competition, emerging technologies, and much else. A *value chain* can be further defined as the additional prices on sale generated by a series of actions carried out on the raw commodity or animal. For agribusiness, it consists of a series of activities that add value to a final product, beginning with production agriculture, continuing with the processing or elaborating of the final product, and ending with the marketing and sale to the consumer or end user – with, increasingly, branding throughout, constituting an ever-rising percentage of the value-added – improving subjective welfare, perhaps, but not diet. Arguably, interdependent linkages of the value chain and the security of a market-driven demand for the final product can provide suppliers, producers, processors and marketing agribusinesses with more secure access to procurement and sale of products. They in turn reduce the costs and risks of doing business and improve access to finance as well as other services needed by those within the value chain (FAO, 2013).

While the literature on *supply* chains tends to emphasise the flow of products or services, by contrast work on *value* chains focuses on the flow and distribution of value (the kind of value involved in a value added tax). For example, Cox *et al.* (2002) were some of the first authors to explore the important ways in which revenues paid by the consumer are distributed to different entities along each stage of the chain – from production through processing and to sale – and the nature of competition for the revenues at each stage of the chain (Cotula & Blackmore, 2014:9). These issues are both important and are clearly interrelated. Combining the two concepts, comparing evolution of the repartition of value-added along the agribusiness supply chain, can then be useful to research the evolution of bargaining power along the chain, e.g. when a particular agribusiness sub-sector faces difficulty in maintaining its value-added faced with, for example, an increase of costs of intermediate inputs (EU, 2009).

Most public policy advocates and analysts agree that increasing agricultural supply chain efficiency, *especially by removing intermediate steps that increase financial value without modifying the product* (i.e.'middlemen') helps to: (i) lower consumer prices, thereby raising the real incomes of poor people everywhere (rural as well as urban), because poor people spend a large share of their income on food, and (ii) raise relative prices received by farmers, providing them additional income as well as incentives to enhance productivity and to diversify (World Bank, 2015:9).

Clearly, the higher the percentage of the value chain seized by 'middlemen', the more advantages both to production agriculture and to retailers there can be. Food processing and retailing firms coming under the agricultural commodity chains are however generally cases of imperfect competition, which can be seen as making every entity guilty of this

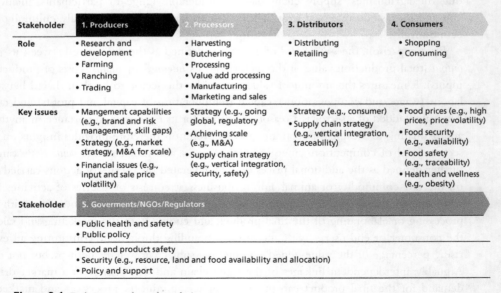

Stakeholder	1. Producers	2. Processors	3. Distributors	4. Consumers
Role	• Research and development • Farming • Ranching • Trading	• Harvesting • Butchering • Processing • Value add processing • Manufacturing • Marketing and sales	• Distributing • Retailing	• Shopping • Consuming
Key issues	• Mangement capabilities (e.g., brand and risk management, skill gaps) • Strategy (e.g., market strategy, M&A for scale) • Financial issues (e.g., input and sale price volatility)	• Strategy (e.g., going global, regulatory • Achieving scale (e.g., M&A) • Supply chain strategy (e.g., vertical integration, security, safety)	• Strategy (e.g., consumer) • Supply chain strategy (e.g., vertical integration, traceability)	• Food prices (e.g., high prices, price volatility) • Food security (e.g., availability) • Food safety (e.g., traceability) • Health and wellness (e.g., obesity)
Stakeholder	5. Goverments/NGOs/Regulators			

• Public health and safety
• Public policy

• Food and product safety
• Security (e.g., resource, land and food availability and allocation)
• Policy and support

Figure 6.1 Deloitte on the value chain
Source: Deloitte (2015)

'middleman' charge to a greater or lesser extent. It must be conceded, however, that eliminating unnecessary elements of the supply chain is only beneficial from a public policy standpoint if the redistributed value lands up somewhere useful, such as investment in new facilities or a reduction in eventual prices to the consumer. Increasing the quasi-monopoly profits and then distribution to shareholders of supermarkets or the ABCD companies is not really much of a benefit by comparison, unless this in turn were to generate increased investment in them and a long-term public policy benefit.

There is a large literature on supply and value chains (e.g. Cotula & Blackmore, 2014; Vorst *et al.*, 2007) but there are problems of theoretical overelaboration, repetition of the limited already-known evidence and a lack of useful empirical analysis, in particular the kind of detailed individual case studies of supply and value chains deriving precise estimates of how they work and how value is allocated (e.g. Cox *et al.*, 2002; Piper, 2007). In fairness, these require large research budgets, which are often not available. A related key problem is the absence of internationally accepted performance indicators for which benchmarks are easily available – benchmarking is never easy in any industry, but it is especially challenging in the case of agribusiness where distortions to establishing a reliable range of comparables are very obvious (Bryceson & Slaughter, 2010; Rosado Júnior *et al.*, 2011). Examples of attempts to establish such indicators do exist but they are usually isolated academic or quasi-academic efforts and never seem to lead to any form of standard approach. This in turn creates investment opportunities from information asymmetry, which private equity can potentially exploit.

Interest in value chains is not new. Businesses have been using value chain analysis and implementation principles for years to formulate and implement competitive strategies. Corporations use value chain analysis to answer questions of the type, 'Where in the value chain should my business be positioned to improve its performance?' The value chain's popularity has been reinforced by many important business strategy themes, including core competencies, comparative and competitive advantage, outsourcing, vertical and horizontal integration, and best practices. This type of analysis has now been supplemented by increased awareness of the importance of reciprocity: that measures taken by a firm might not affect its own competitiveness unless other firms adopt similar or linked practices (e.g. with regard to quality control). This has resulted in the beginning of a more collaborative approach to value chains, attempting to locate and then build on efficiencies and competitiveness both within and among firms, acting on opportunities to build win–win linkages, such as sharing information, that rather goes against traditional notions of cut-throat business competition. In that sense, agribusiness is at the cutting edge of business in the 21st century.

Food processing and the use of chemical preservatives

The agribusiness supply chain is generated by two overwhelming truths of the sector. First, that increasingly agricultural commodities themselves are insufficient as final products. There are some exceptions, such as bananas, but as noted below, they have their own supply chain issues in terms of harvesting, transportation and warehousing. Second – and bananas are an excellent example – most consumers do not live near where the crop is grown or the animal is kept. Foods (and other agricultural products such as cotton and wool) therefore get value-added either just by transport, agglomeration, processing, or by some combination of these activities, and differentiation, including branding. There is no uniform definition of 'processed food', which makes its condemnation by nutritionists especially problematic. Processing and manufacturing cover a range of activities, often performed in rapid sequence or concurrently. Pathogen destruction, the physical modification of a food product and packaging are all examples. Processing also includes canning, chilling, combining, cutting, drying, freezing, juicing and even just washing. Notably, most of these processes are still labour-intensive in most jurisdictions, although this may change. Techniques include thermal processing, irradiation, pressurisation, e.g. pulsed electric field processing (www.pulsemaster.us), pickling and curing. Freezing, for example, is still one of the most effective ways to preserve the majority of nutrients in food. The dictionary definition is foods that have been treated or prepared by a special method, especially in order to preserve them. But some forms of processing, such as curing, cooking, drying, salting, smoking and pickling, have been around for millennia. The real issue is this: ready-to-eat salad greens are often washed and then packed with e.g. nitrogen to prevent them from oxidising and slow down spoilage on the shelf or in the warehouse. That is a form of 'processing' that extends the salad's shelf-life, but has no effect on the benefits of eating it. Problematic forms of processed foods, on the other hand, do remove fibre and vitamins, for example – and add unhealthy ingredients such as sodium, trans fats, and additional sugars. Processed foods such as burgers also multiply the risk of contamination as the content may derive from hundreds of animals, as successive scandals in the UK have demonstrated: first over BSE (Comer & Huntly, 2003), and then over horsemeat (Shrivastava, 2013). In recent decades, partly as a result, emphasis has been placed on 'green' processing techniques, which typically involve less time, water and energy, such as ultrasound-assisted processing, supercritical fluid extraction and processing, microwave processing, controlled pressure drop process, and pulse electric fields (Chemat *et al.*, 2017:357).

For fruits and vegetables, the global value chain is characterised as buyer-driven (Gereffi & Fernandez-Stark, 2016). The buyers are large supermarket chains in both EU, US and increasingly in emerging markets. Stringent quality standards are imposed by these chains upon their suppliers, big or small, worldwide. The horticulture industry is increasingly organised by long-term relationships and tighter links between producers and exporter firms. The latter consist of a few large transnationals, together with domestic firms of varying sizes. Exporters may engage small and medium-size domestic suppliers as contract growers. In the last two decades of the previous century, the low- and middle-income countries have managed to corner a greater share of fresh produce export markets. More recently, developing country exporters are increasingly taking over packing and processing, thereby moving up the value chain. For instance, a wide variety of fruit and vegetables in supermarkets are shipped in as ready-to-eat convenience packs.

Raw animal products, fruit and vegetables, need to be chilled throughout processing – what is termed the *cold chain* (www.coolchain.org) – to avoid bacterial growth. Strict temperature control to precise parts of a degree throughout the process is certainly essential, and there are various methods, such as forced-air cooling, hydrocooling, room cooling, vacuum cooling and icing.

Use of monitoring components in cold chain is particularly increasing. This growth can be attributed to technological advancements and growing need to ensure the integrity, efficiency, and safety of shipments. Advances are equally noticeable in backend IT infrastructure and frontend devices deployed for collecting and reporting real-time shipment information (GrandView Research, 2018).

It is certainly a fertile part of the supply chain for future technical innovation.

Dairy products are usually pasteurised, again to kill bacteria, although milk in some countries is further homogenised: efficient, but with varying consequences for its quality and benefits (Nuora *et al.*, 2018). Best practices for dairies, for example as suggested by the US FDA, include limiting access to shipping, processing and receiving areas, and locking/sealing milk houses and access points to bulk milk, as well as regular inspections of milk transporters. Inventory logs to track products and ingredients in storage, production logs by shift, delivery logs, quality control logs – the list of best practices is long, and getting longer. Water contamination is a major threat, especially for fresh produce, as well as human handling, as the infamous old case of 'Typhoid Mary' demonstrated (Marineli *et al.*, 2013). The supply chain also contains some controversial activities. For example, sometimes, at least in countries such as the USA, India and Australia, meat and poultry is irradiated to kill bacteria (FDA, 2018). The question of chlorinated chicken has even threatened to derail US trade negotiations with the UK (British Poultry Council, 2018).

A distinction is often made between food processing, which is often quite basic, and food manufacturing, which is more complex. Blending, mixing and baking are examples of food manufacturing, all using recipes, some of which develop considerable IP – Coca-Cola is probably the most famous example, but there are many others. Processed foods often go on to be used in food manufacturing: this can make production easier, for example by increasing the range of possible locations for manufacturing locations. Yet still some production activities, notably commercial-scale baking, involve 'inflexible, flow-oriented processes. Their long, sequence-dependent manufacturing processes prod companies to develop product

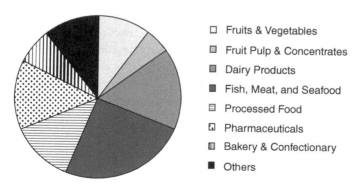

Figure 6.2 Global cold chain market share, by application, 2017 (%)
Source: GrandView Research (2018)

lines with minimal variations' (Pullman & Wu, 2012:188), sometimes with precision sprays (www.tankjet.com) and other technology. On the other hand, other food manufacturing plants are highly modular, able to shift product type with batches (e.g. spreads and dips). Seasonality, input crop price variations and the sensitivity of food products to the processing environment remain serious issues, 'For example, yeast-based breads can be highly impacted by ambient temperatures and humidity, thus creating variations in output yield and timing' (Pullman & Wu, 2012:189). The continuing fragility of these systems and processes must be stressed.

An example: the debate over saturated fats

Saturated fat is found mainly in animal foods – meat and dairy products are often high in saturated fat. Examples include fatty beef, lamb, pork, chicken with skin, whole milk, cream, butter, cheese and ice-cream. Additionally, baked goods and fried foods can be high in saturated fat, as they are made with ingredients such as butter, cream, ghee and lard. Foods with saturated fats may also be high in dietary cholesterol, another negative for health. Even some plant foods – coconut oil, palm oil and palm kernel oil – contain saturated fat, but no cholesterol. Even worse are trans fats (or trans fatty acids), which are found in chips, bakery products, popcorn and other fried foods like doughnuts, and baked goods including cakes, pie crusts, biscuits, frozen pizza, cookies, crackers, margarines and other spreads. These are even worse for human (and animal) health, having powerful biological effects and may contribute to increased weight gain, abdominal obesity, type 2 diabetes and coronary artery disease. Several countries (e.g. Denmark, Switzerland, and Canada) and US jurisdictions have for decades as a result regulated the use of trans fats in food service establishments.

By contrast, unsaturated fats are to be found in plant foods and fish. Monosaturated fat is found in olive oil, peanut oil, canola oil, avocados and most nuts, as well as high-oleic saf-flower and sunflower oils. Corn oil, sunflower oil and safflower oil are common examples of polyunsaturated fats, essential for human health. Oily fish – salmon, tuna, mackerel, herring and trout – contain a type of unsaturated fat called omega-3 fatty acids, while most nuts and seeds contain a type of unsaturated fat called omega-6 fatty acids.

Science is replete with detailed studies on the health effects of each, but essentially it is saturated, bad, unsaturated, good, at least so far as health benefits are concerned. The impact on the industry as a whole is considerable, and still increasing, especially in the developing world where the distinction is still not fully understood. But it is not inconceivable to envisage agribusiness worldwide eventually adapting to the distinction, with higher production of oily fish than today, for example, and more nuts in everyone's diet, and fewer dairy and red meat farms.

Dividing up agricultural commodities

Looking at the supply and value chain from another standpoint, different agricultural commodities can be divided into their components, each of which assumes a position within both the supply and value chain. For example, most rice varieties are composed of roughly 20% rice hull or husk, 11% bran layers and 69% starchy endosperm, also referred to as the total milled rice. In an ideal milling process this will result in the following fractions: 20% husk, 8–12% bran depending on the milling degree and 68–72% milled rice or white rice depending on the variety. Total milled rice contains whole grains or head rice, and brokens. The by-products in rice milling are rice hull, rice germ and bran layers, and fine brokens (IRRI, 2018). The outer hull, though inedible, can be used for fuel or mulch. Though the resultant brown rice can be milled – it has health benefits – the rice bran, the outer layer of the kernel, can then also be removed, leaving white rice behind, which can itself be further polished. Rice bran is used for cereals, baking mixes, vitamin concentrates and, at the lower end, livestock feeds – even oil for cooking. And more: rice is also used extensively in processed foods, cereals, baby food, frozen foods, mixes, snacks, chocolate and energy bars, and canned food products; it is used in beer, replacing traditional malted barley because of a high sugar yield and colour, stability and performance; and pets eat a lot of rice, too, including 'broken rice', what happens when kernels split at any stage in the production process – it is also used in *com tam*, a speciality of Vietnamese cuisine. For crops, infrastructure and processing is frequently found near farms themselves. Again, rice is a good example: small rice mills (<100t/day capacity) are situated close to paddy fields where hulled rice is stored, although there are also small, high quality rice mills for niche products, e.g. California. Large mills (1,000t/day capacity), such as in the USA, require transport of the rice and operate all year.

Another example is dried corn, which can be stored on-farm, which cuts aflatoxin accumulation and provides flexibility for the farmer who can use it as feed. If not, it must be stored in a specialised facility. Field corn is usually processed in a corn refining plant. The raw material is shelled corn, which is then divided into starch, oil, protein and fibre, for use in higher-value products such as sweeteners, co-products, starches and ethanol (Corn Refiners Association, 2018). Today there are over 500 uses for corn in addition to its use for food: plastics, packing material, insulation, adhesives, chemicals, explosives, paint, insecticides, pharmaceuticals, organic acids, soaps and many more (Pullman & Wu, 2012:73). In the USA, an indication of the extent of the corn supply chain is that there are more than two dozen corn refining plants with tens of thousands of suppliers.

A third example: soybean meals and hulls are used as livestock feed, but soybean oil is now also widely used. Together with palm oil it makes up the considerable majority of edible oil used worldwide. Soybean oil is also used for anti-corrosion, diesel fuel and waterproof cement, all of which have separate markets. Soy also finds its way into building materials, cosmetics, clothing, ink and soap, and is becoming more popular as a health food, in particular because of its isoflavones (Ding *et al.*, 2016), although exaggerated claims should be treated with caution (Xiao, 2008). After loading, soybeans are moved to major terminals and processing, but can also be stored in silos. Soybeans end up either whole as soymilk, flours or tofu, or refined further, where they are graded, cleaned, dried and the hull is cracked away from the soybean. The hulls are used for animal feed or fibre; the remainder ends up in animal food flakes or full-flour soy flour. And again, the flakes may be soaked in solvent to extract soybean oil and lecithin, an input in food processing. The residue is used for animal food or other soy flours. Once dry, crops are sold to companies that either use them directly or process them, so mills, extractors, meat grinders or packagers. Refined crops surface

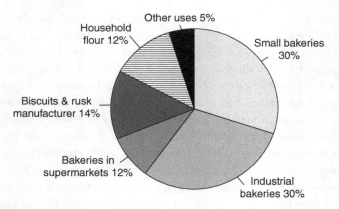

Figure 6.3 Uses of flour, Europe, 2018
Source: European Flour Millers Association (2018)

in other processed foods, both for people and animals, but also find their way out of the food chain into industrial products such as ethanol and plastic (e.g. cellophane). One crop, hundreds of uses – an immensely complex supply and value chain.

What must be remembered in this attractive, environmentally sensitive narrative is that the processing of agricultural bulk commodities requires the transformation of large volumes to reach economies of scale and be profitable. Typically, primary food processors are small margin businesses. The baking industry is a case in point. Wheat accounts for the majority of flour. About 75% of grain emerges from milling. Wheat must be graded (Oregon Wheat Commission, 2018), analysing for protein content, sorted and cleaned. It must then be soaked for several days, spun dry, ground and milled. It is then processed with bleaching and oxidising agents, with vitamins and minerals added for enriched flours. Once milled, the flour is packed, usually in sack bags, and sent to distributors, who then rebag into smaller quantities, label and sell on to retailers and wholesalers (BC Cook Articulation Committee, 2012). US mills grind around 750 million bushels of wheat annually: final demand is driven by commercial bakers' requirements to produce specific bread and cakes. In Europe, the flour milling industry is predictably the leading food industry in grain processing, using around 45 million tonnes of soft wheat and rye plus 2 million tonnes of oats a year to produce around 35 million tons of flour on an annual basis (for the EU-27). The number of flour milling companies is more than 3,800, of which a large majority are small and medium-sized enterprises (SMEs), employing about 45,000 people with a turnover of approximately $20 billion (European Flour Millers Association, 2018).

The flour milling industry plays a central role in the cereal chain, turning safe and good-quality grain from many different farms into a range of flours for human consumption. Flour millers process wheat and other agricultural raw materials, the availability of which is subject to seasonality and climate variations. Flour mills, like any other primary processing plants, have to ensure their continuous supply, as their transformation process cannot be interrupted, but they rarely manage operational efficiency above 70%.

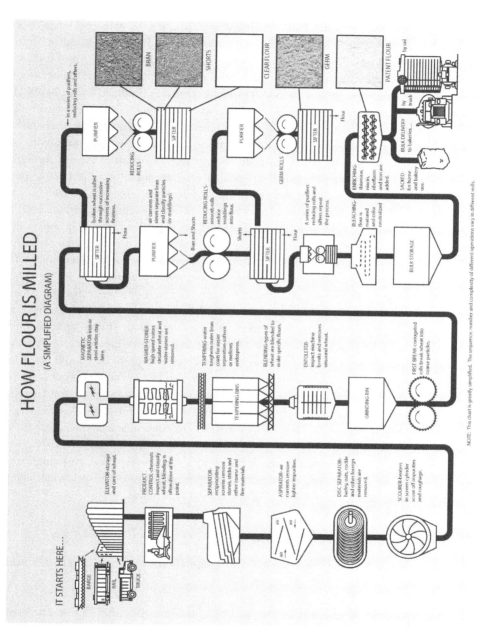

Figure 6.4 A schematic diagram of flour milling

Source: Wheat Foods Council (2015)

To make their task harder, throughout the developed world millers are being challenged by private label brands associated with grocery chains. However, they are retaliating by improving technology and enhancing sustainability practices, aimed at lowering ozone emissions and meeting green standards. Milling is capital-intensive, with real estate, high grain and labour costs, plus energy, packaging, pest control, and equipment repair. To be profitable, as with a farm, these inputs must be managed optimally. 'Large companies have the advantage of advanced milling technology and diversified product lines. Small operations compete by specialising in organic, non-GMO or heirloom grains' (Pullman & Wu, 2012:81). The major millers include Archer Daniels Midland (www.adm.com), Cargill (www.cargill.com/), ConAgra (www.conagrabrands.com/) and General Mills (www.generalmills.com/).

Grains have it a little easier so far as risks are concerned, but there is the possibility of physical contamination (e.g. by insects, or rodents), or bacterial or fungal growth through moisture. Where grains are combined with wet products and yet not fully cooked before sale (e.g. chilled pasta, ready-made dough) has created new avenues for microbial contamination (Pullman & Wu, 2012:26). Traceability is hard because of commingling, as noted for GM crops. Traceability systems, with recordkeeping throughout the value chain, help, especially identity preservation systems, which are more precise, but more expensive, than ordinary segregation. Fruit and vegetables are major sources of food illness, and also require a *cold chain*, where monitored irrigation, cooling and processing are all key points.

Differentiation is of rising importance throughout the agribusiness supply chain. In Japan, for example, the food processing industry produces a wide variety of foods, from traditional Japanese foods such as tofu and natto, to health foods for infants and the elderly. Japanese food producers focus on maintaining market share with traditional product lines while developing creative products to attract consumers who are always on the lookout for new and innovative foods. As a result, Japanese food manufacturing is characterised by high rates of product turn-over. Processed food products that are increasing in popularity include yoghurt, meat, soups and ramen. Popular beverage items include tea, vegetable juice, distilled spirits and energy drinks. Frozen food consumption has grown as well, due to convenience and recent quality improvements. As more people seek single-size portions or claim, at least, that they have insufficient time (and certainly do lack the inclination) to cook every meal, convenience is a keyword for product developers. It is a picture being steadily mirrored worldwide, albeit with national, sometimes local, differences in actual food preferences.

Analysis of the changing value chain

The example of beef in the USA is a good one to show what has changed. The US beef supply chain is:

> …highly fragmented at its outset and highly concentrated at the end. Some ranchers sell weaned calves to the more concentrated stocker operators, who add weight to them by grazing or concentrated feeding in feedlots – the largest market 85–90% of all cattle, the smallest have a capacity of only 1,000 or fewer. For the commodity beef market, fully-grown calves are them sold to feedlots, which finish them, either in open pasture or large enclosed areas (bunkers) with pens of different sizes. Finishing aims at developing flavour,

tenderness and marbling qualities within the beef, and to bulk up the animal. The feed requirements are varied, including dozens of different crops, each for an ideal result carefully adjusted throughout the cow's life (ADHB Beef & Lamb, 2016).

As the forage quality of a particular range or pasture varies depending on rainfall, soil quality and other aspects of the land, there is frequently a complex web of land leasing and feed supply transactions to support the process. Economies of scale are evident within the USA, with large-scale feedlots of up to 100–200,000 cattle capacity, which are known as concentrated animal feeding operations (CAFOs). The next step in the value chain is for the calves to be slaughtered. After that, distribution and processing conclude the value chain. For dairy, it is a similar story, although the average size of farms is growing.

There are, however, still very much in existence middlemen in agribusiness marketing in developing countries. Many are traders. They are usually individuals who buy (take title) commodities, and sell on at what they hope to be a profit, sometimes along established supply chains, sometimes as speculators, although the distinction is never an absolute one. They can be divided into wholesalers, who operate generally on quite a large scale, selling on to retailers or still larger wholesalers, and itinerant traders or village merchants who in bad seasons are often barely wealthier than the farmers from whom they purchase. In addition, agricultural markets in countries such as India are replete with commission agents acting on behalf of larger concerns. The processors (rice millers, oil millers and cotton or jute dealers) and big wholesalers in the consuming markets employ agents for the purchase of a specified quantity of goods within a given price range. In regulated markets, there is often strict control over who can act as an agent. Brokers, on the other hand, do not take title and do not have storage facilities.

The biggest threat to the existence of middlemen in the value chain in the medium to long term may turn out to be the blockchain, or distributed ledger technology. The blockchain describes an ever-growing set of digital records shared, maintained and most importantly verified by multiple participants. Each set of digital records in a blockchain is grouped into sequentially dependent blocks. This makes the data more secure as time goes on and more blocks get added to the chain, especially as records are continuously maintained in multiple places. The potential advantages for farmers in particular are immense, especially given the widespread diffusion of blockchain-tolerant mobile phone technology (Hammerich, 2018; Schmaltz, 2018).

Distribution of value throughout the marketing chain

The trend towards greater value-added in the downstream components of the value chain is unmistakable in developed countries. The input and production stages of the food and agribusiness value chain now supply about 16% of the final food value, with the other 84% coming from post-farm gate stages (Cucagna & Goldsmith, 2018: 294). We know that international agencies and governments, as well as farmers themselves, are deeply and persistently concerned with the low percentage of the total price paid by consumers that ends up in the hands of farmers themselves. In the EU, some data are available. They paint a consistent picture of a downward trend (see Figure 6.5) and are reinforced by subsequent EU data showing a very similar pattern (EU, 2017).

In the USA, the production agriculturalist's share of each dollar spent domestically on food was quite similarly estimated to be about 30 cents in 2003. (Ricketts & Ricketts, 2009:44). The rest went to transportation, processing, marketing and distribution, including retail – and the share fell in the decade after that, with the National Farmers Union highlighting USDA research showing that:

> …for calendar year 2016, farm production and agribusiness value added was 10.0 cents of each food dollar expenditure, implying that 4.8 cents from farm commodity sales (from the 14.8-cent farm share) was used to purchase products from the other industry groups. The 2016 industry group value-added food dollar also indicates that about 48.7 cents of the food dollar value covers the services from food retailers (12.4 cents) and foodservice establishments (36.3 cents). The use of energy throughout the food supply chain accounted for 3.9 cents of every 2016 food dollar expenditure. Advertising accounted for 2.6 cents of a food dollar expenditure (USDA, 2018).

The NFU illustrated the point with a range of indicated farm shares by product (National Farmers Union, 2018). Comparable information in developing countries on the exact distribution of revenue by stage of the marketing chain is, however, relatively rare, hence the prevalence of statements such as the following, written at a time when policymakers were concerned at the effects of rapid price increases both in agricultural commodities and the inputs required to grow them:

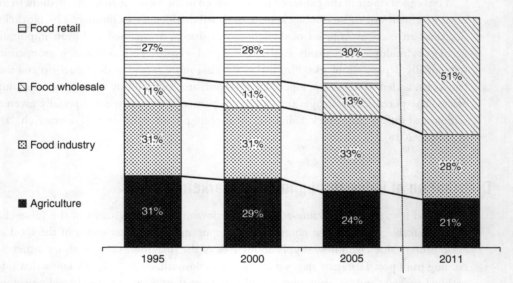

Figure 6.5 Distribution of value-added in the EU food supply chain
Source: Matthews (2015)

Price increases from the first quarter 2007 on occurred weeks after harvesting season. Since most farmers lack either the cash-flow flexibility or the post-harvest handling to store part of the harvest, it's not farmers but traders, store keepers and millers that are likely to have benefitted from the price increases for the 2007 harvest (Hoeffler, 2008:27).

Similarly,

in the case of the Bangladeshi rice market, anecdotal evidence and casual observation support the idea of price asymmetry. Specifically, it is widely believed that price increases emanating at the wholesale level are quickly passed on in terms of higher prices at the retail level. However, it is also widely believed that wholesale price decreases do not lead to similar price decreases at the retail level (Alam *et al.*, 2016:499).

There is little encouragement to take from developed countries so far as the trajectory of farm share in developing countries is concerned – smallholders will always lack bargaining power against monopsony or quasi-monopsony from major retailers.

When agribusiness supply chains reach the consumer

As for *food labelling*, in the USA country of origin labelling law is regulated by the FDA and the Department of Homeland Security. Geographic demarcation (e.g. for wine) is now matched with vigorous legal action to preserve names and trademarks. Manufacturers, distributors and retailers make what have been described as 'credence claims' (Fortin, 2016), sometimes cynically described as 'greenwashing' of products. These divide into three types of claim: first, second and third party. First-party claims are directly from the producer, e.g. humane treatment of animals, with 'humane' self-defined by the producer. Second-party claims are about satisfying a set of guidelines, whether mandatory or voluntary, e.g. ISO 9000 or 14000. Finally, a – hopefully genuine – independent party provides a third-party claim. This includes such organisations as Fairtrade, which aims to ensure that farmers, especially small, poor farmers, receive sufficient income to ensure environmental sustainability and reasonable livelihoods. Other organisations with similar objectives include:

- Food Alliance (http://foodalliance.org), which launched its certification programme in 1998 with a single apple grower selling in three Portland grocery stores. By 2018, FA had certified over 500 farms and ranches in Canada, Mexico and 25 US states that manage a total of over 6.8 million acres of range and farmland. The majority are mid-sized or smaller family-owned and operated businesses. FA has also certified dozens of food processing and distribution facilities.

- Marine Stewardship Council (www.msc.org), which certifies seafood and fish products.

- Rainforest Alliance (www.rainforest-alliance.org/).

- Ecolabel Index (www.ecolabelindex.com), which claims to be the largest global directory of ecolabels, in 2018 tracking hundreds of ecolabels in almost every country, across more than two dozen industry sectors.

- The EU has a wide range of different certification programmes (EU, 2018). Canada has had its own programme since 2009, Japan since 2000. The problem perhaps is that there are so many competing standards that a single optimal route forward is hard to identify.

- Finally, and perhaps most importantly, the Global GAP (Good Agricultural Practice) standards (www.globalgap.org), which sets out to be the internationally recognised standard for farm production. It states that: 'Our core product is the result of years of intensive research and collaboration with industry experts, producers and retailers around the globe. Our goal is safe and sustainable agricultural production to benefit farmers, retailers and consumers throughout the world.

- Global GAP certification covers:

  o Food safety and traceability;
  o Environment (including biodiversity);
  o Workers' health, safety and welfare;
  o Animal welfare; and
  o Includes integrated crop management (ICM), integrated pest control (IPC), quality management system (QMS) and hazard analysis and critical control points (HACCP)' (Global GAP, 2018).

There may also be some false starts and dead-ends. For example, food has also been certified for its CO_2 emissions, notably in Sweden, where the Nutrition Department of the Swedish National Food Administration implemented a carbon footprint labelling programme, which was copied by several Swedish companies. However, the process has only proceeded in fits and starts, even in an advanced market like the UK, where Tesco has dropped carbon labelling at least for the time being, or New Zealand (Guenther et al., 2012), and it has not become universal practice, possibly because research is continuing and there is no agreement on which inputs to include and which not; there are also variations between seasons and across locations, and debate over whether to include specific products only or average scores. Finally, there is a tension between which is more important to label – health impacts on human beings, or overall environmental impact. In sum, progress, but no uniformity. Quite conceivably, the blockchain will make the entire process much easier (Hammerich, 2018).

Finally, in this context, the importance of branding throughout the value chain – but especially at the retail level – should be re-emphasised (Spinelli et al., 2015). Nowhere is easy to create brand differentiation; facing own-brand competition enhances the challenge. In the UK, Retail Economics reported that 48% of 2,000 consumers questioned said they would switch to cheaper own-label alternatives if prices rose by an average 3% (Retail Economics,

2017). Branding can work *against* as well as in favour of eco-labelling and helps offset the costs and slender margins of food processing.

Logistics, transport and machinery

Does how meat, fruit and vegetables are stored and packaged matter for value creation? Yes. As must be evident having read so far, nothing is 'in common' across the range of agri-business products. For example, crops such as dried grains and beans can be stored well if correct temperatures are maintained, sometimes for years. Once dried, only minimal energy is required to store, which makes grains and beans suitable for large-scale, commingled storage. In Africa, the major food crops such as cereal grains and tubers, including pota-toes, are normally seasonal crops, so the food produced in one harvest period, which may last for only a few weeks, must be stored to be consumed until the next harvest, and seed must be held for the next season's crop. In addition, in a market that is not controlled, the value of any surplus crop tends to rise during the off-season period, provided that it is in a marketable condition. So the main objective of storage is to maintain the crop in prime condition for as long as possible. The storage and handling methods should minimise losses, and also be appropriate in relation to other factors, such as economies of scale, labour cost and availability, building costs and machinery cost (Hodges & Stathers, 2012). Training of farmers (producers), such as the 18,000 rice farmers to be trained in the Iringa Region of Tanzania in a project funded by the EU, aims to reduce losses due to harvest and tem-porary storage by strengthening the market linkages between value chain actors, including private and public-sector buyers through inclusive business models, linkage to structured markets, improving organisational management capacities, upgrading post-harvest facilities and coordination (EU, 2018a). The list of goals is now very predictable – what remains is the question of how, without substantial consolidation of agriculture, it is feasible to achieve them.

The FAO has rightly exhibited a decades-long concern with the issue of post-harvest losses (Gustavsson *et al.*, 2011). Although statistical evidence from the FAO varies widely, a general estimate appears to be that, worldwide, food losses and waste account for more than 30% of food intended for humans (FAO, 2018). Food losses and waste are arguably the biggest avoidable cause of death on the planet, and are undeniably a major squandering of resources, including water, land, energy, labour and capital, besides the unnecessary produc-tion of greenhouse gas emissions, contributing to global warming and climate change. Losses amount to roughly $680 billion in industrialised countries and $310 billion in developing countries. Industrialised and developing countries dissipate roughly the same quantities of food — respectively 670 million and 630 million tonnes – because consumer waste occurs at a much higher level in the former. In developing countries 40% of losses occur at post-harvest and processing levels, which translate into lost income for small farmers and into higher prices for poor consumers. The explanations lie mainly in financial, managerial and technical constraints in harvesting techniques, as well as the continued lack of storage and cooling facilities. Even in countries such as Brazil, where agribusiness has developed rapidly and very successfully, for the important crop of soybeans:

Improvements in transportation should accompany the expansion of farm areas originating a new, larger spatial arrangement for the production sectors. The transportation sector thus constitutes a logistical bottleneck. Harnessing the potential of grain production, however, will be possible only through an efficient road system, integrated intermodal transport corridors, and addressing the storage deficit, especially for the segregated cargo (Oliveira & Alvim, 2017:49).

Strengthening the supply chain through the direct support of farmers and investments in infrastructure, transportation, as well as in an expansion of the food and packaging industry, could also help to reduce the amount of food loss and waste. What, on the other hand, commercialised agribusiness cannot prevent, and indeed arguably encourages, is the fact that in industrialised countries more than 40% of losses happen at retail and consumer levels. This despite the fact that logistical services for perishables are increasingly outsourced to specialists, temperature-controlled logistics operators (TCLO) (González-Moralejo *et al.*, 2015). The term 'cold chain' is beginning to give way to 'temperature-controlled logistics', as requirements for exact temperatures become increasing exacting. Outsourcing haulage and storage (basic logistical services) should ensure that products are handled appropriately and delivered on time. This is because the behaviour of consumers plays a huge part in industrialised countries. At retail level, large quantities of food are wasted due to quality standards and buyer preferences that overemphasise appearance. Perhaps raising awareness among industries, retailers and consumers, as well as finding beneficial use for food that is currently thrown away, can play a role in decreasing the amount of losses and waste (FAO, 2018). Although given that preferences are extremely unlikely to be altered, closer alignment of production to standards, better, targeted marketing and, above all, rigorous regulation – transparent waste bins may be a good start – are probably a better bet to reduce this; so is further investment in just-in-time supply chains.

Total per capita food production for human consumption is about 900 kg a year in rich countries, almost twice the 460 kg a year produced in the poorest regions: per capita waste by consumers is between 95–115 kg per year in Europe and North America, while in sub-Saharan Africa and South/South-East Asia, the 'throw away' represents 6–11 kg per capita per year. Fruit and vegetables, plus roots and tubers, have the highest wastage rates of any food: global quantitative food losses and waste per year are roughly 30% for cereals, 40–50% for root crops, fruits and vegetables, 20% for oil seeds, meat and dairy, plus 35% for fish.

The techniques of storage and packaging used in developed countries are key not only to reducing waste, but to the improvements throughout the supply chain that will improve the quality competitiveness of agribusiness in developing countries. In developed countries, fruit and vegetables are often put into large bins and transported swiftly to pack-houses, which are either cooperatives or commercially owned. Different fruits require individual processes, such as waxing for apples, pears and many other fruits and vegetables (although this is being phased out), trimming for broccoli, spring onions and other greens, or spraying, either to postpone germination, as for potatoes, or ethylene to speed up ripening, as for mangoes or tomatoes. They are then transported to distribution warehouses, and finally shipment to retailers. Every individual fruit and vegetable has its own ripening, and therefore transport,

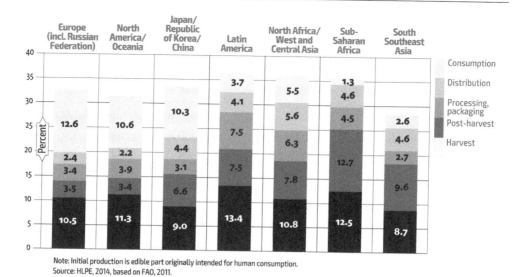

Note: Initial production is edible part originally intended for human consumption.
Source: HLPE, 2014, based on FAO, 2011.

Figure 6.6 Comparative analysis of losses along the food supply chain: regional comparison
Source: FAO (2017:114)

requirements. That for bananas is amongst the most stringent, which makes the subsequent waste at consumer level all the more regrettable.

After nine months, the bananas are harvested while still green. At the packhouse they are inspected and sorted for export. Buyers of fruit in the UK want unbruised bananas and so very high standards are set. If the bananas do not meet these standards they are usually sold locally at a much lower price. The fruit is then transported to ports to be packed in refrigerated ships called reefers (bananas take between six and twelve days to get to the UK/Europe). In order to increase shelf life, they are transported at a temperature of 13.3°C, and require careful handling in order to prevent damage. Humidity, ventilation and temperature conditions are also carefully monitored in order to maintain quality. When the bananas arrive at their destination port they are first sent to ripening rooms (a process involving ethylene gas) and then sent to the shops. Dessert banana production for export (around 15 million tonnes per year) is of huge economic importance for many countries in the Global South. However, it also causes huge environmental issues. For example, banana production relies on intensive monocultures, which are sustained by using massive quantities of toxic chemicals, which are hazardous to both workers and the environment. The use of unsafe chemicals like pesticide can pose serious health problems for workers. In 2011, workers in Latin America won a lawsuit against large corporations who used Nemogon in plantations despite the fact the chemical was banned in 1977. Industrial-scale production also results in problematic waste management issues. Research led by CIRAD (International Agricultural Research for Development Centre) found that significant agrochemical reduction can be achieved while maintaining good levels of productivity and quality (Banana Link, 2018).

What this description does not emphasise is the necessary and extensive capex that the simple phrase 'careful handling' conceals (Catalytic Generators, 2018). Ripening chambers are, however, becoming usual, even in developing countries, as the industry exhibits greater concentration.

Likewise, packaging materials are vital – packing works to slow deterioration of the product, and works with temperature control to extend product life as well as provide protection during transit and deploy the right quantity for sale. The choice between cans, glass jars, foil, cardboard, foam, plastic, mesh, and pallets is dictated by the product, its market and practicality. Some products for example demand waxed boxes, although they are hard to recycle, so recyclable packaging is growing in use, notably RPCs (reusable plastic containers, or 'totes'). PCR (post consumer regrind), PET (polyethylene terephthalate) products are now in use for food packaging, but there are continued challenges, both technical and economic, as explained in articles in the *Packaging Digest* (www.packagingdigest.com) and numerous academic articles and books (e.g. Jung, 2014; Robertson, 2016).

As for meat, the change from a traditional butcher cutting and wrapping the meat in whatever materials are available, perhaps paper or waxed paper, for direct sale to the purchaser to in-store cutting and packaging of meat for refrigerated self-service display cases in developed countries required more advanced forms of meat packaging. Plastics and other polymer forms of materials were used to improve shelf-life, make the meat appear more palatable ('redder') and generate a sense of reassurance about quality. Advances continued in traditional, vacuum (VP) and modified atmosphere (MAP). More recently, active packaging systems that influence the internal environment of packaged products, including oxygen scavengers, antimicrobial agents and bio-based materials, have been introduced, along with intelligent systems that utilise sensors to relay needed changes or communications. It is fair to say, though, that cost and convenience considerations will continue to necessitate improvements in packaging materials, equipment, accessories and systems (McMillin & Belcher, 2012). All this is a far cry from a farmers' market, of the type that still serves consumers directly in some developing countries, but its efficiency – and on the whole reliable delivery of bacteria-free meat – is compelling evidence for its steady encroachment into traditional open sales of meat everywhere in developed countries, albeit that there is still push-back, especially in Asia.

Frozen food packaging has separate demands, and includes the use of aluminium, plastic and paper. Recent techniques enable packages to be put into conventional as well as microwave ovens as dual-ovenable and, as an all-in-one solution, this responds to growing calls for suppliers to create solutions which reduce unnecessary packaging, minimising the use of plastic, helping retailers and food service operators meet sustainable objectives. UK consumers spend £3 billion every year, and rising, on dishes which can be warmed through and served in minutes, and they are increasingly demanding ready meal products which contain fresh, quality ingredients. Consequently, as a number of new premium brands have entered the market, demands on packaging have increased. The packaging solution of ready meals today needs to be sustainable, dual-ovenable, with the ability to customise branding to depict the freshness of the meal within. Answering these increasingly complex packaging requirements, were packaging manufacturers such as Colpac, which in 2018 launched their Cookpac® range. They claimed it was:

…a unique, paperboard solution which can be taken from the fridge or freezer and put straight into the oven or microwave, and features several integral design elements to overcome issues relating to traditional ready meal packaging. For ease of handling during oven or microwave cooking, Cookpac® has integrated heat resistant handles to ensure it is easy to take out of the oven, it features a self-ventilating film which releases slightly during the heating process to enable consumers to open the pack easily. In addition, the shape of Cookpac® will not alter during heating, which frequently occurs with plastic trays, a concern which is particularly important to the elderly market (Packaging Europe, 2018).

And some comparison with the USA, where:

Green Giant Veggie Spirals from B&G Foods, Inc., Parsippany, NJ, takes a big stride in packaged convenience…the Spirals are packed in a first-of-a-kind microwavable PrimaPak…The versatile PrimaPak technology, produced by a joint venture that included Sonoco Flexible Packaging, is a kind of all-in-one, semi-rigid rectangular packaging that acts as a bowl while replacing a bag and or a carton traditionally used for microwavable packaging found across different products and categories in the frozen foods aisle. It is a convenient-for-consumers heat-and-serve format that does not require additional dishes and is resealable. The PrimaPak is produced on modified form/fill/seal machinery (Lingle, 2017).

Competition between different packaging techniques, and brands, is both intense and likely to increase. It is an increasingly important part of the supply chain and there are plenty of further development opportunities, for example in increasing product longevity.

Freezing, chilling especially, and meal manufacturing are gaining in importance, everywhere, and as the generations change this changeover can only consolidate its significance. This is a horizontal shift in the supply and value chain, rather than a vertical one caused by, for example, M&A (mergers and acquisitions). But canning, though declining in importance, is still a significant part of food manufacturing. Although canning is still commonly used for seasonal fruits and vegetables, fish and meat, noodles, complete meals and pet food, it is now recognised that canned foods have certain health risks. The heating process used in canning destroys many antioxidants and certain vitamins like vitamin C and folic acid present in food. Many canned foods have large amounts of sugar and salt, which are used as preservatives; these foods have a high amount of sodium compared to fresh food. Then there is packaging. Bisphenol A or BPA, is a chemical used to make plastics including materials that come into contact with food such as refillable drinks bottles and food storage containers. It is also used to make protective coatings and linings for food and drinks cans. Cans often have a high amount of BPA present in them. The excessive consumption of this chemical has been linked to infertility and heart disease (FSA, 2018). Many brands of canned food products, such as Campbell's, Del Monte and Heinz, have started offering products in BPA-free containers. As to storage, the main advantage of canning, cans can last on the shelf for at least a year, as commercial canning is done under tightly controlled conditions – careful sanitation and the necessary time and temperature under pressure – but there are still limits to how long regulations allow that the process will preserve food, due to rust, the way that natural chemicals in the food eventually react with the can, and the impact of high temperatures on the contents.

The role of cooperatives and intermediaries

Agricultural cooperatives are member-owned, democratically controlled businesses from which the benefits are received in proportion to use. Local farmers who join buy and sell products through the cooperative which becomes a distributor (Barnard *et al.*, 2016:32). Cooperatives in the USA, perhaps surprisingly, are responsible for marketing over a quarter of all agricultural produce. In the US South, for example, rice producers participate in cooperatives. In Africa, agricultural cooperatives focus on agricultural inputs and joint production, as well as marketing. Input supply includes the distribution of seeds and fertilisers to farmers. Cooperatives in joint agricultural production assume that members operate the cooperative on jointly-owned land plots. The third category consists of joint agricultural marketing of producer crops, where farmers pool resources for the transformation, packaging, distribution and marketing of agricultural commodities. However, the most popular use has been for marketing (Sifa, 2014).

There are also for-profit businesses operating at a local level that use economies of scale in purchasing to provide a multitude of services for local agribusiness. In Australia a prime example is Elders (www.elders.com.au), which works across multiple product lines – rural services, financial planning, real estate and insurance. This from a company that proclaims its intention to be Australia's leading agribusiness. The scale of commercial agribusiness and its value-maximising objectives, together with intense use of machinery and fertiliser, has certainly provided plenty of opportunity for firms like Elders.

Variability in prices can have a significant impact on supply chains for a wide variety of commodities. Supply chain managers in developed countries therefore often devote significant resources to forecasting input and output prices and potential sales. This is an approach that remains almost entirely elusive in developing countries: the food grain marketing chains in developing countries tend to be long and complex because of the involvement of many small-scale intermediaries.

There is a widely held belief that the domestic rice market in Bangladesh can be manipulated by private traders operating at wholesale and retail levels leading to increased and unstable rice prices. Such manipulation would have serious economic consequences for poor Bangladeshi households who are net buyers of rice, which accounts for approximately 40–50% of their total annual expenditures. Given this potential impact, government policymakers should be interested in evidence pointing towards the possible existence and sources of price manipulation (Alam *et al.*, 2016:498).

Explanations for the level of vertical integration between sectors

A good starting point is the difference in scale between small and large producers, which, for example in the dairy industry, have different supply chains, and different operational models exist for dairy product manufacturing. Each has its own ownership structure, input sourcing, processing, marketing and distribution practices. Farmsteads, for example, do everything, but they are declining in importance. Contract farmers (see Chapter 8), by contrast, sell raw milk to dairy plants that do all the further processing: pasteurisation, homogenisation, separation (cream, low-fat and non-fat milk), and the manufacture of cheese, ice-cream and yoghurt. The facility itself may be owned by producers, or it may be independent. It has even been suggested that the comparative advantage to be gained by adopting a different supply system and government regulation of it can significantly affect international competitiveness, even between developed countries such as the USA and Canada (McGraw, 2014).

Dairy Farmers of America (DFA)

Through our commercial investments division, DFA is a leading manufacturer of cheese and butter, as well as dairy ingredients, and contract manufacturer for consumer products. Our commercial investments include DFA's Consumer Retail, Ingredients and Beverage and Dairy Foods and Fluid Milk and Ice Cream businesses. This group increases returns for our members through:

- Consumer retail, including Borden® Cheese and Keller's® Creamery
- Dairy foods processing plants that produce American and Italian Cheeses and a wide range of dairy ingredients
- Investments and joint ventures with national companies
- Supply agreements with national and global customers

DFA has an expansive manufacturing footprint and owns 42 plants throughout the country. In addition to our own plants, our members' milk gets delivered to various customers and joint venture partners like Hiland Dairy and Dean Foods.

Source: Dairy Farmers of America (2018)

Pork, apart from fresh meat consumption, has for centuries been preserved (salted) for use as winter food – cured hams, bacon and sausage. But pork's association with diseases such as trichinosis and the power of the US beef industry led to its supersession there. Only in China has pork retained a tenacious grip on the food supply chain. The hog industry in the 21st century has now become highly industrialised, with four distinct elements: the sowing, farrowing, nursing and feedlots of production agriculture, processors, distribution and then further processing – pigs generally after slaughter are divided into final cuts (chops, ribs) or then smoked/cured.

The supply chain for poultry has now divided with – apart from the production specialisms mentioned in Chapter 5 – facilities for egg collection, grading and packing, and separate facilities for slaughtering and processing broilers. Eggs and poultry in developed countries are now arguably the most intensively produced and industrialised of all the animal supply chains: highly controlled environments, huge flocks and few production facilities, all driven by consumer demand for inexpensive, yet high quality and completely uniform products. After collection, eggs are washed, graded and then packed, either at source or by egg marketing companies, to be distributed to retailers the same day as laid. The supply chain for broilers is as a result highly vertically integrated, with most parts owned by subsidiaries of the main broiler company. On receipt of full-sized chickens, they are slaughtered and then, possibly, additionally processed into specific cuts, elements of ready-meals and pet food. The meat is then distributed to wholesalers, retailers or other customer-serving parts of the supply chain. The vertical integration extends to feed mills and veterinary services. Agribusiness companies now exist to provide optimum breeding animals (Hubbard Breeders, 2018).

These specifics are important, but in general analysts envisage there are three basic distribution network designs:

- Line network, where each distributor has its own transport network to outlets.

- Hub and spoke network, where each distributor delivers the goods to a central hub where goods are exchanged aiming for specific network destinations.

- Collection and distribution network, especially suited for international networks, where each distributor delivers the goods to a central collection hub; goods are consolidated in time, regional destination, and product type; and successively transported to a distribution hub, where goods are re-sorted (added with products from other sources) and distributed to specific locations.

Inventory management is one of the design variables in the distribution network. In Figure 6.7 (a) a number of inventory points are presented; however, these could just as well be cross-dock facilities where consolidation activities are performed and no inventory is kept. A hub may perform a consolidation or concentration function to combine many small separate flows into larger flows or split a larger flow into separate smaller flows for different destinations. Thus, hubs are intermediate points along the paths followed by origin-destination flows. It is clear that the network complexity greatly influences the opportunities for improved logistics network designs and roles of logistics.

So much for the theory, which may apply at least in part to developed country supply chains, e.g. ornamental flowers in the Netherlands, or bananas in the UK. In the global fruit and vegetable industry, many companies are vertically integrated throughout the supply chain, especially where there are crucial timings to be observed as well as meticulous temperatures and humidity conditions to be maintained throughout the supply chain, as is notably the case with bananas.

In developing countries, even the diagrams are more straightforward.

Hence in Kazakhstan, the aim is to move from that shown in Figure 6.8 (a) to (b).

Is not the difference quite striking?

A prominent alternative to vertical integration is the development of strategic alliances. These can be in joint R&D programmes, along the supply chain, or economies of scale in production or marketing. Deploying internationally is a good example, for instance for the financing of local agribusinesses.

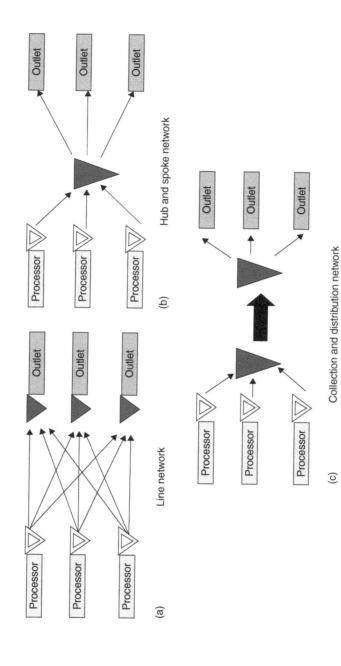

Figure 6.7 Types of distribution network design
Source: Vorst et al. (2007:4)

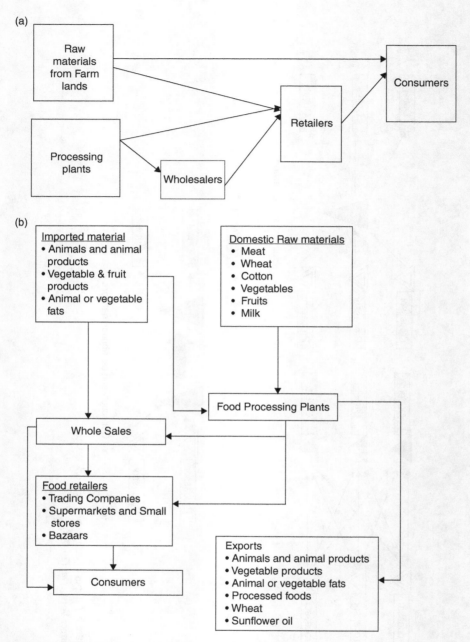

Figure 6.8 Distribution networks in developing countries
Source: Rana (2014)

An example of a strategic alliance: SGS and Kezzler AS

This May 2017 agreement is intended to co-market and execute serialization and tracking and tracing services for global SGS customers in the areas of fast moving consumer goods, food & food safety and pharmaceuticals, as well as tobacco products, alcohol and other beverages.

The technology now exists to give billions of products its own unique digital DNA – a window into information down to the pack/unit level as required by legislative requirements. Assigning a completely unique identity enables brand owners to improve their operations, thus saving costs. For instance, track and trace technology can be used to identify hold ups and inefficiencies in the supply chain by recording the time products spend in warehouse and transit. While unique product identities would best position manufacturers to identify and pre-empt any potential issues such as highly targeted product recalls, including alerting individual consumers that scan the product code using their cell phone. In parallel and for the reasons of fighting illegal trade, public authorities will be able to monitor, record the movement of products through supply chains from manufacturers, through logistics to the end consumers. Subsequently they will be able to trace products back to identify the point of diversion of these into illegal supply chain. Deploying a technology that is multi-functional in nature and that delivers value across several business functions not only facilitates track and trace and brand protection functions, but also enables companies to connect with consumers, exchange information and fulfil research and marketing functions in real time.

Source: SGS (2017)

Transport of agricultural commodities

Land transport is a major feature of the agricultural distribution system, most notably for grains but also livestock. Typically, it involves two components. The first is from farm to the country receival point, and the second from the receival point to the export terminal. There are some exceptions where, for example, some deliveries are made direct from farm to domestic customers, grain merchants or to receival facilities at terminal ports. The transport stage from farm to country receival point has traditionally been undertaken by growers, using their own vehicles, or leased. Grain transport logistics are sometimes coordinated on behalf of the marketing companies by bulk handling companies (BHCs), since they usually have responsibility for handling the grain at both ends of the transport chain. The transport companies, therefore, maintain close operational liaison with the BHCs who in turn must be constantly aware of marketing companies' requirements. The distance travelled depends on the distribution of the local receival points, with the national average being about 17 km in Australia, for example, which is surprisingly short.

Rail transport. Transport from country receival point to terminal port is the more substantial component of the land transport task and, for the most part, this is done by rail. Historically, the expansion of the grain industry has been tied to extension of the rail system, paving the way for subsequent social and economic growth. This has impacted directly on the development of storage and handling infrastructure.

Despite Australia's well-integrated supply chain, concern remains on the significant cost associated with storing and transporting grain from farm paddock to consumer plate. This is compounded through infrastructure that supports a limited 4 month marketing window. Circumventing this requires policy reform and congruent investment decisions by government, industry participants and investors (ANZ, 2016:13).

The average length of haul from receival point to export terminal is about 350 km, but this varies considerably between the states. South Australia, for example, has a comparatively long coastline but it is relatively close to the main grain production areas and has more terminals than other states. As a consequence, average haulage distances are lower (around 160 km) and a greater proportion of growers deliver direct to the terminals. In New South Wales, on the other hand, the average rail haulage distance from receival point to terminal is about 500 km and there is higher use of leased vehicles and haulage companies, as is common in the USA and other developed countries.

Road transport. Over 95% of fresh produce in the USA is moved by truck, and only small amounts are transported by rail, using refrigerated railcars or piggyback trailers. Road is becoming increasingly competitive for the movement of grain, and the probable arrival within the decade of convoys of semi self-driving trucks will only increase the competitive advantage of road transport, both in the EU and the USA. Differences, however, still exist within countries. For example, in South Australia and Western Australia, road transport captures a much larger share. In South Australia, grain terminal ports are much closer to the grain producing areas than in other states, making direct road transport from the farm to port cheaper and more efficient. In Western Australia many country grain receival sites are not serviced by the rail network, due to political arguments about alleged subsidies to rail, making road transport the only alternative.

Sea transport. Internationally, most food is moved by sea – cheap, but slow. Air transport is still only usually used for high-value or extremely perishable products, like exotic fruits – in the UK, mangoes, avocados or pineapples count as exotic, as they cannot be grown domestically – flowers, some seafood such as lobster, or air-flown pork from Australia in Singapore. The shipping industry is changing: over the past few decades, there has been a switch from conventional, direct call reefer ships towards further containerisation, resulting in a shrinking specialised reefer fleet. In 2016 the maritime research consultancy Drewry estimated the perishable reefer cargo split was already 79% in reefer containerships and 21% in specialised reefers.

The percentage of transport cost to exported good prices varies from one country to another. Studies indicate that this ratio is no less than 8% of the goods value and sometimes goes up to more than 20% in some countries. According to a study submitted to the Organisation for Economic Cooperation and Development (OECD) about the impact of maritime costs on agricultural exports, more than 90% of goods exchange between countries is done by sea, although there are exceptions such as Palestine, from which most agricultural exports are made by land and then by air transport. That said, the cost of land transport is higher than the cost of shipping. The study shows that land transport cost of grain imports in some countries is rated between 20–30% of the total value, whereas maritime costs reach 10.5% from the total value in 2007. Generally, the percentage varies according to maritime links between countries, e.g. agriculture import cost for OECD is around 9%, while in developing countries it is around 13% of the goods. Rising freight rates and the increasing likelihood of an occurrence of the La Niña weather phenomenon were among the risks that farmers, investors and commodities traders faced in 2018, according to Rabobank (2017).

Barges are an important part of agricultural transport in the USA, Asia and Europe, though not significantly used in developing countries for the usual reason, lack of reliable infrastructure. The US grain handling report for winter 2017 reported as follows:

> The cost of shipping grain to end users is falling as 2017 winds down. While that has positive benefits for growers selling crops, it's also a case of beware what you wish for. Record 2016 corn production increased rail freight last year, and problems this fall on parts of the river system caused barge freight to spike near record highs. The 2017 corn crop is smaller and traffic is moving again along the Ohio River. Water levels remain low on the lower Mississippi River but the end to the shipping season on northern stretches makes more barges available. Freight costs are falling as a result. But part of the reason for lower costs is due to export demand. It's down overall for corn, soybeans and wheat, causing supplies to back up. That contributed to fairly strong deliveries against corn and wheat futures before December went off the board Dec. 14. Corn basis along the Illinois River, where deliveries focus, weakened last week, with bids also weak along the lower Mississippi River and Ohio River. Average terminal basis dropped around a penny as a result, with the picture mixed elsewhere. Strong ethanol production helped plants boost bids up to six cents, with those costs offset in flat prices as futures made new contract lows. But cash prices at rail terminals weakened across the central and southern Plains, with cattle feeding areas also seeing a reduction. Transportation costs don't look like they'll get much cheaper into spring, which means basis gains may have to come from futures. Carry is running around 4 cents a month, good enough to provide a return for hedgers with on-farm storage. Coupled with tight farmer holding, basis should continue to post modest appreciation though staying below average most places (Farm Progress, 2017).

The Baltic Dry index – an indicator of global bulk commodity freight costs – has increased as much as 66% in 2017 as the availability of new bulk freight supplies has slowed. Bulk freight rates have been trending higher since early 2016, after declining after the 2008 financial crisis, which coincided with the increased delivery of dry bulk vessels.

It is not surprising, therefore, that all participants in the grain trade exhibit not only a concern for logistics and transport means and costs, but are also keenly aware of the transport policies and implications for pricing of their competitors. In 2015, for example, Canadian comparative analysis of the grain supply chain with Australia was picked up the following year by ANZ (see Figure 6.10).

More recently, governments and donors, realising that upgrading the performance of individual firms may have little impact, have shown significant interest in value chain analysis and implementation. In their effort to devise interventions that reposition entire industries,

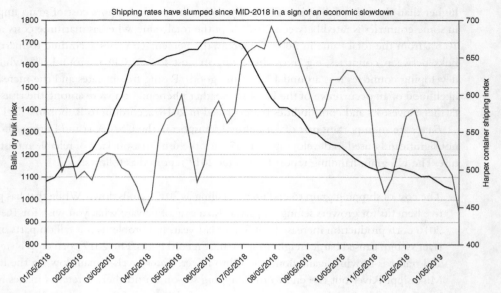

Figure 6.9 Freight rates over time
Source: Gloystein (2019)

Australia vs Canada – Bulk Grain Supply Chain Comparison

	HARVEST	ON-FARM STORAGE	INLAND ELEVATOR	>95% RAIL	PORT TERMINAL	SHIP
CANADA	17.7мт	Capacity to store 73mt – 90-120% of an average harvest	392 primary elevators with a total storage capacity of 6.8mt	Two national rail companies, one rail gauge, 5600km of grain-only track, commonly 110 wagon trains carry 11,000mt	15 bulk terminals at four ports	1500+ ocean vessels and 37mt exported
	30,000 grain producers producing 73mt					
		60-80km Road Transport			37mt Exported	

	HARVEST	ON-FARM STORAGE	RECEIVAL SITE	50% / 50% RAIL & ROAD	PORT TERMINAL	SHIP
AUSTRALIA	44мт	Capacity to store 15mt –20-80% of an average harvest	550 primary elevators with a total storage capacity of 55mt	Eight rail companies operating regionally, three rail gauges, 5400km grain-only track, commonly 60 wagon trains carrying 4500mt	20 bulk terminals at 18 ports	1100+ ocean vessels and 28mt exported
	22,000 grain producers producing 44mt					
		20–30km Road Transport			28mt Exported	

Source: AEGIC The puck stops here – Canada challenges Australia's grain supply chains. May 2015

Figure 6.10 Bulk grain supply comparison
Source: ANZ (2016:14)

build business competitiveness and spur economic growth, governments and donors can use value chain-based approaches as robust tools to protect threatened links, facilitate upgrading of others to generate greater returns, and to promote foreign direct investment (FDI) programmes. Additionally, value chain analysis has been used to examine constraints in the enabling environment in which the chains operate.

Financial criteria

The kind of value chain analysis initially described in this chapter and illustrated with examples from agribusiness has rarely placed sufficient stress on the financial aspects of value addition. A focus on costs, in particular, is rarely likely to generate an adequate investor perspective. Rather, it is necessary at the very least to incorporate traditional accounting information such as return on equity, earnings per share, net operating profit after taxes (NOPAT) and return on investment, all of which are used across industries as common measures or proxies for value. Even these measures may not be sufficient, however, and have been criticised from two flanks. From the right flank comes the criticism that, although widely used, these measures fail both to capture a firm's value creation that results from management actions, and to account for the full cost of capital (Sharma & Kumar, 2010; Cucagna & Goldsmith, 2018). The better alternative, they argue, is to use a harsh criterion based on economic profit, return on capital above the opportunity cost of capital employed. However, there are problems with a formula such as EVA®, which has now been largely abandoned even by consultancy firm Stern Stewart, its originators. It itself may be short-term, and therefore entirely inappropriate to be used for agribusinesses like timber which require long-term investment. It may also bias investment in the direction of 'capital-light' activities such as consultancy at the expense of infrastructure or manufacturing, which may conceivably delight shareholders but will not win favour with government or international agencies. This leads to the criticism of accounting measures from the left flank, such as within the FAO and even the World Bank, where public capital is viewed as a way of transcending the short time horizons that DCF imposes and expanding the opportunities presented by value chains to generate growth employment (the multiplier) and other externalities, as well as to contribute to the welfare of consumers both locally and worldwide.

Conclusion

Studies have consistently found that market power, quality, risk, contracts, technical change, transport and transaction costs, public interventions, perishability of the product and time lags in supply and demand have all affected marketing margins and price transmission along agri-food chains (Morales, 2017:336). The obvious nature of these conclusions demonstrates that whilst value chain analysis is extremely useful, its weaknesses highlight the fact that many other important considerations are necessary to increase value for the entire chain or some of its participants.

Beyond the value chain itself, it is important to understand market dynamics, competitive forces, market concentration and the operational, investment, technological and regulatory landscape, all of which are in permanent flux. Overall, there is a need to focus on fundamentals. Every market segment has key elements and drivers that are important for competing successfully. Policymakers and investors alike now generally agree that investment to build competitiveness should not attempt to make quick, comprehensive improvements throughout a value chain. Rather, investment that aims to build competitiveness should target particular priority parts of the supply chain for improvement. No surprise, therefore, that for success it is crucial to identify success factors and driving forces in the target markets in question and, whilst taking local conditions into consideration, subsequently benchmark these elements against top performers and competitors.

Bibliography

ADHB Beef & Cattle (2016) Feeding growing and finishing cattle for Better Returns. Beef BRP Manual 7. Available at: http://beefandlamb.ahdb.org.uk/wp/wp-content/uploads/2016/12/BRP-Feeding-growing-and-finishing-manual-7-091216.pdf. Retrieved 20 July 2018.

Alam, M.J., McKenzie, A., Begum, I.A., Buysse, J., Wailes, E.J. and Van Huylenbroeck, G. (2016) Asymmetry price transmission in the deregulated rice markets in Bangladesh: Asymmetric error correction model. *Agribusiness* 32(4), 498–511.

ANZ (2016) *Infocus March 2016 The Grains Muster.* Canberra, ANZ. Available at: http://phx.corporate-ir.net/External.File?item=UGFyZW50SUQ9MzI2MTE2fENoaWxkSUQ9LTF8VHlwZT0z&t=1&cb=635924749635933316. Retrieved 24 February 2019.

Banana Link (2018) How Bananas are Grown. Available at: www.bananalink.org.uk/how-bananas-are-grown. Retrieved 11 June 2018.

Barnard, F.L., Akridge, J.T., Dooley, F.J. and Yeager, E.A. (2016) *Agribusiness Management*, 5th edition. New York, Routledge.

BC Cook Articulation Committee (2012) Milling of wheat. *BC Cook Articulation Committee Understanding Ingredients for the Canadian Baker.* Available at: https://opentextbc.ca/ingredients/#milling-of-wheat. Retrieved 16 May 2019.

British Poultry Council (2018) Tag: Chlorinated Chicken. Available at: www.britishpoultry.org.uk/tag/chlorinated-chicken/. Retrieved 21 July 2018.

Bryceson, K. and Slaughter, G. (2010) Alignment of performance metrics in a multi-enterprise agribusiness. Achieving integrated autonomy? *International Journal of Productivity and Performance Management* 59(4), 325–350. Available at: https://core.ac.uk/download/pdf/11038681.pdf. Retrieved 11 June 2018.

Catalytic Generators (2018) Bananas. Available at: www.catalyticgenerators.com/ripening_tips/banana/. Retrieved 11 June 2018.

Chemat, F., Bombaut, N., Meullemiestre, A., Turk, M., Perino, S., Fabiano-Tixier, A. and Abert-Vian, M. (2017) Review of green food processing techniques. Preservation, transformation, and extraction. *Innovative Food Science and Emerging Technologies* 41, 357–377.

Comer, P.J. and Huntly, P.J. (2003) TSE risk assessments: A decision support tool. *Statistical Methods in Medical Research* 12(3), 279–291.

Corn Refiners Association (2018) The Kernel of Innovation. Available at: https://corn.org/kernel-of-innovation/. Retrieved 11 June 2018.

Cotula, L. and Blackmore, E. (2014) *Understanding Agricultural Investment Chains: Lessons to Improve Governance.* London, IIED and FAO. Available at: http://pubs.iied.org/pdfs/12574IIED.pdf. Retrieved 4 September 2017.

Cox, A., Ireland, P., Lonsdale, C., Sanderson, J. and Watson, G. (2002). *Supply Chains, Markets and Power: Mapping Buyer and Supplier Power Regimes*. London, Routledge.

Cucagna, M.E. and Goldsmith, P.D. (2018) Value adding in the agri-food value chain. *International Food and Agribusiness Management Review* 21(3), 293–316.

Dairy Farmers of America (2018) Products. Available at: www.dfamilk.com/products. Retrieved 25 June 2018.

Deloitte (2015) *The Food Value Chain – A Challenge for the Next Century*. London, Deloitte. Available at: www2.deloitte.com/content/dam/Deloitte/ie/Documents/ConsumerBusiness/2015-Deloitte-Ireland-Food_Value_Chain.pdf. Retrieved 22 April 2018.

Ding, M., Pan, J., Manson, A.E., Willett, W.C., Malik, V., Rosner, B., Giovannucci, E., Hu, F.B. and Sun, Q. (2016) Consumption of soy foods and isoflavones and risk of type 2 diabetes: a pooled analysis of three US cohorts. *European Journal of Clinical Nutrition* 70(12), 1381–1387.

El-Namrouty, K.A. (2017) Transportation cost of agricultural exports from Gaza Strip: An exploratory study. *International Journal of Economics, Finance and Management Sciences* 5(6), 276–283.

EU (2009) *Commission Adopts a Communication on a Better Functioning Food Supply Chain in Europe*. European Commission. Available at: http://ec.europa.eu/economy_finance/articles/structural_reforms/article16028_en.htm. Retrieved 11 June 2018.

EU (2017) The Food Supply Chain. Available at: https://ec.europa.eu/agriculture/sites/agriculture/files/statistics/facts-figures/food-chain.pdf. Retrieved 30 July 2018.

EU (2018) Other Ecolabels. Available at: http://ec.europa.eu/environment/ecolabel/other-ecolabels.html. Retrieved 11 June 2018.

EU (2018a) Over 10,000 rice farmers to be equipped with postharvest management skills. European Union/FAO. Available at: https://eeas.europa.eu/sites/eeas/files/press_release_-_fao_eu_rice_project.pdf. Retrieved 11 June 2018.

European Flour Millers Association (2018) Facts and Figures. Available at: www.flourmillers.eu/page/facts-figures-flour-milling-industry/. Retrieved 15 May 2019.

FAO (2013) *Value Chain Analysis for Policy Making. Methodological Guidelines and country cases for a Quantitative Approach*. Rome, FAO. Available at: www.fao.org/docs/up/easypol/935/value_chain_analysis_fao_vca_software_tool_methodological_guidelines_129en.pdf. Retrieved 11 June 2018.

FAO (2017) *The State of Food Insecurity and Nutrition in the World*. Rome, FAO. Available at: www.fao.org/3/a-I7695e.pdf. Retrieved 30 October 2017.

FAO (2018) Key facts on food loss and waste you should know! Available at: www.fao.org/save-food/resources/keyfindings/en/. Retrieved 11 June 2018.

Farm Progress (2017) Grain market week in review. 22 December. Available at: www.farmprogress.com/market-news/grain-market-week-review-dec-22-2017. Retrieved 15 May 2019.

FDA (2018) Food Irradiation: What You Need to Know. Available at: www.fda.gov/food/resourcesforyou/consumers/ucm261680.htm. Retrieved 27 June 2018.

Fortin, N.D. (2016) Credence claims and conditional labeling. In Fortin, N.D. *Food Regulation: Law, Science, Policy, and Practice,* 2nd edition. Hoboken, NJ, Wiley, 107–116.

FSA (2018) BPA in plastic. UK, Food Standards Agency. 12 January. Available at: www.food.gov.uk/safety-hygiene/bpa-in-plastic. Retrieved 12 June 2018.

Gereffi, G. and Fernandez-Stark, K. (2016) *Value Chain Analysis. A Primer*, 2nd edition. Available at: www.researchgate.net/profile/Gary_Gereffi/publication/305719326_Global_Value_Chain_Analysis_A_Primer_2nd_Edition/links/579b6f0708ae80bf6ea3408f/Global-Value-Chain-Analysis-A-Primer-2nd-Edition.pdf. Retrieved 27 July 2018.

Global GAP (2018) Cultivating the Future of the Planet. Available at: www.globalgap.org/uk_en/for-producers/globalg.a.p./. Retrieved 15 July 2018.

Gloystein, H. (2019) Global shipping rates slump in latest sign of economic slowdown. Reuters. 25 January. Available at: www.reuters.com/article/us-shipping-economy/global-shipping-rates-slump-in-latest-sign-of-economic-slowdown-idUSKCN1PJ0BQ. Retrieved 24 February 2019.

González-Moralejo, S.A, Muñoz, P.M. and Miquel, J.F.L. (2015) Firm size, contractual problems and organizational decision-making: Logistics for perishable goods. *International Food and Agribusiness Management Review* 18(4), 189–204.

Grand View Research (2018) *Cold Chain Market Size, Share & Trends Analysis Report By Packaging, By Equipment, By Type (Monitoring Components, Transportation, Storage), By Application, By Region, And Segment Forecasts, 2018–2025*. San Francisco, Grand View Research.

Guenther, M., Saunders, C.M. and Tait, P.R. (2012). Carbon labeling and consumer attitudes. *Carbon Management Journal* 3(5), 445–455.

Gustavsson, J., Cederberg, C., Sonesson, U., van Otterdijk, R. and Meybeck, A. (2011) *Global Food Losses and Food Waste. Extent, Causes, and Prevention*. Rome, FAO. Available at: www.fao.org/docrep/014/mb060e/mb060e00.pdf. Retrieved 11 June 2018.

Hammerich, T. (2018) 5 Potential Use Cases for Blockchain in Agriculture. Futureofag.com [blog]. 4 January. Available at: https://futureofag.com/5-potential-use-cases-for-blockchain-in-agriculture-c88d4d2207e8. Retrieved 30 July 2018.

Hoeffler, H. (2008) *High Commodity Prices – Who gets the Money? A Case Study on the Impact of High Food and Factor Prices on Kenyan Farmers*. Heinrich Böll Stiftung. Available at: https://ke.boell.org/sites/default/files/highfoodprices-whogetsthemoney_kenya.pdf. Retrieved 30 July 2018.

Hodges, R. and Stathers, T. (2012) *Training Manual for Improving Grain Postharvest Handling and Storage*. World Food Programme. July. Available at: https://documents.wfp.org/stellent/groups/public/documents/reports/wfp250916.pdf. Retrieved 11 June 2018.

Hubbard Breeders (2018) Conventional Females. Available at: www.hubbardbreeders.com/products/conventional-females/. Retrieved 25 June 2018.

International Rice Research Institute (IRRI) (2018) Milling. Available at: www.knowledgebank.irri.org/step-by-step-production/postharvest/milling. Retrieved 21 July 2018.

Jung, H. (2014) *Innovations in Food Packaging*, 2nd edition. Amsterdam, Elsevier.

Koigi, R. (2017) Afrexim announces support for development of cotton value chain in West Africa. Africa Business Communities. 13 June. Available at: http://africabusinesscommunities.com/news/afrexim-announces-support-for-development-of-cotton-value-chain-in-west-africa/. Retrieved 27 June 2018.

Lingle, R. (2017) Green Giant creates new twist on microwavable packaging. Microwavable Packaging [blog]. 17 October. Available at: www.packagingdigest.com/microwavable-packaging/green-giant-new-twist-microwave-pkg1710. Retrieved 12 June 2018.

Marineli, F., Tsoucalas, G., Karamanou, M. and Androutsos, G. (2013) Mary Mallon (1869–1938) and the history of typhoid fever. *Annals of Gastroenterology*. 26(2), 132–134.

Matthews, A. (2015) Farmers' share of food chain value added. Available at: http://capreform.eu/farmers-share-of-food-chain-value-added/. Retrieved 11 June 2018.

McGraw, F. (2014) Comparing US and Canadian Dairy Policies and their Impacts. May. Available at: https://static1.squarespace.com/static/51624bdce4b058e82d8a2faf/t/53751bd2e4b000acb068f045/1400183762666/Dairy+Research+Paper+.pdf/. Retrieved 30 July 2018.

McMillin, K.W. and Belcher, J.N. (2012) Advances in the packaging of fresh and processed meat products. In J.P. Kerry (ed.) *Advances in Meat, Poultry and Seafood Packaging*. Abingdon, Woodhead, 173–204.

Morales, L.E. (2017) The effects of international price volatility on farmer prices and marketing margins in cattle markets. *International Food and Agribusiness Management Review* 21(3), 335–349. Available at: www.wageningenacademic.com/doi/pdf/10.22434/IFAMR2017.0020. Retrieved 13 July 2018.

National Farmers Union (2018) The Farmer's Share. Available at: https://nfu.org/farmers-share/. Retrieved 30 July 2018.

Nuora, A., Tupasela, T., Tahvonen, R., Rokka, S., Marnila, P., Viitanen, M., Mäkelä, P., Pohjankukka, J., Pahikkala, T., Yang, B., Kallio, H. and Linderborg, K. (2018) Effect of homogenised and pasteurised versus native cows' milk on gastrointestinal symptoms, intestinal pressure and postprandial lipid metabolism. *International Dairy Journal* 79, 15–23.

Oliveira, A.L.R. and Alvim, A.M. (2017) The supply chain of Brazilian maize and soybeans: The effects of segregation on logistics and competitiveness. *International Food and Agribusiness Management Review* 20(1), 45–61.

Oregon Wheat Commission (2018) Wheat 101. Available at: www.owgl.org/wp-content/uploads/2012/08/Flour-101.pdf. Retrieved 11 June 2018.

Packaging Europe (2018) Colpac launches paperboard solution for ready-meal and take-away market. Packaging Europe. 26 January. Available at: https://packagingeurope.com/colpac-launches-paperboard-solution/. Retrieved 12 June 2018.

Piper, T. (2007). Choosing Between Strategies: Adapting Industry Approaches to Specific Value Chain Analysis Using Three Comparative Commodities [PowerPoint presentation]. Available at: http://stage.technoserve.org/files/downloads/smallenterprisedevelopmentworkshoptimpiperpresentation.pdf. Retrieved 17 September 2015.

Pullman, M. and Wu, Z. (2012) *Food Supply Chain Management*. London and New York, Routledge.

Rabobank (2017) Weather event among threats to global food price stability in 2018. 21 November. Available at: www.rabobank.com/en/press/search/2017/20171121-acmr.html. Retrieved 21 July 2018.

Rana, K. (2014) Kazakhstani agribusiness supply chain: Issues and challenges. *American International Journal of Social Science* 3(7), 92–99.

Retail Economics (2017) Top 10 UK Retailers. Available at: www.retaileconomics.co.uk/top10-retailers.asp. Retrieved 27 June 2018.

Ricketts, K. and Ricketts, C. (2009) *Agribusiness Fundamentals and Applications*. New York, CENGAGE Delmar Learning.

Robertson, G.L. (2016) *Food Packaging: Principles and Practice*, 3rd edition. Bosa Roca, Chapman and Hall.

Rosado Júnior, A.G., Lobato, J.F.P. and Müller, C. (2011). Construção de indicadores consolidados de desempenho para uma empresa do agronegócio: um estudo de caso. *Revista Brasileira de Zootecnia* 40(2), 454–461.

Schmaltz, R. (2018) Blockchain is Coming for Agriculture and You Might Not Even Notice. Agfunder. com. 21 May. Available at: https://agfundernews.com/blockchain-is-coming-for-agriculture.html. Retrieved 30 July 2018.

SGS (2017) SGS signs strategic alliance agreement with Kezzler AS. 14 May. Available at: www.sgs.com/en/news/2017/05/sgs-signs-strategic-alliance-agreement-with-kezzler-as. Retrieved 25 June 2018.

Sharma, A.K. and Kumar, S. (2010) Economic value added (EVA) – literature review and relevant issues. *International Journal of Economics & Finance* 2(2), 200–220.

Shrivastava, S. (2013) Analyzing Horse Meat Scandal, Its Effects, and How it Progressed. The World Reporter. 3 March. Available at: www.theworldreporter.com/2013/03/horse-meat-scandal-effects-and-progress.html. Retrieved 21 July 2018.

Sifa, C.B. (2014) Role of Cooperatives in Agricultural Development and Food Security in Africa. Available at: www.un.org/esa/socdev/documents/2014/coopsegm/Sifa–Coops%20and%20agric%20dev.pdf. Retrieved 12 June 2018.

Spinelli, S., Masi, C., Zoboli, G.P., Prescott, J. and Monteleone, E. (2015) Emotional responses to branded and unbranded foods. *Food Quality and Preference* 42, 1–11. Available at: https://doi.org/10.1016/j.foodqual.2014.12.009.

Statista.com (2018) Consumption of vegetable oils worldwide. Available at: www.statista.com/statistics/263937/vegetable-oils-global-consumption/. Retrieved 11 June 2018.

USDA (2018) Food Dollar Series. Documentation. Available at: www.ers.usda.gov/data-products/food-dollar-series/documentation.aspx. Retrieved 30 July 2018.

Vorst, J.G.A., Duineveld, M.P.J., Scheer, F.P. and Beulens, A.J.M. (2007) *Towards Logistics Orchestration in the Pot Plant Supply Chain Network*. Wageningen University. Available at: www.researchgate.net/publication/40097053_Towards_logistics_orchestration_in_the_pot_plant_supply_chain_network. Retrieved 24 February 2019.

Webber, M. and Labaste, P. (2010) *Using Value Chain Approaches in Agribusiness and Agriculture in Sub-Saharan Africa*. Washington DC, World Bank. Available at: https://openknowledge.worldbank.org/bitstream/handle/10986/2401/524610PUB0AFR0101Official0Use0Only1.pdf?sequence=1. Retrieved [in draft] 20 January 2011.

Wheat Foods Council (2015) How Flour is Milled. Available at: www.wheatfoods.org/resources/how-flour-milled. Retrieved 24 February 2019.

World Bank (2015) *Ending Poverty and Hunger by 2030: An Agenda for the Global Food System*. Washington DC, World Bank.

Xiao, C.W. (2008) Health effects of soy protein and isoflavones in humans. *The Journal of Nutrition* 138(6), 1244S–1249S.

Agribusiness corporates

Introduction: theory

There is an enormous, ever-growing literature on corporate finance and the theory of the firm. The starting point is, for very many, a famous textbook, *Principles of Corporate Finance* (Brealey *et al.*, 2019), to which may be added a complementary book, *Fundamentals of Corporate Finance* (Brealey *et al.*, 2019). It is often the finishing point, too, for many agribusiness managers, who do not either want or need to engage much further with financing methods. This is regrettable, as financing decisions have a huge impact on business success, and finance explains much of why the corporate form dominates agribusiness.

Failing the availability of grants, which most governments make mainly to production agriculture, the pecking order theory of finance (Myers & Majluf, 1984) suggests that internally generated funds (retained profits, low or zero-interest loans from family members, or grants as above) should be the first port of call. This is an extremely important point, frequently completely neglected by textbooks and practitioners alike. Needless to say, neither banks, venture capitalists, nor any other investors, are inclined to reinforce the point either.

A note on cost of capital estimation methods

Granted, then, that internal financing is the cheapest, bank financing the next most expensive, and external equity the most expensive form of finance for the agribusiness, how should we go about calculating the costs in each case? There is, very unfortunately, no adequate way to price internal equity. Opportunity cost is the basic concept in each case, but agribusinesses are frequently 'lifestyle businesses' – as one advertisement put it, the opportunity to buy a 'beautiful 30 acre property with 1500 ft of water frontage. Includes a profitable, lifestyle chocolate farm business in the stunning archipelago of Bocas del Toro, Panama. Own a well-built off-the-grid sustainable home in sheltered Dolphin Bay, and enjoy friendly and safe expat living outside the hurricane zone' (Green Acres, 2018). This kind of benefit is obviously extremely difficult to price. Anyway, internal equity is just that – internal – and the need to price it does not arise. Where it becomes important is when an agribusiness is obviously inefficient, even loss-making, apart from costs drawn by the owner-directors, and decision-making becomes sclerotic and eventually impossible. Many agribusinesses, especially small farms, are unfortunately in that position, with owners caught in the trap of being unwilling, or even unable, to sell up.

When it comes to debt, the calculation of cost is much more straightforward. Interest rates from banks are publicly or semi-publicly available, whilst an agribusiness has only to consult its bank balance and agreement with its bankers to see how much bank debt is costing in terms of interest. A large agribusiness will of course have a whole number of different bank debts, of different maturities and probably with a range of different financial institutions, so any estimate of the cost of bank debt will always be an approximation. It may also be useful to compare the yield on corporate bonds for comparable agribusinesses, although most bonds are issued by large corporates – few of them agribusinesses – which may not be easily comparable with smaller privately-owned concerns. There may also be issues associated with fixing the cost of debt for a period (effectively buying a swap) and foreign currency issues, for agribusinesses involved in multiple currency markets, as many are. The final key observation is that the interest (but not the capital repayment) of a debt is in the overwhelming majority of jurisdictions worldwide deductible against tax, further reducing the relative cost of debt as compared to equity.

As for equity, there are a number of different methods for determining its cost to the business. The essential concept again is opportunity cost, but there are alternatives for calculating it. The most well-known theory is the capital asset pricing model (CAPM), for which the famous formula is:

$$K_e = R_f + (R_m - R_f) * \text{ß}$$

Where:

K_e = The cost of equity

R_f = The risk-free rate (usually, the government bond rate in the jurisdiction where shareholders are mostly located)

R_m = The market rate (the long-term performance of the stock market where shareholders are mostly located), and

ß = The relative volatility of the shares of the company (or, if private, the nearest equivalent public company) compared to the market.

There are numerous academic, as well as business, sources of research on the equity premium, $(R_m - R_f)$ For a recent example of work in the agribusiness space, examining the equity risk premium for Hungarian food businesses, see Gergely & Rózsa (2018). There are other methods, such as arbitrage pricing theory (APT), which are also worth examination.

What again corporate financiers all agree upon is that if the debt burden becomes too substantial, the cost of capital will rise. Eventually, the agribusiness will find itself in financial distress.

Taken together, debt and equity form the weighted average cost of capital (WACC) of the firm. In many agribusinesses, the cost of capital is lower than the required rate of return.

For example, an agribusiness's cost of capital may be 10% but the finance department will use 13% as its target rate of return for investments. A risk-averse agribusiness might raise the discount rate even further, as high as 15–20%. But if the agribusiness is looking to stimulate investments, directors might lower the rate, even if just for a period of time, although this is not necessarily the best way to ensure accurate evaluations of investment opportunities.

The real problem, however, is that identifiable 'investments' are very difficult to locate. Most agribusinesses are ongoing, and it is unlikely that most owners will build a business plan from scratch or estimate the total amount of capital, or returns from it, in the everyday running of their agribusiness. In practice, they often rely on accounting information, which can be very misleading, especially if capital equipment is being run down, for example, sales are separated from cash flow, and above all, if the book value of capital does not match its actual market value. Accounts look backwards, too, whilst corporate finance and investment theory are essentially forward looking.

Agribusiness – the logic for corporates

What Ricketts & Ricketts (2009) described as the 'output sector' – but which in the nomenclature of this book must be a sub-sector – includes:

> ...all agribusinesses and individuals that handle agricultural products from the farm to the final consumer. This includes agribusinesses involved in buying, transporting, storing, warehousing, grading, sorting, processing, assembling, packing, selling, merchandising, insuring, regulating, inspecting, communicating, advertising, and financing (Ricketts & Ricketts, 2009:49).

They also include restaurants, fast-food chains and grocery stores but perhaps these are best considered loosely as the retail sector, even though there is evidently overlap, especially at the wholesale level. Online food retailers and firms such as Deliveroo should surely now also be included.

Perishability dominates the logic of the fruit and vegetable supply chain, so speed is of the essence. Once harvested, fruit and vegetables must be cooled (and kept cool), packed and distributed/stored. Individual supply chains vary enormously, however, depending on local circumstances. Getting locally produced avocados to local markets in Western Australia is easy and they are sold inexpensively by the tray, competing with individually sold more recognised types, such as Haas, imported from other states; getting bananas from Chiquita's plantations to Tesco supermarkets in the UK is an immense task. Ironically, consumers' quality requirements are far higher in the latter case than the former. Even though supply chains are generally getting shorter, in response to environmental considerations and transport cost control, complexities of this kind, and associated economies of scale, not least with branding, mean that industry concentration for food and beverage (F&B) is almost an inevitability, especially in the 'two pillars' of upstream processing such as slaughtering and retailing.

Leading firms in the US beef industry include Tyson Foods (www.tysonfoods.com), Cargill Protein (www.cargill.com/meat-poultry/cargill-meat-solutions) and JBS United States (www.jbssa.com). The markets food processing companies serve are very varied, both in terms of size and geography. Soybean processors, for example, produce soybean oil and soybean meal, the former for many products as different as margarine and cosmetics; the latter is mainly used as a high protein livestock feed supplement. Mergers, alliances and various other types of arrangements are reducing the number of players in output processing and handling and increasing the level of concentration worldwide, and though there are still many more in developing countries than in Europe or the USA, it all combines to make it tough for independent operators. A similar story prevailed for maize: in the 1990s the global market underwent rapid consolidation, mainly through mergers and acquisitions by grain firms. These tend to be relatively new companies; only a few major companies in the 1980s are still active in the trade (Abbassian, 2007).

There is hope for them in a different direction, however. In between these two pillars, AT Kearney noted that the top 25 food manufacturers in the USA had ceded 300 basis points to small and medium-size competitors and had grown more slowly. Their view was changes in consumers' core values – online brand power equalisation between large and small, amplified by social media, celebrity chefs and a myriad of food experts – were rewarding small and medium-size companies with above-average growth and slowing the growth of the top 25 F&B companies (Donnan *et al.*, 2015).

While small, independent farmers only supply a small portion of the US food market, this trend represents a significant amount of growth. Demographics are helping to fuel this shift as consumers, especially Millennials (I suggest born 1990–2000, others sweep up Gen Y into this demographic) and Generation Z (born 2000–2010), are more interested than prior generations in where their food comes from (Stone, 2018).

The trend could cautiously be observed by the end of the 2010s to have reached international markets, with the difficulties faced by companies such as Starbucks in continuing its growth, both domestically and elsewhere in the world, from companies such as Mikel (Mourdoukoutas, 2018) is evidence of the problems faced by 'Big Food'.

Globally, moreover, there is much less concentration, with Nestlé selling only about 3% of processed food worldwide, as, at least for the time being, 'the developing world does not seem to share the industrialized world's taste for highly processed and manufactured goods' (Pullman & Wu, 2012:185). The next decade will see whether this changes, and allows the true globalisation of agribusiness. In developing countries, agribusiness therefore still faces a huge corporate challenge. The Indian food processing segment produces a broad spectrum of products including fruits, vegetables, legumes, spices, meats, poultry, and fisheries, milk and dairy products, alcoholic beverages, grain processing and speciality products such as confectionaries, cocoa products, soya-based and high protein foods, and mineral water, etc., generating around $245 billion in 2015 with an annual growth rate of over 5% for several decades. Yes, but a huge proportion of the Indian food processing industry is formed of SMEs, unable to access finance and land in many cases, and unable also to take advantage of the economies of scale, including brand recognition and loyalty, enjoyed by larger firms, 'giving them more political clout and better access to government credits, contracts, and licenses' (De & Nagaraj, 2014; Ali, 2016:60). Internationally, competition would always be difficult for these firms, and even domestically, as the century wears on they await their fate. Similarly for Malaysian rice mills, large private mills tend to have higher profit margins because of their economies of scale or lower average total costs. Public mills also appear to operate positively because their effective price of whole rice is 5% higher than the market price thanks to the rice miller subsidy. *Small private mills that operate without the miller subsidy and under price controls are most vulnerable*, particularly when a poor harvest results in a shortage of paddy production (Chung *et al.*, 2016 [my emphasis]). Not all parts of the Indian or Malaysian agribusiness landscape would be ideally suited to large multinational enterprises, but there is surely scope for a great deal of upscaling and international investment in the future.

The 70–80 cents of every dollar spent domestically on food in developed countries is spread across thousands of US companies in the agribusiness processing and food manufacturing sub-sectors, and a commensurate number in other developed countries. Large firms account for the majority of the output. Most of these companies exhibit cost profiles much more akin to traditional manufacturing firms rather than farms. Salaries and wages are usually still the most expensive cost item – over 20 million people work in the sector in the USA alone – followed by rent and/or mortgage costs, but the balance is shifting. Communication, transportation, utilities and fuel, as well as taxes, insurance and marketing expenses, are the third category. Inventory management is critical for food processors and manufacturers. For example, the humble Walker's Salt & Vinegar crisps (potato chips) contain Potatoes, Sunflower Oil (25%), Rapeseed Oil, Salt & Vinegar Seasoning. Salt & Vinegar Seasoning contains: Flavouring (from many different sources), Dried Vinegar, Salt, Acid (Citric Acid), Sugar, Potassium Chloride, and Yeast Extract (Walkers, 2018). Inventory required for all these ingredients serves the purposes of localising, supply and demand balance, and buffering. Localising, so transport costs (e.g. of fruit and vegetables in bulk) is minimised. Just-in-time production is now commonplace for agribusiness, so inventories are lower than they were decades ago. Warehousing remains necessary, however, to manage excess demand and supply, and occasional delays (e.g. at ports).

The majority of larger agribusinesses use agricultural commodities as inputs and produce either or both of consumer products or products for further processing. Meat packers, bakers, flour millers, wet corn mills, breakfast cereal companies, brewers, snack firms and tanneries are examples (Barnard *et al.*, 2016:23).

> Major commodity processing industries, such as animal feed, grain milling and meat packing, are dominated by giants such as Smithfield Foods, Cargill, ADM, and ConAgra. Among well-known food processing and manufacturing firms are Nestlé, Kraft [now Kraft-Heinz], General Mills, Mars and Coca-Cola (Barnard *et al.*, 2016:24).

For example, the largest customer for rice in the USA has been Anheuser-Busch, as rice is part of its beer. Some firms, on the other hand, have distinct specialisations. For example, Smithfield Foods, with 50,000 employees (www.smithfieldfoods.com) is the biggest pork producer in the world. Many have complex capital and operating structures: Copersucar, with 11,500 employees (www.copersucar.com), 'consists of forty-seven different companies from twenty-four different groups, management styles, capital ownership arrangements and financial situations' (Neves *et al.*, 2016:234) and is the world's largest originator and trader of cane sugar, and one of the largest ethanol trading organisations.

Obviously enough, the overwhelming majority of these organisations are indeed companies. Some are publicly owned, such as Nestlé, Unilever and Kraft-Heinz. Others, like the Mars Corporation and Cargill, are privately owned and intend to remain so. Major companies of the second rank include Del Monte (www.delmonte.com) and JR Simplot (www.simplot.com), grower cooperatives such as Ocean Spray (www.oceanspray.com), and divisions of larger food companies such as ConAgra (www.conagrabrands.com) and General Mills (www.generalmills.com). Vertical integration is continuing in the sector. Pursuit of value-added revenue has also created markets where none previously existed, for example the development of the mass market for cranberry, pomegranate and even prune juice, the rise of non-alcoholic beer and wine and, in coffee shops everywhere, the omnipresent muffins.

Food manufacturing firms producing branded products figure prominently at the retail level. The top 25 companies generated $741 billion in revenue in 2017 and $86 billion in profits. Even just the top ten accounted for over half of sales of the top 50 across most regions; this group includes familiar brand names such as Nestlé, Kraft-Heinz, Unilever, PepsiCo, Cadbury, Mars, the largest privately-owned food and beverage company, and Kellogg's. The share of the top 50 rose to over two-fifths of food sales in North America, but fell to 17% in Asia Pacific (USDA, 2018), explained by a sizeable presence of large domestic players. In 2008, Dy (2009) counted 19 companies with sales of $1 billion or more in Southeast Asia alone; the biggest of these was Wilmar International (sales of $29 billion, followed by CP Group, over $18 billion, and Sime Darby, over $10 billion. The interdependence of the large agribusiness companies is also very clear: Kellogg's largest customer, Walmart Stores, Inc. and its affiliates, accounted for approximately 20% of consolidated net sales during 2017, comprised principally of sales within the USA. At December 30, 2017, approximately 17% of consolidated receivables balance and 26% of US receivables balance was comprised of amounts owed by Walmart. No other customer accounted for greater than 10% of net sales in 2017. Kellogg's generated 37% of net sales outside the USA in 2017, 35% in 2016 and 37% in 2015. Kellogg's produced its products in 21 countries and had operations in more than 180 countries (Kellogg, 2017).

Food Engineering publishes a more comprehensive list annually (Food Engineering, 2018). *Fortune* magazine also provided a list of the major US agribusiness companies, which Oxfam used to identify what it called 'the Big 10' – Associated British Foods (ABF), Coca-Cola, Danone, General Mills, Kellogg's, Mars, Mondelez International (previously Kraft Foods, now part of Kraft-Heinz), Nestlé, PepsiCo and Unilever. They noted that Mars was not included in the *Forbes* list. These companies, Oxfam noted:

> …collectively generate revenues of more than $1.1bn a day and employ millions of people directly and indirectly in the growing, processing, distributing and selling of their products. Today, these companies are part of an industry valued at $7 trillion larger than even the energy sector and representing roughly ten percent of the global economy (Oxfam, 2013).

Table 7.1 Major agribusiness corporates

	Net sales	Net income
Kellogg's	$12,923m	$1,269m
General Mills	$15,740m	$2,131m
Campbell's Soup	$7,890m	$887m
Kraft-Heinz	$26,232m	$10,999m
Hershey Foods	$7,515m	$783,000
Tyson Foods	$38,260m	$1,778m
Nestlé	CHF89,791 ($89,830m)	CHF7.538 ($7,542m)
PepsiCo	$63,525m	$4,857m
Anheuser-Busch	$56,444m	$7,996m
Unilever	€53,715m ($62,527m)	€6,486 ($7,550m
Coca-Cola Co.	$35,410m	$1,248m

Source: Annual reports

In 2009, it was suggested that 'Few people outside the agricultural industry are aware of the magnitude of the agribusiness input and output sectors' (Ricketts & Ricketts, 2009:52). I doubt that is true any longer. According to official Japanese statistics, the Japanese food processing industry produced $216.1 billion in food and beverage products in 2016. Sales were estimated to have increased to $218 billion in 2017. Close to three-quarters of that total, or $160 billion, were manufactured by the 91 largest food and beverage companies. The largest food processing companies are traditional breweries who have expanded their portfolio to include foods, distilled spirits, health foods and other F&B products. Many of those groups (Kirin Holdings, Asahi Group Holdings, Suntory Ltd. and Sapporo Holdings) are also competing throughout Asia, Europe and the USA, and became international brand names themselves. In addition, a number of companies that emerged from the dairy industry are also among the sector's top 15 companies (e.g. Meiji Holdings, Morinaga Industry Co., Ltd. and Megmilk Snow Brand Co., Ltd.). Other leading food processors including Nippon Ham Foods Ltd. (meats), Ajinomoto Co., Ltd. (food and amino acids), Yamazaki Baking Co., Ltd. (breads), Ito Ham Yonekyu Holdings (meats) are also in the top 15 (USDA, 2018).

The main sources of vegetable oils are oil palm, soybean and rapeseed. The global soybean economy is shaped by a relatively small number of countries and international business conglomerates, although the market remains highly competitive despite high levels of market concentration, and expected consolidation.

For fruits and vegetables, the global value chain is characterised as buyer-driven (Gereffi & Fernandez-Stark, 2016). The buyers are large supermarket chains in EU, US and increasingly in emerging markets. Stringent quality standards are imposed by these chains upon their suppliers, big or small, worldwide. The latter consist of a few large transnationals, together with domestic firms of varying sizes.

In the case of cocoa, processing begins from roasting to grinding, from which a variety of products may result, i.e. cocoa liquor, cocoa butter, cocoa powder and cocoa cake. The cocoa liquor is further processed into industrial chocolate or couverture, which is the raw material for finished chocolate. Two-thirds of grinding are done by just ten firms, with the top three – ADM, Cargill and Barry Callebaut (Switzerland) – dominating the market (40% share in the grinding market). Interestingly, Cargill and ADM have entered the processing segment only in the past few decades; they consolidated the activities of traditional trading companies (such as Gill & Duffus, Berisford and Sucden), by displacement or outright acquisition (UNCTAD, 2008).

For tea, the downstream portion of the supply chain is extremely concentrated (Van der Wal, 2008). World trade is mostly divided across four companies, namely: Unilever (UK), Van Rees (the Netherlands), James Finlay (UK) and Tata/Tetley (UK). About 90% of Western tea trade is controlled by just seven multinational companies. The big tea traders and processors typically own large plantations; however, in the biggest tea exporting countries (Sri Lanka and Kenya), tea is now mostly produced by smallholders (respectively, 65% and 62%).

Meanwhile for livestock, Dyck and Nelson (2003) note that, while hundreds of firms of various sizes participate in the international meat trade, only a few very large firms are market leaders. The global trans-national companies (TNCs) (as of 2001–02) supply both the domestic and foreign markets, with seven of the top ten based in the USA. A high degree of market concentration globally can be inferred given high sales concentration among the top 50; for this sub-group, the top four companies had a market share of 42% and the top five, 60%. Among developing countries, only Thailand (36th) and Brazil (37th and 47th) were able to place at least one domestic firm in the top 50.

Important to note in this context is that these companies are not necessarily as low-risk as might at first sight be imagined. The Coller FAIRR Protein Producer Index (www.fairr. org/coller-fairr-protein-producer-index/), which tracks 60 of the world's largest food companies worth a combined $300 billion, assesses how these companies are managing critical sustainability risks ranging from pollution to the Paris Agreement on climate change, and food safety to worker safety. Antibiotic use in the production of meat and fish is a major risk to human health, according to the report, with 77% of companies failing to adequately manage or disclose antibiotic use, despite growing levels of regulation and international action to combat antibiotic-resistant superbugs. The high-risk companies, worth a combined $152 billion, include major suppliers to McDonald's and KFC, as well as the USA's third-largest poultry producer, Sanderson Farms. Brazil's JBS, which was recently embroiled in a food safety scandal, was also classified as high risk. The food index also revealed the food companies following best practices, including 'medium risk' US meat producer Tyson Foods, which FAIRR's accompanying report highlighted for the launch of its $150 million venture fund to invest in alternative meat start-ups and other sustainability-focused technologies. Norwegian aquaculture group Marine Harvest was the top-ranked company in the initial launch, in large part due to its approach to tracking and using antibiotics (Burwood-Taylor, 2018).

Quality control, the answer to these concerns, can be defined simply as 'maintenance of quality at a level that satisfies the customer and that is economical to the producer or seller' (FAO, 2001). Some aspects of quality are controlled by legislation; for example certain chemical additives or colouring materials may be prohibited in fish and fish products offered for sale or, in some countries, the maximum number of bacteria permitted may be specified (FAO, 2001). There is evidence that a standard such as ISO 9001 offers supply chain management benefits to agribusiness companies (Wilcock & Boys, 2017).

Additional sectors

Mention should be made of the growing sector of agriservices – research and specialised, customised services to agriculture. With the retreat of the public sector from agriculture, the private sector has stepped in. Trade associations are vital to agribusiness; there are many thousands in the USA alone. They work organising sales, promotion, publicity, communications, sales training, auditing and record-keeping, transportation, lobbying, legislative, regulatory and market information, policy-making, collective bargaining and information distribution. A levy system on members is usually their funding method. Private agriservices (and collectively owned groups serving, for example, the wheat market such as CBH, www.cbh.com.au), include shipping, transport and storage, veterinary care, feed grinding and mixing, machine harvesting, contract labour and spraying, and technical support. In the USA more than 30,000 firms provide these services, employing over 100,000 people. All this excludes the many thousands of unpaid workers in the sector, as well as those on farms themselves.

Then, very importantly, there are the major agricultural input suppliers, firms such as Monsanto-Bayer, Dow-DuPont and Syngenta-ChemChina. These giants are the result of recent M&A in the sector: in late 2015, Dow Chemical and DuPont officially announced a $130-billion merger to form ag-chem giant DowDuPont. A few months later ChemChina made a $43-billion move for Swiss ag chemicals and seed giant Syngenta AG. Then, in September 2016, Germany's Bayer took over Monsanto in a $66-billion takeover (although the deal only received US regulatory approval allowing for the delisting of Monsanto in 2018) and Potash Corp. of Saskatchewan merged with Agrium to create the largest fertiliser giant in the world, valued at $36 billion. Feed, supplements, health products, fertilisers and pesticides are all produced by major companies worldwide with very large R&D budgets. Seed firms are now integrated with biotech companies due to GMO. Many major companies use distributors, either in the form of franchises, local cooperatives, or through subsidiaries. The top four companies already account for over half of global sales of pesticides, seeds, farm machineries and animal health products; the market share of the progressively fewer companies in this space has risen substantially over the past two decades, attesting to rising industry concentration at the global level. However, these companies have made only limited diversification moves, for example Monsanto's acquisition of the Climate Corporation (Monsanto, 2017).

Finally, there are agricultural machinery manufacturers. Major manufacturers include firms such as John Deere, which makes farm machinery. Their website (www.johndeere. com) mentions, in addition to their most important product lines of Tractors and Loaders,

Application Equipment, Cutters and Shredders, Harvesting Equipment, Hay and Forage Equipment, Planting Equipment, Precision Ag Technology, Seeding Equipment, Sprayers and Tillage Equipment.

The company's managing director for sub-Saharan Africa said in 2016 that John Deere had expanded its dealer network and now had 32 authorised dealers with 129 outlets across 28 countries, with professional staff and spares. The company was aiming to sell to contractors to smaller-scale farmers, with a policy approach they termed SMART:

S – Smallholder and small contractor solutions, which provides the right portfolio for Africa

M – Mechanisation for yield improvements of two to three times or more

A – Access to finance to empower farmers and contractors to grow

R – Reliability and low overall cost of operation to maximise profits

T – Training and Technology to ensure customers have the knowledge they need (AFFP, 2016).

This is no doubt positive; less encouraging, at least from the perspective of some farmers, is the way in which agricultural machinery manufacturers are following fertiliser and seed producers in copyrighting management software, binding agricultural producers to the company. As with contract farming, this may bring benefits as well as disadvantages, in the blurring of the line between leading and ownership (Wiens, 2015). In the past, in the USA and no doubt in many other countries, production agriculture required more petroleum than any other industry (Ricketts & Ricketts, 2009:48). Energy supply to agribusiness will continue to be vitally significant.

Global agribusiness companies

If concentration is a concern for policymakers in production, they are even more concerned about distribution and trade. The participation threshold appears high enough to limit access to export markets to medium or large companies (or cooperatives). This threshold is set by throughput requirements for shipping and handling. Buyers may be direct retailers (e.g. supermarket chains), or other agents along the market chain. The large companies involved tend to be integrated closely to processing and exert considerable market influence. The threshold is set by throughput requirements for shipping and handling. Buyers may be direct retailers (e.g. supermarket chains), or other agents along the market chain. The large distributors tend to be integrated closely to processing. The global distribution business is dominated by large players: Archer Daniel Midlands (USA), Bunge (founded in the Netherlands), Cargill (USA) and Louis Dreyfus (France), together with Continental Grains (Belgium), CHS (USA) and Wilmar (Singapore).[1] Ownership ranges from family-owned (Louis Dreyfus) to relatively dispersed – i.e. CHS is owned by farmers, ranchers, cooperatives and other preferred stockholders. Activities are usually diversified; aside from the core business in global agricultural logistics. Wilmar is the only newcomer (founded in 1991); the rest are established businesses founded in the 19th or early 20th century. Wilmar is at the vanguard of Asia-based trading houses which launched ambitious expansions, including Noble Group and Olam International, which challenged the ABCD monopoly, but are not opening up trade generally, especially for grains. One study found that, globally, 15% of grain exports are exported by Louis Dreyfus. In the US market just two firms, Cargill and Continental, accounted for 35% of US grain and oilseeds exports in the late 1990s. Back in 2003, it was estimated – in a very widely quoted figure – that the top four grain trading firms, known as Archer Daniel Midlands (USA), Bunge (founded in the Netherlands), Cargill (USA) and Louis Dreyfus (France), already controlled 73% of the world's grain trade (Australian Wheat Board, n.d.), whilst according to Dy (2009), Cargill alone exported 25% of the grain exports of Argentina. Evidently, the global distribution business is, as discussed in Chapter 1, still dominated by large players.

The Pacific Northwest (PNW) wheat market has been very competitive, and most wheat is exported through the port area referred to as CRDIP, or Columbia River District including Portland. There are six export terminals currently operating in the CRD:

CLD Pacific O'Dock (formerly Louis Dreyfus)
CLD Pacific Irving (formerly Cargill)
Columbia Grain in Portland on the Willamette River
United Harvest in Vancouver Washington (formerly United Grain Corp.)
United Harvest in Kalama (formerly Harvest States Cooperatives)
Kalama Export Company in Kalama (formerly Peavey), on the Columbia River.

CLD Pacific is a regional joint venture between Cargill and Louis Dreyfus formed in 2001. Columbia Grain is owned by Marubeni. United Harvest is an equally owned joint venture between CHS and Mitsui set up in 1998. Kalama Export Company is operated by ADM, ConAgra and Mitsubishi. United Harvest has the largest market share of all the exporters, typically around 40% of all exports per year.

Occasionally wheat is moved through PSD, or Puget Sound District (Seattle/Tacoma). There are two terminals there:

Louis Dreyfus Pier 86 (formally Cargill)
Temco (Tacoma Export Marketing Co., a joint venture between Cargill and CHS)

Usually these elevators, as well as the Kalama Export Company facility, are used for corn and soybeans.

These elevators all have the ability to load Panamax-sized vessels and some can do tankers as well (though at some cost to efficiency). They are all serviced by rail links, and all the CRD elevators are serviced by inland barges which travel the Columbia River network. About 80% of all south-west volume is supplied from barges, which primarily move wheat from country elevator river terminals inland.

The PNW exports around 10 million metric tons of wheat annually, to various areas around the world at some point in the past, but primary regular export customers include Japan, the Philippines, Korea and Taiwan. There are several other customers which in a given year, depending on price relationships, will buy from the PNW, including Egypt, Pakistan, Yemen, Sri Lanka, Indonesia, Malaysia, Thailand, Bangladesh, and some South American countries. There have been some exports in the past to African countries, but these tend to be fairly rare cases. Apart from the first group, the PNW must compete in price with wheat offered from other producing countries in order to do exports to most of the latter countries, which is a very important point.

Trading companies play an important role in the PNW as intermediaries and investors. Many of the exports from the PNW are done through Japanese trading companies, notably Mitsui, Mitsubishi, Marubeni, Toyota-Tsusho (formerly Tomen), Itochu, Sojitz (formerly Nissho Iwai and Nichimen), Kanematsu and Sumitomo. The first three companies have stakes in the above-mentioned export terminals. All of these companies have representative offices in Portland, and participate in Japan's Ministry of Agriculture, Forestry and Fisheries (MAFF) business. A large percentage of exports from the PNW are done through trading companies, although there is a growing trend toward more direct sales by exporters to overseas buyers, especially private sector buyers.

Source: Hotgrain (2018)

For rice, volatility in world trade led to a turnover in the major players. Back in the 1990s, the main rice trading firms were Continental, Richco (Glencore) and Cargill; by the 2000s, these had downscaled or abandoned their rice trade operations. The big companies still in rice trading include ADM, Louis Dreyfus and Olam. Unlike maize or wheat, rice is not standardised, hence brokers play an important role in facilitating trade. Examples of brokerage houses are: Jacksons, Marius Brun et Fils (both Europe), Creed Rice (USA) and Western Rice Mills (Canada). But their power is much less than hitherto, as the informational asymmetries on which they relied for their profits have been eroded by plentiful sources of price and volume quotes from the internet, especially over mobile devices.

Case study: Guinea and the international pineapple market

A leading exporter up until the 1970s and recognized for the quality and variety of its pineapples, including the Cayenne Lisse, Baroness of Rothschild and Queen Victoria, Guinea has been absent from major fresh pineapple consumer markets in recent years.

This partnership will allow some 20 producers from the Maferenyah and Kindia areas to receive technical support from the Burquiah Cooperative, which brings considerable experience in exporting pineapples to the European Union, as well as the Cooperative of the Federation of Fruit Planters of the Basse-Guinée region, which will provide technical support and monitoring to the target producers.

The Delivery Unit, under the Office of the Prime Minister of Guinea (DU), the Ministry of Agriculture and main actors in the sector have set a target of 100 tons of fresh pineapple exports targeting international markets, by the end of January 2018. In order to achieve this objective and to remove key bottlenecks in the value chain, a partnership was signed among the Government, pineapple producers in the Basse-Guinée region and French importer VB International. The DU contributed to lifting a key bottleneck by providing fertilizers that are specific to the cultivation of pineapples and by developing payment facilities for farmers. VB International has committed to purchasing 100 tons of quality pineapple from Guinean producers that meet European market standards, between October 2017 and January 2018. 'This partnership marks a key step in initiating the return of Guinean pineapples into international markets', said Mamady Youla, Prime Minister of the Republic of Guinea.

This story – for that is all it amounts to – is a good example of the point that is what is always required in analysing news of this kind is tracking of the initiative, understanding of the investment opportunities it may present, and to learn lessons from its success or failure. This, however, is very unlikely to surface entirely in the public domain.

Source: African Business Communities (2017)

Cargill, for example, operates across a wide range of commodities, products, and services around the globe. It has been organised into five business segments: (1) agricultural services; (2) food ingredients and applications; (3) origination and processing; (4) risk management and financial; and (5) industrial. Each business segment has several business units. In addition to operating as a large grain trader in the USA, Cargill has for decades been one of the largest meatpackers, owning operations that produce poultry, beef, pork and pet foods. Cargill also has, or has had, operations in animal feed, corn, barley, sorghum, vegetable oils, cotton, sugar, petroleum, financial trading, pharmaceutical and health products, sales of crop protection products, biofuels, oils and lubricants, and many other industrial products. In the last decade, Cargill had 142,000 employees in offices that span 66 countries. Its subsidiaries bought and processed grain and beef in Australia, soy in Brazil and Argentina, palm oil and animal feed in Malaysia, palm oil and cocoa in Indonesia, grain, oilseed, coal, and financial services (Murphy *et al.*, 2012:9). The company is constantly evolving to meet new market demands and ensure an adequate return on its investment capital. One analyst went so far – perhaps too far – as to say that food processing is private-company Cargill's world, and everyone else just gets to play in it (Crowe, 2018). He pointed out that Cargill's 2017 estimated revenue ($110 billion) was almost as much as all of the companies in this group combined ($128 billion). More cautiously, one can observe that the larger agribusinesses generally enjoy economies of scale as an inherent advantage, although it is fair to observe that Cargill's cost of capital is low and certainly does have tremendous efficiencies related to scale.

Glencore, a still more diversified company which trades across energy as well as a multitude of commodity markets, similarly characterised Glencore Agricultural Products (Glencore Agri) in 2016 as a differentiated and vertically-integrated business focused on the global agricultural products value chain. Built around a network of high-quality origination and logistics assets worth over $10 billion, comprising over 200 storage facilities, 31 processing facilities and 23 ports in strategic locations around the world, the company claimed that Glencore Agri was well-positioned in key export regions and in the trade of major agricultural commodities including grains, oilseeds products, rice, sugar, pulses and cotton. The salutary fate of Glencore Agri, however, will be a lesson to others attempting this kind of global footprint.

This is the kind of activity in which ABCD firms are involved:

Archer Daniels Midland Company and Cargill have reached agreement to launch a joint venture to provide soybean meal and oil for customers in Egypt. The joint venture would own and operate the National Vegetable Oil Company soy crush facility in Borg Al-Arab along with related commercial and functional activities, including a separate Switzerland-based merchandising operation that would supply soybeans to the crush plant. Cargill is currently expanding the plant from 3,000 metric tons to 6,000 metric tons of daily crush capacity. The plant will be able to produce higher-protein soybean meal while reducing the need for soybean meal imports into Egypt.

The joint venture will be managed as a standalone entity consisting of equal ownership by ADM and Cargill, with a management team reporting to a board of directors appointed by the two parent companies. The joint venture's assets will not include Cargill's grain business and port terminal in Dekheila, or the ADM-Medsofts joint venture at the Port of Alexandria. Each company will continue its separate business activities in the country and region. The deal, which is not yet complete, is subject to regulatory review. The companies hope to formally launch the joint venture in mid-2018.

Ownership of these companies, and others in the same space, ranges from ownership by the Chinese state, as in the case of COFCO (Cereals, Oils and Foodstuffs Corporation), family-owned (Louis Dreyfus), to relatively dispersed (CHS is owned by farmers, ranchers, cooperatives, and other preferred stockholders). Key to their longevity, as well as their success, is that their activities are usually diversified, aside from the core business in global agricultural logistics. On its website, COFCO International describes itself as a global agribusiness with more than 13,000 employees in 35 countries, responsible for delivering 100 million tons of products in 2016 alone.

Information control is key to their operations: traders are often the first to know when crops are falling short or energy cargoes are interrupted, giving them the edge over others, which implies the use of information through their operations to take positions in commodity markets (van Dijk *et al.* 2011; Salerno, 2017). In 2008, when food prices peaked, Cargill reported peak earnings of $744 million. Cargill itself was open about its profits throughout the price swings. As Cargill explained in its annual report from 2009: 'the insights gathered from many activities and places enabled our trading teams to avoid being stung by plummeting commodity prices' (Cargill, 2009). Though it now seems a long time ago, between the years 2006 and 2008 commodity prices were characterised by rapid growth, volatility and unpredictability. Weather extremes thereafter contributed to three world food price spikes between 2008 and 2012 (World Bank, 2015:11). To take one year as an example, '2016 was packed with events that impacted global agricultural markets and prices, including El Niño cutting South American agricultural output, strong FX rate moves, a record decline in French wheat production, China substantially amending its corn support policy and the (by far) largest-ever US grains harvest' (Rabobank, 2016:iii). Yet, as food prices rose and fell, some agricultural and financial actors saw record high profits and increased power over the global agricultural system.

Critical analysis of this kind of market position originally stems from the book *Invisible Giant* (Kneen, 2002) about Cargill, the largest of the ABCD traders, which is nearly twice the size of its publicly held rival in food production and which continues to be privately owned. But it overlooks two critical points about the role of the ABCD companies, and agribusiness in general. First, it is often a marginal business and losses can be easily made. Second, as the case of Nigeria makes amply clear, but equally in shipping rice from Louisiana (Louis Dreyfus, 2018), it is often only the ABCD companies that have the capital and the managerial expertise to make investments. Cross-subsidisation from other parts of the enterprise is frequently necessary.

This trend was mediated in more recent years by the growth of new grain trading firms bidding to break the ABCD monopoly. Wilmar was at the vanguard of Asia-based trading houses which drove competition for the ABCD companies in the first decade of the new century, including until its recent restructuring Noble Group, and Olam International, all of which have tried to challenge the ABCD monopoly, but not opening up trade generally, especially for grains.

Difficult trading conditions towards the end of the decade as part of the cyclical decline in commodity prices, however, severely curbed many of their ambitions, such as Engelhart (www.ectp.com), China's COFCO and CHS of the USA, and brought the Noble Group to the need first to sell the agricultural unit they had built on the foundations of the former trading house Andre & Cie, and then two years later to a need for financial restructuring (Farchy, 2018).

For rice, volatility in world trade led to a turnover in the major players even earlier. Back in the 1990s, the main rice trading firms were Continental, Richco (which eventually became Glencore) and Cargill; by the 2000s, these had downscaled or abandoned their rice trade operations. The big companies still in rice trading include ADM, Louis Dreyfus and Olam. For maize, in the 1990s the global market underwent rapid consolidation, mainly through mergers and acquisitions by grain firms. These tend to be relatively new companies; only a few major companies in the 1980s were still active in the trade by the first decade of the new century (Abbassian, 2007).

Along with the rest of the global economy, global grain trade stagnated due to reduced demand during the Great Recession of 2007–10, as well as the market disruptions from the food price spike that occurred roughly a decade ago. According to FAO data, the quantity of grain exported globally (corn, wheat, rice and other coarse grains) grew only 2.2% annually between 2008 and 2010, while it had grown at an annual rate of 2.7% in the prior ten-year period.

What happened in Brazil

China's COFCO International and ADM climbed the ranks of grain exporters from Brazil in 2017. COFCO exported 9.3 million tonnes of grains including soybeans, soymeal and corn from Brazil, a four-fold increase from 2016, as acquisitions of Nidera NV and Noble Agri and an aggressive approach to farmers boosted volumes. The Chinese firm surpassed ADM and Dreyfus and was closing in on Cargill. ADM reported the second largest growth in volumes from 2016 to 2017, at 140%, reaching 8 million tonnes. ADM completed investments last year of 280 million reais ($86 million) in the port of Santos, expanding its terminal capacity by 33%. It also quadrupled capacity at its northern Barcarena port, a venture with Glencore Plc, cutting the cost of shipping soy and corn from top state producer Mato Grosso. All other commodities traders saw increases in volumes in 2017, as Brazil rebounded from a poor 2016 crop due to drought and delivered a bumper crop in 2017. Stronger Chinese demand for soybeans also boosted numbers, particularly for COFCO.

Source: Gomes (2018)

Commodity exchanges, including trade in grain and oilseeds, were also swept up in the backlash against the role that deregulation of financial markets, especially in the USA, played in the collapse of the housing market in 2007 and 2008. These actions allowed major players in financial markets, both regulated investment banks such as Lehman Brothers and unregulated financial entities such as AIG, to proliferate trade in financial instruments known as swaps or derivatives, which were essentially bets on the financial health of a range of markets and individual business entities. When the housing market began to crater, with defaults spiking as a result of both poor mortgage lending practices and declining home values, it kicked off a cascading decline in the value of those swaps, casting doubts on the ability of the sellers of the swaps to make good on the bets. Lehman Brothers, with estimated assets at more than $600 billion but greater debts, collapsed into bankruptcy in the autumn of 2008, the largest bankruptcy in US history. Within weeks, confidence in the overall global financial system crashed, leading to the years-long financial recession.

In the Dodd-Frank Wall Street Reform and Consumer Protection Act of 2010, Congress sought to rein in these practices by requiring that banks and other financial firms involved in these transactions provide more transparency to regulators and the public by clearing and reporting swap transactions, as well as minimise the systemic risk created by such transactions by imposing margin requirements. It also bars entities which hold customer deposits from engaging in speculative activity.

Entities engaging in swaps based on agricultural products were not pleased to be covered by the new rules, claiming they had not contributed to the problems which caused the Great Recession, and would not do so in the future. However, after the collapse of MF Global, one of the largest commodity brokers on US markets, in 2011, and Peregrine Financial Group, another large swap dealer, a year later, those claims seem a bit optimistic. Under Dodd-Frank, end-users utilising swaps for hedging purposes were exempted from margin requirements. After a federal court vacated the initial effort by the Commodity Futures Trading Commission (CFTC) to establish position limits on speculative trading of physical commodity futures contracts, the CFTC proposed new rules in December 2016. The final rules are not yet in place, but the most recent nominees to the commission pledged to work to complete the rules once they are seated, during their 2017 confirmation hearings.

However, the creation of premium and consumer-facing products still gives a business some additional pricing power from vertical integration and brand recognition. Crowe argued that whilst Archer Daniels Midland and Green Plains have several benefits from vertical integration and finding ways to create value from processing by-products, the products they, and even Cargill, offer do not have the customer-facing component that can command higher margins (Crowe, 2018).

M&A in agribusiness – the logic, facts and results

In the global food products industry, there were about ten M&A transactions in 2002, the market then peaked at nearly 300 transactions in 2007, and settled to around 100+ by the end of the decade (M&A Worldwide, 2017). There are plenty of examples of M&A in recent years, however. For example, in 2013, Shuanghui International (now WH Group) acquired Smithfield Foods, paying $5 billion, a 30% premium for the company. Allegedly, the Bank of China approved the $4-billion loan to buy Smithfield in a single day. WH Group is now the largest meat company in the world – and poses something of an issue for international trade regulation in itself. In 2017, Amazon paid $13.7 billion for Whole Foods Market, an American supermarket chain, and in 2019 it also announced a major investment in international food delivery company Deliveroo. Some deals, though significant, need to be studied carefully before their relevance to agribusiness becomes clear. For example, in September 2017, the UK insurance broker Aon plc agreed to buy the real estate investment management firm the Townshend Group (a $475-million deal). This expanded Aon's property management portfolio, but the significance for agribusiness was that Townshend had been advising institutional investors on agricultural investment.

In August 2017, the Rohatyn Group agreed to buy GMO Renewable Resources, a forestry and agriculture investment manager with 600,000 hectares of assets under management (AuM) valued at $2.1 billion, in rural real estate in eight countries. In June 2017, Domain Timber Advisors agreed to buy Timberinvest's fund management business: 530,000 hectares of timberland (valued at about $1 billion) in the USA. In April 2017, Schroders acquired the private equity investment firm Adveq, which had agriculture investments, especially in permanent crops.

An example of an M&A transaction

Archer Daniels Midland Company (NYSE: ADM) agreed in 2015 to purchase several assets of Eaststarch C.V., ADM's 50-50 joint venture with Tate & Lyle (LSE: TATE) formed in 1992. It owns three corn wet mills – one in Slovakia, one in Bulgaria and one in Turkey – and 50% of a mill in Hungary. The venture deals primarily in corn sweeteners and starches. The EU approved the transaction and it closed in 2015.

Under the terms of the agreement, ADM took full ownership of corn wet mills in Bulgaria and Turkey, and will own a 50% stake in a wet mill in Hungary. Tate & Lyle received a cash consideration of €240 million, which was subject to customary closing adjustments, including for net cash and working capital, to take full ownership of the Eaststarch facility in Slovakia.

The Bulgaria, Turkey and Hungary facilities had in 2015 a combined daily grind capacity of approximately 200,000 bushels. They produce primarily sweeteners and starches; the Hungary facility also produces ethanol for fuel, beverage and industrial uses. This increased ADM's global grind capacity for corn 7.5%, to approximately 3 million bushels per day. As part of the transaction, ADM was to supply Tate & Lyle with crystalline fructose from the Turkey facility. In addition, Tate & Lyle appointed ADM as the exclusive agent for the sale of liquid sweeteners and industrial starches produced by its EU plants.

Predictably enough, it is the USA where the most active agribusiness M&A market can be discerned.

However, other markets such as Europe and Australia are also active, and, as with the development of other M&A markets, the likely eventual trend will be towards first Asia-Pac, and then eventually Africa. In fact, it could be said that the level of M&A in the African agribusiness market will be a good indicator of its maturity and success – whether or not the actual deals themselves end up being successful or not. That will depend on the usual factors of synergies, timing and pricing. Strategies themselves vary hugely. For example, manufacturers often acquire organic brands, e.g. Kellogg's owning Kashi, Coca-Cola owning Odwalla and Kraft owning Boca Foods (Verdant, 2018). Nestlé reported in an annual review that:

> ...we acquired a majority stake in the super premium US roaster and retailer Blue Bottle Coffee in late 2017. Blue Bottle's success is built on three key values: deliciousness, hospitality and sustainability. With 49 cafés and a further 39 to be opened in 2018, future strategic growth focuses on expanding its retail presence in the US and Asia, and accelerating its online and supermarket presence. In late 2017, we also acquired Chameleon Cold Brew, a leading provider of premium crafted coffee. It is the number one organic cold brew brand and one of the top three refrigerated cold brew brands in the US (Nestlé, 2017:16).

To market share and upstream and downstream supply chain motivations can be added potential R&D synergy, hence the giants of agricultural chemicals have reduced from six to four, as noted above.

The trading companies also pursue M&A. During 2014, the Chinese government-owned food and agriculture conglomerate COFCO acquired two multinational grain trading companies, the agricultural trading arm of the Hong Kong-based Noble Group, and the Netherlands-based grain trader Nidera. In 2018, the USA-based grain trading firm Archer Daniels Midland (ADM) and Glencore appear to have entered into a competition to acquire Bunge, another major grain trading firm. Bunge was founded in the Netherlands nearly 200 years ago, and is now headquartered in White Plains, NY. In 2016, Bunge reported revenues of nearly $43 billion. If a deal is concluded by either of Bunge's suitors, a merger of this scope would certainly face major challenges on anti-trust grounds by regulators in a number of major countries (Mercier, 2018).

Another strategy is to integrate up the supply chain. Olam, the Singaporean trading group, is another contender to join the ABCD group. Olam took over ADM's cocoa business

Agribusiness Economic and M&A Landscape: Summer 2018

Commentary

- In 2018, U.S. net farm income is expected to stabilize and finish better than the USDA's initial forecast of a 6.7% decline. The expected stabilization could have 2018 net farm income finishing close to 2017 levels, which would again be below the trailing 10-year average.

- Corn export forecast is up $1.3 billion, to $10.3 billion, as a result of higher prices and larger volumes. U.S. corn export opportunities are expected to continue to improve as South America copes with weather related growing issues.

- The Senate and House have both passed respective versions of the new farm bill. Congress will have to reconcile their differences this summer, as the current bill expires on September 30th.

- According to the USDA trade forecast, FY 2018 exports are up $3.0 billion, to $142.5 billion. The total trade balance is expected to remain at a surplus of $21 billion. Notably, grain and feed exports, along with corn exports, comprise a majority of the growth in exports.

- Reported M&A activity in the Agribusiness sector for 2018 YTD has declined as compared to the same period for 2017 YTD. As more institutional investors continue to make investments in the industry, transaction values are expected to maintain historically high levels.

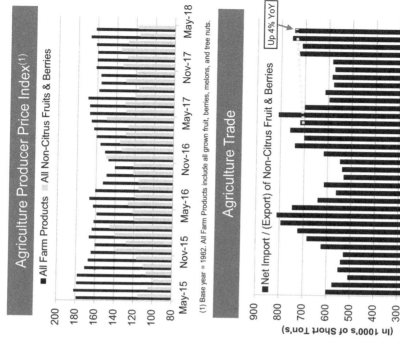

Figure 7.1 Agribusiness economic and M&A landscape: summer 2018

for $1.3 billion, making Olam one of the largest cocoa trading operations, alongside Cargill and Barry Callebaut of Switzerland. The size of the business can be judged from the fact that, after the deal, Olam had a cocoa processing capacity of 700,000 tonnes a year, but this was only 16% of the world's total. The deal meant that Olam has facilities in the UK, Netherlands, Canada, Ghana and Côte d'Ivoire. The purchase was based on Olam's conviction that as incomes rise demand for chocolate, especially in emerging markets, will rise significantly. The conviction is shared by Cargill, which bought ADM's chocolate business for $440 million. (Hazlehurst, 2015).

A similar deal was Glencore's purchase of Canadian grain handler Viterra. Glencore offered Viterra C$16.25 per share ($5.9 billion) for the company, which owned the biggest share of Western Canada's grain storage and farm supply outlets, as well as nearly all grain storage capacity in South Australia. Far from being opposed, the deal was supported by 99.8% of shareholders, far more than the required two-thirds majority (Reuters, 2012). The deal took Glencore within striking distance of the ABCD companies, although trading problems with commodity price falls were to affect all the trading companies in subsequent years. Japanese trading houses such as Mitsubishi are also important participants in global commodity trading, but in agribusiness, they are still below the ABCD companies in size and market reach. Other Asian companies have emerged more recently, such as China's COFCO (which acquired Nidera and Noble), Olam and Wilmar.

Institutional investors have also been involved with some of the major trading companies in recent years, aiming to lever their financial resources to invest in capital-intensive agricultural assets (Vitón, 2018:57). The joint venture between Bunge and the Saudi Agricultural and Livestock Investment Co. (SLIC) that purchased 50.1% of the former Canadian Wheat Board in 2015 for C$250 million was an example. Similarly, when Glencore in particular was eventually forced to dispose of a major minority share in its agricultural trading operations, selling a 9.99% stake in Glencore Agri, it was British Columbia Investment Management which took advantage, for an aggregate consideration of US$624.9 million, payable in cash upon closing, in addition to the sale of a 40% stake to the Canada Pension Plan Investment Board for US$2.5 billion (Glencore, 2016).

Increasing demand for grain in China lay behind two huge deals by COFCO. In 2014 it paid about $1.5 billion (£0.96 billion) for 51% of Dutch trader Nidera, which has access to North and South American grain and oilseed. Just months later, COFCO spent $1.5 billion on a controlling share of Noble Group, a Singapore-based Fortune 500 agricultural supply chain management firm with interests in the Black Sea region. These deals gave China the capacity to import grain without using the ABCD companies.

Family-controlled Brazilian meat company JBS paid $1.5 billion for Northern Irish poultry firm Moys Park. With 8,000 workers, it was Ireland's biggest private-sector employer and made some of the Jamie Oliver-branded chicken products. The deal gave JBS access to markets in the UK, other wealthy European countries and Scandinavia. JBS has been on the acquisition trail ever since the financial crisis hit in 2007, also buying, in 2014, Primo Group, an Australia and New Zealand-based pork producer which exports much of its produce to China, for $1.3 million, and $169 million for Grupo Big Frango, a Brazilian poultry firm.

Deals were not always about taking majority stakes. In 2014 France's Danone paid €486 million to increase its stake in China's biggest milk producer, China Mengniu Dairy, to 9.9%. As part of the deal Danone formed a joint venture with Danish dairy cooperative Arla, which owned 5.3% of the Chinese firm, and COFCO, which owned 16.3%. So, they jointly control about a third of the company. Dairy consumption in China is expected to increase as the country's diet changes. In the mid- 2010s, average per capita Chinese dairy consumption was just 3% of France. Contamination scandals involving Chinese firms have meant many consumers trust foreign companies more. Milk is also a potential growth sector in Africa, which explains the kind of transaction as the June 2014 Dutch dairy cooperative Friesland Campina paying €113 million to increase its stake in its Nigerian subsidiary Friesland Campina WAMCO to 69%.

In March 2015, two of Asia's biggest family-owned groups, Malaysia's palm oil-to-biodiesel group Wilmar, which already processed half of Australia's sugar crop, and Indonesian conglomerate First Pacific, which owns 50% of giant food business Indofood, bought struggling Goodman Fielder in Australia, owner of the Wonder White bread and Meadow Fresh milk brands, for $1.3 billion. The buyers planned to launch Goodman Fielder's brands into Asia to take advantage of increased demand for processed foods in Asia.

Tech-driven M&A in agribusiness

In December 2014, one of the world's largest agricultural and farm equipment manufacturers, Deere & Company, acquired agricultural fleet management provider, Auteq Telematica. John Deere wanted to provide its customers with integrated solutions that enhance the performance and productivity of sugarcane plantations in Brazil.

Trimble bought Finnish forestry & transportation logistics SaaS provider, Fifth Element, aiming to provide solutions that drive integration of business data, improve efficiency and provide better visibility into forest operations to maximise productivity and profitability. Trimble's previous acquisition in this space was for USA-based agricultural equipment pricing provider IRON Solutions.

In January 2015, Munich-based farming, construction and energy supplier, BayWa Ag acquired PC-Agrar GmbH. PC-Agrar provides agricultural enterprise resource planning (ERP), supply chain management (SCM), GIS and farm operations management software, hardware and systems integration services for businesses in the agricultural sector. According to BayWa's acquirer press release: 'Given that the almost revolutionary challenges of "Industry 4.0" also extend to the agricultural sector, this acquisition is [BayWa's] way of arming itself for the digital future.'

Source: https://hampletonpartners.com/agricultural-technology/

Supermarkets and the supply chain

Wholesalers are a hard to pin down sub-sector within agribusiness, not least because of the enormous variation between different agricultural products. A division within the sub-sector has been proposed as follows: Merchant Wholesalers, who 'primarily buy groceries and grocery products from processors or manufacturers, and then resell them to retailers, institutions or other businesses' (Barnard *et al.*, 2016:22). These are the usual entities thought of as wholesalers. In addition, there are manufacturers' sales officers and branches, and whole-sale agents and brokers.

Franchises are commonly observed at the retail level. McDonald's, Wendy's and Domino's are all run on a franchise basis. There are tens of thousands of franchise outlets in the USA alone; McDonald's had 37,241 outlets in more than 120 countries at the end of 2017. Institutional food marketing is another important part of the value chain, including food for hotels, schools, universities and colleges, offices, factories, on aircraft and cruise ships – as well as hospitals, old people's homes, fuel stations and other shops, clubs and many other venues and organisations. After schools, hospitals are the largest institutional food purchaser in the USA. Institutions often hire food service management firms and source nationally. Demands are up, especially for fresh produce, though budgets are tight.

The three largest US food service management companies are Compass Group, Aramark and Sodexo. The Compass Group focuses predominantly on food service in businesses and school. Aramark services more sports and leisure clents and Sodexo, health care. A very concentrated industry in the USA. But less so elsewhere: the five-year food service contract for the new Perth stadium in Australia was given to local firm Mrs Mac's, which specialises in meat pies. The state government noted that Mrs Mac's sources 85% of its ingredients from Western Australia, employs 300 people and is worth A\$50 million a year to the local economy. It purchases \$30 million worth of WA produce each year, including 2,800 tonnes per annum of prime 100 per cent WA beef and 4,800 tonnes of flour produced from premium WA wheat (Murray, 2017). The range of cuisines offered has increased almost everywhere, with notable exceptions in particular rural areas worldwide. Distributors supply these companies in turn and there are thousands of them, either broadline or speciality. Distributors frequently have different prices for their clients. The mark-up depends on 'vendor size, number of delivery windows available, delivery site requirements, order entry mechanism (now almost exclusively electronic), rebate considerations and account type' (Pullman & Wu, 2012:175). Worldwide there are millions of enterprises, ranging from street stalls to national chains with thousands of locations. Hence there are hundreds of millions of food orders annually.

Consumers in developed countries are spending less of their income on food, yet demanding more. The most usual size of food supermarket in the USA carries around 15,000 items in a store of approximately 1,000–2,500 m². Superstores have been defined as those with over 4, 000 m², carrying usually around 25,000 items. Convenience stores, often with extended opening hours, usually carry groceries which account for just under half their sales, with beverages making up the rest. There are also a growing number of specialist food stores, which sell differentiated, often nationally and corporately branded, products such as wines, cheeses or locally produced fruit and vegetables, often organic. Finally mention ought to be made of warehouse club stores, which are wholesale-retail hybrids, 'box stores' that sell approximately 30% groceries, particularly fast-moving non-perishable items such as canned fruit and vegetables. The largest are sometimes described in the USA as 'supacentres' and can range up to 1,700 m². Their share of the market has climbed steadily, achieving roughly one-fifth of food sales by value at the turn of the decade, largely at the expense of supermarkets. The evidence of their success, together with online delivery discussed below, can be seen in the global number of Tesco stores – note the number has tailed off more recently, under the

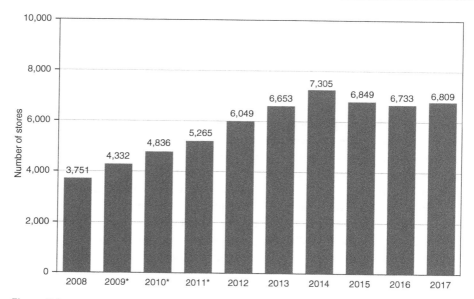

Figure 7.2 Tesco's number of stores worldwide from 2008 to 2017
Source: Statista (2018)

combined pressure of international failures, low-cost stores in domestic markets and the rise of online grocery shopping.

This trend is notwithstanding the consolidation of the market as independent grocery stores and small chains have been acquired by the largest companies. Tesco in the UK most recently concluded a merger with wholesaler Booker, which has created the largest food business in the UK (Tesco plc, 2018). This led analysts to ask whether traditional independent wholesalers could survive in the long term: the merger had already possibly been partially responsible for the collapse of a major UK wholesaler, Palmer & Harvey, which collapsed with debts of more than £700 million, a good illustration of how the agribusiness sector as a whole is certainly not invulnerable to corporate failures and bankruptcies. As a supermarket it remains the largest, with a turnover more than twice its closest competitors, Sainsbury's and Asda (Retail Economics, 2017), although in terms of rate of growth, the discount stores, especially Aldi and Lidl, are outperforming the 'full-service' supermarkets. In the global rankings, Walmart remains the largest food retailer, having experienced fairly meteoric rise since the 1990s, mainly by opening hundreds of supercentres that combine food with other retailing, followed by Carrefour and Costco (Statista, 2018a). *Only about a third of their revenues now come from food retailing.* There are also integrated wholesale-retail operations, such as Kroger.

Not all overseas ventures by supermarkets have been successful by any means: 'Sainsbury's in Egypt, Walmart in Germany, Best Buy in the UK and Marks & Spencer in mainland Europe. The examples are endless and tell the cautionary tale that overseas expansion for major companies is not always a success' (Hopkins, 2015). Supermarket penetration in Asia, however, as Tesco's maladroit ventures showed, has been constrained by cultural issues such as a continued preference for wet markets, for example, in Malaysia and Thailand (Pendrous, 2013), problems with branding, the dominance of convenience stores (e.g. in Japan), and lack of consumer commitment to pre-packaged fresh food. The results of failure have been costly (Wood, 2011).

Notwithstanding these failures, consumers in developing countries purchase an increasing share of their daily food through supermarket chains. Retail sales of fresh products, through supermarkets, already represent two to three times the size of agricultural exports. The supermarket share in food retail was estimated at between 40–70% in Latin America and 10–25% in Africa a decade ago, so now almost certainly 10% more in each case, and increasingly involves middle- and working-class segments of the population in (peri-)urban and even rural regions. Supermarket procurement regimes for sourcing of fruits, vegetables, dairy and meat strongly influence the organisation of the supply chains. The market requires product homogeneity, continuous deliveries, quality upgrading and stable shelf-life. Procurement reliance on wholesale markets is rapidly being replaced by specialised wholesalers, subcontracting with preferred suppliers and consolidated purchase in regional warehouses. These supply chains, which once were largely governed by less formal and often ad-hoc relations between buyers and sellers, are now closely coordinated and 'managed' by their lead players, the supermarkets. In other words, supermarkets thus increasingly control downstream segments of their chains through contracts, private standards and sourcing networks. From the point of view of reliable supply, cleanliness and other quality control issues, and – especially where there is competition – lower prices, this is something to be welcomed, although resistance to the globalisation of agribusiness often targets supermarkets in particular, holding them to far higher standards than their local competitors.

The effect of M&A has been to increase the concentration ratio, so regulators regularly conduct anti-monpoly enforcement investigations into the supermarkets, just as they do for trading companies and international food companies, but the inexorable logic of concentration, intense competition despite the small number of market players, and more recently consumer sentiment moving to local sourcing, has defeated any major diversification of the market.

Supermarkets need their quasi-monopoly positions. They face a bewildering set of choices. They must choose their inventory – a largely data-driven logic in contemporary Western supermarkets – and this varies. Costco stocks some 4,000 items whereas Walmart stocks over 100,000. Product must be allocated to shelves and there are display logics, including consumer pathways around the store, proximate buying, how to deal with discounted and end-of-shelf-life items, choosing between freeform, racetrack or grid layout, slotting fees (which form a substantial part of retail profits), last in first out (LIFO) vs. first in first out (FIFO) purchasing, replenishment, and demand forecasting. Constant innovation in layout and product selection are required, as margins vary between sectors, with higher margins obtainable from in-store bakeries, delis and chilled foods, and the lowest from fresh vegetables. Retailers such as Tesco have responded by creating dining areas, featuring fresh produce, providing non-food sections and services. But they are still losing ground steadily to online deliveries, albeit many of them their own, such as Tesco and Waitrose in the UK. Despite their efforts, now even in some developing and BRIC countries, the supermarkets are already approaching the 70–80% share of total retailing characteristics of developed markets. As noted above,

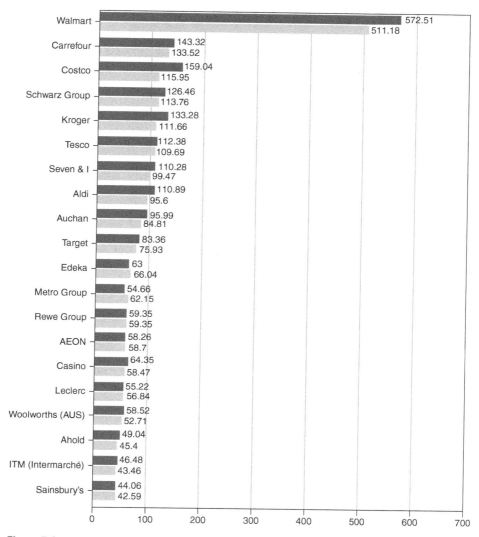

Figure 7.3 Global supermarket chains turnover
Source: Statista (2018)

they are losing market share to food service companies and specialised retailers in developed countries. The historical trend worldwide is towards 'outsourcing' food from the family, *and hence from supermarkets*. In 1960, only 26% of the 'food dollar' in the USA was spent on food away from the home; since 2000, that percentage has been double, steadily rising (Barnard *et al.*, 2016:20). Other countries, though the evidence might only be anecdotal, are evidently following suit, as the success of global chains such as Nando's and many others demonstrates. With the decline in the huge gap between the cost of eating at home and out of it, now that matches up with almost half of food consumed in developed countries being eaten away from home, either in a commercial food service establishment: restaurants (including in hotels), fast-food outlets, vending machines, or in some kind of institutional setting (schools, prisons, hospitals, care homes, recreational locations such as cruise ships, stadiums, parks, casinos, resorts and hotels, and the military and other public services (Grasso, 2013). Public-service food purchases, often outsourced, are subject to strict tendering requirements, and usually end up in contracts. In the USA, there is even an Association of Correctional Food Service Affiliates.

Supermarket procurement and contracts

Certainly, 'The evidence of success for supermarket operations...demonstrates clearly that there are major economies to be made through efficient supply-chain management' (Brookfield & Parsons, 2007:73) but 'Supply-chain management expertise' (Barnard *et al.*, 2016:18) remains one of the key battlegrounds between supermarkets. Just-in-time delivery, even with considerable distances involved, is necessary for the provision of the services that customers expect, especially in developed markets. With air freight, supply chains to retailers have internationalised, to ensure all-year round supplies – e.g. fresh fruit from Chile and South Africa for European supermarkets, from Central to North America.

Supermarkets and other major buyers have a significant impact on farm production practices through the introduction of standards for animal handling in their supply chains. US examples are McDonald's, Kmart, Safeway and Wendy's. In the case of pork, they are encouraging their suppliers not to use sow gestation stalls (basically a crate with a sow and its piglets), and both Maple Leaf Foods and Smithfield Foods, a major processor, intend to source from entirely crate-free sows by 2022. The much-maligned Cargill is aiming for far sooner. A similar story exists for poultry: Unified Grocers announced its intention to transition to 100% cage-free egg procurement by the end of 2025 (Unified Grocers, 2017) joining over 200 major US food companies, including McDonald's and Walmart, that have made 100% cage-free egg commitments, indicating that a significant shift in the industry's production system is under way (Compassion in World Farming, 2018), tracked by Mercy for Animals (2017). In October 2017, the USDA said:

> To date, cage-free commitments stand at 108 grocery chains/distributors, 58 restaurants, 18 foodservice providers, 11 hospitality and travel firms, 14 food manufacturers, 17 convenience/drug chains, and 4 dollar variety stores who, combined, will require 63 billion cage-free eggs per year to meet current and future needs. This will require a cage-free flock of over 227 million hens (73% of the US non-organic flock), indicating a shortage of 198 million hens from the current cage-free flock. The USA is behind the EU – where battery-caged eggs were phased out in 2012, although major UK retailers are taking to 2025 to eliminate caged eggs entirely – but ahead of other Western countries (USDA, 2018a).

Amongst the major Australian supermarket chains Coles no longer sells cage eggs under its own brand, Woolworths has a commitment to end the sale of caged eggs by 2018 and Aldi by 2025. The greatest issue is food production and service, where eight to ten eggs are still battery-farmed, but some companies, for example, Ikea, Grill'd, Lean Cuisine and Leggo's, are already cage-free, whilst McDonald's and Hungry Jack's (the Australian name for Burger King) will be cage-free by 2018, and Mars and Unilever by 2020.

Online delivery and the evolution of consumer behaviour

The first major trend is online delivery. As over 90% of the UK population lives within 30 minutes of a Tesco, online delivery has become routine since its inception as long ago as 1994, especially for an ageing population.

Europe was the battleground in 2017 for the future of grocery. AmazonFresh rolled out one-hour delivery in 10 cities in the UK, as well as in major cities throughout Europe. Carrefour responded with its own one-hour delivery service in France, and likely will be followed by other European grocers. Speed alone, however, will not be enough to compete. Consumers have been conditioned to expect a high-quality, on-demand shopping experience. This includes real-time reviews and local partnerships to provide fresh products. Sprouts Farmers Market, another newcomer on our list this year, has partnered with Amazon to provide fresh products for Amazon Prime delivery in the Dallas area (National Retail Federation, 2017).

Most spectacular of all was the rapid growth in the UK, and then in Europe and Asia, of online delivery firm Deliveroo, whose revenues grew by almost 1,000% between 2013–16. Deliveroo's hotly contested model – ÜberEats and Just Eat are both competitors – provides thousands of restaurants with the ability to send their food from multiple locations (so-called 'dark kitchens') to customers, using self-employed drivers. Its databases alone are extremely valuable IP.

Similarly, the purchase by Amazon in the USA of Whole Foods mentioned above was argued to generate obvious synergies for Amazon as part of its aim to become one of the top five grocers by 2025 (Rosen, 2017); a tidy tie-in with AmazonFresh (providing fresh foods through online ordering), and access to an affluent demographic that is already voting for healthy, clean label food with their food dollars. The purchase also reflects demographic changes: Amazon is how millennials are used to shopping. Most US and UK millennials have no memory of pre-online, and online, together soon with AI such as Amazon's Alexa, is where they think, feel and live. As of 2017, online food and beverage purchases accounted for just 2% of the total food and beverage market in the USA (Connolly & Connolly, 2017:616), but even market research was hard put to capture the rate of growth of the market, so rapidly was it growing. The same year, the Food Marketing Institute (FMI) and Nielsen conducted a survey that found that 49% of US consumers had purchased consumer packaged goods (CPGs) online in the past three months. Special mention should be made of ageing baby-boomers, comfortable with online purchases, but increasingly unwilling to spend time struggling with heavy shopping. Millennials of course need no persuading to go online, and for them the rate was even higher, at 61%, and among Gen Xers, it was 55%. In addition, online grocery shopper numbers have more than doubled in a little over a year: when the FMI and Nielsen ran the same survey in 2016, only 23% of consumers said that they had recently bought CPGs online. These online shopper numbers have been growing so fast that the FMI and Nielsen forecast that 70% of US shoppers could be buying groceries online by as early as 2022. Still, as shoppers tend to make online grocery purchases less frequently than they do in-store grocery purchases, these substantial numbers do not yet translate into a major share of the grocery market for e-commerce (Weinswig, 2018). The demise of 'Big Food' is not yet upon us, however – it would surely be wrong to conflate the rise of online delivery with a move away from established brands. Indeed, quite possibly just the opposite: supermarkets have benefited from the synergistic brand loyalty of the 5Ps (product, price, promotion, place and people), especially place, but online they have no such advantage. Moreover, other countries are still significantly behind: until drones can do the work that currently falls to overly congested highways, for example, Nigeria will not see much in the way of online grocery deliveries. Quality concerns remain, too.

As to restaurants, changing consumer behaviour has meant that full-service establishments, with waiting staff and amenities, are now competing with fast-food outlets, and the gap between them is diminishing. Restaurants and fast-food outlets now compete with retail food sales, and not just in the USA, but worldwide. Fast-food outlets – most obviously McDonald's, but also Taco Bell, Wendy's, Burger King (Hungry Jack's in Australia) have expanded their sales dramatically. Tactics like locating close to residential areas, where planning permits, expanding into retail stores, campuses and hotels have all helped, as did the global financial crisis of 2007–09: in a recession, fast food retains its sales levels, demand being less elastic than for restaurants.

Offerings have increased, partly in response to significant and continuing obesity concerns which have led to, for example, bans on fast-food sponsorship in the Netherlands (Boseley, 2017) or children's meals with toys in California (Allen, 2010) and calorie limits on meals (Weintraub, 2015). Starbucks, for example, has for more than a decade offered healthier meals, including hot oatmeal, a protein plate with a hardboiled egg (cage-free, of course), and whole-wheat bagels and muffins, all providing more protein and fibre and less fat and sugar than other meals. Huge problems have persisted, however: as was argued early in the decade: 'As a result, the supply chain that supports these multi-unit enterprises relies on bulk ingredients…which are processed by a company's central supply facility or a sub-contracting facility into basic products like buns, fries, etc.' (Pullman & Wu, 2012:163). Preservatives, flavourings, additives. Standardised equipment and cooking/preparation procedures. Consider the difficulties Starbucks has in ensuring consistent taste internationally. Consider also the films *Fast Food Nation* and *Supersize Me*. All indicate the food quality problems faced by food service companies and multinational chains.

Although nutrition experts might be able to navigate the menus of fast-food restaurant chains and based on the nutritional information compose apparently 'healthy' meals, there are still many reasons why frequent fast-food consumption at most chains is unhealthy and contributes to weight gain, obesity, type 2 diabetes and coronary artery disease. Fast food generally has a high-energy density, which, together with large portion sizes, induces overconsumption of calories, and people underestimate the calorific content of restaurant meals (Block *et al.*, 2013). In addition, the typical fast-food meal is scarcely identical world-wide. Chemical analyses of 74 samples of fast-food menus consisting of French fries and fried chicken (nuggets/hot wings) bought in McDonald's and KFC outlets in 35 countries in 2005–06 showed that the total fat content of the same menu varied from 41–65 g at

McDonald's and from 42–74 g at KFC. In addition, fast food from major chains in most countries contained then, and still contains, unacceptably high levels of industrially produced trans-fatty acids (IP-TFA). Conclusions that the food quality and portion size of fast food need to be improved before it is safe to eat frequently at most fast-food chains are not unusual (Stender *et al.*, 2007). As long ago as 2003, as noted in Chapter 6, Denmark pioneered the ban on industrially produced trans fats, and cardiovascular disease mortality rates dramatically dropped after a decade. Finland and the UK, early adopters of salt-reduction initiatives, saw a 25–45% reduction of salt content in key foods (Nierenberg & Payne, 2018).

More alarming recent statistics are not hard to find. Organic produce currently forms approximately only 2% of overall UK sales (Gaille, 2017), but growth consistently outpaces the overall market. 'While fruit and vegetables continue to be the most popular choice for shoppers, over the last 12 months the retailer has seen increasing numbers of customers looking to buy organic fish, dairy produce and general grocery items' (Tesco plc, 2017a). Early in the 2010s, the question was still posed: 'The resilience of the organic philosophy, in the face of conventional business pressure, remains an open question' (Pullman & Wu, 2012:113). Now, in developed countries for sure and in middle-class markets in countries such as Brazil, India and South Africa, the question no longer seems open. It is just a question of when the organic market will reach maturity, and at what percentage of the overall market.

The movement towards organic food is not the only change in food retailing. Meanwhile in the USA, 'Customers at full-service restaurants have shifted towards Italian, Mexican, Japanese, Thai, Caribbean, and Middle Eastern foods, as US tastes broaden' (Barnard *et al.*, 2016:20) and this trend has been replicated internationally. Baby-boomers have demonstrated a persistent tendency to spend a higher amount, if not proportion, of income on eating out than their parents ever contemplated. The result is that the restaurant now plays a cultural role in society worldwide far greater than it did even three decades ago.

Some might therefore say the era of the supermarket is being eclipsed. Compare the rates of growth in sales observed in the annual reports of Shoprite and Pick n Pay in South Africa with the results of a supermarket in a developed country, such as Tesco (Tesco plc, 2017). Important questions to ask when reviewing these annual reports are not only return on equity (ROE), turnover and rates of growth of sales and profits, the purely financial ratios that apply to any business, but also questions about sourcing, relationships with farmers, corporate social responsibility, including pricing policy, questions of employment, competition, bricks and mortar vs. online delivery, and long-term strategy. Stockbroking analysts are often the best source of thoughtful answers to these kinds of questions.

Conclusion

All the agribusiness firms described above, from the smallest roadside stall to the largest multinational, share the need for customers, suppliers and funding. Economies of scale dominate major segments of the global agribusiness industry, in particular trading and supermarkets, but also some areas of production. Notwithstanding deep and persistent concerns about their social, environmental and governance performance, global agribusiness companies have had the necessary resources to deliver significant improvements throughout the supply chain, especially in developing countries. All these companies face the need to deliver profits and all have a cost of capital, whether explicitly recognised or not. If they are fortunate, they will survive on internal funding, often aided by state grants. If not, they must seek external financing, which will be the subject of much of the remainder of this book.

Note

1 There may soon be just three if one of the others merges with Bunge.

Bibliography

Abbassian, A. (2007) Background paper for the Competitive Commercial Agriculture in Sub–Saharan Africa. (CCAA) Study. Maize International Market Profile. http://siteresources.worldbank.org/INTAFRICA/Resources/257994-215457178567/Maize_Profile.pdf. Retrieved 20 March 2018.

Africa Business Community (2017) Guinea eyes export of 100 tonnes of pineapple by January 2018. Available at: http://africabusinesscommunities.com/news/guinea-eyes-export-of-100-tonnes-of-pineapple-by-january-2018/. Retrieved 6 June 2018.

African Farming and Food Processing (2016) John Deere launches S.M.A.R.T. campaign to boost productivity in African agriculture. *African Farming and Food Processing*. 30 March. Available at: http://africanfarming.net/technology/machinery-equipment/john-deere-launches-s-m-a-r-t-campaign-to-boost-productivity-in-african-agriculture. Retrieved 27 June 2018.

Ali, J. (2016) Performance of small and medium-sized food and agribusiness enterprises: evidence from Indian firms. *International Food and Agribusiness Management Review* 19(4), 53–63. Available at: www.wageningenacademic.com/doi/pdf/10.22434/IFAMR2016.0024. Retrieved 10 July 2018.

Allen, N. (2010) McDonald's 'Happy Meals' with toys banned to fight childhood obesity. *The Telegraph*. 28 April. Available at: www.telegraph.co.uk/news/worldnews/northamerica/usa/7647021/McDonalds-Happy-Meals-with-toys-banned-to-fight-childhood-obesity.html. Retrieved 28 June 2018.

Australian Wheat Board (n.d.) *Global Wheat Trends*. Melbourne, AWB.

Barnard, F.L., Akridge, J.T., Dooley, F.J. and Yeager, E.A. (2016) *Agribusiness Management*, 5th edition. New York, Routledge.

Block, J.P., Condon, S.K., Kleinman, K., Mullen, J., Linakis, S., Rifas-Shiman, S. and Gilman, M.W. (2013) Consumers' estimation of calorie content at fast food restaurants: Cross-sectional observational study. *British Medical Journal* 346, f2907.

Boseley, S. (2017) Amsterdam's solution to the obesity crisis: no fruit juice and enough sleep. *The Guardian*. 14 April. Available at: www.theguardian.com/society/2017/apr/14/amsterdam-solution-obesity-crisis-no-fruit-juice-enough-sleep. Retrieved 28 June 2018.

Brealey, R., Myers, S. and Allen, F. (2019) *Principles of Corporate Finance*, 13th edition. New York, McGraw-Hill.

Brealey, R., Myers, S. and Marcus, A.J. (2017) *Fundamentals of Corporate Finance*, 9th edition. New York, McGraw-Hill.

Brookfield, H. and Parsons, H. (2007) *Family Farms: Survival and Prospect. A World-Wide Analysis*. London and New York, Routledge.

Burwood-Taylor, L. (2018) Breaking: new food index reveals 'high risk' meat & fish stocks worth $152bn inc McDonalds, KFC suppliers. Agfunder.com. 30 May. Available at: https://agfundernews.com/new-food-index-reveals-high-risk-meat-fish-stocks.html. Retrieved 13 July 2018.

Cargill (2009) *Annual Report 2009*. Minnetonka, Cargill.

Chung, B., Arshad, F.M., Noh, K.M. and Sidique, S.F. (2016) Cost analysis of rice milling: A case study of 7 rice mills in Malaysia. *Journal of Agribusiness in Developing and Emerging Economies* 6(2), 173–190.

Compassion in World Farming (2018) Egg Track 2017 Report. Available at: www.ciwf.com/media/7431604/eggtrack-2017-annual-report.pdf. Retrieved 27 June 2018.

Connolly, K.P. and Connolly, A.J. (2017) When Amazon ate Whole Foods: Big changes for Big Food. *International Food and Agribusiness Management Review* 20(5), 615–622.

Crowe, T. (2018) Top Stocks in Agriculture. Motley Fool [blog]. Available at: www.fool.com/investing/2018/02/02/top-stocks-in-agriculture.aspx. Retrieved 1 July 2018.

De, P.K. and Nagaraj, P. (2014) Productivity and firm size in India. *Small Business Economics* 42(4), 891–907.

Donnan, D., Demeritt, L., Burt, R. and Hokens, D. (2015) Is Big Food in Trouble? Available at: www.atkearney.com/documents/20152/435581/Is%2BBig%2BFood%2Bin%2BTrouble.pdf/fb55f2d2-4c7b-74c9-1503-60b5192735ea. Retrieved 30 July 2018.

Dy, R. (2009). *Food for Thought: How Agribusiness is Feeding the World. (With Special Focus on the ASEAN)*. Manila, University of Asia and the Pacific and Comprehensive Initiative for the Transformation of Organizations Foundation.

Dyck, J. and Nelson, K. (2003). *Structure of the Global Markets for Meat*. Economic Research Service Bulletin Number 785. Washington DC, USDA.

FAO (2001) *Quality Control in the Fish Industry*. Rome, FAO. Available at: www.fao.org/wairdocs/tan/x5934e/x5934e01.htm#TopOfPage. Retrieved 27 June 2018.

Farchy, J. (2018) Rags to riches tale ends in disaster for 'Mini-Glencore'. Bloomberg. 30 January. Available at: www.bloomberg.com/news/articles/2018-01-29/rags-to-riches-tale-ends-in-disaster-for-noble-group-s-elman . Retrieved 5 July 2018.

Food Engineering (2018) The World's Top 100 Food and Beverage Companies of 2017. Available at: www.foodengineeringmag.com/2017-top-100-food-and-beverage-companies. Retrieved 20 July 2018.

Gaille, B. (2017) 31 important McDonald's obesity statistics. Brandongaille.com [blog]. Available at: http://brandongaille.com/29-important-mcdonalds-obesity-statistics/. Retrieved 28 June 2018.

Gereffi, G. and Fernandez-Stark, K. (2016) *Value Chain Analysis. A Primer*, 2nd edition. Available at: www.researchgate.net/profile/Gary_Gereffi/publication/305719326_Global_Value_Chain_Analysis_A_Primer_2nd_Edition/links/579b6f0708ae80bf6ea3408f/Global-Value-Chain-Analysis-A-Primer-2nd-Edition.pdf. Retrieved 27 July 2018.

Gergely, A. and Rózsa, A. (2018) Investigation of equity risk premium in Hungarian food industry. *SEA: Practical Application of Science* 16, 7–19.

Glencore (2016) Sale of additional 9.99% stake in Glencore Agricultural Products to British Columbia Investment Management Corporation. Baar, Glencore. 9 June. Available at: www.glencoreagriculture.com/media/news/p/sale-of-additional-9-99-stake-in-glencore-agricultural-products-to-british-columbia-investment-management-corporation. Retrieved 10 July 2018.

Gomes, J.R. (2018) COFCO, ADM boost Brazil grain exports, close in on Cargill. Reuters. Available at: www.reuters.com/article/brazil-grains-traders/Cofco-adm-boost-brazil-grain-exports-close-in-on-cargill-idUSL2N1QP1BV. Retrieved 5 July 2018.

Grasso, V. (2013) *Defense Food Procurement: Background and Status*. Congressional Research Service. 24 January 2013. Available at: https://fas.org/sgp/crs/natsec/RS22190.pdf. Retrieved 27 June 2018.

Green Acres (2018) Lifestyle home and business for sale. Available at: http://forsale.greenacreschocolatefarm.com/. Retrieved 29 June 2018.

Hazlehurst, J. (2015) M&A fever grips emerging markets. Raconteur. 29 July. Available at: www.raconteur.net/sustainability/ma-fever-grips-emerging-markets. Retrieved 27 June 2018.

Hopkins, K. (2015) Why Tesco failed to crack China. Raconteur. 10 September. Available at: www.raconteur.net/business/why-tesco-failed-to-crack-china. Retrieved 27 June 2018.

Hotgrain (2018) PNW Export Market. Available at: www.hotgrain.com/?tmpl=%2Fsystem%2Fapp%2Ftemplates%2Fprint%2F&showPrintDialog=1. Retrieved 27 June 2018.

Kellogg (2017) Annual Report. SEC Form 10-K and Supplemental Information. Available at: www.kelloggcompany.com/content/dam/kelloggcompanyus/PDF/2017AnnualReport.pdf. Retrieved 11 July 2018.

Kneen, B. (2002) *Invisible Giant: Cargill and Its Transnational Strategies*, 2nd edition. London, Pluto Press.

Louis Dreyfus (2018) The right product to the right location, at the right time. Available at: www.ldc.com/index.php?cID=134. Retrieved 25 June 2018.

M&A Worldwide (2017) Agri Food & Beverages. Available at: www.avvalor.com/MAWW/SECTORS/MAWW_Agri_Food_Beverages_-_Industry_Report_october_2017-Final_version.pdf. Retrieved 15 May 2019.

Marineli, F., Tsoucalas, G., Karamanou, M. and Androutsos, G. (2013) Mary Mallon (1869–1938) and the history of typhoid fever. *Annals of Gastroenterology* 26(2), 132–134.

Mercier, S. (2018) *Changes in Grain Marketing Since the Great Recession*. Farm Futures [blog]. 22 January. Available at: www.agweb.com/mobile/farmjournal/blog/straight-from-dc-agricultural-perspectives/changes-in-international-grain-marketing-since-the-great-recession/. Retrieved 5 July 2018.

Mercy for Animals (2017) List of Cage-Free Egg Companies Grows. Available at: www.mercyforanimals.org/files/MercyForAnimals-CageFreeCompanies.pdf. Retrieved 28 June 2018.

Monsanto (2017) The Monsanto Episode. Big Ag adapts to Climate Change. Podcast. Available at: https://americaadapts.org/2017/10/31/the-monsanto-episode-corporate-agriculture-adapts-to-climate-change/. Retrieved 27 July 2018.

Moss Adams (2018) Agribusiness: Producers, Products and Services. Available at: www.mossadams.com/getmedia/6c930420-3ad2-4113-85ed-c84ba0179377/Agribusiness-Market-Monitor.pdf?ext=.pdf. Retrieved 25 February 2019.

Mourdoukoutas, P. (2018) Starbucks' problems at home and abroad. *Forbes Magazine*. 27 June. Available at: www.forbes.com/sites/panosmourdoukoutas/2018/06/27/starbucks-problems-at-home-and-abroad/#4cca885664b5. Retrieved 30 July 2018.

Murphy, K., Burch, D. and Clapp, J. (2012) Cereal secrets: The world's largest grain traders and global agriculture. Oxfam Research Reports. August. Available at: www.oxfam.org/sites/www.oxfam.org/files/rr-cereal-secrets-grain-traders-agriculture-30082012-en.pdf. Retrieved 14 November 2013.

Murray, M. (2017) Perth Stadium pie contract awarded to WA Company. Government of Western Australia. 22 October. Available at: www.mediastatements.wa.gov.au/Pages/McGowan/2017/10/Perth-Stadium-pie-contract-awarded-to-WA-company.aspx. Retrieved 27 June 2018.

Myers, S.C. and Majluf, N.S. (1984). Corporate financing and investment decisions when firms have information that investors do not have. *Journal of Financial Economics* 13(2), 187–221.

National Retail Federation (2017) 2017 Top 250 Global Powers of Retailing. 16 January. Available at: https://nrf.com/news/2017-top-250-global-powers-of-retailing. Retrieved 28 June 2018.

Nestlé (2017). Good Food, Good Life. Annual Review 2017. Available at: www.nestle.com/asset-library/documents/library/documents/annual_reports/2017-annual-review-en.pdf. Retrieved 12 July 2018.

Neves, M.F., Gray, A.W. and Bourquard, B.A. (2016) Copersucar: A world leader in sugar and ethanol. *International Food and Agribusiness Management Review* 19(2), 207–240.

Nierenberg, D. and Payne, E. (2018) Africa: Why food policy is more important than ever. Available at: https://uncova.com/africawhy-food-policy-is-more-important-than-ever. Retrieved 13 July 2018.

Oxfam (2013) Behind the Brands. Oxfam Briefing Paper 166. 26 February. Available at: www.oxfam.org/sites/www.oxfam.org/files/bp166-behind-the-brands-260213-en.pdf. Retrieved 10 July 2018.

Pendrous, R. (2013) Tesco failed to understand the Chinese consumer. *Food Manufacture*. 5 September. Available at: www.foodmanufacture.co.uk/World-News/Tesco-failed-to-understand-the-Chinese-consumer. Retrieved 27 June 2018.

Pullman, M. and Wu, Z. (2012) *Food Supply Chain Management*. London and New York, Routledge.

Rabobank (2016) *Outlook 2017 – Bear in Mind, Stocks Remain Large*. London, Rabobank.

Retail Economics (2017) Top 10 UK Retailers. Available at: www.retaileconomics.co.uk/top10-retailers.asp. Retrieved 27 June 2018.

Reuters (2012) Shareholders back Glencore takeover of Viterra. 30 May. Available at: www.reuters.com/article/us-glencore-viterra-idUSBRE84S11V20120529. Retrieved 6 June 2018.

Ricketts, K. and Ricketts, C. (2009) *Agribusiness Fundamentals and Applications*. New York, CENGAGE Delmar Learning.

Rosen, E. (2017) Why Amazon bought Whole Foods. Daily Insights. 19 June. Available at: www.l2inc.com/daily-insights/why-amazon-bought-whole-foods. Retrieved 15 May 2019.

Salerno, T. (2017) Cargill's corporate growth in times of crises: How agro-commodity traders are increasing profits in the midst of volatility. *Agriculture and Human Values* 34(1), 211–222.

SGS (2017) SGS signs strategic alliance agreement with Kezzler AS. 14 May. Available at: www.sgs.com/en/news/2017/05/sgs-signs-strategic-alliance-agreement-with-kezzler-as. Retrieved 25 June 2018.

Statista (2018) Tesco's number of stores worldwide from 2008 to 2017. Available at: www.statista.com/statistics/238667/tesco-plc-number-of-outlets-worldwide/. Retrieved 27 June 2018.

Statista (2018a) Leading food retailers worldwide in 2014 and 2019, based on sales (in billion US dollars). Available at: www.statista.com/statistics/240464/global-leading-food-retailers-based-on-food-retail-revenues/. Retrieved 27 June 2018.

Stender, S., Dyerberg, J. and Astrup, A. (2007) Fast food: Unfriendly and unhealthy. *International Journal of Obesity* 31, 887–890.

Stone, D. (2018) Grocers are failing to meet $20bn consumer demand for local food. 25 July. Available at: https://agfundernews.com/grocers-failing-meet-20bn-consumer-demand-local-food.html?goal=0_7b0bb00edf-0843f6b88c-98469273. Retrieved 30 July 2018.

Tesco plc (2017) Annual Report 2017. Available at: www.tescoplc.com/investors/reports-results-and-presentations/annual-report-2017/. Retrieved 28 June 2018.

Tesco plc (2017a) Organic food sales strongest for over a decade. 20 February. Available at: www.tescoplc.com/news/news-releases/2017/tesco-organic-food-growth/. Retrieved 28 June 2018.

Tesco plc (2018) Tesco and Booker Group Merger Archive. Available at: www.tescoplc.com/investors/tesco-and-booker-merger-archive/materials/. Retrieved 27 June 2018.

UNCTAD (2008) *Cocoa Study: Industry Structures and Competition*. UNCTAD, Geneva.

Unified Grocers (2017) Unified Grocers Inc. Cage Free Egg Statement. 24 March. Available at: www.unifiedgrocers.com/EN/AboutUs/Documents/CAGE%20FREE%20EGGS%20UNIFIED%20GROCERS%20STATEMENT.MAR%2024%202017.FINAL.pdf. Retrieved 27 June 2018.

USDA (2018) *Japan Food Processing Sector*. Washington DC, USDA. Available at: https://gain.fas.usda.gov/Recent%20GAIN%20Publications/Food%20Processing%20Ingredients_Tokyo%20ATO_Japan_1-9-2018.pdf. Retrieved 27 June 2018.

USDA (2018a) Egg Markets Overview. 13 April. Available at: https://legacyfoodservicealliance.com/wp-content/uploads/2018/04/Legacy-Market-News-April-13.pdf. Retrieved 15 May 2019.

Van der Wal, S. (2008) *Sustainability Issues in the Tea Sector: A Comparative Analysis of Six Leading Producing Countries*. Amsterdam, Stichting Onderzoek Multinationale Ondernemingen. Available at: https://papers.ssrn.com/sol3/papers.cfm?abstract_id=1660434. Retrieved 15 May 2019.

Van Dijk, B., Berntsen, G. and Berget, I. (2011) *Speculate or Integrate: Rethinking Agricultural Commodity Markets.* AT Kearney Issue Papers and Perspective. Chicago, A.T. Kearney.

Verdant Partners (2018) 2017 Agribusiness M&A Year in Review. 26 January. Available at: www.verdantpartners.com/2017-agribusiness-ma-year-in-review/. Retrieved 27 June 2018.

Vitón, R. (2018) 2018 Global Food & Agriculture Investment Outlook: Investing profitably whilst fostering a better agriculture. Issue 8. Valoral Advisers. Available at: www.valoral.com/wp-content/uploads/2018-Global-Food-Agriculture-Investment-Outlook-Valoral-Advisors.pdf. Retrieved 9 July 2018.

Walkers (2018) Ingredients. Available at: www.walkers.co.uk/crisps-range/walkers-crisps/salt-and-vinegar. Retrieved 30 July 2018.

Weinswig, D. (2018) Online grocery set to boom in 2018 (as Amazon acknowledges online grocery a tough market to crack). *Forbes.* 1 March. Available at: www.forbes.com/sites/deborahweinswig/2018/03/01/online-grocery-set-to-boom-in-2018-as-amazon-acknowledges-online-grocery-a-tough-market-to-crack/#4d398f21520b. Retrieved 12 July 2018.

Weintraub, A. (2015) Will mandating 'Healthy Happy Meals' solve childhood obesity? *Forbes.* 31 August. Available at: www.forbes.com/sites/arleneweintraub/2015/08/31/report-will-mandating-healthy-happy-meals-solve-childhood-obesity/#224376f01f2b. Retrieved 28 June 2018.

Wiens, K. (2015) We can't let John Deere destroy the very idea of ownership. *Wired.* 21 April. Available at: www.wired.com/2015/04/dmca-ownership-john-deere/. Retrieved 27 June 2018.

Wilcock, A.E. and Boys, K.A. (2017) Improving quality management: ISO 9001 benefits for agrifood firms. *Journal of Agribusiness in Developing and Emerging Economies* 7(1), 2–20.

Wood, Z. (2011) Tesco admits defeat and pulls out of Japan. *The Guardian.* 31 August. Available at: www.theguardian.com/business/2011/aug/31/tesco-japan-pull-out-philip-clarke. Retrieved 27 June 2018.

World Bank (2015) *Ending Poverty and Hunger by 2030: An Agenda for the Global Food System.* Washington DC, World Bank.

8

Risk management for agribusiness

Introduction: what risks do agribusinesses face?

It is possible to identify three overlapping stages in the evolution of analysis of agribusiness risk. Half a century ago, agricultural economists focused on production agriculture frequently started with the recognition by Lipton (1968) that 'peasant households' faced a broad range of high risks associated with uneven harvests, explained by climate variability, market volatility and arbitrary political decisions. The argument was that the allocation of scarce household resources was therefore based on the principle of 'safety first'. Resources were allocated in such a way that risks – understood as subjective evaluations of probabilities – were minimised, and therefore subjectively expected utility was maximised on balance in the long-term. This argument spurred a range of development economics perspectives. The second phase may be characterised as 'the rise of the derivatives', although it was never suggested that they were yet dominant in agricultural risk management, including in classic agricultural risk management texts which still owe much to agricultural economics (Hardaker et al., 2004). Derivatives have their place in risk management, certainly, and they are discussed below, but the perception by institutions such as the World Bank that they would solve the risk problems of agriculture proved too optimistic. The third phase, which could be characterised as the shift to agribusiness, perceives risks as primarily corporate, and distinguished between sub-sectors in different dimensions of risk, such as their relative dependence on commodity price volatility, on government support schemes, or on business models that may be threatened by technical advances. The choice an agribusiness makes on whether and which risk management strategies to use is dependent on both risk attitude and risk perception. Risk attitude is the actor's orientation towards or willingness to take risks. It can vary from being risk-averse, which means a business is unwilling to take risks, to risk-seeking where the directors and management are willing to take significant risks (Van Winsen et al., 2016). Analysis of risk in this third phase, both in terms of risks faced and in terms of the response of an agribusiness to risk, is of commercial interest, and is often performed by banks, investors and rating agencies, hence for example the view of a leading rating agency, Standard & Poor's (S&P), of agricultural commodities trading, as practised by firms such as Glencore and their rivals, which they see within the general commodities trading as an inherently 'high-risk' industry.

The key factors underlying S&Ps industry risk assessment were:

- A high degree of confidence sensitivity, as agricultural commodities traders need to sustain the confidence of trading counterparties and creditors, which if weakened, can erode the business franchise and funding flexibility precipitously.
- An inherent complexity and opacity to the business model, including a lack of transparency into risk positions.
- A high degree of dependence of trading results on market price fluctuations and arbitrage opportunities. In S&P's view, agricultural commodities traders typically lack a base of recurring, annuity-like income; to varying extents, their business is transaction-driven and therefore difficult to forecast. In fact, trading companies may do best in periods of economic turmoil. Although earnings are not tied to commodity price cycles, they are nonetheless subject to wide and volatile fluctuations, as the historical performance of rated and unrated industry participants attests.
- Market basis risk, in that agricultural commodities traders set out mostly to exploit market inefficiencies rather than take directional risk positions. However, the extent to which it is possible to hedge price risk varies by commodity, and an agricultural commodities trader can seldom fully hedge market risk. Some basis risk is typically unavoidable, and correlations between markets sometimes break down, leading to wider basis risk than the traders initially anticipated. There can also be volatile changes in market liquidity, and this can have a significant effect on the outcome of trading strategies.
- Hedges, which can give rise to liquidity risks stemming from potential margin calls. Hedges can also give rise to counterparty credit risk relating primarily to in-the-money hedge positions, and agricultural commodities traders also bear credit risk from trade receivables and other sources.
- Performance risk, where even creditworthy counterparties may refuse to honour the terms of contracts if market prices have moved against them, leaving the agricultural commodities trader with unhedged positions.
- The potential for lapses in trading risk management systems that enable, for example, rogue traders who defraud companies or make unauthorised trades that lead to large, unexpected losses, and other more commonplace frauds.
- The risk that catastrophic storage or transportation failures could cause fatalities and economic damages for which an agricultural commodities trader would be liable.
- Relatively loose regulation. Prudential regulatory oversight of agricultural commodities traders is far less extensive than it is for banks. We do not believe regulation is a panacea, but where regulatory oversight is effective and intrusive, it can curb excessive risk-taking and identify defects in enterprise risk management.
- The risk of regulatory sanctions resulting from compliance failures, such as violation of position limit restrictions or of position reporting requirements.

S&P said that there are, however, some mitigating factors:

- Most rated agricultural commodities traders have an arbitrage-based business model and seek to minimise flat price risk through extensive hedging (subject to basis risk, though). This generally allows for at least some degree of profitability when prices rise or fall (but reduces overall profitability).
- S&P believes agricultural commodities traders' emphasis on physical markets, rather than contract/financial markets, makes for relatively less earnings volatility.
- Although agricultural commodities traders are working-capital-intensive (given the need to fund trading inventory), a substantial portion of trading inventory is typically highly liquid and can be easily disposed of on exchanges or in over-the-counter (OTC) transactions, or, at least under normal circumstances, readily financed. Banks have an incentive to extend uncommitted, secured credit facilities to agricultural commodities traders because of traders' favourable capital treatment under Basel 3 and other bank regulations.
- Some investment in logistical assets is generally a competitive requirement, but the agricultural commodities trading industry is not inherently fixed-capital-intensive.
- The cost base is generally highly flexible, and variable compensation costs are among the largest cost components.
- Although agricultural commodities trading is open to new entrants, achieving sufficient mass and scale to be competitive typically requires many years.
- The dynamics of the commodity markets are constantly changing, but there is little risk of secular change or substitution of products, services, and technologies from other industries that could supplant the trading function.
- Continued growth in commodity consumption should support long-term growth in trading volume.
- Firms with well-diversified trading portfolios, global reach, sufficient scale to attract necessary funding, and rigorous trading risk management have generally been able to sustain satisfactory profitability.

Source: Standard & Poor's (2013, 2017)

This analysis should be sharply contrasted with a much more traditional – second stage as suggested above – analysis of agricultural risk, focusing on the risks faced by farmers, such as that developed by the European Union. The EU argued that farmers are exposed to different types of risks that influence their agricultural activity. The EU argues for a distinction of risk between types of risk that have different causes.

Price risks

It is widely recognised that agricultural commodities, which are significant inputs for most agribusinesses and outputs for production agriculture, are characterised by strong price volatility, uncertainty about future prices and co-movement of prices. For agricultural products, in addition, demand occurring at the end of the food supply chain generates delayed price signals for suppliers who will then take decisions that have a deferred effect on the quantities of products. This produces an oscillation in prices, the 'whiplash effect', also known as the cobweb cycle, and is often observed in the livestock sector. High perceived prices for the coming season generate increased stock, and livestock prices rise. Output lags, the market faces oversupply and prices fall. Producers move away from livestock into grains, and the cycle turns again.

The dairy crises of the EU in the early 21st century are a case in point. The first dairy crisis coincided with the financial crisis of 2008, driven by severe world supply constraints from successive droughts in Oceania and the subsequent instant supply response in the EU. Six years later, the 2014 Russian import ban for agri-food products inevitably led to a decrease in dairy prices as a result of oversupply, as Russia was a significant cheese market for the EU, and a drop in Chinese demand pressured the dairy market even more in a context of increased EU production to prepare the end of the milk quotas in 2015. Another view was that:

EU farmers continued to increase production following the end of the EU dairy quota system, while ignoring decreasing world dairy demand. The extension of the 2014 Russian embargo on agricultural imports has added additional downward pressure on dairy markets. In late July, EU dairy farmers joined pig farmers in France and later in Belgium and the United Kingdom in protesting low farm gate prices. Protesters blocked roads and retail distribution centres, and even pulled milk products from retail shelves to donate to bystanders (USDA, 2015).

But, as the EU pointed out, the result of both crises was the same – significant price volatility with negative consequences on farm income and investment (EU, 2017:3). They could have added that the cause was the same as well – exaggerated optimism about prices from farmers, a lack of long- or even medium-term forecasting, a reliance on public funds quite beyond other industries, and even a conviction that the prices for farm products ought to be based on some guaranteed profit in addition to costs, which it has been suggested applies to certain regulated energy markets. In fact, whilst energy markets are regulated, the EU is steadily, if very slowly, moving toward spot market pricing in competitive markets, as has already been achieved in Australia and the USA (Brietschopf *et al.*, 2016).

Production risks

Production risks refer to the possibility that yields and/or outputs are lower than expected. This can be the result of extreme climatic conditions such as drought, hurricanes or floods. An overwhelming majority of the damage and losses caused by droughts is to the agriculture sector. Virtually every continent is affected by increasing drought risk to varying degrees, as noted in Chapter 1. Less systemic events such as pests, diseases and local weather phenomena such as hail, frost and excessive rainfall can have a significant impact on agricultural output. Moreover, the projection of weather events is still subject to high uncertainty, though recent years indicate that, due to climate change, more years turn out to be unfavourable, which in turn increases crop yield variability (EU, 2017). Some of these risks can be mitigated directly through insurance, others through the kind of derivatives described below, whilst still others will remain a constant threat, alleviated only by efficient management, e.g. through diversification, prudent financial policy and good strategy overall.

Economic risks

Agribusinesses also face the same kinds of economic risks as virtually every other business. Their markets may shrink due to competition. Their interest charges may rise due to an increase in interest rates. They may face higher than expected input prices, including land, livestock, grains and fertilisers. If they export or import, even as inputs, exchange rates may affect their financial performance. And as well as potential shortages of labour, poor management decisions, they face adverse consequences from incorrect resource allocation decisions caused by faulty information or decision-making procedures. Some of these risks can be mitigated through derivatives, notably interest costs, although in many markets these are

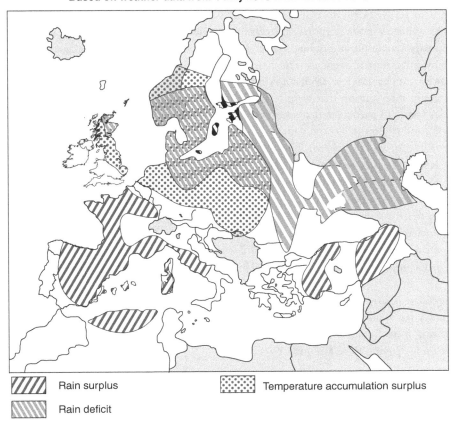

AREAS OF CONCERN - EXTREME WEATHER EVENTS
Based on weather data from 1 May 2018 untill 22 June 2018

Rain surplus   Temperature accumulation surplus

Rain deficit

Figure 8.1 Extreme weather events in the countries of the European Union
Source: EU Science Hub (2018)

either not yet properly available or only available in the form of expensive fixed interest loans. The remaining risks can only be managed.

Foreign exchange risk can serve as an example. Changes in exchange rates do not always have to have negative consequences for agricultural trade, of course. If domestic currency falls in value, exports naturally become more competitive, as the experience of Australia over the period since 2013 clearly shows (see Figure 8.2).

Lower export prices in domestic currency bring their own problems, with increased prices for fertiliser imports, for example, unless they are produced domestically. Agricultural producers can all too easily become accustomed to higher export volumes, too, without making adequate provision for changed circumstances. The importance of managing risk is paramount.

Stocks, price controls and other interventionist strategies

Effective infrastructure helps agribusinesses manage risk. Strategically located warehouses, for example, help stabilise prices by buffering fluctuations in material and product availability and improving transportation efficiency. Agricultural producers can reduce their risks, both in terms of production and pricing. Warehouses are frequently located at transport hubs, whether ports, airports, rail termini or along highways. They can be specialised or compartmentalised, and owned by producers further down the supply chain, independently, or by government agencies. The benefits of warehouses within a commercial system are however quite different from the kind of public stocks, price management and other government intervention that were seriously proposed after the commodity price fluctuations, price spikes in particular, that were seen twice in the past decade. The FAO's Committee on Commodity Problems observed:

> It seems widely recognized that small strategic emergency food reserves can help improve food security. By exploiting synergies with early warning systems and well-designed and well-targeted consumer safety nets, they can reduce the exposure of vulnerable people to price volatility. Many developing countries ran down stocks in 2007–08 to increase availability and maintain food security while stocks lasted, and in some cases, this also moderated consumer price increases. However, using public stocks to specifically manage price volatility is more controversial and its effectiveness is uncertain' (FAO, 2014:2).

Indeed, it is: anyway, the cost involved would be prohibitive and although there was, to be blunt, a lot of talk after the food price hikes of late last decade, that is all it amounted to. So, existing instruments will have to suffice for the foreseeable future for everyone, hence the reason for paying close attention to them.

Public-private partnerships to manage risk

The impracticality of a global or national public-sector response to risk is certainly not to suggest that the public sector has no role in risk management at the level of the individual

Recent developments in Australian agriculture

Agricultural export prices and the Australian dollar

Strong global demand was a major factor behind increases in the prices received for some of Australia's major agricultural exports. This was evident for livestock, when the volume of beef exported to the United States increased sharply in 2013–14 and 2014–15, leading to stronger returns to Australian exporters. Export returns have been more variable for the cropping sector since 2000–01.

Export price indexes for crops and livestock, Australia, 2000–01 to 2015–16

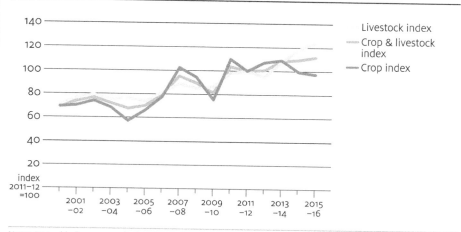

Note: Annual indexes are calculated on a chained-weight basis using a Laspeyres index with a reference year of 2011–12 = 100.
Source: ABARES

From 2013 to the end of December 2016 the depreciation of the Australian dollar relative to the US dollar increased the competitiveness of Australian exports. Because exports are predominately traded in US dollars, depreciation of the Australian dollar increased the amount received by exporters and protected some exporters from bearing the full burden of less favourable price movements. The positive influence of the weaker dollar on export returns is reflected in the index of crop and livestock prices, which accounts for prices received for 11 of Australia's agricultural export commodities.

Figure 8.2 Agricultural export prices and the Australian dollar
Source: ABARES (2017:24)

enterprise. Most obviously these have been managed through different forms of public-private partnerships (PPPs), Collaboration between the public and private sector has been utilised to solve problems ranging from deficiencies in infrastructure, value chain and technology development to the dissemination of finance, information and services to farmers at a local level. An example: in Vietnam, a Public-Private Task Force on Sustainable Agricultural Growth, co-led by government and industry, was formed in 2010 to develop and test agricultural models in priority crops with the potential for rapid scaling up.

The FAO identified a number of different ways in which PPP agreements have been used to manage risk. For example, government agencies may manage the process of transferring some risks from smallholders through risk sharing between the public and the lead private partners. Bank guarantees and subsidised interest on loans to smallholders, when coupled with secure purchasing contracts and business management training for farmer organisations, help to reduce the risk of default. This kind of subsidy to smallholders does run the risk of disguising and then entrenching inefficient production methods, but it is understandable that governments take action to support a numerous and potentially politically significant part of the population – and not just in developing countries. Other potential risk sharing options include agricultural insurance and contingency funds. For example, in Ghana, as part of a contract purchase agreement with smallholder rubber producers, subsidised insurance was made available for wind and fire outbreaks, and an income protection fund was set up in case of low market prices for rubber. A further example: in an Indonesian oil-palm PPP, the public-sector lender and the PPP established a contingency fund, capped at 10% of the farmers' income, to prevent the risk of default on loans during heavy rainy seasons, which may delay harvest and delivery (and thus payment for raw materials) for several months. This was effectively a form of forced savings, replacing inefficient (if understandable) patterns of small-holder spending with rational savings policies. To prevent the potential for private partners to exert undue influence over smallholders, in both the oil-palm case from Indonesia and a similar example of a PPP for bananas in Peru, companies were required to show evidence of previous mutually beneficial partnerships with farmer organisations (i.e. free from unresolved disputes and involving long-term, trust-based relationships) as part of the selection criteria (FAO, 2016:130). The rise of such PPPs is not only proof of the pure private sector approach to derivatives, but also of the need to assess agribusiness risk holistically, including in terms of how much support is and is likely to continue to be forthcoming from the public sector.

Price discovery and open markets

The starting place is the market for each agricultural and processed product. Every market is characterised by trading conditions that range from pure monopoly or monopsony to free, almost perfect competition. For the latter, there must be a large number of roughly equally sized and equally knowledgeable competing institutions on both sides of the market, whilst wrinkles caused by geography, quality differences or market interference (e.g. by government) must be almost completely absent. They are very infrequent markets in real life.

In practice, a range of different trading methods conceal many restrictive practices. Ancient trading methods still exist in some developing countries to trade agricultural products, for example the Hatha, Dara or Moghum Systems in India (Ul-Rehman *et al.*, 2012). But more usually, prices are determined either by private mutual agreement, whereby the individual buyer comes to the shops of commission agents at a time convenient to the latter and offers prices for the produce which, they think, are appropriate after the inspection of the sample. If the price is accepted, the commission agent conveys the decision to the seller, and the produce is given, after it has been weighed, to the buyer. Mention should also be made of open auctions, which are prevalent for certain agricultural commodities such as tea (Tea Board of India, 2018) and fibres. *Open auctions*, at least where there is confidence that the market is not being manipulated, are a clear method of accurate price discovery and serve to dispose of market supply quickly, though they are time-consuming and often rushed. A similar method is closed tender, where bids are invited and submitted privately.

Spot or cash markets trade commodities in exchange for immediate payment. In developed markets, information on spot prices for different varieties of the same commodity is readily available from a number of different sources, notably the ABCD agribusinesses but also cooperatives.

Whichever system operates, the importance of accurate market information in helping to create liquidity and improving the position of the multitude of agricultural sellers is undeniable. Evidence from spot markets demonstrates that production agriculture operates in a fundamentally risky environment, from demand to climate change, from food price oscillations to floods and famines. The FAO points out that as markets take over production agriculture, risks arrive in tandem with opportunities. Links with buyers are not without risks, nor are relationships with other producers. 'Prices at the time of harvest, availability of hired labour, machinery breakdown, technological change, government policy and weather conditions are all examples of factors which affect the level of profits and income on the farm' (Kahan, 2013:48).

Not all risks can, or even should, be eliminated – no risk = no profit – but the key is to take the right risks at the right time. The goal of risk management, therefore, is not to eliminate every risk for an agribusiness but, rather, to balance a farm's risk exposure with increasing profits. This balancing is done after considering the sources of risk, the methods of reducing risk, the ability and the willingness to take risks, and possibly earnings from alternative strategies. The goal of risk-management is not to reduce risk only. Careful risk management can help farmers choose how to best use their limited resources to achieve personal and business objectives. The key to effective risk management is working with up-to-date, accurate factual information of the type described in Chapter 5 for farms, and which firms at other points in the agribusiness value chain would normally collect at least monthly. Risk management strategies are also affected by how deep a farmer or a firm's pockets are. The greater the potential access to financial reserves, the greater the willingness not only to take risks, but unfortunately, also, to pay insurance and for other forms of risk management, such as professional advice and derivative contracts.

Income diversification for agriculture

Managing risks starts at the farm level, where farmers have different strategies to stabilise their income. Farmers have a large variety of options to choose from in order to reduce

BUNGE

Daily Bidsheet   25-Feb-2019

Bunge Agribusiness Australia Pty Ltd
Level 1, 99 Coventry Street,
South Melbourne, Victoria 3205, Australia

2018/19 FIXED GRADE WHEAT (Dec 2018)

Grade	H1	H2	AUH2	APW1	APW2	ASW1	AGP1	FED1
Bunbury Port (Delivered)	$372.00	$362.00	$353.00	$342.00	$322.00	$317.00	$317.00	$302.00
Bunge FIS (Arthur River & Kukerin)	$368.00	$358.00	$353.00	$343.00	$323.00	$318.00	$318.00	$303.00
Kwinana	$368.00	$358.00	$348.00	$343.00	$318.00	$320.00	$320.00	$303.00
Albany	$369.00	$349.00	$349.00	$344.00	$319.00	$323.00	$304.00	$294.00
Esperance	N/A	N/A	N/A	N/A	N/A	N/A	N/A	N/A
Geraldton	N/A	N/A	N/A	N/A	N/A	N/A	N/A	N/A

2018/19 CAN1 ISCC (Dec 2018)

Grade	CAN1	CAG1
Bunbury Port (FIS)	N/A	$511.00
Bunge FIS (AR & KUK)	$566.00	$508.00
Kwinana	$563.00	$493.00
Albany	$563.00	N/A
Esperance	N/A	N/A
Geraldton	N/A	N/A

2018/19 OATS (Dec 2018)

Grade	OAT1	OWAN1	OAT2	OAT3
Bunbury Port (Delivered Jan - March)	N/A	N/A	N/A	N/A
Bunge FIS (Arthur River)	$370.00	$370.00	$355.00	$340.00
Bunge FIS (Kukerin)	$370.00	$370.00	$355.00	$340.00

2018/19 BFED1 (Dec 2018)

Grade	BFED1	Multi - BASS1	Multi - PLANET1	Multi - SPAR1
Bunbury Port (Delivered)	$278.00			
Bunge FIS (AR & KUK)	$276.00	$15.00	$10.00	$15.00
Kwinana	N/A			
Albany	N/A			
Esperance	N/A	*ARTHUR RIVER	*AR/KUK	*BUNBURY

*BDEC1 no discount Bunge sites

2019/20 CAN1 ISCC (Nov/Dec 2019)

Grade	CAN1	CAG1
	N/A	N/A
	N/A	N/A

2019/20 MULTI GRADE WHEAT (Nov/Dec 2019)

Grade	APW1
Bunbury Port (Delivered)	$300.00
Bunge FIS (Arthur River & Kukerin)	$300.00

2019/20 BFED1 (Nov/Dec 2019)

BFED1
$230.00
$230.00

*19/20 Spreads Bunge Sites: APW1 BASE. H1+$10, H2 +$5, APW2 -$10, AUH2 -$5, ASW -$20, AGP -$40, FED1 -$80

*Canola: ISCC Sustainable and CSO-1A only for CAN1/CAN2 bids,CSO-1 for CAG bids.
*Canola bids are basis AOF oil bonifications
^ Freight and Receival Fee to be deducted
Payment terms: 14 days end of week of delivery
All prices quoted GST exclusive
All prices are indicative and subject to confirmation
Prices subject to Bunge contract Terms and Conditions
All bids (excluding those into Bunge sites) are inclusive of CBH receival and grain assessment fee

OPTIONS FOR DELIVERED CONTRACTS 2017/18 (declare at time of contract)
Option 1 : Buyer's Call

For more information and contracting, please contact our Bunbury Office on 1300 4 BUNGE (1300 4 28643)

Christopher Tyson (Regional Manager)   Mob: 0417 999 632
christopher.tyson@bunge.com

Alexander Barber   Mob: 0439 047 452
alexander.barber@bunge.com

Email: bas.enquiries.aus@bunge.com
Alternatively you can reach our Melbourne Office on-
Phone: 03 9275 6555   Fax: 03 9866 0627

Bunge FIS Freight Fees
Arthur River $14.95
Kukerin $20.00

Receival Fees Bunge FIS (Kukerin & Arthur River) & Bunbury Port for Canola only*
Wheat $10.80
Barley $12.20
Oats $12.20
Canola $17.70

Figure 8.3 Bunge daily price sheet
Source: Bunge (2019)

their exposure to risks. They can, for example, diversify their production or income by using different crops or livestock, or by developing non-agricultural income sources for the farm, like agro-tourism, to balance a loss in one of their agricultural activities. Certainly,

> ...achieving scale in agriculture results in reduced volatility in farming returns, due to the benefits scale provides. These include the ability to acquire a portfolio of diversified assets, to negotiate lower unit costs of production, to invest in technology and to acquire highly experienced management teams, as well as providing access to capital for continued growth (Macquarie, 2010:1).

However, diversification comes at a cost because it usually leads to a lower than average income, due to the loss of scale economies. Chasing diversification may also be genuinely difficult if many alternatives exhibit similar sensitivities.

Off-farm employment is another way to diversify the farm household income, together with precautionary savings or cuts in private expenditure and investments in times of hardship. Obviously, this is much easier when employment opportunities are plentiful and when incomes are sufficiently high to enable savings. Even in Australia, farms have little reserves, although many wealthier farmers also have share portfolios and trusts to deal with regular expenses. Over a decade ago it was observed that:

> A great many farm households, large and small, have become pluriactive, so that in many countries, by no means only in the developing world, the larger part of household incomes is now derived off-farm, yet the farm remains a central household activity (Brookfield & Parsons, 2007:213).

Off-farm activity, or at least non-farm earnings, can be derived from numerous different and potentially competing sources. Using the land for alternative income generation may include leasing for wind or solar energy generation, letting properties on the farm, or leasing out land to other farmers. In the UK one of the most famous alternative uses has been the Glastonbury rock festival, which from modest beginnings in 1970 now involves renting land from more than 20 farmers (Rawlinson, 2016).

McKinsey notes that large-scale commercial farming has taken off in places such as Brazil, where commercial farms can top 100,000 acres (Goedde *et al.*, 2015). On the other hand, it was suggested two decades ago that 'Farmers are the original vertical integrators in that they frequently own the means to produce the feed supply, the grind and mix facilities to produce feed, the animal production processes and the trucking needed to take the finished animals to market' (National Farmer, 2019). Quite possibly it is a motive of food security, and hence supply security, that drives vertical integration in agribusiness, rather than the traditional drivers of economic efficiency (DiPietre, 1999). One factor that definitely remains is the frequent absence of price-driven intermediate markets, with transfer pricing remaining opaque. More recently, smaller- and medium-size family farms are increasing their purchasing (for example, seeds, crop protection, fertiliser and machinery) and selling grains, sugar and ethanol through cooperatives, lowering transaction costs significantly. Well-organised farms in Australia are following exactly this trend, partly through equity ownership by farmers in cooperatives that handle sales, for example CBH, which describes itself well on its website (CBH, 2018). There is also emerging interest in Africa as a production basin: major agribusiness companies are increasingly integrating vertically as more traders extend into production and processing, while retailers are moving into production and sourcing of key input commodities. One author who deplored Chinese government pressure for major agribusiness firms to dominate Chinese agriculture even argued that if Chinese family farms are to survive, it will require vertical integration (e.g. through cooperatives) from cultivation to processing to marketing, albeit without horizontal integration for farming (Huang, 2011). There is evidence that farmers may benefit from vertical integration in terms of gross sales and overall farm profitability (in terms of relative profit differences). Moreover, integration does not affect the burden of variable and fixed costs: vertical integration seems not to significantly change farms' production organisation. Thus, results may suggest that farms establishing integration relations with the processing industry are more committed to exert effort to pursue quality improvement of their products and, consequently, to benefit from higher prices on their market. This goal seems to be reachable without a deterioration of the costs structure and/or a reduction in yields (Carillo *et al.*, 2016). Before completely acceding to the principle, however, a note of caution should be sounded that it is all in the contract, or the equity sharing agreement as the case may be: a bad deal will always be a bad deal, however attractive the theory (Liesveld, 2016).

On-farm, there is the possibility for technical improvements such as using drought-resilient varieties, optimising the scale of the farm or to increase the value added of the product by on-farm processing or sales.

Contract farming

This is partly a question of risk management, and partly of marketing. But it also relates to how a farm is managed. Developed countries have seen close relationships between farmers and their customers, amounting to what is now called contract farming, for half a century or longer. Sharecropping, effectively a version of contract farming, has been around for centuries. In the USA, farmers produced for canneries, packers and food wholesalers. In the USA, and in Europe and for several decades also Latin America and parts of Asia, it has been the supermarkets and fast-food companies themselves which have been at the other end of contract farming contracts. The numbers of farmers involved in each scheme are usually relatively few, in the hundreds unless a parastatal is involved (Brookfield & Parsons, 2007:75).

Contract farming supporters, such as the World Bank and even, since the publication of its guide (Eaton & Shepherd, 2001), the FAO, stress the efficiency and security for farmers that it can provide. For hog farming, for example, the life-cycle specialisation has encouraged a chain of contracts, each with required inputs and compensations, so different growers can specialise in specific parts of an animal's life – farrow to wean, wean to feeder pig, and feeder pig to finish, with ownership transferring at the farrow to feeder point. Contracts can be priced using spot market, formula and fixed price methods, either on a live weight basis or yield/trade. And contracts typically outline producers' standards for care and quality, e.g. no use of herbicide within 50 ft of any building housing hogs covered by the contract (Pullman & Wu, 2012:46–47). Some examples can fail, especially if purchasing companies are rapacious

- The Government of India's National Agriculture Policy envisages that "Private sector participation will be promoted through contract farming & land leasing arrangements to allow accelerated technology transfer, capital inflow & assured market for crop production especially of oilseeds, cotton & horticultural crops"

- The promotion of the agritech sector has led to a heavy investments of over USD10 million in 2017 by companies like Accel India, IDG ventures, etc.

Foreign companies practicing contract farming in India		
Company	State	Crop
Cargill India Pvt Ltd	Madhya Pradesh	Wheat, Maize & Soya bean
Hindustan Lever Ltd	Madhya Pradesh	Wheat
ITC – IBD	Madhya Pradesh	Soybean
Appachi	Tamil Nadu	Cotton
Nestle India Ltd	Punjab	Milk
Pepsi Foods Pvt Ltd	Punjab, TN	Chillies, Groundnut, Seaweed, Tomato & Basmati Rice

Source: Company reports, Assorted articles, TechSci Research

Contract Farming in India

- Companies provide R&D & agricultural implements to farmers
- Regular & timely payments to farmers & credit facilities
- Reduces the price risk fluctuations & saves land investments for companies
- Lesser logistics cost for both, farmers and companies
- Stable and steady supply of quality farm output for companies

The government is planning to revamp the old model Agriculture Produce Marketing Committee Act (APMC Act) & carve out the provisions on contract farming into a separate law to form a new Contract Farming Act.

Figure 8.4 Indian government position on contract farming
Source: India Brand Equity Forum (2017:39)

and unscrupulous. In India, it was argued over a decade ago that 'contract farming only helps corporations get a handle on farm operations and make profit' (Sharma, 2006). The government remains committed as the diagram in Figure 8.4 shows.

Criticism continues: in Punjab, the Amarinder Singh government's obsession with crop diversification has exposed farmers to the vagaries of corporate interests; farmers, it is claimed, now resent a system that has put them under the total control of corporations. The growing incidents of predetermined prices being reduced on the pretext of inferior quality of the grain or crop, have added to the resentment among farmers. Another pertinent development objection is that 'true smallholders only rarely participate' (Brookfield & Parsons, 2007:75).

On the other hand, a report from the Netherlands Foreign Affairs Ministry on Ethiopian contract farming from 2010 suggested this:

Contract farming is acknowledged as one of the effective institutional arrangements to minimize transaction costs and risks. Apart from enhancing smallholders' commercialization, it can also serve as a means of developing partnership spirit between smallholders and the private sector as it is crucial to recognize smallholders as trading partners, beyond mere producers. Both contracting parties depend on each other and are equally required for the success of a contract. The importance of choosing the right type of contract has been discussed. Products like horticulture require stringent contracts that detail high quality standards, grades which require close supervision and monitoring while other products like cotton require less strict contracts. However, any contract needs to detail the important clauses in an unambiguous language and during the process of contract design all contracting parties should be allowed to participate. Pricing mechanisms and enforcement mechanisms during default need to be clearly spelled out (Melese, 2010:28).

This is a view also taken by more recent research: contractual arrangements are likely to help structure markets and provide producers with market options that offer better prices, but the arrangements need to be accompanied by clear terms and conditions. For instance, issues regarding grading and pricing as well as mechanisms governing the terms of the contract need to be clearly defined and understood by the buyer and the seller (Mwambi et al., 2016:15). At root is willingness to pay, whether for security or externalities (Mhuriro-Mashapa et al., 2017).

Forecasting commodity prices – methodologies, software and institutions

Despite the fact that forecasting techniques and software have been available for many decades, forecasting remains rather like the rain god in many institutions: a very necessary part of life, but entirely inexplicable to most and the actual responsibility of no one. It is deeply regrettable. Partly this is explained by the many failures of forecasting itself, partly by its undoubted complexity, at least if done properly, which explains why in larger agribusinesses few will step up to take responsibility for it, and partly it is because many participants in agribusiness, especially compulsive optimists, believe that they either cannot forecast at all, or that even if they could, it would not greatly benefit them as they would have to continue with their operations in any event. Mostly this is a misperception: accurate, or even approximately correct, predictions of future prices assist decision-making, especially investment decision-making, to deliver better returns.

But how can forecasting be done?

Qualitative techniques are subjective estimates from informed sources, but the argument frequently expressed that they should only be used when historical data are scarce or non-existent is incorrect. Qualitative methods should be used wherever possible and it is in fact the shortage of opportunities to use them that is the main constraint rather than the absence of data, especially when good data is a pre-requisite for effective qualitative forecasting anyway.

Put simply, it is about consulting experts. There is a need, however, for the experts to be on a level playing field: they need not only the same data to work from, but the same time at which to be consulted and the same task of forecasting set before them. For example, it is quite usual to want to ask a minimum of eight experts and take an average of the middle six, to eliminate the outliers of the most and least optimistic amongst them, as this process has been found to generate better forecasts than straight averages. A variant, or modification, of this approach of averaging is known as the Delphi technique. Here, a group of experts is asked the same questions and the results of their individual opinions (forecasts) are presented, anonymously, to all the experts. They are then invited to forecast again, a second round, with the anonymous results available to them. Hopefully, the result is a progressively narrower gap between the experts.

Second, *time series analysis*. This forecasting methodology uses only historical data as the forecast variable, such as crop output, yields or commodity prices, to find patterns that are then projected forwards. There are several different examples of time series forecasting models: for example, moving averages, exponential smoothing or ARIMA models. In stock market analysis the equivalent is technical analysis. Both are based on the premise that the factors that influenced patterns of activity in the past will continue to do so in the future. Shocks, therefore, are bad news for time series analysis generally. Time series forecasting also relies on data, the more the better (Amin *et al.*, 2014), frequently needing seasonal adjustment.

Finally, there are *regression models* which, at least in their simplest form, are neither especially complex nor particularly difficult either to construct or use. They are based on the idea that any given variable can be explained by the performance of other variables which must, therefore, themselves be forecast. Linear regression involves presenting two sets of variables – the dependent variable, such as farm values, agricultural commodity prices, or retail profits – and the independent variables, such as economic growth, labour costs or agricultural commodity prices themselves (e.g. to forecast processor profit).

The accuracy of forecasts. How far time series forecasts can go badly wrong is illustrated by the chart in Figure 8.5.

But we should not be surprised: commodity price forecasts based on simple econometric modelling will usually tend to produce smoothed outcomes, as the charts in Figure 8.6 show.

U.S. farm-level prices: Corn, wheat, and soybeans

Dollars per bushel

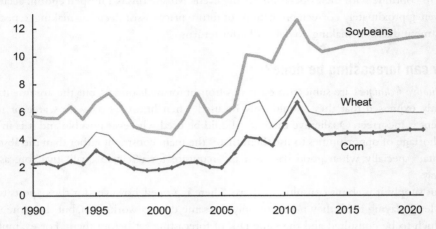

Figure 8.5 Commodity forecasts by the USDA
Source: USDA (2012)

The temptation to smooth out the future is apparently irresistible, and it is not *always* wrong, as the World Bank commodity price forecast for 2017 compared to the actual outcome demonstrates.

Forecasting techniques

Forecasting is not easy, but it is not impossible. Obviously the need to forecast is not confined to agricultural product prices: inputs such as fertilisers, labour and other costs need to be forecast as well, all of which are worth considering, and very few of which are ever actually used by farmers. This despite the fact that there are plenty of tutorials on how to conduct time series forecasting using software such as R (which is free).

A typical example of a commodity forecast was that produced by ABARES (the Australian equivalent of the USDA) for the global milling wheat market in March 2017. Discussing the medium term, ABARES had this to say:

In the medium term, prices are projected to decline further in real terms. The area planted to wheat is projected to fall in high-cost producing regions in response to continued low prices. However, global production is projected to continue to increase over the medium term because of productivity improvements, particularly in Argentina and the Black Sea region. Ample exportable supplies are expected to be available to satisfy increasing import demand from a growing world population unless there is a major disruption to supply over the next five years. A strong US dollar over the outlook period will continue to affect the competitiveness of US wheat exports and place downward pressure on the world indicator price (ABARES, 2017:29).

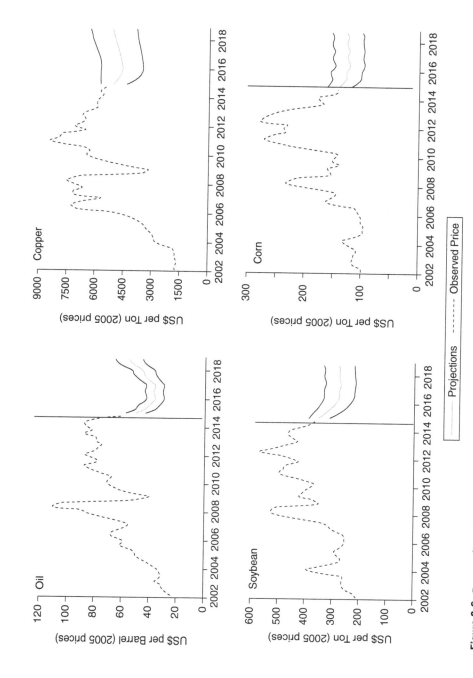

Figure 8.6 Commodity price projections based on simple econometric modelling
Source: Powell (2015)

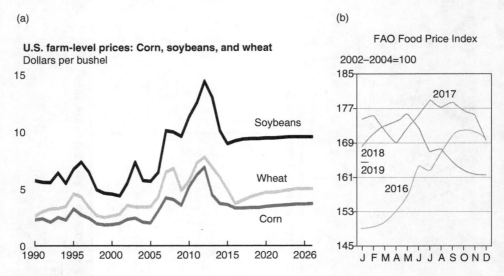

(a)

U.S. farm-level prices: Corn, soybeans, and wheat
Dollars per bushel

(b)

FAO Food Price Index
2002–2004=100

Figure 8.7 Outcomes of forecasts
Source: USDA (2017); FAO (2019)

Thomson Reuters Eikon forecasts:

…a variety of data sources to produce production forecasts of corn, soybean, wheat, canola/rapeseed, and palm oil and monitor the flows of imports/exports. To produce the forecasts, we process and analyze global weather data and remotely sensed satellite imagery, monitor news and forums, talk with grain elevators and industry experts, and directly collect information from hundreds of crop fields spread across the globe, stretching from the Americas to Asia (Redo, 2019).

How accurate have these forecasts been?

Qualitative and general predictions are not immune to error, either. In 2009, Agricultural economic experts expected US exports of value-added commodities to increase significantly from about 2010 to 2015, but also foresaw raw commodity exports gaining as livestock production takes place nearer to the end consumer. This forecast evidently did not anticipate the global economic crisis of those years.

There are too many commodity forecasts to list: the World Bank, the USDA amongst many international and national organisations, as well as firms such as Goldman Sachs and ABN Amro and Rabobank. The important point is to determine what and how these organisations forecast (local or international prices, time series or regression modelling, etc.), and to be aware of the potential pitfalls involved in the particular methodology they happen to use. Most recently research has questioned the analytic basis of even USDA forecasts (Cumming *et al*, 2017).

There is also the question of which software to use. Excel is cumbersome for the purpose; R or its competitors like Stata, E-views, require considerable training and are not very user-friendly. For most purposes, a half-way house such as Forecast Pro or Smart Forecast is all that is needed.

Risk management techniques

Besides these different on-farm practices, farmers can also make use of private and/or public risk management techniques. The claim that:

> …risk management is dealt with by providing financial contributions for (a) insurance against economic losses to farmers caused by adverse climatic events and animal or plant diseases, for instance; (b) mutual funds that pay financial compensation for economic losses; and (c) an income stabilisation tool that supports mutual funds and compensates farmers in case of serious income losses' (EU, 2014:23)

may however be somewhat exaggerated. The perception of risk relates to how large management estimates the threat of the risk and can be influenced by previous events. The EU argues that the relation between risk attitude and the choice for risk management strategies is paradoxical. More risk-averse farmers adapt less ex-ante strategies to prevent risks but rather use ex-post mitigating measures. On the other hand, risk-seeking farmers make more use of ex-ante measures. A possible explanation for this is that risk-seeking farmers take more risks and hence have more need to protect them against these risks. Since farmers operate in a risky environment, they have been found to be in general more risk-averse. They are sometimes reluctant to engage in risk management schemes for different purposes. Some of these problems are to pay money upfront for ex-ante schemes without knowing what their 'return on investment' will be, or because it is hard to cooperate with other farmers to pool risks because of personal, cultural or regional differences. It is also possible that participation in risk management schemes changes the risk perception or attitude of farmers, creating moral hazard (i.e. reducing farmers' incentive to protect themselves properly against the risk since they are protected from its consequences by, for example, buying insurance). Further, ex-post payments provided by public institutions can crowd out the incentive for farmers to protect themselves ex-ante against risk through the private market if they know that their losses will be covered anyway.

Non-subsidised insurance

Crop or livestock insurance works similarly to any other insurance. The farmer pays a premium and, in case of losses covered by the insurance, receives compensation for these losses. Insurance allows the farmer to transfer part of the risks to a third party. In the EU, insurance addresses mainly production risk; insurance protection against price risks, revenue losses and income losses, whether related to crops or livestock, is uncommon in the EU. The amount of indemnities is generally calculated on the basis of results of individual farms. Significant reserved amounts of losses before payment. may apply.

The insurance market is dominated in each member state by a limited number of players active on the national market. Private-based insurance schemes are difficult to establish. Firstly, as in all insurance schemes, the asymmetric information (adverse selection and moral hazard) needs to be managed. In particular, it is difficult to foresee and calculate the costs of phytosanitary outbreaks and livestock epizootics. Second, the occurrence of systemic risks causes problems for insurance, and may require the insurance company to set very high premiums, which can cause a death spiral for the product, especially when reinsurance options for insurance companies to cope with these challenges, such as covering themselves on the futures market or reinsurance by global players with a more diversified portfolio, may be very limited. Crop insurance (both of private and public-private nature) covering climatic risks is largely available in Europe. The most extended type of insurance is the single-peril crop insurance covering hail. Multi-peril risk insurance, securing against a larger range of weather events (e.g. frost, storm, excessive rain, drought), is only available to a lesser extent. In a few member states, phytosanitary risk insurance is proposed, mainly for potatoes. Compensation covers direct losses resulting from quarantine actions, limited to 60–90% of the value of crops destroyed, but rarely to consequential losses in income. Livestock insurance schemes covering diseases are commonly available in the EU, although not as yet in all member states. While direct losses, i.e. the value of the deceased animal, are compensated, few schemes also cover consequential losses from livestock epizootics. Endemic diseases are also rarely covered. In general, livestock insurance covers death and emergency slaughter due to illness (sanitary risks), risk of accident, theft, contamination of products, fire and storm. Even in the advanced countries of the EU, take-up of insurance remains limited, mainly because of the high premiums, the high deductibles and the mismatch between demand and supply, in particular with regard to multi-peril crop insurance and the absence of revenue/income insurance.

Non-subsidised mutual funds and cooperatives

Mutual funds require farmers to contribute, usually with a fixed amount independent of the risk, to a common financial reserve. In case of losses, the farmers concerned receive full or partial compensation, when necessary with an additional collection from participants to the fund. Mutual funds are set up mainly at a sector-specific level or regional level, where farmers experience similar risks. Mutual funds are based on a solidarity principle with a pooling of risks amongst farmers and over time. Its effectiveness depends largely on the available funds in case of losses. Indeed, one of the main issues with mutual funds is when too many farmers incur losses at the same time. Mutual funds may provide protection against climatic and sanitary risks, but also against income risks. Set-up and uptake of mutual funds remain limited. This is partly explained by the availability of public support, but specific difficulties to setting up mutual funds may also encourage farmers to turn to other available risk management tools, in particular insurance. The challenges for setting up a mutual fund include the administrative requirements, behavioural biases (individualism, lack of trust among farmers), and the need for sufficient reserves and possible reinsurance to mitigate risks. [1]

Derivatives

Forward contracts. To address price risks, in many developed countries farmers can use forward contracts. These are non-standardised (over-the-counter) contracts between a farmer and a buyer or trader. The farmer agrees to sell a specified quantity and quality of a particular agricultural product at an agreed price at a specified future date. The farmer can then plan on the basis of fixed cash flows, at least so long as the counterparty actually pays. When it works well, the system allows farmers to manage cash flow, reduce risk and thereby encourage them to make investments. The actual agreed price can be the market price prevailing at the moment of delivery (benchmark), based on an index of some close correlation with the actual product, an average market price over a certain period (known as a pool contract), or with any amount of complexity in setting the price, although the more complexity, the less predictability. In sectors where firms are vertically integrated, contracting is unnecessary because of the full integration of producers and processors. At the other end of the spectrum, individual farmers can negotiate contracts with downstream partners, but in general have a lack of bargaining power.

In sectors with only a few downstream partners, for example, in the dairy or pig sector in the EU (and other developed countries), processing companies can exert a certain amount of negotiating advantage over producers with respect to prices or quality. Therefore, the higher use of forward contracts is mostly observed in sectors and member states which have cooperative structures in place that are able to lower transaction costs and increase the market power of farmers. Forward contracts are widely developed in the grain and oilseed sectors in France, in the pig sector in Denmark, and benchmark contracts are used for dairy and poultry in Hungary and Slovenia. But aside from these individual examples, again even in advanced countries such as the EU, and despite centuries of use and widespread opportunities, the use of forward contracts in the EU for both crops and livestock is not widespread.

The Glanbia fixed milk price scheme

Glanbia, an Irish dairy cooperative that processes milk, launched its new scheme in December 2016. This voluntary fixed milk price scheme allows milk suppliers to lock in a minimum milk base price based on a given quantity for either one year or three years. This base milk price consists of the milk costs plus a farmer's margin that moves in line with the Consumer Price Index. A market adjuster applies to the scheme to increase the base price per litre with 0.5c/l when the milk price gets 1 cent above a predefined threshold. In a similar manner, the base price will decrease when the milk price gets below a lower threshold. By locking in a minimum milk price, farmers have more predictability for the duration of the scheme in exchange for accepting a price that might not be as attractive as the current market price. The scheme has a 60% participation rate among the suppliers of the dairy cooperative.

Source: EU (2017:9)

Derivatives (options, swaps, futures and others) and their use

For thousands of years markets have been more sophisticated than just spot trading. The very nature of agricultural commodities, with production extended over a season, lends itself to *derivative* trading.

Forward contracts. The most well-known, simplest and most frequently used derivative in agricultural products, this is a market in which the purchase and sale of a commodity takes place at time 't=0' but the exchange of the commodity, or settlement in cash or its equivalent takes place on some mutually contracted date 't' in the future. Although for the most part forward contracts are over-the-counter (OTC) products contracted individually, they can be integrated into a sequence, forming a series of marketing contracts, with their own legal and commercial challenges. In California, for example, 80% of rice is sold through contractual arrangements called paddy pools, where rice is committed to one mill, usually owned by the mill association. The price, however, is not determined until sale. The remaining 20% is sold privately, without a mill association.

Futures contracts (or simply 'futures') by contrast are standardised, binding agreements in which a buyer and a seller agree to trade a specified quantity of an (agricultural) commodity at an agreed price on a given future date. They are frequently traded on the derivatives markets of stock exchanges. Used sensibly, they can reduce some of the contractual risks that occur with forward contracting. The benefit of using an exchange for any derivative contract always used to be that there is a clearing house standing behind it. Should any member of the exchange fail, then their contracts would be automatically distributed to other members and the client would not lose. More recently, even OTC contracts have been able to take advantage of clearing houses, which are themselves now in competition with one another.

Farmers can use futures markets to hedge their risk in order to protect themselves against an unforeseen decrease in prices. In this way the farmer is securing a price at the cost of losing some potential gains in case the price at the moment of delivery has gone up. To participate in the futures market, farmers need to pay a small margin that serves as collateral to minimise credit risk. To make hedging work, the price on the futures market and the market price should converge. The difference between these two prices measures the value of the basis risk.

Nor are futures markets especially well established worldwide. Whereas in the USA futures markets for cereals have a long history, the first futures markets started to develop in Europe in 1992 with the reduction in price support under the Common Agricultural Policy (CAP). There are contracts available for different products. The institutional picture keeps changing with M&A amongst derivative exchanges and the emergence of new ones, but as of the end of the decade, the Euronext stock exchange (based in Paris, London, Brussels and Amsterdam) provides contracts for different cereals, fertilisers and dairy products. The European Energy Exchange (EEX) offers contracts for hogs and piglets, potatoes, dairy products and fertilisers.

However, trade activity on the market is different across commodities. Rapeseed and wheat are the most traded commodities on the futures market with respectively 19% and 10% of the crop production in 2016. For skimmed milk powder (SMP), butter and whey it is lower than 1%, so the market is characterised by low liquidity. However, more market participants appear to be using derivatives, at last. But for the other commodities concerned, the shares traded on the futures market are close to zero. As futures are standardised contracts, future contracts are adequate precisely for standard products. The characteristics of some agricultural products are thus less favourable to be traded on the futures market. Particularly in Europe products such as cheese or hogs are not as homogeneous as cereals are. Also, for some agricultural products, the price in the local market is not strongly correlated with the prices on the EU futures market. For these producers, futures may not be appropriate to offset their price risk.

Options markets. Option contracts give the holder the right but not the obligation to buy or sell. Options are attractive to hedgers because they protect against loss in value but do not require the hedger to sacrifice potential gains.

Futures contracts have five standardised elements in these contracts:

(1) The type of commodity (for example, cotton, wheat, corn, meat...);
(2) The quantity of the commodity (the number of bushels of grain, pounds of livestock...);
(3) The quality of the commodity (using specific grades);
(4) The delivery point (the location at which the product should be delivered); and
(5) The delivery date (the day at which the product should be delivered; there are typically no more than four or five delivery dates per year).

These standards are determined by futures exchanges (or futures markets), which are the public marketplaces where people can buy or sell futures contracts. This differentiates futures from forward contracts, which are private bilateral agreements ('over-the-counter') between two parties who can freely decide on the terms of the contract themselves.

These futures markets add a time dimension to the physical market (or 'spot market') for agricultural products. Nevertheless, a key difference with the physical market is that the contract is traded on futures exchanges, and not the actual product itself. Therefore, futures are derivatives, as the value of the contract is derived from the underlying (agricultural) commodity. The price of the futures contract is determined through an auction process at the futures exchange, based on the balance between demand and supply for these contracts. Because these futures contracts are continuously traded on the futures exchanges, they pass through many hands, and in the end the contract will have a different buyer ('short position') and seller ('long position') than the original ones. The courses of these contracts are monitored on a daily basis, and buyers and sellers pay or receive *variation* margins on their future contracts, which are executed by a brokerage firm. When the price of the futures drops, the broker will compensate for this price change by withdrawing the corresponding amount of money from the buyer's margin account and depositing this amount on the seller's margin account. Similarly, when the price of the futures contract rises, the gains will be deposited to the account of the buyer and the seller will lose this money on their account. When the buyer or seller is required to deposit more money on their account to cover the losses on their futures contract, this is known as a variation margin call. In theory, the price of the futures contract and the price in the physical market ('spot price') should converge when the delivery date of the contract is approaching. This occurs through arbitrage: if there is a difference between the price on the futures market and the spot price of the commodities on the cash market, traders will buy and sell in these markets to profit from these differences, which will lead to a convergence in both prices. Nevertheless, the commitment to deliver the physical commodity remains crucial, as it guarantees that the price of the futures contract will converge towards the 'real' price of the commodity (spot price) when the end of the contract approaches. For this reason, the delivery points, i.e. the locations where the products need to be delivered when the futures contract expires, also play a key role. The distance between the physical market and the delivery points of the futures market can require significant transportation and storage costs, and will thus largely dictate the affordability of futures for farmers. Because of these costs, there can be a structural gap between the futures price and the spot price, which is called the base. In practice, however, there are issues associated with delivery that may impede this exact convergence.

On the agreed delivery date ('at maturity'), the contract expires and needs to be 'settled' in two possible ways: by actually delivering the goods or where permitted through a form of cash settlement. It is estimated that fewer than 2% of the futures contracts are eventually settled through physical delivery, in which the seller actually delivers the agreed amount of goods to the buyer. In the large majority of the contracts, the seller simply offsets the contract by buying another futures contract, and receives or pays an amount of money for the expired futures contract (this is often done even before the date of expiration). Because the seller buys back the same amount of futures, his selling position is cancelled out and only the price will vary.

It is vital to stress that the quality and success of a futures market is determined by its liquidity, or the frequency at which contracts are traded and the ease at which they can be exchanged. When liquidity is low, there are not enough market participants, it is difficult to exchange futures contracts and neutralise trading positions, and the price of the futures contracts do not reflect the actual price of the underlying product.

Futures markets perform two key functions which can be helpful for farmers and other agribusinesses: risk management and price discovery. First and foremost, futures (and associated options) are, or should be, a risk management tool (see below, hedging). Secondly, futures can also be valuable as an instrument for price discovery. As futures markets reflect the price expectations of both buyers and sellers, they allow farmers to estimate the future spot prices for their agricultural products. In the context of unstable agricultural markets, being able to estimate the selling price at the beginning of the production process is especially valuable for farmers.

Derivatives are a complex risk management tool which requires a significant amount of technical know-how of the markets and regular information on daily price changes. However, individual farmers are often not aware of how this instrument functions in practice, and can therefore sometimes make limited use of it. Although they may hire advisors or advisory bodies who can help them with the use of futures by offering training and/or personalised monitoring of their transactions, this represents a considerable investment for farmers in terms of time and money. Forward, future and options contracts are the main private instruments available to manage price risks. Farmers can decide to individually hedge their risk on the futures market, but this very rarely happens.

More often, cooperatives provide forward contracts to farmers and base the price of these contracts on the futures market. Other private initiatives by cooperatives such as the fixed milk price scheme of Glanbia can also reduce the price risk of farmers. Nevertheless, farmers require more education and training, in particular about how future markets work. Public authorities can provide support to farmers on how to use future markets.

Traditionally, European agricultural markets were highly protected through the guaranteed price system of the original Common Agricultural Policy (CAP). Given that public interventions limited the impact of downward price fluctuations on their incomes, futures contracts were initially not considered as necessary for farmers. However, the subsequent CAP reforms towards a reduction of market support gradually exposed the European agricultural sector to price variations. Faced with price volatility, farmers became increasingly interested in derivative markets for agricultural products. As a result, a number of futures exchanges were developed in Europe, and futures contracts can now be traded for a variety of agricultural products.

How good is the fit between agribusiness and derivatives?

The proper functioning of futures markets thus requires a sufficient number of actors, both hedgers who want to protect themselves against price changes and speculators who want to bet on these price changes, as this should guarantee that the prices of futures are a good reflection of the 'real' prices of the (agricultural) commodities. On the other hand, if the futures market is illiquid, a small number of actors will be able to manipulate the prices of futures and the use of futures markets will become unattractive. When a farmer wants to sell a contract on the futures market, there must also be a counterparty to buy a contract to create liquidity. Speculators involved to bear the risk and willing to take the opposite position on the futures market are essential. One of the main issues for the development of derivative markets is to increase the liquidity in the market. To increase liquidity, more market information and price transparency is required, to incentivise investors. The problem is acute: in India, for example, there is substantial evidence to suggest that futures markets are unfortunately moving away from their role of rationalising growers' price expectations. Until and unless the futures markets are being participated in by a large number of producers and traders, including small and marginal ones, the benign role of these markets cannot be realised (Dey & Maitra, 2016).

The experience of futures markets in Europe has also revealed that not every agricultural commodity is equally suitable for a derivative market. Because of the nature of futures contracts, it is necessary that the underlying products can be standardised, and not every agricultural sector has the same possibilities to do this. Futures contracts are considered to be a very appropriate instrument for crops, and grains and oilseeds in particular, since it is relatively straightforward to standardise plant products. This is due to the fact that commodities such as wheat, corn, soybeans and rapeseed are easy to store and deliver, which also reduces the risk that the quality of the product will fall short of the standards required in the futures contract. The standardisation process is even easier for feed grains, which are seen as the most appropriate commodities for futures contracts. As a result, ICE Futures Europe in London and Euronext in Paris offer good hedging opportunities for grains, as these markets have a high level of liquidity, have transparent prices which are accepted as European benchmarks, and farmers can easily access these markets through grain merchants or cooperatives. Moreover, efforts have been made to expand these futures markets, as ICE Futures Europe then added a second delivery point for wheat in Dunkirk to the traditional delivery point in Rouen. Other plant products also have well-functioning European futures markets. For instance, ICE Futures Europe has a liquid exchange for refined white sugar and all types of cocoa and provides reliable price benchmarks for these products. These markets are liquid because both of these products can be stored for a relatively long period, which enables smooth exchanges and higher trading volumes.

On the other hand, certain crops also suffer from very poor liquidity levels on their European futures markets due to limited trading volumes, such as barley and potatoes. And in general, creating standardised contracts poses more difficulties for animal products, due to their specialised nature, differences in species and quality, and the perishability of these products, which complicates their storage. As mentioned in the previous section, there are no longer any European futures markets for pigs, as they suffered from very poor liquidity. Futures are also not available for beef products, as the production of multiple breeds of beef makes it difficult to standardise these products. The trade volumes for lamb products are also deemed to be insufficient to create a well-functioning futures market. Likewise, dairy products are so perishable that they require complex storage procedures, which leads to illiquid futures markets with prices unrepresentative of the physical market. In particular, a futures market for milk is likely to have limited liquidity as it is highly vulnerable for spoiling. However, this does not apply to milk powder, which is easier to store and is thus more suitable for futures trading.

It is clear that the extent to which agricultural products can be standardised is a major determinant for the liquidity, and therefore the success, of their futures exchange markets. Crops, and especially grains and oilseeds, are particularly suitable for a futures approach, while this risk management instrument may have little value for the meat and dairy sectors, and in other minority sectors such as jute or hemp there are no such markets. In still others, such as tea, spot auctions still largely prevail.

Because of the increase in the trade of (agricultural) commodity contracts and the risks associated with speculation, policy-makers have paid growing attention to the regulation of their derivatives markets. Following the financial crisis of 2008, which was largely caused by problems with these derivatives, jurisdictions such as the EU have introduced a range of legislative measures aimed at reforming and strengthening European financial markets. These include:

■ Long (buy) and short (sell) positions should be netted to determine the effective size of a position a person controls at any time.

■ Any positions held by other persons on behalf of a person should be included in the calculation of that person's position limit, which should be aggregated at both an entity level and at a group level, using a methodology to convert options into delta equivalent futures (based on data produced by Euronext) (Allen, 2012).

- The limit for all other months applicable to the combined positions on futures and options will however be based on the open interest of futures only (i.e. excluding option) (Raevel & Porte, 2017).

However, the use of futures also has several compelling disadvantages. The very nature of this instrument prevents farmers from benefiting from positive price developments for their products, as these prices are fixed by the futures contract. Engaging in futures contracts is also a rather expensive undertaking for farmers, as they need to pay commissions and fees to brokerage firms and advisors to manage these complex financial products on their behalf. Moreover, if the futures market is not functioning adequately, it is likely that the futures price will be different from the price on the physical markets, leading farmers to receive a lower price than the one agreed in the futures contract.

Most importantly, futures do not reduce price volatility for agricultural products as such, since fluctuations in prices are a necessary condition for the proper functioning of their exchanges. On the contrary, excessive speculation on futures can lead to artificial short-term price increases and thus even higher levels of price volatility, which is detrimental to both producers and consumers of agricultural products. In short, futures are not an instrument that can reduce price volatility, but remain at best a useful financial tool to manage its negative consequences. Moreover, trading volumes and the number of farmers using futures in the rest of the world remain far more limited than those in the USA. The recent experiences of European futures markets and the dismal failure of exchanges across Africa as a whole, with a few exceptions such as South Africa (www.jse.co.za/trade/derivative-market/commodity-derivatives/agricultural-derivatives), is indicative, but notice how agricultural derivatives are just one product line amongst many. The JSE took over SAFEX, the South African Commodity Exchange, and Ethiopia (www.ecx.com.et/) has an exchange worth studying. The Ethiopian Exchange is a major achievement, though not without its critics, and also shows that a futures approach is not equally suitable for all agricultural sectors. In Asia-Pac, apart from contracts in Australia, where again the stock exchange runs the derivative markets, there are a number of innovative exchanges, such as the Indonesian Commodity and Derivative Exchange (www.icdx.id) and the Multi-Commodity Exchange of India (www.mcxindia.com), both of which list commodity contracts. As with the experience of the Pakistan derivatives exchange (www.pmex.pk), more lucrative business is to be found with financial derivatives, even with gold, as they are easier to list and far easier to find liquidity for, so a policy gap remains that organisations such as the World Bank continue to try to fill.

How should agribusinesses hedge?

The starting point is to recognise that, overwhelmingly, 'individual farmers have little control over the price of their production' (Barnard et al., 2016:27). The same applies to the vast majority of agribusinesses. Not only do output prices exhibit considerable volatility, but production expenses such as fuel and fertiliser are also highly sensitive to macroeconomic changes. Derivative markets enable farmers and others exposed to commodity price risk to fix their prices for the future, reduce their risks, and should enable them better to plan their production and investment decisions.

As an example of hedging, suppose a wheat producer has planted a crop in his field in May, when the price on the physical market ('spot price') for wheat is $4 per bushel. However, the farmer will only be able to harvest and sell this wheat in September, and is not certain which price he will receive for his products at harvest time. If the price of wheat rises between May and September, he will have higher earnings, while he will have less profit if the price drops in the coming months. In order to protect himself against the possibility of a price drop, he can secure the current selling price by selling a number of bushels of wheat in the futures market in May, and buying a futures contract with the same number of bushels back in September, when he will sell his crops on the physical market. This will enable him to plan his investments over a longer term and limit potential losses. This is a producer hedge. By entering into a futures contract, the farmer will receive the price mentioned in the futures contract in September, as any losses on the physical market will be compensated by a gain on the futures market. For instance, let's assume that when the farmer buys the futures contract in May, the spot and future prices are identical at $4 per bushel of wheat. Because the futures market is assumed to function perfectly, these two prices should also continue to change identically.

If in September the price of wheat has dropped by $1 to $3 per bushel, the farmer will make a loss of $1 per bushel on the sale of his wheat on the cash market. However, the value of his futures contract is now $1 per bushel higher than other futures contracts ($4 compared to $3). Therefore, if he sells his futures contract of $4 per bushel and buys another futures at $3 per bushel, he makes a profit of $1 per bushel. Because the profits on his future position equal his losses on the physical market, his net selling price will still be $4 per bushel. Likewise, if the price of wheat rises by $1 to $5 per bushel, the net selling price that the farmer receives would still be $4 per bushel, as the additional $1 per bushel he receives for selling his crops on the physical market are offset by the loss of $1 per bushel on the futures contract. In both cases, gains and losses on the two markets cancel each other out, and the 'locked in' price target is achieved: a selling price of $4 per bushel of wheat in September.

Meanwhile, in this hypothetical, balanced example of hedging, a bakery may also try to secure a fixed buying price for wheat in order to determine its future production and profits. The bakery will take an opposite position, buying the futures contract. In this scenario, the farmer holds a short position (agreeing to sell) while the bakery holds the long position (agreeing to buy). As an exchange traded futures contract is anonymous, neither farmer nor baker knows the other, and indeed they may not be holding similar sized positions, but the liquidity of the exchange permits each to buy and sell what they need, when they need to. There are many analyses available of different hedging strategies: a good place to start is what is available from the exchanges themselves (e.g. www.cme.com).

Black-Scholes works here as a method of options valuation, at least (Geman, 2005; Clark, 2014). Exchange-traded futures prices are publicly available.

Products	Features and Advantages	Disadvantages and Risks
Forwards[1]	• An over-the-counter (OTC) instrument; • Customised contract between the two parties, in terms of size, quality and delivery date; • Usually involves no 'upfront' payment and 'cash' changes hands only at the expiry of the contract;	• It is negotiated between two parties and is not marketable; • OTC markets, where forward contracts are traded, are generally opaque, as trades are not compulsorily reported and transaction prices are unknown to the outside world; • Closing out the position to limit the losses may not be unilaterally possible;
Futures[2]	• Standardised contract in terms of contract size, delivery dates, quality, trading hours, tick size, and maximum daily price limits; • Exchange traded; hence, zero counterparty risk; • Involves a 'down payment' known as the initial margin[3]; • Transparent pricing • Contract can be closed out prior to its maturity (giving an opportunity to cut losses);	• Requires active portfolio management as loosing positions leads to margin calls; • Standardisation can have an impact on hedging, as delivery dates and terms are not flexible; • Do not cover basis risk[4];
Options[5]	• Helps to lock-in the price but without the compulsion to honour the contract, especially to benefit from favourable price movements; • No margin calls for options buyers; • Risk is limited for the buyer of options contract, i.e., he/she can at the most lose the contracts premium; • More suitable for risk averse participants such as farmers and small commercial players; • Options can be exercised or offset before expiration; • Generally, a very liquid market allowing the producer to quickly reverse positions.	• Does not cover basis risk; • Premium requires to be paid upfront by options buyer; • Premium payable for the options contract may at times be "too high" as compared with the rights granted by the contract; • Options are in specified quantity (contract size) and represent some standard quality; • Using options requires thorough understanding of futures and options markets
Swaps[6]	• Traded in OTC markets; • Customised transactions, perfectly suiting hedging needs; • Provides a choice to set the currency you require; • Useful for hedging against the spread between prices of the final product and that of raw materials; • Generally no upfront payment	• Transaction may turn costly if the swap is terminated before the expiry of the contract; • Generally, the contract sizes are large, hence, not suitable for small commercial players; • Challenge to achieve an agreement among different parties; • Time consuming commerce due to the long negotiations process;

[1] A cash market transaction in which delivery of the commodity is deferred until after the contract has been made. Although the delivery is made in the future, the price is determined on the initial trade date. http://www.investopedia.com/terms/f/forwardcontract.asp#axzz1yyAvjrlu

[2] Futures contracts are exchange traded legal agreements to buy or sell goods for a specified delivery future date at a price agreed today. http://www.lme.com/what_contracts_futures.asp

[3] The initial margin is primarily a deposit to ensure both parties to the contract do not default

[4] Basis is the difference between the price of a futures contract and the spot price of the underlying commodity.

[5] Options contract is a financial derivative that represents a contract sold by one party (options writer) to another party (options buyer). Options contracts give trade hedgers and investors a more flexible alternative to futures exchange trading. When buying an options contract, the purchaser (taker) does not enter into a firm obligation. He/she simply purchases a choice of action. This choice gives the genuine trade hedger an opportunity to lock in a fixed price while maintaining the ability to abandon the option in order to take advantage of favourable price movements. http://www.lme.com/what_contracts_options.asp

[6] Commodity swap refers to a transaction wherein one party pays (once or periodically) floating amounts in a specified currency calculated from a notional amount in the given currency and a floating price, and a second party pays (once or periodically) fixed amounts in the same currency calculated from the same notional amount at a fixed price. This product serves to hedge risks resulting from price fluctuations for the given commodity. Only the price difference is settled monetarily, not the notional amounts. http://www.unicreditbank.cz/en/web/corporate-public-sector/treasury/commodity-risk/commodity-swap

Figure 8.8 Advantages and disadvantages of different types of derivative
Source: MCX (2013:6)

Yield, revenue and weather insurance

Western jurisdictions such as the USA and the EU provide financial support to farmers, generally when market conditions are unfavourable. The degree of government intervention varies across crops and between countries, but the policy objective is usually the same – to keep farms in business.

Improved technology can in turn raise accuracy in yield insurance. Some yield insurance schemes, covering yield losses due to meteorological events, use indices based on meteorological data or area and yield to trigger compensation.

Arguably one of the most efficient ways to deploy agricultural risk management is through weather derivatives, as they do not have the moral hazard problems inherent in yield insurance (i.e. they provide no disincentives to optimise production) (CGIAR, 2012).

An example of a weather derivative trial: MicroEnsure's entrance into Zambia's rural microinsurance market:

In 2014, MicroEnsure – a large global microinsurance company – began serving the Zambian market with its FarmerShield life and weather insurance product in partnership with NWK Agriservices. NWK is an agribusiness that operates a cotton out-grower programme that engages 100,000 smallholder farmers and has diversified into input distribution and commodity storage and trading. Faced with famer loyalty and side-selling problems, NWK partnered with MicroEnsure to offer weather index and life insurance to its farmers. The companies planned to build weather stations across Zambia to record weather events, but faced with high construction and operation costs, decided to use satellite imaging to monitor regional weather. Prior to its first season of operation in 2013–14, 6,610 farmers signed up for weather index insurance, covering 7,600 hectares. This particular weather index product was designed so that benefits payouts were modelled on the impact of various climatic events, such as drought or floods, on cotton yields. Data was collected at a local level and benefits were automatically paid out if the weather event crossed the predetermined level of severity.

In 2014, weather events triggered $42,000 of payouts, thus demonstrating the value of the product in its first season. Further, the FarmerShield life insurance product covered 25,165 farmers' lives, who paid a total of $5,536 for coverage. The net loss ratio for this product was 48%, which is a positive outcome for a life microinsurance product. It attracted even further demand from farmers to cover additional lives in their households. As a result of this coverage, farmers valued both the weather index and life insurance products and appreciated both direct (for example, claim payouts) and indirect (for example, integration into the value chain) benefits of the insurance products. NWK noticed a positive impact on its business with increased deliveries and reduced side-selling (pending final conclusions of this pilot study) and the products are expected to be sustainable and profitable for the insurers and reinsurers. From the initial product with NWK Agriservices, MicroEnsure is diversifying its product offerings to rural Zambians, which is vital for the development of rural Zambian financial markets (World Bank, 2015:12).

Smallholder farmers in Zambia are vulnerable to weather-related shocks such as drought, flooding and irregular rainfall. Insurance can be a good risk management tool for these farmers, but the traditional insurance market largely fails to meet their demand for affordable insurance. Index insurance provides an innovative and more efficient solution for them to protect their crops against losses and encourage investment.

In March 2016, the World Bank's Global Index Insurance Facility signed a capacity building grant with Mayfair Insurance, a private insurer registered in Zambia. The grant enabled them to build their capacity to develop and sell weather-based insurance products that would be used to cover vulnerable farmers against weather-related crop losses. Mayfair has demonstrated the effective use of a distribution strategy to deliver sustainable premium volumes by working with select aggregators (NWK Agriservices, the Zambia National Farmers Union, and the World Food Programme). Following a competitive bidding process in November 2017, Mayfair was contracted by the government of Zambia to develop insurance products that would be bundled together with the government input subsidy package under the Farmer Input Subsidy Program (FISP). This way, farmers benefiting from FISP would receive compensation equal to the value of the inputs in case of drought, thereby improving their resilience. The Global Index Insurance Facility (GIIF) extended support to Mayfair for additional product development, training, and awareness-raising activities (Index Insurance Forum, 2016).

The problem of basis risk

There are two senses in which the term 'basis risk' is used. The first is the relationship between cash/spot and derivative prices. Futures markets prices often track spot markets closely, as the diagram in Figure 8.9 reveals.

However, it is always wise to recognise that there may be significant exceptions to this general rule, at which point basis risk becomes a real problem.

The second sense of basis risk relates much more specifically to agricultural commodities. Unfortunately, the need to generate liquidity within a derivative market is in conflict with the multiplicity of different species and varieties of agricultural products, each with their own particular price trajectory. The consequence of this clash is that using a derivative, whether based on a specific grade and quality of an agricultural commodity or an index, may not produce an exact correlation between the price of the particular species or variety that the user has physically. The resultant difference in price trajectory is known as basis risk, and it can be fatal to a hedging strategy. Basis risk can also derive from different locations or trading dates.

Tax and accounting treatment of derivatives

Generally, for an agribusiness, the taxation test for the proceeds (or losses) from a derivative are – or should be – in connection with their use in the course of ordinary business, and therefore taxable as business income. The exception to this general rule would be where the asset itself was being held for capital purposes, the most obvious example being land.

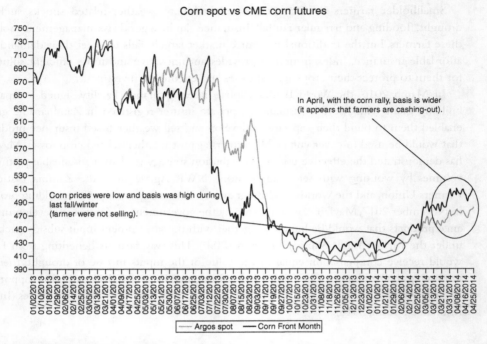

Figure 8.9 Basis risk illustrated
Source: Jacques (2014:8)

As for accounting, in most jurisdictions, such as the USA, when the underlying commodity being hedged is available for sale or is valued on the balance sheet at its fair (or market) value, marked-to-market gains or losses as of the date of financial statement are recognised with respect to net income and reported on the income statement as hedging gains or losses. If the hedged commodity is normally sold in the course of business, as would be the case for grain on a farm, for example, the reported gain or loss is shown in the revenue section of the income statement and, if purchased, such as rice for a breakfast cereal manufacturer, then in the expense section of the income statement – all quite logical (Neiffer, 2013; Index Insurance Forum, 2016).

Fair value hedge: example

As of 1/3/20:

- Assume producer has 100,000 bu of unpriced commodity inventory on hand;
- The forward price for May 2020 delivery is $6.8/bu;
- Producer buys (goes long) 100,000 bu (however many contracts this represents) of July 2020 commodity options with an out-of-the-money strike price of $6.5 for $0.35/bu, i.e. $35,000.

On 5/2/20:

- Producer sells 100,000 bu of commodity inventory to local trader or warehouse for $6.5/bu;
- Producers sells (goes short) 100,000 bu (an equal number of contracts) of July 2020 commodity for $0.2/bu, i.e. $20,000.

Result:

- Producer receives $650,000 for selling the commodity;
- The loss from the options premium is $-0.11/bu ($0.2-$0.35), i.e. -$15,000.

The net price received by the farmer is $635,000.

Particularly important is determining whether a commodity contract is within the scope of IAS 39, as contracts to which IAS 39 applies will mainly be derivatives measured at fair value, whilst contracts to which IAS 39 does *not* apply will not usually be recognised in the financial statements until delivery takes place.

Key derivative market institutions

The major institutions involved in derivative markets are, first and foremost, the commodities exchanges. The main European futures exchanges for agricultural commodities are situated in London and Paris. The Intercontinental Exchange Futures Europe (ICE Futures Europe) in London offers futures and so does Euronext. There are many other exchanges, most of which are members of either or both of the Association of Futures Markets (www.afm.org) or the Federation of World Exchanges (www.world-exchanges.org).

However these days, more accurately, we should speak of those exchanges where commodity contracts are traded, not of commodity exchanges, as the majority of commodities contracts are traded on exchanges like the Chicago Mercantile Exchange (www.cme.org), where the dominant form of contract is financial, e.g. interest rates, exchange rates and share derivatives of one kind or another. The consequence of this imbalance is that commodity contracts, both in terms of development, marketing and management, have become the Cinderella of the derivative markets. Often exchanges cannot make money launching them, and only do so as a result of regulatory pressure and/or the need at least to appear to be acting in the interests of commodity market participants, especially farmers, whilst their significant income lies with traders and investment institutions which are much easier to reach and much more significant players when they do. Furthermore, there are doubts over transparency. In 2018, the CME Group, which is the largest commodity and derivatives exchange in the world, announced plans to offer its customers so-called block trades in agricultural commodities. 'These instruments are large, privately negotiated deals struck away from the broader market by phone or otherwise and cleared by the exchange. The National Grain and Feed Association opposes this move, asserting that it would threaten market transparency' (Mercier, 2018).

This in turn places stress on government and quasi-government institutions, as well as innovative marketplaces in developing countries that are constantly developing new products and new ways of reaching out to producers and wholesalers. Agribusinesses in the public sphere, especially the World Bank, the OECD, CGIAR, USDA and now very importantly also the FAO, as well as many others, are also active in promoting a range of agricultural derivatives, following extensive development work in past decades. The OECD, for example, claims that its analysis takes a holistic approach to risk management that focuses on the interactions between different types of risks, of strategies undertaken by farmers, and of government policies that impact on risk management. The studies undertaken by the OECD cover a wide range of areas, from livestock diseases that impact at both the international and national levels, climate change, food security, and on risks that affect, in particular, farmers working in developing countries (OECD, 2018).

Use of derivatives by agribusiness: the evidence

In the past, there have also been a limited number of futures exchanges in which contracts for animal products were traded, in particular for pork. An early example was the Commodity Exchange ('Warenterminbörse') in Hanover, which was created in 1998 and had a significant trading volume in the early 2000s, but was closed due to insolvency in 2008. Likewise, contracts on live pigs and piglets were created in Amsterdam in 1980 and 1991, yet these markets disappeared in 2003. A major problem for these exchanges was the lack of market participants: only producers were positioning themselves, while there was limited interest from buyers (e.g. slaughterhouses, processors and manufacturers).

In general, the number of futures contracts traded on European exchanges and the use of futures by farmers has increased steadily in recent years. Nevertheless, the number of trading activities is still significantly lower than in the USA, even for commodities which are largely produced and consumed inside the EU. European farmers also make less use of commodity futures: it is estimated that between 3% and 10% of them have used this risk management tool, compared to 33% in the USA.

This remarkable difference can be explained by the fact that US agricultural policy has traditionally focused more on a free market approach, which led US farmers to search for risk management instruments such as futures a lot earlier than their European counterparts. Other reasons for the limited development of futures markets by European farmers include a lack of information and knowledge on futures, the bad image of the instrument due to its association with speculation, and the various costs related to the use of futures.

Risk management along the supply chain

Supply chains, as the name suggest, are about interlocks between different agents, each with their own tasks. The need to share information, manage inventories, maintain food safety and add value characterises all agribusiness supply chains.

We should now revisit contract farming from the standpoint of the large retailer and fast-food chain. The potential advantages of a supply chain that achieves the benefits of vertical integration without the pitfalls of M&A and a conglomerate are clear. Markets are not good at ensuring continuous supply at a predetermined price. Quality control is hard to achieve without real involvement with production: with most fresh produce from flowers to fruit having a short shelf-life and discerning customers, strict systems of grading and inspection

Table 8.1 Who should use derivatives and how

Category	Who	Way of involvement	Motives
Commercial entities ('Commercials')	• Farmers and other agricultural producers • Merchants • Silo operators • Agricultural processors • End-users of agricultural products, exporters	• Bona-fide hedging • May hedge for clients • May speculate, including for treasury financing activities	Protection against agricultural price changes/volatility, smooth convergence of futures prices into spot prices as contracts approach their expiration date
Banks	• Investment banks • Large banks with commodity trading desks • Banks focusing on agricultural clients	• Providing OTC contract to hedgers and speculators • Trading futures and options for clients on regulated trading venues • Speculating (through proprietary trading) • Market making • Operating as brokers or broker-dealers • Operating (informal) trading venues • Issuing exchange traded commodity (index) products (ETPs) • May design and operate indexes • May own, mostly non-agricultural, physical commodity operations	Profits from earning management or servicing fees, and from proprietary trading to careful manage price risks, especially when prices are volatile are high
Hedge funds	• 'Alternative investment funds' (EU definition) • Managed money (US definition) • Commodity trading advisors (CTAs, US) • Commodity pool operators (US)	• Pursue a variety of speculative trading strategies, e.g. technical modelling, fundamental approaches, algorithmic programming and high frequency trading • Are funded by rich and institutional investors • Hedge funds may borrow (operate with leverage)	Aiming at very high profit making from speculative trading strategies and large fees
Providers of commodity index products and commodity (index) exchange traded products (ETPs)	• Banks • Limited liability investment corporations • Hedge funds and securities brokers • Other investment firms	• Tracking the returns on the commodity futures specified in the index • US (not EU) ETF and other regulated fund managers may buy related futures on trading venues • Trading strategies to reduce risks of ETPs • May use OTC derivatives (swaps)	Lucrative fees and commissions from the sales of commodity (index) ETFs, ETNs and investment funds for institutional investors

(continued)

Table 8.1 (Cont.)

Category	Who	Way of involvement	Motives
Pension funds and other institutional investors	• Private pension funds • Portfolio managers for rich clients or other investors • Other institutional investors	• Speculating by tracking commodity indices and buying related derivatives on trading venues • Participate in commodity index funds or buying other ETPs • Directly trading speculatively on trading venues • Trading 'passively', i.e. rolling-over 'long' futures contracts • Invest in hedge funds speculating in commodity derivatives	'Investing' in commodities as portfolio diversification strategy to get long-term overall stable and profitable returns to their total assets. When investing passively, they do not need to act according to price developments
Broker-dealers, brokers, dealers	• Persons • Companies • Sometimes divisions of banks or other firms	• Intermediaries buying and selling orders and trade on behalf of their clients (brokering) and /or engage in trading for their own account (dealing)	Profits from fees from the brokerage services and careful management of price risks when dealing for own account
OTC commodity derivatives traders; US swap dealers and swap dealers and swap execution facilities	• Banks • Broker-dealer firms • Institutional investors and others • Regulated platforms for swap trading (US)	• Trading OTC derivatives/swaps • Providing a bilateral OTC derivative/swap for hedging or speculative purposes • Facilitating OTC/swap trading offering trading platforms	Make profits by relying on careful price risk management and fees, including embedding fees within the offered OTC product
Agricultural commodity exchanges and other regulated trading venues	• Publicly listed firms operating exchanges (trading agricultural futures and options) • EU firms operating regulated multilateral trade facilities (MTFs) • EU firms operating regulated organised multilateral trade facilities (OTFs)	• Operating venues for commodity futures and options trading • May offer also related services (e.g.) clearing • May aggressively promote trading to all potential participants	Fees from (large volumes of) trading and related activities on their trading venues
Clearing houses and central counter parties (CCPs)	• Firms specialised in clearing • May be banks • May be corporations operating commodity exchanges or other trading venues	• Provide settlement risk mitigation and management services related to OTC and on-venue trading operations	Profits from fees for clearing services. May make profits from proprietary managing of collateral ('margins')

Source: European Union (2017)

may be required. Quality standards are frequently contained within contract farming contracts, for example Cargill, Hormel and Smithfield all have policies requiring growers and their employees to be certified by the US National Pork Board Quality Assurance Plus programme (Pullman & Wu, 2012:47). Some contract farming is the prerogative of freezers, canners, packers, manufacturers of soups and sauces, and processors; others by retailers – and the difference may be important, especially in spatial terms. For example, in Mexico, whereas the big retailers are of course located close to major population centres, food-processing firms are largely concentrated around their source of supply – they may even receive their inputs from farmers directly (Brookfield & Parsons, 2007:70–71). This approach certainly has advantages by comparison to open source, where no source information is available about the product.

Conclusions

Risk for agribusiness is here to stay. Conventional derivative markets have only filled part of the risk management function for the majority of agribusinesses. There are still some ways to improve their operation. For example, a possibility for the future is a fund that consists of a set of contracts – credit, insurance, warrant and forward – that enables producers to tackle specific agricultural risks and gain access to market finance. In a trial with cotton cooperatives in Argentina, these financial contracts proved to be successful at guaranteeing the fund as issuer of state-contingent debt securities in the capital markets. The fund, as an intermediary, then lent on to cooperatives to help finance small cotton producers (Alem & Elias, 2018).

This kind of solution may well work for smallholders, but what time has shown is that no amount of derivatives can substitute as a key risk management solution for *sheer scale*, including the ability to diversify, cross-subsidise, access capital markets and maintain cash reserves in order to survive periodic market downturns and volatility without adversely affecting the efficiency of resource allocation. In the 21st century, agribusiness can do much better than function as optimising peasants.

Note

1 This text is drawn from the EU but the explanation is generic. Similar analysis is to be found in Kang & Mahajan (2006) and in numerous other sources, e.g. Madre & Devuyst (2016), many of which take divergent views on the usefulness or otherwise of these financial instruments for agriculture.

Bibliography

ABARES (2017) Agricultural Commodities. March Quarter 2017. Available at: www.agriculture.gov.au/ abares/Documents/agricultural-commodities-report-march-2017.pdf. Retrieved 4 October 2018.

Alem, M. and Elias, J.J. (2018) Allocating production risks through credit cum insurance contracts: The design and implementation of a fund for small cotton growers to access market finance. *International Food and Agribusiness Management Review* 21(2), 237–248. Available at: www.wageningenacademic. com/doi/pdf/10.22434/IFAMR2017.0116. Retrieved 10 July 2018.

Allen, S. (2012) *Financial Risk Management: A Practitioner's Guide to Managing Market and Credit Risk,* 2nd edition. Hoboken, NJ, Wiley.

Amin, M., Amanullah, M. and Akbar, A. (2014) Time series modelling for forecasting wheat production in Pakistan. *Journal of Animal and Plant Sciences* 24(5), 1444–1451.

Barnard, F.L., Akridge, J.T., Dooley, F.J., Foltz, J.C. and Yeager, E.A. (2016) *Agribusiness Management,* 5th edition. London and New York, Routledge.

Breitschopf, B., Wachsmuth, J., Schubert, T., Ragwitz, M. and Schleich, J. (2016) *Prices and Costs of EU Energy. Annex 2 – Econometrics.* Available at: https://ec.europa.eu/energy/sites/ener/files/documents/annex2_ecofys2016.pd. Retrieved 22 July 2018.

Brookfield, H. and Parsons, H. (2007) *Family Farms: Survival and Prospect. A World-Wide Analysis.* London and New York, Routledge.

Bunge (2019) Daily Bidsheet. Available at: http://bunge.com.au/wp-content/uploads/2019/02/Cash-Pricing-25-February-2019-New-Format.pdf. Retrieved 25 February 2019.

Carillo, F., Caracciolo, F. and Cembalo, L. (2016) Vertical integration in agribusiness. Is it a bargain? *Rivista di Economia Agraria, Anno LXXI* 1 (Supplemento), doi:10.13128/REA-18624. Available at: www.fupress.net/index.php/rea/article/view/18624/17342. Retrieved 28 February 2018.

CBH (2018) Available at: www.cbh.com.au/

CGIAR (2012) Weather index insurance: new age risk management solution in South Asia. 22 April. Available at: https://ccafs.cgiar.org/es/weather-index-insurance-new-age-risk-management-solution-south-asia#.WrTKHohubIU. Retrieved 28 June 2018.

Clark, I.J. (2014) *Commodity Option Pricing: A Practitioner's Guide.* Chichester, Wiley.

Cooper, C. and FitzGerald, V. (eds.) (1989) *Development Studies Revisited: Twenty-five Years of The Journal of Development Studies.* London, Cass.

Cumming, K., Mattos, F. and Etienne, X.L. (2017) Evaluating crop forecast accuracy for corn and soybeans in the United States, China, Brazil, and Argentina. *Proceedings of the NCCC-134 Conference on Applied Commodity Price Analysis, Forecasting, and Market Risk Management.* St Louis, MO. Available at: www.farmdoc.illinois.edu/nccc134. Retrieved 5 February 2018.

Dey, K. and Maitra, D. (2016). Can futures markets accommodate Indian farmers? *Journal of Agribusiness in Developing and Emerging Economies* 6(2), 150–172.

DiPietre, D. (1999) Vertical Integration – Sometimes a Solution to Market Failure. Available at: www.nationalhogfarmer.com/mag/farming_vertical_integration_sometimes Retrieved 11 June 2018.

Eaton, C. and Shepherd, A.W. (2001) *Contract Farming: Partnerships for Growth: A Guide.* FAO, Rome.

European Union (2014) *Financial Instruments and Legal Frameworks of Derivatives Markets in EU Agriculture: Current State of Play and Future Perspectives.* Brussels, European Union. Available at: www.europarl.europa.eu/RegData/etudes/STUD/2014/514008/IPOL_STU(2014)514008_EN.pdf. Retrieved 18 March 2018.

European Union (2017) *Risk Management Schemes in EU Agriculture. Dealing With Risk and Volatility.* EU Agricultural Market Briefs Number 12. Brussels, European Union. Available at: https://ec.europa.eu/agriculture/sites/agriculture/files/markets-and-prices/market-briefs/pdf/12_en.pdf. Retrieved 28 June 2018.

European Union Science Hub (2018) Crop monitoring in Europe. Yield forecasts revised downward. *JRC MARS Bulletin* 26(6). Available at: https://ec.europa.eu/jrc/sites/jrcsh/files/jrc-mars-bulletin-vol26-no06.pdf. Retrieved 19 March 2019.

FAO (2014) Food Stocks and Price Volatility. Committee on Commodity Problems. Seventieth Session. 7–9 October. Rome, FAO. Available at: www.fao.org/3/a-mk895e.pdf. Retrieved 18 March 2018.

FAO (2016) *Public–Private Partnerships for Agribusiness Development – A Review of International Experiences.* Rome, FAO. Available at: www.fao.org/3/a-i5699e.pdf. Retrieved 29 June 2018.

FAO (2019) FAO Food Price Index. Available at: www.fao.org/worldfoodsituation/foodpricesindex/en/. Retrieved 26 February 2019.

Geman, H. (2005) *Commodities and Commodity Derivatives Modeling and Pricing for Agriculturals, Metals and Energy.* Chichester, Wiley.

Goedde, L., Horii, M. and Sanghvi, S. (2015) Global agriculture's many opportunities. *McKinsey on Investing* 2. Available at: www.mckinsey.com/~/media/McKinsey/Industries/Private%20Equity%20and%20Principal%20Investors/Our%20Insights/Global%20agricultures%20many%20opportunities/Global%20agricultures%20many%20opportunities.ashx. Retrieved 9 July 2018.

Hardaker, J.B., Huirne, R.B.M., Anderson, J.R. and Lien, G. (2004) *Coping With Risk in Agriculture,* 2nd edition. Wallingford, CABI Books.

Huang, P.C. (2011) China's new-age small farms and their vertical integration: Agribusiness or co-ops? *Modern China* 37(2), 107–134.

Index Insurance Forum (2016) Zambia. Available at: https://indexinsuranceforum.org/project/zambia. Retrieved 28 June 2018.

India Brand Equity Forum (2017) Agriculture. April. Available at: www.ibef.org/download/Agriculture-April-2017.pdf. Retrieved 25 February 2019.

Jacques, S. (2014) Grain Cash Market and Logistics Report. Available at: www.slideshare.net/SimonJacques1/grain-cash-markets-logistics-freight-34174562. Retrieved 26 February 2019.

Kahan, D. (2013) *Managing Risk in Farming.* Rome, FAO. Available at: www.fao.org/uploads/media/3-ManagingRiskInternLores.pdf. Retrieved 17 March 2018.

Kang, M.G. and Mahajan, N. (2006) *An Introduction to Market-Based Instruments for Agricultural Price Risk Management.* Rome, FAO. Available at: www.fao.org/3/ap308e/ap308e.pdf. Retrieved 19 May 2019.

Liesveld, J. (2016) Vertical integration: Pros and cons to farmers. *Fremont Tribune.* 6 May. Available at: https://fremonttribune.com/business/vertical-integration-pros-and-cons-to-farmers/article_868aa720-14b3-5a4e-a607-2f404efec7de.html. Retrieved 11 June 2018.

Lipton, M. (1968) The theory of the optimising peasant. *The Journal of Development Studies* 4(3), 327–351.

Macquarie (2010) *The Case for Investing in Agriculture.* Macquarie Agricultural Fund Management. Available at: www.macquarie.com/dafiles/Internet/mgl/com/agriculture/docs/white-papers/case-for-investing-in-agriculture.pdf. Retrieved 9 July 2018.

Madre, A. and Devuyst, P. (2016) *Are Futures the Future for Farmers?* Available at: www.farm-europe.eu/travaux/are-futures-the-future-for-farmers-2/. Retrieved 15 May 2019.

Mercier, S. (2018) Changes in grain marketing since the great recession. Farm Futures [blog]. 22 January. Available at: www.agweb.com/mobile/farmjournal/blog/straight-from-dc-agricultural-perspectives/changes-in-international-grain-marketing-since-the-great-recession/. Retrieved 5 July 2018.

Markham, R. (2016) *Breaking the Mango Disease Cycle.* Australian Centre for International Agricultural Research. Available at: http://aciar.gov.au/files/partners1606_pakistan_p14_breaking.pdf. Retrieved 12 July 2016.

MCX (2013) *Importance and Benefit of Hedging.* Occasional Paper 3/13. Mumbai, MCX. Available at: https://pdfs.semanticscholar.org/ccc3/748df4603ad1d53ce5ef784a9cb0a2a8e6c8.pdf. Retrieved 25 February 2019.

Melese, A.H. (2010) Contract farming in Ethiopia: An overview with focus on sesame. Development Cooperation, Netherlands Ministry of Foreign Affairs. Available at: www.wur.nl/upload_mm/4/5/9/5753d95f-5d41-4872-9a68-b4520d3a5cfa_Report5Tiruwha28062010a.pdf. Retrieved 17 July 2018.

Mhuriro-Mashapa, P., Mwakiwa, E. and Mashapa, C. (2017) Determinants of communal farmers' willingness to pay for human-wildlife conflict management in the periphery of Save Valley

Conservancy, South-Eastern Zimbabwe. *The Journal of Animal & Plant Sciences* 27(5), 1678–1688. Available at: www.thejaps.org.pk/docs/v-27-05/36.pdf. Retrieved 2 March 2018.

Mwambi, M.M., Oduol, J., Mshenga, P. and Saidi, M. (2016) Does contract farming improve smallholder income? The case of avocado farmers in Kenya. *Journal of Agribusiness in Developing and Emerging Economies* 6(1), 2–20. Available at: www.emeraldinsight.com/doi/pdfplus/10.1108/JADEE-05-2013-0019. Retrieved 10 July 2018.

National Farmer (2019) Vertical integration – sometimes a solution to market failure. Midwest Digest. 15 May. Available at: www.nationalhogfarmer.com/mag/farming_vertical_integration_sometimes. Retrieved 15 May 2019.

Neiffer, P. (2013) Accounting for Hedging Transactions. Clifton Larsen Allen. Presentation. Available at: http://cdn2.hubspot.net/hub/116265/file-1510362824-pdf/docs/hedging–paul_neiffer.pdf. Retrieved 18 March 2018.

OECD (2018) Risk Management in Agriculture. Available at: www.oecd.org/tad/agricultural-policies/risk-management-agriculture.htm. Retrieved 28 June 2018.

Powell, A. (2015) Commodity prices: Over 100 years of booms and busts… IDB Blog. Available at: https://blogs.iadb.org/ideasmatter/2015/05/04/commodity-prices-100-years-booms-busts/. Retrieved 18 March 2019.

Pullman, M. and Wu, Z. (2012) *Food Supply Chain Management*. London and New York, Routledge.

Raevel, O. and Porte, L. (2017) *New Regulations: Impact on Commodities Futures Markets*. Paris, Euronext. Available at: https://ec.europa.eu/agriculture/sites/agriculture/files/cereals/commodity-expert-group/2017-09-20/euronext.pdf. Retrieved 28 June 2018.

Rankin, M., Gálvez Nogales, E., Santacoloma, P., Mhlanga, N. and Rizzo, C. (2016) *Public–Private Partnerships for Agribusiness Development – A Review of International Experiences*. Rome, FAO.

Rawlinson, K. (2016) Glastonbury festival to move from Worthy Farm in 2019, says founder. *The Guardian*. 20 December. Available at: www.theguardian.com/music/2016/dec/19/glastonbury-festival-to-move-from-worthy-farm-in-2019-says-founder. Retrieved 6 July 2018.

Redo, D. (2019) Refinitiv. Available at: www.linkedin.com/in/daniel-redo-783a1a38/?original Subdomain=uk. Retrieved 16 May 2019.

Sharma, S. (2006) Corporate agriculture: Transplanting failure. *India Together*. 3 May. Available at: http://indiatogether.org/contract-agriculture--2. Retrieved 17 July 2018.

Standard & Poor's (2013) *Key Credit Factors for The Agribusiness and Commodity Foods Industry*. New York, Standard & Poor's.

Standard & Poor's (2017) *Commodities Trading Industry Methodology*. London, Standard & Poor's.

Tangermann, S. (2011) Risk Management in Agriculture and the Future of the EU's Common Agricultural Policy. Available at: https://pdfs.semanticscholar.org/b885/3dc6eece1b55a32389c5e dee22f6d027c0be.pdf.

Tea Board of India (2018) Tea Auctions. Available at: www.teaauction.gov.in/eAuctionReports/Reports.aspx. Retrieved 28 June 2018.

Ul-Rehman, S., Selvaraj, M. and Syed Ibrahim, M. (2012). Indian agricultural marketing – A review. *Asian Journal of Agriculture and Rural Development*, 2(1), 69–75.

USDA (2012) *Agricultural Projections to 2021*. 1 February. Washington DC, USDA. Available at: www.usda.gov/oce/commodity/archive_projections/USDAAgriculturalProjections2021.pdf. Retrieved 25 February 2019.

USDA (2015) A Perfect Storm for EU Dairy Prices. Gain Report E15033. 14 August. Available at: https://gain.fas.usda.gov/Recent%20GAIN%20Publications/A%20Perfect%20Storm%20for%20EU%20Dairy%20Prices_Brussels%20USEU_EU-28_8-19-2015.pdf. Retrieved 22 July 2018.

USDA (2017) *USDA Agricultural Projections to 2026.* Washington DC, USDA. Available at: www.usda. gov/oce/commodity/projections/USDA_Agricultural_Projections_to_2026.pdf. Retrieved 19 March 2019.

USDA (2018) Risk in Agriculture. Available at: www.ers.usda.gov/topics/farm-practices-management/ risk-management/risk-in-agriculture.aspx. Retrieved 28 June 2018.

Van Winsen, F., de Mey, Y., Lauwers, L., Van Passel, S., Vancauteren, M. and Wauters, E. (2016) Determinants of risk behaviour: effects of perceived risks and risk attitude on farmer's adoption of risk management strategies. *Journal of Risk Research* 19(1), 56–78.

World Bank (2015) *Agricultural Lending: A How-To Guide.* Washington DC, World Bank. Available at: https://elibrary.worldbank.org/doi/abs/10.1596/25897. Retrieved 22 July 2017.

9

Agribusiness lending

Grants and the role of the public sector

A key point of differentiation between farms, in particular, is the potential availability of grants or subsidised loans, usually from government but sometimes from international agencies and donors, which can dramatically reduce the cost of capital for a production agribusiness. In the USA, for example, state governments play a role; hence, for example in Delaware, the state government has a programme of Specialty Crop Block Grants to enhance the competitiveness of speciality crops. The Delaware Department of Agriculture manages a competitive solicitation process to award Specialty Crop Block Grant Program – Farm Bill (SCBGP-FB) funds for projects that solely enhance the competitiveness of Delaware's speciality crop industry. The department explained that projects should benefit the speciality crop industry as a whole and be able to provide a positive impact with measurable outcomes. Speciality crops are defined by the USDA as fruits, vegetables, tree nuts, dried fruits, horticulture and nursery crops (including floriculture). Individual producers, producer groups, organisations and associations, as well as state and local organisations, academia and other speciality crops stakeholders, are eligible to apply, either as single entities or in combined efforts. The Delaware Department of Agriculture looked for grant projects that solely increase the competitiveness of Delaware-grown speciality crops in respect of the following priorities specified by the USDA:

■ Enhancing food safety;

■ Improving the capacity of all entities in the speciality crop distribution chain to comply with the requirements of the Food Safety Modernization Act, for example by developing 'Good Agricultural Practices', 'Good Handling Practices', 'Good Manufacturing Practices', and in cost-share arrangements for funding audits of such systems for small farmers, packers and processors;

■ Investing in speciality crop research, including research to focus on conservation and environmental outcomes;

- Developing new and improved seed varieties and speciality crops;

- Pest and disease control;

- Increasing child and adult nutrition knowledge and consumption of speciality crops;

- Increasing opportunities for new and beginning farmers;

- Improving efficiency and reducing costs of distribution systems;

- Protecting and improving pollinator health;

- Developing local and regional food systems; and

- Improving food access in underserved communities and among veterans.

Source: Delaware Department of Agriculture (2019).

Sometimes other agribusinesses can receive subsidised loans, e.g. A$5 million for a sheep processing facility in Western Australia (MacTiernan, 2018).

Financing an acquisition

Let's suppose a farming family is currently farming 600 hectares. Their neighbour proposes to sell a nearby 400 hectares farm for $1,500 per hectare, i.e. $600,000. How can the family finance the purchase? They may be fortunate enough to have saved up the required amount from previous profits: the retained profits may be currently in shares and bonds, perhaps. The family decides that a better, more effective use of funds (notwithstanding the diminution in diversification) is to sell up these other investments and buy the farm. Few farmers, or other agribusinesses, however, are in that fortunate position. Most agribusinesses are already indebted and do not have diversified investments. Another possibility is for the family to make an offer of sharecropping, or some other partnership arrangement, to enable a gradual withdrawal from the farm for the vendor. However, most vendors want out immediately, and such arrangements are very much the exception rather than the rule. A third possibility is that the family can go to the bank and try to borrow the required money. A private company or even a major corporation is in no different a dilemma as to how to fund expansion, except that it has one final option, which is to raise additional monies through issuing more shares. So, finally, the family can consider creating a corporate entity of some description, in which outsiders become shareholders, in order to raise the necessary capital to buy the 400 hectares; in which case the family, of course, eventually becomes a minority shareholder in the company that will own their land, and they will become managers of the firm and minority shareholders, no longer the exclusive owners. All four methods of finance, and various combinations, have been seen in practice, so what does theory and practice tell us about which is preferable?

Corporate finance theory – in essence, the branch of academic analysis concerned with how firms finance themselves – is uncertain about how much cost should be ascribed to the family's first option, but there is unanimous agreement that worldwide (with the exception of Nigeria) equity is cheaper than debt and that therefore the farmer, or agribusiness generally, ought to borrow before issuing more equity, until its debt burden starts to become troublesome, a position that many overly aggressive expansion strategies followed by agribusinesses have in fact created. Almost every corporate finance textbook as well as practitioners are agreed, therefore, that the next least expensive form of finance for the agribusiness will be a bank loan, which goes a long way to explaining why 'Decisions about credit often are the most important judgements that people in the agricultural industry must make' (Ricketts & Ricketts, 2009:143). After senior bank debt, the next form of debt finance is mezzanine, which is usually unsecured, and sometimes comes with a small equity 'kicker' as a way to improve its return. Only if it proves impossible to raise sufficient finance through the banking and other debt providers should the farmer contemplate seeking external equity. Simply put, the explanation lies in increasing risk throughout the pecking order.

Borrowing from banks has its own issues, however. Moral hazard means borrowers undertake higher risk projects with borrowed funds than they would with their own money, since the lender bears part of the cost of failure. Consequently, the lender treats the willingness to pay a higher interest rate as a signal of poor loan quality and often prefers to ration credit rather than raise interest rates to a market clearing level. In these circumstances an agribusiness with adequate cash flow may make an investment where a firm dependent on external finance (and unable to issue new equity) will not. Financial quantities such as cash flow can therefore influence real investment decisions and the price mechanism cannot clear the market (Hayes, 2003).

What financing methods do farms use?

What does the diagram in Figure 9.2 tell us? That the IFC's pessimistic view is that, as the document explains:

> ...lower-risk farmers in relatively low-risk value chains at the bottom left corner of the graph can be financed with more direct approaches. While the financing reaches

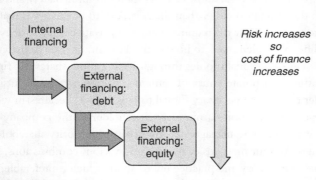

Figure 9.1 The pecking order hierarchy
Source: efinancemanagement.com (2019)

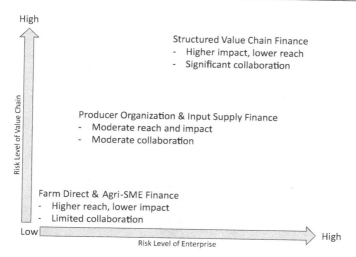

Figure 9.2 How the IFC sees agribusiness finance
Source: IFC (2015:13)

the farmer directly, this approach is limited in its impact on the single farmer directly financed. In contrast, farmers that fall into the higher risk categories, concentrate on commodities that are riskier, or live in areas that have higher risk profiles, are more successfully financed through structured value chain finance approaches [e.g. cooperatives, contract farming]. This type of financing is concentrated on larger organisations that work with farmers (IFC, 2015:13).

It's quite a strong argument: in the IFC's view, direct (e.g. bank) financing is really only suitable for farmers who have relatively diversified sources of income, do not experience overmuch seasonality, use irrigation or at least have limited exposure to weather risks, use good agricultural practices, and have strong access to markets. They have to be reachable, too, either through the internet or bank branches. Loan sizes have to be large enough to justify individual credit assessments and the other overhead costs that come with direct lending (IFC, 2015:14). *Unfortunately, on this basis, it would be hard to find any farmer anywhere who could really be extended direct credit: compromises are always being made by lenders.*

In reality, most farms do find themselves forced to use some form of credit, whether supplied by banks or less scrupulous, and much more poorly regulated, local money-lenders or traders. Most retail fresh produce trade (in developing countries) takes place in cash, but individual retail traders, as distinct from the supermarkets, frequently offer credit to customers. Most market traders have limited capital, and lend on the basis that they know that the debtors will repay, at least in part, or ultimately' (Brookfield & Parsons, 2007:67–68). With no, or few banks, creditors are plentiful, but small operators. Wholesaling always involves credit, especially where one wholesaler supplies another or forwards goods to distant places (Brookfield & Parsons, 2007:69).

What farm financial management seeks to obtain, viz. growth in net worth (equity) in real terms, exceeding the cost of equity for farm performance, retaining credit lines to use

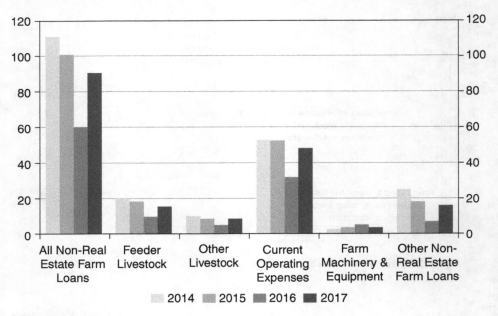

Figure 9.3 Where loans go to
Source: USDA (2018)

when required, keeping debt cost down, managing risk effectively, maintaining liquidity and solvency, and continuing the farm's ability to repay debt – are all laudable objectives. But they may not always match with the requirements of lenders. When things go wrong, the results are frequently final for the farmer's equity, and occasionally tragic. There is no doubting the importance of getting it right.

Farms (and agribusinesses more generally) usually adopt a range of debt financing types.

■ Mortgages – long-term (10+ years) credit. Land, buildings and some types of IP can be financed through mortgages, either Western or Islamic. Some loans are not repaid, and land is transferred with the mortgage attached. 'Mortgaging of land can be a dangerous business in times of rising costs and unstable prices, and many developed country farmers lost land in this way during the agricultural downturn of the last 20 years of the twentieth century' (Brookfield & Parsons, 2007:33). Yet because in advanced economies capital increasingly substitutes for labour on farms, as well as in manufacturing and retail agribusinesses, mortgage loans are a reluctant necessity for most farmers in developed countries. The steady shift in farm assets towards real estate, noted in Chapter 5, has caused secured lending to emerge as an increasingly attractive, and important, form of farm financing. Around 90% or more of costs are capital now in US farming.

Most of these loans are financed using the amortisation system, whereby payments are fixed monthly or quarterly. In the initial years, most of the payment is for interest, but subsequently more capital is repaid. Loans can be at fixed interest rates for a number of years, or variable interest rates; changes in interest rates affect the amount payable every month or quarter. Interest costs *matter*. Farms in the West are no exception to the general rule that the cost of capital should be seen in terms of a pecking order.

- Intermediate – ranging from one to ten years. Generally, these are used to finance depreciable assets such as vehicles, machinery and equipment, livestock, irrigation systems, and modernisation of farm facilities. Almost all these loans are financed with security, creating liens on the items financed. Most of these loans are regularly amortised term loans, sometimes with a bullet element, as would be typical for land or buildings acquisition.

A bullet is a way to structure the repayment of a loan in which the borrower does not pay the principal over the life of the loan, but rather makes a lump sum payment at maturity. This is relatively common in mortgage loans; the borrower pays the interest each month and refinances the security (a farm, an agribusiness) in order to make the bullet repayment at the end of the mortgage term. There are also bullet and other loan types that differ from the standard amortisation repayment profile.

In some cases, there may be lines of credit issued, allowing the borrower to acquire assets up to a specific amount. This is often available for the purchase of production inputs such as fertiliser, feed, or feed calves, and is generally repayable within a year. A revolving credit, on the other hand, although it too allows borrowing up to a limit, can fluctuate with seasonal credit needs, and amortisation is not required. Often these loans are more expensive, but they are more flexible and can be amended, e.g. to raise the amount of the credit.

- Short-term – less than a year. The most obvious need is for working capital on the farm: for financing operating inputs such as fuel, fertiliser, chemicals and seeds, for example. Generally, these are bullet repayments at the end of the financing period. 'Short term credit is an almost unavoidable requirement of farming, given the need for expenses early in each season long before any crop can be harvested. Only the relatively affluent can get by on their own. Quite apart from farming expenses, farm families also have to meet regular expenses…and life-crisis events' (Brookfield & Parsons, 2007:33).

SPVs and other special forms of financial structure

Most farms, whether held corporately or not, have no reason to seek financing for part of the enterprise, rather than the whole. From producers to haulage providers, developed country agribusiness has traditionally relied on conventional, usually bank, debt financing. Being captive to variable factors such as climate and cyclical business cycles, financial institutions often take a conservative approach to lending which has restricted the flow of funds. When adverse trading conditions limit revenue and compound debt levels, alternative sources of finance may be used to clear debt, remove unfavourable assets from the balance sheet and adjust cash flow forecasts.

- A *joint venture* (JV) is a method to expand operations without necessarily taking on increased debt funding or investment. A new business, or special purpose vehicle (SPV), is developed with each JV entity sharing revenue and expenses. As agribusinesses in countries such as Australia are increasingly adding value by vertically integrating, however, such capital expenditure would require taking on higher debt levels or searching for outside direct investment. By engaging another entity and forming a JV, businesses can vertically integrate up or down the supply chain, lending no more than their current capabilities to the SPV. For example, a business operating road haulage may want to add warehouse facilities to its supply chain. Equally, a warehouse business may wish to add transport to increase its service offering. The two businesses within a JV scenario could leverage each of their current assets and capabilities to provide an end-to-end warehouse and delivery service, maximising each of their assets. Parties should be aware of any imbalances between the skill set and asset offering of each party when coming together to form the SPV. Objectives need to be clear and ownership of assets, including intellectual property, should be clearly defined. JVs are rarely long-term business arrangements, more commonly established to target a particular business opportunity or goal. Therefore, termination provisions are important clauses to draft in a JV agreement, encompassing the rights and responsibilities of each party on dissolution of the SPV. However, where vertical integration exists, for example between processors and input suppliers, there may be a need to create an SPV, which has been supported by lenders such as Rabobank: 'An SPV is a stand-alone company, jointly owned by the processor, input providers, and any other equity investors.' The SPV then contracts with farms, and often also with off-takers. The SPV is then financed by the bank. All participants in the SPV structure share the risk of contract breach, which may encourage participation by smaller enterprises, even farms themselves. SPVs may also be required for public-private partnerships in agribusiness, advocated for some decades by organisations such as the FAO (2016) and the OECD (Moreddu, 2016), as the government will need to contract with a private sector party, usually comprised of several different private sector organisations, which together form an SPV.

- *Project finance.* In very exceptional circumstances, in particular very large projects, financing in the $1 billion+ range, equity investors will not be willing to invest unless the project is ringfenced in an SPV so that their risk extends only to the equity they invest into the SPV. This is project finance, which is commonly used in the oil and gas sector but only rarely in agribusiness. For project finance, the bank's security is confined to the assets and the cash flows of the project, without recourse to the equity providers, so reducing the project's exposure to commercial risks and sources of cash flow volatility will increase the leverage potential and improve the equity returns of the project. In project financing, the proposed economic/revenue model is crucial, with the cash flow structure (including tenor and volatility risks) ultimately driving the debt sizing and the debt sizing methodology adopted. For large-scale greenfield agricultural projects, there are direct parallels in the completion risk structuring that banks require for mining (and infrastructure) greenfield project financing. However, since the global financial crisis, banks no longer have to accept pure project finance, and usually demand corporate guarantees, so it may never spread to even the largest of agribusiness projects, with a few exceptions, perhaps even ironically some major start-ups (Clarke, 2014).

■ *Lease back.* Lease backs are attracting an increasing amount of interest in Australia, both from asset owners and agribusiness investors. They are ideally suited to entities looking to finance manufacturing plants, heavy equipment or rural land. A lease back encompasses the sale of an asset, and a simultaneous lease agreement entered into between the vendor/lessee and purchaser/lessor for a period of time, leasing back the relevant asset. This frees up capital in the asset while retaining the operations. Lease backs are favourable for agribusinesses which have significant equity in an asset but however have inadequate cash flow and escalating debt. The sale of the asset unlocks capital for debt reduction and reduces the cost of debt service. Lease backs are also advantageous for entities seeking to benefit from investment in the sector as the lease allows experienced operators to remain with the asset, providing management expertise to the investor. A lease back involves a liquidity event, which may be unfavourable depending on the prevailing market conditions. However, an agreement can be drafted to allow the lessee/vendor to participate in any subsequent sale, whether as a first right of refusal to purchase the land or to participate in any gain in value of the land if there is a subsequent sale to a third party. Understandably, for this to occur there would be additional commercial costs to the lessee to facilitate this optionality. Sale and leasebacks also improve corporate finance ratios such as return on assets, as the business appears to be running leaner, although this is an illusion which rating agencies and banks do cause to evaporate when they examine the business for lending purposes.

■ *Cow banks.* Cow banks are utilised extensively by charities in developing countries, where a 'bank' of cattle is retained to lend to people for use in breeding programmes or to work fields. However, cow banks are gaining traction in commercial dairy operations, giving farmers the ability to increase herd size without the necessity to purchase stock outright. Cow banks suit producers seeking herd finance in order to expand operations. Cow banks commence as either an agreement for new stock or to refinance an existing herd. In contrast to purchasing and financing cattle outright, a cow bank agreement allows the farmer to increase and decrease herd size to suit the needs of the business. Alternatively, a producer could utilise equity in their current stock by selling the cattle for their full value before leasing back. The ability to unlock full equity held in the cattle in this manner is advantageous over conventional cattle financing. A lender in the conventional scenario will only finance against the value of the cattle on a depreciating scale, leaving a margin of value which the producer must bridge. This is not the case in a cow bank agreement. A cow bank may not suit a producer, however, who is focused on herd improvement and breeding programmes. Further, it may not be a viable option for older cattle where a producer is looking to refinance the herd. For the owner of the cow bank, the wellbeing of the cattle is taken out of their control and into the control of the producer. To mitigate the risk of adverse care, a cow bank agreement can provide for benchmark requirements on the producer, such as body condition scoring, pasture improvement targets and best practice animal handling requirements.

■ *Forward sales finance.* Agribusinesses dealing in soft commodities, such as grain, livestock and fruit, generally receive revenue on delivery of the product. Agricultural commodities tend to have lengthy growth cycles, therefore the time between capital expenditure to produce the commodity and the time of delivery (and therefore receipt of funds) generally requires finance to bridge the operational gap. Most commodity markets, even some in developing countries, albeit informal, offer exchange or physical based forward contracts (as discussed in Chapter 8) and so provide a known value of the revenue expected (dependent on yield). This known value provides an underlying security for advanced payments, prior to delivery. This is effectively a loan and will be either charged with interest, or the face value of the contract will be discounted to accommodate the finance costs. Even traders in developing countries offer this kind of finance, albeit often at exorbitant rates of interest. The main benefit of financing against future contracts compared to traditional finance is that the funding is transaction based and is focused on the borrower's performance, rather than the borrower's balance sheet. The security for the finance is the underlying commodity. Streaming facilities further allow financiers to purchase additional volumes of the commodity, depending on the yield outcome. Adversely, the unknown component of yield can place the seller in an exposed position if production falls short of expectation. Lower than anticipated production results in a shortfall of security against the cash advance. Financing against forward sales should be undertaken on a conservative basis and managed diligently. More complex forms of forward financing can involve *structured finance*, whereby interest rates and other borrowing terms can be linked to the performance of the underlying asset, e.g. the price of wheat. Much as borrowers might want these kinds of arrangements, however, they are hard to come by, not least because the resultant debts are almost impossible to *syndicate*, i.e. divide up amongst other lending institutions.

Principles of corporate lending

Key ratio analysis for agribusiness transactions (including DSCR, LLCR and others)

'About the worst thing you can do is go into a banker's office and ask, "How much can I borrow?" This shows the banker that you do not have a budget or any clear understanding of your cash needs' (Klonsky, 2012). How much an agribusiness can borrow depends, predictably enough, on two things: what is the value of assets, and what the business can afford to repay.

First, asset values. Some lenders may lend on – or more usually set a maximum of – a *debt-equity ratio basis*.

A bank always has a policy of advance rates for specific collateral. Our bank loan policy has our advance rates at 65% of growing crops, 50% of used equipment and 80% of farm real estate. Essentially, advance rates are the percentage of your collateral a bank will lend (Louder, 2018).

Asset ratios are critical – in the example below, 50% is the allowable ratio for second-hand machinery.

A bank website provides an example. A borrower finds a 2010 John Deere 7330 on Tractorhouse.com for $75,000. If we estimate the market value of that tractor at its purchase price, the Farmers and Merchants Bank advance rates allow a maximum loan of $37,500. The balance will be required as a down payment, or it may be able to be negotiated with the vendor, provided the agreement allows for title of the vehicle to pass to the borrower and for the bank to take first charge, i.e. ahead of any claim by the vendor.

Leverage (solvency) ratios

Net Capital Ratio = Total Assets / Liabilities

(the inverse is the Debt/Asset (D/A) Ratio)

This ratio represents the level of debt to assets for an agribusiness. This type of ratio is often referred to as a leverage ratio. It is a good indicator of the level of financial risk associated with the agribusiness. Often this ratio is expressed as the inverse:

Debt to Asset Ratio = Total Liabilities/Total Assets

Either way, this ratio is a measure of how much of the firm is debt financed.

The D/A ratio can be difficult to interpret. There is nothing inherently wrong with a high debt, provided the operation is very efficient and can service the debt. Also, in an ideal world where farming is a choice, not a birthright, young farmers who start out will tend to be highly leveraged and are just as likely to support their operation with off-farm income. These producers may have efficient operations with a high return on assets. It is just that by the time they make their interest and principal payments, there may be little income left to provide for living expenses. A high D/A ratio is therefore not necessarily bad if there is a real prospect of reducing it over time.

Nor is having a D/A ratio of zero is necessarily a desirable goal either. Corporate finance theory, discussed above, suggests that equity investors get higher returns than debt providers, as they are lower down the pecking order. Assuming that the operation is efficient and has a high return on assets, then it is desirable to assume an acceptable level of debt in order to 'lever up' return on equity. However, for every agribusiness, a high D/A level involves a higher degree of financial risk. Furthermore, it is clear that higher debt levels will require a higher return on assets to service the debt.

Equity / Asset Ratio = Total Farm Equity/Total Farm Assets

This ratio is a variant of the D/A ratio. Caution is advised in using this ratio in that it is extremely sensitive to low equity levels and/or situations where large amounts of leased assets are employed.

Total Liabilities / Net Worth = Debt / Equity

When this ratio is greater than one, the lender has more invested than the borrower, and more debt will definitely not be forthcoming except under the most exceptional circumstances, such as forthcoming external equity (e.g. a flotation) and then only very rarely. This is also a variant of the D/A ratio and subject to the same cautions as with the equity/asset ratio.

Debt Payout = Total Liabilities / Net Income

This ratio represents the number of years it would take to reduce the debt level to zero if all of the income of a farm could be directed towards principal reduction. It relates the level of debt to the ability of the agribusiness to generate income to repay the debt. Many of the same issues that relate to the debt to asset ratio also apply to debt payout. The real strength in the debt payout ratio is in trend analysis. If the trend is upward, this implies that the debt load is increasing at a greater rate than income. This trend cannot be sustained over the long run and is a warning signal of future financial stress. The comparative analysis is useful here in that it can help to determine if the farm's trend is due to individual farm factors or is caused by general economic or weather factors.

Second, simply put, the amount of borrowing possible is a matter of available cash flow. Generally, the available cash flow for an agribusiness is income after operating expenses, family living expenses, where relevant, and those taxes which do not depend on debt levels for their amount (e.g. basic property taxes). That number will be the amount of cash available to service debt. In a historical analysis, that number should be sufficient to cover all debts that year. When considering a proposed loan, projected cash flow should cover current debts as well as proposed debts.

'The repayment ability or cash flow requirement may differ from each bank. At some banks the ratio is 1 to 1, whereas some banks are 1 to 1.25 as the minimum of what you can afford. As a loan officer, I look at how are you going to pay for it (the new loan) as well as service your other debt' (Johnston, R. quoted in Louder, 2018). Following up on that, another US banker observed: 'The borrower must have the ability to service debt with free cash flow, above operating expenses, to keep them from being put in a position in which they could fail. I must have proof of repayment capacity to move forward' (Hanger, K. quoted in Louder, 2018).

Debt coverage

Ratios in this category are designed to measure a firm's ability to generate funds to meet debt obligations.

Debt service coverage ratio (DSCR)

A firm's cash available for debt service divided by the cash needed for debt service. It is a measure of a firm's ability to service its debt obligations. A DSCR of 1:1 means the agribusiness is operationally breaking even with no margin for deteriorating operating conditions. Less than 1:1 indicates that the agribusiness is generating less income than required to support its debt. This is the most important ratio examined by banks, although the interest coverage ratios explained immediately below are gaining traction in lending analysis as more loans tend towards, in effect, revolving credits.

Interest Coverage Ratio (ICR) = (Net Farm Income + Interest Expense) / Interest Expense

This ratio is similar to the interest expense ratio, but it relates interest expense to earnings before interest. It provides a truer picture of debt servicing ability than the interest expense ratio as it accounts for expenses. The trade-off is in the reliability. Net farm income includes non-cash expenses, such as depreciation, that are estimated. An associated inverse ratio is times interest earned ratio (TIE) – a firm's earnings before interest and taxes (EBIT) divided by its interest charges. It shows a firm's ability to meet its interest payments. A related ratio is:

Interest Expense Ratio = Interest Expense / Gross Income

This ratio relates the interest expense to a farm's ability to generate income. This is a particularly useful ratio as it can be measure accurately. This is a ratio where the trend is vitally important. A trend upward will lead to eventual financial stress.

Term Debt Coverage Ratio = (NFI + Depreciation – Unpaid Operator & Family Labour + Term Interest) / Scheduled Annual Term Interest & Principal Payments

This is another variation on the ICR. The earnings are adjusted to account for cash flow by adding back in depreciation and subtracting out unpaid labour (which is used as a proxy for family withdrawals). Principal payments are included with the interest payments to get a clearer picture of cash flow obligations of debt. The weakness of this ration is the estimate of unpaid labour and reduces the reliability of the values. A variation of this may be calculated to incorporate non-farm income and capital leases. This may be particularly significant in showing the potential reliance on income from not-farm sources in retiring debt.

A final variant on the ICR is the loan life coverage ratio (LLCR), which takes a long-term view, providing lenders with a measure of the number of times the project cash flow over the scheduled life of the loan can repay the outstanding debt balance, but this really only makes sense for a term loan, especially to an SPV, rather than to a continuing agribusiness.

Debt Payment / Income Ratio = Scheduled Annual Term Interest & Principal Payments (NFI + Depreciation + Interest on Term Debt)

The debt payment/income ratio measures the ability of a business to service debt over the term of the loan. Once again, this ratio can provide an indication of the reliance on income from non-farm sources in retiring debt.

Significance and application of conventional corporate finance ratios

The bank will, or anyway should, also look at the overall health of the agribusiness. The following ratios are generally regarded as indicative of this.

Liquidity measures

Liquidity is a measure of how easily a business can meet its upcoming short-term debts with its current assets without disrupting the normal operation of the business, i.e. does the business have enough liquid assets to cover any debts or upcoming payments within the next year. Liquidity ratios are designed to measure an agribusiness's ability to pay its obligations by generating cash.

Current Ratio = Total Current Assets / Total Current Liabilities

The current ratio gives an indication of a farm's ability to meet its cash obligations coming due within the next year. A value below one could indicate a developing cash flow problem. Having a very high value may not be desirable either. It may indicate that too high a level of assets is tied up in conservative investments that have lower rates of return. A current ratio, say US bankers, should be at least 1:1. This means that the agribusiness has a dollar in liquid assets for each dollar it will need to pay over the next year.

Valuation problems are not usually significant given the liquid nature of the assets. However, the time of the measure is important as the time of year may have an influence on inventory amounts and values.

Working Capital = Total Current Assets − Total Current Liabilities

Working capital and current ratio have similar issues. A positive value is desirable, but too large a value may indicate too many relatively unproductive assets are being held. Hence:

Working Capital Rule = Working Capital / Total Farm Expenses

This ratio enables an assessment of adequacy of working capital relative to business expenses. Care should be taken in adjusting for large inventories and/or valuation issues.

In an excellent article on liquidity in agribusiness, the author suggests that:

> the most common measure of liquidity is the current ratio, and that benchmarks for the current ratio vary, depending on the industry. For agriculture I usually like to see a current ratio between 1.5 and 3.0. In other words, I like to see an agribusiness have at least $1.50 in current assets for every $1.00 of current liabilities. Personally, I do not like to see this ratio go above 3.0 – this tells me that the firm may have too much of their assets in liquid, non-earning assets, and this can hurt your profitability (White, 2008).

These ratios may move around, however, depending on the state of the economy and even, now, on technology.

Profitability measures

Ratios in this category are designed to measure a firm's ability to generate profit.

Income = Cash Receipts + (Change in Value of Product Inventory + Change in Value of Accounts Receivable) – Capital (e.g. livestock) Purchases

This amount represents the accrued value of agricultural products (whether raw or processed) sold during the fiscal (or calendar) year. For a retail agribusiness this may include other non-food items.

Net Farm Income (NFI) = Gross Income – Direct Costs – Capital Costs

This is not a ratio by definition, but it is included as it represents the bottom line for farms and a starting point for analysis. The problem with net farm income is that it does not relate the income to the size of the investment. This is the advantage of using return on assets (ROA) as a measure of profitability. A very similar ratio, net income more generally, can be applied to any agribusiness.

Gross Margin = NFI (or net income) – Depreciation

This margin represents the excess of revenue over the cost of goods sold. Gross margin indicates funds available to cover unallocated fixed costs, returns to unpaid operator and family labour, and returns to owners/shareholders' equity.

Cash Operating Margin = (Income – Production Inventory Change – Accounts Receivable Change) – (Direct Costs – Supplies Inventory Change – Accounts Payable (Change) – (Capital Costs – Depreciation)

The cash operating margin essentially 'un-accrues' (i.e. rescues from the financial statements) the farm income statement. It represents the actual cash available to cover principal payments; net cash capital acquisitions; and, where relevant, i.e. in the case of a family-owned agribusiness, the family's living withdrawals.

Return on Assets = (NFI (or net income) + Interest Expense – Unpaid Operator & Family Labour / Total Farm Assets (or total assets generally)

This ratio shows the total income generated from the farm or other agribusiness divided by the total assets employed to generate this income. It shows the ability of the firm's assets to generate net income. Interest expense is added back to net income because interest is a form of return on debt financed assets.

Unpaid family labour is subtracted as it represents a non-cash expense. This adjustment helps to compare farms which pay family wages to those that do not.

Notice that in the case of a farm it is not so much the actual ratios that differ, as the emergence of specific, very considerable difficulties in calculating them accurately. The cash withdrawals from any family business pose difficulties for lenders at the best of times – farm withdrawals are notoriously difficult for the bank to assess accurately as to what are actually required for the farm's operation and what are lifestyle withdrawals.

Return on Farm Equity = (NFI − Unpaid Operator & Family Labour) / Total Farm Equity = Return to Farm Equity / Total Farm Equity

This ratio represents the income generated from the owner's investment in the farm business. As is the case for return on assets, the estimate of market values will have a large impact on the value. In fact, the effect will be even more exaggerated for return on equity than for return on assets.

The return on equity should be higher than the return on assets over the long-run. This assumes that the manager is using debt leverage for an advantage. There is a trade-off here between a high return on equity and high risk as the two are positively correlated.

Operating Profit Margin Ratio = (NFI + Interest Expense − Unpaid Operator & Family Labour) / Income = Return to Equity / Gross Income

This ratio measures the portion of each dollar of revenue in the income statement which become profits. A low profit margin can be compensated for with a higher asset turnover. Thus, this ratio must be viewed in the context of the capital turnover. Highly capitalised operations tend to have a higher profit margin combined with a low capital turnover.

Net Farm Income − Net Government Transfers = NFI − (Government Programme Receipts − Government Programme Premiums)

This ratio is a measure of a farm's dependence on government transfers for income. As the level of government support continues to drop, this ratio will become less significant.

Financial efficiency measures

Ratios in this category are designed to measure a firm's ability to generate revenues and control costs.

Capital (Asset) Turnover Ratio = Gross Income / Total Farm Assets

This ratio is a measure of capital intensity. A lower value is acceptable if it represents a capital-intensive operation with a higher profit margin. If a lower value is combined with a low profit margin, it signifies an inefficient operation. As is the case with return on assets, the valuation of the assets will have a large impact on the value. As market values are used, the value for capital turnover will be lower than if cost was used. Beware of this fact if comparing against capital turnover values based on cost.

Operating Expense Ratio (OER) (excludes depreciation and interest) = Operating Expenses (excluding interest and depreciation) / Income

This ratio represents the percentage of operating expense that will consume every $1 of revenue. A useful way to view the ratio is that the residual represents the amount of money left on a dollar of revenue that remains to:

Service debt (both interest and principal);
Provide for reinvestment in capital assets such as machinery, equipment and buildings; and
Provide for family living withdrawals.

For example, a 75% ratio would indicate that there remain 25c from every dollar of revenue generated left to cover debt servicing, reinvestment and withdrawals. In general, the lower the OER, the better. This will result in more cash from every dollar of revenue generated left to cover debt servicing, reinvestment and withdrawals. However, it should also be recognised that farms that have low debt levels can get by with a higher OER. Their mix of debt servicing, reinvestment and family withdrawals can lean more heavily towards withdrawals without sacrificing debt servicing or reinvestment. Conversely, farms that are highly leveraged will require a lower OER to be able to service the debt and maintain an adequate level of investment. This states an obvious truth: to take on more debt requires greater efficiency in the operation. Another major consideration in the analysis relates to the operating strategy of the farm. If the farm has a low cost-of-production strategy, or if the farm does not require high levels of reinvestment to maintain productivity, then it can operate at a higher level of OER and still be as profitable as other operations.

Depreciation Expense Ratio = Depreciation Expense / Gross Income

A lot depends on how depreciation is calculated, and it is often difficult to do so for a farm, less so for an agribusiness further along the value chain. In principle, depreciation is based on an imputed cost based on market values. Ideally, depreciation expense should be based on the original cost of the assets and reflect the actual use of the asset. If the appropriate cost base were available, a properly calculated depreciation expense ratio provides an important measure of the capital costs incurred by a farm.

It must be remembered that a ratio is nothing more than one number divided by another, so there is nothing inherently revealing about the value of one, or even several, ratios. Ratio analysis is nothing more than a tool to help understand the business, so it is never usually right to make snap judgements about ratios being too high or too low. This will depend upon the circumstances of the operation and the overall strategy of the farm or other agribusiness. Moreover, a value must be viewed within the context of the other ratio values.

There are many inherent measurement problems. There are, for example, persuasive arguments for the use of both cost and market values. With market valuation, the confidence in the value will depend upon the accuracy of the appraisal of the property. Allow for a certain amount of 'slack' in comparisons to account for this. A strength of ROA is in that it does not differentiate on how the operation is financed as interest payments are included in income.

Again, seasonality hampers comparability. As ratios are calculated at a point in time, the timing of the calculations with respect to the seasonal pattern on the farm is important.

In conclusion, these ratios are all useful for an analyst, but unfortunately banks often do not forecast long term, nor do they examine industries or individual businesses for their future profitability. All too often, banks with poor internal governance and lending procedures adopt a 'follow-my-leader' approach and end up lending to agribusinesses that, on careful reflection and after proper due diligence, represent very poor lending opportunities.

Comparative ratio analysis – evidence from international agribusiness

Adjustments necessary to generate comparability (peer groups)

For most banks and other lenders, these adjustments are not an issue. Their agribusiness units operate primarily at a national level, with portfolios being managed regionally or at an even smaller geographic level. Clients are known personally, quite unlike retail banking. The principles of making adjustments to achieve comparability are, moreover, quite complex, based on regression analysis, and most lenders eschew them as a result. Academics are very keen to promote it, however, and the theoretical arguments in favour of identifying variables and weighting them in terms of their impact on default are highly persuasive (Durguner, 2007). A writer from the Asian Development Bank (ADB) reported that:

> Loan contract performance determines the profitability and stability of the financial institutions and screening the loan applications is a key process in minimizing credit risk. Before making any credit decisions, credit analysis (the assessment of the financial history and financial backgrounds of the borrowers) should be completed as part of the screening process. A good credit risk assessment assists financial institutions on loan pricing, determining amount of credit, credit risk management, reduction of default risk and increase in debt repayment. The purpose of this study is to estimate a credit scoring model for the agricultural loans in Thailand. The logistic regression and Artificial Neural Networks (ANN) are used to construct the credit scoring models and to predict the borrower's creditworthiness and default risk. The results of the logistic regression confirm the importance of total asset value, capital turnover ratio (efficiency) and the duration of a bank–borrower relationship as important factors in determining the creditworthiness of the borrowers. The results also show that a higher value of assets implies a higher credit worthiness and a higher probability of a good loan. However, the negative signs found on both capital turnover ratio and the duration of bank–borrower relationship, which contradict with the hypothesized signs, suggest that the borrower who has a long relationship with the bank and who has a higher gross income to total assets has a higher probability to default on debt repayment (Limsombunchai et al., 2005).

From even that abstract the lack of empathy between academics and multinational bank officials on the one hand, and lenders on the ground in developing – or even developed – countries on the other, should be obvious enough. This probably explains why regression has not attracted so many discussions or explanations in the past decade as in the two decades before, when hopes were higher of a faster dissemination of ideas from theory to practice. More generally, lenders, especially in developing countries where automated credit criteria are still relatively scarce, typically still look at CAMPARI – Character, Ability to pay, Margin of
profit, Purpose of the loan, Amount being requested, the terms of Repayment and the Insurance in case of default – or a version of it for the assessment of borrower repayment capacity (Owusu-Dankwa & Badu, 2013). The most commonly known variant for agricultural lending are the '7 Cs', which were originally advanced by the Farm Credit Corporation in the USA.

- *Credit*: this refers to the macroeconomic, sectoral and bank-specific credit environment in which loans are demanded and credit supplied.

- *Character*: this refers to the borrower and is defined in the context of moral hazard and adverse selection. What is in the human character of the borrower that makes him (her) a good credit risk? In recent times, credit risk analysis based on algorithms has rather reduced the significance of independent judgement on this point in particular.

- *Capacity*: this refers to the ability of the farmer to service and ultimately repay the loan. This is often also referred to as 'Cash flow' but capacity is broader because it not only includes cash flow from farming operations but also cash flow from off-farm sources of income as well as cash available in near or intermediate liquid assets. This has become less significant in recent times, as rising land prices have enabled regular refinancing.

- *Capital*: this refers to the amount of capital available to pledge against the loan. Capital and Collateral are often included as one, but capital is a much broader definitions of assets that include assets that can or cannot be pledged as security against the loan.

- *Condition*: this deals with the conditions for granting and repaying the loan. It deals primarily with the attributes of the economy in which the borrower operates. Does the farmer compete in the marketplace, have access to forward contracts, or provide a niche product? Does the farmer-borrower face low, moderate or high production and market risks? What conditions (lending covenants), if any, should be placed on the loan to ensure that repayment can be met in accordance with the specific needs (timing and sequencing of cash flow, for example) and risks?

- *Capability*: Capability to repay a loan is often included with the Capacity to repay a loan, but at times it is convenient to keep the two apart analytically. For example, if Capacity were to be measured in terms of the cash flow from production of agricultural products, household consumption, medical issues, schooling and other extraneous factors may affect the household's capability to do so.

- *Collateral*: Collateral refers to the value of assets and the specific itemisation of assets that can be pledged against a loan. This has always been a vital point, but with rising land prices, banks have on many occasions relied on collateral to allow for regular refinancing irrespective of cashflow.

(Modified from Turvey *et al.*, 2011:101–102)

Commodity cycles and income

Net farm income is determined by commodity prices, yields and expenses. As discussed in Chapter 1, commodity prices are relatively volatile. And generally farmers are price-takers, with little influence over farm gate prices. Expenses, also driven in some cases by commodity prices, can also be volatile. Fertiliser prices are a good example.

A lender's policies and procedures should also address risks posed by individual loans as well as aggregate agribusiness portfolio risk. Even when individual farm and other agribusiness loans are prudently underwritten, groups of loans that are similarly affected by internal and external market factors may expose the bank to a heightened level of risk and warrant increased board and management attention.

What is perhaps striking about banking documentation in developing countries is really how simple and straightforward it is. Lending to agribusinesses, especially farms, in developed countries is really not so different in principle from in developing countries. It is the execution which differs so very radically.

Refining ratio calculations for agribusiness by sector

The debt service ratio, rather than the DSCR, indicates *the proportion of the value of farm production* that is used to meet principal and interest payments. The TDSCR calculation is an income-statement-driven measure of the borrower's ability to service debt. TDSCR uses adjusted net income as the numerator and is calculated as follows:

Adjusted Net Income Available to Service Debt
Net income
+ Noncash expenses or − Noncash income
+ Interest expense
- Dividends/distributions
= Adjusted net income available to service debt
Debt Service
Current maturities of long-term debt
+ Interest expense
= Debt service (Grady, 2017).

According to the USDA's ERS, in the late 2010s around 27% of the value of farm production is consumed by principal and interest payments. This ratio has clearly been higher in the past, but the times in which it was higher were generally characterised by difficult financial times in agriculture (USDA, 2018). The average DSCR in agribusiness is almost certainly, in fact, much less attractive than this, as DSCR is calculated after operating expenses, on net income, not gross income. In fact it is hard to see that debt service ratios based on gross income tell us much useful.

A DSCR of 4, on the other hand, would be extremely low by comparison to, for example, the average person's domestic mortgage figure, let alone that of an SPV in a typical PPP, oil and gas transaction or other project financing, and would suggest a large reservoir of unused lending capacity in the industry. Compare: lenders today are looking for a DSCR measured on an annual historical basis of 1.25:1. Stated another way, you must have 1.25 times more net operating income (NOI) than you have existing and proposed debt in order to qualify for a loan. NOI is a real estate term, most agribusinesses would use net income, but the ratios are usually similar.

Market-based covenants

Business loan covenants or undertakings are terms set out by the lender when they approve an agribusiness loan. Essentially, the borrower must meet certain benchmarks or take certain actions regularly so the bank can be confident that the agribusiness is profitable and that you can continue making your repayments. Meeting the reporting requirements can be difficult and time-consuming but there are ways to negotiate agribusiness loan covenants, which may often be waived to preserve a banking relationship. There are numerous analyses of bank covenants generally (e.g. Demiroglu & James, 2010; Sagner, 2009) and the rise of covenant-lite loans for major transactions (Billett *et al.*, 2016). What is lacking is detailed empirical analysis in countries other than the USA, Australia and a handful of others of how banks actually deal with their agribusiness customers' loan requests. All we have are examples, and most of them, unfortunately, from developed countries.

Here is one – loan covenants for the firm Murray River Organics:

MRG's rising gearing levels and earnings uncertainty places pressure on the company's financial covenants. We understand MRG's covenants are based on statutory results and its key metrics are:

- *Interest cover ratio of 1.5x* measured quarterly on a 12-month rolling basis for the period ending 31 December 2016 and thereafter an interest cover ratio of 2.0x measured quarterly on a 12-month rolling basis. This ratio excludes interest incurred on the Colignan vineyard finance lease;
- *Minimum stock/debtors/inventory to working capital debt of 1.25x* (with fruit grown by the company being excluded from the stock/inventory calculation) to be calculated monthly and confirmed 45 days after quarter end; and
- *Maximum dividend payout or shareholder/beneficiary loans to be 50% of NPAT* [Net Profit After Tax] as measured for the financial year end (30 June) annually for the company (Morgans, 2017).

Taking and enforcing security

The lender will require protection against business failure. It will need a security package to protect it as a last resort if things go badly wrong with the financing and the business cannot be sold as a going concern.

Farms generally possess the following assets:

- Land (a very valuable asset for investors, as well as for lenders);
- Buildings. Examples include dairy barns, hay sheds, grain elevators and farmhouses;
- Machinery and equipment (M&E). Generally M&E has a shorter life expectancy than land or buildings. These include combine harvesters, tractors, drones, and other equipment; and
- Fixtures and tools

In some cases, especially larger corporate entities, they may also possess limited amounts of:

- Intellectual property (e.g. from seed banks) which, although they pose valuation difficulties (as noted in Chapter 5) may also be able to be used as security for farm debt; and
- Goodwill, and brand value.

In all cases, but especially in developing countries, the registration, let alone the enforcement, of security may not be easy or quick. The best solution, as strongly advocated and supported by the World Bank, for example in Nigeria, is a land registry together with a credit bureau system that allows M&E to be 'tagged' with attached debt – in future, the blockchain, especially combined with GPS tracking systems, may make this much easier and more effective. However, in many developing countries neither of these systems is as advanced as it could, or certainly should, be, and lenders must price the disappearance of some of their assets into every agribusiness loan.

Carryover debt refers to the portion of an agricultural operating line that the borrower cannot repay from operating production revenue (for example, from crop, livestock or milk sales). It represents a substitute for investment capital and must be serviced through future cash flow, sale of unencumbered assets, or other sources. The presence of significant carryover debt may require restructuring the borrower's overall debt exposure. Depending on variables including the borrower's leverage position, projected cash flows, and balance sheet, it may be appropriate to restructure carryover debt into amortising medium-term loans while continuing to finance current operations with short-term loan

Agricultural credit administration and loan documentation standards will, or ought to, include:

- Financial documentation and repayment capacity analysis, including updates on outside debt;

- Budget or cash flow projection analysis;

- Liquidity monitoring;

- Stress testing;

- Guarantor analysis, when applicable;

- Crop and livestock inspection requirements, including appropriate frequency and timing of inspections and valuations;

- Equipment inspections and valuation expectations;

- Expectations for the content and frequency of real estate evaluations and appraisals;

- Title and lien verification;

- Insurance policy requirements; and

- Regular credit checks.

The conditions under which a loan is advanced should include provisions for default in the event that one or more of these conditions are failed. However, default does not necessarily mean the bank will immediately step in to enforce its security. In fact, most banks are averse to calling in loans and seizing property if they can avoid it, for a host of reasons, not least the risk that they themselves may end up not being able to secure a quick and satisfactory sale of the assets to cover their own loan, let alone the reputational issue and potential problems with government. They would much rather the borrower work out their loan arrears through a *restructuring* (changing the time period for repayment, allowing a standstill of interest payments, etc.), and may even advance additional funds to tide borrowers over difficult periods. That said, there are many notorious cases of bank repossessions of farms and other agribusinesses, often with tragic consequences (Tiwary, 2017).

The terms of purchase for a repossessed property (the property is being put up for sale by the bank, following the bank having obtained a court judgment against a prior owner of the property against whom the bank instituted legal proceedings) may differ from those of a normal property, for example:

> ...should the court judgment which the bank obtained be set aside or become unenforceable for any reason, the bank will no longer be able to sell the property. Should you therefore conclude a sale agreement with the bank for the purchase of a bank repossessed property, and the court judgment in terms of which the bank has repossessed the property is set aside, or becomes unenforceable for any reason, the bank will be entitled in its sole discretion to cancel the agreement, and you will have no claim against the bank of any nature arising from the bank's cancellation of the agreement (Standard Bank, 2018).

Warehouse receipts finance

Farmers in developing countries often face difficulty obtaining financing due to the inability to provide creditors with acceptable collateral. Most common types of collateral, such as land and/or machinery, are usually not available for short-term finance and in many cases farmers, or cooperatives, do not have adequate title. Export objectives compound the difficulty with strict requirements for quality and deliverables. As a result, farmers often have to make hard choices, and liquidity shortages lead to inefficient investment and lower productivity than technically possible. Post-harvest, only a robust system of public warehouses for harvested crops, as supported by IGOs such as the World Bank and the European Bank for Reconstruction and Development (EBRD), would allow farmers to use the stored crops as collateral.

Most well-known are warehouse receipts (WHR), which consist of a collateralised commodity transaction where the stored crop provides security for the loan. The financing cycle begins after the harvest. The harvested crop is stored in a licensed warehouse which issues a receipt proving that the commodity is physically in the warehouse and meets quality standards. On this basis, financing is extended. The warehouse manager is also obliged to issue periodic reports – eventually available in real time – which ensure that the bank can monitor the total value of the goods in stock and the accounts receivables, thereby effectively keeping an eye on its credit risks. Stock will be released from the warehouse only upon the instructions of the bank. Likewise, movement of stock from one storage facility to another will require prior authorisation of the bank and will be subject to the supervision of the collateral manager. It is pertinent to note that in addition to the appointment of a collateral manager to issue warehouse receipts, in order to guarantee the effectiveness of the bank's security, the creation of a pledge over the warehoused goods, the assignment of offtake contracts for the sale of the goods to the bank and the creation of a charge over an account (maintained with the bank) into which proceeds of sales of the goods will be remitted, are essential.

With respect to import finance collaterised with warehouse receipts, it is common for banks to secure the financing of international trade by taking pledges over the goods purchased by the importer with the credit advanced. However, since the bank cannot actually take physical possession of the goods, the bank would usually take a pledge over the bills of lading and appoint an independent collateral manager, who is knowledgeable about the nature of the goods, to monitor the goods. For this purpose, the bank, the collateral manager and the importer would enter into a tripartite collateral management agreement. Under this agreement, the collateral manager assumes, on behalf of the bank, custody of the goods until they are sold to final off-takers and the proceeds of sale, used to offset the importer's outstanding loan with the bank. Importantly, upon importation of the goods, same are transferred to a warehouse under the control of the collateral manager. The collateral manager then issues warehouse receipts, made out in the name of the bank, which state the quality of the goods, the quantity received, and the value at time of receipt. These warehouse receipts will serve as a security for the loan advanced to the importer.

The problem is that for the system to work, many moving parts must interact successfully.

If properly designed, the system provides benefits for farmers through enhanced access to credit, and the possibility to delay their sales and take advantage of the seasonality of prices. Lenders gain by decreasing their risk exposure, as they have collateral which is easier to enforce and usually recognised by central banks operating the Basle or other capital management systems as low risk, in turn enabling lower pricing.

The EBRD has supported warehouse receipts reform in Slovakia, Bulgaria, Romania, Poland, Lithuania, Moldova, Kazakhstan and more recently Serbia, Turkey and Russia. Reforms are often followed or accompanied by investment projects, in particular with partner financial institutions where the risk of lending against warehouse receipts would

Table 9.1 Warehouse receipts – allocation of responsibilities

Organisation	Task
Farmers	Must deposit crop of sufficient quality and trust the warehouse owners and operators.
Warehouse owners and operators	Need to be independent of government pressures and with good governance, providing quality storage without contamination or separation problems.
Banks	Need to trust the warehouse system and be prepared to act quickly once crops are deposited.
Government	Must step aside from the control of the crop and regulate the warehouses and their receipts fairly.

be shared between the EBRD and the partner institutions. Since 2010, the EBRD has promoted a new instrument, referred to as crops receipts. The instrument originated in Brazil as a private sector initiative. A crops receipt system is structured around a specific law – in Brazil, in 1994 the Cedulo de Produto Rural (CPR) was created through Law 8,929 – providing a standardised obligation to supply agricultural products or to make payment in future (to the holder of the receipt) in return for received pre-harvest finance (monetary or in kind). This obligation cannot be altered or evaded under any possible debtor's defence (force majeure included) and can be incorporated as a tradable paper, further increasing its market value. The obligation is also secured by collateral, in particular collateral over future agricultural products (perhaps those that the financing precisely permitted to grow, but not exclusively). The CPR system has achieved great success in Brazil and is now totally integrated into the agricultural finance sector, financing approximately US$20 billion a year. There are now crop receipts reform projects under way in Serbia, Ukraine and Russia (EBRD, 2018).

Credit enhancements

Before the global financial crisis, commercial credit enhancement was possible through the use of insurance companies (the monolines). Now, credit enhancement is still possible for the largest deals through the use of World Bank/IFC products (Multilateral Investment Guarantee Agency, 2015), and there are some financial engineering techniques such as credit enhancements that may be applicable, especially to larger agribusinesses, but their application is highly limited, especially since the global financial crisis, and the overwhelming majority of commercial lending does not have that opportunity. More promising, but still relatively rarely applied, are structured lending solutions to agribusiness that take account of the cyclical nature of agricultural markets.

In this model, lenders work around existing products and techniques to engineer the products into tailor made products or process meeting unique conditions of a borrower.

As a result, structured loans allow lenders adapt a flexible repayment structure best suiting farm conditions hence boosting demand for credit and inputs (Kitaka & Kalio, 2015:575).

Agricultural lending institutions

Public agencies are supplemented in many countries by additional private sector market players. These include:

■ Life insurance companies, which primarily provide farm real estate financing to larger agricultural enterprises, generally borrowers financing amounts greater than $1 million.

■ Captive lenders: vendors such as equipment manufacturers, seed companies and retailers normally provide limited-purpose vendor financing to enhance market penetration for their products.

■ Other lenders: these include parents financing their children's farming or other agri-business operations, property owners providing self-financing for their tenant farmers, and individuals financing the sale of land and other capital assets using a contract for deed or sales contract.

■ Offtakers. Cooperatives and farm output purchasing processors may also offer loan agreements to farmers as part of contract farming or other similar arrangements.

In its 2015 document, the IFC set out what process a potential lender should follow before entering the agribusiness lending space. They noted, first, that agriculture is an area that receives political attention, so there may be certain government policies that will need to be watched, such as subsidies or grants, and perhaps exploited (such as loan guarantees) (Cowley & McCoy, 2018). Will the financial institution be able to charge adequate interest to cover its expenses, including projected loss rates as well as the marketing cost of reaching dispersed populations? Second, is there demand? Third, can the organisation cope? The IFC noted several levels at which agribusiness loans can impact the organisation:

■ Senior management should be open to restructuring the organisation and aligning staff to implement agricultural lending effectively. This may obviously involve training. Obviously, the credit department should be capable of implementing adequate process across the region or country's branches. There may be a need for adjustment of roles and responsibilities, both of field and head office staff, to assess, approve and manage agricultural loan applications, and to train branch managers on the approval and monitoring of agricultural loans using the new processes.

■ The lender's risk department should adjust its policies to address the additional risks involved with the agricultural sector, and to implement new processes and tools to manage and monitor agricultural portfolio risks.

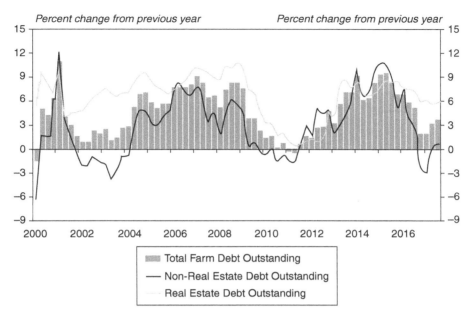

Figure 9.4 Farm debt outstanding at commercial banks
Source: USDA (2016:Table B1)

- The IT department needs to be able to incorporate the flexible loan schedules, grace periods and other aspects of agricultural loans that match farmer cash flows.

- Perhaps most important of all, although the IFC do not mention this, the timescale of agricultural loans needs to be extended.

In the USA, farms accessed $6 billion in new credit in 2017, either directly or guaranteed through commercial lenders, in addition to working capital and other non-real estate backed debt. Most funds required were for farm expansion, and higher-cost production items, such as machinery and motor vehicles (Ricketts & Ricketts, 2009:156). The cyclical nature of US farm debt levels is quite evident from USDA data.

The USDA's ERS data show the current on-farm debt to asset ratio at 14%. Compare that to its highest point of 22.2% in 1980 and its lowest point of 11.3% in 2012, nowhere near the levels seen in the 1980s – prior to the 1980 agricultural economy crash, farm income was very volatile and producers did not have much opportunity to stockpile assets. Going into the current very modest downturn, commodity markets hit record highs and producers had several good years to get their financial houses in order (Wilson & Bjerga, 2018).

In Australia, farm debt seems to have stabilised. ABARES (www.abares.gov.au) is the main source of information about agriculture, and it estimated that broadacre debt increased by only 7% during 2015–16 to average a very modest A$560,500 per farm as at 30 June 2016, after much more rapid growth during the previous decade when land values increased considerably. Dairy industry debt also increased by around 7% to average A$937,600 per

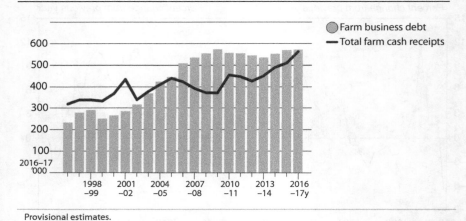

Figure 9.5 ABARES Australian farm debt analysis
Source: ABARES (2017)

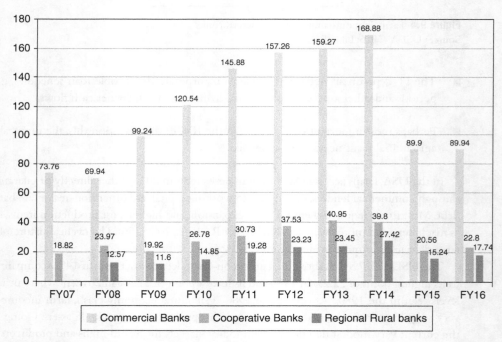

Figure 9.6 Institutional credit to Indian agriculture (US$ bn)
Source: Reserve Bank of India (2016)

farm. Most new borrowing during 2015–16 for broadacre and dairy farms funded new on-farm investment. Farm business equity on average is strong for broadacre farms. The average equity ratio for broadacre farms at 30 June 2016 is estimated at an extremely high 88%, an increase from 87% at 30 June 2015 (Martin *et al.*, 2018).

The major sources of credit for those in the agricultural industry are the Farm Credit System (FCS), commercial banks, the Farm Service Agency (FSA), the Commodity Credit Corporation, life insurance companies and HNWIs (high-net-worth individuals). Not all these lend throughout the value chain. Back in 1995 commercial banks supplied only 50% of US farm credit, but this percentage is now far higher.

A comparison may be made with the volume and division of lending by type of institution in India which has been regularly published by the Reserve Bank of India (Subbarao, 2012).

According to official figures, institutional credit to the agricultural sector in India increased at an annual rate of 3% between 2007–15. Farmers are able to access crop loans at a subsidised 7% interest rate. In FY2015, institutional credit to the agricultural sector was US$90 billion, $21 billion from cooperative banks and US$15 billion from regional rural banks. For academic analysis of the problems facing agricultural credit in India, see Seena (2015), Solanki (2016) and Kumar (2017), all of whom do a good job of presenting the current lending environment and its problems. The cost of borrowed capital is a significant part of most growers' budgets. Ideally, producers should shop for loans just as they look for the best price for fertiliser, seed and all other production inputs. Deregulation in the banking industry worldwide has increased competition (for the USA, see Morris, 2015), which has caused more precise pricing of loans, except in developing countries where local monopolies unfortunately continue. This means that banks are competing with each other by offering lower interest rates, lower loan fees, or other services. See also the IFC's 2014 report on the success and problems experienced by microfinance lenders to agriculture in Latin America (Varangis *et.al.*, 2014). One of the key indicators of competition amongst lenders has been found to be the degree of concentration in the banking industry (Davcev & Hourvouliades, 2013), technical analysis of which is relatively forthcoming (e.g. Soares, 2014), although the exact relationship by industry is not clear and therefore it would be premature to draw conclusions for global agribusiness. Arguably the deep knowledge base of large international banks such as Rabobank actually enables them to price more accurately, as well as serve more clients.

In South Africa, the key lenders to the South African agricultural sector are the Land and Agricultural Bank (Land Bank), commercial banks, agricultural cooperatives, private persons and other relatively small financial institutions such as merchant banks, insurance companies, trust companies, etc. The commercial banks lent the most, 62%, followed by the Land Bank with a share of 27%, agricultural cooperatives with a share of 7%, and the rest being private persons and other financial institutions (Sihlobo, 2018).

The problem, however, is the disparity of banking services between developed and developing countries, as it has been for decades. The availability of lending services to agribusiness from leading banks in developed countries is clear from their websites, e.g. Barclays in the UK (www.barclays.co.uk/business-banking/sectors/agri-business/) or ANZ in Australia (www.anz.com.au/business/industries/agribusiness/). Both of these banks still equate agribusiness essentially with farming. Notably, too, borrowing terms even for agricultural mortgages are quite short. Barclays showcase the following key attributes of their agricultural mortgages:

■ Borrow up to 80% of the value of farm buildings or land;

■ Choose repayments to suit your business cashflow, either monthly, quarterly or annually;

■ If you take the interest-only period, interest will be charged to your current account;

■ Choose a variable or fixed-interest rate, with the option to change your selection during the mortgage term;

■ Fixed rate terms are available from 1 to 10 years;

■ Lending fees and associated borrowing costs apply and can be added to the loan;

■ Prepayment fees may apply if you repay all or part of your loan before the expiry of the agreed term;

■ For fixed rate loans, if you decide to pay early or cancel the fixed interest rate, you may have to pay breakage cost in addition to other fees such as prepayment fees (Barclays, 2018).

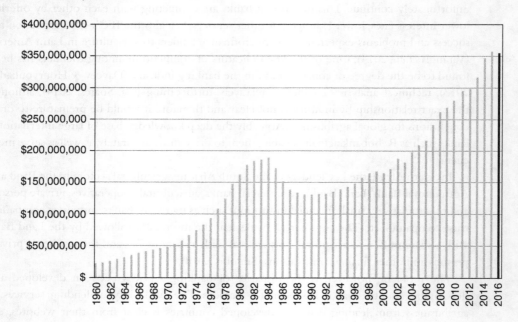

Figure 9.7 Farm debt (US$ 000s)
Source: Zerohedge (2016)

Lending to agribusiness in developed countries is exhibiting solid growth, as the data from the USA shown in Figure 9.7 demonstrate.

It would be a great mistake to imagine that because the theory of bank lending to agriculture is clear enough, and the evidence from the West is that it works, and works well, lending is successful in developing countries. It is not. A recent evaluation of agricultural lending by banks in Pakistan identified the following problems, generating inefficiency, which are quite typical for developing countries generally.

One of the main difficulties faced by the farmers in obtaining agricultural credit from the formal institutions is documentation and cumbersome procedure; it is considered the prime impediment in securing loans from institutional sources. There are several groups of documents that farmers should be prepared to provide when applying for a loan.

- The directors or owners need to put together a resume describing their background, including experience working on other farms and agribusinesses, and even education.

- The business's tax returns for at least the last three years should be included, as well as financial statements for each of the last three years.

- Financial statements for each of the last three years. These include a balance sheet which lists all of the agribusiness's assets and liabilities, including all existing debts as well as such assets as debts payable. The next financial statement is the income statement, which is a profit and loss statement for the past year developed on an accrual basis. Finally, there should be a cash flow statement that shows sources and use of funds on a monthly basis for the past year at least.

- There will be a business plan, accompanied by a cash flow budget for the period over which the loan is payable. This will include a marketing plan, which is another essential part of a loan package.

- All contracts, including sales contracts and membership of cooperatives. Include any sales contracts you might have and co-op membership if applicable.

- Other documents the lender may insist on seeing include titles to real estate and personal property particularly if these assets are securities for the loan. Include serial numbers and identification of any new equipment purchases.

- In the case of a farm, the lender may also ask for a third-party opinion on the yield and value of growing crops if they are listed as assets. Any crop loan application must include a map of the fields and cropping plans for the farm operation. All lease agreements will need to be shown, so that it is clear what crops are to be grown where, what the ownership status is for the properties to be farmed, and what the cash rent or crop-share agreement is.

- Insurance policies for equipment, liabilities and crops may be a requirement for the loan. The agribusiness must be prepared to provide complete insurance information including carrier, policy number and amount of coverage.

There are several questions the directors of an agribusiness should ask a lender when applying for a loan. First, is real estate a security? If so, is there an appraisal fee? Is there an application fee or commitment fee and is it returned if the loan is made? There may also be closing costs, inspection fees or charges for documents that may be recorded. Who pays these and when? What covenants will be required? What latitude for further investment, changes in personnel or other business decisions?

There are several questions the agribusiness directors must be prepared to answer. The lender may want to know if the directors are co-signers, endorsers or guarantors for debts incurred by others. Questions about corporate and even personal income tax owed on assets already sold or income received should be expected. Tax liabilities should match with balance sheets. Any potential lawsuits or other threats to value, compliance with existing and even potential laws (e.g. on water, environment, employment). Many lenders ask for an environmental questionnaire to be completed by the business to determine if further investigation is necessary. In order to complete the questionnaire, the borrower must know the history of the property being farmed. For example, questions may be asked about the existence of underground fuel tanks, prior use of herbicides and pesticides and past pollution problems on the property, all of which would affect value negatively and hence the strength of the security.

There is no substitute for a good working relationship between an agribusiness and its lender. Creative financing such as restructuring a loan, refinancing or rolling over production loans are done at the discretion of the lender and not as a matter of course. A long-term relationship with a lender increases the financing options of the agribusiness. Financing is critical to any farming operation. Remember that complete and accurate records are the building blocks for any financial decision.

However, there are plenty of obstacles to effective agricultural lending in developing countries.

- There is lack of timely availability of credit.

- There is considerable political pressure in disbursement of the agricultural credit. Institutional credit is not offered according to the relative efficiency of the farmer but according to the economic and political power of the credit recipient.

- Formal institutions always ask for collateral when they issue credit. However, most developing country farmers are resource poor, they do not have anything to offer. This makes cheap credit accessibility difficult for marginal, sub-marginal and small farmers.

- Banking institutions have difficult credit rules which obstruct small and marginalised farmers from accessing the loan. Because the credit rules and regulations are very complicated, they are not clearly apprehended by illiterate and partially educated farmers.

- There is risk involved in lending to the farm sector because of the associated uncertainties and probability of default. So banks try to avoid it and find other lucrative investments.

■ Despite the fact that Zarai Taraqiati Bank Limited (ZTBL) in Pakistan, and similar institutions in other countries, have played a crucial role in advancement of agricultural credit to farmers, rural farmers still hesitate to apply for loans. There are various reasons that explain this. For example, high interest rates, the distance from home to bank (which mobile banking has only very partially overcome), delays in disbursement of loans, complex procedures, and corruption and inefficiency on the part of the public sector. Taken together it is scarcely an enticing prospect for farmers, even in the second decade of the 21st century.

■ The operation of banks has not been extended and so the farmers are provided expensive financial support.

■ There is no proper research and no specific policy from the government side on the agriculture credit requirement. No specific database is available on the current credit needs of the farmers.

■ The rate of interest is high on such loans, which despite benefiting farmers can harm them. Sometimes it leads to bankruptcy and even suicide. In the last 20 years in India, nearly 300,000 farmers have ended their lives by ingesting pesticides or by hanging themselves. The suicide rate among Indian farmers was 47% higher than the national average, according to a 2011 census. An average of 41 farmers commit suicide every day, leaving behind scores of orphans and widows (Umar, 2015). However, it is quite noticeable that suicides, in particular, are closely correlated with low education levels and are often found amongst agricultural workers, not owners of farms. A 2013 study in Australia found that the suicide rate for agriculture workers was 1.6 times higher than the average for all employed people. Official Indian data published in April 2016

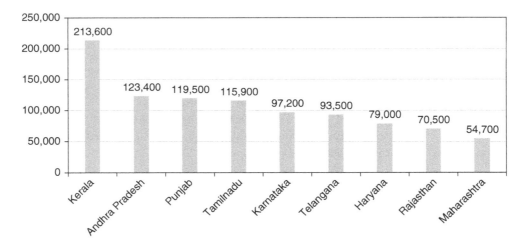

Figure 9.8 Total amount of outstanding loan per agricultural household, by state
Source: Deshetti (2015)

on the basis of a national survey carried out by the National Sample Survey Office (NSSO) during July 2012–June 2013 suggested that about 52% agricultural households in rural India were in debt, with an average amount of outstanding loan per agricultural household of Rs47,000. This can be compared to average annual income of Rs77,112. Agricultural households in rural India are estimated to be 90.2 million, about 57.8% of the total estimated rural households in the country (NSSO, 2013). Conclusions are not entirely easy to draw from these data: the Indian state with the largest problem, Maharashtra, was also the state with the lowest average bank debt per farmer, at least in 2012.

Sometimes the cause of repossessions is a change in policy, as in the case of South Africa (Le Cap, 2009). In other cases, it is adverse weather, or a change in market conditions. It is a grim tally, against which institutions such as USAID and the State Bank of Pakistan are doing their utmost to improve the situation. The IFC noted in 2012, consistent with its own generally negative evaluation of commercial lending opportunities to the agriculture sector, especially SMEs, that:

Agriculture is very seasonal, from planting or livestock birth to harvest or slaughter with long gestation periods. The result is that cash flows are highly seasonal and sometimes irregular, with earnings concentrated in certain times of the year. As such, there is a slow rotation of the invested capital as investments are spread over longer time horizons than for non-seasonal businesses. For the banker, this means that short-term agricultural credit may need to be repaid in 'lumpy instalments' sometimes over multiple seasons. It also means that farmers require flexible and targeted savings and term finance products to meet their specific needs. From the banker's point of view, irregular repayment schedules make liquidity management more challenging and require costly investments in developing customized loan products in an unfamiliar sector (Varangis et al., 2012).

Hence,

In countries where agriculture has [a] substantial role in generating domestic product, sustainable agro-finance can seriously increase economic development. It is well known that agriculture is perceived as too risky to be financed by commercial banks. Therefore, creating specific agro-credit lines within state development banks is a key element in enhancing agricultural activities. These state development banks, operating in close collaboration with the Government, have a significant role in accelerating the economic welfare of farmers and the rural poor (Kovachev, 2013).

In many jurisdictions – including the USA – the perceived market failure of commercial banks has led to the persistence of similar public sector agencies providing loans to farmers and other parts of agribusiness. One of the huge advantages to farming in a developed country, especially the USA, is therefore the deep reservoir of potential funding sources. These certainly include mutual lending institutions:

- Farm Credit System (FCS): the FCS comprises cooperative institutions regulated by the Farm Credit Administration. FCS institutions lend money to farmers through local FCS associations. Wholesale lending (to FCS institutions) is shared between the Farm Credit System Funding Corporation and the regional farm credit banks. The FCS relies exclusively on selling farm credit bonds to fund lending operations. The liability for FCS bond underwriting is jointly and severally shared by the farm credit banks and is guaranteed by the Farm Credit System Insurance Corporation. Primarily, financial institutions purchase the bonds. FCS lenders traditionally are most competitive in the agricultural real estate market, because they can issue long-term bonds to offset their interest rate exposure on long-term mortgages. Other products include operating loans, intermediate term debt for capital purchases, rural home mortgage loans, leases, credit-related life insurance, crop insurance, commercial real estate loans, and accounting/income tax preparation.

- Farm Service Agency (FSA): the FSA, formerly known as the Farmers Home Administration (FmHA), is the agency within the USDA that administers federal agricultural lending programmes. FSA loans are funded from the USDA's budget and from funds repaid by borrowers. The FSA focuses resources on serving small, less-experienced and disadvantaged farmers.

Evidence on international bank lending and agricultural leverage ratios

Both the World Bank and its commercial arm, the International Finance Corporation (IFC) are significant players in the international bank lending market for major agricultural projects. Indeed, for those projects that are not directly commercially viable they are often the only potential source of finance (World Bank, 2018). Hence, for example, a loan agreement of US$318 million was signed between the Government of India, the Government of Tamil Nadu and the World Bank in December 2017 for the Tamil Nadu Irrigated Agriculture Modernization Project, which is expected to benefit around 500,000 farmers in the state. Some projects are much smaller.

ADB Irrigation Project in Jalalpur to Increase Food Production in Punjab, Pakistan
    ISLAMABAD, PAKISTAN (24 November 2017) — The Asian Development Bank's (ADB) Board of Directors has approved a $275 million loan to help build a surface irrigation system to increase agricultural production and improve food security in the Jhelum and Khushab districts in Punjab province in Pakistan. The project is expected to benefit 384,000 people.
    The Jalalpur Irrigation Project will build a new seasonal irrigation system and convert over 68,000 hectares (ha) of less productive, predominantly rain-fed land to irrigated land by drawing water from the Jhelum River, one of the tributaries of the Indus River. The

project will construct a diversion structure, a 117-kilometer (km) main canal, 97-km secondary and tertiary canals, and 485 watercourses. The project will also assist in forming 485 water user associations (WUAs) and involve them in planning, designing, and constructing watercourses. The WUAs and the farmers will be trained to improve their agriculture and water management capacity. Advanced technologies like laser land leveling and high-efficiency irrigation systems will be introduced by the project. About 660 agricultural demonstration plots will be established, and 6,000 farm households will learn climate-smart agriculture practices and more profitable farm management.

Source: The Financial (2018)

A second recent example:

The African Development Bank Group (AfDB) is supporting Namibia's Agriculture Sector with the approval of One Billion South African Rands (*ZAR 1 billion) loan to finance the country's Agricultural Mechanisation and Seed Improvement Project (NAMSIP). The NAMSIP was approved by the AfDB Board, on Monday, 4th December 2017 in Abidjan, and aims to enhance agricultural productivity in order to reduce annual importation of staple cereal crops/grains, facilitate job creation, and enhance household incomes which will improve the lives of rural people.

The Project's two key components comprise Value Chain Improvement, (with agricultural mechanization and certified seed systems as sub-components), and Institutional Support through Capacity Building, and Project Management. The Project is aligned to the Bank's High-5 priorities of Feed Africa, and Improve the quality of life for the people of Africa; Ten Year Strategy (2013–2022); Namibia Country Strategy Paper (CSP: 2014–2018), and Gender Strategy (2014–2018). The Project is also in line with Namibia's Fifth National Development Plan 2017/2018–2021/2022); Harambee Prosperity Plan (2016/2017–2019/2020), and Growth at Home Strategy for Industrialization, which identify agriculture as a priority area with enormous potential to contribute to economic progression, social transformation and environmental sustainability. The Project will be implemented by Namibia's Ministry of Agriculture, Water and Forestry over a period of 5 years, in all 14 Administrative Regions of Namibia. It will directly benefit 294,500 crop farmers, and 10,000 livestock farmers. In addition, the project will fully support 111 smallholder farmer cooperatives, and indirectly benefit about 800,000 people along the cereal crops and livestock value chains. The Project is estimated to cost ZAR 1.42 billion. The ADB Loan will finance 70.5% of the total project cost while the Government and beneficiaries will contribute the remaining 25.5% and 4.0%, respectively.

Source: African Business Communities (2017)

Some projects are much smaller.

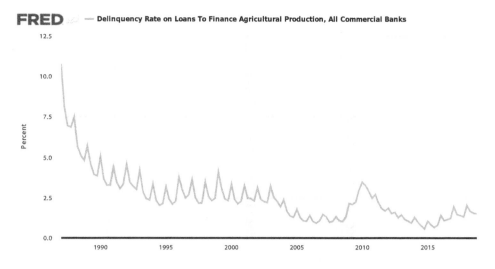

FRED — Delinquency Rate on Loans To Finance Agricultural Production, All Commercial Banks

Source: Board of Governors of the Federal Reserve System (US)myf.red/g/naUE

Figure 9.9 Delinquency rate of agricultural loans
Source: Federal Board of Governors (2019)

In 2018, 'Nigeria has been selected alongside two other African countries (Ethiopia and Tanzania) to benefit from the World Bank Group's Livestock and Micro Reforms in Agribusiness (L-MIRA) program. The L-MIRA program's objective is to improve the competitiveness of the dairy and poultry sectors in the agribusiness value chain in the selected countries. The International Finance Corporation – a member of the World Bank Group, recently signed the cooperation agreement with the Federal Government to implement the $2 million initiative… The partnership which is expected to streamline the regulation of animal feed and remove overlapping or redundant regulatory requirements related to the standards and quality control mechanism in the country, as well as the registration and renewal process for drugs and vaccines.'

Source: Owoeye (2018)

Information on actual D/E ratios for international bank lending are extremely hard to find. National information is available only for the advanced economies. As for debt service ratios, having peaked at just shy of 50% in the early 1980s, US debt service ratios seem to have achieved relative stability at around 25% for the last two decades. Similar effects have been observed in Europe, all largely caused by macroeconomic effects, in particular declines in interest rates, which have affected all sectors.

Default ratios are likewise difficult to locate, although again some national agencies do publish annual data. In 2017, for example, 'Danish banks had losses for kr. 392 million on

						Yield-to-worst	Yield-to-worst
Issuer	Issuer rating[1] (S&P's / Moody's)	Currency	Coupon	Date of issue	Maturity	as of 1 year ago	as of today
EMEA SÜDZUCKER	BBB / Baa2	EUR	1.250%	Nov-16	8-year	1.2%	0.5%
TATE&LYLE	BBB / Baa2	USD	6.750%	Nov-09	10-year	1.3%	1.1%
Tereos	BB / NA	EUR	4.125%	Jun-16	7-year	4.0%	2.8%
Americas BUNGE	BBB / Baa2	USD	3.250%	Aug-16	10-year	3.7%	3.6%
cosan	BB / NA	USD	5.950%	Sep-17	7-year	NA	5.2%
Ingredion	BBB / Baa2	USD	3.200%	Sep-16	10-year	3.5%	3.3%
Total average						2.7%	2.8%

② Focus on sugar sector ... despite positive sentiment from debt investors

Figure 9.10 Rating of sugar companies
Source: Taurins (2017)

their loans to Danish agriculture etc. This corresponds to approximately 0.6 per cent or kr. 6,000 per lent million to the industry' (Danmarks Nationalbank, 2018). US data from the Federal Reserve shows the extent to which the delayed effects of macroeconomic factors dominated default rates for agricultural loans over the past decade, occluding the commodity price boom which ironically took place over exactly the same period as the spike in defaults.

Liquidity and refinancing

Significance of commodity prices in agribusiness profitability and debt repayment capacity

There is little doubt of the long-term relationship. But commodity prices are only one part of a larger picture, which includes land prices (Farm Futures, 2017) as well as commodity input prices (Barnard et al., 2013). Credit Suisse reported in November 2017 that, despite uncertainty over prices and even regulatory concerns, debt providers were relatively upbeat about sugar companies, which can be measured by the rating of their debt issuance by rating agencies (see Figure 9.10).

Deloitte Africa in fact identifies a whole series of reasons why agribusiness debts can end up in arrears, none of which concern commodity prices:

■ Insufficient cash flow/income due to climatic reasons (this is normally a short-term problem);

■ Inefficiency of enterprise or enterprises due to lack of resources, managerial ability and lack of industry knowledge;

■ High overhead costs, for example labour costs or number of dependants/families relying on income from the agribusiness;

■ Incorrect alignment between debt repayment maturities and cash flow;

■ Overzealous changes in strategy that actually worsen cash flow;

■ Lack of risk management; and

■ Poor use of assets.

Source: Deloitte Africa Agribusiness Unit (2011)

Lending to intermediary companies and the bank role in the value chain

International lending institutions such as Afrexibank are also looking to achieve synergies with their lending; for example, to connect cotton processing activities and proposed fabric production in Burkina Faso with garment manufacturing plants, the bank is assisting in setting up in the West Africa region, extending lines of credit to local banks and financing for industrial parks, special economic zones and logistics parks, as part of its Intra-African Trade Strategy (Koigi, 2017). These initiatives are slow to come to fruition and are often beset by numerous delays and other problems, but they do at least provide evidence that multilateral lending institutions are aware of the need to understand and promote agribusiness value chains, especially in developing countries.

When a turnaround is required, three to five years should be expected before the agribusiness returns to profitability. Whilst most farms have credit lines that are funded from *relatively* stable cashflows, larger agribusinesses further along the value chain can easily find themselves needing to refinance. The drama can be quite intense, with the entire future of the company at stake.

Aryzta's need to refinance €600 million of debt in the next year has become more difficult in the wake of the latest profit warning this week from the Swiss-Irish food company, according to analysts at two of the world's most influential banks…Aryzta faced higher interest rates when refinancing the debt with its banks before it is due in February, as declining earnings will push its debt burden close to what's allowed under its banking covenants…The company's net debt is likely to be 3.4 times the size of its earnings before interest, tax, depreciation and amortisation in 2018, close to its covenant limit of 3.5 times agreed with its banks (Brennan, 2017).

Good luck, Aryzta.

They succeeded:

'The Group's new five-year unsecured €1,800m refinancing, comprising a €1,000m amortising term loan and a €800m revolving credit facility, was utilised on 22 September 2017 to repay in full the revolving credit and term loan facilities put in place in September 2016 and all amounts outstanding as of 31 January 2018 have been classified between current and long-term, in accordance with the terms of this new financing agreement. The refinancing was underwritten by four of the Group's key relationship banks and general syndication was successfully completed during the period ended 31 January 2018. In order to provide enhanced financial flexibility, the Group has increased the covenant to a maximum 4.75x Net Debt: EBITDA at 31 January 2018, reducing to a maximum of 4.00x at 31 July 2018 and a maximum of 3.50x from 31 July 2019. The Group has also reduced the interest cover covenant to 3.0x EBITDA: Interest' (Aryzta AG, 2018).

Establishing bank security interests/collateral management/pledges

In most emerging markets, the lack of acceptable collateral is often cited as a key constraint on the provision of credit to agriculture. Three main types of collateral are typically used to finance agriculture: farmland, equipment and agricultural commodities. In many economies, however, the ability to use farmland as collateral is hindered by the absence of land titles or by inefficient land markets. Likewise, mortgaging or leasing out equipment is not always possible due to the lack of mechanisation in agriculture, the absence of a legal and regulatory framework conducive to leasing, or limited secondary markets for equipment in case of default. As a result, the third option, use of agricultural commodities as collateral, is increasingly being explored in various countries, particularly in Latin America, South Asia, and East Africa (Varangis & Saint-Geours, 2017).

In common with most other developing countries, the Indian agri-commodity market, being highly fragmented, is characterized by a large number of participants including farmers, several layers of aggregator, processors and traders. Before the advent of professional Collateral Management entities, access to finance and consequentially holding capacity for the above entities was difficult due to poor balance sheet quality and credit history. While banks were keen to identify lending opportunities within this segment to meet their priority segment obligations, a high level of non-performing assets and heavy supervisory costs dissuaded their efforts. Moreover the flow of credit remained skewed in favour of the developed and urban pockets. Over the past 8 years collateral management services have brought about a transformation by allowing banks to almost ignore the borrower's financial strength and rely solely upon the warehouse receipt issued by the agency. This form of lending by banks is in contrast to the traditional lending in the form of working capital, with credit facility based on the balance sheet of the borrowing entity, and is more secure due to the collateral manager's services. The current collateral management processes in India are rudimentary but effective and more importantly in line with the domestic market practices. The collateral manager after a survey enters into a lease agreement and takes custody of the storage facility containing the commodities. The collateral manager guarantees the quality and quantity of the agri-based collateral, provides price information required for margin call and aids in disposal of the commodities, if necessary. The collateral manager also ensures that the commodities are adequately insured for natural calamities and burglary, though these risks are not underwritten by the collateral agency. The loans against agri-collaterals are typically short term (8 months to 1 year), self-liquidating, and one of the most secure products in a bank's portfolio. For the borrowers the willingness of a collateral manager to provide services in a variety of storage facilities, including the godown in his backyard (field warehousing), makes this the easiest method of procuring low cost finance (Thoopal, 2013).

Conclusion

Debt, as corporate finance theory teaches, is a double-edged sword: prudent borrowing can be highly profitable and wealth-creating. However, there are negative aspects to debt financing – from the smallest farm to the largest multinational – that have consequences for liquidity, solvency and profitability (Greig, 2010). The rise of new lending techniques derived from finance tech (FinTech) may improve access to finance even for smallholder farmers: whereas US farm loans start around $300,000, it is possible to sponsor a 7-acre rice farm in Nigeria for $250 via Farmcrowdy (www.farmcrowdy.com), a digital platform that connects sponsors to farmers to increase food production. Other FinTech for agricultural start-ups are enabling smallholders to get credit to purchase higher quality inputs like seeds, while others are selling their own products via in-house asset financing. As these platforms mature, commercial banks will have serious competition in funding debt for agribusinesses, which can be no bad thing in the decades ahead.

Bibliography

ABARES (2017) *Financial Performance of Grain Farms, 2014–15 to 2016–17.* Canberra, ABARES. December. Available at: http://data.daff.gov.au/data/warehouse/9aas/2017/FarmPerformance Grains/AustGrainFinPerf_2014-16_2016-17_v.1.0.0.pdf. Retrieved 23 February 2019.

African Business Communities (2017) AfDB supports Namibia's agriculture sector with one billion South African Rands. 6 December. Available at: https://africabusinesscommunities.com/news/afdb-supports-namibia%E2%80%99s-agriculture-sector-with-one-billion-south-african-rands/. Retrieved 30 June 2018.

Aryzta AG (2018) 2018 Interim Report and Accounts. Available at: www.aryzta.com/wp-content/uploads/2018/03/2018-HalfYear-Results.pdf. Retrieved 30 June 2018.

Barclays (2018) Agricultural Mortgages: Finance for land and buildings. Available at: www.barclays.co.uk/business-banking/borrow/agricultural-mortgages/. Retrieved 30 June 2018.

Barnard, F.L., Yeager, E.A. and Miller, A. (2013) Repayment capacity sensitivity analysis using Purdue Farm financial analysis spreadsheet. *Journal of the ASFMRA (American Society of Farm Managers and*

Rural Appraisers). Available at: https://ideas.repec.org/a/ags/jasfmr/161502.html. Retrieved 30 June 2018.

Billett, M.T., Elkamhi, R., Popov, L. and Pungaliya, R.S. (2016) Bank skin in the game and loan contract design: Evidence from covenant-lite loans. *Journal of Financial and Quantitative Analysis* 51(3), 839–873.

Brealey, R., Myers, S. and Allen, F. (2016) *Principles of Corporate Finance*, 12th edition. New York, McGraw-Hill.

Brealey, R., Myers, S. and Marcus, A.J. (2017) *Fundamentals of Corporate Finance*, 9th edition. New York, McGraw-Hill.

Brennan, J. (2017) Aryzta €600m refinancing 'more difficult' after profit warning. *Irish Times.* 26 January. Available at: www.irishtimes.com/business/agribusiness-and-food/aryzta-600m-refinancing-more-difficult-after-profit-warning-1.2951324. Retrieved 30 June 2018.

Brookfield, H. and Parsons, H. (2007) *Family Farms: Survival and Prospect. A World-Wide Analysis.* London and New York, Routledge.

Carroll, M. (2015) A perspective on risk & the farm enterprise. ABARES Outlook 2015 Conference, Canberra, 3 March. Available at: www.agriculture.gov.au/abares/outlook-2015/Documents/mcarroll.pdf. Retrieved 30 June 2018.

Clarke, M. (2014) Large scale greenfield agri-business development. 13 June. Available at: https://business.nab.com.au/large-scale-greenfield-agri-business-development-6758/. Retrieved 29 June 2018.

Cowley, C. and McCoy, J. (2018) Farm Business: Ag Loans Up as Interest Rates Rise – Fed Reserve Kansas City. 2 February. Available at: https://agfax.com/2018/02/02/farm-business-ag-loans-up-as-interest-rates-rise-fed-reserve-kansas-city/. Retrieved 30 June 2018.

Danmarks Nationalbank (2018) Fewer Losses on Bank Loans to Agriculture (2018). Available at: www.nationalbanken.dk/en/statistics/find_statistics/Pages/2018/Fewer-losses-on-bank-loans-to-agriculture.aspx. Retrieved 30 June 2018. Similar data are available for other developed countries.

Davcev, L. and Hourvouliades, N. (2013) Banking Concentration in FYROM: Evidence from a country in transition. *Procedia Economics and Finance* 5, 222–230.

Delaware Department of Agriculture (2019) *Specialty Crop Block Grant Program.* Available at: https://agriculture.delaware.gov/communications-marketing/specialty-crop-block-grant-program. Retrieved 29 June 2019.

Deloitte Africa Agribusiness Unit (2011) *Prosper and Grow.* Johannesburg, Deloitte. Available at: www.afrilogic.co.za/downloads/pdf/Agribusiness%20Management%20of%20risk%20accounts%20.pdf. Retrieved 30 June 2018.

Demiroglu, C. and James, C.M. (2010) The information content of bank loan covenants. *The Review of Financial Studies* 23(10), 3700–3737.

Deshetti, S. (2015) Total Amount of Outstanding Loan per Agricultural Household – Indian Farmers loans. Available at: https://factly.in/indian-farmers-loans-more-than-half-agricultural-households-indebted-quarter-loan-taken-from-money-lender/total-amount-of-outstanding-loan-per-agricultural-household-indian-farmers-loans/. Retrieved 23 February 2019.

Durguner, S. (2007) A Panel Data Analysis of the Repayment Capacity of Farmers. Available at: https://pdfs.semanticscholar.org/9303/1c98486d0437f6c096e4bf06458939ad3380.pdf. Retrieved 16 April 2018.

EBRD (2018) Agricultural Finance. Available at: www.ebrd.com/what-we-do/legal-reform/access-to-finance/agricultural-finance.html. Retrieved 6 June 2018.

efinancemanagement.com (2019) Pecking Order Theory. Available at: https://efinancemanagement.com/financial-leverage/pecking-order-theory. Retrieved 23 February 2019.

FAO (2016) *Public–Private Partnerships for Agribusiness Development – A Review of International Experiences.* Rome, FAO. Available at: www.fao.org/3/a-i5699e.pdf. Retrieved 29 June 2018.

Farm Futures (2017) Ag lenders concerned about decline in commodity prices. 1 May. Available at: www.farmfutures.com/capital/ag-lenders-concerned-about-decline-commodity-prices. Retrieved 30 June 2018.

Federal Board of Governors (2019) *Agricultural Loans*. Washington DC, Federal Board of Governors. Available at: https://fred.stlouisfed.org/series/DRFAPGACBN. Retrieved 23 February 2019.

Fegarty, T., Edwards, C. and Gitman, L.J. (2005) Cost of Capital. Presentation. Available at: http://slideplayer.com/slide/7737468/. Retrieved 27 March 2018.

Gergely, A. and Rózsa, A. (2018) Investigation of equity risk premium in Hungarian food industry. *SEA: Practical Application of Science* 16, 7–19.

Grady, J.T. (2017) Debt service coverage ratio: Two views are better than one. *The RMA Journal Philadelphia* 92 (7), 52–60.

Green Acres (2018) Lifestyle home and business for sale. Available at: http://forsale.green acreschocolatefarm.com/. Retrieved 29 June 2018.

Grieg, B. (2010) New Zealand Dairy Farm Debt. Available at: https://researcharchive.lincoln.ac.nz/bitstream/handle/10182/3700/2010_side_greig.pdf?sequence=1/. Retrieved 30 June 2018.

Hayes, M.G. (2003). Investment and finance under fundamental uncertainty. PhD thesis. University of Sunderland.

IFC (2015) *Agricultural Lending: A How-To Guide*. Washington DC, IFC. Available at: www.ifc.org/wps/wcm/connect/88d4a7004a42ef7c800fbb10cc70d6a1/Agricultural+Lending-A+How+To+Guide.pdf?MOD=AJPERES. Retrieved 28 March 2018.

Kitaka, A.N. and Kalio, A.M. (2015) assessing influence of structured loans on agribusiness borrowing at First Community Bank, Kenya. *International Journal of Economics, Commerce and Management* 3(6), 574–586.

Klonsky, K. (2012) How to finance a small farm. Available at: http://sfp.ucdavis.edu/pubs/Family_Farm_Series/Farmmanage/finance/?search=yes. Retrieved 29 June 2018.

Koigi, R. (2017) Afrexim announces support for development of cotton value chain in West Africa. Africa Business Communities. 13 June. Available at: http://africabusinesscommunities.com/news/afrexim-announces-support-for-development-of-cotton-value-chain-in-west-africa/. Retrieved 27 June 2018.

Kovachev, G. (2013) Financing agribusiness by state development banks – The case of Macedonia. *Journal of Governance and Regulation* 2(3), 107–116.

Kumar, A. (2017) Institutional Versus Noninstitutional Credit to Agricultural Households in India Evidence on Impact from a National Farmers' Survey. Discussion Paper 01614 March 2017. Washington DC, IFPRI. Available at: www.indiaenvironmentportal.org.in/files/file/Institutional%20versus%20noninstitutional%20credit%20to%20agricultural%20households.pdf. Retrieved 23 February 2019.

Le Cap (2009) Land repossessions threaten hundreds of black farmers. 24 July. Available at: www.irinnews.org/report/85423/south-africa-land-repossessions-threaten-hundreds-black-farmers. Retrieved 30 June 2018.

Limsombunchai, V., Gan, C. and Lee, M. (2005) An analysis of credit scoring for agricultural loans in Thailand. *American Journal of Applied Sciences* 2(8), 1198–1205. Available at: www.researchgate.net/publication/274769928_An_Analysis_of_Credit_Scoring_for_Agricultural_Loans_in_Thailand. Retrieved 16 April 2018.

Louder, E. (2018) How Much Can I Borrow? 31 January. Available at: www.progressiveforage.com/forage-production/management/how-much-can-i-borrow. Retrieved 29 June 2018.

MacTiernan, A. (2018) Loan to help sheep processor grow exports. 20 July. Available at: www.mediastatements.wa.gov.au/Pages/McGowan/2018/07/Loan-to-help-sheep-processor-grow-exports.aspx. Retrieved 20 July 2018.

Martin, P., Levantis, C., Shafron, W., Philips, P. and Frilay, J. (2018) Farm debt: broadacre and dairy farms, 2014–15 to 2016–17. ABARES. 18 April. Available at: www.agriculture.gov.au/abares/research-topics/surveys/debt. Retrieved 30 June 2018.

Moreddu, C. (2016) *Public-Private Partnerships for Agricultural Innovation: Lessons from Recent Experiences.* OECD Food, Agriculture and Fisheries Papers, No. 92. Paris, OECD Publishing. Available at: www.oecd-ilibrary.org/docserver/5jm55j9p9rmx-en.pdf?expires=1530297124&id=id&accname=guest&checksum=07326546FF7B748B0F009D96B5E4B5F4. Retrieved 29 June 2018.

Morgans (2017) Murray River Organics. 22 May. Available at: https://my.morgans.com.au/research/5E6AC860-6A05-492A-AFBC-97BCF14091B2.pdf?u=9b6e4620-b777-4faa-824c-18d547e2ca31. Retrieved 30 June 2018.

Morris, C.S., Wilkinson, J. and Hogue, E. (2015) Competition in local agricultural lending markets: The effect of the Farm Credit System. *Federal Reserve Bank of Kansas, 2015 Economic Review.* Available at: www.kansascityfed.org/~/media/files/publicat/econrev/econrevarchive/2015/4q15morriswilkinsonhogue.pdf. Retrieved 17 March 2018.

Multilateral Investment Guarantee Agency (2015) MIGA: Cultivating Agribusiness Growth. Available at: www.miga.org/Documents/agribusinessbrief.pdf. Retrieved 30 June 2018.

NSSO (2013) *Income, Expenditure, Productive Assets and Indebtedness of Agricultural Households in India.* New Delhi, National Sample Survey Office, Ministry of Statistics and Programme Implementation. Available at: http://mospi.nic.in/sites/default/files/publication_reports/nss_rep_576.pdf. Retrieved 23 February 2019.

Owoeye, F. (2018) World Bank says it is investing $2 million in Nigeria's agribusiness value chain. 12 March. Available at: https://nairametrics.com/world-bank-says-it-is-investing-2-million-in-nigerias-agribusiness-value-chain/. Retrieved 30 June 2018.

Owusu-Dankwa, I. and Badu, G.P. (2013) Principles and practice of lending in the banking sector: A case study of some selected banks in Ghana. *Journal of Contemporary Integrative Ideas* 1(2), 9–21. Available at: www.onghana.org/wp/Journal/wp-content/uploads/2014/07/Vol-1-No-2-Paper-2-Owusu-Dankwa.pdf. Retrieved 16 April 2018.

Reserve Bank of India (2016) *Handbook of Statistics on Indian Economy.* New Delhi, Reserve Bank of India.

Ricketts, K. and Ricketts, C. (2009) *Agribusiness Fundamentals and Applications.* New York, CENGAGE Delmar Learning.

Sihlobo, W. (2018) How Indebted is the South African Farming Sector? Wandilesihlobo.com [blog]. 24 March. Available at: https://wandilesihlobo.com/2018/03/24/how-indebted-is-the-south-african-farming-sector/. Retrieved 30 June 2018.

Subbarao, D. (2012) Agricultural credit – Accomplishments and Challenges. *RBI Bulletin.* 10 August. Available at: www.rbi.org.in/scripts/BS_ViewBulletin.aspx?Id=13468. Retrieved 30 June 2018.

Sagner, J. (2009) Bank loan covenant measures and mis-measures. *North American Journal of Finance and Banking Research* 3(3), 55–68.

Seena, P.C. (2015) Management of agricultural credit and the impact of Indian banking sector reforms on agriculture. *International Review of Research in Emerging Markets and the Global Economy* 1(3), 378–391.

Shalmani, A., Zhou, D., Khan, S.A. and Asad, A. (2015) Agricultural credit in Pakistan: Past trends and future prospects. *Journal of Applied Environmental and Biological Sciences* 5(12), 178–188.

Soares, M. (2014) *An Assessment of Competition and Concentration in the Brazilian Credit Market.* Banco Central do Brasil IX Annual Seminar on Risk and Financial Markets. 15 August. Available at: www.bcb.gov.br/pec/depep/Seminarios/2014_IXSemRiscosBCB/Port/MarcosSoares.pdf. Retrieved 30 June 2018.

Solanki, R. (2016) A study of agricultural finance by commercial banks in India: A case study of Central Bank of India. *Abhinav National Monthly Refereed Journal of Research in Commerce & Management* 5(4),

1–7. Available at: http://abhinavjournal.com/journal/index.php/ISSN-2277-1166/article/view/1008. Retrieved 16 April 2018.

Standard Bank (2018) Terms and Conditions for the purchase of repossessed property. Available at: www.myroof.co.za/Standard-Bank. Retrieved 30 June 2018.

Taurins, S. (2017) Understanding the way in which sugar, starch and sweetener companies' debt and equity is being assessed by the market. Presentation by Credit Suisse at the International Sugar Organisation 26th International Seminar, London, 29 November.

The Financial (2018) ADB Irrigation Project in Jalalpur to Increase Food Production in Punjab, Pakistan. Available at: www.finchannel.com/business/69830-adb-irrigation-project-in-jalalpur-to-increase-food-production-in-punjab-pakistan. Retrieved 16 May 2019.

Thoopal, V. (2013) Collateral Management in Agriculture Finance in India. Available at: http://agrifinfacility.org/resource/collateral-management-agriculture-finance-india. Retrieved 6 June 2018.

Tiwary, D. (2017) In 80% farmer-suicides due to debt, loans from banks, not moneylenders. *Indian Express.* 7 January. Available at: www.indianexpress.com/article/india/in-80-farmer-suicides-due-to-debt-loans-from-banks-not-moneylenders-4462930/. Retrieved 30 June 2018.

Turvey, C.G., Guangwen, H., Kong, R., Ma, J. and Meagher, P. (2011) The 7 Cs of rural credit in China. *Journal of Agribusiness in Developing and Emerging Economies* 1(2), 100–133.

Umar, B. (2015) India's shocking farmer suicide epidemic. Aljazeera.com. 18 May. Available at: www.aljazeera.com/indepth/features/2015/05/india-shocking-farmer-suicide-epidemic-150513121717412.html. Retrieved 30 June 2018.

USDA (2016) *Agricultural Finance Databook.* Washington DC, USDA.

USDA (2018) Farm Sector Financial Ratios. Available at: https://data.ers.usda.gov/reports.aspx?ID=17838. Retrieved 30 June 2018.

US Government (2018a) Agricultural Export Financing. Available at: www.export.gov/article?id=Trade-Finance-Guide-Chapter-13-Government-Backed-Agricultural-Export-Financing. Retrieved 6 June 2018.

Varangis, P. and Saint-Geours, J. (2017). *Using Commodities as Collateral for Finance (Commodity-Backed Finance).* Washington DC, World Bank. Available at: https://openknowledge.worldbank.org/handle/10986/28318. Retrieved 6 June 2018.

Varangis, P., Hess, U., Teima, G., Khan, A. and Van der Velde, P. (2012) *Innovative Agricultural SME Finance Models.* Washington DC, World Bank Group. Available at: http://documents.worldbank.org/curated/en/133761468338532319/pdf/949100WP0Box380l0SME0Finance0Models.pdf. Retrieved 18 April 2018.

Varangis, P., Kioko, M., Spahr, M., Hishigsuren, G. and Miller, H. (2014). Access to *Finance for Smallholder Farmers: Learning from the Experiences of Microfinance Institutions in* Latin America: [*Acceso a las finanzas para pequenos productores agropecuarios: lecciones de las experiencias de instituciones microfinancieras en America Latina*]. Washington DC, World Bank Group.

White, A. (2008) Financial Analysis of an Agricultural Business – Liquidity & Solvency. Virginia Cooperative Extension Newsletter. Available at: www.sites.ext.vt.edu/newsletter-archive/fmu/2007–12/FinancialAnalysis.html. Retrieved 29 June 2018.

Wilson, J. and Bjerga, A. (2018) US Farm Income to Hit 12-Year Low. Bloomberg. 7 February 2018. Available at: www.bloomberg.com/news/articles/2018-02-07/u-s-farm-income-to-hit-12-year-low-as-agriculture-rout-persists. Retrieved 1 July 2018.

World Bank (2018) Agriculture Finance & Agriculture Insurance. 2 February. Available at: www.worldbank.org/en/topic/financialsector/brief/agriculture-finance. Retrieved 30 June 2018.

Zerohedge (2016) USDA Sees 2016 Farm Income Crashing as Farmer Leverage Spikes to 34 Year Highs. Zerohedge.com. 9 January. Available at: www.zerohedge.com/news/2016-08-30/usda-sees-2016-farm-income-crashing-farmer-leverage-spikes-34-year. Retrieved 23 February 2019.

10

Agribusiness trade finance

Issuance and re-issuance of international guarantees

Banks operating in international agricultural trade, such as Stanbic, issue irrevocable reimbursement undertakings, which can be used as security when the nominated confirming/negotiating bank engages itself to Stanbic's customer's letter of credit. This service is suitable for high-value transactions and particularly for situations where: the exporter's preferred confirming bank requires security before adding its confirmation and has no line availability; the letter of credit issuing bank does not wish to encumber cash unnecessarily in a collateral account with the exporter's preferred confirming bank; the exporter's preferred confirming bank wishes to syndicate a deal among a number of banks that may have appetite on the issuing bank and chooses not to offer the risk under a risk participation structure. It must of course be stressed that these kinds of transactions are mostly for large deals – it is vital not to seize on the complexity of international trade structures and imagine that the majority of agricultural trade functions this way, it does not. However, for these larger transactions, the bank is able to enter into risk sharing on both the buy and sell side of trade transactions. The major banks exchange trade-related risks with each other, there is a master agreement for the transactions (Devilbiss, 2014). Banks like Stanbic can reissue guarantees against a correspondent bank's counter-guarantee through a central gateway. Customers can either register as an authorised user of the programme or use it on an ad hoc basis. Or a customer can use Stanbic at both ends of the transaction, as the bank can provide re-issuance on the same service principles as the gateway, except that re-issuance will be directly through the bank's respective operations in each country (Bank of China, 2018).

Working capital financing

A good example is factoring, which has been used for centuries in agricultural export financing but which for over three decades has also been supported by the World Bank and other IGOs. In essence, this is how it works.

Step 1: Small Supplier, S, sells US$1 million in tomatoes to its customer Big Buyer, B, a large multinational exporter. S, in a competitive gesture, offers B 30 days' trade credit. S records the sale as US$1 million in accounts receivable and B records the purchase as US$1 million in accounts payable.

Step 2: S needs working capital to produce more inventory. A factor, F, purchases S's accounts receivable (S 'assigns' its accounts receivable from B to F). S receives today 70% of the face value of the accounts receivable (US$700,000). B is notified that S's receivables have been factored.

Step 3: In 30 days, F receives the full payment directly from B, and S receives the remaining 30%, less interest (on the US$700,000) and service fees.

Source: Klapper (2005)

In reverse factoring, the lender purchases accounts receivable only from high-quality buyers. This way, the lender only needs to collect credit information and determine the credit risk for large, very transparent, accredited firms.

Commodity letters of credit (title, documentation including letters of indemnity, open account, consignment)

International trade is, as yet, still an old-fashioned place.

The documentary credit system has been used for over a hundred and fifty years, and still plays a major role in international trade. Letters of credit have been estimated to represent more than US$100 billion in banking obligations annually. At least 60% of commodity trading is conducted through letters of credit. Documentary credit is an essential part of the export process. It is a trade finance mechanism that was developed to add a measure of security to trade transactions, particularly between buyers and sellers from different countries, and to assert sufficient pressure in case of any violation or non-performance to the trade contract. The letter of credit calls for the participation of a third party, which is the bank. The bank provides additional security for both parties; it plays the role of an intermediary, by assuring the seller that he will be paid if he provides the bank with the required documents, and by assuring the buyer that his money will not be paid unless the shipping documents evidencing proper shipment of his goods are presented. There are initially three parties involved in documentary credit, the issuer (issuing bank), the account party (buyer/applicant), and the beneficiary (seller). Three agreements represent the relationship between the parties, a trade contract between buyer and seller, the documentary credit between the issuing bank and the seller, and a reimbursement agreement between the issuing bank and the buyer (UNCTAD, 1998).

Although the three agreements are related to the same transaction, each of them is independent, and the breach of one agreement may not constitute breach of another agreement. The terms letters of credit (L/C) (USA, Asia) and documentary credit (D/C) (mainly

Europe) mean the same thing. In an *irrevocable letter of credit*, the importer's bank agrees to the exporter ('the beneficiary') that the exporter will get paid if it can prove it has shipped the proper goods by providing the corresponding documents required by the letter of credit. Exporters like letters of credit because the advance assurance of payment ensures the seller that it will not waste time preparing or shipping an order to a buyer who ultimately refuses to accept or pay for the goods. An irrevocable letter of credit cannot be amended or cancelled without the consent of all parties.

The global law firm DLA Piper has argued that when considering performance security requirements to support export contracts, parties often wonder what form of performance security is appropriate – a performance bond, parent company guarantee (where there are subsidiaries involved in funding an SPV, for example), financial institution guarantee or letter of credit. However, such securities normally carry fees and charges, which may add to the overall cost of the transaction. Such securities can also be difficult to obtain if the contract party has poor credit or if the secured amount is too great, and will typically specify a maximum cap. Such securities can be issued by insurers as well as banks. The three principle existing financial institution-issued instruments are letters of credit, guarantees and performance bonds.

- Standby letters of credit and bank guarantees are both methods of providing assurance to a vendor of payment on credit. They are often used for international trade transactions where the financial risk is high (HSBC, 2018)

- A bank guarantee is a commitment by a bank to pay its client's obligation up to a certain amount, while a standby letter of credit is a more formal document that details the obligations of both parties.

- Performance bonds are provided by a third party for up to a stated amount, payable in the event that the beneficiary incurs loss as a result of the contract party's breach. There are two main forms of performance bonds: a 'default' bond and an 'on demand' bond. A 'default' bond imposes a secondary obligation on the grantor. Similar to a guarantee, the beneficiary must prove that the contract party has breached the contract and caused damage in order to cash the bond.

Insurance issues

An exporter of agricultural commodities or processed foods will need to be aware of and consider insuring against the risks of:

- Loss of or damage to goods in transit;

- Non-payment for goods or services;

- The cost of returning to premises any goods that a buyer abroad refuses to accept;

- Political or economic instability in the buyer's country;

- A new customer's credit-worthiness;

- Currency fluctuations; and

- A defect that causes an end-customer to sue (worst case – a major food safety issue).

An importer may need to take into account:

- Possible loss of or damage to goods in transit;

- Supplier problems, including failure to supply transport delays and potential hold-ups at ports;

- The risk of performance or health and safety problems;

- Import duties;

- Storage of goods in bonded warehouses; and

- Currency fluctuations.

The responsibility for organising insurance can be shared between the importer and exporter, or be taken on by just one of them. Trade credit insurance, for example, covers payment risks resulting from trade with buyers. If the seller or policyholder decides to only insure his exports, i.e. their trade with buyers situated in other countries than their own, the cover is referred to as export credit insurance. There are many additional risks if payment is due from a buyer in another country. Not only is it more difficult to determine the buyer's current status, many instances may occur that prevent payment taking place. Political events, exchange restrictions or changes in import regulations can determine whether payment can be expected or not. An export credit insurance policy addresses all these and other risks.

Pledges of warehoused goods – legal aspects (including collateral management agreements)

ACE Global Depository explained that collateral management operations envisage the use of storage premises which are owned and operated by an independent third party without the influence of the depositor of the goods. The inventory collateral or pledged goods are therefore placed at third party premises such as independent, public or terminal warehouses. In such cases the collateral controller, is required to enter into an arrangement with the storekeeper/warehouseman in order for it to devise a methodology for maintaining control, custody and possession, and for effecting release within the premises, all of which binds the third party to the collateral controller as per the mechanism agreed by the bank/financier. Such an arrangement would allow the collateral controller to be the eyes and ears of the bank/financier within the independent premises. It is therefore critical for the success of such operations that the collateral controller devise a methodology for maintaining control, custody and possession and effecting release (where legally and practically permissible), all of which binds the third party to the mechanism agreed by the bank. In such collateral management operations, it is this third party which is deemed to be the original goods father in respect of such goods i.e. the first bailee of the goods.

From the lender's point-of-view, the legal title in the goods is unquestioned if the collateral management is properly established and maintained on its behalf and possession of the goods is maintained in the hands of an independent third party. As a pledgee the lender is a secured creditor pursuant to the financing documents and is in constructive possession of the goods placed as security and listed on the warehouse receipts. A lender secures its interest in the goods and perfects the pledge via:

- Constructive possession and monitoring of pledged goods;

- Accurate reporting and accounting by the collateral controller of all movements and balances;

- Deliveries to the depositor/third party and releases being made only in accordance with the lender's instruction;

- The collateral controller ensures accurate reporting over the condition of the goods described in the warehouse receipts; and

- The lender as the holder of the warehouse receipts is protected against professional negligence and fraud under the collateral controller's comprehensive professional indemnity insurance.

From the depositor's perspective, facilities are provided for the convenient deposit and withdrawal of goods for processing or sale, a condition which may be essential to the proper conduct of the business. The establishment of a collateral management agreement may be the least costly method of enabling a business to obtain credit and to carry on productive operations that would otherwise be impossible to do with goods being placed at third party/independent premises. Collateral management operations may also be set up to effect savings in storage rates and to avoid storage costs.

Documentary discount/pre-export finance

Pre-export finance (PXF) is a type of finance product specifically aimed at commodities producers, including agricultural exporters. The reasoning behind these facilities is so that it can make the underlying producer a credible partner to finance; so that the product is available. A PXF is very different to the more vanilla type of facilities, such as corporate loans against the balance sheet of the borrower. In a PXF funds are provided directly from the lender or a syndicate of financiers directly to producers in order to assist with the working capital needs of the company. Raw materials can be purchased along with processing, storage costs and transportation. Usually a PXF will be valid for between one to five years, but it is common for facilities to be amended and restated throughout their life. Clauses within agreements will focus on the borrower being able to produce commodities and sell product.

Alternative methods of commodity trade finance

It should also be noted that in addition to commercial organisations, national schemes are in place to support international agricultural exporters, notably in the USA (US Government, 2018).

The world of trade finance is about to change, and agricultural trade is set to be a major potential beneficiary. Existing trade finance contracts are typically loaded with optionality, frequently linked to information provision, and agricultural trade finance is no exception. This can be financial, as in the case of structured finance agreements or rating agency decisions, legal, such as signatures on other contracts or confirmation of payments made, or commercial: the results of due diligence, important notifications about goods having arrived in warehouses, confirmation of quantity and quality certification from a company like SGS or of successful loading from a shipping company. What global trade finance infrastructure lacked were means to conduct complex instantaneous, secured, linked, cross-border, verifiable multi-party transactions electronically. Until now, it seems.

After years of promising, held back both by technology gaps and corporate policy, the development of real-time payment schemes (RTP) is finally – thanks mainly to distributed ledgers and open application programming interfaces (APIs) launched by firms and alliances like the global payment innovation initiative (GPII) created by SWIFT – about to transform global trade finance operations in much the same way that the internet did for airlines. The key, though, is to see national systems interlink: trade finance courses provide a global assessment of the viability of different systems and their speed of implementation, as dozens of countries are adopting RTP, with the first line Single Euro Payments Area (SEPA) instant payment trials planned as in 2019, albeit at an initially very low level of €15,000, and developing countries drawing level for example India's UPI. Even firms in the USA are now adopting ISO Standard 20022, more conformity with which – and fewer local variations – are both required for true globalisation of the systems.

Trade financiers envisage that RTP will have keys and gateways installed to accommodate optionality and multiple party legally enforceable smart contracts, all accessible on mobile devices, once there are interoperable, low-cost platforms with minimum standards that are universally available, including to the digital trade finance banks that will base their business on them. These will cover a wide range of trade finance essentials, generating e-bills of lading, enforceable liability and security standards and data conformity, e.g. with the World Custom Organization's (WCO) data model, down to common IT formatting standards for international readability, with trade finance training now incorporating fine-grained explanations of how they will work.

The extraordinarily old-fashioned nature of international trade is painfully apparent from the list of documents above. Smaller firms, which have the most difficulty in accessing trade finance, will clearly benefit most – whilst RTP will deliver significant efficiency benefits for manufacturers and shippers, e.g. cheaper letters of credit and more ability to deliver just-in-time ordering and supply, so customers will receive greater choice and faster delivery.

Table 10.1 Summary of trade finance options

Extended terms	Importer pays over time, sometimes years but not frequently with agricultural products. Promissory notes cover potential default, along with terms for repossession.
Open account	Exporter ships and receives payment directly, documents sent directly by exporter when invoiced, draft may proceed between banks.
Time or date draft documents	Exporter ships, presents draft and documents to bank, documents to be released to importer on acceptance of the draft, which constitutes a promise to pay.
Consignment, retention of title	Exporter ships and is paid when goods are sold by importer. Sales contract and other documentation provides right of repossession.
Sight draft, cash against documents/delivery on payment	Exporter ships and gives documents to a bank, to be released to importer on payment of draft.
Cash in advance	Importer sends funds before shipment.
Irrevocable letter of credit	Importer's bank in favour of exporter, payable on presentation of checked documents, either on inspection or with guaranteed financing.
Confirmed irrevocable letter of credit	Importer's bank asks advising bank to add confirmation. Payable upon receipt of checked documents to the confirming bank, either on inspection or with guaranteed financing.
Cash against goods, shipment into bonded warehouse	Goods shipped to warehouse operated by exporter in importer's jurisdiction. Goods released in stages from warehouse by local agent of exporter.

Source: Author

Banks that are ahead on digitalisation are also likely winners. But there will be losers, too. Imminent now is the replacement of daily cut-off times by real-time cash balances for corporates – giving treasurers cash forecasting problems and demanding predetermined cash management strategies. Any entity that has thrived on information asymmetry and inconsistencies – agricultural trade brokers, especially, but also those banks that have profited from deposit cash and lent to trading firms with the type of significant working capital needs that RTP erodes. But the change is irreversible. The effect on agricultural trade will be slower than the implications for other agricultural commodities, but they will happen nonetheless.

Freight forwarders

Mention finally should be made of freight forwarders, or non-vessel operating common carriers (NVOCCs). These are independent companies which handle export shipments. At the request of the shipper/exporter, the NVOCC makes the actual arrangements and provides the necessary services for expediting the shipment to its overseas destination. The NVOCC acts as a substitute for a truly efficient blockchain process, creating, managing and transferring the documentation needed to move the shipment from origin to destination, including for submission to the bank on behalf of the exporter. The NVOCC arranges for marine insurance, makes the necessary overseas communications and advises the shipper on the relevant destination's requirements for marking, phytosanitary inspections and labelling.

It usually provides a full range of services including: tracking inland transportation, preparation of shipping and export documents, warehousing, booking cargo space, negotiating freight charges, freight consolidation, cargo insurance, and filing of insurance claims. Freight forwarders usually ship under their own bills of lading or air waybills (called house bill of lading or house air waybill) and their agents or associates at the destination (overseas freight forwarders) provide document delivery, deconsolidation, and freight collection services (Rao, 2014).

The NVOCC operates on a fee basis paid by the exporter or importer, depending on the terms of sale. It is an excellent example of contracting out, but their days may eventually be numbered, depending on how efficiently major international firms can make distributed ledger solutions work in their place.

Obtaining a loan

In any loan application that is considered by the bank/financier, there are a number of pre-loan considerations which must be taken into account by the bank prior to agreeing to grant a credit facility to its client. Know Your Client's Client (KYCC) due diligence has to be conducted and certain decisions have to be taken, such as:

- The maximum amount of credit to be made available against warehouse receipts;

- The percentage of the advance to be made against the value of the collateral;

- The pricing system in valuing the collateral (i.e. borrower cost, sales price less percentage, etc.);

- The frequency with which reporting on the borrowing base would be required and the nature of the documentation to be presented by the collateral controller; and

- The reporting mechanism prior to the goods being released by the collateral controller, or under their supervision, the independent third party storer, to the depositor/relevant off-taker.

Bibliography

Bank of China (2018) Re-issuance of Letter of Guarantee. Available at: www.bankofchina.com/nl/en/cbservice/cb2/cb23/201110/t20111022_1567734.html. Retrieved 6 June 2018.

Devilbiss, P. (2014) BAFT Releases Master Loan Agreement for Bank-to-Bank Trade Loans. Available at: www.baft.org/about-baft/news-and-press-releases/2014/05/08/baft-releases-master-loan-agreement-for-bank-to-bank-trade-loans. Retrieved 6 June 2018.

HSBC (2018) A bank guarantee in case of non-payment of commercial import or export transactions. Available at: www.hsbc.fr/1/2/en/entreprises-institutionnels/international/importing-and-exporting/standby-letter-of-credit-details. Retrieved 6 June 2018.

Klapper, L. (2005) *The Role of 'Reverse Factoring' in Supplier Financing of Small and Medium Sized Enterprises.* Background paper prepared by the Development Research Group for Rural Finance Innovations. Washington DC, World Bank.

Rao, R. (2014) What Does a Freight Forwarder Do and Do You Need One? Universal Cargo [blog]. 9 December. Available at: www.universalcargo.com/what-does-a-freight-forwarder-do-do-you-need-one/. Retrieved 21 July 2018.

UNCTAD (1998) *Documentary Risk in Commodities Trade.* Geneva, UNCTAD. Available at: http://unctad.org/en/docs/itcdcommisc31_en.pdf. Retrieved 1 May 2018.

US Government (2018) Agricultural Export Financing. Available at: www.export.gov/article?id=Trade-Finance-Guide-Chapter-13-Government-Backed-Agricultural-Export-Financing. Retrieved 6 June 2018.

Varangis, P. and Saint-Geours, J. (2017). *Using Commodities as Collateral for Finance (Commodity-Backed Finance).* Washington DC, World Bank. Available at: https://openknowledge.worldbank.org/handle/10986/28318. Retrieved 6 June 2018.

Agribusiness marketing

Introduction: principles of marketing

Agribusinesses have several important stakeholders with which they must establish and maintain relations conducive to a positive operating environment and their eventual success as businesses. These stakeholders include such diverse groups as consumers, suppliers, neighbours, members of the channel of distribution, voters and/or the general public, shareholders, competitors and government. In short, stakeholders are all those individuals or groups who affect and/or are affected by, the operations of the agribusiness. The management of those relationships is part of an agribusiness's overall marketing effort, although the ultimate aim is to increase sales as a route to greater shareholder value, at least for a private firm.

Marketing, as a general concept, therefore concerns how an agribusiness, whether a farm, wholesaler or supermarket chain, will produce, what price it will charge, how its products (and services) will be delivered to the customer and how it will convey information to them. Marketing is, then, what the Chartered Institute of Marketing says it is: the management process responsible for identifying, anticipating and satisfying customer requirements profitably. Traditionally, marketing gurus like Philip Kotler talked of the 4Ps – Product, Price, Place and Promotion. Now marketers have added People, Process and Physical Evidence, and they also talk of the 4Cs: Customer, Cost, Convenience and Communication.

The 7Ps model, however, has endured and more than adequately incorporates today's customer-first marketing world. Figure 11.2 shows my personal, only slightly humorous, view of marketing.

Where I completely agree with the marketing profession is that, except for regulated markets – and agribusiness still has more than its fair share of those, such as rice in India – there is no point in developing a product or service that no one wants to buy, yet that is exactly what so many agribusinesses still do: make it, and they hope, consumers will buy. On the contrary, successful agribusinesses put marketing first, find out what customers want, and what they will pay, and then produce with the right level of quality to meet their current and future willingness to pay. Hence McDonald's, for example, has adapted its

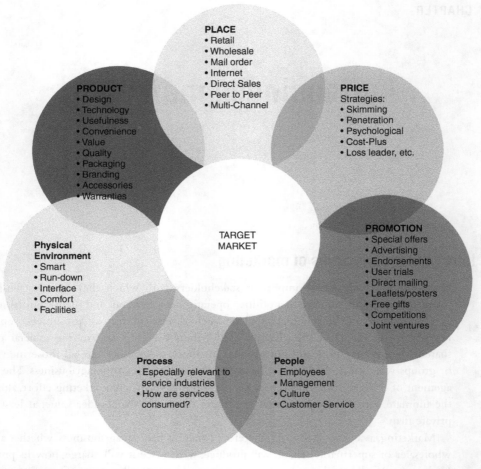

Figure 11.1 Marketing: originally there were four Ps, now there are seven
Source: http://genzmarketing.blogspot.com/2009/03/7ps-of-marketing-mix.html

Invent – if you are cynical

Identify – crucial we know who

Investigate – critical we know amarp

Interest – attract them to us

Inspire – make them desire

Isolate – block our competition

Invite – launch the proposition

Interact – do not let them go

Inveigle – get them to buy

Figure 11.2 The nine Is of marketing
Source: Author's own (Amarp = as much as reasonably possible, actually a key concept in marketing)

menu to local tastes, such as Japan serving a pork patty teriyaki burger and 'Seaweed Shaker' or chocolate-drizzled fries, Germany serving shrimp cocktail, Italy's burger being topped with Parmigiano-Reggiano cheese, Australia offering a guac salsa or a bacon cheese sauce as a topping for fries, and French customers being able to order a caramel banana shake (Rosenberg, 2018). As with every product or service, the output from an agribusiness, except in a regulated market, is only worth what customers are prepared to pay.

Marketing channels are routes through which agricultural products move from producers to consumers. The length of the channel varies from commodity to commodity, depending on the quantity to be moved, the form of consumer demand and degree of regional specialisation in production.

Competitor analysis and pricing strategies

Competitor analysis is essential for every agribusiness; there is none that is an absolute monopoly, if only because agricultural products have substitutes. Competitor analysis provides both an offensive strategy, which allows firms to more quickly exploit opportunities and capitalise on strengths, and a defensive strategy which allows them to more effectively counter the threat posed by rival firms seeking to exploit the firm's own weaknesses. Through competitor analysis, firms identify who their key competitors are, develop a profile for each of them, identify their objectives and strategies, assess their strengths and weaknesses, gauge the threat they pose, and anticipate their reaction to competitive moves. Firms that develop systematic and advanced competitor profiling have a significant competitive advantage. All of this is a well-known part of standard marketing analysis; what makes competitor analysis so difficult to do in an agribusiness context is that some competitors may be on the other side of the world, completely beyond the capacity of the firm to analyse, whilst others may equally be tight-lipped neighbours, unwilling to share much information about their planting plans for next season. This leads to a range of different pricing strategies for agribusinesses, discussed below.

Where possible, to identify their current and potential competitors, firms have to use both a sectoral approach as well as a market approach. The sectoral approach will yield insights on the structure of the sector and the products offered by all market participants – which variety of avocado (Haas, Shepherd, etc. (Dorantes-Alvarez *et al.*, 2012; Simpsons Farms, 2018), what imports, what pricing points. The market approach, on the other hand, focuses on the customer need and the firms attempting to satisfy those needs, which will provide the firm with a wider view of current and potential competitors. Who is buying what variety of avocado, what are the price differentials and the quality requirements? Above all, what brands are being built? Sources of potential competitors include (but are not limited to) firms which compete in a related fruit or vegetable, use related technologies, already target the same market even if with unrelated products, operate in other geographical areas to sell avocados and, last but not least, new start-ups aiming to produce and sell avocados. With a growing market for avocados, not least in the USA, this is a constantly evolving competitive landscape (Ferdman, 2015).

Evolution of marketing analysis

Over the century or more of marketing analysis, there have been plenty of developments. Traditionally the history of marketing has been divided into major stages (Bartels, 1976); as they apply to agribusiness, they can be characterised approximately thus:

The local production/exchange era: production consisted in locally produced agricultural commodities that were limited and generally traded through exploration.

The production orientation era: this saw the rise of processed foods. Marketing was entirely subordinate to production. The percentage of bankruptcies was, by contemporary standards, prodigious. The expression 'ruined' is so often found in novels of the time.

The sales orientation era: gradually, agribusinesses began to recognise the importance of professional selling – branding and sales became an important corporate function. Farms were generally left out of this development, however (Louth, 1966).

The marketing orientation era: from the second half of the 20th century onward, the saturation of markets in developed countries led to a need to know customers in detail. Marketing, at least in successful companies, became involved throughout the production process – in what the company would produce, its distribution channels and pricing strategy.

The relationship marketing era: the focus of companies shifts towards building customer loyalty and developing relationships with clients. Marketing gurus were instigators of the importance of creating bonds between customer and company, considering Kotler's mantra that the cost of attracting a new customer is estimated to be five times the cost of keeping a current customer happy (Kotler & Armstrong, 2017).

The social/marketing era: now, marketing concentrates on social interaction and a real-time connection with clients. Businesses are connected to current and potential customers 24/7 and engagement is a critical success factor (Brian Jones & Shaw, 2018). The significance of social media for marketing success is now so well known as to be a commonplace, and nowhere more significant is it than for agribusiness products and services – at the tip of the verbal spear, the reputation of supermarkets and restaurants, easily damaged by critical references online, but equally reinforced by good evaluations on Facebook, TripAdvisor and many other social media platforms.

Know your customer: consumption trends and consumer attitudes

Clearly, agribusinesses as much as any other business must know their customers. A good example is a report on the future of food consumption in Canada in the period to 2020, originally produced in 2004. The report concluded, predictably, that the Canadian population will continue to age, with more seniors than ever before and actually fewer children projected in real numbers in 2020 than there were in 2004. Other socio-demographic drivers identified as affecting food choices included the shrinking household size, participation in the workforce, globalisation, environmental awareness and media fragmentation. Brands, they said, will become less of a status symbol and more an expression of individual taste. Consumers will become even more disconnected from food preparation. Shopping and eating habits will be sporadic; meal planning cycles will be shorter; snacking will replace courses as well as whole meals and food will become even more portable. These trends will have implications for both food and package waste. The move to spending less of our disposable income on food will continue. Retail food purchases will still dominate, while food service will see only modest growth in expenditures. The real shift will be in prepared meals and takeouts. All this was undoubtedly right, though scarcely difficult to predict – but the report also suggested that health foods would start to become a significant proportion of the Canadian diet by 2020, and, perhaps unfortunately, that seems still a long way off. Analysing customers in such large segments has its specific difficulties, too – firms can make colossal marketing mistakes by ignoring issues of elasticity (described below) or niche markets, such as the elderly, specific demographics, or those with strong individual preferences. Supermarkets probably have the toughest marketing proposition of all, as the numerous empty spaces next to discounted foods demonstrate.

Pricing strategies

All of the decisions made with respect to the elements of the marketing mix are critical, not least the decisions as to what price to ask for the product or service. The task of pricing is reiterative because it takes place within a dynamic environment: shifting cost structures affect profitability, whilst new competitors and new products alter the competitive balance, changing consumer tastes and increases in disposable income modify established patterns of consumption. This being the case, an agribusiness must not only continually reassess its prices, but also the processes and methods it employs in arriving at these prices.

It can happen that an enterprise designs its marketing mix around its prices. It may be, for instance, that marketing research identifies a market segment for cheaper, smaller avocados. The agribusiness might set a target selling price and then select a growing and selection which will keep the product within this target range. In such circumstances price is the principal determinant of product positioning, product formulation, packaging, promotional strategy and, perhaps, distribution. On other occasions, price will be determined by the other elements of the marketing mix. The agribusiness may decide that in order to achieve a given level of market penetration the product must be promoted through the mass media. The price of the product would have to be set to cover the cost of this relatively expensive channel of communication, and if the project fails, it fails. Similarly, if the agribusiness's initial decisions centred around creating a particular product image or gaining access to a specific channel of distribution or in making use of an innovative form of packaging, then the price would be greatly influenced by these decisions. Whatever the starting point, marketers – who are often, with agribusinesses, the business owners with no special marketing knowledge – must take into account all of the elements of the marketing mix when developing marketing strategies. It is invariably the case that pricing decisions will be central to those strategies.

However, pricing decisions are not made by agribusinesses in a vacuum. When making pricing decisions agribusiness decision-makers have to take into account a range of factors. Some of these are internal to the agribusiness, such as its marketing objectives, its marketing mix strategy and the structure of its costs. Then there will be external factors such as the state of market development, the pattern of supply and demand, the nature and level of competition and a host of environmental considerations (e.g. legislation, political initiatives, social norms and trends within the local, regional, national or international economy). And as with any other marketing decision, pricing decisions must take into account the current behaviour of competitors and seek to anticipate the future behaviour of those competitors. In particular, an agribusiness will wish to anticipate competitors' likely reactions if the pricing strategies and tactics it is considering are actually implemented.

- Going-rate pricing: competing firms will sometimes set out to match the industry leader's prices. The net result is to take the emphasis away from price competition and refocus competition onto other elements of the marketing mix.

- Anti-competitive pricing: on occasion, a firm will price its products with a view to discouraging competitors from entering the market or to force them out of the market

- Prestige objectives are unrelated to profitability or volume objectives. These involve establishing relatively high prices to develop and maintain an image of quality and exclusiveness that appeals to status-conscious consumers.

- Price stabilisation: the objective of stabilising prices is met in the same way as that of removing price as the basis of competition.

- Supporting other products: pricing decisions are often focused upon the aim of maximising total profits rather than maximising profits obtained from any single product within the portfolio.

- Maintaining cash flow: many businesses fail not so much because there is an inadequate demand for their products and services, but due to cash outflows running ahead of cash inflows.

- Target markets: the sensitivity of buyers to prices can vary across different market segments. Some consumers will view products as commodities and therefore purchase mainly, or wholly, on price. Others will perceive differences between competing brands and will perhaps make their choice on the basis of characteristics such as quality, freshness and convenience rather than on price. This applies very much to the comparison between producing for local markets in developing countries, which may be very price sensitive, as opposed to producing for export, where quality concerns will predominate.

Prospective buyers also differ in their perceptions of what the actual price is that they are being asked to pay. They may have little or no appreciation of discount rates or even the effects of interest. Some farmers, for instance, will focus on the retail price of a piece of agricultural equipment when considering a purchase. Others will take into account the credit terms available on the item. Yet others will calculate the trade-in value for used equipment that one dealer is offering in competition with another dealer. Skilled equipment vendors make best use of these informational asymmetries in developing their marketing plans.

■ Product positioning: the category into which a product is placed by consumers, and its relative standing within that category, is generally known as its position within the market. The same product can hold different positions depending upon which segments of its market are under consideration. In 1997, the FAO issued its first guidance on marketing agricultural products. Whilst most of the marketing *arrangements* described in the book have long been superseded, the *principles* of marketing that are illustrated remain entirely relevant.

An example: take Hodzeko-Amasi, a brand of fermented milk marketed in Zimbabwe. This product is popular among low-income groups who perceive it to be a cheap relish to flavour their staple food of maize porridge (or *sadza*). But it is also purchased by consumers in the higher income groups, among whom it is used as a substitute for soured cream in baking. These varying perceptions of the product can allow differential pricing according to the position in the market. Hodzeko-Amasi's price as a relish for the staple food has to be held at fairly low levels, but with some repackaging, and a different brand identity, the more affluent consumers can be persuaded to pay a higher price for a product which still undercuts the price of soured cream.

Source: FAO (1997:159)

■ Price setters have also to take account of perceived price-quality relationships: the product has to be priced at a level commensurate with the target quality image and market positioning.

■ Channel of distribution members: the interests of all participants in the channel of distribution for the agribusiness's products have to be taken into consideration when making pricing decisions. By developing pricing policies and structures which assist intermediaries to achieve their own profit objectives, an agribusiness is better able to retain the loyalty of channel members. Where there is intense competition for distributive outlets it is the agribusiness which proves most knowledgeable and sensitive about the needs of intermediaries that will fare best.

■ Suppliers: just as the agribusiness must take account of the interests of its distributors, so it must be concerned about the welfare of suppliers. Agribusinesses have to be careful in the way they report prices and profits since these can easily be perceived as being excessive.

■ Government: governments often take a keen interest in the prices charged, particularly if the product is a staple food. This is true even where agribusinesses have been freed from government control over prices, because the price of basic foods is a politically sensitive issue in most countries. The government will wish to be seen to be vigilant in preventing profiteering at the expense of the common people. The situation can be particularly difficult for agribusinesses such as agricultural marketing parastatals who after years of suppressed prices find it necessary to raise prices substantially to become commercially viable. Market liberalisation may give them greater freedom in price setting, but substantial price increases have to be 'marketed' to both government and the wider public.

Two broad alternatives are open to agribusinesses launching new products on to the market: skimming or penetrating. Skimming strategies involve setting high prices and heavily promoting the new product. Profit objectives are achieved through a large margin per unit rather than by maximising sales volumes. By contrast, penetration strategies aim to achieve entry into the mass market. The emphasis is upon volume sales. This facilitates the rapid adoption and diffusion of the new product. Profit objectives are achieved through gaining a sizeable sales volume rather than a large margin per unit. Other possibilities are discriminatory pricing, which involves the agribusiness selling a product/service at two or more prices, where the differences in prices are not based on differences in costs and time pricing, which involves varying prices seasonally. Typically, this is done to encourage, e.g,. demand for avocados by reducing prices at times when sales are seasonally low and by raising prices to contain demand when it is strong and likely to outstrip supply. Retailers face a much more complex pricing environment than farms, and may therefore carry out a further range of pricing strategies, such as loss leaders. It is generally accepted that, in common with many other products and markets, the price of a product or service sold by an agribusiness conveys many diverse messages to consumers. Some consumers will see price as an indicator of product quality; others will perceive the price as a reflection of the scarcity value of the product or service; some others will view price as a symbol of social status; and yet others will simply see price as a statement by the supplier about the value he/she places on the product or service. This being the case, consumers will perceive a given price in a variety of ways: as being too high or too low, as reflecting superior or inferior quality, as indicating ready availability or scarcity of supply, or as conveying high or low status.

Vertically integrated agribusinesses also face the issue of *transfer pricing*, that is, the pricing strategies open to agribusinesses when transferring goods and services between different departments, divisions and/or subsidiaries belonging to the same parent agribusiness.

E-marketing and other recent trends (e.g. social media)

In the USA, 'Typically, cattle producers sell their livestock through local or remote auctions conducted by video or over the Internet' (Pullman & Wu, 2012:36). Prices are determined by a multitude of factors of the calf (size, weight, breed, genetics, health, location, time of year, whether organic, cost of bringing to market). Loads of cattle with similar characteristics are forward purchased with delivery anywhere from one to ten weeks ahead. Other examples of e-markets can be readily found worldwide. For example, in the late 2010s, www.liv-ex.com/ for fine wine, www.sellmylivestock.co.uk/ and www.livestock-live.com/ for livestock in the UK.

Globalisation is, however, having a significant impact on agribusiness marketing, especially of food products. Migration means that 'people bring their cultures, their traditions and religions, their needs, their connections and networks with them from the lands from which they came' (Barnard, 2016:104). Whether marketing basmati rice in the UK, couscous in France or Chinese vegetables in Australia, awareness of international markets is now crucial. Firms such as Tilda Rice now export worldwide, their consumers becoming aware of the brand in part from conversations and social media exposure from migrants, both permanent and temporary.

These factors, including the use of e-marketing and social media campaigns, do not differentiate agribusiness from other sectors. Indeed, the bulk nature of basic agricultural commodities and the fact that sales take place predominantly at wholesale level actually mean that the impact of new media (as opposed to e-marketing or online markets) is much less for farms, in particular, than it is for other goods and services that sell directly to consumers, notwithstanding the hype (Edia, 2018). At the other end of the value chain, however, the position is quite different, supermarkets live and die by Facebook and other social media (Felix *et al.*, 2017), so we can formulate an approximate rule: *the significance of social media for an agribusiness depends on its relative position within the value chain.* This is not to say that social media is not used by farmers, just that they use it for leisure, not work (McConnell, 2015), although this of course may start to change in coming decades.

Sectoral and international differences in agricultural marketing

Agricultural marketing has very specific qualities that set it aside from manufacturers, for example, or most services.

(1)   The product itself is frequently perishable: storage mechanisms, especially for fruit and meat, are exceptionally limited as well as expensive.

(2)   Seasonality, although this may be mitigated by multiple sourcing. Hence, for example, many of California's fruit and vegetables are highly perishable, and production is seasonal. A major challenge in marketing is to ensure both the high quality of these products and their availability to consumers year-round.

(3)   The maturity of developed markets for agricultural products. Both their population growth rates and and their income elasticity of demand for food are low, meaning that the market for domestic food consumption expands only slowly over time, and firms are essentially competing for a share of a relatively stable market. This competition has intensified given the high rate of new product introductions and expanded year-round availability of formerly seasonal items, often through imports. Both of these factors have led to a greater array of substitute products, frequently dampening demand for large-volume staples like oranges and apples. Agricultural product marketing has for over two decades now as a result targeted specific consumer segments rather than employing the mass marketing strategies of the past — which also explains the demise of many state-based marketing arrangements, such as used to exist in the UK for potatoes. Retailers now look to their suppliers and customers themselves to assist them in understanding and better serving different types of consumer segments, rather than to the government to organise a collective marketing system.

(4)   Difficulties of transportation, especially but by no means exclusively in developing countries.

(5)   Variation in quality and, one might add, a multiplicity of different sub-markets caused by local tastes and differences in species, e.g. the demand for Indian mangoes, as opposed to those from any other location, demonstrated by local Indian communities worldwide. In developing countries, these problems are exacerbated by the huge dispersion of production still amongst millions of producers, rendering production estimates difficult.

(6)   The need for processing for many agricultural commodities, with the percentage of processed foods rising all the time, especially in newly developing countries.

In theory, efficient agricultural marketing can reduce the impact of these problems – reducing the layers of merchants and other intermediary institutions between farm and fork can evidently increase returns to farmers and supermarkets alike, creating more investment opportunities throughout the supply chain and allowing agricultural products to reach wider markets, in turn reducing price fluctuations and supply gluts and shortages.

The reality remains far from the dream, however. Village and primary wholesale markets, known as mandis in Southern Asia, still predominate as basic marketing mechanisms for agricultural produce worldwide. The bulk of transactions in rice, or chilli, take place between local village traders and wholesalers, some of them operating only for very restricted working hours, dealing with such perishable commodities as fish, fresh fruit and vegetables and milk. Others can operate more extensively to trade less perishable commodities, notably grains. Of course, international markets of a much more conventional kind exist for fertilisers, farm equipment, land and agribusinesses themselves.

The multiple ingredients of successful agricultural marketing range widely. Appropriate packaging is an important component for most agricultural products, helping in quality identification, advertising and branding, both at a generic and firm-specific level. Transportation forms part of the process too, a careful balance being required between distance, product quality, perishability, fragility and other risks. Standardisation and then grading based on quality issues such as size, colour, taste, freedom from blemishes, etc. is another component. Storage and processing are also part of the marketing calculation.

Market research and market segmentation

In developed countries, prices are readily available, for example in the UK through Farmers Weekly (www.fwi.co.uk/market-prices) and in the USA through Agweb (www.agweb.com/markets/). Even in developing countries, information is readily available, in particular through mobile phone delivery. Esoko (www.esoko.com/) for example, started as long ago as 2005, as an experiment to see how the emergence of mobile technology in Africa could work in agriculture. Its first project enabled the delivery of market prices via SMS, in support of work that FoodNet was doing with the telecommunications operator MTN in Uganda. In addition, Esoko set up a call centre to support local languages and address issues with literacy. Over time Esoko has added weather alerts, crop advice and linking buyers with sellers. The company then leveraged its technical platform and field force for the collection of information, using tablets and smartphones. This technology,

Insyt, has been used in social protection programmes in Ghana. More recently, in 2016, Esoko incubated and launched Tulaa – a mobile commerce platform for rural consumers and producers in Africa. As of the end of the decade, its blog still focused on prices, however, as this remains the core of mobile services in developing countries. Similar initiatives exist in Kenya. The surge in smartphone ownership is riding on the back of the over 90% mobile penetration in the country, according to data from the Communications Authority of Kenya. Agriculture, along with health and transport, are among the economic sectors that have attracted the development of a large number of apps. Agriculture has increasingly attracted the attention of young tech-savvy people due to the sector's profitability, hence the development of applications that make farming easier. Here are some of the apps:

iCow: developed a few years ago, this voice-based WAP-enabled application allows farmers to get vital information on animal breeding and feeding methods. Farmers register their cows free of charge through the iCow portal and get regular SMS on breeding and production patterns. 'We found out that most dairy farmers do not get the most out of their livestock because they depend on rudimentary livestock management methods,' said Sue Kahumbu, the creative director of Green Dreams, the company behind the application. iCow's objective is to increase farmer productivity through access to knowledge and experts and to encourage the development of a younger generation of farmers.

M-Shamba is an interactive platform accessible in smart- and low-end phones. A regular SMS provides the subscriber with information on production, harvesting, marketing, credit, weather and climate. The information is customised based on location, allowing farmers to know what to grow within the season in their region. Farmers can also share information on various platforms. The info is stored in a chip in the phone memory and enables the farmer to obtain the latest information on various aspects of farming. Subscribers pay a monthly fee for the service.

MbeguChoice: with the challenges of climate change, app developers are also creating solutions to help farmers adapt to the effects of changing weather patterns. MbeguChoice, seed choice in Swahili, is a free app developed jointly by the Kenya Agricultural and Livestock Research Organisation, the Kenya Plant Health Inspectorate Service, seed companies and Agri Experience, with support from the Kenya Markets Trust. If a farmer searches for drought-resistant crop varieties to plant during the rainy season, the app will show the best five kinds of seeds, depending on the area and the altitude. The database that powers the app has information on more than 200 crop varieties. The developers intend to expand the app to keep farmers updated about market information on crop and fertiliser prices as well.

M-Farm: M-Farm Ltd is a software solution and agribusiness company. The investors say M-Farm is a transparency tool for Kenyan farmers where they simply SMS the number 20255 (for Safaricom users) to get information pertaining to the retail price of their products, buy their farm inputs directly from manufacturers at favourable prices and find buyers for their produce. M-Farm, works as a transparency tool for farmers. M-Farm was launched after winning the IPO48 competition – a 48-hour bootcamp event aimed at giving web/mobile start-ups a platform to launch their initiative.

VetAfrica: the VetAfrica app, which is a developed by Cojengo, enables vets, animal health workers and rural farmers to quickly and accurately diagnose livestock illness and identify which drugs are most effective. The app offers a support system not just for livestock farmers but veterinary experts and animal health professionals (Standard, 2018).

Not all of these apps are likely to survive indefinitely, at least in their current format, but the direction of implementation is absolutely clear.

For more detailed market research, reference is often made to detailed sectoral reports costing several thousand dollars each, although these too have a distinct tendency to dwell on developed markets at the expense of those parts of the world where there are more risky agribusiness opportunities. It cannot be stressed too much that the global agribusiness market is, in fact, not one market but many thousands, segregated principally by product, by geography and by stage in the value chain. Individual market analysis is required for each particular agribusiness – and worse still for the cost of the task, frequently markets are fast-moving, which means that *agribusiness marketing reports more than three months old are generally unreliable*.

Marketing and the value-add chain

Table 11.1 How the Dutch international agricultural outreach organisation envisages explaining and teaching the marketing of agricultural products in developing countries

	Market and consumers survey	**Market prospection**	**Marketing intelligence***	**Promotion**
What does this term mean to you?	Mechanism that helps to understand the buyers' demand	Identify possible buyer(s) of a given product in a given market, and the way to promote it	Mechanism that enables to get strategic information to be able to anticipate and organise trade of a given product	Series of operations designed to publicise a product, to give visibility to a specific audience
Which question/ issue does it meet?	Buyers and consumers' needs in terms of quality, quantity, period, price, etc.? Who are the potential buyers? The environment: formal and informal barriers, standards, infrastructures, competitors, etc.	Who can be interested in our product? And at which conditions?	Risk management (price, production) Market and competition anticipation Maintaining its commercial position	Facing competition, how to bring buyers/ consumers interested in my product and buy it?

Table 11.1 (Cont.)

	Market and consumers survey	Market prospection	Marketing intelligence*	Promotion
How to operationalise it (action)?	Meet potential buyers (traders, consumers, providers), state bodies (regulation, control, market information), see and visit infrastructures, etc.	Cluster's representative (with communication and commercial skills) meet potential buyers; it can be done during a trade fair (best) Two important previous conditions: i) A good knowledge of the product; and ii) Prepare and present samples + docs	Focal points' network in strategic places Access to management information systems (national and external) Explore various sources of information within literacy, media, internet, etc. Data collection, treatment and analysis Information distributed to cluster's members	Develop a consensus within ABC (possibly also between ABC and buyer) Develop and implement a communication and marketing plan Participate in trade events Developing a brand, etc.
Which output can be expected from its implementation?	Analysis of the targeted market helps to determine the interest to develop marketing actions	Cluster has identified the buyer(s) whom the product can be sold to	Strategic commercial information	Visibility, reputation, development of sales and turnover
When is the best moment in 'value chain life' to operate it?	As soon as possible, in order to organise production according to the market requirements (*demand-driven approach*)	After a market survey, which brings information about the market	Once the market is known, in order to control a maximum of commercial elements	When the supply is controlled (quantity, quality), when the product's characteristics are established, and when the product begins to have success
What are the possible bottlenecks for its implementation?	A poor organisation and then low quality result A survey realised by under-skilled person The poor quality of official data The cost	An inadequate preparation: limited knowledge of the supply's potential, of buyers' demand, weak market study Financing issue to organise it Wrong choice of the cluster's representative	Cost: level, funders Network implementing (find focal points), quality of the focal points Sustainability (technically and financially) Quality of analysis Weak interest from members	Inability to control supply in quantity, quality, deadlines, etc. Cost Insufficient knowledge of the product standards

Source: ICRA (2014)

The emphasis on practical measures, and an understanding of the business environment, is both clear and absolutely correct. To see how far agribusiness marketing has come in the past two decades, it is only necessary to see how the FAO saw the landscape more than two decades ago (FAO, 1997). The change in emphasis away from agricultural marketing boards that were still prevalent then, and the evident novelty of marketing concepts that are now taken for granted pretty much worldwide, is really striking. Much of the text remains relevant: it is the tone, and the emphasis, which has changed so much in the intervening decades.

Differences between sectors

A constant value creation theme of this book has been the importance of market knowledge. For example, the Chinese prefer to sell fish, crab or most seafood that is still alive in order to appeal to customer's 'mind of freshness'. The same can be seen in Kisumu town harbours along Lake Victoria, where small traders catch live fish then deep-fry them in oil in order to lure customers (Participatory Ecological Land Use Management, 2014). Another good example is bananas, where the colour preferred on UK supermarket shelves – yellow, no black, with green tops – would be in turn unacceptable in most African markets where the fruit is expected to be much riper. It is *not* just about difference in quality.

Several actions geared toward the Brazilian marketplace were part of continuing efforts to spur domestic agribusiness: partnering with brands and fashion stylists, point of sale actions, projects with fashion universities and colleges, reinforcement of digital media coverage, public relations announcements, improvement of website content and other initiatives (Castro *et al.*, 2018:678).

Difference in agribusiness marketing depends on which sector. For John Deere, a manufacturing business, individual ticket size is large, financing offered by the company is critical,

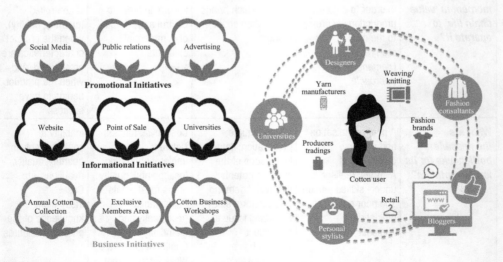

Figure 11.3 The marketing strategy developed by the Brazilian cotton industry to raise its domestic market share
Source: Castro *et al.* (2018:675)

competitors are generally global firms, potential and existing clients and the decision-makers within them are all known by name, and a conventional customer relations management (CRM) software suite works well. For a roadside stall selling fresh produce, none of the above applies. One of the key difficulties with agribusiness marketing is that it is so sectorally and even product specific: you can sell fruit and vegetables from a wholesale roadside warehouse direct to the public in Australia, but in the UK, apart from pick-your-own (Pochin, 2016) and regular/'pop-up' farmers' markets and small stalls in city centres, such a venture would be very unlikely to succeed.

Managing the product and new product development

The challenge arises from the difficulty in identifying gaps in the extensive line-up of already available products and developing and marketing a new product, or variation of an existing one, that fills that gap. Meeting this challenge is the role of market research. Would-be food entrepreneurs typically fall into one of two categories. One is the producer who has a very specific idea or prototype of a product and needs to assess the most effective way to sell it. A common example of this entrepreneur is the individual who believes that he or she possesses the recipe for the world's absolute best barbecue sauce, wine, cheese, etc., and wishes to discover the most effective way to go about marketing it. The second type of entrepreneur is one who produces a raw product such as tomatoes, grapes or milk and desires to pinpoint the most profitable method for adding value to his or her raw product. Their research may, therefore, not be limited to answering questions about the best way to market cheese, but whether milk should be processed into cheese, butter, ice-cream or simply bottled and sold in its original form.

Johnston Dairy began operations in the 1940s and followed the model of most dairies in the USA by selling its milk through a farmer-owned cooperative. Johnston's milk was delivered to a large corporate dairy processor who commingled it with the milk of many similar dairies and marketed it under a number of well-known brands and store labels. The second generation of Johnston dairy farmers became interested in capitalising on the growing interest in locally produced foods and began to research the idea of launching a family brand in 2005. The quest to determine whether the venture could be financially feasible led dairyman Russell Johnston through a series of steps involving analysis of customer perceptions of currently available milk products, desired attributes such as container types, fat content, flavour and shelf-life, as well as their willingness to pay a premium for his product.

Source: Shepherd & Kane (2008:6)

Every agribusiness needs a marketing plan. As the Nova Scotia Farm Board reminds us, a plan reminds you and informs your people of your business vision and the goals to be achieved. Everyone knows where the business is headed. A marketing strategy will help the agribusiness be competitive with other producers that have their own individual marketing strategies. Key elements include:

■ What products or services do you intend to sell, and what are their USPs? A SWOT analysis, in essence, for each product. This should include an analysis of competitive products, as well as potential synergies with other businesses.

■ Who are your existing and potential customers and what are their profiles? This involves regular surveys and profiling. In developed countries, accurate demographic information is available from public and private sources. This will include income and wealth statistics. Professional surveys can also indicate willingness to pay, which has always been a problem with, for example, insurance products.

■ What is your competition and what are they up to? Information about market share and competitors' plans, e.g. to introduce new products, will be vital in developing your own plan. Specific aspects of competitor products – for agribusiness, such issues as country of origin, distribution networks, quality issues, as well as the usual elements of pricing, will be relevant

■ How will new technology affect your future business? In the past, most agribusinesses did not need to worry especially about the impact of technology, but as Chapter 4 has hopefully established, this is no longer true. From drone deliveries to new freezing techniques, technology and any resultant necessary capex now has an impact on how marketing for agricultural products will be designed.

■ How will changes in legislation and other circumstances beyond your control affect your future business? Much the same goes for regulation. Planning ahead for certain and likely changes in accounting and taxation, as well as phytosanitary regulations, will improve the effectiveness of marketing spend.

■ The advertising plans. Wholesalers and those selling to them may not need any; supermarkets and all those selling directly to consumers are in constant need. Deploying advertising across the many different possible channels – conventional media (TV, radio, print), the internet, and social media, requires a careful balance of investment, both of time and money. A Google search for 'Chiquita bananas' immediately reveals the benefit of search engine optimisation (SEO). The AI behind SEO is currently one of the most important aspects of online marketing in every area of business. The Nova Scotia Farm Board suggests an annual advertising budget of 1–2% of projected sales, but this cannot be anything other than the most general of guidelines.

Another important component of the marketing plan is the choice of marketing channel(s). A marketing channel is, in essence, the chain of intermediaries through which the various grains pass from producers to consumers that constitutes their marketing channels. Marketing channels for agricultural products naturally vary between products, size of enterprise, by country and over time. The course taken in the transfer of the title of a commodity constitutes its channel of distribution. Different marketing alternatives for farmers include, e.g., roadside stalls, local markets, contract farming or sales on the internet. For example, marketing cooperatives are often successful. Some process agricultural products (e.g. milk, vegetables) and sell directly to consumers and retailers. In the USA, examples of marketing cooperatives are fruit growers' cooperatives, such as Sunkist, and dairy marketing co-ops, such as Dairy Farms of America (DFA), Land O'Lakes and Mid-America Dairy. Most recently, Land O'Lakes has introduced what it describes as a new entrepreneurship programme aimed at developing a new wave of USA-based dairy food start-ups. Through its Dairy Accelerator Program, the farmer-owned cooperative and Arden Hills-based agribusiness will invite a select group of food entrepreneurs to a three-month bootcamp to be held in the Twin Cities. The programme will focus on finance, brand-building, manufacturing, sales, distribution and leadership development (Williams, 2017). Evidently, they intend to generate their own customers. Which is possible, given that cooperatives are exempt from income tax under US law. A different case: much of the grass-fed beef sold in recent years has been marketed via direct sale from farmer to consumer on the farm or via farmers' markets, as well as via direct sale to restaurants and grocery stores. As the market for grass-fed beef continues to expand, many of the larger-scale grocery stores and restaurants with interest in carrying grass-fed beef products are likely to desire to purchase it in larger quantities than most grass-fed beef producers working alone can provide. This will likely lead to increased interest in unique strategic alliance arrangements, where producers market their product together with other producers, perhaps sharing common processing and distribution systems. Whether such alliances are organised as cooperatives, formal contracts, or through 'looser' verbal agreements will depend upon the preferences of the firms involved (Gillespie *et al*, 2016:185).

Supermarkets by comparison, face a rather more limited choice of marketing channel – they can either sell in retail outlets, online or a combination of both. Their marketing channel choices relate more to how they structure their investments in online sales, decisions about where to site retail outlets (and when to close them), how to advertise and how to manage stocks. Coffee chains like Starbucks, Tim Hortons or local firms face an even more straightforward question about locations, but are also confronted with a myriad other marketing choices, including questions of discounts, loyalty cards and range of products on offer.

Frequently, agribusiness marketing plans are also enacted at a government level, ranging from national sector plans down to quite local arrangements. Contrary to widespread perceptions, the USA's extensive public sector has detailed planning for specific agribusinesses as well as the sector generally. This kind of detailed planning is the 'secret weapon' of US agribusiness, and this kind of plan is very definitely a model for public authorities to follow in developing countries, to help level the playing field.

Analysing the results of marketing strategies

Any proper business plan, of which the marketing plan forms a component, will include as its centrepiece sales forecasts. All forecasts, but especially sales, ought to be reviewed at least monthly and a feedback system set up so that the plan is not driven forward irrespective of necessary changes: forecasts must be changed on the basis of actual experience as well as changes in predicted values, such as interest rates, or regulations. Every piece of advice about marketing plans makes the same point. Hence, for example, this from Li (2015):

There are many simple ways that you can assess which types of advertising generate the best results for your business. You can:

- Ask your customers how they found out about your business;
- Motivate customers to mention/bring in an advertisement for a discount;
- Use a separate phone number or email address for specific advertisements to track the response;
- Monitor the enquiries from customers just after a new advertisement is published – for example, you might advertise a new product on the radio on Friday and find that you have an increase in customers the next day;
- Capture customer postcode information to determine the best locations for advertising;
- Review your goals;
- Comparing the results of your advertising with your initial goals will tell you whether your advertising has reached or exceeded your expectations.

For example, you might research whether:

- Enquiries and sales have increased;
- Your business image has improved;
- Your marketing goals have been met;
- Feedback from customers has been positive.

After reviewing your goals and results you are in a strong position to set new goals and strategies for your next advertising campaign. There is nothing particular about agribusiness in this respect except that a much smaller percentage of agribusinesses sell directly to consumers than in some other sectors.

Further, it is highly desirable to establish marketing success metrics. Again, nothing particular about agribusiness here, although it is fair to observe that, with the notable exception of supermarkets, agribusiness marketing worldwide is decades behind other sectors, e.g. telecoms. Unfortunately, one of the most well-observed characteristics of marketing plans is that this does not happen, in agribusiness as much as any other business sector (Li, 2015).

Bibliography

Acharya, S.S. and Agarwal, N.L. (2006) *Agricultural Marketing in India*. New Delhi, Oxford & IBH Publishing Co. Pvt. Ltd.

Barnard, F.L., Akridge, J.T., Dooley, F.J., Foltz, J.C. and Yeager, E.A. (2016) *Agribusiness Management*, 5th edition. London and New York, Routledge.

Bartels, R. (1976) *The History of Marketing Thought*, 2nd edition. Columbus, Ohio, Grid.

Bohl, M.T., Groß, C. and Weber, S.A. (2017) German Dairy Futures: Quality of Price Signals and Hedging Effectiveness. Brussels, European Commission, Expert Group on Agricultural Commodity and Spot Markets. 20 September. Available at: https://ec.europa.eu/agriculture/sites/agriculture/files/cereals/commodity-expert-group/2017-09-20/dg-bohl-weber-dairy-futures.pdf. Retrieved 26 January 2018.

Brian Jones, D.G. and Shaw, E.H. (2018) Avoiding academic irrelevance in the marketing discipline: the promise of the history of marketing thought. *Journal of Marketing Management* 34(1–2), 52–62.

Castro, L.T., Neves, M.F., Downey, W.S. and Torres, M.K. (2018) The Brazilian cotton marketing initiative: 'Sou de Algodão' case. *International Food and Agribusiness Management Review* 21(5), 669–678.

Dorantes-Alvarez, L., Ortiz-Moreno, A., García-Ochoa, F. (2012) Avocado. In Siddiq, M. (ed.) *Tropical and Subtropical Fruits: Postharvest Physiology, Processing and Packaging*. Chichester, Wiley, 435–454.

Edia, H. (2018) The Role of Social Media in Agribusiness. Available at: www.farmcrowdy.com/social-media-agribusiness/. Retrieved 29 June 2018.

FAO (1997) *Agricultural and Food Marketing*. Rome, FAO. Available at: www.fao.org/docrep/004/w3240e/W3240E00.htm#TOC. Retrieved 28 June 2018.

Felix, R., Rauschnabel, P.A. and Hinsch, C (2017) Elements of strategic social media marketing: A holistic framework. *Journal of Business Research* 70, 118–126.

Ferdman, R.A. (2015) The rise of the avocado, America's new favorite fruit. *Washington Post*. 22 January. Available at: www.washingtonpost.com/news/wonk/wp/2015/01/22/the-sudden-rise-of-the-avocado-americas-new-favorite-fruit/. Retrieved 28 June 2018.

Gillespie, J., Sitieneib, I., Bhandaric, B. and Scaglia, G. (2016) Grass-fed beef: How is it marketed by US producers? *International Food and Agribusiness Management Review* 19(2), 171–188.

ICRA (2014) Introduction to marketing for agricultural products. Available at: www.icra-edu.org/file.php/458/module%204_3volumes.pdf. Retrieved 26 March 2018.

Jackson, E., Quaddus, M., Slam, N. and Stanto, J. (2007) Wool industry stakeholder opinions on the pros and cons of forward contracts. *International Journal of Sheep and Wool Science* 55(1). Available at: http://sheepjournal.net/index.php/ijsws/article/view/690. Retrieved 22 March 2018.

Kahan, D. (2013) *Managing Risk in Farming*. Rome, FAO. Available at: www.fao.org/uploads/media/3-ManagingRiskInternLores.pdf. Retrieved 17 March 2018.

Kotler, P. and Armstrong, G. (2017) *Principles of Marketing (Global Edition))*. London, Pearson.

Li, J. (2015) *Tracking Sales Activities in Agribusiness*. Open Access Thesis. 475. Available at: http://docs.lib.purdue.edu/open_access_theses/475. Retrieved 23 March 2018.

Louth, J.D. (1966) The Changing Face of Marketing. McKinsey Quarterly. September. Available at: www.mckinsey.com/business-functions/marketing-and-sales/our-insights/the-changing-face-of-marketing. Retrieved 28 June 2018.

McConnell, A. (2015) Farmers Making Use of Social Media. Available at: www.agriculture.com/news/technology/farmers-making-use-of-social-media_6-ar50861. Retrieved 29 June 2018.

MCX (2013) *Importance and Benefits of Hedging*. Occasional Paper Series No 3. New Delhi, MCX. Available at: www.mcxindia.com/docs/default-source/education-training/occasional-papers/benefits_of_hedging.pdf?sfvrsn=2. Retrieved 10 October 2015.

Participatory Ecological Land Use Management (2014) Production Economics, Value Chain, Market & Entrepreneurship Development Workshop. 24–26 June. Available at: http://pelum.net/wp-content/uploads/2014/09/PELUM-Value-Chain-Final-Report.pdf. Retrieved 17 March 2018.

Pochin, C. (2016) Ten places in Norfolk where you can pick your own fruit and veg. *Eastern Daily Press*. 5 July. Available at: www.edp24.co.uk/going-out/ten-places-in-norfolk-where-you-can-pick-your-own-fruit-and-veg-1-4604806. Retrieved 29 June 2018.

Pullman, M. and Wu, Z. (2012) *Food Supply Chain Management*. London and New York, Routledge.

Rosenberg, M. (2018) Number of McDonald's Restaurants Worldwide. Thought Co. 11 February. Available at: www.thoughtco.com/number-of-mcdonalds-restaurants-worldwide-1435174. Retrieved 20 July 2018.

Shepherd, T.L. and Kane, S.P. (2008) *A Do-It-Yourself Producer's Guide to Conducting Local Market Research*. Agricultural Marketing Resource Center, Value-added Agriculture Profile, Iowa State University. Available at: www.agmrc.org/media/cms/UofGeorgiaorg_7EE4EE6C3DABF.pdf. Retrieved 16 May 2019.

Simpsons Farms (2018) Varieties. Available at: www.simpsonfarms.com.au/FreshProduce/Avocado/Varieties.aspx. Retrieved 28 June 2018.

Standard (2018) Top mobile applications transforming farming. Standard (Kenya). 26 May 26. Available at: www.standardmedia.co.ke/business/article/2001281733/top-farming-apps-in-kenya. Retrieved 29 June 2018.

Williams, N. (2017) Land O'Lakes launching a dairy-startup bootcamp (but not for butter). *St Paul Business Journal*. 6 June. Available at: www.bizjournals.com/twincities/news/2017/06/05/land-olakes-launching-a-dairy-startup-bootcamp-but.html. Retrieved 29 June 2018.

Private equity and venture capital investment in agribusiness

Introduction: how do private equity and venture capital work?

Both private equity (PE) and venture capital (VC) investment constitute shares representing ownership of or an interest in an entity which is not publicly listed or traded on an exchange. The somewhat blurred difference lies in the state of development of the investee company – generally, if it has positive cashflow and can bear some debt, the investment is classified as private equity; if not, and the main value of the company lies in the future, then it is venture capital. Ultimately, most private equity is derived from pension funds, insurance companies, banks and HNWIs, 'Limited Partners' (LPs) – who channel their money into funds to attract such investment set up by private equity firms – and 'General Partners' (GPs). As the basis of private equity investment is direct investment into a firm, which in turn provides GPs with a significant level of influence over the firm's operations, significant capital is required, which is why larger funds with deep pockets dominate the industry. VC investments, being generally less in amount, can come from more varied sources, including established companies themselves as well as funds. The minimum amount of capital required for investors can vary depending on the firm and fund. Some PE and VC funds have a $250,000 minimum investment requirement; others can require much more. IRRs of well into double figures are usually sought, though not always obtained, with an investment horizon of anywhere between three and 30 years (e.g. for timber), although at the latter end private equity shades off into fund management (Gompers et al., 2016).

In the West, much private equity, at least in past decades, has been about taking companies private, removing them from exchanges and turning them around – or at least restructuring private companies – rather than growth investment (Demaria, 2013). Very specific criteria are required for these kinds of investments (Street of Walls, 2013) and few agribusinesses, at least as yet, are potentially attractive targets, although publicly listed trading conglomerates might eventually represent possibilities, especially if they can be dismembered after their acquisition by a private equity firm.

Compare this focus on dealmaking with this quote about the situation in India from Ashish Dhawan, co-founder of ChrysCapital, which manages $2.5 billion in six funds and has completed over 60 deals:

We're starting from a low per capita income and we've yet to reach middle income status. If you look at that macro backdrop – 8% real growth, 13% or 14% nominal growth – the appropriate role for private equity is really to provide growth capital for companies that are serving the consumer…Our belief has been that over the last decade, the sweet spot for private equity is really not what it is in the Western world, which is leveraged buyouts, financial re-engineering, taking family-owned businesses and professionalizing them. Instead it's working with entrepreneurs who have a mid-sized business, putting in capital and helping the business to become three or four times its size over a five-year period of time (O'Callaghan, 2012).

The legal environment further shapes the industry. Turnarounds are not especially attractive in India, for example, as the country's bankruptcy laws are inefficient and complex, so there is no real distressed market. The banks also have healthy capital ratios, so they're not looking to sell off loans, and nor is there an active market in distressed investments. *This difference is of obvious importance to agribusiness, as many agribusinesses very much fall within the category of company Dhawan identifies.* But even in the West, private equity has increasingly turned to this kind of deal as opportunity, although turnarounds are still popular.

On the other hand, VC investment has always been about maximising investment return from spectacular growth in value, usually due to rapid growth of the company, intellectual property, optimistic views of potential sales driving high NPVs, synergies with an acquiring third party, or some other factor that can lead to rapid, substantial growth in value. The problem for venture capital is, and always has been, its low success rate, which drastically reduces overall fund performance, and has driven many firms out of the business. Venture capitalists are therefore always seeking a class of investment that promises both high returns and low failure rates. *One of the latest candidates is agtech.*

Success criteria for private equity and venture capital

Generally, private equity and venture capital companies measure their success by IRR. The comparison between IRR and the cost of capital for the private equity firm – WACC, usually, as most are levered with some debt, at least – will indicate a priori how attractive to measure the investment is, and ex post how successful it has been. Simple to describe – but very difficult in practice. For example, private equity funds do not invest all their cash at once. They have to select companies in which to invest. What happens to the remaining funds? What happens to the remaining funds? Usually they are not drawn up and remain with the LPs. What conclusions can be drawn from this? That they will not necessarily match the performance of individual investments. As academics trying to analyse the problem observed, 'One problem in using the IRR is the assumption that capital not yet drawn down from or already distributed to the investor would be invested at the same interest rate as the private equity investment' (Aigner *et al.*, 2008; Jegadeesh *et al.*, 2009), which evidently might not be the case with agtech investments. There is also critical analysis of the alleged opacity of private equity performance (Brown *et al.*, 2016).

We do know that PE returns have fallen since last century when investment banks and Wall Street could apparently do no wrong. The minimum expected return that private equity companies have on their portfolios has definitely decreased in the past decade. In 2002 private equity companies on average expected a minimum return of 25%. By 2011 this expected return fell to almost 19%. However, more recently returns have fallen generally, yet there may be some evidence that private equity has done relatively well. Data analysed in the April 2017 Rothschild/AVCAL report examining weighted average returns for all initial public offerings since 2015 with an offer size of $100 million or more showed that the performance of private equity-sponsored businesses delivered a return in excess of 14%. This would certainly compare favourably with a benchmark return of just over 5% for the ASX Small Industrials Index for the same period (El-Ansary, 2018).

A note on business valuation

What underlies both VC and PE success is valuation. For both, the objective is to buy cheap and sell dear. Business valuation is a huge subject with a long pedigree, and is now the subject of AI-driven software even in the agribusiness sector (Digital Agriculture Services, 2019). This section is meant as an introduction and summary focused on agribusiness; much more detailed discussion of the topic is available (e.g. the classic analysis by Koller *et al.*, 2015, and recent business-friendly texts with a more practical focus (e.g. Shields, 2018).

The main methods of business valuation, either for reporting or investment purposes, are as follows:

Discounted cash flow (DCF). The value of a company, it has been said by practitioners for many years, is determined by the cash flows net of expenses it can generate in the future, discounted at a suitable cost of capital – discounted cash flow or DCF. These cash flows will be generated as a result of the available success factors of the agribusiness as of the valuation date, e.g. its products, market position, internal organisation, innovative strength, employees and management. Provided that only financial objectives are pursued, the value of the agribusiness will be attributed solely to its capacity to generate financial surpluses for shareholders (PwC, 2006, 2018). Sometimes DCF uses overall firm cash flows to different stakeholders, and sometimes just cash flows to equity (shareholders), after subtracting cash flows to others, e.g. lenders. Theoretically the results should be the same, but in practice they can diverge. Either way, this method assumes that future cash flows can somehow be forecast, and discounts them at the cost of capital of the firm (or of equity shareholders, depending on which cash flows are to be discounted) to produce net present value (NPV), which we met in Chapter 5 as a decision-making tool. There are a plethora of resources surrounding DCF (e.g. Morningstar, 2013) in a variety of formats, including video tutorials (e.g. Corporate Finance Institute, 2018), but there is no doubt that although the introductory principles above are generally agreed, there are fierce, sustained and possibly intractable arguments over the details. A discounted cash flow analysis is often the methodology of choice for an income-producing agribusiness, but there are many potential pitfalls, and it is absolutely the case that small changes in inputs will result in potentially very large changes in value. Here are some of the main potential issues and pitfalls with using DCF to value an agribusiness.

Actually, what determines value using this method is projected cash flows, agreed between buyer and seller, but this is frequently overlooked in presentations of the method in order to create an aura of objectivity (Roche, 2005). The main culprit is usually an exaggeration of projected sales, together with an underestimate of how long sales will take to transpire. If proper cyclical forecasting based on the techniques described in Chapter 8 is not followed, and a single growth rate is used, then the effect can be very significant indeed.

An example of how different sales projections can change value in a DCF model: $1 million starting revenues, projected over ten years – 2% growth rate = $1,220,000; 4% growth rate = $1,480,000.

The price level for wheat, blueberries or whatever commodity prices are relevant to the agribusiness. Exaggerated demand can be derived from a host of different misperceptions, but this one is a leading error. Without detailed qualitative, time series and regression forecasting the chance of getting future prices right is slight. This makes far more difference to production agriculture than it does to an agribusiness further along the supply chain, because retail prices are much more stable than commodity inputs, and whereas those inputs do undoubtedly form a significant part of the cost base for firms selling processed agricultural commodities they are balanced by other costs, notably labour and rent, which are less volatile.

The level of competition. Firms, especially those with new products, often underestimate the scale of their competition in a number of ways, also leading to exaggerated demand forecasts. They may underestimate the ability of competitors to reach with comparable products, or the elasticity of substitution. There are exceptions in the other direction, too – few expected Innocent smoothies to be the success it was: Coca-Cola bought an 18% stake in the company in 2009, £76 million for a further 38% in 2010 and then full control in 2013 (Neate, 2013). The company has now become the subject of many business school-type analyses, as it has now successfully expanded into Europe. A SWOT analysis is a reasonable approach to such a company (Business Teacher, 2018).

Especially in emerging markets, an incorrect inflation estimate can make a big difference to a DCF valuation. Generally, inflation favours more highly levered companies, assuming their debt burden does not drive them into financial distress.

Underestimating expenses. The most well-known example is a failure to include necessary capex, either for expansion or to replace existing machinery.

Accounting issues. The rating agencies are quite careful to ensure that all leases, for instance, are capitalised on the balance sheets of companies they rate. The accounting profession has responded by following their example with IFRS 16 (Deloitte, 2016).

The exit. One of the old bugbears of DCF analysis is that unless some reasonable methodology is applied, companies can theoretically endure forever (Goodburn, 2015). They do not. Indeed, there is some evidence that the average length of a company's life is declining (Perkin, 2015).

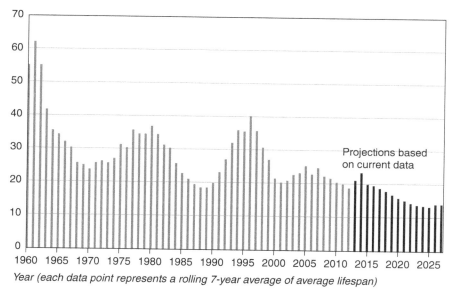

Figure 12.1 Average company lifespan on the S&P index in years (rolling seven-year average)
Source: Perkin (2018)

One might expect this life expectancy to be sector-specific, although research suggests otherwise (Thurston, 2015). Farms, however, were not included in this analysis. There is as yet insufficient evidence to draw a conclusion as to whether the corporate form for agriculture itself results in firms of great longevity, given the enduring nature of their resource, or whether although the resource itself endures, the specific corporate proves as transient as in other sectors, such as food processing, delivery or transport. In any event, unfortunately, this is not a methodology used for DCF generally. Rather, as a result of uncertainty surrounding the life expectancy of the business, analysts often only run out the DCF for five years or so, with the remainder of the company's value incorporated in one single exit number, itself based on a projected comparable, usually the price/earnings ratio or similar.

Manipulation of the cost of capital. Whilst investors themselves are not likely to make this mistake except deliberately, as they should know their own cost of capital, the question of what constitutes a reasonable cost of capital for the market to use is always a matter of doubt.

There are plenty of examples of the problems and issues with creating a set of principles that can overcome these kinds of difficulties and effectively harmonise valuation approaches for one particular sector. The problem, however, is that although this may work well for professional valuers, who are bound by their own standards, it does not apply to the to-and-fro of negotiations between investors and companies, where *caveat emptor* is never a bad maxim to apply.

Real options. The main idea is that an investment decision can be treated as the exercise of an option, analytically akin to the financial options met in Chapter 8. The firm has option to invest. The firm need not exercise the option now — it can wait for more information. If the investment is irreversible (sunk cost), there is an opportunity cost of investing now rather than waiting. This opportunity cost (the value of the option) can be very large. Importantly, the greater the uncertainty (e.g. of commodity prices), the greater the value of the firm's options to invest, and the greater the incentive to keep *these options open*. The theory is described by Pindyck (2008).

The idea that land represents an option for its owner makes sense. Real options have also been used in agriculture to value high risk investments as well as investment-related government policies. For example:

- Evaluate the potential returns from investment in either precision agriculture technology or conventional sowing and harvesting technology;

- Assess the impact of different agricultural policies (such as price floors, investment subsidies and production ceilings);

- Evaluate the potential returns from investment in either new perennial pastures for beef-trading or volunteer annual pasture for Merino ewes after extreme drought conditions in Western Australia reduced pasture availability and herd numbers;

- Assess the potential value of increased drought tolerance in genetically modified (GM) canola;

- Assess whether farmers in wheat-dominant agriculture will adjust their practices and technologies as a result of climate change;

- Evaluate profitability and market success of GM crops in volatile market and regulatory environments, comparing developing countries with industrialised GM-adopting countries.

There are plenty of other applications of real options theory to agribusinesses generally, in fact, (e.g. Turvey, 2001; Duku-Kaakyire, 2003; Macedo & Nardelli, 2011; Nardelli & da Silva, 2011). To be cynical about it, however, this may be because of its theoretical attractiveness rather than its practical application. According to Deloitte (Wynn, 2018), real options are best used for planning high risk investments, such as genetically modified crops – although should they even count as risky any more, one wonders? Agtech, perhaps? Real options, argues Deloitte, can help deal-makers more effectively target crucial opportunities to accelerate, redeploy, delay, modify or even abandon capital-intensive investments as events unfold and new information comes to light, especially for investments in agriculture that involve large sums of money, long investment lives and that are not easily valued using a market-based approach. While it has not seen – and will not see – widespread adoption because of its complexity, real options have been considered the most accurate for high risk investment planning than the more commonly used tools (such as DCF). In particular, investments can be rejected using DCF but accepted using real options.

How much of this argument to accept? It is hard to disagree with Deloitte that investments in agriculture can be risky, with uncertainties such as weather and the incidence of pests and disease. This is on top of the more common investment uncertainties, such as demand, regulatory and commercial uncertainties, that apply to most industries and investment situations. So, too, many agribusiness investments facing uncertainty – new technology, research and development, product and geographical expansion – often involve multiphased decisions where management bases its decision to continue to the next phase on new information. But real options do not mean that, in some magical fashion, decision-making is improved; I think Deloitte is wrong there. They were also very much the product of the pre-financial crisis era of optimism about valuations. Moreover, these applications may be much more questionable than to land itself (Moreno *et al.*, 2009). This is because every business has choices and options, all the time – they are not necessarily *valuable* options. On the contrary, they may well already be incorporated into the DCF valuation, and in particular through risk analysis such as the development and weighting of different scenarios. Real options proponents also sometimes suggest using risk-free discount rates on the perhaps mischievous grounds that all but that risk has been included in the real options analysis, which is again questionable. *You do not have to believe in real options as a valuation technique, although Deloitte argue real options analysis could help you proactively manage or get more out of your existing investments, or help you identify investment opportunities that others have passed over.* Just possibly, however, real options can give investors a genuine edge in deciding how much to pay for investment opportunities, hence the detailed discussion above.

Comparable valuation. The idea is straightforward, which is that the value of a company (or anything) is best obtained by studying what has recently been paid for something very similar. The usual ratios analysed are price to earnings (P/E), which is dependent on financing structure, enterprise value/earnings before interest, tax, depreciation and amortisation (EV/EBITDA), which is not (it adds debt to share price and payment on debt to earnings), and price/sales. The methodology is easy to perform unless done well, in which case regression analysis is required which in turn requires using subjective judgements about the values of the independent variables (though some, like turnover, should be objective). Comparables should reflect industry trends, business risk, market growth, etc. (Street of Walls, 2013a). They come in two forms: the share prices of publicly traded companies – although these are often larger than the smaller, private companies where valuations are most usual, and most difficult – and deal data, which is often held by private companies such as BDO. It has also been suggested that the methodology is best used when a minority (small, or non-controlling) stake in a company is being acquired or a new issuance of equity is being considered, i.e. where there is no control premium. There are plenty of problems and potential distortions in comparable company analysis, for sure.

(1)   Large numbers of comparable deal information may be unobtainable and the stock market may contain few, if any, agribusinesses. In the USA one may be spoilt for choice, but not much elsewhere.

(2)   Even where comparables are obtainable, no two companies are identical, so ratios will never be completely appropriate or accurate.

(3)   Valuing land and property on a farm using a regression model may seek to determine price based on the qualities of a property as well as acreage. But what should be the independent variables: land area, location, the quality of the farmhouse, size of herd and capital quality? Depending on the type of farm there will be many more. Have we caught all the relevant variables? Are the four independent variables really linearly correlated with value, or is the story more complex? And what about time – are all these transactions within the same time-frame, or should we consider introducing another variable, that of when the transaction occurred? This approach assumes that recent sales of properties that are nearby and are comparable to the subject provide the best indicators as to the value of the subject, but is that always the case? When used properly, regression analysis is the best way to value *anything*, including a farm, but it is critically dependent on accurate inputs, including assessments of quality which may be regarded as subjective, especially when the modeller already knows the 'answer', the value of the property – derived from past transactions. Unfortunately, regression analysis is often avoided in favour of clumsy and inaccurate rough averages.

(4)   Takeovers may distort valuation multiples. It has been suggested that the methodology is best used when a minority (small, or non-controlling) stake in a company is being acquired or a new issuance of equity is being considered, i.e. where there is no control premium.

Evidently, there are plenty of risks using comparables to value agribusinesses.

Short-cuts. In practice, business valuers and dealmakers often use short-cuts, and then sculpt DCF models in particular to fit those short-cuts. They should not do this, it is not in anyone's interests except for successful business vendors, and it may very well contradict fiduciary duty, but it happens, even for very large transactions.

> *…valuing Cargill turns out to have required little more than an envelope, a pen and a cheap calculator. The charitable trust owns 17% of the company. For its portion of Cargill, the trust will receive 110 million shares of Mosaic. Assume that for this exchange, the trust is surrendering its whole stake in Cargill. Those 110 million shares, at Mosaic's undisturbed price, are worth $9.4 billion. And voila, scaling up from the trust's stake in Cargill implies the company is worth about $55 billion.*
>
> *That number sounds familiar. Before the spin-off was announced, one of the only reasonable ways to value Cargill was by comparing it with ADM. In the last 12 months, Cargill posted $114 billion of revenue and $4 billion of net income. Slapping ADM's price-to-earnings multiple on Cargill led to a suggested market capitalization of $49 billion (Reuters, 2011).*

The short-cuts themselves are often based on turnover, to avoid difficulties associated with the accounts of different firms, or even very specific industry ratios or numbers. Textbooks, and formal valuation teaching generally, tend to eschew discussion of rules as they threaten, and often do, demolish carefully crafted narratives about DCF valuation. Examples of rules of thumb for different industries (admittedly in the USA, where there are plenty of transactions) are found at various sources (e.g. BizStats, 2011; Gabehart Valuation Services, 2018). One expert comments that: 'Interestingly, there is little geographic deviation in the value of businesses. A gift shop in Alabama with similar financial performance is worth about the same as one in California' (Bruce, 2010) – although that kind of argument should probably not be stretched across too many national boundaries, despite the use of US and other developed country market data as benchmarks in many developing countries.

Dividend valuation method. This is really a specific application of DCF, tailored for a company that pays out most, ideally all, of its income as dividends. Known as the dividend discount model, or dividend growth model, the most straightforward form is called the Gordon growth model. For this methodology, all future dividends represent all future cash flows of that share. The value of the stock is equal to the sum of the net present value of all future dividends.

Costs. Finally, a very few agribusinesses can be valued on the basis of how much it cost to produce their output, and/or how much the assets (e.g. land, machinery) are worth. Some agribusinesses may also have unproductive assets, such as land, that can be added to the value of a DCF.

Due diligence on agribusiness investments

Crucial to private equity is due diligence on investments and their business plans.

A summary of the key due diligence areas correctly identified the following (Frese, 2012 – concerns aquaculture but generally applicable):

■ *Top management is key* – as with all investments, finding a strong management team that has a solid mix of technical expertise and agribusiness business management skills is critical to success. An inexperienced, unbalanced or incomplete team is usually a recipe for disaster unless the business strikes it lucky, when 'a rising tide lifts all boats'. Invest in people you believe in, replace or fill-in the weak or missing links with key hires, give management the tools and resources they need to succeed, and let them do their job. Promises of annual returns in the order of 30%+ will probably remain just that – promises – and their very existence suggests either inexperience or a lack of belief in the competence of the due diligence process. The sorry story of Hampton Creek is a good illustration of what can go wrong, and very expensively, when this advice is not heeded, in agribusiness as much as in other sectors. In that case, the company, one of four new Silicon Valley-style food-tech start-ups looking at replacing animals in food and other products, itself specialising in mayonnaise and then cultured meat, had by 2014 aised $120 million in four rounds of funding (Kowitt, 2014). But it was then subject to multiple lawsuits, found itself targeted by existing institutions, lost most of its board members (Zaleski, 2017), and had its products pulled from the shelves (Sosa, 2017). However, it has survived (it is now called JUST).

■ *Location, location, location* – superior sites yield superior biological results and when it comes to farms and aquaculture, an appropriate supply of water, the right climate and, where appropriate, good soil, are all key ingredients. Site analysis is an essential component of due diligence for farms and aquaculture: it is less important for processors, but essential again for bricks-and-mortar retail. Then there are transport costs: proximity to traditional infrastructure, infrastructure and strong markets for the farm-raised products are all important ingredients for success. 'Cost-to-market analysis is a fundamental element of any agricultural investment, not just in considering long-haul freight rates, but also the practicalities of getting large quantities transported in and out of ports or countries with very limited roads and ports facilities' (Atkin, 2013:172).

■ *Picking the right segment* of the industry for a particular investor's profile is also an excellent way to reduce risk, while still maintaining the desired exposure to agribusiness as a sector. Agfunder suggests the following categories within agribusiness, but these need not necessarily be regarded as definitive.

Fishfarming.com, for example, suggests investing in an aquaculture feed company, a new aquaculture technology with wide-ranging application, or even an established aquaculture

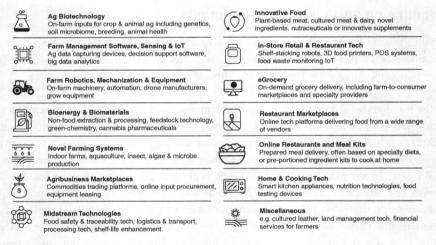

Figure 12.2 Agrifood tech category definitions
Source: Agfunder (2018b)

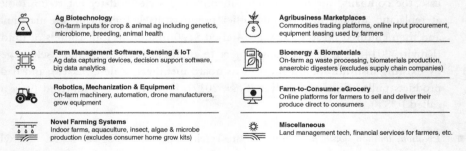

Figure 12.3 Farm tech category definitions
Source: Agfunder (2018b)

equipment manufacturer, as ways to reduce exposure to farming-specific risks like disease yet still achieve the desired industry exposure (Frese, 2012). Careful selection of the sub-sector is equally essential. Not all farms or aquaculture are created alike. For more risk-tolerant investors who prefer to be involved in the production end of the industry, selecting the right species is one way to mitigate some of the risk associated with growing live animals. Farm-raised species like salmon, shrimp and tilapia all have well established farming methods in place and markets for these species are well established, all of which serves to lower overall risks. Conversely, the farming methods for relatively new aquaculture species like amberjacks, groupers, snappers and tunas are still being refined and subsequently carry greater investment risks, but potentially higher returns on investment are achievable for successful first movers in these farm-raised fish. Farm animals are even cyclical in their investment appeal: llamas, ostriches and other species have all enjoyed their place in the investment sun.

The need for capital is frequently underestimated by entrepreneurs and managers alike. One of the most common causes of failure in the aquaculture industry, just as with farming projects, is a lack of capital to see the project through the early development and first few years' operational phases. Prospective investors are well advised to use conservative projections and be prepared to inject cash into the actual aquaculture operations for the first few years and most likely longer depending on the type of species and details of the expansion plan. Wise private equity investors know this, and will insist that the business plan includes cash reserves set aside for unexpected events such as disease, seasonal contractions in wholesale prices, a sudden need to expand production, delays in full payment of accounts receivable, and other threats to cash flow. It is a central maxim of PE and VC investment never to risk the project, and therefore the investment, by having insufficient cash for operational expenses, any loan payments and tax. The PE or VC investor does not always believe what entrepreneurs or managers tell them about these calls on cash, and makes their own forecasts and provisions. *One of the best ways to identify competent managers and entrepreneurs in any industry is to find out whether their forecasts turn out correct.*

Frese (2012) further suggests that, while not required for profitability, the greatest returns on investment in the aquaculture industry are achieved by maximising economies of scale and internally controlling all the major components that go into producing the final form of the farm-raised product being grown. At each level, incremental higher returns are achieved by investing in research and development, hatcheries, aquaculture feeds, grow-out operations, processing plant operations, seafood sales, marketing and distribution. Fully integrated companies that control all phases of aquaculture operations are well positioned to return the greatest profits. Investments in fully integrated aquaculture operations are not insignificant and can easily exceed $50 million. Most qualified investors start with much smaller and more conservative investments and initially focus on one particular segment of the industry. Fishfarming.com advises its qualified clients to consider investments of no less than $1 million in new or existing projects and preferably in the range of $10–15 million for important new commercial projects (Frese, 2012), which are similar amounts to most PE and VC investments in agribusiness, with the caveat that investing in really sizeable farms or major firms may involve even larger sums.

More recently, hybrid investment opportunities have been offered to investors, such as private funds utilising a limited liability company (LLC) or a limited partnership with

Table 12.1 Criteria applied in private equity investment decisions

Cash flow	Sustainable EBITDA; Look to boost this number; Then on-sell the business at a premium.
Profitability	Documented strategies and business plan; Initiatives already taking place to get there.
Growth prospects	Certain industries identified as too risky; Some investors avoid start-ups and turnarounds; Check competitors and industry specific metrics; Benchmarking.
Industry	In the sector specified by the private equity company; Where private equity executives have experience.
Management	Avoid non-profitable contracts; Look at the margins in each product; Key executives encouraged to take equity stake.
Product analysis	Check expense control measures; Cost management.
Investment	25–50% equity position; Investment size ranges; Will normally require a funding component; Active involvement and representation on the management board.

Source: Miller (2015) and author

diversified investments. One such US company is Farmfolio Holdings (FFH) (https://farmfolio.net/) which advertises both to investors and agribusinesses, acting as a gateway and consolidator between the two. The assets are secured by a Delaware-based LLC, and investors pool their resources by acquiring participatory shares in a property-owning LLC, in this case farmland. Unlike other forms of incorporation, LLCs usually do not have limitations on the quantity of participants within the company. Likewise, LLCs and LPs can avoid double taxation on income by passing most of the yields directly through to the investors and only being taxed at the individual level. Similar to private equity, Farmfolio's Farmshares programme functions as crowdfunding. However, Farmshares have much smaller unit sizes than private equity, giving them a wider appeal. True, they allow access to several points along the agricultural supply chain, Farmshares give investors the opportunity to participate in projects usually reserved to institutional investors. And Farmshares offer potential liquidity, at least, through membership in an investor exchange network, which is an attempt to resolve one of the main problems of PE and VC investment, illiquidity. But they do *not* provide for actual ownership of the land, the way the modern timeshare industry does, and are therefore inherently more risky than actual land investment, so the main appeal of this kind of fund should logically be not for land, but for investments further along the supply chain.

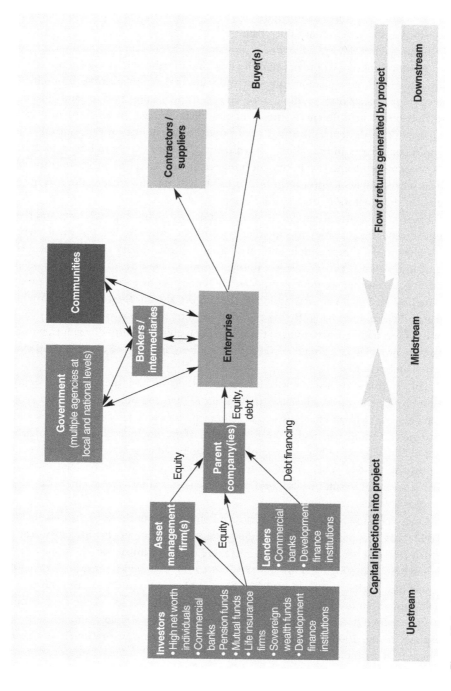

Figure 12.4 The investment value chain

Source: Cotula & Blackmore (2014:2)

Strategic issues in investment – a top-down perspective

It is of value to compare the approach above with what the FAO has set out in what it described as the 'investment value chain'

In the view of the FAO, the idea of 'investment chains' captures the multiplicity of actors and relations linked to a project, and the flow and distribution of value among those actors. Any given investment chain involves multiple sites of decision-making, resourcing and operation, often spread over multiple geographies. Capital contributions and financial returns are distributed in different segments of the chain. Money flows from project financiers ('upstream') to the enterprise that leads project implementation ('midstream'), through to various contractors and suppliers ('downstream'). It also flows from buyers back up through the investment chain. The notion of 'pressure points' refers to sites along the investment chain where public action can influence the behaviour of actors, or the nature of relations between those actors' (Cotula & Blackmore, 2014:1–2).

The FAO puts the argument in terms of disparate ownership structures and the resultant opportunities for government and other quasi-public entities to become involved in agribusiness investment. One example enterprise it cites is a subsidiary of an Ethiopian investment company, which is part of a larger business group owned by a billionaire Saudi-Ethiopian national. In another example from Mali, the enterprise is part of a business group directly owned by a Malian national, although the project also involves significant lending from a Malian development bank. Before the Mali venture, the business group was mainly known for its grains trading operations, so the group's branching out into direct agricultural production also provides an example of vertical integration in the value chain. A third example was from Cambodia (see Figure 12.5).

This is really an argument about externalities, or else there would be no issue to raise: investment into agribusiness, perhaps more than any other sector of the economy, can generate employment effects as well as influence other sectors of the economy and generate strategic and political issues for the government of the day. Individual investments by the private sector, whether public or private, is not guaranteed to produce the desired result. Hence the involvement of government, which can generate equally complicated investment value chains, with significant possibilities for inefficiencies in their own right, notably corruption but also slowness of response.

One such issue is the question of how much investment there ought to be in agricultural R&D. That it is profitable seems unquestionable: investments in this sub-sector appear to return IRRs of between 20–80%, whilst there is also an impact on the value of production, somewhere in the region of 6–12% (FAO, 2017:53) although it must be reserved that much of this time-series data includes both the period before the GFC and even that of higher yield growth. In the previous century, and even the first decade of the new century, investment remained flat, however: after a brief rise in overseas development assistance (ODA) in response to the 2007–08 food crises, ODA for agriculture was relatively flat from 2011. It is hard to resist the conclusion that these arguments need concrete support in terms of evidence regarding actual private sector investment.

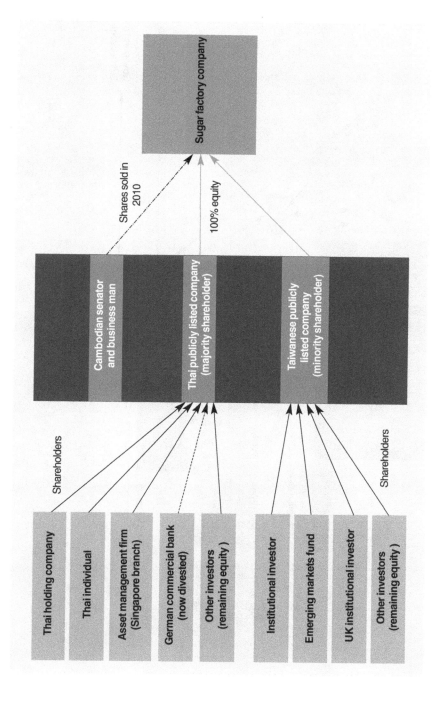

Figure 12.5 Corporate structure

Source: Cotula & Blackmore (2014:22)

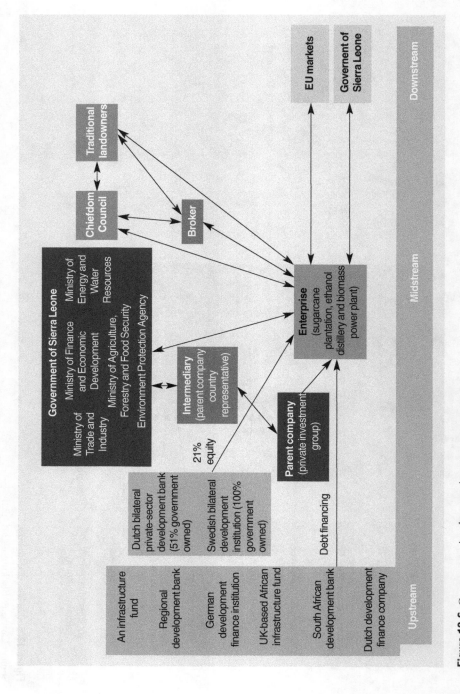

Figure 12.6 Government involvement in corporate structure
Source: Cotula & Blackmore (2014:24)

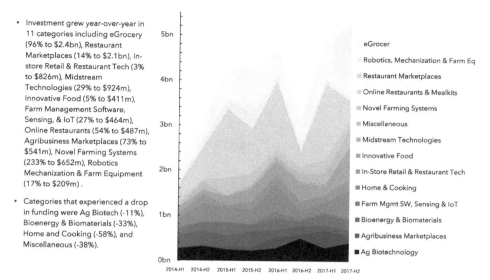

- Investment grew year-over-year in 11 categories including eGrocery (96% to $2.4bn), Restaurant Marketplaces (14% to $2.1bn), In-store Retail & Restaurant Tech (3% to $826m), Midstream Technologies (29% to $924m), Innovative Food (5% to $411m), Farm Management Software, Sensing, & IoT (27% to $464m), Online Restaurants (54% to $487m), Agribusiness Marketplaces (73% to $541m), Novel Farming Systems (233% to $652m), Robotics Mechanization & Farm Equipment (17% to $209m).

- Categories that experienced a drop in funding were Ag Biotech (-11%), Bioenergy & Biomaterials (-33%), Home and Cooking (-58%), and Miscellaneous (-38%).

Figure 12.7 Investment by category, 2014–2017
Source: Agfunder (2018)

Evidence of private equity investment in agribusiness worldwide

Fortunately, the attention of private equity companies has now been well and truly drawn by agribusiness. Agfunder data present the picture seen in Figure 12.7.

Australia is per capita the most advanced private equity market for agribusiness; in their review of the prospects for private equity for 2018, Allens and Linklaters in Australia commented:

The Agri & Food sector is continuing to get significant attention from sponsors, attracted by strong macro trends driving demand from Asian markets for quality branded Australian food and beverage products. Pacific Equity Partners (PEP) has been at the forefront of this activity, and, in 2017, acquired Allied Mills, Australia's leading manufacturer of flour, bakery premixes and speciality frozen par-baked bread products. Allied Mills has subsequently been integrated with PEP's Pinnacle Bakery and Integrated Ingredients business. Quadrant Private Equity has also been active in this space, recently acquiring the iconic confectionery manufacturer Darrell Lea. We expect to see further buy and sell-side sponsor activity in the Agri & Food sector in 2018. European sponsor Terra Firma may look to exit its trophy cattle business Consolidated Pastoral Company, which it has held for the past nine years. This process is expected to be a highly competitive auction, led by both Australian and offshore superannuation and pension funds seeking exposure to a sizable and high-quality Australian pastoral asset. On the buy-side, sponsors will continue to seek out opportunities to acquire unloved branded food or beverage businesses sitting within multinational portfolios'(Allen & Linklaters, 2018).

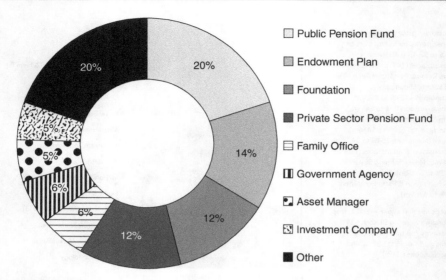

Figure 12.8 Sources of land investment by type of investor
Source: Prequn (2016)

And from India, similar mid-size investments:

In January 2018, India Agri Business Fund II (IABF-II), co-sponsored by Rabobank, the UK's CDC Group and Asian Development Bank (ADB), made an investment worth US$10 million for a minority stake in Global Gourmet Pvt. Ltd., a frozen food products exporting company.

Source: Susmit (2018)

Private equity, sovereign wealth funds and land grabs

What underlies much private equity investment in agribusiness, however, is land. Land prices have soared in the past two decades amid worries about financial stability globally. In the late 2000s, the world experienced what was widely described as a 'land grab'. Motivated by high food prices, the wish to acquire guaranteed food supplies, rising land prices and energy costs, the increasingly important sovereign wealth funds (SWFs) of wealthy credit nations such as Norway, China, Abu Dhabi and Singapore (PwC, 2016), private equity and corporates all plunged into land acquisition. Farmland investors turned to crop exporting hubs like the USA, Australia and Eastern Europe to snap up farmland as a long-term investment. Some of the large US private equity funds bought land particularly in the USA, Brazil and Argentina, and there have been similar successes in Canada.

Amongst many other examples, Almarai Co. bought land that roughly doubled its holdings in California's Palo Verde Valley, an area that enjoys first dibs on water from the

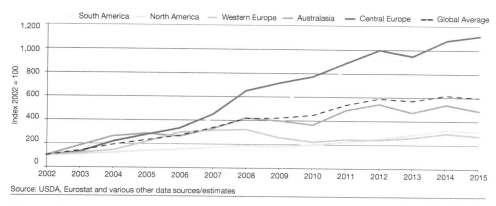

Figure 12.9 Comparative land price trends by region
Source: Savills (2016:2)

Colorado River. The company also acquired a large tract near Vicksburg, Arizona, becoming a powerful economic force in a region that has fewer well-pumping restrictions than other parts of the state. As John Szczepanski, director of the US Forage Export Council, said at the time: 'It [the deal] flies in the face of economic reason. You've taken on all of the risk a farmer has. The only way you can justify that is that they're really not trying to make a profit. They're trying to secure the food supply' (Associated Press, 2016). Qatar's SWF has invested in Australian farmland through Hassad Food, although interestingly, they are not necessarily prepared to stay invested definitely, announcing a plan to redirect investment away from pure primary production to a strategic blend of both farming and investments across the sheepmeat and grain supply chains (Cranston, 2017). ANZ agreed: they argued in 2016 that although globally the flow of institutional investment in farming has been largely into row crops, skewed by investments into US and Brazilian soy and wheat, while in Australia the focus has been on beef production, investors are increasingly seeking new opportunities. They suggested that with pension funds in particular having patient timelines, the result is likely to be the increased acquisition of grain operations (ANZ, 2016:14). Another example: Al Dahra, an Abu Dhabi-based firm, which owns 81,000 hectares of cultivated farmland worldwide and has a presence in Egypt, Greece, Morocco, Namibia, Saudi Arabia, the UAE, India, Pakistan and Serbia, linked in 2017 with the Saudi Agriculture and Livestock Investment Company (Salic), a state-owned group which already owns 46,000 hectares of land in western Ukraine, to develop farmland in ten countries around the Black Sea. And in February 2018 a group of Dubai companies outlined plans to make up to $1 billion of investment in a 77,000-hectare beet and grains farm in Egypt. The examples keep coming. In July 2018 the Investment Corporation of Dubai partnered with Optimum Agriculture, a Miami-based investment company, to acquire a 38,453-acre ranch in Florida, which they intended to be the first of several US farmland-based deals. Again: in 2018 UK-based Cibus Fund (owned by ADM Capital) purchased an almond orchard in Victoria, Australia. The almond orchard has a planted area in excess of 1,000 acres and is located in Victoria's prime horticultural district of Sunraysia. The mature orchard is expected to generate target production of approximately 1,400 metric tonnes of almonds per annum. The acquisition was aimed to take advantage of Australia's counter-cyclical almond production to the USA and to benefit from a mature, high-yielding asset that, the investor hopes, will deliver near-term cash flows over a long duration investment (Australian Government, 2018). Elsewhere, some private equity companies are also open about their intention to continue to invest in farmland, for example US real estate investment trusts (REITs) and Agcapita in Canada. According to Agcapita:

> We believe that farmland is an excellent long-term investment. We believe the world is in a period of elevated demand for crops due to the combined requirements for 'food, feed, and fuel' – the population grows every year requiring each acre to produce more; emerging economies are moving to a high meat diet driving livestock feed demand; and biofuels are diverting crops from food us. We believe Canadian farmland has some highly unique and useful characteristics – low volatility, low correlations to traditional asset classes, high risk adjusted returns, strong linkage to emerging market growth with limited political risk, reliable cash-flow generation, if structured correctly, minimal counter-party risk and in certain markets a margin of safety due to discounted prices (Agcapita, 2018).

Investment in land has by no means been confined to OECD countries. In Eastern Europe, there have been a number of Western-backed agribusinesses, such as Landkom, Alpcot Agro, Trigon Agri and Black Earth Farming Ltd. Similarly, the Russian Direct Investment Fund and TH Group, Vietnam's largest agricultural conglomerate, agreed jointly to invest in dairy farming and milk processing projects in Russia (Preqin, 2018:6).

A diverse landscape of agricultural funds has emerged with unique strategies; however, the frontier of smallholder finance remains very difficult to serve from private equity, which has minimum investment sizes, only medium-term investment strategies and high expectations of returns, even if they are not always met. Pension funds have also become investors: in 2017, the Ontario teachers' pension plan closed a A$180-million deal to purchase a privately owned avocado farm, with the owner retained as manager for an interim period, probably in an earn-out arrangement (final fee dependent on post-acquisition performance). There had been competition for the deal from the ASX-listed Costa Group, and Chinese-based livestock and stockfeed company Shenzhen Kondarl (Brammer, 2017).

The list of deals is long, and still growing

Information on SWF and private equity land deals is plentiful, if often very sketchy, although opinions on how much land has been the subject of deals varies from 49 million hectares and 1,356 deals (Land Matrix, 2018) to Oxfam's 2011 claim that an area the size of Western Europe had been leased or sold since 2001 (Oxfam, 2011), a claim, if not the surrounding rhetoric, that had been scaled back by 2016 to the size of Germany (Oxfam, 2016). Not-for-profit groups like Oxfam (www.oxfam.org), GRAIN (www.grain.org) and the Oakland Institute (www.oaklandinstitute.org) object in principle to the deals – to the potential job losses, the impact on small farmers and the environment, and the overseas repatriation of profits from land. For a flavour of the debate, see the plethora of websites (e.g. Bouckley, 2013; Harrison-Dunn, 2013). It should be noted, though, that, 'Far from being coerced into these land deals, many developing country governments welcome them – and even lobby aggressively for them. Pakistan, for example, has staged "farmland road shows" across the Arab Gulf to attract investor interest, offering lavish tax incentives' (Kugelman, 2012:5). Developing country governments want the infrastructure, the employment, and the technology that successful deals can bring. Since 2011 the FAO has had a code of conduct for land deals, which may have helped establish a standard for them going forward (FAO, 2012).

So, land deals have been popular – but have they been profitable? US land prices have seen boom and bust: the average farm land value ($/acre) was $196 in 1970, $737 in 1980 but only $683 in 1990. Since then, however, growth has been both steady *and* dramatic, defying the financial rule book: $844 in 1995, $1,090 in 2000, $1,610 in 2005, $2,150 in 2010 and in 2017, $3,080 per acre, compared to $3,010 per acre in 2016.

Similarly in the UK, farm land values have soared more than 200% in eight years as of 2012, according to Global AgInvesting. There are established UK listed farmland investment companies that therefore have performed well, for example Braemar. As has been pointed out, investing in agricultural land and forestry in the UK has many tax advantages. Owners of agricultural land and forestry pay no inheritance tax, provided the land has been held for at least two years prior to death. There are also ways of mitigating the capital gains tax. There is also reason to invest in land because it is widely considered that the residential property market is overheated so there may be further 'concreting over' the greenbelt. Chartered surveyors and global property consultants Savills publish research on UK and international farmland prices (Savills, 2016). There are no guarantees of perpetual annual positive returns – for example land values fell by 3% in the three months to March 2016 according to chartered surveyors and property consultants Knight Frank, the largest quarterly drop since the end of 2008, 'ending a bull run of spectacular returns on farmland' (Pickford, 2016). But considering the dramatic nature of the global financial crisis, and the falls in commodity prices experienced in 2015, these are very slight changes. Knight Frank data suggest that average values in the UK have risen nearly 180% in the past decade. It is almost impossible to find any other investment that has performed so well, so consistently, so globally, so uniformly. Land has certainly outperformed other commodities (Savills, 2016). And in terms of regions – Central Europe has seen the best results since the turn of the century, an average 20%+ annual rise.

The success of farmland investment was described by the TIAA-CREF Center for Farmland Research at the University of Illinois thus: no matter how you cut the data to examine different time periods, agricultural investment outperformed all other asset classes. For example, US Farm Land returned 10.27% per annum in the period from 1970 to 2016 and 8.58% per annum in the period from 2000 to 2016. This compared with S&P500 index returns of 6.79% per annum and 2.48% per annum respectively for the same periods (Sherrick, 2016). There were slight falls in the USA: between 2008 and 2009, from $2,170 per acre to $2,090 per acre, and from 2015 to 2016, a dip of $10 per acre, which led to unfulfilled Cassandra-like predictions of a slump (Caldwell, 2015) that took no account of long-term fundamentals in the relationship between demand and supply. To date, land investment has proved extremely profitable. US farmland has relentlessly outperformed both stocks and bonds since 1970 (USDA, 2017).

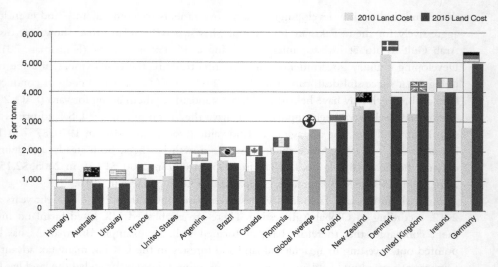

Figure 12.10 Cost of land per tonne of wheat
Source: Savills (2016:3)

The result of this rapid land price rise worldwide is that the cost of land required to produce agricultural commodities has risen steadily, as the chart in Figure 12.10 demonstrates.

Comparables are the usual valuation method for land, but the application of real options to agricultural land is definitely plausible, as:

Cashflow generation does not drive land valuation anywhere, and especially in developed locations that are cash rich and potentially subject to development alternatives. Real options represent a more accurate way to estimate land, and hence agribusiness, valuations in most such jurisdictions. If it is not real development propping up land valuations, it is the government with grants and regulations. In North Dakota, for example, agricultural land values for tax purposes are regulated as the landowner share of gross returns divided by the prevailing capitalisation rate. Landowner share of gross returns is the portion of revenue generated from agricultural land that is assumed to be received by the landowner, and is expected to reflect current rental rates (Rauschenberger, 2014).

Yes, the idea works well when applied to land valuation. Moreno *et al.* (2009) modelled the potential selling decision of the land owner as a put option. They showed that theoretical prices are close to market land prices and that the value of the put option accounts for, at least, 25% of the total land value.

Forecasting land prices

Agricultural land derives its value from three particular characteristics: (i) scarcity; (ii) physically immobility; and (iii) durability (Dasso *et al.*, 1995). The scarcity of land is not only a consequence of its physical scarceness, but also the scarcity of the products that emanate from

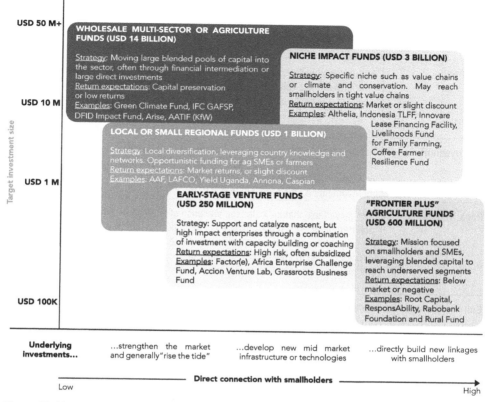

Figure 12.11 A diverse landscape of funds have emerged with unique strategies
Source: RAF Learning (2017)

it. However, being an immobile factor that cannot be reproduced, the economic scarcity of land is caused by its low elasticity of production and substitution, which can be privately appropriated by some agents. Nevertheless, the development of technologies that increase its productivity, as well as administrative measures such as land reform, for example, can substantially modify the level of land scarcity in a region (Plata, 2006). It is also assumed that a land market is created when the ownership of the region is accepted in general terms, regardless of the way it is maintained or the guaranties for its maintenance (Binswanger *et al.*, 1993).

Reydon *et al.* (2014) are typical of academic approaches to land valuation questions, basing their analysis on a multiple regression model with the logarithm of the rural land price per acre as a dependent variable and, as explanatory variables, physical characteristics of the land (soil, climate, landscape), production (sstems of production, location, approach), the infrastructure of the property and expectations (regional situation and local investments) (Reydon *et al.*, 2014:403).

The problem with this kind of analysis is that it works very well as an ex post analysis to explain why, given a general level of land prices, any particular piece of land is worth more, or less, than its neighbour. What it fails to do, and the problem is encapsulated in

Table 12.2 Depiction of key regression variables for land valuation

Variable	Description	Expected sign of the estimated coefficient
Electricity	Dummy variable that indicates access to electricity. It has a value of 1 when the farm has access to electricity, otherwise 0.	Positive, as besides representing benefits from electricity itself, this variable may be a proxy of other characteristics of infrastructure, which usually come together with electricity.
Improvements	Dummy variable that indicates the existence of improvements on the farm, such as barns, for example. It has a value of 1 if there are improvements on the farm, otherwise 0.	Positive, since improvements increase production options.
Rock fragments	Dummy variable that indicates the presence of rock fragments, which is considered to be good (1): soil with no mechanisation restrictions due to rocks, or bad (0): soil with rock fragments that makes mechanisation impossible.	Positive, since it is expected that the property, where rocks do not interfere with the use of mechanisation, have higher prices. Those in which rock fragments make mechanisation impossible have lower prices.
Soil	Composite index that considers soil's physical properties, such as depth and texture. This index varies in a range from 10 to 100.	Positive, as soil with better physical properties permits greater land productivity and rent.
Subsistence	Dummy variable; value 1 when the system of production of the property is agriculture and cattle-raising related to subsistence and trade of surplus, and 0 in the opposite situation.	The sign depends on the group of production systems in the homogeneous zone in question.

Source: Reydon *et al.* (2014:399)

the term 'expectations', is to provide an adequate forecasting tool. This is simply because in order to do so, all the independent variables must themselves be forecast, together with any changes in their relative weighting. Reducing the problem to this shows how circular the regression reasoning can become: of course, if the relative importance of rock fragments, for example, increases, then land without them will rise in relative value; and equally of course, if expectations rise, then land values will rise generally. But how are future expectations to be known in the first place? As a forecast, a regression, though by far the best way to project land prices (Roche, 2013), is still more advocated theoretically than used in practice, even if basic comparables are a crude version.

Some agribusiness deals to ponder

Aside for pure land plays, private equity investors generally believe that they can target specific links in the agribusiness value chain and secure investments in companies that:

■ Develop innovative products to increase crop yields and improve economics for farmers;

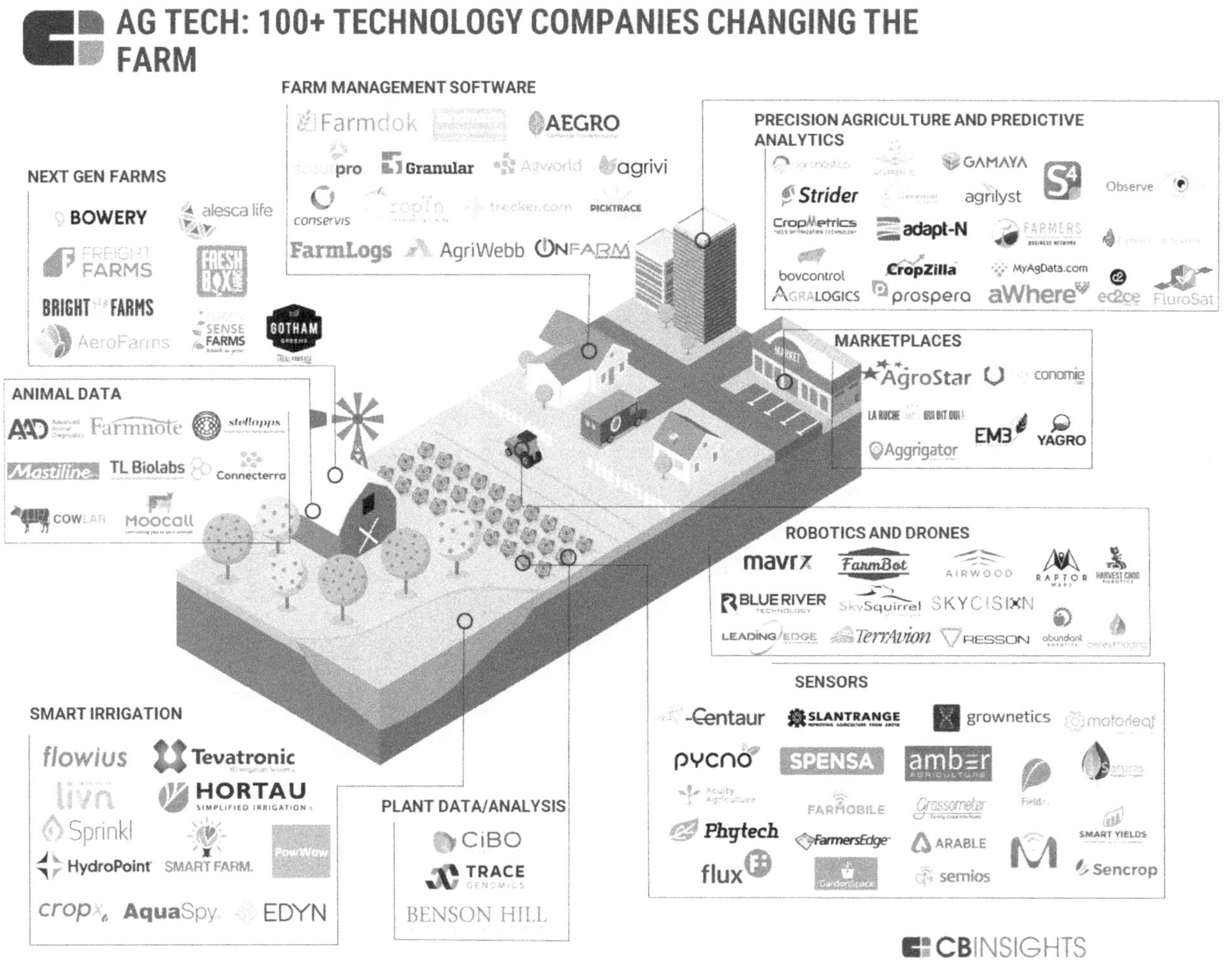

Figure 12.12 100+ technology companies changing the farm
Source: CB Insights (2017)

- Harness big data for more exacting crop production;

- Develop environmentally-friendly agricultural inputs;

- Pursue novel production systems, such as urban fisheries and vegetable farms located in warehouses and on rooftops;

- Improve food safety and traceability; and

- Increase production of fruits, vegetables and nutritional products that capitalise on continued growth in health and wellness trends.

This has resulted in deals of the following type:

- Paine & Partners' acquisitions of Suba Seeds Company, a leading speciality vegetable and legume seed producer, and Spearhead International, a leading European agricultural producer and supply chain partner, and its growth equity investment in AgBiTech Pty. Ltd., an Australia-based provider of biological pest control solutions.

- AGR Partners' investment in Tru-Test Ltd., a dairy and livestock equipment company that manufactures and markets critical farm equipment into over 100 countries around the world.

- Sun Capital Partners' acquisition of UK-based Finlays Horticulture Holdings, a grower, seller and distributor of cut flowers and fresh vegetables.

- Five Point Capital Partners' financing of WaterBridge Resources, a Houston, Texas-based acquisition platform focused on water infrastructure for upstream producers in North America.

- GenNx360 Capital Partners portfolio company Salford Group's acquisition of the AerWay aeration products line from SAF-Holland.

- American Securities' and P2 Capital Partners' acquisition of Blount International, a Portland, Oregon-based maker of replacement parts and equipment for the garden, agriculture, and forestry markets.

These are just representative examples of many hundreds of such deals worldwide.

The development of private equity agribusiness funds

To start with an example. In 2017, Phatisa was aiming to raise $300 million for the Phatisa Food Fund II, a successor fund to the Africa-focused private equity firm's African Agriculture

Fund. The new fund will target opportunities in the food and fast-moving consumer goods value chain in sub-Saharan Africa. Phatisa announced the launch of the ten-year PFF2 in 2017. The second-generation fund was established with an initial commitment of $75 million from the Overseas Private Investment Corporation (OPIC), the development finance institution of the US government, and a focus on investment opportunities along the food and consumer goods value chain in sub-Saharan Africa. The African Development Bank (AfDB) then approved a $10-million investment in the Phatisa Food Fund 2 (PFF2) to forward the mission of boosting agriculture and nutrition across Africa. The fund expected to deliver its returns, predictably, by backing mid-sized fast-moving consumer goods (FMCG) and agribusiness-related companies well-positioned to modernise and grow the continent's domestic food production industry. Phatisa Food Fund II's predecessor fund, the $246-million African Agriculture Fund targeted investments that range between $5–24 million in size. It focuses on businesses which field experienced management teams and have proven financial and operational track records. The fund had eight companies in its portfolio, located across sub-Saharan Africa. The fund acquired a significant stake in Kanu Equipment in a $31-million deal in November 2016, which gave Phatisa a controlling stake in the sub-Saharan African equipment agricultural and construction equipment supplier (Global Ag Investing, 2017). This is the kind of fund that is already delivering the capital required to make companies in developing markets competitive.

At present, however, capital invested in emerging markets agribusiness through private equity has increased, but remains a modest share of the emerging market private equity industry (<2%). Investors remain wary of the unpredictability of agricultural markets and inherent risks that affect returns. Most probably they always will be: relative to other sectors, agricultural investments are seen to have much broader risk exposure across farmer segments and value chains, as such many investors in these markets tend to focus on larger investment classes in sectors such as infrastructure, extractive industries and major manufacturing. The importance of land investment to complement downstream, riskier investments and reduce portfolio volatility is therefore clear.

Amidst this very mixed and uncertain context, the market has seen the emergence of a diverse landscape of impact-driven agricultural funds, combining public and private capital totalling approximately $19 billion to execute unique strategies in the agricultural sector. Amongst 80 impact-orientated agribusiness and related sector funds, a range of strategies can be observed, all intended to reach smallholders, cultivate a pipeline, align technical assistance and match sources of capital to return expectations. In some due to the large size of each fund. The total capital available among this group of funds has been estimated at approximately $14 billion, and the target investment size typically falls between $5–50 million or even more. Examples of wholesale multisector or agriculture funds include the African Agriculture Trade Investment Fund (AATIF), Norfund, the Green Climate Fund, DFID Impact Fund, ARISE and the IFC's Global Agriculture and Food Security Program (GAFSP). Note that a number of these are facilities, programmes or windows of multilaterals or development finance institutions rather than stand-alone investment funds. Typically, these funds have concessional return expectations, with some or all of the underlying investors willing to take on higher risk or lower returns to leverage additional private capital for their cause or address the impact thesis of the fund. The principal investors are typically a mix of development finance institutions and multilaterals, and may include some private investors.

A number of these funds are multisector in focus, and even when they have a stated inclusive agriculture focus, it is impossible for them to directly reach smallholder farmers or small rural enterprises due to their high minimum investment size. When they do reach small farmers and small rural enterprises, it is indirectly through intermediaries or project-based funding cases, these funds blend public support and private capacity. While every fund is different, their general characteristics typically align to one of five archetypes shown in Figure 12.11, although some funds may align to multiple archetypes.

Financial intermediation is a commonly used approach for these funds, in which investors target local financial institutions that serve smallholder farmers and rural enterprises through on-lending or risk sharing. Niche impact funds are defined by a specific and well-thought-out thesis around the impact they are trying to achieve and their use of an investment strategy and partnership structure to achieve it. This may revolve around, for example, developing a specific value chain (e.g. a West African cocoa fund), product class (e.g. equipment financing) or impact thesis (e.g. preventing deforestation). These funds are fairly heterogeneous in nature, but one estimate suggested that they had roughly $3 billion in available capital with target investment size typically falling between $1–$20 million. Examples of niche impact funds include Althelia, an impact investment manager working for agroforestry and sustainable land use, and Innovare's Lease Financing Facility, which aims to make equipment financing more readily available to African agribusinesses.

Most of these funds have a ready-made pipeline of investees – defined by the particular value chain, product, or market segment in which they invest – with some having LPs and even GPs who can feed the investment pipeline. In many cases, there is some de-risking of the investment pipeline due to the complementary activity of other actors alongside the investor. For example, a supply chain focused fund can identify pipeline by looking at the

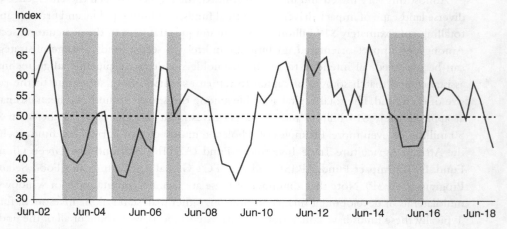

Figure 12.13 Agbiz/IDC confidence index
Source: Agbiz (2019)

agribusinesses and farmers from which major companies are sourcing, while also benefiting from off-take agreements and supply chain strengthening activities of the companies working in that supply chain. Though the investors in these funds are typically seeking market returns, they may involve some concessional or first-loss investors because their involvement helps to further a particular impact thesis or strategic goal. The Livelihoods Fund for Family Farming, for example, combined investment from Danone, Mars and other companies along with donor grants and investments, in the kind of synthetic public-private investment partnership of which the World Bank so approves. to provide upfront financing to a project developer or NGO that carries out supply chain strengthening and ecological preservation projects that include smallholder farmers.

The result can certainly be a win for all parties, generating cost-effective results and impact. But it can equally be disastrous, with no party satisfied with the outcome, if proper forecasting is not done and it is not combined with rigorous governance.

Local or small regional funds are defined by their local or regional focus, with locally embedded fund managers, which gives them an ability to source local investment opportunities efficiently. Many of them have a diversified sector focus in order to spread risk, but there are some dedicated agriculture funds. The target investment size typically falls between US$500,000 and US$5 million. Examples included the African Agriculture Fund (AAF), Lending for African Farming (LAFCo), Yield Uganda, Annona in Latin America and Caspian in India. For the most part, these funds provide capital to growth stage enterprises and they raise capital at market-based returns, which makes them relatively risk-averse. However, in some cases they may also blend concessional or first loss capital from donors or development finance institutions seeking to promote investment in higher-risk geographies or commodities. They typically have in-country investment officers with strong local networks through which they identify investment opportunities. Reaching smallholder farmers is not necessarily a core focus, though they may invest in agribusinesses that engage farmers and thus have an indirect smallholder farmer benefit through general strengthening of the agricultural sector.

Most of these funds offer some light in-house technical assistance for investees in the form of financial and operational advisory services. More intensive capacity building is typically too expensive for their operating model and available resources, but in some cases they may pair up with a separate grant-based fund to offer a more holistic suite of services that strengthen impact. The African Agriculture Fund, for example, has an associated grant-based facility with independent technical assistance fund managers who direct grants toward programmes that strengthen portfolio companies in the investment fund.

Some funds, for example in India, may go smaller still in their target market. Samunnati, for example, provides access to financing to farmers and SMEs in the agricultural sector that would find it hard to get credit or adapted financial services otherwise. It is estimated that only 30% of the total agriculture demand in India is met by institutional credit. Samunnati helps meet the market need by going through aggregator producer companies and buyers. This approach allows farmers to benefit from better prices, access to formal credit and technical know-how. The company has so far reached about 15,000 small holder farmers and is expected to grow its client base to more than 100,000 in the coming five years (responsAbility, 2018). These are surely impressive numbers – the question is how effective the financial assistance turns out to be.

Venture capital for agribusiness

What governments failed to do, however, venture capital finally rose to the challenge in the subsequent decade.

Hence it is not surprising to hear Jorge Heraud, founder of Blue River Technology, which according to Agfunder achieved one of the best exits yet seen in agribusiness, observing in a podcast to investors that:

> When I started enterpreneuring in agtech it was a weird thing; no-one was doing it. We had to explain to every single investor what it is that we did and why it made sense. One of the things that has helped accelerate agtech is AgFunder; you guys have been phenomenal in educating the market, both the VCs and the entrepreneurs, and I'm really thankful for the help you guys are bringing to this space (Heraud, 2018).

Similarly, the director of research at Agfunder observed that:

> When I first started covering agribusiness investment in late 2013, agtech was just a small portion of the overall ag investing landscape, with more activity taking place in farmland and private equity fund management. Today in 2018, agtech has blossomed into a fully-fledged venture capital industry, with some agtech funds reaching $250 million in size and well-funded startups reaching unicorn status. While it will take some time for agriculture to become a mainstream sector for venture capital investment – not least due to the widely varied types of technology coming to bear across the convoluted space – the need for innovation in this most essential global industry cannot be underestimate' (Burwood-Taylor, 2018).

Major funds include Anterra (Netherlands), SHIFT Invest, Five Seasons (France), AgFunder (US), Cultivian, Finistere, Germin8S2G (US), New Protein Capital (Singapore) and Bits x Bites (China). It is now impossible to gather together a list of all VC investments in agriculture, agribusiness and agtech. More happen every day. In Israel, for example, the agrifood tech space is bustling with at least 800 start-ups out of a total 8,000 Israeli start-ups from a population of 8 million (Agfunder, 2018a). Brazil is a similar location of hundreds of start-ups. Even Agfunder (www.agfunder.com) and CB Insights (www.cbinsights.com) find it hard to track them all, and interactive maps of investments, though very welcome, can never hope to be comprehensive (Forward Food, 2018).

To be added to the roll-call are the venture capital investment arms of the major corporates: Bayer's 'Lea' programme has favoured larger investments via joint ventures like Joyn Bio, a $100-million JV with Ginkgo Bioworks, although it has made a few dispersed start-up investments off its balance sheet. In addition to forming joint ventures, Bayer has also chosen to be a limited partner in several agribusiness-related venture funds, including Cambridge, MA-based Flagship Pioneering (formerly Flagship Ventures), Israel's Trendlines, and San Diego, CA-based Finistere Ventures. Monsanto's venture arm, Monsanto Growth Ventures (MGV), has been more aggressive in funding start-ups, so a combined strategy of MGV's more traditional VC investment tack with Bayer's preference for grander schemes could be the result of the merger. Syngenta, too, has been very active in this space.

A good example of VC investment from 2018 was the announcement that Crop One Holdings, a Silicon Valley food start-up, and Emirates Flight Catering (EKFC), one of the world's largest airline catering operators, plan to build a 130,000-square-foot vertical farm in Dubai, twice the size of AeroFarms 69,000-square-foot warehouse in Newark, USA. The Dubai facility will grow greens and herbs all year round, and indoors, without natural sunlight or soil, under LEDs (which mimic natural sunlight) located inside climate-controlled rooms, which are each set to optimal temperature and oxygen levels depending on the crop. Instead of soil, greens sprout in nutrient-rich water beds on trays stacked from the floor to the ceiling. Sensors in the trays will track how the plants are doing in real time. There are real advantages in a location like Dubai, and a customer like Emirates. The facility was planned be the largest of its kind, and will produce 6,000 pounds of crops daily. Crop One already operated a vertical farm in Millis, Massachusetts, delivering to Boston metro area grocery stores under the Fresh Box Farms brand name. Not all vertical farm projects have been successful, however: Panasonic and Google have abandoned vertical farming projects, and Farmed Here – once the largest vertical farm in the USA –shut down in 2017. The reason: vertical farms rely on large amounts of electricity from the LEDs, so high energy costs can make it harder for them to compete in regions where cheap produce is still available (Garfield, 2018).

Another example: Stellapps Technologies, the Indian IoT and data analysis stack for the dairy supply chain raised $14 million in Series B funding in a round led by IndusAge Partners alongside the Bill & Melinda Gates Foundation and two strategic corporate venture investors: Qualcomm Ventures and ABB Technology Ventures, the venture arm of the industrial technology company. Existing investors also participated in the funding round including Omnivore Partners, the Indian agtech-focused VC, and two local tech VCs Blume Ventures and Venture Highway, and Asia-focused venture group BEENEXT. The Indian dairy industry stands in great need of improved access to data and analysis. This venture aims to optimise the entire dairy supply chain, including milk production, procurement and cold chain logistics through the deployment of 26 different types of sensors, automation and machine learning. On the farms, wearable devices collect animal-specific data from the cows and buffalos. At the dairy collection sites, quality analysis sensors measure fat content to assess the quality of the milk to help with pricing. These records are sent automatically to the dairy company's headquarters and the farmer's phone via SMS (Nair, 2018; Burwood-Taylor, 2018). This kind of AI in agriculture is already established in developed countries: berries are very water-sensitive, so farms often have someone physically monitoring water levels four times per day. Sensors could monitor them every 15 minutes, and once a database is established, AI can identify patterns and determine when plants need to be watered. Agnov8 in Australia provides AI to do just that (Kinch, 2018).

Vertical farms and agtech are examples of the way in which the simultaneous availability of multiple new technologies – genetics, cheap energy, and AI – can achieve a breakthrough in terms of commercial success. Certainly, the multiplicity of different technologies required for future agribusiness, the many opportunities that they generate, and the importance of agriculture and agribusiness for national policies, have now generated a steadily rising drumbeat of international interest. One of the most obvious manifestations of this kind of interest has been the rise in conferences devoted to the issues analysed in this book. Another is the willingness of Governments to dispense grants to SMEs developing agtech (Goodland, 2018).

Early-stage venture funds support early stage but high impact enterprises that bring new and scalable technologies or business models to market. These funds typically use a combination of high-risk equity, grants and debt, along with capacity building or coaching for entrepreneurs. The target investment size typically falls between $500,000 to $2 million. Examples included Factor[e], the Africa Enterprise Challenge Fund, Accion Venture Lab and the Grassroots Business Fund. There is a sad, but probably inevitable, tendency for these funds to come and go, which is accounted for by the risky nature of their investment model. They are usually among the first institutional investors to support any given investee, which makes them high risk and means they seek high return potential or scalable impact from rapid growth. Most of these funds cultivate their investment pipeline through global relationships and networks. Some funds, fortunately, are also underpinned by donor support and concessional capital that seeks to catalyse new ideas. For example, the Africa Enterprise Challenge Fund offered both regular grants and repayable grants to assist young enterprises. Some of these funds may diversify revenue streams by offering incubation, acceleration or other fee-based services for start-ups. Smallholders themselves may not be the focus of these funds, but services for smallholder farmers may be an important part of the incubated enterprise by bringing new models or technologies to market that make smallholders more productive.

Two examples of investment areas for VC funds:

Data analytics. Farmers across the world are turning to remote sensing, data analytics and machine learning to monitor their acreage and optimise their yields. However, while growers in North America are using internet of things (IoT) solutions to automate pumping in across hundreds of acres of rice fields, companies like Kitovu are collecting, analysing and aggregating soil and geolocation data from remote smallholder farmers across Nigeria to provide them with the right fertilisers, agrochemicals, and seedlings for their fields.

Cold storage. Worldwide, about 45% of fruits and vegetables are lost or wasted every year. In emerging markets, this is largely due to spoilage before crops can make it to markets because the infrastructure is not there to support the transportation of fresh produce. In developed countries where the cold chain is established, food waste at the consumer end is the primary culprit. In Sub-Saharan Africa, start-ups like Wakati are developing innovative methods of storage that require minimal space and resources to preserve crops and increase farmer income.

Some further examples from Africa:

- *Kitovu* (www.kitovu.com.ng) is a web/mobile-based decentralised fertiliser/seedling warehousing system based in Nigeria that matches the right inputs to different farm locations owned by smallholder farmers in distant pocket locations, using geolocation and soil data collected by the mobile app.

- *Wakati* (www.wakati.co) developed the world's first standalone solution for the preservation of fruits and vegetables without using cooling. Smallholder farmers could store their produce on their farms in a protective microclimate inside a tent with a storage of 200–1,000 kg, using one litre of water per week and powered by a small solar panel.

- *Illuminum Greenhouses* (www.illuminumgreenhouses.com) – an agri-tech green-house and drip installation company in Kenya working with smallholder farmers to improve production and increase efficiency through the use of new modern technologies. They constructed affordable modern greenhouses and install automated drip irrigation kits for smallholder farmers by using locally available materials and solar-powered sensors.

- *Apollo Agriculture* (www.apolloagriculture.com) helps farmers in emerging markets increase their profits. They use agronomic machine learning, remote sensing and mobile technology to help farmers access credit, high-quality farm inputs and customised advice. Their first product is a customised package of farm inputs, farming advice and credit delivered to farmers in Kenya.

- *AMIntegrated Aerial* (www.gsvc.org/project/amintegrated-aerial-limited/) designed a simple spray boom accessory, called the FiKapSy – short for 'Flying Knapsack System' – for agriculture drone applications in the precision dispersal of agro-inputs on farm fields, reducing excessive use/waste of agrochemicals that lead to the degradation of the soil and environment across Africa.

- *Pula* (www.pula-advisers.com) set up as an insurance intermediary that implements data-driven agricultural insurance. Pula assists hundreds of thousands of small-scale farmers across six countries in Africa. Farmers can safeguard their crops and invest in their farms through financial tools that take advantage of the rising use of mobile technology.

- *Futurepump* (www.futurepump.com) developed solar-powered irrigation technologies to help the 500 million one-acre farmers around the world. Based in Kenya, it offers smallholder farmers a cheaper, cleaner and more sustainable alternative to costly and polluting petrol or diesel pumps. Irrigating crops on demand leads to more reliable harvests. It also gives farmers the opportunity to grow and sell crops out of season, bringing huge economic benefits to the farmers, their families and the wider community.

- Thermogenn (www.smallholderfortunes.uga.edu/) developed high-performance, off-grid, portable, evaporative coolers to expand smallholder farmers' marketable dairy products in sub-Saharan Africa, mitigating spoilage to allow farmers to sell their dairy products later in the day instead of only in the morning.

- *Syecomp* (www.syecomp.com) specialised in the acquisition, processing, analysis and synthesis of imagery from remotely sensed satellites and multispectral image data from drones to monitor field crops/vegetative status and identify and mitigate potential diseases across fields in sub-Saharan Africa on farms in Ghana.

Agtech faces obstacles, however, which must be recognised. For example, some start-ups face a backlash from the industries they aim to disrupt, including legal actions with established players, e.g. Phytelligence, a biotech micropropagation business, and food assistance app developer Propel (Agfunder, 2018). Second or third rounds of financing are not guaranteed, competition may be too severe to overcome, or the technology may not upscale satisfactorily. Not all these bold initiatives will succeed. Ultimately, too, the markets for the SMEs that even these funds are supporting will be more commercial enterprises that can fully utilise the technological and market improvements that they offer. *The list of African agtech companies above was compiled in July 2018. A worthwhile exercise will be to check their eventual success or failure at the point you read this.*

The importance of local knowledge, and the synergies that bringing companies together and even assembling a portfolio that is geographically and sectorally close enough for one portfolio manager to understand and add value to, has never been disputed in the VC space. So, although technology is pushing them together, agtech solutions for farmers in North America and other developed markets are still not necessarily relevant to smallholders in Africa, where many agribusiness start-ups and technologies aim at assisting smallholders to increase efficiencies and hopefully move many from subsistence farming to farming for profit. Many of these smallholder-focused start-ups loosely fit into three categories: finance tech (FinTech), data analytics and storage technology.

Frontier plus agriculture funds are focused on reaching underserved segments of small-holder farmers and rural enterprises with capital that can connect them to markets. The Omidyar Network classifies the 'frontier plus' as investments that support unproven business models that are also asset intensive, serving only lower-income customers and/or operating in a country with an underdeveloped capital market. The frontier plus funds deploy approximately US$600 million per year and the target investment size typically falls between $50,000 and $2 million. Examples include Root Capital, responsAbility, Oikocredit, the Rabo Rural Fund and all the members of the Council on Smallholder Agricultural Finance (CSAF).

'Frontier plus' investments in agriculture are difficult due to the high cost to serve and high risks (e.g. weather, price, production risks) of smaller agro-enterprises and producer organisations. Smaller loans (under $200,000) are particularly difficult because operations and due diligence costs are relatively fixed and thus become a large relative portion of small loans. The funds that push this frontier typically use low-cost capital coupled with lean operations and may include internal cross-subsidy from larger loans and/or external subsidies from philanthropic funders. Impact must be carefully evaluated for small loans in order to justify subsidies.

These funds cultivate their pipeline through local loan officers and exporter relationships. For technical assistance to investee companies, they often piggyback on donor supported technical assistance or value chain strengthening programmes.

Deal structuring for private equity and venture capital

When the private equity investor has decided to invest, and decided their preference for yield or capital gain, it is possible to decide how to incentivise management. In terms of how much equity management can provide, a traditional rule-of-thumb for management buyouts (where the management is buying the business from the existing owners) suggested 1.5 times existing salary if no member of the management team is already independently wealthy. Determining the split between preference (paid first) and ordinary shares is the last step – the institutional share will be reached by investing an appropriate proportion of ordinary shares; the balance, usually the bulk of the institutional capital, will be in the form of preference shares or loan stock. The incentive for management could operate through a 'ratchet'. The principle is that the management team may start with a fairly low percentage of the equity (perhaps around 5–10%) but, if they meet certain targets, their percentage interest increases to up to, say, 25–30%. or even higher. This kind of deal is in everyone's interests: the management are given the maximium possible incentive, whilst the private equity company gets its return and can then afford to be generous with additional returns. Another rule-of-thumb is that the proportional entry price paid by management should not generally be less than a third of that paid by institutions, whilst the return on exit should give management approximately a maximum of eight to ten times private equity investment returns given realised cash flows. This has been called the 'envy ratio'. Incentivising management is crucial, and the point is private equity investors should not be too envious – it will not benefit them.

Preference shares are a convenient way of organising this kind of deal. One way such an increase can be effected is by a redemption of the convertible preference shares held by the investors. For example, as certain target cash flows are achieved or if a certain target valuation is met when the company is sold within a given period, part of the investor's equity will be redeemed at par (or perhaps with a small premium) resulting in an increase in the percentage held by management. A second possibility is by issuing to management deferred shares which will acquire the rights of ordinary shares only when certain profit targets have been met. Whichever method is deployed, full details will be set out in the articles of association of the new operating company and the drafting of the articles will need to be absolutely precise.

Almost every private equity deal requires bank finance, simply because companies themselves cannot deliver the required returns. Companies can be levered themselves, if they have sufficiently stable cash flows. In addition, the private equity houses themselves can be levered. If all goes well at the corporate level, the bank will be paid first, but because so much less equity will have been invested in the company, the return to that equity will be far greater than it would have been in the absence of the debt. This is the tremendous advantage of leverage. If things go badly, however, the effect of leverage works in the reverse direction, with equity perhaps receiving nothing at all.

Finally, agribusiness debt itself can be sold on by banks and other debt providers and rated, providing investment opportunities in itself. If sufficient of these debts are gathered together, the possibility might just exist of securitising them, although the securitisation market has been severely depressed since the global financial crisis and does not show much sign of life a decade on.

A *term sheet* is how the mutual intentions of a private equity investor – the lead investor if there are several – and a target coalesce. The terms and conditions under which a private equity company will invest in an agribusiness will normally be set out in a term sheet. One of the key problems with investment in agribusinesses in developing countries is the relative inability of both owners and management to understand the legal liabilities they undertake when accepting investment into their company. There are few more important services that accountants, lawyers, bankers and other professionals can render to growing companies than to make them understand the importance both of external equity generally, and how important it is to conform to the rules, both legal and administrative, that PE and VC companies will expect to be rigorously enforced. The term sheet is a perfect example of the problem. It is unfortunately as if two different languages are being spoken.

A typical term sheet will, or at least should, contain, *inter alia*, details of the control which the private equity company will demand in exchange for its investment, exclusivity, conditions precedent for investment and conversion of any preference shares, and rights of sale (including so-called 'tag-along' rights which ensure the private equity company is never disadvantaged). Once agreed, the term sheet forms the basis for the legally binding sale and purchase agreement for the investment as well as any amendments to the company's articles of association and by-laws. It should contain, in clear and unequivocal language, all the major terms of the transaction. These include the quantity of financing, assets or shares, agreed pricing structures pre- and post-money, the capital structure of the company pre- and post- financing, including existing share issuance and whether new shares will be issued, so a proposed vesting time-scale, dilution such as share splits, antidilution clauses for additional share issuance after the deal, pre-emptive investment rights such as tag-along and drag-along rights for subsequent funding rounds or rights issues, liquidation preferences, IPO registration rights and share options with associated conversion provisions. Critical valuation questions many years later will be heavily dependent on technical drafting here: path-dependent options valuations, for example, and earn-out provisions for another.

Other clauses will cover who pays fees and other costs and when, negotiation exclusivity clauses and their duration – typically between one to three months – and all the proposed rights of investors, including to information, such as in advance to the annual operating plan, decision-making, the size and composition of the board and board participation by the investor. Private equity investors need confidence that they can intervene when they deem necessary in business plans, investment, disposal, any dividends payable, key HR decisions and even social or environmental goals. The term sheet must contain all of these control issues, hence the proposed allocation of rights to different classes of shares. Finally, most term sheets contain a timetable (with time limits) for the transaction and allocate tasks between the parties. Understandably, PE and VC firms generally outsource drafting to their lawyers; the use of templates, especially in cross-border transactions, can pose significant problems. It is very easy to see how all this represents a completely baffling new world for the majority of agribusiness owners and managers.

Term sheets themselves used to be immune from the law, especially in England, where there has been a longstanding presumption against negotiation in good faith, and the term sheet itself does not constitute an agreement in itself, only 'an agreement to agree', usually 'subject to contract'. Hence any risk related to misrepresentation of and negligent misstatements should be minimised in term sheets, although there is uncertainty about whether clauses relating to confidentiality and exclusivity should always be considered as binding. The wider perspective provided by private equity indicates, however, that they are, and can be used as the basis for claims of damages. If documents are not properly drafted, this rule is now even applying in English courts (e.g. *New Media Holding LLC vs. Kuznetsov 2016*). This, and the additional vigilance entailed from the minority stakes most private equity investments outside Europe and the USA involve, is now moving to settle the debate about how detailed a term sheet should be in favour of tightly negotiated, detailed term sheets, with all terms explicitly spelled out, rather than the old practice of a rather vague term sheet with the significant terms left for agreement in the actual asset or share purchase agreement.

Exit strategies and options

Table 12.3 Exit strategies

EXIT (i.e. how the private equity firm gets its return)	Time horizon of five to seven years; May be either to original owner, trade buyer, another private equity firm or an initial public offering (IPO); Aim at double-digit annual returns.

Source: Miller (2015) and author

Valuation and investment strategies

Finding the right investment opportunity is not easy. It comes as no surprise that McKinsey pointed out mid-decade, before the real VC rush began, that investing in the food and agribusiness sectors requires a high level of understanding of specific crops, geographies and sometimes-complex value chains that encompass inputs, production, processing and retailing. Additionally, many of the relevant investment opportunities are in geographies that are unfamiliar to a number of investors, and their profitability rests not only on crop yields but also on how different parts of the value chain perform (Goedde *et al.*, 2015). It is a safe bet that understanding of these markets, and indicators that will serve effectively as predictors of success or failure in farm and corporate agricultural businesses, will become more prominent as VC and PE agribusiness investment gradually increases. It has been argued that large agricultural producing countries, such as the USA and Australia, may be adversely affected by this growing phenomenon, as the flow-on effects of any failures could negatively impact relationships with prominent agricultural trading partners (Purves *et al.*, 2015).

Perhaps. However, sensing an opportunity, investors have been trying for decades now to capture value from technological innovations and improved efficiencies in food and agriculture. Since 2004, global investment in the food-and-agribusiness sector grew threefold to more than $100 billion in 2013, according to McKinsey analysis, and this was just a beginning. There are already numerous indices available to assist decision-makers in this regard, for example of confidence in the sector.

Conclusion

Investors seem increasingly prepared not only to enter the agribusiness space but to do so directly, managing their investments in-house rather than committing to funds. Disappointing returns from tax-driven farmland, and timber, investments, such as the managed investment schemes (MIS) in Australia, and scepticism about the management of funds, especially when it comes to the use of derivatives, have driven this move. The 'land grab' by sovereign wealth funds, club deals and co-investments being offered to family offices and HNWIs, and direct investment by limited partners, sometimes in deal-by-deal fundraising, are all symptoms of both rising interest in the sector but concern about how private equity has managed its agribusiness exposure in the past. In a sector with both significant environmental, social and governance aspects and, of necessity, considerable reliance on the actual asset managers themselves, the evolution of investment protocols towards established norms can be expected. Even by the second decade of the new century, however, they are some way in the future.

Bibliography

Agbiz (2019) Agbiz/IDC Agribusiness Confidence Index falls to the lowest level in 9 years. Available at: https://agbiz.co.za/economic-intelligence-1/agribusiness-confidence. Retrieved 26 February 2019.

Agcapita (2018) Farmland Basics. Available at: www.farmlandinvestmentpartnership.com/farmland-basics/. Retrieved 1 July 2018.

Agfunder (2018) Disruptive agrifood tech start-ups face industry backlash. *Agfunder*. 7 June. Available at: https://agfundernews.com/2-disruptive-agrifood-tech-startups-face-industry-backlash.html?utm_source=AgFunder+Updates&utm_campaign=4c33a0c929-June_7&utm_medium=email&utm_term=0_7b0bb00edf-4c33a0c929-98469273&mc_cid=4c33a0c929&mc_eid=8e4f6ed816. Retrieved 10 June 2018.

Agfunder (2018a) Breaking: Gates Foundation Invests in Dairy Tech Stellapps $14m Series B, First in India. Agfunder.com. 31 May. Available at: https://agfundernews.com/gates-foundation-invests-in-dairy-tech-stellapps.html. Retrieved 13 July 2018.

Agfunder (2018b) Year in Review. AgFunder AgriFood Tech. Available at: https://agfunder.com/research/agrifood-tech-investing-report-2017. Retrieved 23 February 2019.

Aigner, P., Albrecht, S., Beyschlag, G., Friederich, T., Kalepky, M. and Zagst, R. (2008) *Analyses of Success Factors for Private Equity Funds*. HVB Stiftungsinstitut für Finanzmathematik, Technische Universität München. Available at: www.risklab.com/media/aigneretal_08_-successfactorsforprivateequity.pdf. Retrieved 9 May 2018.

Allen and Linklaters (2018) Private Equity Horizons. Available at: www.allens.com.au/pubs/pdf/pe/PrivateEquityHorizons2018Feb18.pdf. Retrieved 1 July 2018.

Alston, J. (2010) *The Benefits from Agricultural Research and Development, Innovation and Productivity Growth*. OECD Food, Agriculture and Fisheries Working Papers Number 31. Paris, OECD.

ANZ (2016) *Infocus March 2016 The Grains Muster*. Canberra, ANZ. Available at: http://phx.corporate-ir.net/External.File?item=UGFyZW50SUQ9MzI2MTE2fENoaWxkSUQ9LTF8VHlwZT0z&t=1&cb=635924749635933316. Retrieved 24 February 2019.

Associated Press (2016) Saudi Arabian dairy buys 14,000 acres in California to take advantage of US water laws. 29 March. Available at: http://nationalpost.com/news/world/saudi-arabian-dairy-buys-14000-acres-in-california-to-take-advantage-of-u-s-water-laws. Retrieved 1 July 2018.

Atkin, C. (2013) Regional Perspectives: Central and Eastern Europe and the Former Soviet Union. In Kugelman, M. and Levenstein, S.L. (eds.) *The Global Farms Race: Land Grabs, Agricultural Investment, and the Scramble for Food Security*. Washington DC, Island Press, 169–180.

Australian Government (2018) Australian almond plantation acquired by London private equity firm. 9 February. Available at: www.austrade.gov.au/international/invest/investor-updates/2018/australian-almond-plantation-acquired-by-london-private-equity-firm. Retrieved 1 July 2018.

Binswanger, H.P., Deininger, K. and Feder, G. (1993) Agricultural land relations in the developing world. *American Journal of Agricultural Economics* 75(5), 1242–1248.

BizStats (2011) Valuation Rule of Thumb. Available at: www.bizstats.com/reports/valuation-rule-thumb.php. Retrieved 1 July 2018.

Bouckley, B. (2013) Oxfam tackles PepsiCo-Coke over disastrous impact of sugar land grabbing. Beverage Daily.com. 1 October. Available at: www.beveragedaily.com/Ingredients/Oxfam-tackles-PepsiCo-Coke-over-disastrous-impact-of-sugar-land-grabbing. Retrieved 1 July 2018.

Brammer, J. (2017) Canadian-based Ontario Teachers' pension plan emerges as likely buyer for avocado producer Jasper Farms near Busselton. *The West Australian*. 20 October. Available at: https://thewest.com.au/news/wa/canadian-based-ontario-teachers-pension-plan-emerges-as-likely-buyer-for-avocado-producer-jasper-farms-near-busselton-ng-b88632785z. Retrieved 1 July 2018.

Brown, G.W., Gredil, O.R. and Kaplan, S.N. (2016) Do Private Equity Funds Manipulate Reported Returns? NBER Working Paper No. 22493. August. Available at: www.nber.org/papers/w22493. Retrieved 1 July 2018.

Bruce, W. (2010) Using rule-of-thumb guidelines to estimate business value. williambruce.com [blog]. 13 August. https://williambruce.org/2010/08/13/what-is-a-business-really-worth/. Retrieved 1 July 2018.

Burwood-Taylor, L. (2018) E-mail to the author. 13 June 2018.

Business Teacher (2018) Innocent SWOT analysis. Available at: https://businessteacher.org.uk/swot/innocent.php. Retrieved 1 July 2018.

Caldwell, J. (2015) Worst Investment Out There? Farmland, Investor Says. *Successful Farming*. 23 January. Available at: www.agriculture.com/news/business/wst-investment-out-re-farml-invest-says_5-ar47162. Retrieved 1 July 2018.

CB Insights (2017) The Ag Tech Market Map: 100+ startups powering the future of farming and agri-business. Available at: www.cbinsights.com/research/agriculture-tech-market-map-company-list/. Retrieved 26 February 2019.

Committee on World Food Security (2018) Responsible Investment in Agriculture and Food Systems. Available at: www.fao.org/cfs/home/activities/rai/en/. Retrieved 1 July 2018.

Corporate Finance Institute (2018) Guide to the Discounted Cash Flow DCF Formula. Available at: https://corporatefinanceinstitute.com/resources/knowledge/valuation/dcf-formula-guide/. Retrieved 1 July 2018.

Cotula, L. and Blackmore, E. (2014) *Understanding Agricultural Investment Chains: Lessons to Improve Governance.* Rome, FAO.

Cranston, L. (2017) Strategy change: Qatar's Hassad taking next $80m Australian farm sell down. 28 August. Available at: www.farmlandgrab.org/post/view/27426-strategy-change-qatar-s-hassad-taking-next-80m-australian-farm-sell-down. Retrieved 21 July 2018.

Dasso, J., Shilling, J. and Ring, A. (1995) *Real Estate,* 12th edition. Englewood Cliffs, New Jersey, Prentice Hall.

Deloitte (2016) A guide to IFRS 16. Available at: www.iasplus.com/en/publications/global/guides/ifrs-16. Retrieved 21 July 2018.

Demaria, C. (2013) *Introduction to Private Equity Venture, Growth, LBO & Turn-Around Capital,* 2nd edition. Chichester, Wiley.

Digital Agriculture Services (2019) New Generation Rural Intelligence. Available at: https://digitalagricultureservices.com/. Retrieved 26 February 2019.

Duku-Kaakyire, A. (2003) *Evaluation of the Real Options Approach to Agribusiness Valuation: A Pork Investment Case Study*. Calgary, University of Alberta.

El-Ansary, Y. (2018) Private equity offers two bites of the cherry. *Investment Magazine*. 4 April. Available at: https://investmentmagazine.com.au/2018/04/private-equity-offers-two-bites-of-the-cherry/. Retrieved 1 July 2018.

Fan, S., Yu, B. and Saurkar, A. (2008) Public spending in developing countries: trends, determination and impact. In Fan, S. (ed.) *Public Expenditure: Growth and Policy*. Baltimore, John Hopkins Press.

FAO (2012) *Voluntary Guidelines on the Responsible Governance of Tenure of Land, Fisheries and Forests in the Context of National Food Security*. Rome, FAO. Available at: www.fao.org/docrep/016/i2801e/i2801e.pdf. Retrieved 1 July 2018.

FAO (2017) *The Future of Food and Agriculture: Trends and Challenges*. Rome, FAO. Available at: www.fao.org/3/a-i6583e.pdf. Retrieved 5 February 2018.

Forward Food (2018) The Global FoodTech Map. Available at: http://forwardfooding.com/globalfoodtechmap. Retrieved 20 July 2018.

Frese, T. (2012) Fishing for solid returns: a few keys to successful investments in aquaculture. 13 July. Available at: www.fishfarming.com/fishing-solid-returns-few-keys-successful-investments-aquaculture.html. Retrieved 1 July 2018.

Gabehart Valuation Services (2018) Business Valuation Rules of Thumb and Service Companies. Available at: http://business-valuation.biz/artrulesofthumb.asp. Retrieved 1 July 2018.

Garfield, L. (2018) Dubai is getting the world's largest vertical farm – and it will grow produce for the world's largest international airport. *Business Insider*. 6 July. Available at: www.businessinsider.com.au/dubai-emirates-airlines-world-largest-vertical-farm-2018-7?r=US&IR=T. Retrieved 9 July 2018.

Global Ag Investing (2017) Phatisa Secures $10m for Phatisa Food Fund 2. 27 November. Available at: www.globalaginvesting.com/phatisa-secures-10m-phatisa-food-fund-2/. Retrieved 1 July 2018.

Goedde, L., Horii, M. and Sanghvi, S. (2015) Pursuing the global opportunity in food and agribusiness. McKinsey. 24 July. Available at: www.mckinsey.com/industries/chemicals/our-insights/pursuing-the-global-opportunity-in-food-and-agribusiness. Retrieved 15 May 2019.

Gompers, P., Kaplan, S.N. and Mukharlyamov, V. (2016) What do private equity firms say they do? *Journal of Financial Economics* 121(3), 449–476.

Goodburn, M. (2015) What is the life expectancy of your company? 24 January. Available at: www.weforum.org/agenda/2015/01/what-is-the-life-expectancy-of-your-company/. Retrieved 1 July 2018.

Goodland, A.D. (2018) Innovative agribusinesses could drive agriculture modernization in Sri Lanka. World Bank blogs. 17 May. Available at: https://blogs.worldbank.org/endpovertyinsouthasia/innovative-agribusinesses-could-drive-agriculture-modernization-sri-lanka.

Harrison-Dunn, A. (2013) Associated British Foods responds to Oxfam land grab criticism. Food Navigator.com. 2 October. Available at: www.foodnavigator.com/Market-Trends/Associated-British-Foods-responds-to-Oxfam-land-grab-criticism. Retrieved 1 July 2018.

Heraud, J. (2018) E-mail to the author. 14 June 2018.

Jegadeesh, N., Kräussl, R. and Pollet, J. (2009) Risk and Expected Returns of Private Equity Investments: Evidence Based on Market Prices. NBER Working Paper No. 15335. September. Available at: www.nber.org/papers/w15335. Retrieved 1 July 2018.

Katchova, A.L., and Enlow, S.J. (2013) Financial performance of publicly-traded agribusinesses. *Agricultural Finance Review* 73(1), 58–73.

Kinch, S. (2018) Agriculture: A cash cow for Wi-Fi-based IoT? *Wi-Fi Now*. 2 June. https://wifinowevents.com/news-and-blog/agriculture-a-cash-cow-for-wi-fi-based-iot/. Retrieved 13 July 2018.

Koller, T., Goedhart, M. and Wessels, D. (2015) *Valuation: Measuring and Managing the Value of Companies*, 6th edition. Hoboken, Wiley.

Kowitt, B. (2014) More money for mayo: Food startup Hampton Creek raises $90 million in funding. *Fortune Magazine*. 18 December. http://fortune.com/2014/12/18/hampton-creek-funding/. Retrieved 16 May 2019.

Kugelman, M. (2012) Introduction. In Kugelman, M. and Levenstein, S.L. (eds.) *The Global Farms Race: Land Grabs, Agricultural Investment, and the Scramble for Food Security*. Washington DC, Island Press, 1–21.

Land Matrix (2018) The Online Public Database on Land Deals. Available at: http://landmatrix.org/en/. Retrieved 1 July 2018.

Luhrmann, H. and Theuvsen, L. (2016) Corporate social responsibility in agribusiness: Literature review and future research directions. *Journal of Agricultural and Environmental Ethics* 29(4), 673–696.

Macedo, M.A.S. and Nardelli, P.M. (2011) Teoria de Opções Reais e viabilidade econômico-financeira de projetos agroindustriais: o caso da opção de abandono. *Organizações Rurais & Agroindustriais* 13(1), 109–123.

Macquarie (2010) The case for investing in agriculture. Macquarie Agricultural Fund Management. Available at: www.macquarie.com/dafiles/Internet/mgl/com/agriculture/docs/white-papers/case-for-investing-in-agriculture.pdf. Retrieved 9 July 2018.

Miller, S. (2015). Private Equity Investment Criteria. Available at: www.spectrifin.co.za/Member/spectrifin/Files/Article%20Private%20Equity%20Investment%20Criteria.pdf. Retrieved 1 July 2018.

Moreno, M., Navas, J.F. and Todeschini, F. (2009) Land valuation using a real option approach. *Revista de la Real Academia de Ciencias Exactas, Fisicas y Naturales. Serie A. Matematicas* 103(2), 405–420.

Morningstar (2013) The Discounted Cashflow Method. 20 February. Available at: www.morningstar.co.uk/uk/news/65385/The-Discounted-Cash-Flow-Method.aspx. Retrieved 1 July 2018.

Nair, A.A. (2018) Binny Bansal-backed Stellapps raises $14 million from Gates Foundation, others. Yourstory.com. Available at: https://yourstory.com/2018/06/binny-bansal-backed-stellapps-raises-14-million-gates-foundation-others/. Retrieved 13 July 2018.

Nardelli, P.M. and Marcedo da Silva, M.A. (2011) Análise de um Projeto Agroindustrial Utilizando a Teoria de Opções Reais: a opção de adiamento. *Revista de Economia e Sociologia Rural* 49(4), 941–966. Available at: https://ageconsearch.umn.edu/record/154697. Retrieved 7 May 2018.

Neate, R. (2013) Coca-Cola takes full control of Innocent. *The Guardian*. 22 February. Available at: www.theguardian.com/business/2013/feb/22/coca-cola-full-control-innocent. Retrieved 1 July 2018.

O'Callaghan, T. (2012) How does private equity work in India? *Yale Insights*. 18 October. Available at: https://insights.som.yale.edu/insights/how-does-private-equity-work-in-india. Retrieved 1 July 2018.

Oxfam (2011) Land and Power: The growing scandal surrounding the new wave of investments in land. 22 September. Available at: www.oxfam.org/sites/www.oxfam.org/files/bp151-land-power-rights-acquisitions-220911-en.pdf. Retrieved 1 July 2018.

Oxfam (2016) Land Grabs. 26 September. Available at: www.oxfam.org/en/tags/land-grabs. Retrieved 1 July 2018.

Perkin, N. (2015) Is the life expectancy of companies really shrinking? Onlydeadfish.com [blog]. 1 September. Available at: www.onlydeadfish.co.uk/only_dead_fish/2015/09/is-the-life-expectancy-of-companies-really-shrinking.html. Retrieved 1 July 2018.

Pickford, J. (2016) English farmland prices hit by Brexit fears. *Financial Times*. 8 April. Available at: www.ft.com/content/62930f14-fd7a-11e5-b5f5-070dca6d0a0d. Retrieved 1 July 2018.

Pindyck, R. (2008) Lectures on Real Options. Part One – Basic Concepts. Available at: http://web. mit.edu/rpindyck/www/Courses/RO_P1_Handout%20Slides.pdf. Retrieved 1 July 2018.

Plata, L.E.A. (2006) Dinâmica de preços da terra rural no Brasil: uma análise de co-integração. In Reydon, B.P. and Cornélio, F.N.M. (eds.) *Mercados de Terras no Brasil: estrutura e dinâmica*. Brasília, NEAD, 125–154.

Preqin (2016) Natural Resources. Available at: www.preqin.com/item/natural-resources-online/17/ 12610. Retrieved 13 July 2018.

Preqin (2018) *The Preqin 2018 Sovereign Wealth Review*. New York, Preqin.

PriceWaterhouseCoopers (2006) *Business Enterprise Valuation Survey*. Johannesburg, PwC.

PriceWaterhouseCoopers (2016) Sovereign Investors 2020. A Growing Force. Available at: www.pwc. com/ee/et/publications/pub/sovereign-investors-2020.pdf. Retrieved 21 July 2018.

PriceWaterhouseCoopers (2018) Enterprise value as present value of expected future free cash flows. Available at: www.pwc-evaluation.com/en/approach. Retrieved 9 July 2018.

Purves, N., Niblock, S.J. and Sloan, K. (2015) On the relationship between financial and nonfinancial factors: a case study analysis of financial failure predictors of agribusiness firms in Australia. *Agricultural Finance Review* 75(2), 282–300. Available (in postprint) at: https://epubs.scu.edu.au/ cgi/viewcontent.cgi?referer=https://www.google.com/&httpsredir=1&article=1451&context= bus_tourism_pubs. Retrieved 10 May 2018.

RAF Learning (2017) Fund management and inclusive agribusiness: A global perspective. Available at: www.raflearning.org/post/fund-management-and-inclusive-agribusiness-global-perspective. Retrieved 15 May 2019.

Rauschenberger, R. (2014) Property Tax Valuation Concepts – Agricultural Property. March. Available at: www.nd.gov/tax/data/upfiles/media/valuationconceptsagriculturalproperty.pdf?2018 0702003739. Retrieved 1 July 2018.

responsAbility (2018) First Private Equity Investment into Agricultural Value Chains. Available at: www. responsability.com/en/first-private-equity-investment-agricultural-value-chains. Retrieved 1 July 2018.

Reuters (2011) Cargill valuation validates Wall St. rules of thumb. 20 January. Available at: http://blogs. reuters.com/breakingviews/2011/01/20/cargill-valuation-validates-wall-st-rules-of-thumb/. Retrieved 15 May 2019.

Reydon, B.P., Plata, L.E.A., Sparovek, G., Goldszmidt, R.G.B. and Telles, T.S. (2014) Determination and forecast of agricultural land prices. *Nova Economia Belo Horizonte* 24(2), 389–408.

Roche, J. (2005) *The Value of Nothing: Cashflow and Business Valuation*. London, 40 Lessons.

Roche, J. (2013) *Agribusiness Investment Valuation and Modelling*. London, Euromoney Publications.

Rural and Agricultural Finance Learning Lab (2017) The Fund Manager Perspective: Moving the Needle on Inclusive Agribusiness Investment. Available at: www.raflearning.org/sites/default/files/ may_2017_isf_briefing_15_fund_landscape_1.pdf?token=IhUEyEZk. Retrieved 19 March 2019.

Savills (2016) Market in Minutes. Global Farmland Index. Available at: http://pdf.euro.savills.co.uk/ uk/rural---other/global-farmland-index.pdf. Retrieved 1 July 2018.

Schwartz, K. (2015) Why Shrewd Investors Feel Optimistic About Agribusiness Opportunities Despite the Current Down Cycle. Available at: http://capitalroundtable.com/masterclass/CapitalRoundtab leAgribusiness2016.html. Retrieved 1 July 2018.

Shankar, S., van Raemdonck, F. and Maine, D. (2016) Can Agribusiness Reinvent Itself to Capture the Future? Bain Brief. 24 March. Available at: www.bain.com/publications/articles/can-agribusiness-reinvent-itself-to-capture-the-future.aspx. Retrieved 1 July 2018.

Sherrick, B.J. (2016) Quoted in *BDO, Global Aginvesting Conference Insights*. Available at: www. valoral.com/wp-content/uploads/2018-Global-Food-Agriculture-Investment-Outlook-Valoral-Advisors.pdf. Retrieved 29 May 2018.

Shields, G. (2018) *Business Valuation: The Ultimate Guide to Business Valuation for Beginners, Including How to Value a Business Through Financial Valuation Methods.* CreateSpace Independent Publishing Platform.

Sosa, C. (2017) A vegan mayo company was attacked in a malicious hoax – then Target kicked its products off the shelves. Alternet. 2 September. Available at: www.alternet.org/2017/09/vegan-mayo-company-was-attacked-malicious-hoax-then-target-kicked-its-products/. Retrieved 16 May 2019.

Street of Walls (2013) Private Equity Investment Criteria. Available at: www.streetofwalls.com/finance-training-courses/private-equity-training/private-equity-investment-criteria/. Retrieved 1 July 2018.

Street of Walls (2013a) Valuation Techniques Overview. Available at: www.streetofwalls.com/finance-training-courses/investment-banking-technical-training/valuation-techniques-overview/. Retrieved 1 July 2018.

Susmit, S. (2018) India Agri Business Fund II invests $10 million in Global Gourmet. Livemint.com. 26 January. Available at: www.livemint.com/Companies/dMeYe7S9UA1rsoHqYCLwMO/India-Agri-Business-Fund-II-invests-10-million-in-Global-Go.html. Retrieved 15 May 2019.

Thurston, S. (2015) The typical lifespan of a business, according to science. 8 April. Available at: www.businessadministrationinformation.com/news/the-typical-lifespan-of-a-business-according-to-science. Retrieved 1 July 2018.

Turvey, C. (2001) Mycogen as a case study in real options. *Review of Agricultural Economics* 23(1), 243–264.

USDA (2017) Farmland Value. Available at: www.ers.usda.gov/topics/farm-economy/land-use-land-value-tenure/farmland-value/. Retrieved 11 June 2018.

Wynn, K. (2018) Demystifying real options in agribusiness investment. Deloitte. Available at: www2.deloitte.com/tl/en/pages/consumer-industrial-products/articles/demystifying-real-options.html. Retrieved 1 July 2018.

Zaleski, O. (2017) Demystifying real options in agribusiness investment. Bloomberg News. 18 July. Available at: www.bloomberg.com/news/articles/2017-07-17/hampton-creek-s-entire-board-is-said-to-leave-except-for-ceo. Retrieved 16 May 2019.

13

Listed investments in agribusiness

Introduction: principles of public equity listing

Publicly-traded agribusinesses may be defined as those that trade on the open market (a stock exchange or, conceivably but less usually, an over-the-counter (OTC) market). The owners of publicly-traded companies are individual and institutional shareholders, frequently pension funds, insurance companies and other funds, and sometimes also management and original owners, who hold stocks issued by the company.

Why would any agribusiness seek a public listing? Tech company advisers often advance the following kinds of arguments as to why any business might want to do so:

> We've seen the public markets force valuable discipline on companies. There are other benefits, such as opening up a permanent and liquid source of capital that bypasses negotiations with VCs and LPs and having a currency to use for acquisitions. The Initial Public Offering (IPO) process also gives companies an unprecedented branding opportunity that allows them to broadcast their corporate narrative to investors, to potential employees and most importantly to their enterprise customers, for whom being public suggests added legitimacy and stability (Bou-Saba, 2018).

These arguments are very similar to the traditional arguments for a listing. First, that increased liquid assets will be available to the company, either to increase working capital, invest in corporate infrastructure, do more R&D, retire expensive debt or grow the business generally. Second, that a public company will enjoy greater prestige and reputation. Listing works effectively as marketing. Third, public companies may become more valuable. *Entrepreneur* (2005) reported – some time ago now – that the public companies that compose Standard & Poor's 500 were valued at about 17 times their earnings, while private companies are typically bought and sold at one to five times cash flow. That is a very significant difference, had it been maintained. These are overall averages – agribusinesses themselves may differ, as noted below. Fourth, a public company may be able to recruit higher quality staff, not least because the prudent but ambitious corporate executive may prefer the higher standards of governance at a public company. They are often larger, with more promotion prospects, and finally may also be able to use share options as a retention incentive. Finally, a public company may find it easier to go on the acquisition trail, as it can potentially use a rights issue (an issue of new shares) to fund part of the purchase cost. Whether it should or not is, of course, another matter.

All strong arguments, perhaps, but the evidence suggests that they are not *persuasive* arguments any longer for most senior management in the most developed markets of the USA and the UK. Since the 1990s, the number of US IPOs has plummeted – now around a quarter of the figure at that time, with fewer than half the number of US public companies in the late 2010s than two decades before. Similarly, in the UK, in August 2000, the total market capitalisation of the LSE's main market was £5.3 trillion. In 2017 it was 26% lower than that, at £3.9 trillion – in real terms the fall would be even starker. Why? Although publicly traded companies have greater access to financing because they can issue more shares to a wider range of investors, the attractions of private equity are often sufficient to outweigh this issue of range. Moreover, public companies are also subject to more regulation in terms of filing requirements and corporate taxes. Fewer US and UK companies now perceive the advantages as decisive, when compared to the tighter governance standards of the 2002 Sarbanes-Oxley Act brought in after the Enron scandal, laws such as those aimed at curbing bribery of foreign officials, and the 'blood diamonds' section of the 2010 Dodd-Frank Act, let alone activist investors following the rise in interest in corporate governance since the 1990s. Listing is also expensive: an IPO can cost a significant chunk of the company's equity – no less than 25% and perhaps a great deal more – and fees and expenses can climb to as much as 25% of the deal. It is also resource-intensive and time-consuming, involves a great deal of public disclosure, and is not guaranteed to succeed. There are anyway more competitive jurisdictions in which to list with competitive advantages over the traditional exchanges of the USA and UK, even than their secondary, less regulated markets. Perhaps even more important eventually, digital technology is driving down the cost of transactions; the blockchain may even accelerate this trend. Lean business models reduce capital requirements (Davis, 2016). Finally, more recent evidence is that public companies no longer enjoy substantial valuation premiums – in 2017, investors paid on average 12.5 times multiples for private companies compared with 9.5 times multiples a year earlier. This compares with 16.8 times multiples paid for public companies in 2016 versus 19.5 times multiples a year earlier (Hammoud et al., 2018).

Elsewhere in the world, however, the message has not yet sunk home. The residual status attraction of going public, less stark distinctions in relative costs – in Nigeria, extraordinarily, public equity is cheaper than bank debt – less availability of significant private equity, fewer onerous regulations and government encouragement of stock markets and exchanges in countries such as Hong Kong, China, Singapore, Malaysia and Russia, have all served to see quite the reverse trend. For example, US$18 billion was listed on the Shanghai and Shenzhen stock exchanges in the first half of 2017, so they became the second and third most valuable IPO markets in the world (behind the New York Stock Exchange). For the time being, at least, public equity markets overall are still growing. Global market capitalisation rose from around $30 trillion in 2004 through $80 trillion in 2017 and still seems to have a way to go, in a prolonged bull run of share prices that has lasted since the global financial crisis of 2007–09.

Listed agribusiness entities worldwide

In this expanding universe of publicly traded companies, how much space has there been for agribusinesses? There is no doubt that agribusinesses are providing an ever-growing pool of investment opportunities worldwide. At present, over 440 funds are operating in the food and agriculture sector, against 38 in 2005, with more planned. As of 2017, these funds managed around $73 billion in assets. The sector has attracted private and institutional investors – pension funds, endowments, family offices and particular investment structures such as Luxembourg specialised investment funds, are steadily increasing allocations to this sector. Agribusiness is also, quite logically given the importance of agriculture in developing countries, becoming an important sector for social impact-related investments (Vitón, 2018), as is already the case for unlisted agribusiness investments. Already, two-thirds of impact investors said they were putting their dollars into food and agriculture, and impact investment in the sector grew at over 30% per annum in the 2010s (GIIN, 2017), although finding suitable companies in which to invest for impact investment, however, is even more difficult than agribusiness investment overall.

Investing in equity funds or individual stocks of listed agribusinesses is clearly the logical way to gain access to the sector whilst retaining liquidity. Mention should also be made of exchange-traded funds (ETFs) that invest in agribusiness, especially in the USA which is still the only market really large enough to make sense for them and there are fewer than a dozen of them even in the USA (ETFdb, 2018). The advisory firm Valoral Advisers tracked as of 2018 38 funds and ETFs with a total AuM of around $4.6 billion. Of these, ten were ETFs, AuM of $1.5 billion, or a third of the assets tracked in listed equities (Vitón, 2018). Funds include Deutsche Bank's DWS Global Agribusiness Fund and 3F Asset Management's Food and Fibre Fund.

Public equities are part of a range of potential agribusiness investments.

Of these, 'The most direct and pure exposure is achieved through investing in real agricultural assets and gaining exposure to farming operations and the underlying land. Listed equities have the advantage of providing liquidity, but [they] are more highly correlated to equity markets' (Macquarie, 2010:1). Macquarie also argued that agricultural assets provided an inflationary hedge, on the grounds that food and related items form a significant proportion of the consumer price index, a quarter in Europe and 15% even in the USA – more elsewhere. The price inelasticity of demand for wheat, for example, is a factor driving this hedging capability. However, public equities do not, as yet, provide much access to agricultural assets overall. This is because the number of agribusiness companies is limited, with the universe still being less than 2% of the MSCI World Index. As with REITs, too, high correlation with overall equity performance means that buying public equities inevitably means exposure to broader equity trends.

Third, for a range of reasons, listed equities in the sector have had a very mixed performance in the decade,

reflecting the broader issues that arise from lower farm income and lower trading and processing margins across many producing regions, including [that] food-and-agribusiness companies on average have demonstrated higher total returns to shareholders (TRS) than

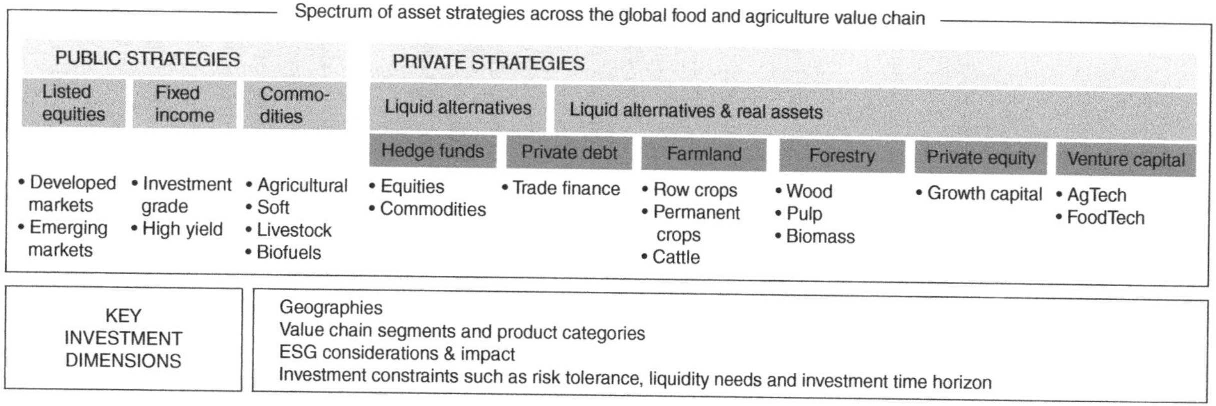

Figure 13.1 The spectrum of opportunities in the global food and agriculture class

Source: Vitón (2018:13)

Metric	Range	Average
Fund Life (Years)	4-21	11
Investment Period (Years)	2-10	5
Management Fee of Committed Funds (%)	0.5-2.5	1.7
Carry to GP (%)	0-20	12.4
Preferred Return (%)	0-8.5	5.3

Figure 13.2 Listed agribusiness performance snapshot
Source: Albert Partners (2017)

many other sectors: the TRS of more than 100 publicly traded food-and-agribusiness companies around the world increased on average by 17% annually between 2004 and 2013, compared with 13% for energy and 10% for information technology companies (Goedde *et al.*, 2015).

In terms of fund performance, at the 2017 AgInvest conference in the USA scarcely stellar performance data were presented (see Figure 13.2).

For a list of the top 100 (Ranker, 2018). M&A, changes in currencies, and alterations in corporate performance can affect these lists annually, especially at the bottom end. For US data, see InvestSnips (2018). For Africa, Harding (2011). One of the best websites for critical analysis of quoted companies is the Motley Fool. Tyler Crowe (2018) produced a list of companies that are pure-play investments in agriculture, are listed on the US exchanges and have market capitalisations greater than $300 million.

Tyler Crowe divided the list of companies above into two neat categories: input providers and food producers and processors. A comparable measure of earnings is earnings before interest tax, depreciation and amortization (EBITDA), which enables companies' operating performance to be compared independently of financing decisions, accounting decisions or tax environments.

He suggested that agricultural inputs such as seeds and fertilisers, and agricultural chemicals such as herbicide and pesticide, are incredibly valuable products for the industry. Combined, they all help to improve crop yields, which continue to be a critical challenge for the industry. But he rightly pointed out that the market for these products acts very much like other critical commodities, like oil or minerals, that tend to move in a cyclical nature because of changes to the supply-and-demand dynamic. On the other hand, companies like Monsanto and Syngenta have patent protection on several of their seeds and agricultural chemicals, which give them some modicum of pricing power compared to more basic products like potash or nitrogen fertiliser. Or in the case of Scotts Miracle-Gro, a company can cater more to smaller retail customers and leverage other advantages, such as brand recognition. Selling to customers directly through retail networks was one of the driving factors behind the merger of Potash Corp of Saskatchewan and Agrium into Nutrien.

For an alternative view of these questions – equally interesting – see Jones (2017, 2017a).

There are other listed agribusinesses outside the USA, of course, notably in Australia, Brazil, Russia and the EU, but increasingly everywhere. In Australia, for example, Graincorp (www.graincorp.com.au) was a A$2-billion grains company, listed since 1998, focused on

Company	Market Capitalization	Products	Return on Equity (Five-Year Median)	Dividend Yield
CF Industries	$9.8 billion	Fertilizer	21.9%	2.85%
Monsanto (NYSE:MON)	$53.6 billion	Seeds, agricultural chemicals	23.5%	1.77%
Mosaic	$9.7 billion	Fertilizer	9.4%	2.17%
Nutrien	$18 billion	Fertilizer	N/A*	1.86%
The Scotts Miracle-Gro Company (NYSE:SMG)	$6.1 billion	Seeds, fertilizers, agricultural chemicals	27.6%	1.92%
Syngenta AG	$43 billion	Seeds, agricultural chemicals	16.7%	1.09%
Terra Nitrogen Company (NYSE:TNH)	$1.54 billion	Fertilizer	90.9%	6.16%
Green Plains	$749 million	Ethanol, livestock feed, distiller grains, food ingredients	6.2%	2.64%
Archer Daniels Midland	$24.1 billion	Ethanol, livestock feed, supplements food ingredients	8.1%	2.97%
Calavo Growers	$1.5 billion	Fresh, packaged, and processed vegetables	14.5%	1.09%
Fresh Del Monte Produce		Fresh, packaged, and processed fruits and vegetables	7.1%	1.26%
Tyson Foods	$29 billion	Beef, pork, poultry	14.2%	1.14%
Dean Foods	$969 million	Dairy products	18.7%	3.38%
Sanderson Farms	$2.9 billion	Poultry	21.8%	0.86%
Cal-Maine Foods (NASDAQ:CALM)	$2.1 billion	Eggs	17.5%	0%
Pilgrim's Pride (NASDAQ:PPC)	$7.3 billion	Poultry	42.1%	0%

Tyler Crowe divided the list of companies above into two neat categories: input providers and food producers and processors. A comparable measure of earnings is Earnings Before Interest Tax, Depreciation and Amortisation, or EBITDA, which enables companies' operating performance to be compared independently of financing decisions, accounting decisions or tax environments.

Figure 13.3 US publicly quoted agribusinesses
Source: Crowe (2018)

[b]

Company	EBITDA Margin	Return on Capital Invested (Five-Year Median)	Financial Debt to EBITDA
CF Industries	18.2%	10%	8.1
Monsanto	28.8%	15.7%	2.1
Mosaic	16.2%	7.4%	3.5
Nutrien	29.3%	N/A	3.5
Scotts Miracle-Gro	17.8%	10.1%	3.4
Syngenta	11%	11.3%	3.9
Terra Nitrogen Company	48%	113.4%	0.1

Crowe suggested that agricultural inputs such as seeds and fertilizers, and agricultural chemicals such as herbicide and pesticide, are incredibly valuable products for the industry. Combined, they all help to improve crop yields, which continue to be a critical challenge for the industry. But he rightly pointed out that the market for these products acts very much like other critical commodities, like oil or minerals, that tend to move in a cyclical nature because of changes to the supply-and-demand dynamic. On the other hand, companies like Monsanto and Syngenta have patent protection on several of their seeds and agricultural chemicals, which give them some modicum of pricing power compared to more basic products like potash or nitrogen fertilizer. Or in the case of Scotts Miracle-Gro, a company can cater more to smaller retail customers and leverage other advantages, such as brand recognition. Selling to customers directly through retail networks was one of the driving factors behind the merger of Potash Corp of Saskatchewan and Agrium into Nutrien.
For an alternative view of these questions –equally interesting (Jones, 2017; 2017a).

Figure 13.3 Continued

storage and logistics, marketing and processing. It was the subject of an intense but eventually unsuccessful takeover bid, eventually blocked by the government, which then led to a drop in the share price from which it struggled to recover. Earnings were highly cyclical, less so after diversification into other areas such as malt and oil. The company said of itself that it was

> …the largest integrated edible oils business in Australia and New Zealand, producing a wide range of quality food and animal feed products including specialist ingredients for infant nutrition. We have also invested $125 million to create a state-of-the-art processing hub in Victoria for refining and distributing oilseed products. Ongoing innovation and investment ensures we are creating new opportunities for growers and customers in Australia and around the world. In a joint venture with the Zen-Noh Grain Corporation

[c]
Food producers and processors

Company	EBITDA Margin	Return on Invested Capital (Five-Year Median)	Financial Debt to EBITDA
Green Plains	5.8%	2.9%	5.3
Archer Daniels Midland	4.8%	5.8%	2.4
Calavos Growers	6.2%	11.5%	0.7
Fresh Del Monte Produce	5.6%	6.4%	1.0
Tyson Foods	9.6%	9.1%	2.2
Dean Foods	3.8%	6.1%	3.0
Sanderson Farms	15.7%	18.4%	0.01
Cal-Maine Foods	(3.2%)	15.6%	N/A
Pilgrim's Pride	15.6%	24.3%	1.3

Figure 13.3 Continued

of Japan, we are developing a game-changing supply chain model in Western Canada that builds on global demand for quality grain and oilseed products. Closer to home, GrainCorp continues to set the pace for the Australian grains industry with innovative technology and marketing initiatives connecting Australian growers and customers to a world of opportunity (Grain Corp, 2018).

A second example from Australia: the Costa Group (not to be confused with Costa coffee). Costa Group (www.costagroup.com.au) listed in 2016, and in two years more than doubled its market capitalisation to nearly A$1.5 billion. Costa Group is involved in produce, logistics and farming. Results are dependent on factors such as berry volumes and tomato pricing.

Two more Australian examples. The A2 milk company (www.theA2milkcompany. com): its milk and related dairy products contained a strain of protein known as A2 instead of a combination of A1 and A2. Its sales were mainly in high-price quality-conscious markets – Australia, New Zealand and the UK – but it was also seeking to make more infant formula sales to China. And Treasury Wine Estates (www.tweglobal.com) which held a portfolio of well-known Australian brands such as Penfolds, Lindemans, Wolf Blass and Rosemount Estate. They sold to more than 70 countries around the world, including the USA and China.

Designing and maintaining an investment strategy that included Grain Corp would therefore involve, *inter alia*, an understanding of grain and the animal feed market, oilseeds, the capital position of Zen-Noh and the Canadian market. Analysts worried whether the company could continue that rate of growth, and also about its Chinese joint venture, the Chinese market always carrying plenty of risks. As to Costa, there were questions regarding its leasing arrangement with farms privately owned by the Costa family, and the rapid growth of its avocado business, combined with exiting such areas as stone fruits and potatoes. The memory of Timbercorp, another Australian company that grew very rapidly, diversified into many areas (including avocados), took on heavy debts, and became a huge bankruptcy might weigh on investors' minds. Timbercorp, however, was a managed investment scheme company, very dependent on a particular tax structure, which has since been abolished (ATO, 2018). Whether all stockbrokers or fund managers actually perform the necessary due diligence on these companies seems doubtful, but investors would certainly benefit by consulting analysts who do the detailed analysis really required.

An example of an agribusiness IPO

Bojun Agriculture Holdings is based in Jiangxi province in China, producing vinegar beverages and a variety of fruit-based snack foods for Chinese consumption from Nanfeng mandarins. In December 2017, the company listed on the Australian Securities Exchange. Shares rose modestly after listing to raise A$7.6 million. Bojun Agriculture had proposed issuing from 24 million to 40 million shares to raise from A$7.2 million to A$12 million through the IPO. Another 96 million shares had previously been issued to Chinese investors, including the company's founder Bo Zhu. At the time of the listing, Bojun Agriculture was capitalised at A$38.2 million. The Australian chairman of the company observed: 'Bojun Agriculture's listing on the ASX will enable the company's collaboration and research with Australian agricultural entities and allow us to source Australian agriculture products for distribution in China and to provide capital to continue to invest in the development of new products to expand distribution.'

Source: Hemphill (2017)

Agribusiness investment strategies

In 2019, the agribusiness IPO story refocused to lab-grown (clean) meat. Along with Hampton Creek (now JUST), the other three original US clean (or cultured) meat companies were Beyond Meat, Impossible Foods and Modern Meadows. 'You will have to have been living under a rock not to have seen Beyond Meat's blockbuster IPO and stock market listing…that's pushed the company's valuation beyond $3 billion. Impossible Foods will no doubt follow suit soon. To say the industry is having a moment is an understatement' (Leclerc, 2019). The charge continues: in 2019 Motif Ingredients, a spin-off of Ginkgo Bioworks, a major player in synthetic biology, raised $90 million in funding, the largest Series A round ever for a food technology company. This made Motif the largest company focused on cellular agriculture, at least for a while. Research has now indicated growing acceptance of the new technology. According to even the pessimistic analysis of YouGov (2018), 26% of Chinese consumers said they would eat clean meat, which was amongst the lowest rate of acceptance compared to other countries in Asia. This series of surveys yielded evidence of substantial differences between countries. For example, 34% of Thai consumers said they would eat clean meat and 52% of Vietnamese consumers said they would eat clean meat. Further academic analysis for India suggested that investment strategies are perhaps predictably almost as numerous as the funds themselves, and may frequently stretch across listed and unlisted investments, depending on the mandate of the fund. For example, lower commodity prices and resultant lower farm income has increased the comparative potential attractiveness of wholesale, food processing and other downstream investments. In the 2010s, funds also targeted fertiliser companies and agribusiness supply chain managers, with arguments such as 'The market is underestimating the value of companies that can ship surplus wheat from North America to Europe or elsewhere. These are difficult assets to replicate' (Featherstone, 2015). There may be short-term factors, such as good growing conditions worldwide, that create value for international exporters and importers.

Geographically, Brazil has long been a destination of choice for agribusiness investors, but now South America as a whole is gradually turning to a more market-friendly political and economic environment which seems quite likely to offer the regional food and agriculture sector an opportunity to become an ever more important supplier of food to the world and a source of sustainable development for the region (Vitón, 2018:2). Combining geography with sector, protein producers in emerging markets are another preferred theme, especially when a devaluation of local currency, as in Brazil, increases the competitiveness of the local agribusiness sector further. Minerva Foods, listed on the São Paulo Stock Exchange, has been cited as an example (Carrera *et al.*, 2017).

Australia is another favourite potential destination for investors, with big local listed companies such as Elders and Nufarm providing liquidity as well as opportunities generated by restructuring and local demand, whilst other listed stocks such as Incitec provide growth plays. As yet, there are only a handful even of Australian funds that specialise in global agribusiness. The Colonial First State Global Soft Commodity Share Fund is one example, and the Ironbark GTP Global Equity Agribusiness Fund, managed by Global Thematic Partners, is another. There are also a few ASX-quoted exchange-traded funds (ETFs) that provide exposure to soft commodities. For example, the BetaShares Agriculture ETF and ANZ ETF Securities gives access to a basket of commodities, specifically corn, grains and wheat. BetaShares' Agriculture ETF offered leverage to soybeans, corn, wheat and sugar, and was claimed to be hedged against currency movements. Actually, this was technically a synthetic ETF: it employed derivative instruments to provide access to those commodities, because physical storage is not possible. The managers argued that the main benefit of an agriculture ETF were portfolio diversification and an offset against rising inflation.

Finally, mention should be made of real estate investment trusts (REITs) that specialise in investment in farmland. Hence, for example, the Rural Funds Group, Australia's first listed agricultural property trust, owned poultry farms, almond orchards and viticulture. It bought farms and leases them, and its manager, Rural Funds Management, is one of Australia's oldest agricultural investors. However, unlike many Australian REITs in this market, Rural Funds Group tended to trade at a discount to its net asset value (NAV). In the USA, Gladstone Land Corp., one of the first publicly-traded farmland REITs – which act as property owners and managers — was launched in January 2013. REITs are a great success: they are highly liquid since they are tax free, trade as a share so can be bought and sold quickly, and so can provide a way for retail investors to get into land ownership. Gladstone acquired 1,800 acres in three US states, where berries and ground crops such as lettuce were grown. The REIT investment universe, along with all other public equity opportunities, is constantly changing, in part through M&A. For example, in February 2017, Farmland Partners merged with the American Farmland Company, which created the largest and most diverse public farmland REIT with 144,000 acres across 16 US states. It seems very likely indeed that as the sector and the investment strategies evolve, there will be further consolidation, not just in developed but also in developing markets.

Valuation in public markets

Obviously, information on traded values is in principle much more readily available in public markets than for private equity. The problem is that there are, at least as yet, few national markets where there are sufficient numbers of traded agribusinesses to provide a reliable basis for comparison with the market as a whole. Compounding this problem is the very diversity of agribusinesses themselves, which had meant that different analysts divide up the sector in different, incompatible ways.

There are, further, some pitfalls. For example, frequent changes in DCF assumptions result in stockbrokers altering target prices: here is an example from Align Research covering the African agribusiness, Obtala Limited, which is an Africa focused forestry and agriculture company with a goal of becoming one of sub-Saharan Africa's largest sustainable food and timber producers.

Forecasts updated following Q4 statement and talks with management. At the top line, for 2017 we have pared back our forecasts for the agriculture division due to the slower than expected year, which was affected by prolonged rains. We also modestly reduce forecasts in the forestry production and trading businesses. The overall effect is to reduce group revenue forecasts for 2017 from $10.2 million to $9.4 million. Due to higher costs we now expect an underlying pre-tax loss (excluding the gain made on the purchase of Woodbois) of $5.8 million, up from $0.3 million. For 2018 we also pare back our revenue forecasts across the divisions and look for $41 million at the group level, down from $45.9 million. Higher costs and investments take pre-tax profits down from $20.8 million previously to $7.1 million. We also update our model for the recent strengthening of sterling against the US dollar. Our forecasts for 2019 and beyond, used in the DCF analysis, are unchanged.

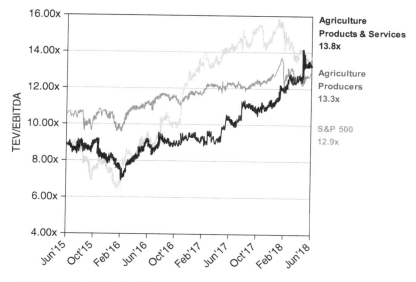

Note: The indices in the chart above are composed using the public companies included on the following two pages.

Source: Capital IQ

Figure 13.4 Public market valuations: EV/EBITDA
Source: Moss Adams (2018)

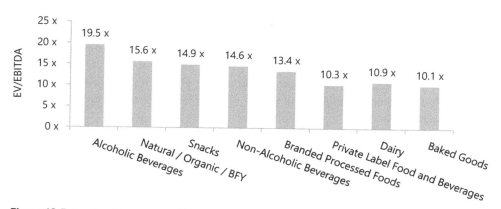

Figure 13.5 Food and beverage public company average EBITDA multiples by segment
Source: Capstone Headwaters Partners (2018)

Despite the revision our target price only falls from 38.18p to 38.09p. This is due to the lower forecast profits and negative exchange rate movements being offset by removing the loss making 2017 numbers from the DCF analysis and by adding additional funds received from preference share issues in H2 2017 (Align Research, 2018).

Compare this to the following internally generated presentation, which presents the company's own view of its prospects. Notice how much more difficult it is to devise an accurate DCF model from outside the company than from within, and how much more influenced it will be by such issues as M&A, valuation changes in assets, alterations in business plans and trading conditions.

Dividend valuation. Agribusinesses are often fairly stable, generating reliable dividends. In that way some, at least, can be considered in the same way as bonds and valued using their projected future dividend stream and a market-based cost of capital.

Combining methods. When combining methods and recognising risk, the best way to approach valuation is as a range that changes over time, as shown in Figure 13.6.

Analysis of agribusiness transactions: global evidence of comparables. 'Good agribusiness valuers like Knight Frank, CBRE, Colliers or their competitors, as well as specialised agents with national expertise, are intuitive regression experts, balancing different advantages and disadvantages against one another to produce an eventual number that meets our initial criterion – it turns in a number that reflects what potential purchasers will actually pay' (Roche, 2018). There are also private databases, often only available on subscription (e.g. for the UK, www.caav.org.uk).

There are some academic analyses, which are worth examining. For example, Goh *et al.* (2015) used the 'Plantation Index' of the Malaysian Stock Exchange as the basis for identifying agribusiness firms. They reported 41 firms and used 2003–09 data. They took equity prices from the Bursa Station database, and financial and outstanding shares data from annual reports. They found that the agribusiness industry typically employs homogenous business models and produces standardised products, thus rendering excellent empirical settings to reveal the value drivers of such traditional industries. It was discovered that commonly adopted methodologies in valuation multiples are associated with pitfalls which may hamper the reliability of the valuations. Their findings also showed that price-to-earnings multiples led to the best valuation performance, while price-to-sales multiples produced the worst results. Moreover, this research showed that growth prospects are an effective control factor in multiples valuation. I suspect that using public company data is always likely to produce this kind of result. Small private companies with doubtful earnings data may be a different story.

Business valuation software: application to agribusiness

It should be noted that in many jurisdictions, but notably the USA, there are specialist valuers, including for agribusiness (Capital Valuation Group, 2018). Although the majority of valuations are still carried out using Excel, business valuations, and in particular DCF, lends themselves to bespoke software. For example,

Business Valuer software works by simply taking the key financial information from your business accounts and uses one or all of the widely accepted business valuation methods to calculate a guide price value for your business. The software also has several in-built industry specific valuation methods as well, so if your business is in one of these industries then an additional valuation can be produced. The business accounts can be

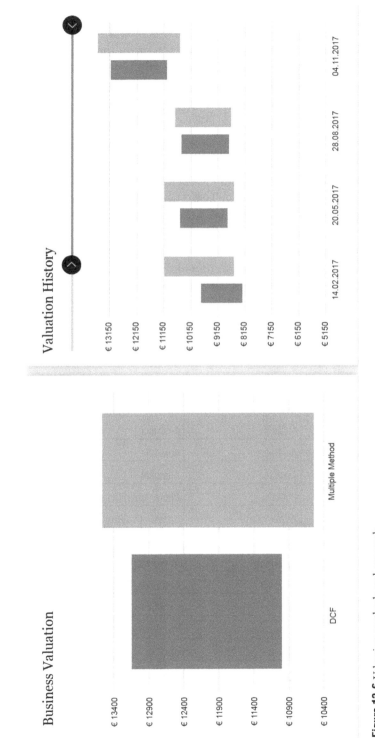

Figure 13.6 Valuation methods and approach
Source: PwC (2019)

statutory accounts, management accounts, forecasts, or a mixture of them all. And, for those people that are novices to business valuations, there is comprehensive in-built help to keep you on track... The objective of entering in all the information on all of the data input screens is to calculate the sustainable or maintainable profits of the business in order to provide as reliable and fair a guide price valuation as possible (Business Valuer, 2018).

Why do land prices matter so much to investors?

Because land is such an important part of most production agribusinesses, is the simple answer. The result is, major investors hold vast tracts of land. There are only so many countries where this is possible, thanks to a combination of land shortages and restrictive land ownership laws.

Sheer size is not the only issue by far. Not all soil is equally productive and different soils fit different crops. If land costs were undifferentiated, a commercial land investor would seek to acquire what the USDA categorises as mollisol areas (that is, areas with naturally nutrient-rich surface soils that run deep with organic matter, e.g. in the pampas in Latin America, or the Russian steppes). But where market forces price land, the lower

Table 13.1 Agroholdings with largest land banks

Name	Origin	Countries of production	Land bank
S. Kidman & Co.	Australia	Australia	10.1 mill. ha
Australian Agricultural Co.	Australia	Australia	7.0 mill. ha
North Australian Pastoral	Australia	Australia	5.8 mill. ha
Consolidated Pastoral Co.	Australia	Australia	5.7 mill. ha
Beidahuang Group	China	China, Argentina...	5.4 mill. ha
Ivolga Holding	Kazakhstan	Kazakhstan, Russia	1.5 mill. ha
KazExportAstyk	Kazakhstan	Kazakhstan	1 mill. ha
El Tejar	Argentina	Argentina, Brazil...	1 mill. ha
Cresud	Argentina	Argentina, Brazil...	1 mill. ha
NCH Capital	USA	Ukraine...	820 tsd. ha
Agrocenter Astana	Kazakhstan	Kazakhstan	700 tsd. ha
UkrLandFarming	Ukraine	Ukraine	670 tsd. ha
Kernel Group	Ukraine	Ukraine	420 tsd. ha
MHP	Ukraine	Ukraine	360 tsd. ha
Razguliay Group	Russia	Russia	350 tsd. ha

Source: Balmann *et al.* (2015:6)

nutrient levels required are already priced in. Investors often seek agronomic areas where there is natural contribution to nitrogen binding, e.g. soybean production. Soil is only one part of the package investors seek – water is equally important. With some experts, at least, projecting that half the world will live in areas of acute water shortage as soon as 2030 (UNESCO, 2015) investors want a guaranteed supply. Finally, investors seek relatively competitive livestock production areas, such as CAFOs in South America, the USA, Europe and even China. Environmental and animal rights activists are not keen (Steier & Patel, 2017).

Public agribusiness investment funds and their performance

There are few such funds, and their performance to date has been underwhelming. The largest, DWS, has succeeded in *losing* money over a five-year period. Of their own socially sustainable fund, RobecoSAM, the promoter says:

> The aim of the fund is to provide long term capital growth by taking exposure of at least two thirds of its total assets to equities of companies all over the world which operate within the agricultural industry or profit from developments within the agricultural industry, which includes companies that operate in mature economies (developed markets) as well as companies that operate in developing economies (emerging markets) and which show an elevated degree of sustainability. Sustainability means striving to achieve economic success, while at the same time considering ecological and social objectives (Morningstar, 2018).

Social responsibility is a double-edged sword so far as fund investment in agribusiness is concerned. It may increase demand, but it drastically reduces the potential supply of firms in which to invest, unless the term is taken so generously that it is denuded of virtually all meaning.

Comparison with other sectors

Less than a decade ago, it was reasonably contended that publicly-traded agribusinesses have not received much attention in the literature even though substantial indicators point to their economic strength as a market sector (Katchova & Enlow, 2013:5). To make comparisons it was necessary for academics to get involved and create sub-sectors themselves. They found that agribusinesses outperformed the market significantly, as measured by financial ratios and as determined, they argued, by higher operating efficiency than the market average.

It is a convincing argument, and no doubt correct as it was based on empirical data. As such it represents a good basis for analysing the performance of publicly-traded agribusinesses, but it has the following drawbacks for practical purposes.

■ *It is dated.* The reduction in commodity prices observed subsequently will undoubtedly have had a negative impact on the relative performance of agribusinesses compared to markets as a whole.

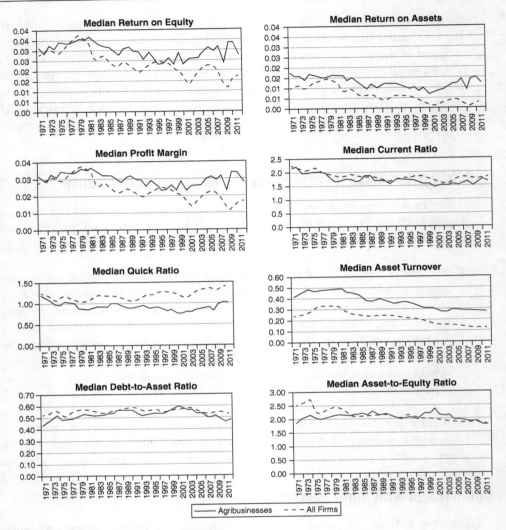

Figure 13.7 Comparing agribusiness with other sectors
Source: Katchova & Enlow (2013: 25–26).

■ *It is US-based.* As usual, data are better available for the USA than elsewhere, both generally and in terms of the number of agribusinesses listed on stock exchanges. What may have been true of the USA need not necessarily be true of other markets.

It remains the case that the standard categorisations of equities do not identify agribusiness separately. Fidelity, for example, do not identify 'technology' separately either, although both energy and real estate get separate categories (Fidelity, 2018). The very diversity of agribusiness – its great strength as a repository of knowledge and investment opportunity – militates against it.

The difficulty of developing an adequate public equity agribusiness investment strategy is illustrated by the risk/opportunity matrix presented by McKinsey in 2015 (Goedde *et al.*, 2015).

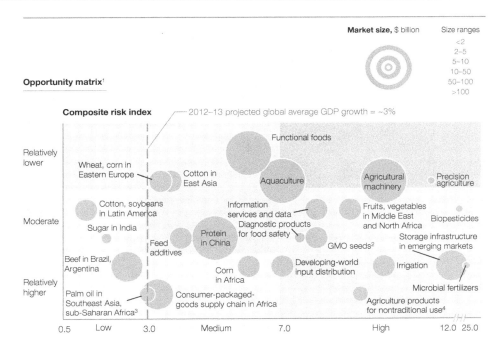

Figure 13.8 Risk/opportunity matrix of agribusiness investment
Source: Goedde *et al.* (2015)

Corporate social responsibility (CSR), impact investment and agribusiness

There is wide recognition that meeting the UN's 2030 sustainable development goals (SDGs) will require a smart blend of public and private sources of capital. The Business and Sustainable Development Commission estimates that business opportunities for the SDGs in food and agriculture have the potential to reach $2.3 trillion annually by 2030, generating up to a seven-fold return on investment. Personally, I doubt investment will reach anywhere near that level, but even if it reached a tenth of that amount, it would shift the balance of equity investment fundamentally, and quite possibly for all intents and purposes irreversibly, in favour of agribusiness (and related technologies).

The current state of corporate social responsibility (CSR) in agribusiness was reviewed by Luhrmann & Theuvsen (2016). There are, perhaps in part as a result of CSR, a number of voluntary guidelines for agribusiness investment.

- In 2010, the World Bank, the Food and Agriculture Organisation (FAO) and the United Nations Conference on Trade and Development (UNCTAD) sponsored the Principles for Responsible Agricultural Investment (PRAI) (UNCTAD, 2018).
- In 2011, a number of investment funds associated with the UN Principles for Responsible Investment (PRI) unveiled the Principles for Responsible Investment in Farmland (UNPRI, 2015).

Figure 13.9 The United Nations' 17 sustainable development goals and their linkages to the F&A sector
Source: FAO (2015)

- The Voluntary Guidelines on the Responsible Governance of Tenure of Land, Fisheries and Forests in the Context of National Food Security were adopted by the FAO in 2012 (FAO, 2012a).

- In 2014, the CFS adopted the Principles for Responsible Investment in Agriculture and Food Systems (PRIAFS) (FAO, 2018).

- In 2015, member countries of United Nations adopted a set of 17 Sustainable Development Goals (SDGs) to end poverty, protect the planet and ensure prosperity for all as part of a new sustainable development agenda. No industry is as relevant to the successful implementation of the SDGs as agriculture: almost every single SDG has some linkage to agriculture. The development of sustainable agricultural practices, the efficient use of water, the protection of biodiversity, the development of rural areas, the reduction of food loss and food waste are among key challenges and opportunities achieving this agenda, as illustrated in Figure 13.9.

All of these guidelines are not without criticism:

> …voluntary responsible investment initiatives for agriculture are likely to face similar weaknesses to those experienced in responsible investment initiatives more generally. These include vague and difficult to enforce guidelines, low participation rates, an uneven business case, and confusion arising from multiple and competing initiatives. In addition, the large diversity of investors and high degree of complexity of financial investments further complicate efforts to discern who bears the burden of responsibility in practice (Clapp, 2017:223).

The global climate agreement that came out of the COP21 meeting held in Paris in late 2015 perfectly illustrates the scale of the climate change challenge. According to its conclusions, the decarbonisation of the world economy, essential to keep global warming to below the fateful 2°C, would require considerable investment.

Issues of concern with listed agribusiness investment

Firstly, relevant to both local and international investors alike, is the important distinction between investing in commodities and in agribusiness. Soft commodities historically have a lower relationship to other asset classes, such as equities and bonds. As such, fund managers argue, introducing soft commodities to a portfolio can potentially improve its risk-adjusted return. Also, they suggest, it can operate as an inflation hedge (PIMCO, 2018). One adviser suggested that investors who want better portfolio risk diversification should allocate 5–10% a portfolio to agricultural and minerals commodities.

> Australian investors, generally, have very low or no exposure to soft commodities, despite a large, growing middle class in China, and later in India, needing more food. Investors tend to group all commodities together, but soft commodities dance to a different tune compared to bulk or base metals or energy prices (Featherstone, 2015).

Yes, perhaps so – but this is an argument for direct exposure to commodities, not necessarily an argument for investment in agribusinesses, which, it must be clearly understood, are a different sector with a range of risks and opportunities, of which commodity risk is only one.

Second, for international investors in both countries, the conundrum of local, including currency, risk versus increased local competitiveness may act as a disincentive to investment. The potential weakness of this kind of strategy is dependence on the performance of the local stock market *overall*. Hence, for example, when investors decided that risks in the Brazilian economy had been underestimated, the currency depreciation of the real actually worked *against* sentiment (Burgess, 2018). On the other hand, BetaShares Agriculture ETF as a currency-hedged ETF did not benefit from the Australian dollar's fall.

Third, compounding this problem, there is an imbalance between the growth of agribusiness in regions such as Latin America, the countries of the former Soviet Union and Asia-Pac, and the necessities of listed agribusiness investment which ties investors to North America, home to most of the constituents of different equity indices and related funds and ETFs (Vitón, 2018:14). Much the same problem has been seen for several decades with the REIT market, including for farmland – only by the end of the 2010s did significant liquid investment opportunities start to emerge elsewhere.

Fourth, what we also know is that stock picking is essential for successful agribusiness investment. In the years 2004–14, according to Bain & Company analysis, the top five companies in each of four segments (crop inputs, crops, animal products, and trading and logistics) achieved average total shareholder returns (TSR) that ranged from 7% to 42%. However, this is an industry with a huge variation in returns. Their research showed that the best performer among the largest crop companies enjoyed a TSR of 53%, and the worst performer, negative 34%. A similar pattern played out in the animal products segment: The best performer saw TSR of 67% while the worst delivered negative 29% (Shankar *et al.*, 2016). Evidently, access to the sector overall is no guarantee of success: what is needed is detailed due diligence, exactly as with private equity or venture capital investment.

Fifth, the difficulty of diversification owing to the small number of agribusiness companies available in many markets. Difficulties with stock picking usually give rise to passive investment strategies, with no attempt to stock-pick or even decide on a sub-sector. One option would therefore be to use an index. The S&P Commodity Producers Agribusiness Index includes the main publicly traded companies in the global agribusiness sector, subject to specific requirements for investors. The other principal index is the DAX Global Agribusiness index, which aims to replicate the performance of the globally most important listed agribusiness companies, ranging across agriproduct operations, livestock operations, agrichemicals, agricultural equipment and ethanol/biofuel. *The problem with these indices is the undue concentration on massive primarily US companies such as DowDuPont. Achieving a reasonable level of diversification by including only the companies within these indices is practically impossible, especially for non-US investors.* In Nigeria, for instance, there were only five companies that were classified as 'agriculture' listed on the Nigerian Stock Exchange, although there was clear groundswell of opinion behind further listings in the future, and it is certainly an important market to watch in the future.

A related problem is the issue of gaining access to farmland through listed equities. In principle, investors are interested in gaining access to diversified portfolios of farmland. And again, in principle, land ownership is a lower-risk play on agribusiness compared to, e.g., investing in farm producers or soft commodities. Operating risk is dismissed, with the only risks remaining being land prices and currency. Diversification is also possible: for example, Rural Funds Management in Australia owns farmland used for almonds, poultry and viticulture. But even the CEO himself admitted that 'things can change quickly in agriculture, which is why you should invest through diversified funds', and therein lies the problem. In the UK, for example, where many investors would dearly like to gain access to highly productive farmland in East Anglia, there are drastically few and often no opportunities available: farmers own all the land. Meanwhile listed farmland owners in Africa are still as yet virtually unknown. Most opportunities that do exist in farmland investment are unlisted, with all the attendant problems of illiquidity and difficulties of due diligence. Australian farmland may well consolidate further over the coming decades, and other countries, even developing countries, may start to follow suit, but institutional and retail investors insisting on a public equity strategy may well find themselves frozen out of the opportunities by their insistence.

Sixth, but in this agribusiness is no exception to general rules of investment, it is also necessary to get the timing right, so an understanding of all the factors that are responsible for high and low stock market valuations generally, the rules of economic cycles, such as interest rates and exchange rates, government expenditure and private sector net investment, will all be necessary if investment is to be successful.

Conclusion

It is straightforward enough to conclude that listed agribusiness investment is emerging from its infancy to become a valuable and potentially important part of international fund management strategies. What fund managers need is a greater range of companies, in more jurisdictions, at different levels of the food and fibre production process, in which to invest. Generating these companies is not likely to be a swift process, and it cannot be hurried.

Bibliography

Albert Partners (2017) Table Three. Agricultural Fund Investment Landscape. In *BDO, Global Aginvesting Conference Insights*. Available at: www.valoral.com/wp-content/uploads/2018-Global-Food-Agriculture-Investment-Outlook-Valoral-Advisors.pdf. Retrieved 29 May 2018.

Align Research (2018) Obtala Limited Forecasts and DCF model update. 29 January. Available at: www.alignresearch.co.uk/wp-content/uploads/2018/01/Obtala_Update_Align_Research_29th_January_2018.pdf. Retrieved 1 July 2018.

Australian Tax Office (2018). Collapse and restructure of agribusiness managed investment schemes – participant information. Available at: www.ato.gov.au/General/Tax-planning/In-detail/Collapse-and-restructure-of-agribusiness-managed-investment-schemes–participant-information/. Retrieved 26 July 2018.

Balmann, A., Chaddad, F. and Hermans, F. (2015) Agro-holdings and other types of mega-farming operations in developed and emerging economies. Pre-conference workshop of the 29th International Conference of Agricultural Economists, 8 August. Available at: www.iamo.de/fileadmin/user_upload/Bilder_und_Dokumente/06-veranstaltungen/icae-mailand_2015/icae-workshop_presentations/Agroholdings_Introduction.pdf. Retrieved 26 February 2019.

Bou-Saba, J. (2018) Why it's time to go public – even when staying private has never been easier. *Forbes*. 23 February. Available at: www.forbes.com/sites/valleyvoices/2018/02/23/why-its-time-to-go-public/#760d9412694d. Retrieved 6 July 2018.

Burgess, R. (2018) Markets do the samba as Brazil comes under attack. A flight to quality leads commentary on stocks, bonds, currencies and more. Bloomberg.com. 8 June. Available at: www.bloomberg.com/view/articles/2018-06-07/markets-convulse-as-brazil-comes-under-attack. Retrieved 21 July 2018.

Business Valuer (2018) How it works: Generate a business valuation report in 3 simple steps. Available at: www.thebusinessvaluer.co.uk/how-it-works/. Retrieved 1 July 2018.

Capital Valuation Group (2018) Agri-business. Available at: www.capvalgroup.com/agriculture-business-valuation.php. Retrieved 1 July 2018.

Capstone Headwaters Partners (2018) Food and Beverage Q1 2018. Available at: capstoneheadwaters. com/sites/default/files/Capstone%20Food%20%20Beverage%20MA%20Coverage%20Report_ Q1%202018.pdf. Retrieved 1 July 2018.

Carrera, H., Filgueiras, S., Ayres, M. and Romano, F. (2017) *Private Equity Strategies for Brazil's New Economic Reality*. Boston Consulting Group. 26 July. Available at: www.bcg.com/en-gb/ publications/2017/principal-investors-winning-emerging-market-private-equity-strategies-brazil- new-economic-reality.aspx. Retrieved 21 July 2018.

Clapp, J. (2017) Responsibility to the rescue? Governing private financial investment in global agricul- ture. *Agriculture and Human Values* 34, 223–235.

Crowe, T. (2018) Top stocks in agriculture. Motley Fool [blog]. Available at: www.fool.com/investing/ 2018/02/02/top-stocks-in-agriculture.aspx. Retrieved 1 July 2018.

Davis, G.F. (2016) *The Vanishing American Corporation*. Oakland, Berrett-Koehler.

Entrepreneur (2005) Going public. Available at: www.entrepreneur.com/article/81394. Retrieved 15 May 2019.

ETFdb (2018) Agribusiness ETF List. Available at: http://etfdb.com/type/sector/agribusiness/. Retrieved 1 July 2018.

FAO (2012) *Voluntary Guidelines on the Responsible Governance of Tenure of Land, Fisheries and Forests in the Context of National Food Security*. Rome, FAO. Available at: www.fao.org/docrep/016/i2801e/ i2801e.pdf. Retrieved 1 July 2018.

FAO (2012a) *Voluntary Guidelines on Tenure*. Rome, FAO. Available at: www.fao.org/tenure/voluntary- guidelines/en/. Retrieved 1 July 2018.

FAO (2015) *Food and Agriculture in the 2030 Agenda for Sustainable Development*. Rome, FAO. Available at: www.fao.org/sustainable-development-goals/overview/en/. Retrieved 9 July 2018.

FAO (2018) *The CFS Principles for Responsible Investment in Agriculture and Food systems*. Rome, FAO. Available at: www.fao.org/policy-support/resources/resources-details/en/c/1151242/. Retrieved 15 May 2019.

Featherstone, T. (2015) How to profit when agribusiness booms. *Financial Review*. 17 October. Available at: www.afr.com/personal-finance/shares/how-to-profit-when-agribusiness-booms-20151012- gk6qtu. Retrieved 9 July 2018.

Fidelity (2018) Sectors and Industries Overview. Available at: https://eresearch.fidelity.com/eresearch/ markets_sectors/sectors/sectors_in_market.jhtml. Retrieved 1 July 2018.

Global Impact Investment Network (2017). Impact Investing Trends. Evidence of a Growing Industry. Available at: https://thegiin.org/assets/GIIN_Impact%20InvestingTrends%20Report.pdf. Retrieved 25 July 2018.

Goedde, L., Horii, M. and Sanghvi, S. (2015) Global agriculture's many opportunities. *McKinsey on Investing* 2. Available at: www.mckinsey.com/~/media/McKinsey/Industries/Private%20 Equity%20and%20Principal%20Investors/Our%20Insights/Global%20agricultures%20many%20 opportunities/Global%20agricultures%20many%20opportunities.ashx. Retrieved 9 July 2018.

Goh, C.F., Rasli, A., Dziekonski, K. and Khan, S. (2015) Market-based valuation multiples: Evidence from agribusiness sector. *Pertanika Journal of Social Sciences and Humanities* 23 (1), 209–222. Available at: www.academia.edu/11775881/Market-based_Valuation_Multiples_Evidence_from_ Agribusiness_Sector. Retrieved 7 May 2018.

Grain Corp (2018) Our History. Available at: www.graincorp.com.au/about-graincorp/company. Retrieved 26 July 2018.

Hammoud, T., Schneider, A., Öberg, J., Brigl, M., Bellehumeur, K. and Brummer, M. (2018) *Private Equity Is Hot but Not Overheating*. Boston Consulting Group. 25 April. Available at: www.bcg.com/ en-us/publications/2018/private-equity-hot-but-not-overheating.aspx. Retrieved 6 July 2018.

Harding, C. (2011) Ranked: Africa's top 20 agribusiness companies. *Africa Business Insight*. 24 November. Available at: www.howwemadeitinafrica.com/ranked-africas-top-20-agribusiness-companies/13532/. Retrieved 1 July 2018.

Hemphill, P. (2017) Bojun Agriculture Holdings lists on Australian Securities Exchange. *Weekly Times*. 1 December. Available at: www.weeklytimesnow.com.au/agribusiness/bojun-agriculture-holdings-lists-on-australian-securities-exchange/news-story/d06153817dd07c1ac055fc93bc3e3d2e. Retrieved 9 July 2018.

InvestSnips (2018) Publicly Traded Agricultural Stocks. Available at: http://investsnips.com/publicly-traded-agricultural-companies/. Retrieved 1 July 2018.

Jones, A. (2017) What Investors are Paying for Agribusiness Stocks Part One. Available at: https://marketrealist.com/2017/12/investors-paying-agribusiness-stocks-december-2017-part-1. Retrieved 1 July 2018.

Jones, A. (2017a) What Investors are Paying for Agribusiness Stocks Part Two. Available at: https://marketrealist.com/2017/12/agribusiness-stocks-valuation-december-2017-part-2. Retrieved 1 July 2018.

Katchova, A.L. and Enlow, S.J. (2013) Financial performance of publicly-traded agribusinesses. *Agricultural Finance Review* 73(1), 58–73.

Kugelman, M. and Levenstein, S.L. (2013) Introduction. In Kugelman, M. and Levenstein, S.L. (eds.) *The Global Farms Race: Land Grabs, Agricultural Investment, and the Scramble for Food Security.* Washington DC, Island Press, 1–20.

Leclerc, R. (2019) We're only in the second innings of plant-based meats. Agfunder News. 9 May. Available at: https://agfundernews.com/were-only-in-the-second-innings-of-plant-based-meats.html. Retrieved 16 May 2019.

Luhrmann, H. and Theuvsen, L. (2016) Corporate social responsibility in agribusiness: Literature review and future research directions. *Journal of Agricultural and Environmental Ethics* 29(4), 673–696.

Macquarie (2010) The case for investing in agriculture. Macquarie Agricultural Fund Management. Available at: www.macquarie.com/dafiles/Internet/mgl/com/agriculture/docs/white-papers/case-for-investing-in-agriculture.pdf. Retrieved 9 July 2018.

Morningstar (2018) RobecoSAM Sustainable Food Equities D €. Available at: www.morningstar.co.uk/uk/funds/snapshot/snapshot.aspx?id=F00000243V. Retrieved 1 July 2018.

Moss Adams (2018) Agribusiness: Producers, Products and Services. Available at: https://mossadams.com/getmedia/6c930420-3ad2-4113-85ed-c84ba0179377/Agribusiness-Market-Monitor. Retrieved 1 July 2018.

Nardelli, P.M. and Marcedo da Silva, M.A (2011) Análise de um Projeto Agroindustrial Utilizando a Teoria de Opções Reais: a opção de adiamento. Brazilian Journal of Rural Economy and Sociology (Revista de Economia e Sociologia Rural-RESR) 49(4), 941–966. Available at: https://ageconsearch.umn.edu/record/154697. Retrieved 7 May 2018.

Perkin, N. (2017) Is the Life Expectancy of Companies Really Shrinking? Available at: www.onlydeadfish.co.uk/only_dead_fish/2015/09/is-the-life-expectancy-of-companies-really-shrinking.html. Retrieved 7 May 2018.

PIMCO (2018) Commodities. Available at: www.pimco.co.uk/en-gb/resources/education/understanding-commodities/. Retrieved 21 July 2018.

PwC (2019) Enterprise value as present value of expected future free cash flows. Available at: www.pwc-evaluation.com/en/approach. Retrieved 25 February 2019.

Ranker (2018) List of Agriculture Companies. Available at: www.ranker.com/list/agriculture-companies/reference. Retrieved 1 July 2018.

Roche, J. (2018) How to Value an Agribusiness. Available at: https://redcliffetraining.com/banking-category/agribusiness-valuation/. Retrieved 7 May 2018.

Shankar, S., van Raemdonck, F. and Maine, D. (2016) Can Agribusiness Reinvent Itself to Capture the Future? Bain Brief. 24 March. Available at: www.bain.com/publications/articles/can-agribusiness-reinvent-itself-to-capture-the-future.aspx. Retrieved 1 July 2018.

Steier, G. and Patel, K.K. (eds.) (2017) *International Farm Animal, Wildlife and Food Safety Law*. Dordrecht, Springer.

UNESCO (2015) *The UN World Water Development Report 2015, Water for a Sustainable World*. New York, Unesco. Available at: www.unesco.org/new/en/natural-sciences/environment/water/wwap/wwdr/2015-water-for-a-sustainable-world/.

UNCTAD (2018) The Principles for Responsible Agricultural Investment (PRAI). Available at: http://unctad.org/en/Pages/DIAE/G-20/PRAI.aspx. Retrieved 1 July 2018.

UNPRI (2015) Responsible investment in farmland. 1 July. Available at: https://www.unpri.org/64.tag. Retrieved 1 July 2018.

Vitón, R. (2018) 2018 Global Food & Agriculture Investment Outlook Investing profitably whilst fostering a better agriculture. Issue 8. Valoral Advisers. Available at: www.valoral.com/wp-content/uploads/2018-Global-Food-Agriculture-Investment-Outlook-Valoral-Advisors.pdf. Retrieved 9 July 2018.

YouGov (2018) No demand for fake meat. Available at: https://china.yougov.com/en-cn/news/2018/02/22/no-demand-for-fake-meat/. Retrieved 16 May 2019.

Conclusions

Introduction: food security and international policy

Global pessimism about how to feed the world is nothing new, from Malthus in 1798, onwards to the present day. Looking ahead, the core question is whether today's agriculture and food systems are capable of meeting the needs of a global population that is projected to reach more than 9 billion by 2050 and may peak – assuming it does – at more than 11 billion as soon as 2100. Can we achieve the required production increases, even as the pressures on already scarce land and water resources and the negative impacts of climate change intensify? The UN has warned that global water use is growing at twice the rate of global population growth. Unless this trend is reversed, two-thirds of the world's population will face so-called 'water stress' by 2025. The consensus view is that current systems are likely capable of producing enough food, but to do so in an inclusive and sustainable manner will require major transformations (FAO, 2017).

Food security will remain an important global priority. The experience of rapid food price escalation in 2007–09, with its serious effects on the urban poor in low income countries, is not likely to be easily forgotten by policymakers, especially when:

> This resulted in civil unrest in some countries and an increase in protectionist trade policies in others. In developing countries, where populations faced declining physical availability of food as well as sharply deteriorated affordability, many people were forced to reduce nutritional intakes and defer expenditures on essential items, such as health and education, to survive (Sheales & Gunning-Trant, 2009:iii).

A mass of policy recommendations followed the crisis, but as we have seen, few if any of them have been implemented or show any sign of being implemented.

Meeting demand

How might we increase the supply of food to match burgeoning and apparently uncontrollable demand?

First, one obvious route is more farmland. Syngenta has argued that the land available for farming will also have to expand by approximately 120 million hectares in developing countries, mainly sub-Saharan Africa and Latin America. These 120 million hectares should, they suggest, come primarily from a change in land use, for example pastures to arable land, which will require significant investment, knowledge transfer and education. However, the area suitable for agriculture is only available in limited geographies: remarkably, Brazil represents about 60% of this opportunity, with approximately 70–85 million hectares that could be brought into production in the future without impacting natural ecosystems such as the rainforest (Syngenta, 2015:13).

Second, yield growth, which is the main direction of both animal and plant research. Jaggard et al. (2010) asked if yields in industrialised countries have reached a ceiling but concluded no, both in the short and long term, although the matter is far from settled. Conventional animal breeding is still capable of increasing yields, and will be important in addressing other goals such as sustainability and better welfare. Modern genomic approaches to breeding will undoubtedly produce further gains, perhaps supplemented by the prospect of genetic modification. Not only will animals be bigger, with less fat, and be more suitable for their environment and the tasks humans set them (e.g. bees pollinating plants) but they will grow faster and produce more twins. Milk output will rise. New breeds will cope better with drought and disease. This is the positive argument. Ray et al. (2013) concluded, however, (on the basis of a linear regression analysis, with all the benefits and limitations of that methodology) that yields of four key global crops – maize, rice, wheat and soybean – that currently produce nearly two-thirds of global agricultural calories are increasing at 1.6%, 1.0%, 0.9% and 1.3% per year, non-compounding rates, respectively, which is less than the 2.4% per year rate required to double global production by 2050: not enough to feed the world if consumption patterns do not change.

Third, yields for existing major crops and more land for agriculture are not the only possibility. Many advances have involved novel crosses, and preserving rare breeds may be a valuable investment for the future. We already have a much better understanding of animal nutrition than last century, but further research is required to develop robust animal growth models to help optimise livestock production. More importantly, poor nutrition and general livestock practices are a particular problem in developing countries, where livestock often represent a critical component of household and community capital. In developed countries there has been a general decline in endemic diseases, although major epidemics, including new emergent diseases, continue to be a major threat. Less progress has been made in tropical countries, although with some success such as, for example, steps towards the eradication of rinderpest. Animal breeding and veterinary advances, as well as better diagnosis and surveillance, will all help farmers keep pace with evolving pathogens and hopefully reduce the burden of disease. Even modest increases in livestock management practices in developing countries will bring significant benefits.

Animals are already being used for human health projects, and pig organs in particular seem suitable for transplant. Xenotransplantation, swapping organs and tissues between species, has been actively pursued for decades, and with technical advances it may be possible either to grow organs inside animals or use animal organs for transplant increasingly over future decades, notwithstanding that we have been promised this future many times before and it is yet to come to pass. Other pharmaceutical products derived from animals, such as TPA or blood-clotting agents from cows' milk, skin grafting, and vaccine production, have made less spectacular but valuable progress. As this part of science develops, agribusiness will develop an entirely new, if very specialised, sub-sector.

Fourth, not to be forgotten in this plethora of opportunities are those potentially offered to agribusiness by robots. Raising, shipping and transplanting vegetables and tree seedlings, picking fruit, and even herding animals, are all potential opportunities for the next generation of robots, which will reduce the demand for labour on farms, as has already happened in progressively more food processing plants and retail stores. The use of robots to plant, reap and process grains would make the process more efficient. Robots could also be used to monitor plant health and growth. There are already proposals to use micro-robots for this purpose, to swarm fields to monitor the crops. Employment opportunities in agribusiness can reasonably be expected to fall over the next few decades, posing significant challenges for government but potential opportunities for farmers and investors alike.

Fifth, hydroponics is also very likely to expand. Likewise, a gradually adopted solution is vertical urban farming – creating stacked hydroponic farms inside buildings, especially skyscrapers. This would address the problem of high land prices, and also reduce transport costs to the mega-cities. Vertical farms are already there, in places like Michigan, in the USA, as well as London and Japan, where there is little space. Crops are grown inside in multi-storey buildings such as high rises and skyscrapers, in rooms with artificial lighting or in vertical greenhouses. As urbanisation and global population size increases, this trend will most likely increase. It is likely we will see more of this approach in the decades to come.

Indoor agriculture may also be beneficial, in other ways, since it creates a more controlled environment where the environmental conditions can be engineered to be just right for optimal crop growth. For example, scientific research has shown that light of different wavelengths has different effects on crop growth and the health of the plants. Thus, being able to grow the plants under specific lighting would be an advantage of indoor, vertical agriculture. Although critics suggest hydroponics is way too energy intensive, technological developments in energy may neutralise even this criticism in coming years.

Finally, improvements in artificial meat may end up being the most promising advance of all, given the comparative inefficiency of animal husbandry by comparison to crops. If – and it is a big if – the world's middle class can be persuaded to eat lab-grown meat, then the use of resources by agribusiness can be improved dramatically. The environmental benefits may be complex to calculate (Lynch & Pierrehumbert, 2019), but recent IPOs have suggested that this trend will be of real significance in coming decades.

Combining much of this is what the World Bank refers to as 'Agriculture 2.0', an agricultural technology revolution aimed at using IoT and data analytics to render crop production more precise and reliable. This is primarily due to advancements in technology as it applies to sensors, devices, machines and information technology. Today's agriculture operations routinely use sophisticated technologies that allow businesses to be more profitable and efficient, safer and more environmentally friendly. Oliver Wyman likewise opined that the kind of technical developments discussed in Chapter 4 will no longer depend on applying water, fertilisers and pesticides uniformly across entire fields. Instead, farmers will use the minimum quantities required and target very specific areas. Farms and agricultural operations will have

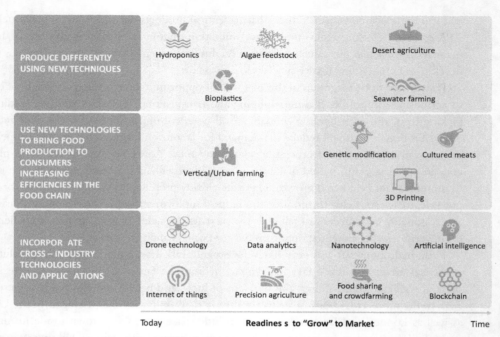

Figure 14.1 An integrated view of the future of agriculture
Source: Oliver Wyman (2018)

to be run very differently, primarily due to advancements in technology such as sensors, devices, machines and information technology, which are already in use in many advanced, large production agribusinesses. Future agriculture will use sophisticated technologies such as robots, temperature and moisture sensors, aerial images, and GPS technology. These advanced devices and precision agriculture and robotic systems will allow farms to be more profitable, efficient, safe, and environmentally friendly (Oliver Wyman, 2018).

Sixth, some of us at least may have start eating differently. Remarkably few plant and animal species dominate global agriculture and food production. As noted in previous chapters, cattle, sheep, pigs and poultry make up most of the livestock sector, while wheat, maize, rice and soya account for 60% of the world's total crop output. Fewer than 30 species account for more than 95% of human food needs. Food security experts are pressing for diversification, not least because of the threat of disease to staple crops (e.g. black sigatoka to bananas). Academics are therefore urging greater use of. underexploited food sources – sometimes known as orphan, neglected or underutilised crops – that could be grown more widely, particularly in the developing world., e.g. the Bambara groundnut, which is traditionally grown by female subsistence farmers in west Africa.

It is a so-called 'complete food', containing a healthy combination of carbohydrate, protein and fat. The nuts are versatile; they can be eaten whole after boiling or roasting – or dried and milled to yield a flour for making dumplings, cakes and biscuits. Although Bambara groundnut is easily cultivated in poor, arid soil, it only grows well in the tropics…because development of the nuts depends on the amount of daylight in any given day, which should not change much over the year. However, cross-breeding is now producing Bambara varieties that will do well in places further from the equator that have significant seasonal changes in the length of night and day, such as the Mediterranean (Cookson, 2017).

Likewise, Cookson explains, the FAO is urging the cultivation of crops that have been largely forgotten over the last century, in collaboration with the African Orphan Crops Consortium. Examples include the African yam bean, desert date, prickly pear cactus, baobab tree, teff (a grain native to Ethiopia and Eritrea) and ber (a stocky tree with a vitamin-rich berry). The collaboration aims to enhance Africa's food security, providing information to allow breeders to use the same strategies and technologies as those for Western crops, such as maize, to make rapid improvements in African crops.

As for diversifying from livestock to new sources of food from animals, insects usually top the list of alternatives, followed by lab-grown meat. In parts of central Africa as much as half of dietary protein has historically come from insects; their market value is often higher than other sources of animal protein. They are eaten raw, fried, boiled, roasted or dried and ground into meal. Even a relatively small increase in entomophagy, for example by using insects as ingredients in some pre-packaged foods, would bring environmental benefits. However, in practice, the aversion of many Western consumers to eating insects – and the infrastructure investment that would be required – mean that this will not happen on such a large scale. By contrast, lab-grown meat is at least for the time being no more sustainable in environmental terms than poultry production, although this may improve. But technology, even including new foods, alone cannot achieve the necessary increase in production.

To all of these possibilities should be added changes in consumption patterns such as a gradual shift towards sheep milk in dairy production (Lees & Lees, 2018), and a continuation of the general move away from red meat and sugar consumption, both of which will have significant effects on agribusinesses as varied as farms in Denmark and Nestlé itself. What cannot be prevented, however, is the continuation of dietary change, with all its consequences in terms of employment, health and corporate value, that has already been observed. Just the size of the cold chain has been forecast to reach \$382 billion by 2025 (GrandView Research, 2018), and even that may prove an underestimate.

Finally, the drift towards the legalisation of cannabis worldwide means that an entirely new legal crop, and with it a very significant new part of the agribusiness industry, is on its way to being incorporated into business activity in many countries, starting in 2018 with Canada. Deloitte forecast that Canadians would spend as much as C\$7.17 billion on cannabis products in 2019 and increase their overall consumption by up to 35% once recreational cannabis is properly legalised. Other countries may follow suit. Already in 2018, Canadian ETFs had been formed, with firms readying for IPOs, such as Acreage (O'Hara, 2018; Janiec, 2018).

Agribusiness and energy

One reason is that agriculture is producing more energy, as well as using far more, and it can even be said that the energy and agribusiness sectors are converging, at least temporarily, and dependent on technology and regulation. Some of this is entirely positive, of course, such as wind farms on farming land, notwithstanding some alleged negative health effects on animals and people, and some real damage to wildlife.

Another aspect to the changing relationship between agribusiness and energy is that as global energy requirements continue to rise, agricultural crops will themselves be utilised for energy. Whereas the first generation of biofuels have come from maize and other crops such as rapeseed, a second generation may be produced from plant material whose production does not compete for resources with food supplies, e.g. waste material from food plants or from plants grown on non-arable land. This in turn may change the type and distribution of crops grown worldwide (Cap Gemini, 2010).

Agribusiness: the right solution

Access to technology remains the main inhibitor of business growth, with modern farms and agricultural operations working much differently from a few decades ago. In order to achieve Agriculture 2.0 (or any other number), as well as to improve the multitude of supply chain issues, quality deficiencies, and lack of investment in agribusiness, especially in developing countries, the main change has to be that agribusiness replaces farming, as has been consistently argued in this book. As long ago as 2007, it was estimated by the FAO that to meet food demand by 2050, no less than $9.2 trillion of investment will be required (Koohafkan *et al.*, 2011). And yet the gap in financing for smallholders and rural enterprises persists. The problem is partly a tremendous uncertainty about infrastructure development rates, prices and price volatility, domestic governance regimes (including taxation, competition from parastatals or local firms backed by domestic authorities), concerns about transportation bottlenecks and rapid changes in the availability of competitive products. These are all legitimate investment concerns that government policy should be designed to overcome. But there is another effect, which is that the gap in value between agribusiness winners and losers is likely to broaden as markets continue to internationalise – albeit more slowly than was expected a decade or two decades ago. Substitutes, changes in demand caused by economic growth and greater market access contribute to this process, and there is nothing, or very little, that cash-strapped governments can do to prevent it in the long-term. It is over to the private sector from here on, collaborating with government and international agencies for sure, but with a profit motive, as it it has been in other sectors such as transport and for the most part, housing as well.

A good example is the need for irrigation. The World Bank estimated that the global investment requirement in irrigation through 2050 is estimated to be $960 billion. They noted that in the previous 60 years, most irrigation projects were led and financed by governments. But the rate of public irrigation investment has slowed due to high and increasing construction costs, fiscal constraints limiting both capital expenditure and operation and maintenance, limited cost recovery through tariffs, and poor management and supervision due to lack of technical expertise and changing political agendas. In the view of the World Bank, budget constraints and poor public management track record, however, call for new financing tools and greater private sector involvement (World Bank, 2017:15).

At the same time, as the World Bank has noted, the agriculture sector is fragmented and there is a large presence of SMEs. There are still those who argue that family farms will be better able to cope with the withdrawal of subsidies to farms generally, on the grounds that they have 'adaptable flexibility…competitive ability…and [make a] contribution to sustaining wider rural economies' (Brookfield & Parsons, 2007:217). Yet in the following paragraph, these authors call for continued *subsidies* to family farms, a privilege not usually extended to family firms in other industries. The reality is that SMEs in agriculture are particularly vulnerable to climate and natural hazards. They often have limited access to effective risk management tools, are often non-compliant with industry norms and regulations, and cannot afford marketing, both of which limit the growth of their customer and supply base. Similarly,

> Smallholders often have limited access to land, credit, technical advice, basic knowledge of the market system, and current information on market prices and conditions – all of which restrict their capacity to invest, expand their market surplus, and add value to their produce. The limited market surpluses of individual smallholders raise the unit cost of assembling, handling, and transporting their products (Devaux *et al.*, 2018:111).

Above all, they often – one may even say, with the exception of VC investment in potentially high return agtech and other fast-growing SMEs, *usually* – face severe constraints on their access to timely, affordable and appropriate types of finance, access to knowledge and technology, and consistent access to stable and high-value markets (World Bank, 2017:15). A frequent response has been to argue that 'These common attributes of smallholders highlight the importance of policies and programs that strengthen farmer associations and collective marketing' (Devaux *et al.*, 2018:111), in line with the argument advanced earlier that: agriculture 'can play a significant role in the livelihoods of rural populations by providing work opportunities related to agribusiness. Indeed, agribusinesses at any scale, even micro-enterprises, begin to provide a path to economic well-being' (Raj, 2011).

The African Development Bank (AfDB) similarly put out a mixed message, no doubt constrained by politics. On the one hand, the AfDB says that, since 2015, it has made a shift in its approach to the development of the agriculture: *the new approach embarks on viewing agriculture as a business rather than a means of survival* [my emphasis] (AfDB, 2016:1). On the other, however, the AfDB president emphasised that African smallholders *were* the largest component of the private sector in Africa.

> By seeing agriculture as business, smallholders as customers and entrepreneurs, and companies as organizations that want smallholders as customers and suppliers, policymakers and investors can leverage the continent's existing assets to catalyze economic transformation rather than trying to create it from whole cloth (AfDB, 2016:1).

This seems right up to a point: but agribusiness at a scale large enough to overcome the obstacles evident for SMEs and smallholders, introduce agtech and take the steps so vitally necessary to drive up yields, has had a bad press for far too long, whether in India, Africa or anywhere else. Critics, for example in NGOs, often want to use agricultural production, farming in particular, as a political weapon, writing quixotically as if either international capitalism can be ignored, treated as an ephemeral phenomenon, or somehow bypassed. But in fact, the question of how food and agricultural *production* generally should be organised is one thing; how the economic rewards of that production should be distributed is another. Agribusiness, especially large international firms as well as agtech start-ups, are well-placed to deliver the former; it is the responsibility of governments to deliver the latter, and it is unfair on agribusiness to blame it, for example, for seeking to minimise its tax burden. Any responsible management should do that; and any responsible government should decide how far they should be allowed to do so.

The two issues are reciprocally related, which is why the World Bank and other enthusiasts for global agribusiness want to see them solved concurrently. It remains imperative for agribusinesses to keep up with the latest technology in order to grow. This is, however, expensive. Predictions that IoT device installations in the agriculture world will increase from 30 million in 2015 to 75 million in 2020 may turn out to be overoptimistic, and those that do, may end up in the developed world to a far greater extent than the World Bank and its bloggers would want (World Bank, 2018).

So, too, the new focus on technology that has permeated agribusiness in recent years must not be allowed to obscure traditional business concerns. In 2017, KPMG's global survey of agribusiness identified key challenges that would have been familiar half a century before: low commodity prices, price volatility, the evolving political landscape, access to finance and working capital, issues of HR, and the ability to innovate (KPMG, 2017:6). Lessons from throughout the business world are, and clearly will continue to be, relevant to agribusiness. The skill of agribusiness investment over the coming decades will be in blending highly specific sectoral expertise, whether in avocados or packaging, with a relentless focus on shareholder value and stakeholder satisfaction.

Opportunities and risks for agribusiness investment

In the first decades of the 21st century, opportunities for agribusiness investment, from farmland to agtech and from R&D to retail delivery strategies, have never been greater. To be successful, however, investors must do much more than study financial ratios and trust management's DCF forecasts. The lessons of the dotcom bubble from the late 1990s should be recalled and studied carefully. Answers are needed, to start with, as to how global macroeconomic factors and technologies are driving growth opportunities. For example, whilst delivery services such as Deliveroo and Amazon have grown rapidly in the food sector in recent years, the potential of drone delivery is ultimately disintermediating, and their business model may be placed under threat in the future. Macroeconomics analyses global trends, agricultural economics concerns production functions, and consumer microeconomics analyses demand and supply curves. The need for business is a discipline that integrates all three, technological and policy analysis, into one coherent economic and business discipline with a view to informing value creation decisions at the microeconomic, firm level. *The gap between high-level analysis of markets and business analysis of firms needs to shrink*. We could call the new discipline *Agribusiness Economics*. Central to agribusiness economics will be forecasting and risk management.

Then, what changes lie ahead for agribusiness investors in the medium term – when value within a business will be created or destroyed – what specific sub-sectors within the agribusiness industry are likely to provide the best returns (e.g. from export opportunities, changes in dietary preferences, the registration of intellectual property, or other forms of value growth), what competitors may be already heavily invested, and about to reap returns, in the same technology or application, how will exits look in the medium term (for a VC or PE investment) and what regulatory threats may exist? Due diligence in agribusiness will become harder to do, and more expensive, as the rewards from successful investment climb.

Concluding remarks

Governments will not, and SMEs cannot, provide the required level of investment to feed around 10 billion people by 2050. Food and agribusiness already form a $7-trillion global industry that increases in size annually by more than even population growth. Assuming current trends in population, GDP and food demand approximately continue, it needs to grow at least 70% larger in real terms by then. Fortunately, there is no shortage of investors working to invest in rural economic growth and inclusive agriculture, and nor is there a shortage of global liquidity interested in funding the agriculture sector. Now the challenge is to bring the investment requirements and investors together profitably.

The world needs dynamic, but well-regulated, agribusiness, and if this book has made even the smallest of contributions towards its acceptance, as well as its understanding, it will have had some merit.

Bibliography

African Development Bank (2016) Evaluation of Bank's Support to the Agricultural Value Chains Development. Available at: http://idev.afdb.org/sites/default/files/documents/files/AVCD%20 Draft%20Approach%20Paper.pdf. Retrieved 30 July 2018.

Brookfield, H. and Parsons, H. (2007) *Family Farms: Survival and Prospect. A World-Wide Analysis*. London and New York, Routledge.

Cap Gemini (2010) *Food for Thought: The Future of Agribusiness*. London, Cap Gemini. Available at: www.capgemini.com/wp-ontent/uploads/2017/07/tl_Food_for_Thought__the_Future_of_ Agribusiness.pdf. Retrieved 20 July 2018.

Cookson, C. (2017) Scientists see role for insects and 'orphan crops' in human diet. *Financial Times*. 7 December. Available at: www.ft.com/content/ab7092b2-c545-11e7-b30e-a7c1c7c13aab. Retrieved 15 July 2018.

Deloitte (2018) *A Society in Transition, An Industry Ready to Bloom*. Deloitte Canada. Available at: www2. deloitte.com/ca/en/pages/consulting/articles/deloitte2018cannabisreport.html. Retrieved 21 July 2018.

Devaux, A., Torero, M., Donovan, J. and Horton, D. (2018) Agricultural innovation and inclusive value-chain development: a review. *Journal of Agribusiness in Developing and Emerging Economies* 8(1), 99–123.

FAO (2017) *The State of Food Insecurity and Nutrition in the World*. Rome, FAO. Available at: www.fao. org/3/a-I7695e.pdf. Retrieved 30 October 2017.

Goedde, L., Horii, M. and Sanghvi, S. (2015) Pursuing the global opportunity in food and agribusiness. McKinsey. July. Available at: www.mckinsey.com/industries/chemicals/our-insights/pursuing-the-global-opportunity-in-food-and-agribusiness. Retrieved 11 June 2018.

Grand View Research (2018) *Cold Chain Market Size, Share & Trends Analysis Report by Packaging, By Equipment, By Type (Monitoring Components, Transportation, Storage), By Application, By Region, And Segment Forecasts, 2018–2025*. San Francisco, Grand View Research.

Jaggard, K.W., Aiming, Q. and Ober, E.S. (2010) Possible changes to arable crop yields by 2050. *Philosophical Transactions of the Royal Society B* 365, 2835–2851. Available at: http://rstb.royalsocietypublishing.org/content/royptb/365/1554/2835.full.pdf. Retrieved 20 July 2018.

Janiec, C. (2018) Cannabis investor acreage raises $119m ahead of Canadian list. *Agri Investor*. 24 July. www.agriinvestor.com/cannabis-investor-acreage-raises-119m-ahead-canadian-listing/. Retrieved 24 July 2018.

Koohafkan, P., Salman, M. and Casarotto, C. (2011) Investments in land and water. SOLAW Background Report 17. Rome, FAO. Available at: www.fao.org/fileadmin/templates/solaw/files/thematic_reports/TR_17_web.pdf. Retrieved 15 July 2018.

KPMG (2017) *Global Agribusiness Survey 2017*. London, KPMG. Available at: https://home.kpmg.com/au/en/home/insights/2018/01/global-agribusiness-survey-2017.html. Retrieved 10 July 2018.

Lees, N. and Lees, I. (2018) Competitive advantage through responsible innovation in the New Zealand sheep dairy industry. *International Food and Agribusiness Management Review* 21(4), 505–523.

Lynch, J. and Pierrehumbert, R. (2019) Climate Impacts of Cultured Meat and Beef Cattle. *Sustainable Food Systems*. 19 February 2019. Available at: https://doi.org/10.3389/fsufs.2019.00005. Retrieved 29 June 2019.

O'Hara, C. (2018) New pot fund to take on Canada's most popular ETF of 2018. *The Globe and Mail*. 31 January. Available at: www.theglobeandmail.com/globe-investor/funds-and-etfs/etfs/redwood-to-enter-haze-of-canadian-pot-etfs/article37798355/. Retrieved 27 July 2018.

Oliver Wyman (2018) Agriculture 4.0 – The Future Of Farming Technology. Available at: www.oliverwyman.com/our-expertise/insights/2018/feb/agriculture-4-0–the-future-of-farming-technology.html. Retrieved 20 July 2018.

Raj, S.P. (2011) Editorial. *Journal of Agribusiness in Developing and Emerging Economies* 1(1).

Ray, D.K., Mueller, N.D., West, P.C. and Foley, J.A. (2013) Yield trends are insufficient to double global crop production by 2050. PLOS One. Available at: https://journals.plos.org/plosone/article?id=10.1371/journal.pone.0066428. Retrieved 20 May 2019.

Sheales, T. and Gunning-Trant, C. (2009) *Global Food Security and Australia*. Canberra, ABARES.

Syngenta (2015) Annual Review 2015. Available at: http://annualreport2015.syngenta.com/assets/pdf/Syngenta-annual-review-2015.pdf. Retrieved 10 June 2018.

World Bank (2017) *Options for Increased Private Sector Participation in Resilience Investment. Focus on Agriculture*. Washington DC, World Bank.

World Bank (2018) World Bank Blogs: Agribusiness. Available at: https://blogs.worldbank.org/category/tags/agribusiness. Retrieved 13 July 2018.

Index

Note: **Bold** page numbers indicate tables, *italic* numbers indicate figures.

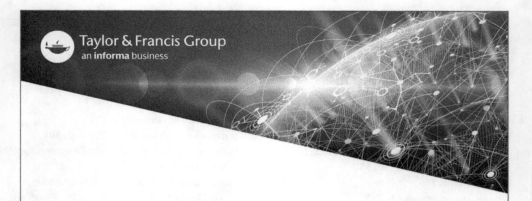